University of Edinburgh

In Memory of the late

A. G. Carmichael

the University Court have the honour
to present to

Miss Carmichael

this copy of the

ROLL OF HONOUR
1914-1919

UNIVERSITY OF EDINBURGH
ROLL OF HONOUR
1914—1919

EARL KITCHENER OF KHARTOUM
Lord Rector of the University
1914-1916

UNIVERSITY OF EDINBURGH

ROLL OF HONOUR
1914—1919

EDINBURGH
Printed and Published for the University by
OLIVER AND BOYD, TWEEDDALE COURT
LONDON: 33 PATERNOSTER ROW, E.C.
1921

EDITOR

MAJOR JOHN E. MACKENZIE

CONTENTS

	PAGE
INTRODUCTION BY THE PRINCIPAL	ix
EXTRACT FROM SPEECH BY RUDYARD KIPLING	xii
ROLL OF THE FALLEN	1
RECORD OF WAR SERVICE	117
ORDERS, DECORATIONS AND DISPATCHES	753

INTRODUCTION

THIS volume has been compiled to meet a strong and general desire that the names should be recorded of those members of the University of Edinburgh who took part in the war, as well as those whose service cost them their lives. At first it was intended that the Record should comprehend all forms of national service; but as the collection of material proceeded it was found impracticable to obtain particulars from more than a small proportion of the great number who contributed to win the war by one form or another of civilian effort. It was, moreover, realised that such services, important as many of them were, stood in a different category from services in the field. Any attempt to mention them was therefore abandoned, and the Record of War Service which is now presented relates only to those who served in the Forces of the Crown. For similar reasons no account is included here of the work—some of it of notable consequence—which was done in the laboratories of the University with a definitely military aim.

The Record comprises, first, a "Roll of the Fallen," on which are the names of 944 members of the University, with a brief account of their military careers, and with photographs, when these could be obtained. The University desires to thank the relatives of those whose names appear in this list for their ready and careful response to enquiries as to service, and for the photographs which have been sent in about eight hundred and fifty instances. All the photographers concerned have

Introduction

generously waived any claim to copyright in respect of the reproduction of photographs in this volume. The Roll is arranged alphabetically. It gives for each individual his date of birth and his school, his athletic and military record at school, the Faculty in which he studied and his degree (if any), his athletic and military record at the University, the record of his war services, with promotions, dates, places of service, decorations, honours, and mentions in dispatches.

The next list, which is entitled "Record of War Service," gives details, necessarily in a very concise form, of service in the Navy, Army, or Air Force, on the part of about seven thousand members of the University. Names which are included in the "Roll of the Fallen" are not repeated in this list. The particulars which are given have in general been furnished by the persons concerned, in reply to a circular issued by the University, and have been checked and supplemented by reference to Army and Navy Lists.

Then follows a list of Orders, Decorations, and Mentions in Dispatches, which includes, with many other honours, five awards of the Victoria Cross.

On the outbreak of hostilities about six hundred students and young graduates who had been members of the Officers' Training Corps at once received commissions in the Army. The Officers' Training Corps, which in this University includes Artillery, Engineer, Infantry, and Medical Units, continued to be an active training centre for Cadets during the whole of the war. It will be seen from the lists that a large proportion of the graduates of the University took service as medical officers. In many instances medical students who had joined the Forces as combatants were returned at a later stage to the University to complete their professional training in view of the urgent needs of the Royal Army Medical Corps.

Introduction

The work of editing the volume has been carried out by Major John E. Mackenzie. The University desires to thank the Editor for the labour and care he has expended in compiling it, and in passing it through the press. To gather, select, and verify the particulars of service of so many persons has not been a short or easy task. Among Major Mackenzie's qualifications for the Editorship was the fact that he had served as Adjutant of the Officers' Training Corps throughout the War. He has spared no pains to secure accuracy and completeness, and in this he has had efficient help from a staff of assistants and from several voluntary workers, among whom Mr J. G. Gilbertson, Dr Thomas Mackenzie, Dr Samuel Walker, and Mr George Wilson, should especially be named. Much of the initial work of collecting particulars was carried out by the former Secretary of the Senatus and Court, Professor Sir Ludovic Grant, with the assistance of the clerical staff, and the material was indexed under the supervision of Dr James Walker.

Mr Rudyard Kipling has allowed us to print the sentences which follow on the next page. They formed part of a speech delivered in July 1920, on the occasion of his receiving from the University the honorary degree of Doctor of Laws. His words are felt to be a peculiarly fitting introduction to the Roll of Honour of the University in which they were spoken.

J. A. EWING,
Principal and Vice-Chancellor.

THE UNIVERSITY,
EDINBURGH, *January* 1921.

"HERE as elsewhere, the sins of the fathers were visited on the children, and the sons of your University were once again constrained, like their forebears, so to use themselves in matters of conscience as they should answer to their Maker. All earth is witness that they answered as befitted their ancestry; they endured as the strong influences about their youth had framed them to endure. That they willingly and wittingly laid down the unachieved purposes of their lives in order that all life should not be wrenched from its purpose; that they turned without fear or question from these Gates of Learning to those of the Grave in order that free men might still continue to learn freedom, is their glory but not their glory alone. It is the glory also of their severe and beloved mother, who, while she gave them learning, dowered them with that wisdom without which all learning is folly."

RUDYARD KIPLING.

From a Speech at the University of Edinburgh, 7th July 1920.

ROLL OF THE FALLEN

ABERNETHY, WILLIAM (*b.* 1893).
   Anderson Institute, Lerwick. Student of Science, 1914-15. R.E. (Special Brigade), Pioneer Feb. 1916. France. Wounded on 29th and died of wounds on 30th June 1916 at Fricourt on Somme.   Pl. II.

ADAMSON, GEORGE ADDIS (*b.* 1898).
   Ardrossan Academy; Dux; First XV. and XI. Cadet Corps 1909-12. Student of Arts, 1916-17. O.T.C. Infantry, July to Dec. 1916, Cadet; Officer Cadet Dec. 1916. 6th King's Own Scottish Borderers, 2nd Lieut. Jan. 1917. France. Fell in action at Passchendaele on 12th October 1917.   Pl. II.

ADAMSON, ROBERT THORBURN (*b.* 1893).
   Ardrossan Academy. Cadet Corps 1903-6. Student of Arts, 1911-14; M.A. O.T.C. Infantry, Oct. to Dec. 1914, Cadet. 13th Royal Scots, Private Dec. 1914; Lieut. and Acting Captain Dec. 1916. France. Fell leading his Company at the Battle of Arras on 23rd April 1917.   Pl. II.

AINGER, HERBERT CECIL (*b.* 1895).
   Giggleswick. O.T.C. 1910-11. Student of Science, 1913-14. O.T.C. Engineers, Dec. 1913 to Nov. 1914. 15th Royal Scots, Private Sept. 1914. 3rd Royal Scots, 2nd Lieut. March 1915; Lieut. 1916. R.F.C. Observer, 1916; Pilot March 1917. France. Killed in Flanders on 4th October 1917.   Pl. II.

AINSLIE, ARCHIBALD (*b.* 1893).
   Launceston Church Grammar School, Tasmania. Student of Medicine, 1913-14. Scottish Horse, Private Dec. 1914. 3/4th King's Own Scottish Borderers, 2nd Lieut. Aug. 1915. Palestine. Killed in action in Egypt on 19th April 1917.   Pl. II.

AITKEN, IAN MALCOLM (*b.* 1899).
   Edinburgh Academy; First XV. and XI. Edinburgh University O.T.C. Artillery, April to Dec. 1917, Cadet. R.F.A., 82nd Brigade, 2nd Lieut. May 1918. France Sept. 1918. Wounded near Le Cateau, Battle of Cambrai, on 10th and died on 12th October 1918.   Pl. II.

AITON, WILLIAM (*b.* 1890).
   George Watson's College. O.T.C. 1905-9. Student of Arts, 1909-14; M.A. 1912. O.T.C. Infantry, Oct. 1909 to Jan. 1914, Cadet. Lothians and Border Horse, Private Aug. 1914; Corporal 1916. 3rd Rifle Brigade, 2nd Lieut. Oct. 1917. France and Macedonia. Killed in action on 21st March 1918.   Pl. II.

Roll of the Fallen

ALEXANDER, JOHN ALEXANDER ELLIOT (*b.* 1894).
George Watson's College. O.T.C. 1908-12, Cadet Corporal. Shooting VIII. Student of Science, 1912-14. O.T.C. Infantry, Oct. 1912 to Sept. 1914, Cadet. 12th Highland Light Infantry, 2nd Lieut. Sept. 1914; Lieut. March 1915. France. Treacherously shot while trying to save a German on 15th August 1915 near Bethune. Pl. II.

ALEXANDER, THOMAS MALCOLMSON (*b.* 1899).
George Watson's College. O.T.C. 1913-16. Student of Medicine, 1916-17. O.T.C. Artillery, April to Oct. 1917, Cadet. Royal Air Force, 41st Squadron, 2nd Lieut. Sept. 1917. France July 1918. Killed in action in Flanders on 17th August 1918. Pl. II.

ALEXANDER, THOMAS MITCHELL (*b.* 1885).
Selkirk High School. Student of Law, 1903-4; Procurator, 1908. 1/4th King's Own Scottish Borderers, Lieut. Aug. 1914. Killed at the Dardanelles on 12th July 1915.

ALLAN, ARTHUR GORDON (*b.* 1898).
George Watson's College. O.T.C. 1913-16, Cadet Drummer. First XI. Student of Medicine, 1916-17. O.T.C. Artillery, Oct. 1916 to May 1917, Cadet. R.F.A., Officer Cadet June 1917. 106th Brigade, 2nd Lieut. Oct. 1917. France Feb. 1918. Wounded on 4th Nov. near Valenciennes and died on 8th December 1918. Pl. III.

ALLAN, JAMES GRANT (*b.* 1895).
Merchiston Castle. O.T.C. 1908-13, Cadet Sergeant. First XV. Student of Arts, 1913-14. O.T.C. Infantry, Sept. to Oct. 1914, Cadet. 9th Gordon Highlanders, 2nd Lieut. Sept. 1914; Lieut. Nov. 1914. Regimental Lewis Gun Officer. France. Killed in action at Hill 70, Loos, on 25th September 1915. Pl. III.

ALLEN, STEPHEN DEXTER (*b.* 1899).
Bedford Modern School. Student of Arts, 1915-17. O.T.C. Infantry, Oct. 1916, to Aug. 1917, Cadet; Officer Cadet Aug. 1917. 4th Bedfordshire Regiment, 2nd Lieut. Dec. 1917. Attached 7th Royal Fusiliers, Aug. 1918. France. "Killed while gallantly leading his men" at Ligny Thilloy on 27th August 1918. Pl. III.

ALLISON, JAMES (*b.* 1881).
George Watson's College. Student of Law, 1900-1; Law Agent. 8th and 9th Royal Scots, Private March 1916; 2nd Lieut. March 1917. Killed in action in France on 20th September 1917. Pl. III.

ALLISON, T.
Former Student. Solicitor. 4th Cameron Highlanders, Captain. Killed in action in France on 18th May 1915.

PLATE II.

R. T. ADAMSON.   W. ABERNETHY.   G. A. ADAMSON.

H. C. AINGER.   A. AINSLIE.   IAN M. AITKEN.

J. A. E. ALEXANDER.   T. MALCOLMSON ALEXANDER.   W. AITON.

PLATE III.

A. G. ALLAN.

STEPHEN D. ALLEN.

J. G. ALLAN.

A. D. ANDERSON.

JAMES ALLISON.

J. DOUGLAS ALSTON.

JAMES ANDERSON.

DAVID ANDERSON.

C. G. ANDERSON.

Roll of the Fallen

ALSTON, J. DOUGLAS (*b.* 1890).
  Edinburgh Academy. Student of Law, 1907-9. 2nd and 3rd Scottish Rifles (S.R.), 2nd Lieut. Aug. 1914; Lieut. Feb. 1915. Killed in action at the Battle of Neuve Chapelle on 10th March 1915. Pl. III.

ANDERSON, ALEXANDER DAVID (*b.* 1882).
  George Watson's College. Student of Arts; M.A. 1904. Chartered Accountant (London). Inns of Court O.T.C. 1905-9. 1st Grenadier Guards, 2nd Lieut. Dec. 1917. France. Killed in action near Maubeuge on 6th November 1918. Pl. III.

ANDERSON, COLVIN GIBSON (*b.* 1889).
  Boroughmuir School; First XV. Student of Science, 1916-17. 15th and 18th Highland Light Infantry, Private March 1917. France March 1918. Wounded 2nd June 1918. Killed in action on 28th September 1918. Pl. III.

ANDERSON, DAVID (*b.* 1893).
  Daniel Stewart's College; First XV. Student of Medicine, 1911-14. 1/5th Royal Scots (Machine-Gun Section), Private Sept. 1914. Killed in action in Gallipoli on 2nd May 1915. Pl. III.

ANDERSON, JAMES (*b.* 1893).
  Forfar Academy. Student of Arts, 1911-15; M.A. 1914. O.T.C. Infantry, Nov. 1911 to Feb. 1915, Cadet. 10th Scottish Rifles, 2nd Lieut. May 1915; Lieut. June 1916. Died on service on 20th August 1916. Pl. III.

ANDERSON, JOHN GEORGE. (See p. 115.)

ANDERSON, JOSEPH EDMUND ALEXANDER (*b.* 1892).
  Student of Law, 1912-14; Law Agent, 1914. 24th Royal Fusiliers (2nd Sportsman's Battalion), Private Feb. 1915. France. Killed in action at Beaumont Hamel on 13th November 1916. Pl. IV.

ANDERSON, ROBERT BALLANTINE (*b.* 1890).
  St Mary's, Melrose; Edinburgh Academy; First XV. Academicals, 1909-13. Student of Law, 1908-12. Writer to the Signet, 1913. 1st Lovat Scouts, Private Sept. 1914. 4th King's Own Scottish Borderers, Lieut. Jan. 1915. Gallipoli July 1915; Egypt and Palestine. Killed at Gaza on 19th April 1917. Pl. IV.

ANDERSON, SAMUEL STEPHEN (*b.* 1882).
  George Heriot's School; Captain XV. and XI. Student of Arts, 1899-1905; M.A. (Hons. Mod. Lang.) 1903. Schoolmaster's Diploma, 1904. 5th Royal Scots Fusiliers, Private Aug. 1914; Sergeant 1915; 2nd Lieut. Nov. 1915. Interpreter. Killed in action in Gallipoli on 30th December 1915. Pl. IV.

ANDERSON, WALTER KINLOCH (*b.* 1885).
  George Watson's College. Student of Law. Chartered Accountant, 1913. 9th Royal Scots, Private Aug. 1914. 5th Royal Highlanders (Black Watch), 2nd Lieut. March 1915; Lieut. Aug. 1915; Acting Captain 1916; Captain 1918. Attached 6th Black Watch, 51st Highland Division, July 1918. France. Killed in Bois de Courtrai, near Rheims, on 22nd July 1918. Pl. IV.

Roll of the Fallen

ANDERSON, WILLIAM JAMES (*b.* 1888).
    Daniel Stewart's College. Student of Law, 1907-9. Chartered Accountant, 1911. 14th Argyll and Sutherland Highlanders, Private May 1915. France June 1916. Wounded Sept. 1916. Killed in action near Bethune on 23rd October 1916.   Pl. IV.

ANDERSON, WILLIAM STEWART (*b.* 1884).
    George Heriot's and Boroughmuir Schools. Student of Arts, 1905-8; M.A. 1908. R.G.A., Gunner Sept. 1916. France. Wounded on 29th Sept. and died of wounds on 9th October 1917 near Etaples.   Pl. IV.

ANDREW, WILLIAM DICKIE (*b.* 1894).
    Linlithgow Academy. Student of Law, 1913-14. Lothians and Border Horse, Private 1912. 1/10th and 15th Royal Scots, 2nd Lieut. May 1917. Killed in action on 22nd March 1918.   Pl. IV.

ANGUS, STEWART (*b.* 1890).
    Edinburgh Academy. Student of Science, 1908-12; B.Sc., 1912. O.T.C. Artillery, March 1909 to Jan. 1910. Engineers 1910-12, Cadet. R.E. City of Edinburgh (Fortress) Engineers, 2nd Lieut. April 1915. Egypt Dec. 1915, and France. Killed in action near Hebuterne on 1st July 1916.   Pl. IV.

ARCHIBALD, JAMES (*b.* 1890).
    West Calder and Boroughmuir Schools. Student of Arts, 1908-11; M.A. 1911. 16th Highland Light Infantry, Corporal May 1916. France. Died of wounds received near Albert on 26th August 1918.   Pl. IV.

ARMIT, NAPIER (*b.* 1880).
    George Watson's College. Student of Law, 1901-3. Advocate, 1904. 16th Royal Scots, Private Dec. 1914; Captain Jan. 1915. France. M.C. July 1916. Killed in action at Bazentin-le-Petit on 4th August 1916.   Pl. V.

ARMSTRONG, HENRY LESLIE (*b.* 1892).
    George Watson's College; First XV. Student of Arts and Law, 1911-15; M.A. 1914; LL.B. 1915. 4th King's Own Scottish Borderers, 2nd Lieut. March 1915; Lieut. 1917. Dardanelles Nov. 1915; Egypt Spring 1916; France April 1918. Killed in action at Kemmel on 25th April 1918.   Pl. V.

ARMSTRONG, HENRY LOUIS WINTHROP (*b.* 1880).
    Haileybury. Student of Law, 1902-4. 7th Somerset Light Infantry, 2nd Lieut. Killed in action in December 1915.

AUBEL, WILLY VAN.
    Student of Arts, 1914-15. Belgian Army, Adjutant. Killed in action on October 1916.   Pl. V.

AUSTIN, JOHN HENRY EDWARD.
    Student of Medicine. L.R.C.P. & S. (Edin.) and L.F.P.S. (Glasgow) 1887; M.R.C.S. (Eng.) 1892. Army Medical Service, Colonel. Died on service on 21st April 1917.

PLATE IV.

R. B. Anderson.

S. Stephen Anderson.

J. E. A. Anderson.

W. K. Anderson.

Wm. J. Anderson.

Wm. S. Anderson.

W. D. Andrew.

James Archibald.

Stewart Angus.

PLATE V.

W. van Aubel.   J. M. Bain.   A. P. Baker.

H. Leslie Armstrong.   Napier Armit.   D. H. Bailey.

Roy F. Balmain.   J. E. Balfour-Melville.   C. J. Banks.

Roll of the Fallen

BAILEY, DERMOT HARVEY (*b.* 1884).
 George Watson's College. Swimming. Student of Medicine, 1901-2. Tea Planter, Ceylon. 1/8th Royal Scots, 2nd Lieut. 1915. France July 1915. Killed in action on 23rd May 1917. Pl. V.

BAIN, JOHN MEIKLE (*b.* 1880).
 Buccleuch and Wilton Schools, Hawick. Student of Arts and Science, 1900-4; M.A. 1904; B.Sc.(London). Schoolmaster. 12th Scottish Rifles, 2nd Lieut. April 1915. Killed in action on 14th July 1916. Pl. V.

BAKER, ALBERT PARKES (*b.* 1886).
 George Watson's College; First XV. Gold Medalist, Exhibition Marathon, 1908. Student of Law. Malay States Volunteer Rifles, Sergeant. 2nd Highland Light Infantry, attached 10th Durham L.I., Lieut. Dec. 1916. France Jan. 1917. Killed in action on 27th August 1917. Pl. V.

BALFOUR, ISAAC BAYLEY. (See p. 115.)

BALFOUR-MELVILLE, JAMES ELLIOT (*b.* 1882).
 Edinburgh Academy and Malvern; First XI. B.A. (Oxford). Association "Blue." Student of Law. Chartered Accountant, 1912. 3rd attached 2nd Black Watch, 2nd Lieut. Nov. 1914. France. Killed in action at Loos on 25th September 1915. Pl. V.

BALMAIN, ROY FREDERICK (*b.* 1895).
 George Watson's College. Student of Medicine, 1913-14. O.T.C. Artillery, Oct. 1913 to Aug. 1914, Cadet. R.F.A., 2nd Lieut. Aug. 1914; Lieut. Sept. 1915; Captain Aug. 1917. Adjutant 51st Brigade R.F.A., 1915-18. France May 1915; Somme 1916; Arras April, and Ypres Sept. 1917. Dispatches Jan. 1917 and Jan. 1918. M.C. June 1918. Died of wounds on 1st October 1918 near Passchendaele. Pl. V.

BANKS, CHARLES JAMES (*b.* 1896).
 Lanark Grammar School; George Watson's College. O.T.C. 1912-14. Student of Medicine, 1914-15. O.T.C. Artillery, Oct. 1914 to April 1916, Cadet. 7th Seaforth Highlanders, Private April 1916. France. Killed at High Wood on 12th October 1916. Pl. V.

BANNERMAN, ROBERT GILROY (*b.* 1894).
 George Heriot's School; Dux; First XV. O.T.C. 1909-12, Cadet Corporal. Student of Arts, 1912-15. O.T.C. Artillery, Oct. 1912 to June 1915, Cadet Bombardier. R.F.A., 157th Brigade, 2nd Lieut. June 1915; Lieut. July 1916. France 1916. Killed in action on 25th July 1916 near Montauban on the Somme. Pl. VI.

BARCLAY, IVAN CURROR CHRISTIE (*b.* 1895).
 Dunfermline High School. Student of Medicine, 1912-17. R.N.V.R., H.M.S. *Mary Rose*, Surgeon-Probationer. Jutland Battle. Dispatches Aug. 1918. Killed in action on 17th October 1917. Pl. VI.

Roll of the Fallen

BARRIE, CHARLES DAVID OGILVY (*b.* 1881).
  Dumfries Academy. Student of Arts, 1898-1903; M.A. (Hons. Classics) 1903. 14th London Regiment (London Scottish), Corporal. France. Killed in action at the Somme on 1st July 1916. Pl. VI.

BARRIE, WILLIAM COWAN OGILVY (*b.* 1882).
  Dumfries Academy; George Watson's College. Student of Arts, 1900-4; M.A. (Hons. Classics) 1904. Royal Highlanders (Black Watch), Lieut. Sept. 1914. France. Neuve Chapelle and Festubert. Twice wounded. Killed in action on 14th October 1916. Pl. VI.

BARRON, JAMES (*b.* 1877).
  Royal Academy, Inverness. Student of Arts, 1896-8. 7th Cameron Highlanders, Captain Sept. 1914; Major Jan. 1915. France. Wounded at the Battle of Loos on 25th and died on 27th September 1915.

BARTLEMAN, THOMAS EDWARD (*b.* 1897).
  George Watson's College; First XI. O.T.C. 1909-14, Cadet Corporal (Piper). Edinburgh University O.T.C. Infantry, Nov. 1914 to Nov. 1915, Cadet. 5th Royal Scots, Private Nov. 1915. 5th Seaforth Highlanders, 2nd Lieut. April 1917. France June 1917. Killed in action on 6th September 1917. Pl. VI.

BAXENDINE, JOHN YOUNG (*b.* 1893).
  George Watson's College. Edinburgh University O.T.C. Infantry, March 1914 to April 1915, Cadet. 1st Border Regiment, 2nd Lieut. April 1915. Suvla Bay, Dardanelles, Sept. 1915; Egypt and France. Killed in action in France on 1st July 1916. Pl. VI.

BAXTER, ALEXANDER KIDD (*b.* 1869).
  Student of Medicine, 1896-1902; M.B., Ch.B. 1902. Medical Officer of the War Office Emigration Agency, Wei-hai-wei, 1917. Died there from typhus on 14th March 1918. Pl. VI.

BAXTER, ANGUS CAMERON (*b.* 1894).
  Rothesay Academy; Hillhead High School, Glasgow. Student of Science, 1912-14. 4th Cameron Highlanders, Private Aug. 1914; 2nd Lieut. Sept. 1915. France. Killed in action at Ypres on 31st July 1917. Pl. VI.

BEATTY, GUY (*b.* 1870).
  Newry Intermediate School and Wesley College, Dublin. Student of Medicine, 1889-94; M.B., C.M. 1894. L.D.S., R.C.S.I. 1908; D.P.H., D.T.M. West African Medical Staff, Medical Officer. South Africa, 1900-2; German Cameroons, 1915. Died at Belfast on 7th February 1916. Pl. VI.

BEDELL-SIVRIGHT, DAVID REVELL (*b.* 1880).
  Fettes College; First XV. B.A. (Cambridge); Student of Medicine, 1905-10; M.B., Ch.B. 1910. Rugby Scottish International, 22 "Caps." Royal Navy, Fleet Surgeon, 1914. Dardanelles April 1915. Died of acute septicæmia on 5th September 1915. Pl. VII.

PLATE VI.

C. D. OGILVY BARRIE.

W. C. OGILVY BARRIE.

R. G. BANNERMAN.

I. C. C. BARCLAY.

T. E. BARTLEMAN.

J. Y. BAXENDINE.

A. KIDD BAXTER.

ANGUS C. BAXTER.

GUY BEATTY.

PLATE VII.

WILLIAM BEGG.

D. R. BEDELL-SIVRIGHT.

C. M. BEGG.

J. H. BEILBY.

A. HERBERT BELL.

A. M^C. BELL.

T. H. S. BELL.

J. A. TERRAS BELL.

J. MURRAY BELL.

Roll of the Fallen

BEGG, CHARLES MACKIE (*b.* 1879).
    Otago High School, N.Z. Student of Medicine, 1898-1905; M.B., Ch.B. 1903; M.D. 1905; F.R.C.S. (Edin.) 1906; F.R.C.P. 1915. N.Z. Medical Corps, Captain 1907; Colonel and A.D.M.S. 1914; D.D.M.S. Oct. 1916. Gallipoli 1915. France. C.M.G. Nov. 1915; C.B. Jan. 1918. Croix de Guerre, second Battle of the Marne, 1918. Died of pneumonia at Twickenham on 2nd February 1919.   Pl. VII.

BEGG, WILLIAM (*b.* 1889).
    Brechin High School. Student of Law, 1909. Law Agent. 5th Royal Highlanders (Black Watch) Sergeant Aug. 1914; 2nd Lieut. Summer 1915. France. Nov. 1914. Killed in action at Beaumont Hamel on 13th November 1916. Pl. VII.

BEILBY, JULIUS HENRY (*b.* 1868).
    Edinburgh Collegiate School. Student of Medicine, 1885-9; M.B., C.M. 1889. R.A.M.C. (T.), attached Worcester Yeomanry, Captain Nov. 1914. Dispatches June 1917. Killed in action at Katia, Egypt, on 23rd April 1916.   Pl. VII.

BELL, ALFRED HERBERT (*b.* 1880).
    George Watson's College. Student of Law, 1898. Chartered Accountant, 1904. Royal Scots (College Coy.) 1898-1906, Sergeant. 8th Royal Scots, 2nd Lieut. 1906; Captain 1911. 11th Royal Scots, Captain Nov. 1914. France May 1915. Wounded in July 1915. Missing, reported killed at Loos on 25th September 1915.   Pl. VII.

BELL, ARCHIBALD McCUTCHEON (*b.* 1899).
    Royal High School. Edinburgh University O.T.C. Infantry, Feb. to Nov. 1917, Cadet. Royal Air Force, Nov. 1917; Pilot Nov. 1918. Died of influenza and pneumonia on 29th March 1919.   Pl. VII.

BELL, JAMES ALEXANDER TERRAS (*b.* 1871).
    Grammar Schools in New Zealand. Student of Medicine, 1891-5; M.B., C.M. 1895; M.D. 1902. N.Z. Medical Corps, Captain Aug. 1914. Egypt. Died of apoplexy at Cairo on 29th December 1914.   Pl. VII.

BELL, JOHN MURRAY (*b.* 1882).
    George Watson's College; Glenalmond. Cadet Corps 1896-8. Student of Law, 1902-3. Chartered Accountant, 1905. O.T.C. Infantry, June 1909 to Dec. 1914; Captain 1913. Barry Officers' Camp, Aug. to Sept. 1914. 9th Royal Highlanders (Black Watch); Captain Dec. 1914. France July 1915. Killed in action on 25th September 1915 near Loos.   Pl. VII.

BELL, THOMAS HENRY STANLEY (*b.* 1890).
    High School, Dunfermline. Student of Medicine, 1909-15; M.B., Ch.B. 1914. O.T.C. Medical, Oct. 1912 to Sept. 1914; Cadet. R.A.M.C. (S.R.), Lieut.; Captain. France. Killed in action on 1st October 1915 near Vermelles. Pl. VII.

BENTLEY, CHARLES ARTHUR CAMPBELL (*b.* 1878).
    Student of Medicine. Edin. City Vol. Art. Univ. Coy. Scots Greys, Private 1896; Corporal. South African Campaign, 1898-1901. 1st Royal Warwickshire Regiment, Captain. Killed in action at Armentières on 23rd October 1914. Pl. XCII.

Roll of the Fallen

BEST, STEPHEN WRIOTHESLEY (*b.* 1889).
    Christ College, Brecon. Student of Law, 1912-14. O.T.C. Infantry, Jan. 1913 to Oct. 1914, Cadet. 4th (Brecknockshire) and 7th South Wales Borderers, 2nd Lieut. Sept. 1914; Lieut. Aug. 1916. Aden 1914; India 1915; Mesopotamia 1916. Dispatches Oct. 1917. Wounded March 1917. Killed at Battle of Bund-i-Adhaim, Mesopotamia, on 30th April 1917.   Pl. VIII.

BEVERIDGE, DAVID ALEXANDER (*b.* 1886).
    Loretto; First XV. and Hockey XI. B.A. (Cambridge) 1908. Student of Law, 1908-9. O.T.C. Infantry, Sept. to Oct. 1914. R.F.A., 54th Brigade, 2nd Lieut. Oct. 1914. Gallipoli 1915. Died of dysentery at Malta on 13th September 1915.   Pl. VIII.

BEZUIDENHOUT, PETER H. S.
    Student of Medicine, 1914-15. O.T.C. Artillery, Oct. 1914 to Aug. 1915, Cadet. R.F.A. (S.R.), 2nd Lieut. Aug. 1915. France. M.C. Killed in action in 1917.
     Pl. XCIV.

BINGHAM, JOHN WARNOCK (*b.* 1880).
    Campbell and Queen's Colleges, Belfast. Student of Medicine, 1899-1907. M.B., Ch.B. 1907. R.A.M.C., 10th Field Ambulance, Lieut. Feb. 1915; Captain. Died on service 1919.

BINKS, HERBERT WALTER (*b.* 1884).
    Exeter College. Student of Medicine, 1900-7; M.B., Ch.B. 1907. R.A.M.C., Lieut. May 1915; Captain May 1916. Died from pneumonia following influenza in October 1918.   Pl. VIII.

BINNING, WILLIAM BARCLAY (*b.* 1896).
    Dunfermline High School; Dux. Student of Medicine, 1914-15. O.T.C. Infantry, Oct. to Dec. 1914, Cadet. Scottish Rifles 2nd Lieut. Dec. 1914. Died of wounds on 24th April 1916.   Pl. VIII.

BIRNIE, ROBERT (*b.* 1881).
    Mount Pleasant, Gretna, and Girvan Schools. Student of Arts and Science, 1906-15; M.A. 1911; B.Sc. 1915. R.E. (Special Brigade), March 1916, Pioneer. France. Died of gas poisoning on 28th June 1916.   Pl. VIII.

BIRRELL, GEORGE HENRY GORDON (*b.* 1893).
    Loretto. Edinburgh University O.T.C. Artillery, Jan. to Dec. 1911, Cadet. 9th Argyll and Sutherland Highlanders (T.), 2nd Lieut. Nov. 1914. France Feb. 1915. Killed at the second Battle of Ypres on 10th May 1915.   Pl. VIII.

BIRRELL, WILLIAM GEORGE (*b.* 1860).
    Edinburgh Academy. Student of Medicine; M.B., C.M. 1880. R.A.M.C., Surgeon 1881; Major-General (Retired). Sudan, Burmah, Egypt, Nile Campaigns. Surgeon-General, Dardanelles, 1915. D.D.M.S., Salisbury. Dispatches (Burmah). Died at Lochboisdale on 23rd August 1918.   Pl. VIII.

PLATE VIII.

H. W. BINKS.

D. A. BEVERIDGE.

STEPHEN W. BEST.

W. B. BINNING.

D. C. BLACK.

ROBERT BIRNIE.

WM. G. BIRRELL.

G. H. G. BIRRELL.

ANDREW BLACK.

PLATE IX.

John Black.

E. J. Blair.

John Blair.

G. S. Blandy.

P. A. Blair.

William Blair.

P. Dick Booth.

G. V. Bogle.

F. Borda.

Roll of the Fallen

BLACK, ANDREW (*b.* 1896).
Royal High School. Student of Arts, 1915-16. Orkney and Zetland Bursar. O.T.C. Infantry, Oct. 1915 to March 1916, Cadet. 7th Seaforth Highlanders, April 1916, Private. Killed at the Battle of Arras on 9th April 1917. Pl. VIII.

BLACK, DAVID CHRISTIE (*b.* 1889).
Alva Academy and Dollar Institution. Student of Arts and Law, 1908-10; M.A. 1910; LL.B. 1911. O.T.C. Infantry, Oct. 1908 to Jan. 1912, Cadet. Barrister in Calgary, Alberta. 10th Battalion Canadian Infantry, Private Aug. 1914; Lieut. July 1915; Captain Aug. 1916; Acting Major. M.C. Dispatches April 1917. Killed in action on 28th April 1917. Pl. VIII.

BLACK, JOHN (*b.* 1894).
Edinburgh Academy. Student of Law, 1913-14. 4th Royal Scots, Private Aug. 1914. 6th Battalion Tank Corps, 2nd Lieut. April 1917; Lieut. 1918. Gallipoli, Egypt, and France. Dispatches Nov. 1917. Wounded twice at Cambrai Nov. 1917. Wounded again and died on 23rd August 1918 at Courcelles. Pl. IX.

BLACK, MAURICE CHARLES OSBORNE (*b.* 1894).
Merchiston Castle. O.T.C. 1909-12. Edinburgh University O.T.C. Infantry, Sept. 1914, Cadet. 7th Border Regiment, attached Trench Mortar Battery, Lieut. Sept. 1914. France. Killed in action on the Somme on 24th August 1916.

BLAIR, EDWARD JAMES (*b.* 1885).
Kirkcaldy High School. Student of Medicine, 1909-14; M.B., Ch.B. 1914. 5th Royal Scots (T.), Captain. R.A.M.C., Lieut.; Captain 1915. Wounded 1915 and 1916. M.C. Nov. 1916. Killed in action in April 1917. Pl. IX.

BLAIR, JOHN (*b.* 1889).
Ardrossan Academy. Cadet Corps. First XI. Student of Arts and Science, 1907-12; M.A. 1910; B.Sc. 1912. 6th Royal Scots (College Coy.) for four years, Private. 8th, 2/8th, and 20th Durham Light Infantry, March 1915; 2nd Lieut. Nov. 1915; temp. Captain May 1916; Lieut. Oct. 1918. France. Wounded twice in April 1918. Wounded on the 2nd and died of wounds on the 12th of October 1918. Pl. IX.

BLAIR, PATRICK ALEXANDER (*b.* 1880).
Sedbergh. Student of Law, 1900-1. Chartered Accountant, 1904. 9th Royal Scots previous to 1914; Captain Dec. 1912. France 1915. Dispatches 1916. M.C. 1917. Killed in action on 23rd April 1917. Pl. IX.

BLAIR, WILLIAM (*b.* 1893).
George Heriot's School. Student of Law, 1914. 2/9th Royal Scots, Private 1914. 8th Seaforth Highlanders, 2nd Lieut. March 1915. Killed in action on 23rd April 1917. Pl. IX.

BLANDY, GURTH SWINNERTON (*b.* 1878).
Sheffield Royal Grammar School. Student of Medicine, 1895-1902; M.B., Ch.B. 1902; M.D. 1912. R.A.M.C., Lieut.; Captain. M.C. Died of wounds in May 1917. Pl. IX.

Roll of the Fallen

BOGLE, GILBERT VERE (*b.* 1884).
    Napier High School. B.A. (New Zealand). Student of Medicine, 1908-12; Buchanan Scholar. M.B., Ch.B. 1912. Athletics. O.T.C. Artillery, Feb. 1909 to April 1910, Cadet Bombardier. R.A.M.C. (S.R.), Lieut. April 1910. N.Z. Medical Corps, attached 1st Battalion N.Z. Rifle Brigade, Jan. 1915; Captain. Killed in action on 17th September 1916.   Pl. IX.

BOOTH, PATRICK DICK (*b.* 1886).
    Daniel Stewart's College; First XV. Student of Science, 1902-7; B.Sc. 1907. Trevelyan Scholar. Edin. City Art. Vol. Univ. Coy. 1906-8. Canadian R.A., 32nd Howitzer Battery, Lieut. R.F.A., 2nd Lieut. Aug. 1914; Lieut. Jan. 1915; Captain. Gallipoli, 29th Division, 1915-16. France 1916-17; Somme, Arras, Ypres, and Cambrai. M.C. June 1915. Dispatches Nov. 1915 and May 1918. D.S.O. (posthumous) Cambrai 1917. Wounded at Dardanelles and Cambrai. Died of wounds near Les Rues Vertes on 1st December 1917.   Pl. IX.

BORDA, FORTUNATO (*b.* 1898.)
    Student of Medicine, 1915-17. O.T.C. Infantry, May 1915 to June 1917, Cadet. Enlisted Feb. 1917, Private; L/Corporal. Killed in action in France on 28th September 1918.   Pl. IX.

BOSWALL, JAMES DONALDSON (*b.* 1870).
    Edinburgh Academy and Fettes College; First XV. Student of Law, 1890-4. Writer to the Signet, 1894. Q.R.V.B. Mtd. Infantry, 1893-8. C.I.V. Mtd. Infantry, South African Campaign 1900-2. 9th Royal Scots, Private Sept. 1914. 10th Seaforth Highlanders, attached 1st Essex Regiment; Captain Jan. 1915. Killed in action at Gallipoli on 6th June 1915.   Pl. X.

BOTHA, THE RIGHT HON. LOUIS (*b.* 1863).
    LL.D. 1907. Privy Council. Premier of the Union of South Africa. Commander-in-Chief of the Boer Forces, 1899-1903. General in British Army. Commander of the Union Forces in German South-West Africa, 1914-15. Died of influenza on 26th August 1919.   Pl. X.

BOW, JOHN MACKENZIE (*b.* 1863).
    Loretto. Student of Law, 1880. Q.R.V.B. Royal Scots, 2nd Lieut. 1887. 10th Canadian Exp. Force, Private. Killed in action in France on 15th August 1917.   Pl. X.

BOWHILL, JAMES SHOLTO ELLIOT (*b.* 1888).
    George Watson's College. Student of Law, 1908-13. Chartered Accountant, 1913. 9th Royal Scots, Private May 1916. France. Died of wounds on 1st June 1917.   Pl. X.

BRASH, JAMES (*b.* 1893).
    West Calder and Boroughmuir Schools. Student of Arts, 1911-14; M.A. 1914. 16th Royal Scots, Private 1914. Seaforth Highlanders, Captain. France. Dispatches 1917. D.S.O. April 1917; M.C. (posthumous) Dec. 1918. Died of wounds at Wimereux on 9th November 1918.   Pl. X.

PLATE X.

J. M. Bow.   J. D. Boswall.   Louis Botha.

J. S. E. Bowhill.   James Brash.   George Bremner.

J. H. Brink.   G. S. Brock.   Alex. Brook.

PLATE XI.

A. C. BROWN.

D. D. BROWN.

D. M. BROWN.

G. L. BROWN.

JOHN BROWN.
12th Highland Light Infantry.

JOHN BROWN.
4th Royal Scots.

WM. S. BROWN.

WILLIAM BROWN.

WILLIAM BROWNLIE.

Roll of the Fallen

BREMNER, GEORGE (b. 1893).
    Grove Academy, Broughty-Ferry. Student of Science, 1910-13; B.Sc. 1913. R.E. 80th Field Coy., 2nd Lieut. Oct. 1914; Lieut. July 1915; Captain Sept. 1916; Major Jan. 1917. Dispatches Nov. 1917 and April 1918. M.C. July 1916; D.S.O. March 1918. Killed in action on 23rd March 1918.   Pl. X.

BRINK, JOHANNES HIERONYMUS (b. 1893).
    Somerset West School; South African College, Cape Town. Student of Medicine, 1912-14. O.T.C. Artillery, Oct. 1913 to Oct. 1914, Cadet. R.F.A., 2nd Lieut. Aug. 1914; Lieut. July 1915. Royal Flying Corps, Jan. 1916. France; St Julien, St Jean, Hill 60, and second Ypres. Dispatches. Wounded Aug. and Nov. 1915. Wounded at Cambrai on 9th and died on 11th April 1917.   Pl. X.

BROCK, GEORGE SELBY (b. 1886).
    Uppingham; First XV. St Andrews University; First XV. Student of Medicine, 1904-10; M.B., Ch.B. 1910. O.T.C. Infantry, Feb. 1909 to Jan. 1911, Cadet Corporal. Indian Medical Service, attached 9th Bhopal Infantry; Captain. France 1914. Dispatches (Givenchy). Died at Rawal Pindi on 12th October 1918.   Pl. X.

BROOK, ALEXANDER (b. 1865).
    Knox Institute, Haddington. Student of Arts, 1883-7; M.A. 1887. Writer to the Signet, 1891. 8th Royal Scots, June 1886. Mobilised Aug. 1914, Major; Lieut.-Colonel. France Nov. 1914. Dispatches. Died of wounds in France on 21st May 1915.   Pl. X.

BROWN, ARCHIBALD CAMPBELL (b. 1884).
    Royal High School; First XV. and XI. Student of Law, 1902-5. Writer to the Signet, 1908. R.F.A., 2nd Lieut. Dec. 1915; Lieut. June 1916. 95th Battery, France, Sept. 1916. Killed in action at Berry-au-Bac on the Aisne on 27th May 1918.   Pl. XI.

BROWN, DAVID DOUGLAS (b. 1894).
    Broughton and George Heriot's Schools. O.T.C. 1909-11, Cadet L/Corporal. Student of Arts and Divinity, 1911-14; M.A. 1915. 6th Royal Scots, 1912-14, Private. 13th Royal Scots, 2nd Lieut. Dec. 1914. France. Killed in action on 26th September 1915.   Pl. XI.

BROWN, DONALD MORTON (b. 1897).
    Daniel Stewart's College; Dux. Student of Arts, 1914-15. Jamieson Bursar. O.T.C. Infantry, Oct. 1914 to July 1915, Cadet. 2/7th Lancashire Fusiliers, 2nd Lieut. July 1915. 8th, 7th, 3rd and 1st Battns. Cameron Highlanders, Lieut. July 1917. France 1916. Wounded at Arras April 1917. Killed in action near Vaux-Andigny on 17th October 1918.   Pl. XI.

Roll of the Fallen

BROWN, G. L. (*b.* 1886).
    Bedford County and University College School. Student of Medicine, 1906-7. 14th London Regiment (London Scottish), Private Sept. 1914. 10th and 1st Loyal North Lancashire Regiment, 2nd Lieut. Nov. 1914; Lieut. April 1917. France March 1917. Killed in action at Passchendaele on 15th November 1917.   Pl. XI.

BROWN, JOHN (*b.* 1884).
    Dalkeith High School. Student of Arts, 1904-6. 4th Royal Scots, Private Sept. 1914; Corporal; 2nd Lieut. May 1917; Lieut. Nov. 1918. Palestine and Egypt. Invalided home Feb. 1919 and died on 27th June 1919.   Pl. XI.

BROWN, JOHN (*b.* 1889).
    North Berwick and Dairsie Schools. Student of Arts, 1908-11; M.A. 1911. 16th Royal Scots, Private Dec. 1914; L/Corporal May 1916. 12th Highland Light Infantry, 2nd Lieut. June 1917. France. Died of wounds on 26th March 1918.   Pl. XI.

BROWN, WILLIAM (*b.* 1889).
    Boroughmuir School. Student of Arts, 1908-12; M.A. 1912. Shooting XI. 1911. 6th Royal Scots, Sergeant Aug. 1914; 2nd Lieut. April 1915; Lieut. 1917; Acting Captain. Egypt. Killed in action on 11th August 1918.   Pl. XI.

BROWN, WILLIAM SANDILANDS (*b.* 1891).
    High School, Glasgow; Athletics. M.A. (Glasgow) 1912. Student of Law, 1912-14. 15th Royal Scots, Private Sept. 1914. 3rd North Staffordshire Regiment, 2nd Lieut. March 1915; Lieut. Jan. 1916; Captain July 1917. France Feb. 1916. Killed in action in Flanders on 14th October 1918.   Pl. XI.

BROWNLIE, WILLIAM (*b.* 1881).
    High School, Invercargill, N.Z. M.A., B.Sc. (New Zealand). Student of Medicine, 1911-16; M.B., Ch.B. 1915. R.A.M.C., attached 13th Yorkshire Regiment; Captain Jan. 1917. France. M.C. (posthumous) for gallantry near Cambrai, Nov. 1917. Killed in action on 25th March 1918.   Pl. XI.

BRUCE, ALEXANDER CHARLES ARBUTHNOT (*b.* 1899).
    Edinburgh Academy. Student of Science, 1911-12; Mem. Inst. Mech. Eng., 1914. A.S.C. 1/1st Lowland Mounted Brigade, T. and S. Column, Jan. 1910; Lieut. 1914; Captain Jan. 1915. Mediterranean Sept. 1915; Gallipoli, Cape Helles, Mudros and Egypt. Dispatches (Egypt) June 1916. Killed in action on 23rd April 1916 at El Derweidar, Suez.   Pl. XII.

BRUCE, JOHN RUSSELL (*b.* 1884).
    Edinburgh Academy. Student of Law; M.A. 1907, LL.B. 1910; Advocate, 1911. O.T.C. Infantry, May 1907 to Oct. 1914; Captain and O.C. 1912. 15th Royal Scots, Major Dec. 1914. France. Killed in action at La Boiselle on 1st July 1916.   Pl. XII.

PLATE XII.

J. R. BRUCE.

GEORGE BRUNTON.

A. C. A. BRUCE.

J. M. BRUNTON.

J. E. BRYDON.

R. B. BUCHANAN.

E. H. BURGH.

J. RATTRAY BURNS.

R. M. BUNCLE.

PLATE XIII.

A. B. BURTON. R. M. BURNS. R. BURNS-BEGG.

WM. A. CAIRNS. G. M. CAIRNS. E. T. CAIRD.

JOHN HUNTER CAMERON. JAMES M. CAMERON. JAMES HUNTER CAMERON.

Roll of the Fallen

BRUCE, VINCENT CONNELL (*b.* 1888).
> George Watson's College. B.A. (Oxford). Student of Law, 1911-13; LL.B. 1913; Advocate, 1914. O.T.C. Infantry, Nov. 1911 to June 1914. 15th and 13th Royal Scots, Private Sept. 1914; 2nd Lieut.; Lieut. 1/5th Gordon Highlanders. France. Killed at Neuville St Vaast on 26th March 1916.

BRUNTON, GEORGE (*b.* 1881).
> Daniel Stewart's College. Edinburgh University O.T.C. Infantry, Aug. to Sept. 1915, Cadet. 4th and 8th Royal Scots, 2nd Lieut. Sept. 1915; Lieut. Jan. 1917. France. Died of wounds on 11th April 1918. Pl. XII.

BRUNTON, JAMES MACLEOD (*b.* 1885).
> Daniel Stewart's College. Edinburgh University O.T.C. Infantry, Oct. 1915 to March 1916, Cadet; Officer Cadet March 1916. 6th attached 4th Royal Scots, 2nd Lieut. Aug. 1916. Egypt Nov. 1916; Palestine. Killed in action on 1st August 1917 near Gaza. Pl. XII.

BRYDON, JOHN EARNSCLEUGH (*b.* 1886).
> Darlington; Richmond School, Yorks. Student of Medicine, 1903-8; M.B., Ch.B. 1908. R.A.M.C. (Vol.) Univ. Coy., 1904-8; R.A.M.C., Lieut.; Captain Jan. 1914. Attached Northumbrian Division, Ammunition Column. Gassed and died in France on 27th June 1917. Pl. XII.

BUCHANAN, RICHARD BRENDAN (*b.* 1894).
> Foyle College, Londonderry; Bedford Grammar School. O.T.C. 1909-11. Student of Medicine, 1911-14. O.T.C. Medical, Oct. 1911 to Sept. 1914. 5th Royal Scots Fusiliers, 2nd Lieut. Aug. 1914. Killed in action in Gallipoli on 20th June 1915. Pl. XII.

BUNCLE, RONALD MACDONALD (*b.* 1896).
> Epsom College. O.T.C. 1909-12. Student of Medicine, 1913-15. O.T.C. Artillery, Oct. 1914 to Oct. 1915, Cadet. R.F.A., 2nd Lieut. Sept. 1915. Died of injuries at Edinburgh on 16th October 1916. Pl. XII.

BURGH, EDWARD HENRY (*b.* 1896).
> Kendal Grammar School; St Bees School, Cumberland. Student of Medicine, 1914-15. O.T.C. Artillery, May to Sept. 1915, Cadet. R.F.A., 4th East Lancashire Brigade, 2nd Lieut. Sept. 1915; Lieut. 223rd Brigade, attached Royal Naval Division, France and Flanders. M.C. Oct. 1917. Died of wounds near Ruyualcourt in France on 4th January 1918. Pl. XII.

BURNS, JAMES RATTRAY (*b.* 1888).
> Student of Law, 1907-8. Solicitor. R.F.C., 2nd Lieut. Sept. 1914; Lieut. April 1915. M.C. April 1917. Accidentally killed in June 1918. Pl. XII.

BURNS, RICHARD MORRIS (*b.* 1881).
> Royal High School. Student of Law, 1901-4. Writer to the Signet, 1905. 3rd Royal Scots Fusiliers, Private Aug. 1914; Corporal. France Nov. 1914. Killed in action at Neuve Chapelle in March 1915. Pl. XIII.

Roll of the Fallen

BURNS-BEGG, ROBERT (*b.* 1872).
  Stranraer School, Bournemouth. M.A. 1892. Advocate, 1895. King's Counsel, Transvaal. South African Campaign, 1899-1902. Transvaal Police, Colonel 1908. W.O., General Staff, Colonel 1915. Town Commandant, Folkestone. Dispatches Feb. 1917. Died at Edinburgh on 9th January 1918. Pl. XIII.

BURTON, ALEXANDER BROWN (*b.* 1888).
  Newton School, Dalkeith. Student of Arts and Science; M.A. 1910; B.Sc. 1912. 14th Highland Light Infantry, attached 13th East Surrey Regiment, Private Nov. 1914; 2nd Lieut. Dec. 1914; Lieut.; Captain. France June 1916. M.C. Missing, presumed killed, on 9th April 1918. Pl. XIII.

CAIRD, ERNEST THOMSON (*b.* 1898).
  George Watson's College O.T.C., 1912-16; Edinburgh University O.T.C. Infantry, June 1916 to Jan. 1917, Cadet. 11th Royal Scots, 2nd Lieut. March 1917. France June 1917. Killed in action near Combles on 24th March 1918. Pl. XIII.

CAIRNS, GEORGE MORTON (*b.* 1881).
  Edinburgh Academy. B.A. (Oxford) 1905. Student of Law, 1905-8. Writer to the Signet, 1908. A.S.C. (M.T.), Private June 1915; Corporal. Royal Highlanders (Black Watch), 2nd Lieut. Nov. 1915. France Sept. 1916. Killed at Beaumont Hamel on 13th November 1916. Pl. XIII.

CAIRNS, WILLIAM ANDERSON (*b.* 1892).
  George Watson's College. Student of Science, 1911-15. 15th attached 17th Royal Scots, 2nd Lieut. Sept. 1915; Lieut. Dec. 1915. France June 1916. Killed in action at Cambrai on 30th September 1918. Pl. XIII.

CALVERT, WILLIAM HALL (*b.* 1862).
  Royal High School. Student of Medicine, 1878-82; M.D. 1889. R.A.M.C., attached 2/6th Seaforth Highlanders, Lieut. April 1915; Captain. Died at London on 16th June 1917. Pl. XCII.

CAMERON, JAMES HUNTER (*b.* 1895).
  Morrison's Academy, Crieff; Dollar Institution. O.T.C. Sept. 1909 to April 1914, Cadet Sergeant. Student of Medicine, 1913-14. O.T.C. Infantry, April to Sept. 1914, Cadet. 9th Royal Highlanders (Black Watch), 2nd Lieut. Sept. 1914; Lieut. Dec. 1914. Gallipoli and France. Killed at Loos on 25th September 1915. Pl. XIII.

CAMERON, JAMES M. (*b.* 1890).
  Glen Urquhart and Strichen Schools. Student of Arts, 1908-11. O.T.C. Artillery, Dec. 1908 to Nov. 1913, Cadet. R.F.A., Lieut. Aug. 1914. Gallipoli 1915, 29th Division. Killed in action at the Dardanelles on 7th May 1915. Pl. XIII.

Roll of the Fallen

CAMERON, JOHN HUNTER (*b.* 1888).
    Cheltenham College. Student of Science, 1905-10; B.Sc. 1910. O.T.C. Infantry, May 1909 to 1910, Cadet. Civil Engineer, India. I. A. Reserve of Officers, attached 5th Light Infantry, 2nd Lieut. Aug. 1914; Lieut. East Africa. Dispatches Aug. 1918. Died at Fatehgarh, India, from pneumonia following malaria, on 14th March 1918.   Pl. XIII.

CAMERON, ROBERT ALLAN (*b.* 1889).
    Royal High School; Dux. Student of Arts, 1906-10; M.A. (Hons. Classics) 1910; B.A. (Oxford) 1914. 7th Cameron Highlanders, Sergeant Sept. 1914. France. Missing since September 1915.   Pl. XIV.

CAMERON, WILLIAM MACKENZIE (*b.* 1891).
    Daniel Stewart's College; Merchiston Castle; Shooting VIII.; First XV. O.T.C., 1905-11, Cadet Sergeant. Student of Arts, 1910-14; M.A. 1915. O.T.C. Infantry, Dec. 1911 to Aug. 1913, Cadet Sergeant. 1st Cameron Highlanders (S.R.), 2nd Lieut. Aug. 1913; Lieut. June 1915. France Aug. 1914. Wounded at Loos on 25th Sept. and died at London on 27th October 1915.   Pl. XIV.

CAMPBELL, ALEXANDER (*b.* 1891).
    Anderson Institute, Lerwick; School Champion. Gordon Highlanders (Vol.), Private 1907-8. Student of Arts, 1908-12; M.A. (Hons. Classics) 1912. O.T.C. Artillery, Nov. 1909 to April 1912, Cadet. Volunteered, medically unfit, Aug. 1914. Royal Scots, Private July 1917. R.G.A. Gunner. Died of influenza at Plymouth on 9th November 1918.   Pl. XIV.

CAMPBELL, ALEXANDER CHARLES PENN (*b.* 1894).
    City of London School; First XI; First "Fives." O.T.C. 1909-13, Cadet Sergeant. Student of Arts, 1913-14. O.T.C. Infantry, Oct. 1913 to Sept. 1914, Cadet. 9th East Surrey Regiment, 2nd Lieut. Sept. 1914; Lieut. France. Killed at Hulluch on 28th September 1915.   Pl. XIV.

CAMPBELL, DANIEL G. (*b.* 1888).
    Miller Institution, Thurso. Student of Law, 1909-10. Scottish High Jump Champion, 1910-13. Rugby and Hockey International. Barrister in Canada. 16th Canadian Regiment, Captain Aug. 1915. France. Wounded at the Battle of the Somme. Killed in action on 9th April 1917.   Pl. XIV.

CAMPBELL, DONALD (*b.* 1887).
    Pitlochry; George Watson's College. Student of Arts and Medicine, 1906-13; M.A. 1910; M.B., Ch.B. 1913. Macdougall Bursar in Arts; Vans Dunlop Scholar in Medicine. O.T.C. Infantry, May 1909 to Feb. 1912, Cadet. R.A.M.C., attached 2nd East Yorkshire Regiment, Lieut. Dec. 1914. Killed in action in France on 17th February 1915.   Pl. XIV.

Roll of the Fallen

CAMPBELL, EWEN JOHN (*b.* 1891).
George Heriot's School. Student of Medicine, 1911-14. Scottish Horse Field Amb., Private; Corporal Sept. 1914. 3rd Argyll and Sutherland Highlanders (S.R.), 2nd Lieut. Jan. 1915. Died at Cape Town on 21st February 1917. Pl. XIV.

CAMPBELL, ROBERT BURNS (*b.* 1893).
Christ's Hospital. Student of Science, 1911-14. O.T.C. Infantry, May 1912 to Oct. 1914, Cadet. 5th King's Own Scottish Borderers, 2nd Lieut. Dec. 1914; Lieut. Killed in action on 3rd May 1917. Pl. XIV.

CAMPBELL, ROBERT GILLIES (*b.* 1868).
Blairlodge. Student of Law, 1887-92. Writer to the Signet, 1893. 10th Seaforth Highlanders, Captain Aug. 1914; Major. Died at Cromarty on 1st February 1915.

CAMPBELL, WILLIAM BARTON (*b.* 1890).
Lockerbie Academy. Student of Arts and Divinity, 1909-15; M.A. 1913. O.T.C. Infantry, Oct. 1910 to Feb. 1914, Cadet. Probationer, Church of Scotland. 2/5th King's Own Scottish Borderers, 2nd Lieut. May 1915. Killed in action on 19th April 1917. Pl. XIV.

CARMICHAEL, ANDREW (*b.* 1897).
Lasswade School. Student of Arts, 1915-16. 3/9th Royal Scots, Private April 1917; Officer Cadet Jan. 1918. King's Own Scottish Borderers, 2nd Lieut. May 1918. Killed in action on 12th October 1918. Pl. XV.

CARMICHAEL, ANDREW GEMMELL (*b.* 1894).
Student of Medicine, 1910-14. O.T.C. Infantry, June 1911 to July 1914 and Nov. 1915, Cadet. 6th Cameron Highlanders, 2nd Lieut. Killed in action on 11th April 1917. Pl. XV.

CARNAGHAN, JAMES (*b.* 1889).
North Berwick High School. Student of Law, 1912-13. 15th Royal Scots, Private Oct. 1914. 12th Scottish Rifles, 2nd Lieut. Aug. 1915. Wounded and missing on 23rd October 1916. Pl. XV.

CATHCART, FRANCIS JOHN (*b.* 1894).
Loretto. Student of Science, 1912-14. O.T.C. Artillery, March 1913 to Oct. 1914, Cadet Bombardier. R.F.A., 2nd Lieut. Aug. 1914. Gallipoli; Egypt. Killed in action in Mesopotamia on 3rd June 1916. Pl. XV.

CATTANACH, JOHN (*b.* 1885).
Newtonmore and Kingussie Schools; George Watson's College. Student of Arts and Medicine, 1903-12; M.A. 1907; M.B., Ch.B. 1912. Australasian Cup. International Hockey; Long Jump. R.A.M.C., attached Warwickshire Regiment, Lieut. Sept. 1914. Dardanelles. Died of wounds in July 1915.
Pl. XV.

PLATE XIV.

Wm. M. Cameron.

R. A. Cameron.

Alex. Campbell.

Donald Campbell.

A. C. P. Campbell.

D. G. Campbell.

W. B. Campbell.

R. Burns Campbell.

E. J. Campbell.

PLATE XV.

Andrew Carmichael.

James Carnaghan.

A. G. Carmichael.

S. McA. F. Cesari.

F. J. Cathcart.

John Cattanach.

Harry Cheyne.

Eric Chalker.

J. J. P. Charles.

Roll of the Fallen

CENTER, WILLIAM RUDOLPH (*b.* 1870).
    Aberdeen Grammar School; Charterhouse; Aberdeen University. Student of Medicine, 1889-93; M.B., C.M. 1893. M.R.C.S. (Eng.), L.R.C.P. (Lond.) 1896. Royal Navy, H.M.S. *Russell*, Staff Surgeon, 1896; Fleet Surgeon, 1912. Injured in sinking of H.M.S. *Russell* and died at Malta on 28th April 1916.   Pl. XCII.

CESARI, SYDNEY McALPINE FRASER (*b.* 1889).
    Perth Academy. Student of Medicine, 1907-14; M.B., Ch.B. 1913. O.T.C. Medical, April 1908 to April 1913, Cadet Corporal. R.A.M.C. (S.R.), Lieut. April 1913; Captain July 1915. France Aug. 1914. Killed in action in France on 4th October 1915.   Pl. XV.

CHALKER, ERIC (*b.* 1893).
    Elstow School, Bedford; Oundle. Student of Science, 1911-14. O.T.C. Artillery, Nov. 1912 to Oct. 1914, Cadet Bombardier. R.F.A. (S.R.), 67th Battery, 2nd Lieut. Sept. 1914; Lieut. St Eloi, Ypres, Hooge, Loos, and the Somme. Dispatches April 1915. Wounded at Ypres May 1915. Killed near Caterpillar Wood, the Somme, on 20th July 1916.   Pl. XV.

CHARLES, JOHN JAMES PERCIVAL (*b.* 1884).
    Cork Grammar School. Student of Medicine, 1903-9; M.B., Ch.B. 1909. R.A.M.C., Lieut. Aug. 1914; Captain 1915. France Sept. 1914. First Battle of Ypres. Dispatches 1914. M.C. Died of wounds received at the third Battle of Ypres on 6th October 1917.   Pl. XV.

CHEYNE, HARRY (*b.* 1882).
    Edinburgh Academy; First XV. B.A. (Oxford) 1905. Student of Law, 1905-8. Writer to the Signet, 1908. R.F.A., 1st Lowland Brigade, 2nd Lieut. 1909; Lieut. Mobilised Aug. 1914; Captain Dec. 1916; Major April 1917; Lieut.-Colonel 1917. France Oct. 1915. Killed in action on 10th July 1917.   Pl. XV.

CHILTON, FRANK (*b.* 1892).
    West Christ Church, and Waitaki High Schools, N.Z. Student of Medicine, 1912-14. O.T.C. Infantry, Oct. 1913 to Aug. 1914, Cadet. 3rd and 13th Argyll and Sutherland Highlanders, 2nd Lieut. Aug. 1914; Lieut. Jan. 1915. Attached 2nd Hampshires, 29th Division. Killed in action at Gallipoli on 4th June 1915.
  Pl. XVI.

CHRISTIE, ALLAN LESLIE (*b.* 1887).
    Wanganui College, N.Z. Student of Medicine, 1906-12; M.B., Ch.B. 1912. R.A.M.C., Lieut. France. Died of influenza in 1919.   Pl. XVI.

CHRISTIE, ROBERT MAIN (*b.* 1865).
    Dunblane School, and High School, Stirling. Student of Arts, 1882-4. Association "Blue" and International, 1884 and 1885; International Curler. Solicitor. Royal Highlanders (Black Watch), Lieut. South African War, 1899-1902. 13th Highland Light Infantry, attached 8th Royal Scots Fusiliers, Captain 1914; Major 1915. Killed in France on 15th May 1918.

Roll of the Fallen

CLARK, CHARLES INGLIS (*b.* 1889).
George Watson's College. Student of Science, 1905-10; B.Sc. 1910. O.T.C. Artillery, Oct. 1908 to May 1910 and Aug. 1914, Cadet. A.S.C. (M.T.), 2nd Lieut. Sept. 1914; Lieut. Jan. 1915; Captain Dec. 1915. France Sept. 1914 to May 1916. Admiralty, 1916-17. Mesopotamia from Sept. 1917. Dispatches 1915. Wounded at Givenchy Dec. 1914; died of wounds at Baghdad on 6th March 1918. Pl. XVI.

CLARK, GEORGE MACKAY (*b.* 1895).
George Watson's College. O.T.C. 1909-13, Cadet Sergeant. Student of Medicine, 1912-14. O.T.C. Artillery, April 1913 to Oct. 1914, Cadet. 4th Royal Scots, Lieut. Oct. 1914; Captain June 1915. Gallipoli July 1915; invalided home Oct. 1915. Mediterranean Feb. 1916. Killed in action at Burkah in Palestine on 12th November 1917. Pl. XVI.

CLARK, JAMES (*b.* 1859).
Paisley Grammar School, and Lycée, Pau. M.A. (Glasgow). Student of Law, 1881; LL.B. 1884. King's Counsel. Deputy Lieutenant, City of Edinburgh. 9th Royal Scots, Colonel 1904-12. 9th Argyll and Sutherland Highlanders, Lieut.-Col. Aug. 1914. C.B. (Civil). France. Dispatches 1915. Killed in action at Hooge near Ypres on 10th May 1915. Pl. XVI.

CLARK, JAMES SMITH (*b.* 1880).
Royal High School. Student of Arts and Law, 1897-1902; M.A. 1900; LL.B. 1902; Advocate, 1902. 6th Gordon Highlanders, attached 5th Cameron Highlanders, 2nd Lieut. Sept. 1915. Killed in action on 3rd May 1917. Pl. XVI.

CLARK, SAMUEL CLARKSON (*b.* 1898).
Edinburgh University O.T.C. Infantry, April to Oct. 1916, Cadet. Gordon Highlanders, 2nd Lieut. Feb. 1917; Lieut. July 1918. Wounded on 23rd Aug. 1918 and died at London on 17th September 1918. Pl. XVI.

CLARKE, IAN ALEXANDER MURRAY-MITCHELL (*b.* 1893).
Dunfermline High School; Football. Student of Medicine, 1910-15; M.B., Ch.B. 1915. Association "Half Blue." O.T.C. Infantry, Oct. 1911 to July 1915, Cadet Sergeant. Red Cross Hospital, Rouen, Sept. 1914 to March 1915. R.A.M.C. attached 1st Dorset Regiment, Captain 1915. Killed in action in France on 16th November 1916. Pl. XVI.

CLARKE, JAMES HENRY FISHER (*b.* 1894).
King Edward VII. School, Sheffield. O.T.C. 1908-13, Cadet Sergeant. Edinburgh University O.T.C. Infantry, Oct. to Dec. 1914. 7th Battn. Alexandra Princess of Wales' Yorkshire Regiment, 2nd Lieut. Jan. 1915. France July 1915. Wounded Aug. 1915. Killed at Fricourt, the Somme, on 1st July 1916.

PLATE XVI.

C. Inglis Clark.

Frank Chilton.

A. Leslie Christie.

G. M. Clark.

James Smith Clark.

James Clark.

I. A. M.-M. Clarke.

S. C. Clark.

A. J. Cleghorn.

PLATE XVII.

H. A. CLEMENT.

H. S. CLEGHORN.

T. H. CLOW.

J. A. H. COATS.

G. K. H. COCHRANE.

R. P. COLE.

D. O. CONSTABLE.

P. F. CONSIDINE.

C. F. G. COLES.

Roll of the Fallen

CLEGHORN, ALLAN JAMES (*b.* 1895).
Dundee High School; Dux. Student of Arts, 1913-15. O.T.C. Infantry, Nov. 1913 to March 1915, Cadet Corporal. 11th attached 1st Gordon Highlanders, 2nd Lieut. March 1915. France Sept. 1915. Died of wounds at 58th Casualty Clearing Station on 7th September 1916. Pl. XVI.

CLEGHORN, HERBERT STUART (*b.* 1891).
Dundee High School. Student of Science, 1909-12; B.Sc. 1912. O.T.C. Engineers, 1910-12, Cadet. R.E., attached R.F.C., Oct. 1914; Captain 1915. France. Died of wounds on 2nd September 1917. Pl. XVII.

CLEMENT, HUBERT ARNOLD (*b.* 1893).
Edinburgh Academy; O.T.C. 1908-9; Wellington; Bedford Grammar School. Student of Science, 1910-12. O.T.C. Engineers, 1910-11. 19th Royal Fusiliers, Private Sept. 1914; Sergeant. 3rd attached 8th Royal Highlanders (Black Watch), 2nd Lieut. July 1915. France April 1916. Wounded twice on the Somme July 1916. Dispatches Jan. 1917. Killed in action on 3rd May 1917. Pl. XVII.

CLOW, THOMAS HOWIE (*b.* 1887).
George Heriot's School. Student of Arts, 1908-12; M.A. 1912. 1/6th attached 4th Royal Scots, Private Sept. 1914. Killed in action at Dardanelles on 28th June 1915. Pl. XVII.

COATS, JOHN ALEXANDER HAMILTON (*b.* 1896).
Daniel Stewart's College; Athletics. 1st Highland Cadet Battn. Royal Scots, Coy. Sgt.-Major. Student of Medicine, 1914-15. Royal Navy, March 1915, Chief Petty Officer. 3/10th Royal Scots, 2nd Lieut. Oct. 1915. 2/5th Lancashire Fusiliers, attached 4th Loyal North Lancashire Regiment, 164th Trench Mortar Battery. Missing, believed killed near Ginchy in France on 8th August 1916. Pl. XVII.

COCHRANE, GEORGE KING HICKS (*b.* 1895).
George Watson's College. Student of Arts, 1912-14. 9th Royal Scots, Private Sept. 1914. 1st Highland Light Infantry, 2nd Lieut. Nov. 1915. 1/1st Gurkha Rifles, Jan. 1917. Severely wounded in Mesopotamia March 1916. Killed in action in Mesopotamia on 25th March 1917. Pl. XVII.

COLE, REGINALD PRICE (*b.* 1895).
Greenock Academy. Student of Medicine, 1913-14. Royal Scots, Private Oct. 1914. Highland Light Infantry, 2nd Lieut. Oct. 1915. Killed in action on 20th May 1917. Pl. XVII.

COLES, CECIL FREDERICK G. (*b.* 1888).
George Watson's College. Student of Music, 1905-6; Bücher Scholar. 9th London Regiment, Queen Victoria's Rifles, Private Sept. 1914; Sergeant and Bandmaster. France. Killed in action near Hangar Wood on 25th April 1918. Pl. XVII.

Roll of the Fallen

CONSIDINE, PATRICK FRANCIS (*b.* 1893).
Merchiston Castle School; First XV. and Shooting VIII. Cadet Corps 1906-12, Coy. Sgt.-Major. Student of Law, 1913-14. 4th Royal Scots, 2nd Lieut. 1912; Lieut. 1913. Dardanelles. Wounded at the Gully Ravine on 28th June and died at Malta on 11th July 1915. Pl. XVII.

CONSTABLE, DOUGLAS OLIPHANT (*b.* 1890).
Traquair School; St Mary's, Melrose. Student of Arts, 1907-10; M.A. 1910. Inns of Court O.T.C., Private Feb. 1915. Grenadier Guards, 2nd Lieut. France. Killed in action on 25th September 1916. Pl. XVII.

COOK, CECIL HADDON (*b.* 1896).
George Watson's College; Captain First XI. 1914. Student of Medicine, 1914-15. 23rd Manchester Regiment, 2nd Lieut. Jan. 1916. Killed in action on 22nd October 1917. Pl. XVIII.

COOPER-MARSDIN, A. C. (*b.* 1867).
Totteridge Park, Herts. Student of Divinity, 1890-1; B.A. (Cambridge); D.D. (Dublin). Canon of Rochester. Army Chaplain at Portsmouth, Shoreham, and Harwich, 1915-17. Invalided out 1917 and died on 16th August 1918. Pl. XVIII.

COTTERILL, DENIS (*b.* 1881).
Edinburgh Academy; First XV. Student of Medicine, Cambridge University (two years); First XV. Student of Medicine, Edinburgh University, 1902-6; M.B., Ch.B. 1906; F.R.C.S. (Edin.). Surgeon, Red Cross Hospital, Rouen, Nov. 1914 to Jan. 1918. R.A.M.C., Lieut.; Captain July 1918. 50th Casualty Clearing Station, Bohain, France, where he died of influenza on 2nd December 1918. Pl. XVIII.

COULTHURST, ROBERT ALLAN (*b.* 1896).
Leith Academy. Student of Arts, 1914-16. O.T.C. Artillery, May 1914 to Dec. 1915, Cadet. R.F.A., 4th Lowland Brigade, Gunner Dec. 1915. Discharged medically unfit 1st Aug. 1916 and died at Leith on 26th September 1918. Pl. XVIII.

COUTTS, JOHN KERR (*b.* 1890).
Royal High School; First XV. Student of Law, 1910-12; Law Agent, 1913. 15th Royal Scots, Private Oct. 1914; L/Corporal March 1916. France Jan. 1916. Killed at the Battle of the Somme on 1st July 1916. Pl. XVIII.

COUTTS, ROBERT DISHER (*b.* 1888).
George Watson's College. Student of Law, 1908-10. 4th Gordon Highlanders, 2nd Lieut. April 1914; Lieut. Oct. 1914. Missing, believed killed, at Loos on 25th September 1915. Pl. XVIII.

COWAN, GEORGE DEAS (*b.* 1884).
Edinburgh Academy. B.A. (Oxford) 1904. Infantry 1900-2. Student of Law, 1906-10. Writer to the Signet, 1911. 9th Royal Scots, 1903; 2nd Lieut. 1905; Captain 1908. Mobilised Aug. 1914; Major June 1916. France Feb. 1915. Wounded 1916. Dispatches May 1917. Died of wounds on 22nd April 1918.
Pl. XVIII.

PLATE XVIII.

A. C. COOPER-MARSDIN.

C. H. COOK.

DENIS COTTERILL.

R. D. COUTTS.

J. K. COUTTS.

R. A. COULTHURST.

G. D. COWAN.

ARCHIBALD COWE.

JOHN CRABBE.

PLATE XIX.

JOHN CROCKET.

J. H. CRESSWELL.

T. F. CRAIG.

D. C. CROLE.

D. R. CROMB.

W. J. CROSBIE.

A. J. CUNNINGHAM.

J. C. B. CROZIER.

W. G. L. CULLEN.

Roll of the Fallen

COWE, ARCHIBALD (*b.* 1889).
  Penicuik School; George Watson's College. Student of Medicine, 1908-13; M.B., Ch.B. (Hons.) 1913. R.A.M.C., Lieut. Feb. 1915; Captain 1916. Served overseas for 18 months. Invalided home. Returned Sept. 1917. Killed in action on 2nd December 1917. Pl. XVIII.

COX, PERCY. (See p. 115.)

CRABBE, JOHN (*b.* 1891).
  Lasswade School. Student of Arts, 1910-13; M.A. 1913. 4th, 6th, and 13th Royal Scots, Private 1910; Sergeant; 2nd Lieut. Dec. 1914. France. Killed in action on 6th May 1916. Pl. XVIII.

CRAIG, THOMAS FORREST (*b.* 1884).
  Kelso High School. Student of Medicine, 1905-10; M.B., Ch.B. 1910. R.A.M.C., Captain July 1915. Died of wounds on Hospital Ship on 2nd February 1918. Pl. XIX.

CRESSWELL, JAMES HENRY (*b.* 1890).
  George Heriot's School. Student of Arts, 1910-15; M.A. 1914. Schoolmaster. 3/9th Royal Scots, Private. France. Killed in action on 10th April 1917. Pl. XIX.

CROCKET, JOHN (*b.* 1886).
  George Watson's College. Student of Medicine, 1902-7; M.B., Ch.B. 1907; M.D. 1914. Resident, Royal Infirmary, Sick Children and Chalmers Hospitals. R.A.M.C., attached Cameron Highlanders, Lieut. 1913. Killed at the Battle of the Aisne on 25th September 1914. Pl. XIX.

CROLE, DAVID CLEMENT (*b.* 1885).
  Royal High School. Student of Medicine, 1900-5; M.B., C.M. 1905. Resident, Royal Infirmary. Golf. R.A.M.C., attached 19th Hussars, Lieut. May 1916; Captain. France Nov. 1916. Killed in action on 23rd March 1918. Pl. XIX.

CROMB, DAVID RANKIN (*b.* 1896).
  Daniel Stewart's College; Bursar and Scholar; First XV. Student of Arts, 1913-16; M.A. 1916. Dundas Bursar; Crichton Bursar in Medicine. O.T.C. Infantry, Dec. 1914 to March 1916, Cadet; Officer Cadet March 1916. 3rd and 13th Royal Scots, 2nd Lieut. Aug. 1916. France Sept. 1916. Killed in action on 23rd April 1917. Pl. XIX.

CROSBIE, WILLIAM JAMES (*b.* 1894).
  Wilton and Buccleuch Schools, Hawick. Student of Arts, 1912-15; M.A. 1915. O.T.C. Infantry, Nov. 1914 to July 1915, Cadet. Army Cyclist Corps, attached R.E. (Special Brigade), Corporal July 1915. France. Killed at Mazingarbe near Loos in October 1915. Pl. XIX.

CROZIER, JAMES CYRIL BAPTIST (*b.* 1890).
  Loretto; First XV.; "Fives" and Hockey. Student of Medicine, 1909-10. O.T.C. Artillery, Jan. 1911 to July 1912, Cadet. 2nd Royal Munster Fusiliers, 2nd Lieut. July 1914. France. Killed in action on 27th August 1914. Pl. XIX.

Roll of the Fallen

CULLEN, WILLIAM GEOFFREY LANGLEY (*b.* 1894).
: Edinburgh Academy. O.T.C. 1909-11. Student of Law, 1914. 2/9th Royal Scots, 2nd Lieut. Sept. 1914. Died of pneumonia at Edinburgh on 30th March 1915.   Pl. XIX.

CUMMING, COLIN EDWARD (*b.* 1890).
: Royal High School; Dux. Student of Arts, 1908-11; M.A. (Hons. Classics). O.T.C. Artillery, Oct. 1908 to Sept. 1909, Cadet. R.F.A. (S.R.), 2nd Lieut. Sept. 1909. 103rd Battery, R.F.A., Sept. 1914; Lieut. Dec. 1914. France and Flanders Oct. 1914. Died of wounds received near Ypres on 24th February 1915.   Pl. XCIII.

CUNNINGHAM, ARCHIBALD JOHN (*b.* 1886).
: Royal High School; Dux. Student of Arts and Divinity; M.A. (Hons. Engl.) 1908. Probationer of U.F. Church. O.T.C. Artillery, July to Nov. 1915, Cadet. R.F.A. (S.R.), 2nd Lieut. Nov. 1915; Lieut. Killed in action on 24th March 1918.   Pl. XIX.

CUNNINGHAM, JAMES SANDEMAN (*b.* 1884).
: Bradford College, Berkshire. B.A. (Cambridge). 1st Trinity Boat. Student of Law, 1909-10. Chartered Accountant, 1912. 73rd Royal Canadian Highlanders, Sergeant Aug. 1915 Killed in action on 31st October 1916.   Pl. XX.

CUNNINGHAM, JOHN CRAIGIE (*b.* 1885).
: George Watson's College. Student of Arts, 1902-5; M.A. (Hons. Classics) 1906; B.A. (Oxford). Canadian Mounted Rifles, Corporal Feb. 1915; Princess Patricia's Canadian Light Infantry, Sergeant. France Oct. 1917. Killed at Monchy on 26th August 1918.   Pl. XX.

CUNNINGHAM, ROBERT ALEXANDER (*b.* 1888).
: George Heriot's School; University Bursar. Student of Science, 1907-11; B.Sc. 1910. Lecturer, Chemistry (Agriculture), Manitoba Agricultural College. 46th Canadian Infantry, Lieut. Wounded. Died on 27th September 1918.

CURR, THOMAS (*b.* 1890).
: East Linton and Dunbar Schools. Student of Arts and Science, 1909-14; M.A. (Hons. Maths.) and B.Sc. 1914. 9th Royal Scots, Private Oct. 1914. 18th Highland Light Infantry, 2nd Lieut. Sept. 1915. Wounded 1915. Killed in action on 4th October 1916.   Pl. XX.

CUTHBERT, DAVID WILSON HARPER (*b.* 1892).
: Alloa Academy; First XI. Golf. Student of Law, 1910-13. O.T.C. Infantry, May 1910 to April 1913, Cadet. 7th Argyll and Sutherland Highlanders, Private Sept. 1914; Sergeant. 1st attached 9th Royal Highlanders (Black Watch), 2nd Lieut. France. Died of wounds at Arras on 9th April 1917.   Pl. XX.

CUTHBERT, JOHN GEORGE GUNN (*b.* 1890).
: Hownam School; Woodside School, Glasgow. Student of Arts and Divinity, 1910-15; M.A. (Hons. Engl.) 1913. O.T.C. Infantry, Oct. 1914 to March 1915, Cadet Corporal. 9th Royal Scots Fusiliers, March 1915. M.G.C., 2nd Lieut. Wounded in July and Oct. 1916. Died of wounds on 19th October 1916.   Pl. XX.

PLATE XX.

J. S. Cunningham.

J. C. Cunningham.

Thomas Curr.

D. W. H. Cuthbert.

J. G. G. Cuthbert.

E. I. Cuthbertson.

A. D. Darbishire.

D. A. Davidson.

J. E. Davidson.

PLATE XXI.

JAMES DAVIE.   R. C. DAVIE.   JOHN DAVIDSON.

H. M. DEANS.   J. M. DEWAR.   JAMES DAWSON.

W. H. DIXON.   WILLIAM DICKIE.   N. A. DOGGART.

Roll of the Fallen

CUTHBERT, ROBERT LANCELOT (*b.* 1869).
    Edinburgh Collegiate School. Student of Law, 1889-91. Chartered Accountant, 1891. 2nd King Edward's Horse, Trooper, attached 1st Canadian Division. Killed in action in France on 6th July 1915.

CUTHBERTSON, ERIC IAN (*b.* 1898).
    Edinburgh Academy. O.T.C. 1913-14. Edinburgh University O.T.C. Artillery, Nov. 1915 to Dec. 1916, Cadet Corporal. R.G.A. (6" Howitzers), 2nd Lieut. 1916. France June 1917. Killed in action on 23rd October 1917.   Pl. XX.

DALLAS, THOMAS CURRIE (*b.* 1886).
    Royal High School. Student of Medicine, 1907. O.T.C. Medical, May 1911, Cadet. 38th Canadian Infantry, Private May 1916. France. Killed at Bourlon Wood on 30th September 1918.

DANZIG, MORRIS WILLIAM (*b.* 1882).
    South African College, Capetown. Student of Medicine, 1909-15; M.B. 1915. R.A.M.C., Lieut. Lost at sea on 15th April 1917.

DARBISHIRE, ARTHUR DUKINFIELD (*b.* 1879).
    Magdalen College School. M.A. (Oxford). Demonstrator and Lecturer in Zoology, Oxford and Manchester Universities and Royal College of Science. Lecturer, Genetics, Edinburgh University. 14th Argyll and Sutherland Highlanders, Private July 1915. R.G.A., 2nd Lieut. Dec. 1915. Died at Kilmarnock on 26th December 1915.   Pl. XX.

DAVIDSON, DAVID ADAMS (*b.* 1898).
    George Heriot's School; First XV. O.T.C. 1912-16, Cadet Coy. Sgt.-Major. University Bursar. Edinburgh University O.T.C. Artillery, Aug. 1916 to Jan. 1917, Cadet Bombardier; Officer Cadet Jan. 1917. R.G.A., 179th Siege Battery, 2nd Lieut. May 1917. France on the 15th, and killed at Spoilbank, Ypres, on 28th July 1917.   Pl. XX.

DAVIDSON, JAMES EADIE (*b.* 1893).
    Daniel Stewart's College. Student of Science, 1911-14; B.Sc. 1914. O.T.C. Engineers, Oct. 1911 to Sept. 1914, Cadet. R.E., Sapper Sept. 1914. R.G.A., 2nd Lieut. Sept. 1914; Lieut.; Captain; Major May 1917. France May 1915; Flanders. Croix de Guerre and Chevalier de l'Ordre de la Couronne (Belgian) Dec. 1917. D.S.O. Sept. 1918. Dispatches Dec. 1918. Wounded in March and Oct. 1918. Died of wounds in France on 16th October 1918.   Pl. XX.

DAVIDSON, JOHN (*b.* 1885).
    Ayr Academy; Dux. Student of Arts, 1902-6; M.A. (Hons. Hist.) 1906. Argyll and Sutherland Highlanders, Private Aug. 1915; Corporal, Border Regiment; 2nd Lieut. May 1917. France. Killed in action on 15th October 1917.   Pl. XXI.

DAVIE, JAMES (*b.* 1886).
    George Heriot's School. Student of Medicine, 1903-9; M.B., Ch.B. 1909. Australian Army Medical Corps, Captain Aug. 1916. France Aug. 1917. Died of wounds on 6th October 1917.   Pl. XXI.

Roll of the Fallen

DAVIE, ROBERT CHAPMAN (*b.* 1886).
   Glasgow High School. M.A. 1907; B.Sc. 1909 and D.Sc. 1915 (Glasgow). Lecturer in Botany, Edinburgh University. R.A.M.C. (4th Water Tank Coy.), Lieut. May 1917; Captain, Senior Chemist, May 1918. Died of pneumonia while on leave from France on 4th February 1919. Pl. XXI.

DAWSON, JAMES (*b.* 1892).
   Broughton School. Student of Arts, 1910-13; M.A. 1913. R.A.M.C. (T.), 1908-12. 11th Gordon Highlanders, Corporal Nov. 1914; Sergeant. 3rd Royal Highlanders (Black Watch), 2nd Lieut. June 1915. Mesopotamia. Invalided home and died on 2nd April 1917. Pl. XXI.

DEA, JAMES TOD KEDSLIE (*b.* 1887).
   George Heriot's and Boroughmuir Schools. Student of Arts, 1905-9; M.A. 1909. 7th Argyll and Sutherland Highlanders, Private. France. Killed in action at Ypres on 25th April 1915.

DEANS, HAROLD MACKENZIE (*b.* 1892).
   Bournemouth School; King's School, Canterbury. Student of Medicine, 1912-14. O.T.C. Infantry, April to Aug. 1913, Cadet, and Aug. 1913 to Aug. 1914, 2nd Lieut. 3rd attached 7/8th King's Own Scottish Borderers (S.R.), 2nd Lieut. Aug. 1914; Lieut. Feb. 1915; Captain March 1915. France from 1914 to 1917. Instructor, British Military Mission to America, Oct. 1917 to July 1918. France 1918. Killed in action on 17th September 1918. Pl. XXI.

DEWAR, JAMES MELVILLE (*b.* 1890).
   Lochgelly School. Swimming. Student of Arts, 1908-12; M.A. 1912. O.T.C. Infantry, Sept. to Oct. 1914, Cadet. 11th Royal Highlanders (Black Watch), Lieut. Oct. 1914. France 1914-15; Macedonia 1916-17. France 1918 with 51st Highland Division. Killed in action on 16th October 1918. Pl. XXI.

DICKIE, WILLIAM (*b.* 1892).
   Dumfries Academy. Student of Arts, 1910-13; M.A. (Hons. Classics) 1913. Scholar of Oriel College, Oxford, 1913-14. Oxford University O.T.C. 9th and 1st King's Own Scottish Borderers, 2nd Lieut. Oct. 1914; Lieut. Gallipoli and France Aug. 1915 to July 1916. Killed at Beaucourt-Sur-Ancre on 1st July 1916. Pl. XXI.

DIXON, WILLIAM HUTTON (*b.* 1891).
   George Heriot's School; First XV. Edinburgh University O.T.C. Infantry, Feb. to June 1916, Cadet. 3rd and 8th Seaforth Highlanders, Officer Cadet June 1916; 2nd Lieut. Oct. 1916. France Dec. 1916. Wounded and died there on 22nd April 1918. Pl. XXI.

DOBSON, J. ROBINSON (*b.* 1880).
   Student of Medicine, 1912-13. Royal Irish Fusiliers, Lieut. Died of wounds on 19th February 1917.

Roll of the Fallen

DOGGART, NORMAN ALEXANDER (*b.* 1891).
Kirkcaldy High School; Dux 1908; Captain of School. O.T.C. 1903-6. Student of Arts and Medicine, 1909-14; M.A. 1912. O.T.C. Infantry, Nov. 1909 to March 1912, and in Sept. 1914, Cadet. 3rd and 12th Scottish Rifles, Lieut. Sept. 1914; Captain Oct. 1915. Transferred to Royal Air Force. Died of injuries at Witney, Oxford, on 11th October 1918. Pl. XXI.

DON, ALEXANDER DUFF BROWNLEE (*b.* 1893).
George Watson's College. Cadet Corps 1904-8, Sergeant. Student of Science, 1909-12; B.Sc. 1912. O.T.C. Engineers, Feb. 1910 to Sept. 1914, Cadet Sergeant. R.E., 2nd Field Coy., 8th Division, 2nd Lieut. Sept. 1914; Lieut. July 1915. France July 1915. Killed in action at Les Bœufs on 22nd October 1916. Pl. XXII.

DONALDSON, SIR HAY FREDERICK (*b.* 1856).
Eton. Trinity College, Cambridge. Former Student (Research). Chief Superintendent Ordnance Factories. Brigadier-General on Lord Kitchener's Staff. Ministry of Munitions, Technical Adviser. C.B., K.C.B. Drowned in sinking of H.M.S. *Hampshire* on 5th June 1916. Pl. XXII.

DONALDSON, SAMUEL RITCHIE. (See p. 115.)

DONALDSON, STUART (*b.* 1889).
Royal High School; First XI. Student of Law, 1908-9. Chartered Accountant, 1912. Highland Light Infantry, 2nd Lieut. Feb. 1916. Killed in action on 28th September 1918. Pl. XXII.

DOUGHTY, GORDON GRAY (*b.* 1893).
Royal High School. Student of Arts, 1911-15; M.A. 1914. 6th Royal Scots, Private Jan. 1915. 1st King's Own Scottish Borderers, 2nd Lieut. May 1917. Served in Egypt (Senussi Campaign) 1915-16, and in France 1916-18. Killed in action in April 1918. Pl. XXII.

DOUGLAS, IAN VICTOR (*b.* 1897).
Grammar School and Royal Agricultural College, Cirencester. Student of Science, 1915-16. O.T.C. Artillery, May to Nov. 1916, Cadet Bombardier; Officer Cadet Nov. 1916. R.F.A., 2nd Lieut. Feb. 1917. France May 1917. M.C. Oct. 1917. Killed in action on 25th October 1917. Pl. XXII.

DOUGLAS, R. ROSS (*b.* 1891).
George Watson's College; O.T.C.; First XV. Student of Arts, 1909-13; M.A. 1913. 5th Royal Scots, Private. Mobilised Aug. 1914. 7/8th King's Own Scottish Borderers, Lieut. Aug. 1916. Gallipoli. France. Killed in action on 30th August 1917. Pl. XXII.

DOW, JOHN (*b.* 1894).
Stanley School. Student of Arts, 1912-15. 51st (Grad.) Training Reserve Battalion, Highland Light Infantry, July 1916. Royal Scots, Corporal; 12th Battalion King's Royal Rifle Corps, 2nd Lieut.; Acting Adjutant, Sept. 1917. Killed near Arvillers in France on 25th March 1918. Pl. XXII.

Roll of the Fallen

DOW, JOHN MITCHELL (*b.* 1890).
    Dunfermline High School. Student of Arts, 1908-11; M.A. 1911. 9th Royal Highlanders (Black Watch), Private Aug. 1915; L/Corporal. Killed in action in France on 29th April 1916.   Pl. XXII.

DRENNAN, ROBERT HUGH (*b.* 1866).
    Academical Institution, Coleraine. Student of Medicine, 1887-92; M.B., C.M. 1892. Voluntary Medical Officer, Gravesend, 1914-15. R.A.M.C., Captain May 1915. Died on service at Gravesend on 26th July 1917.   Pl. XXII.

DRUMMOND, ROBERT KENNETH (*b.* 1894).
    George Watson's College; First XV. Student of Arts, 1912-13. 9th Highland Light Infantry (Glasgow Highlanders), Private Aug. 1914. Cameron Highlanders, 2nd Lieut. Sept. 1915; Captain. France Nov. 1914 to May 1915, and May 1916 to July 1918. M.C. Sept. 1916; Bar to M.C. Nov. 1916. Wounded at Richebourg in May 1915. Wounded on 23rd and died of wounds near Pierrefonds in France on 24th July 1918.   Pl. XXIII.

DRUMMOND, WILLIAM YOUNG (*b.* 1894).
    George Watson's College. Student of Arts, 1911-15; M.A. (Hons. Ment. Phil.) 1915. O.T.C. Infantry, Oct. 1914 to March 1915, Cadet. 13th attached 10th Argyll and Sutherland Highlanders, Lieut. March 1915. France. Ypres Aug. 1915. Killed at Montauban on 11th July 1916.   Pl. XXIII.

DUGGAN, CHARLES WILLIAM (*b.* 1866).
    Daniel Stewart's and George Watson's Colleges. Student of Medicine; M.B., C.M. 1887. R.A.M.C., Lieut. 1891; Major 1903. Sofia Expedition, 1898. Mention Feb. 1917. Drowned through torpedoing of the *Leinster* in the Irish Sea on 10th October 1918.   Pl. XXIII.

DUNCAN, RONALD WINGRAVE.
    Edinburgh Academy. Student of Medicine; L.R.C.P. & S. (Edin.); L.F.P.S. (Glasgow) 1907. R.A.M.C., attached 2nd Royal Highlanders (Black Watch), Captain. France and Mesopotamia. Killed in action on 8th March 1916 in Mesopotamia.

DUNLOP, GEORGE HARRY MELVILLE.
    Student of Medicine, 1875-80; M.B., C.M. 1880; M.D. 1884; F.R.C.P. R.A.M.C., Major June 1915. Died at Etaples in France on 3rd July 1916.   Pl. XXIII.

DUNLOP, WILLIAM J. (*b.* 1889).
    Coleraine Academical Institution. Student of Medicine, 1912-14. O.T.C. Artillery, Oct. 1912 to Oct. 1914, Cadet. R.A.M.C., Scottish Horse Brigade, Private Sept. 1914. R.F.A., 2nd Lieut. 1915. Killed in action on 21st September 1916.   Pl. XXIII.

PLATE XXII.

STUART DONALDSON.

A. D. B. DON.

SIR H. F. DONALDSON.

G. G. DOUGHTY.

R. ROSS DOUGLAS.

I. V. DOUGLAS.

J. M. DOW.

JOHN DOW.

R. H. DRENNAN.

PLATE XXIII.

C. W. DUGGAN.

W. Y. DRUMMOND.

R. K. DRUMMOND.

G. H. M. DUNLOP.

THOMAS DUNN.

W. J. DUNLOP.

J. J. DYKES.

W. J. DUNN.

A. B. DURWARD.

Roll of the Fallen

DUNN, THOMAS (*b.* 1892).
    Castle Douglas School and Dumfries Academy. Student of Arts and Law, 1909-14; M.A. 1912. O.T.C. Infantry, Jan. 1911 to July 1913, Cadet. 4th Royal Scots (S.S.C. and Banking Coy.), Private Aug. 1914. 5th King's Own Scottish Borderers, Lieut. Nov. 1914; Gallipoli 1915; Captain Feb. 1916. Killed in action at Gaza in Palestine on 19th April 1917.   Pl. XXIII.

DUNN, WILLIAM JOHN (*b.* 1895).
    Dumfries Academy. Student of Medicine, 1913-15. O.T.C. Infantry, Jan. 1914 to March 1915, Cadet Sergeant. 6th King's Own Scottish Borderers, 2nd Lieut. Feb. 1915. Killed in action in France on 17th July 1916.   Pl. XXIII.

DURWARD, ANDREW B. (*b.* 1888).
    George Heriot's School. Student of Arts, 1908-11; M.A. 1911. 14th Royal Scots, Private April 1915. 6th King's Own Scottish Borderers, 2nd Lieut. Aug. 1915. Wounded at the Somme in Oct. 1916. Captain Aug. 1918. M.C. July 1918. Killed in action at the River Lys in France on 16th October 1918.   Pl. XXIII.

DYKES, JAMES JOHNSTONE (*b.* 1886).
    Dumfries Academy. Student of Medicine, 1908-9; L.R.C.P. & S. (Edin.), L.F.P.S. (Glasg.), L.D.S. (Edin.). 1/5th King's Own Scottish Borderers (T.), Captain 1913. Mobilised Aug. 1914. Dispatches (Gallipoli) 1915. Killed in action on 12th July 1915 in Gallipoli.   Pl. XXIII.

EDGAR, JOHN MAXWELL (*b.* 1887).
    Stirling High School; First XV. and XI. Student of Arts, 1904-9; M.A. 1908; (Hons. Classics) 1909. First XI. (Assoc.). Schoolmaster. Sheffield University O.T.C., Jan. to March 1915. 4th South Staffordshire Regiment, 2nd Lieut. March 1915; Lieut. March 1916; Captain Aug. 1917. France. Killed in action on 22nd March 1918.   Pl. XXIV.

EDWARDS, ALFRED JOSEPH A. (*b.* 1896).
    Durban High School. Student of Medicine, 1912-15. O.T.C. Infantry, Oct. 1914 to Feb. 1915, Cadet. Royal Scots, 2nd Lieut. Feb. 1915. Attached 6th Loyal North Lancashire Regiment, Lieut. Gallipoli and Mesopotamia. Died of wounds on the Tigris Line on 10th April 1916.   Pl. XXIV.

ELLIOT, EDWARD JOHN (*b.* 1881).
    George Watson's College. Student of Medicine, 1899-1904; M.B., Ch.B. 1904. R.A.M.C., Lieut. July 1906; Captain July 1910; Adjutant; Major. No. 10 Stationary Hospital. France 1914. Dispatches Jan. 1916. Killed at St Omer on 23rd May 1918.   Pl. XXIV.

EVERETT, WILLIAM (*b.* 1863).
    Kettering Grammar School. Student of Medicine, 1885-9; M.B., C.M. 1889; M.D. 1893. Royal Navy, H.M.S. *Persia*, Surgeon. Killed by torpedoing of the *Persia* on 30th December 1915.   Pl. XXIV.

Roll of the Fallen

FAIRWEATHER, PRIMROSE (*b.* 1889).
Leith Academy. Student of Arts, 1906-9; M.A. 1909. 16th Royal Scots, Private Jan. 1915; L/Corporal. France. Killed at the Battle of the Somme on 1st July 1916. Pl. XXIV.

FALCONER, JAMES BISSET (*b.* 1886).
Blairgowrie School. Student of Law, 1910-11. 275th Siege Battery, R.G.A., Bombardier, July 1916. France. Killed in action near Ypres on 27th September 1917. Pl. XXIV.

FARQUHAR-THOMPSON, DOUGLAS (*b.* 1889).
Cheltenham College. Student of Medicine, 1912-15. O.T.C. Infantry, Oct. to Dec. 1914, Cadet. 10th Gordons, attached 1st Cameron Highlanders, 2nd Lieut. Dec. 1914. Missing, presumed killed in action on 13th October 1915.

FARQUHARSON, ALEXANDER McNAUGHTON (*b.* 1894).
Musselburgh Grammar School. Student of Arts, 1912-16; M.A. (Hons. Engl.) 1916. 9th Royal Scots, 51st Division, Signaller, April 1916. France. Killed near Roeux on 25th May 1917. Pl. XXIV.

FENTIMAN, FREDERICK WILLIAM (*b.* 1899).
Royal High School; First XV. Edinburgh University O.T.C. Infantry, March to Aug. 1917, Cadet; Officer Cadet Aug. 1917. 8th Battn. Border Regiment, 2nd Lieut. Dec. 1917. France Feb. 1918. Wounded and missing on 24th March 1918. Pl. XXIV.

FENTON, EBENEZER (*b.* 1893).
Dundee High School. Student of Arts and Divinity, 1910-14; M.A. 1912. U.F. Church Guild Tents, April to Nov. 1915. A.S.C., Private March 1916. Died at Hounslow Military Hospital on 17th March 1916. Pl. XXIV.

FENTON, JOHN ALFRED (*b.* 1895).
Royal High School. Student of Law, 1916-17. R.F.C., Air Mechanic, April 1917. Killed accidentally in France on 28th June 1917. Pl. XXV.

FERGUSON, ARTHUR DOUGLAS (*b.* 1881).
Edinburgh Academy. Student of Law, 1901-3. Chartered Accountant, 1904. O.T.C. Infantry, Nov. 1915 to Jan. 1916, Cadet. Seaforth Highlanders, 2nd Lieut. Jan. 1916; Lieut. France Jan. 1917. Killed in action on 12th October 1917.
Pl. XXV.

FERGUSON, GEORGE DOUGLAS (*b.* 1889).
Edinburgh Academy; First XV.; Academicals, First XV. Student of Medicine, 1907-13; M.B., Ch.B. 1913. O.T.C. Artillery, Oct. 1908 to Nov. 1911, Cadet. R.A.M.C., Lieut. Aug. 1914; Captain. France. Dispatches Jan. 1916. D.S.O. Nov. 1916. Killed in action at Vimy Ridge on 22nd April 1917. Pl. XXV.

PLATE XXIV.

J. M. Edgar.

A. J. A. Edwards.

E. J. Elliot.

Primrose Fairweather.

J. B. Falconer.

William Everett.

F. W. Fentiman.

A. M'N. Farquharson.

Ebenezer Fenton.

PLATE XXV.

J. A. Fenton. A. D. Ferguson. G. D. Ferguson.

James Ferguson, Jun. John Ferguson. W. P. Ferguson.

C. C. Fleming. I. G. Fleming. J. S. Fleming.

Roll of the Fallen

FERGUSON, JAMES, *Senior* (*b.* 1857).
 Craigmount, Edinburgh. Student of Arts and Law, 1875-6; M.A. 1876. K.C. Sheriff of Forfar. "Buchan Rifles," 1874. 9th Royal Scots, Lieut.-Col. 1900. With assistance organised 9th Royal Scots, 1900; 2/9th 1914-15; and 3/9th in 1915. Trained over 2000 officers and men. Died at Edinburgh on 25th April 1917.

FERGUSON, JAMES, *Junior* (*b.* 1886).
 Edinburgh Academy and Charterhouse. Student of Arts and Law, 1904-10; M.A. 1910; LL.B. 1913; Advocate, 1913. 9th Royal Scots (Highlanders), 2nd Lieut. May 1904; Lieut. Feb. 1907; Captain Dec. 1908; Major Sept. 1915. France Feb. 1915. Dispatches Jan. 1916. Missing since 23rd July 1916.
Pl. XXV.

FERGUSON, JOHN (*b.* 1897).
 Daniel Stewart's College. 1st Highland Cadet Battn. Edinburgh University O.T.C. Infantry, March to June 1916, Cadet. 1/7th Gordon Highlanders, Private June 1916. Killed at Courcellette on 19th December 1916.
Pl. XCIII.

FERGUSON, JOHN (*b.* 1892).
 MacLaren High School, Callander; Athletics. Student of Arts, 1911-14. 4th and 6th Royal Scots, Private Aug. 1914. 4th Scottish Rifles, 2nd Lieut. Nov. 1914. France. Dispatches Oct. 1916. Killed near Le Transloy, the Somme, on 23rd October 1916.
Pl. XXV.

FERGUSON, WILLIAM PERCIVAL (*b.* 1896).
 Daniel Stewart's College. Student of Law, 1914. O.T.C. Infantry, Jan. to July 1915, Cadet. 9th Royal Scots, 2nd Lieut. July 1915. France July 1916. Wounded at the Somme. Killed at Vimy Ridge near Arras on 9th April 1917.
Pl. XXV.

FLEMING, CHARLES CHRISTIE (*b.* 1864).
 Edinburgh Collegiate School. Student of Medicine; M.B., C.M. 1888. R.A.M.C., 1892. Sudan Campaign, 1896-9. D.S.O. Dec. 1898. South African Campaign, 1899-1901. Colonel and A.D.M.S., May 1915. With 51st (Highland) Division in France, 1915. Dispatches 1916. Died of wounds on 24th December 1917. Pl. XXV.

FLEMING, IAN GRANT (*b.* 1892).
 Keith Grammar School and Glenalmond. Student of Law, 1912-14. 6th Gordon Highlanders, 1910. Mobilised Aug. 1914; Captain Jan. 1916. With 51st Division in France. M.C. and Dispatches June 1915. Killed in action on 31st July 1917.
Pl. XXV.

FLEMING, JAMES SWORD (*b.* 1895).
 Royal High School. Edinburgh University O.T.C. Infantry, Oct. 1915 to May 1916, Cadet. Seaforth Highlanders, Private Dec. 1915. Gordon Highlanders, 2nd Lieut. June 1917. Died of wounds at No. 20 General Hospital on 29th September 1917.
Pl. XXV.

Roll of the Fallen

FLETT, ARTHUR DAVID (*b.* 1880).
Leys School, Cambridge; Edin. Wanderers First XV. and XI. Student of Law, 1901-3. Chartered Accountant, 1904. Treas. Edin. Univ. Athletic Club; Sec. Scottish Football Union. 7th Royal Scots, 2nd Lieut. Killed at Arras on 9th April 1917.   Pl. XXVI.

FLETT, HENRY WILLIAM (*b.* 1882).
Leys School, Cambridge; First XV., First XI., and Lacrosse; Edin. Wanderers First XV. Student of Law, 1905-8. Chartered Accountant, 1908. 6th Royal Highlanders (Black Watch), 2nd Lieut.; Lieut. M.C. April 1916. Died of wounds on 19th April 1916.   Pl. XXVI.

FORBES, ALEXANDER BRUCE (*b.* 1888).
Madras College, St Andrews, and Morrison's Academy, Crieff. Student of Science, 1906-10; B.Sc. 1910. Board of Agriculture till July 1917. Inns of Court O.T.C., July 1917. Argyll and Sutherland Highlanders, 2nd Lieut. April 1918. Died of wounds on 29th October 1918.   Pl. XXVI.

FORBES, ALEXANDER FISHER (*b.* 1889).
George Heriot's School. Student of Arts, 1908-11. 6th attached 1/4th Royal Scots, Private Aug. 1914. Gallipoli. Wounded on 28th June and died at the Dardanelles on 1st July 1915.   Pl. XXVI.

FORD, ERNEST GEORGE (*b.* 1875).
Hull College and Bath College. Student of Medicine, 1892-9; M.B., Ch.B. 1899. R.A.M.C., Lieut. April 1900; Captain April 1903. South African Campaign, Sept. 1900 to May 1902. Major. Retired 1911. Died on 7th October 1915.   Pl. XXVI.

FORD, GEORGE TURNER (*b.* 1879).
George Watson's College; Athletics. Student of Arts, 1897-1901; M.A. (Hons. Classics) 1901. Licentiate ès Lettres (Geneva). 1/4th Royal Scots, Private Nov. 1914. Dardanelles. Killed in action at the Gully Ravine, Gallipoli, on 28th June 1915.   Pl. XXVI.

FORREST, BERTRAM THOMAS ALEXANDER (*b.* 1882).
George Watson's College. Banker. Edinburgh University O.T.C. Artillery, Feb. to July 1916, Cadet; Officer Cadet. Yeomanry, 2nd Lieut. Egyptian Expeditionary Force, Jan. 1917. Killed at Beitunia near Jerusalem on 27th December 1917.   Pl. XXVI.

FORRESTER, JAMES DAVID (*b.* 1888).
Peebles High School and George Watson's College. Student of Medicine, 1906-12; M.B., Ch.B. 1912. R.A.M.C., Lieut. Jan. 1915; Captain Feb. 1916. France Aug. 1915. Attached Royal Naval Division. Killed in action on the Somme on 4th November 1916.   Pl. XXVI.

PLATE XXVI.

A. B. Forbes.

H. W. Flett.

A. D. Flett.

E. G. Ford.

G. T. Ford.

Alex. F. Forbes.

J. D. Forrester.

B. T. A. Forrest.

W. A. Forsyth.

PLATE XXVII.

I. Forsyth-Grant.

G. B. Foulkes.

Alex. Fraser.

Rowland Fraser.

G. D. Fraser.

A. C. Fraser.

G. S. Freeman.

Grant Gall.

J. W. Frew.

Roll of the Fallen

FORSYTH, WILLIAM (b. 1864).
    Cockburnspath School, and Wellfield Academy, Duns. Student of Law, 1887-8. Solicitor. 2nd V.B. King's Own Scottish Borderers, 1879; Lothians and Berwickshire Yeomanry, twelve years. 2nd V.B. Royal Highlanders (Black Watch), eight years. 7th Gordon Highlanders, Captain. V.D. 1907; T.D. 1914. Killed in action in October 1915.

FORSYTH, WILLIAM ALLAN (b. 1895).
    Montrose Academy; First XV. Student of Science, 1913-14. O.T.C. Artillery, Oct. 1913 to Aug. 1914. R.F.A., 2nd Lieut. Aug. 1914; Lieut. June 1915; Captain June 1917. Transferred to Royal Air Force. Mesopotamia, Gallipoli, and France. Dispatches Aug. 1917. Killed in air fight at Armentières on 27th June 1918.   Pl. XXVI.

FORSYTH-GRANT, IVOR (b. 1888).
    Edinburgh Academy; Athletics. Student of Arts and Law, 1907-11; M.A. 1911; LL.B. 1913; Advocate, 1913. 2nd Lovat Scouts, 2nd Lieut. 1910; Lieut. July 1914. Gallipoli. Dispatches March 1916. Wounded and died at Suvla Bay on 19th October 1915.   Pl. XXVII.

FOULKES, GEORGE BOYD (b. 1891).
    Bede Collegiate School, Sunderland. Student of Arts, 1909-14; M.A. (Hons. Classics) 1914; Black Scholar. Oxford O.T.C. 6th Royal Scots Fusiliers, 2nd Lieut. Sept. 1914; Lieut. Dec. 1915; Captain March 1916. France. Wounded at the Battle of Loos Sept. 1915. Killed at Martinpuich on 13th August 1916.   Pl. XXVII.

FRASER, ALEXANDER (b. 1865).
    The College, Inverness. Student of Arts and Law, 1880-9. Solicitor. 1st Cameron Highlanders (Vol.), 2nd Lieut. 1890; Hon. Lieut.-Colonel April 1907. 4th Cameron Highlanders, Lieut.-Colonel 1909-13. Reserve Battn. 4th Cameron Highlanders, Sept. 1914. France. V.D. Dispatches May and Oct. 1915. Killed in action at Festubert on 18th May 1915.   Pl. XXVII.

FRASER, ALEXANDER CHARLES (b. 1897).
    Daniel Stewart's College. Edinburgh University O.T.C. Infantry, March to Sept. 1914, Cadet. 1/4th Royal Scots, Private Sept. 1914. Gallipoli. Killed in action at the Dardanelles on 28th June 1915.   Pl. XXVII.

FRASER, DONALD REGINALD. (See p. 115.)

FRASER, GEORGE DICK (b. 1898).
    Inveraray Grammar and George Heriot's Schools. O.T.C. 1914-15. Student of Medicine, 1915-17. O.T.C. Infantry, Nov. 1915 to Aug. 1916 and Feb. to May 1917, Cadet; Officer Cadet May 1917. 13th Rifle Brigade, 2nd Lieut. Sept. 1917. France Oct. 1917. Died of wounds at Rouen on 3rd June 1918.   Pl. XXVII.

Roll of the Fallen

FRASER, ROWLAND (*b.* 1890).
    Merchiston Castle. Cadet Corps 1903-8, Cadet Colour-Sergeant. First XV. and XI. B.A. (Cambridge) 1911; Student of Law, 1911-14. First XV. Scottish International, four "Caps." 1st Rifle Brigade, 2nd Lieut. Aug. 1914; Lieut. Aug. 1915; Captain Nov. 1915. France Jan. 1915. Killed in action on 1st July 1916.   Pl. XXVII.

FREEMAN, GERALD STEWART (*b.* 1895).
    Perth Academy, and Gordon Schools, Huntly. Student of Medicine, 1913-16. O.T.C. Infantry, Oct. 1914 to Dec. 1915, Cadet. Gordon Highlanders. R.N.V.R., H.M.S. *Lassoo*, Surgeon-Probationer, Jan. 1916. Killed in action on 13th August 1916.   Pl. XXVII.

FREW, JOHN WILLIAMSON (*b.* 1884).
    George Heriot's School; Athletics. Student of Medicine, 1901-6; M.B., Ch.B. 1906. South African Medical Corps, Captain Aug. 1914. Attached Hartigan's Horse in German S.-W. Africa. R.A.M.C., Captain 1915. Egypt 1915-17; France 1917-18. M.C. Sept. 1918. Died of wounds, No. 8 General Hospital, on 8th October 1918.   Pl. XXVII.

GALL, GRANT (*b.* 1892).
    Daniel Stewart's College. Student of Music, 1909-14; Mus. Bac. 1914. Bücher Scholar. O.T.C. Infantry, Nov. 1909 to April 1913, Cadet. 3rd Royal Scots, 2nd Lieut. March 1915; Lieut. Sept. 1916; Acting Captain July 1917. 3rd Field Survey Coy., R.E. France July 1915; Loos and St Eloi. Killed in action on 21st March 1918.   Pl. XXVII.

GALL, WILLIAM JOHN REID (*b.* 1878).
    George Heriot's School. Student of Arts, 1898-1901; M.A. 1901. R.G.A., Gunner 1916; 2nd Lieut. 1918. France 1916. Wounded in France on 18th and died on 19th April 1918.   Pl. XXVIII.

GALLETLY, IAN (*b.* 1889).
    Edinburgh Academy; First XV. and XI.; Academicals First XV. B.A. (Oxford) 1913. First XV. London Scottish. Student of Law, 1912-14. R.F.A., 1st Lowland Brigade, 2nd Lieut. June 1913; Lieut. 1915. France Oct. 1915. Killed at Mametz near Albert on 3rd August 1916.   Pl. XXVIII.

GARDEN, DUNCAN (*b.* 1899).
    Fordyce Academy. Student of Science, 1916-17. O.T.C. Artillery, Oct. 1916 to Nov. 1917, Cadet Corporal. R.F.C., Flight Cadet, Sept. 1917. Accidentally killed at Thetford on 24th July 1918.   Pl. XXVIII.

GARDINER, GEORGE ARCHIBALD VICTOR (*b.* 1897).
    Garmouth School and Elgin Academy. Student of Medicine, 1915-16. O.T.C. Infantry, Feb. to July 1916, Cadet. 3rd, 5th and 6th Cameron Highlanders, Private July 1916. Missing, presumed killed, on 6th May 1917.   Pl. XXVIII.

PLATE XXVIII.

DUNCAN GARDEN.   W. J. R. GALL.   IAN GALLETLY.

G. A. V. GARDINER.   A. C. GARVIE.   J. L. GAUDIE.

A. C. B. GEDDES.   J. S. GELLATLY.   ROBERT GELLATLY.

PLATE XXIX.

ALEX. GEMMELL.

D. H. GEORGESON.

R. F. GERRARD.

ALEX. GIBB.

ALEX. REID GIBB.

ARTHUR J. GIBB.

R. J. GIBSON.

W. E. GIBBONS.

W. A. GIBB.

Roll of the Fallen

GARVIE, ALEXANDER COCKBURN (*b.* 1897).
Trinity Academy, Leith, and Daniel Stewart's College. Student of Medicine, 1915-16. O.T.C. Infantry, Feb. to Aug. 1916, Cadet Corporal; Officer Cadet Aug. 1916. 6th Royal Highlanders (Black Watch), 2nd Lieut. Killed in action in France on 23rd April 1917. Pl. XXVIII.

GAUDIE, JOHN LOGIE (*b.* 1894).
Montrose Academy. Student of Law, 1913-15. Solicitor, July 1915. Highland Cyclist Battalion, Private Oct. 1915. 1st Royal Highlanders (Black Watch), July 1916. France. Killed in action at Flers on 25th September 1916. Pl. XXVIII.

GAVIN, NEIL MURPHY.
Student of Medicine; L.R.C.P. & S. (Edin.); L.F.P.S. (Glasgow) 1901. R.A.M.C., Lieut. Accidentally killed in France on 12th March 1916.

GEDDES, ALASTAIR COSMO BURTON (*b.* 1891).
Edinburgh Academy. Student of Science, 1908-14; B.Sc. 1914. Vans Dunlop Scholar. R.N.A.S., July 1915; Kite Balloon Service, R.F.C., 1916; Major Dec. 1916. France Aug. 1915. M.C. Jan. 1917. Chevalier Legion d'Honneur April 1917. Killed in action on 19th April 1917. Pl. XXVIII.

GELLATLY, JOHN STEWART (*b.* 1893).
George Watson's College and Edinburgh Institution. Student of Law, 1912-14. 9th Royal Scots (Highlanders) 1911. Mobilised Aug. 1914, Private; L/Corporal; 2nd Lieut. Sept. 1915. France. Killed in action on 31st July 1917. Pl. XXVIII.

GELLATLY, ROBERT (*b.* 1886).
George Watson's College; Gymnastics; First XV. Watsonians. Student of Law, 1907-9. Solicitor. Lothians and Border Horse, Private Nov. 1914. 13th Royal Scots, 2nd Lieut. 1916. France. Wounded 1917. Killed in action on 23rd April 1917. Pl. XXVIII.

GEMMELL, ALEXANDER (*b.* 1889).
George Watson's College. Student of Science, 1905-8; B.Sc. 1908; D.Sc. 1915; F.I.C. O.T.C. Infantry, Nov. 1908 to Nov. 1911, Cadet Corporal. Unattached List, T.F. Edin. Univ. O.T.C. Infantry, 2nd Lieut. Jan. 1915; Lieut. July 1915; O.C. March to Sept. 1916; O.C. Scot. Comd. Anti-Gas School Sept. 1916; Captain April 1917. R.E. (Chemical Research) Feb. 1918. Died at Murtle, Aberdeenshire, on 3rd January 1919. Pl. XXIX.

GEORGESON, DAN HORACE (*b.* 1894).
Edinburgh Academy; O.T.C. Student of Arts and Law, 1910-14; M.A. 1913; LL.B. 1914. O.T.C. Infantry, Oct. 1910 to June 1914, Cadet. 9th and 8th Seaforth Highlanders, 2nd Lieut. Sept. 1914; Lieut. Jan. 1916; Captain Feb. 1918. France June 1915. Dispatches 1916 and 1917. Killed at Monchy near Arras on 9th March 1918. Pl. XXIX.

Roll of the Fallen

GERRARD, ROBERT FINLAY (*b.* 1887).
    Moray House School, Edinburgh. Student of Arts, 1906-12; M.A. (Hons. Engl.) 1912. 9th Royal Scots (Highlanders), Private 1902. Unattached List, T.F. George Watson's College. O.T.C., 2nd Lieut. 1912; Lieut.; Captain and O.C. 1914. 4th Royal Scots, attached 1/6th Gloucestershire Regiment, June 1915; Captain; Major. France 1916. Dispatches April 1917. Killed in action on 18th April 1917.   Pl. XXIX.

GIBB, ALEXANDER (*b.* 1896).
    Edinburgh Institution. Student of Science, 1913-15. O.T.C. Artillery, Sept. 1914 to Jan. 1915, Cadet. R.F.A., 4th Northumbrian (Howitzer) Brigade, 2nd Lieut. Jan. 1915; Lieut. Oct. 1915. France. Attached 2/63rd Heavy Trench Mortar Battery. Killed in action near Arras on 5th June 1917.   Pl. XXIX.

GIBB, ALEXANDER REID (*b.* 1874).
    George Watson's College; Athletics. Student of Law, 1893-5. Solicitor 1904. R.F.A., 2nd Highland Brigade, 2nd Lieut. 1912; Lieut. and Captain Oct. 1914. France with Forfarshire Battery, May 1915. Wounded Sept. 1916. Killed at Ploegsteert, Belgium, on 12th October 1916.   Pl. XXIX.

GIBB, ARTHUR JOHN (*b.* 1892).
    Arbroath High School; Athletics. Student of Arts, 1910-14; M.A. (Hons. Engl.) 1914. 6th Royal Scots (College Coy.) three years. 4th Royal Scots, Private July 1911; Corporal. Dardanelles June 1915. Killed in action at Gallipoli on 28th June 1915.   Pl. XXIX.

GIBB, WILLIAM ALEXANDER (*b.* 1872).
    Ipswich Grammar School. M.B., C.M. 1895; M.D. 1900. R.A.M.C. (T.), Lieut. April 1902; Lieut.-Col. 1914. 1st East Anglian Casualty Clearing Station. Died of pneumonia on 10th March 1915.   Pl. XXIX.

GIBBONS, WILFRED ERNEST (*b.* 1869).
    Charterhouse and Liverpool University College. Student of Medicine, 1890-6; M.B., C.M. 1896; M.D. 1900. R.A.M.C., 5th Northern General Hospital, Leicester, Captain. Died on 20th December 1917.   Pl. XXIX.

GIBSON, REGINALD JAMES (*b.* 1894).
    George Watson's College; First XV. Student of Arts and Law, 1912-14. O.T.C. Artillery, Feb. 1913 to Oct. 1914, Cadet. 4th Royal Scots, 2nd Lieut. Oct. 1914. Gallipoli, May 1915. Killed in action on 28th June 1915.   Pl. XXIX.

GIBSON, ROBERT GRAY NICHOL (*b.* 1891).
    George Watson's College; O.T.C., Cadet. Student of Law, 1912-14. 4th, 6th and 2nd Royal Scots, Private Aug. 1914; 2nd Lieut. May 1915; Lieut.; Acting Captain. Attached 5th Liverpool Regiment. France 1915-18. M.C. July 1917. Wounded Sept. 1917. Killed in action in France on 21st March 1918.   Pl. XXX.

Roll of the Fallen

GILLISON, ANDREW (*b.* 1868).
George Watson's College. Student of Arts, 1885-9; M.A. 1889. New College, Edinburgh, 1889-93. U.F. Church Minister. 2nd Australian Expeditionary Force, Chaplain. Twice Mentioned in Dispatches. Died of wounds in Gallipoli in September 1915. Pl. xxx.

GILMOUR, DAVID (*b.* 1890).
George Watson's College. Student of Medicine, 1907-13; M.B., Ch.B. 1913. O.T.C. Medical, April 1910 to May 1912, Cadet. R.A.M.C. (S.R.), Lieut. 1912; Captain. France Aug. 1914 to May 1915. Invalided out in May 1915. Died at Kingussie on 19th August 1916. Pl. xxx.

GLANVILL, ERNEST MURE (*b.* 1877).
Royal High School. Student of Medicine, 1895-1901; M.B., C.M. 1901. R.A.M.C. 1903; Captain 1907. France Aug. 1914. Attached Scots Greys. Dispatches Jan. 1915. Killed in action on 2nd November 1914. Pl. xxx.

GOODFELLOW, ERIC HECTOR (*b.* 1892).
Auckland Grammar School, N.Z. First XV. Student of Medicine, 1913-14. Vans Dunlop Scholar in Botany and Zoology, 1914. N.Z. T.F., Lieut. Australian Hospital, Aug. to Dec. 1914. R.F.A., 28th Battery, 9th Brigade, Meerut Division, 2nd Lieut. Dec. 1914. France, Mesopotamia. Wounded Sept. 1915. Dispatches 1916. Killed near Kut on 8th March 1916. Pl. xxx.

GORDON, ALISTAIR CAMPBELL MILLER (*b.* 1891).
Charterhouse. Student of Science, 1913-14. O.T.C. Infantry, Oct. 1913 to Aug. 1914, Cadet. Middlesex Regiment (Pub. Sch. Battn.), Private 1914. Royal Scots Fusiliers, Lieut. Three times wounded. Killed in action in March 1917.

GORDON, REGINALD GLEGG (*b.* 1878).
Edinburgh Academy. Student of Medicine, 1897-1903; M.B., Ch.B. 1903. Univ. Battery, E.C.A.V., 1897 to 1903; 2nd Lieut. March 1903; Lieut. Feb. 1904; O.T.C. Artillery, Captain July 1908; O.C. till Oct. 1909. 6th Royal Highlanders (Black Watch), Captain 1913. R.G.A., Lowland Heavy Battery, Aug. 1914; Major March 1915. France 1916. Dispatches Oct. 1917. D.S.O. Jan. 1918. Killed in action in France on 25th March 1918. Pl. xxx.

GORRIE, ALEXANDER KEITH (*b.* 1884).
George Watson's College; First XI. Student of Law, 1903-5. 9th Royal Scots. Private Sept. 1914. 11th Highland Light Infantry, 2nd Lieut. Sept. 1915. France March 1915. Killed in action on 26th April 1916. Pl. xxx.

GRACIE, WILLIAM JAMES (*b.* 1895).
North Berwick High School; Golf. Cadet Corps 1912-13, Cadet Sergeant. Student of Science, 1913-15. O.T.C. Engineers, Oct. 1914 to July 1915, Cadet. 9th and 10th North Staffordshire Regiment, 2nd Lieut. July 1915. France July 1916. Killed at the Battle of Arras on 26th April 1917. Pl. xxx.

Roll of the Fallen

GRAHAM, HENRY BALFOUR (*b.* 1894).
 Edinburgh Academy. O.T.C. 1910-12, Cadet. Student of Science, 1913-14. 7th Royal Highlanders (Black Watch), 2nd Lieut. Oct. 1914; Lieut. July 1915; Captain Aug. 1915; 2nd Lieut. (Regulars) July 1916. With 51st Division and wounded in France in Nov. 1915. With 10th Battn. at Salonika. Killed in action near Lake Doïran on 8th May 1917. Pl. XXX.

GRAHAM, HUGH CHRISTISON (*b.* 1893).
 Dumfries Academy; Athletics. Student of Arts, 1911-15; M.A. 1915. O.T.C. Infantry, Nov. 1911 to March 1915, Cadet Sergeant. 8th Royal Scots Fusiliers, attached M.G.C., 2nd Lieut. April 1915; Lieut. Aug. 1916. France. Killed at Messines on 8th June 1917. Pl. XXXI.

GRAHAM, MALCOLM (*b.* 1891).
 Uig, Skye, and Kingussie Schools. Student of Arts, 1909-14; M.A. 1913. Sec. Celtic Soc. O.T.C. Infantry, Feb. 1910 to April 1915. 2nd Gordon Highlanders, 2nd Lieut. Jan. 1916; Captain Oct. 1917. M.C. April 1917. Killed in action on 28th October 1917. Pl. XXXI.

GRANT, CHARLES WILLIAM (*b.* 1891).
 St George's College, Mussoorie, India. Athletics. Mussoorie Vol. Rifles. Student of Science, 1911-14. 11th Royal Scots, 2nd Lieut. Aug. 1914; Lieut. 1915; Captain Aug. 1917. France, Loos, Somme, Festubert, first and second Ypres, Longueval. Killed at Passchendaele on 12th October 1917. Pl. XXXI.

GRANT, JOHN PETER (*b.* 1880).
 Dundee High School. Student of Medicine; B.Sc., M.B., Ch.B. 1902. South African Medical Corps, attached Natal Light Horse, Captain Dec. 1914. With 6th Mounted Rifles during the Rebellion. Died of influenza on 19th October 1919. Pl. XXXI.

GRANT, PERCY KENMURE (*b.* 1890).
 George Watson's College. Student of Law, 1910-12. C.A. 1914. 1/14th City of London Regiment (London Scottish), Private Feb. 1915. A.S.C., 2nd Lieut. Oct. 1915. France. G.H.Q., 2nd, 4th and 5th Armies. Dispatches. Wounded at Loos on 25th Sept. 1915. Died at Lille of pneumonia following influenza on 6th November 1918. Pl. XXXI.

GRANT, RONALD CAMERON (*b.* 1891).
 Dover College and Daniel Stewart's College; Dux. University Bursar. Student of Science, 1908-12; B.Sc. 1912. O.T.C. Infantry, March 1909 to Jan. 1910; Engineers, 1910-12. R.E., 2nd Lieut. Dec. 1914; Lieut. June 1916. France. Attached Canadian Corps. Died at Amiens on 16th October 1916. Pl. XXXI.

GRANT, THOMAS FRANCIS (*b.* 1892).
 Royal Academy, Inverness. Student of Medicine, 1909-14. O.T.C. Infantry, Nov. 1911-14, Cadet. Highland Mtd. Bde. Field Ambulance. Private, Aug. 1914. 5th Seaforth Highlanders, 2nd Lieut. July 1915; Lieut. Dec. 1916. With 51st (Highland) Division in France for two years. M.C. May 1917; Bar to M.C. March 1918. Killed in action on April 1918. Pl. XXXI.

PLATE XXX.

R. G. N. Gibson.

David Gilmour.

Andrew Gillison.

E. M. Glanvill.

R. G. Gordon.

E. H. Goodfellow.

Wm. J. Gracie.

H. B. Graham.

A. K. Gorrie.

PLATE XXXI.

C. W. GRANT.

H. C. GRAHAM.

MALCOLM GRAHAM.

J. P. GRANT.

R. C. GRANT.

P. K. GRANT.

F. C. GRAY.

J. J. E. GRAY.

T. F. GRANT.

Roll of the Fallen

GRAY, DOUGLAS WILLIAM (*b.* 1894).
　Royal High School; First XV. Student of Science, 1914-15. O.T.C. Infantry, Oct. to Dec. 1914, Cadet. Royal Scots, Private. M.G.C., 2nd Lieut. Killed in action on 18th November 1916.   Pl. XCIII.

GRAY, FRANCIS HENRY TURNER (*b.* 1881).
　Elgin Academy and George Watson's College. Student of Arts; M.A. (Hons. Classics) 1901. A.S.C., 2nd Lieut. 1915; Lieut.; Captain. Sicily and Salonika. Intelligence Dept. War Office, Spring 1918. Serbian Order of White Eagle. Drowned while on leave at Prawle, South Devon, in July 1918.

GRAY, FREDERICK COLIN (*b.* 1892).
　Kirkcaldy High School. Student of Arts and Divinity, 1911-14; M.A. 1914. U.F. Church Guild Tent for six months. 1/7th Argyll and Sutherland Highlanders, Private Nov. 1915. France with 51st (Highland) Division. Killed at Beaumont Hamel on 15th November 1916.   Pl. XXXI.

GRAY, JOHN JAMES EMSLIE (*b.* 1876).
　Daniel Stewart's College. Student of Law, 1898-1900. No. 4 (University) Coy. Q.R.V.B., Royal Scots, 1900, Private. Sharp-Shooters' Corps and Imperial Yeomanry; South African War, 1901-3. King's Royal Rifle Corps, Private Nov. 1914. Duke of Cornwall's Light Infantry (S.R.), 2nd Lieut. July 1915. France Dec. 1914. Wounded at Longueval, France, in July 1916. Killed in flying accident at Gosport on 18th March 1917.   Pl. XXXI.

GRAYFOOT, BLENMAN BUHÔT.
　Student of Medicine; L.R.C.P. & S. (Edin.); L.F.P.S. (Glasg.) 1885; M.R.C.S. (Eng.) 1886. Indian Medical Service, Colonel. Dispatches. C.B. 1916. Died on 30th September 1916.

GREEN, CHARLES LAYTON (*b.* 1893).
　Swanage and St Bees, Cumberland. Student of Medicine, 1913-15. O.T.C. Infantry, Sept. to Oct. 1914, Cadet. 11th Essex Regiment, 2nd Lieut. Oct. 1914. Royal Fusiliers, Sportsman's Battalion. France 1915-16, Ypres. Transferred R.F.C., 1916. Killed in action in France on 9th June 1917.   Pl. XXXII.

GREENE, REGINALD DOWNES LATIMER (*b.* 1883).
　Trinity College, Stratford-on-Avon. Student of Medicine; M.B., Ch.B. 1908. P.M.O., Sarawak, 1915. R.A.M.C., Lieut. May 1916. France June 1916, Battle of the Somme. Invalided home Nov. 1916. Died of malaria at Labuan on 21st July 1919.

GREY, PATRICK RIDDLE (*b.* 1892).
　Avenue Academy, Berwick. Student of Science, 1911-15. O.T.C. Engineers, Nov. 1914 to June 1915, Cadet. 8th Northumberland Fusiliers, 2nd Lieut. June 1915. Killed in action in France on 26th September 1916.   Pl. XXXII.

Roll of the Fallen

GRIERSON, JOHN CHARLES (*b.* 1893).
George Heriot's School. Student of Arts, 1911-15; M.A. (Hons. Hist.) 1915. O.T.C. Artillery, Oct. 1913 to Dec. 1915. Middlesex Regiment, Private (Lewis Gunner) Spring 1916. Died of wounds in France on 23rd October 1916.
Pl. XXXII.

GRIEVE, DAVID CLARK (*b.* 1891).
Breadalbane Academy, Aberfeldy. Student of Arts, 1908-10. O.T.C. Artillery, Oct. 1909 to Dec. 1910. 13th Battn. 5th Royal Canadian Highlanders, Private Aug. 1914; Corporal and Sergeant 1915; Lieut. 1916. France. Killed at Vimy Ridge on 9th April 1917.
Pl. XXXII.

GRIGOR, THOMAS ALEXANDER (*b.* 1893).
George Heriot's School. O.T.C. 1908-10. Edinburgh University O.T.C. Infantry, Oct. 1910 to Dec. 1912, Cadet. Law Apprentice. Lothians and Border Horse, Private Dec. 1912. Mobilised Aug. 1914; Corporal 1916. Transferred to 11th Royal Scots, July 1917. France. Killed at Passchendaele on 12th October 1917.
Pl. XXXII.

GROENEWALD, ALBERT (*b.* 1885).
Student of Medicine, 1906-11; M.B., Ch.B. 1911. S.A. Medical Corps, Captain. German S.-W. Africa and German E. Africa. Attached 3rd South African Horse. M.C. at Kondoa-Waugi (East Africa) 1916. Died at Johannesburg in 1916.

GUNSON, LESLIE ROBERT SCHRADER (*b.* 1895).
St Bees, Cumberland. Shooting. O.T.C. 1909-13. Student of Medicine, 1912-14. O.T.C. Artillery, Oct. 1913 to Sept. 1914, Cadet. R.G.A., 31st Heavy Battery, 2nd Lieut. Sept. 1914; Lieut. Sept. 1915. France. Wounded in July 1916. Killed in action on the Somme on 18th July 1916.
Pl. XXXII.

GUTHRIE, GEORGE WATSON (*b.* 1877).
George Watson's College. Student of Medicine, 1895-1900; M.B., Ch.B. 1900. R.A.M.C., attached Naval Division, Lieut. Killed at Beaumont Hamel on 13th November 1916.
Pl. XXXII.

GUTHRIE, THOMAS ERROL (*b.* 1887).
Boys' High School, Christchurch, and University, N.Z. Student of Medicine, 1904-9; M.B., Ch.B. 1909. N.Z. Medical Corps, attached 3rd Ambulance, The Rifle Brigade, Captain Feb. 1916. France. Killed in action at Armentières on 4th July 1916.
Pl. XXXII.

GYLE, ERNEST WOODS (*b.* 1898).
Perth Academy; Athletics; First XV. Student of Medicine, 1916. 6th Royal Highlanders (Black Watch), L/Corporal July 1916; Officer Cadet Nov. 1917. 7th attached 1st Royal Highlanders (Black Watch), 2nd Lieut. March 1918. Killed in action at Wassigny, France, on 18th October 1918.
Pl. XXXII.

PLATE XXXII.

J. C. GRIERSON.

P. R. GREY.

C. L. GREEN.

T. A. GRIGOR.

D. C. GRIEVE.

L. R. S. GUNSON.

G. W. GUTHRIE.

T. E. GUTHRIE.

E. W. GYLE.

PLATE XXXIII.

John Handyside.   J. G. Hamilton-Grierson.   Henry Hall.

J. H. M. Hardyman.   N. E. J. Harding.   R. M. Hardy.

A. T. Harris.   R. J. P. Harle.   A. B. Hare.

Roll of the Fallen

HALL, HENRY (*b.* 1891).
  Edinburgh Academy; Football. O.T.C. 1906-9. Student of Science, 1910-14. O.T.C. Artillery, Oct. 1910 to Aug. 1914, Cadet Corporal. Royal Horse Artillery, 1/1st Ayrshire, 2nd Lieut. Aug. 1914; Lieut. June 1916; Captain. Egypt Sept. 1916. Attached Anzac Mounted Division, Palestine. Killed near Jerusalem on 25th September 1918. Pl. XXXIII.

HAMILTON-GRIERSON, JAMES GILBERT (*b.* 1887).
  Edinburgh Academy. B.A. (Oxford). Student of Law, 1908-9. Writer to the Signet, 1911. 4th Royal Scots, Private Aug. 1914. 5th Royal Scots Fusiliers, 2nd Lieut. Oct. 1914. Gallipoli May 1915. Killed in action near Cape Helles on 15th July 1915. Pl. XXXIII.

HANDYSIDE, JOHN (*b.* 1883).
  Royal High School; Dux. Student of Arts, 1899-1903; M.A. 1903 (Hons. Ment. Phil.); Hamilton Fellow and Ferguson Scholar. Balliol College, Oxford, 1903-8; Fellow of St John's College, Oxford, 1908; B.A. (Oxford). Assistant in Logic and Metaphysics, Edin. Univ.; Lecturer in Philosophy, Liverpool Univ. 16th Liverpool Regiment, 2nd Lieut. July 1915. Died of wounds on 18th October 1916.
  Pl. XXXIII.

HARDIE, FREDERICK (*b.* 1876).
  High School, Kirkcaldy. Student of Medicine, 1895-1900; M.B., Ch.B. 1900. R.A.M.C., Captain April 1915. 26th Field Ambulance, France. Died of wounds on 20th September 1917.

HARDING, NORMAN ERNEST JASPER (*b.* 1875).
  Merchant Taylor School, Crosby, and Cambridge House, Liverpool. Student of Medicine, 1895-1900; M.B., Ch.B. 1900; Diploma in Public Health. R.A.M.C., Lieut. 1901; Major 1914; Lieut.-Colonel. South African Campaign, 1901-3. France 1914. Severely wounded. No. 12 Stationary Hospital. India. Died of cholera at Bombay on 10th August 1916. Pl. XXXIII.

HARDY, RALPH MILLER (*b.* 1894).
  Daniel Stewart's College; First XV. Student of Law, 1913-15. 14th Argyll and Sutherland Highlanders, Private July 1915; Corporal; Sergeant; Coy. Q.M.S. 5th Highland Light Infantry, 2nd Lieut. Jan. 1917; Lieut. July 1918. France Dec. 1917. Killed near Ors, France, on 4th November 1918.
  Pl. XXXIII.

HARDYMAN, JOHN HAY MAITLAND (*b.* 1894).
  Fettes College. Student of Arts, 1912-14. 4th Somerset Light Infantry, Private Aug. 1914. Flight Cadet, Dec. 1914. 9th and 8th Somerset Light Infantry, 2nd Lieut. Feb. 1915; Lieut. Nov. 1916; Captain and Major April 1917; Brigade Major (Staff) 1917-18; Lieut.-Colonel May 1918. France 1916-18 with 37th Division. M.C. July 1917; D.S.O. Aug. 1918. Dispatches Nov. 1917 and Nov. 1918. Wounded three times. Killed in action at Biefvillers on 24th August 1918. Pl. XXXIII.

Roll of the Fallen

HARE, ALEXANDER BALFOUR (*b.* 1890).
  Leith Academy. Student of Arts, 1908-14; M.A. (Hons. Hist.) 1913. O.T.C. Artillery, Nov. 1909 to Jan. 1913, Cadet Bombardier. Schoolmaster; George Watson's College. O.T.C., 2nd Lieut. 1913. R.F.A. (S.R.), 2nd Lieut. Sept. 1915. France, the Somme, Feb. 1916. Killed in action on 31st October 1916. Pl. XXXIII.

HARLE, RICHARD JOHN PATERSON (*b.* 1896).
  Berwickshire High School. Shooting. Edinburgh University O.T.C. Infantry, March to Sept. 1914, Cadet. Royal Scots, Private Sept. 1914. 7th Argyll and Sutherland Highlanders, Private; 2nd Lieut. Feb. 1915. France Feb. 1915. Lieut. 1916; Captain Dec. 1916. Transferred to Regulars, King's Own Scottish Borderers, in 1917. M.C. (11th to 13th April 1917) Vimy Ridge. Wounded at Roeux on 23rd and died at Etaples on 26th April 1917. Pl. XXXIII.

HARLEY, ALLAN LANGLANDS. (See p. 115.)

HARRIS, ANTROBUS TAFT (*b.* 1890).
  Morrison's Academy, Crieff. Student of Arts and Music, 1906-12; Mus. Bac. 1912; London Scottish, Private Sept. 1914. France from 1914. 4th Bedford Regiment, attached 1st Lincolns, 2nd Lieut. Feb. 1915. Killed at Armentières on 19th March 1916. Pl. XXXIII.

HARROWER, WILLIAM (*b.* 1893).
  Falkirk High School. Student of Arts, 1911-15; M.A. (Hons. Classics) 1915. 3rd Gordon Highlanders, Private April 1915. R.E., Sergeant. France Aug. 1915. Died from gas poisoning near Bailleul, Battle of the Somme, on 1st July 1916. Pl. XXXIV.

HARTE, JOSEPH FRANCIS. (See p. 116.)

HARTLEY, ARTHUR CONNING (*b.* 1865).
  Student of Medicine; M.B., C.M. 1888; M.D. (Hons.) 1891; F.R.C.S. (Ed.) 1893. No. 4 (University) Coy. Royal Scots for eleven years. R.A.M.C., attached East Anglian R.E., Major. Died at Bedford on 5th March 1919. Pl. XCIII.

HARVEY, ALEXANDER SCOTT (*b.* 1896).
  Daniel Stewart's College; First XV. and XI.; Athletics. 1st Highland Cadet Battn. 1913-15, Cadet Corporal. Student of Medicine, 1915-16. O.T.C. Infantry, Oct. 1915 to Jan. 1916, Cadet. 2nd attached 1st Gordon Highlanders, 2nd Lieut. Jan. 1916; Lieut. March 1917. France Aug. 1916-18. Wounded twice. Wounded at Aubigny near Arras on 28th and died on 29th March 1918. Pl. XXXIV.

HASTINGS, JOSEPH EDWARD (*b.* 1894).
  George Heriot's School. Student of Arts, 1913-14. 11th Royal Highlanders (Black Watch), 2nd Lieut. Sept. 1915. France. Killed in Delville Wood, Longueval, on 20th July 1916. Pl. XXXIV.

Roll of the Fallen

HAWKS, AUBREY MELDRUM WOOD (b. 1896).
> George Watson's College; Dux 1914; University Bursar. Student of Arts, 1914-15. O.T.C. Infantry, Jan. to Oct. 1915, Cadet L/Corporal. 1/4th Royal Scots, 2nd Lieut. Oct. 1915; Lieut. April 1917. 1/6th Gloucestershire Regiment and 7th Field Coy. R.E., 52nd Division. France Sept. 1916 to Feb. 1917; Egypt Feb. 1918; France March 1918. Killed in action at Canal du Nord, east of Moeuvres, on 27th September 1918. Pl. XXXIV.

HAYHURST, THOMAS (b. 1888).
> King William's College, Isle of Man; First XV. and Athletics. Student of Medicine, 1905-11; M.B., Ch.B. 1911. O.T.C. for one year. R.A.M.C., Lieut. Aug. 1914; Captain March 1915. 2/1st East Lancs. Field Ambulance. Drowned by torpedoing of H.M.S. *Royal Edward* in Ægean Sea on 14th August 1915. Pl. XXXIV.

HEARD, FRANCIS GEORGE.
> Student of Medicine; L.R.C.P. & S. (Edin.) and L.F.P.S. (Glasg.), 1889. R.A.M.C., Lieut. Died on service on 15th March 1917.

HEGGIE, DAVID (b. 1874).
> Grammar School, Larne, and Royal High School. Student of Arts and Divinity, 1894-1902; M.A. 1899. Minister Church of Scotland. Chaplain. 7th and 8th Royal Scots, Captain Oct. 1916. Died at The Curragh, Ireland, on 23rd October 1917. Pl. XXXIV.

HELM, HENRY PAUL DUNDAS (b. 1894).
> Repton. O.T.C. 1909-12. Trinity College, Cambridge. Student of Medicine, 1913-15. O.T.C. Infantry, April to Sept. 1914, Cadet. 3rd and 2nd Border Regiment, 2nd Lieut. Aug. 1914; Lieut. May 1915; Captain March 1916. R.F.C. and Royal Air Force, Wing Adjutant, 1917. France Nov. 1914 to 1916 and also in 1918. First Battles of Ypres and Somme. Dispatches Jan. 1919. Died at Carlisle on 6th November 1918. Pl. XXXIV.

HELM, JOHN HUNTER (b. 1856).
> Castle Douglas School. Student of Medicine, 1879-85; M.B., C.M. 1885. R.A.M.C., Captain. Killed in action on 26th June 1916.

HENDERSON, ANDREW HUBERT MILLIN (b. 1895).
> St Mary's School, Melrose, and Edinburgh Institution; Athletics. 1st Highland Cadet Battn. Royal Scots, 1911-13, Cadet Sergeant and Hon. Lieut. Student of Medicine, 1913-14. 1/4th King's Own Scottish Borderers, 2nd Lieut. May 1913. Killed in action at Gallipoli on 12th July 1915. Pl. XXXIV.

HENDERSON, MICHAEL WILLIAM (b. 1871).
> Cargilfield and Rugby. Cadet Corps, 6th V.B. Royal Warwicks, Cadet. Student of Law, 1891-4. Chartered Accountant, 1894. 8th and 10th Royal Scots, 2nd Lieut. 1890; Lieut.-Col. (Retired). South African Campaign, 1900-1. 9th Royal Highlanders (Black Watch), Major Nov. 1914. Killed in action in France on 25th September 1915.

Roll of the Fallen

HENDERSON, WILLIAM (*b.* 1894).
   Ayr Academy; Dux. Student of Arts, 1911-15; M.A. (Hons. Mod. Lang.) 1915; Carnegie Travelling Scholar. Royal Scots, Private Jan. 1916. 1st and 14th Highland Light Infantry, 2nd Lieut. Dec. 1916. France Dec. 1917. Killed in action near Laventie on 9th April 1918. Pl. XXXIV.

HENDERSON-HAMILTON, JAMES CAMPBELL (*b.* 1884).
   Glenalmond; Shooting and Cricket. Cadet Corps 1901, Cadet Sergeant. Student of Law, 1902-6; LL.B.; Advocate, 1907. 9th Royal Scots, Lieut. Nov. 1902 to June 1906. 9th Royal Highlanders (Black Watch), 2nd Lieut. Sept 1914; Lieut. France. Killed in action at Loos on 25th September 1915. Pl. XXXV.

HENDRY, PETER GEDDES (*b.* 1897).
   Berwick Grammar School; Dux; Athletics. Student of Medicine, 1916-17. O.T.C. Artillery, Dec. 1916 to April 1917, Cadet. R.G.A., Gunner April 1917. France Dec. 1917. Accidentally killed near Arras on 6th February 1918. Pl. XXXV.

HENDRY, RALPH WILFRID (*b.* 1899).
   George Watson's College. Student of Science, 1916-17. 8th Royal Scots, Pioneer Battalion, Private April 1917; 2nd Lieut. France. Killed in action in woods near Epernay on 23rd July 1918. Pl. XXXV.

HENNEY, HERBERT NORMAN (*b.* 1892).
   Daniel Stewart's College; Rugby; L.D.S. (Edin.) Edinburgh University O.T.C. Artillery, July to Oct. 1915, Cadet. R.F.A., 26th Battery, 17th Brigade, 2nd Lieut. Oct. 1915. France June 1916; Somme. Killed in action at Monchy-le-Preux on 25th April 1917. Pl. XXXV.

HERFORD, BERNARD HENRY (*b.* 1886).
   George Watson's College and Fettes College. Student of Arts, 1904-9; M.A. (Hons. Classics) 1909. Schoolmaster. O.T.C. Infantry, Sept. 1914, Cadet. R.N. Division, 9th Royal Marine Brigade, 2nd Lieut. Sept. 1914; Lieut. Jan. 1915. Gallipoli April 1915. Wounded on 29th April and died at Gaba Tepe on 2nd May 1915. Pl. XXXV.

HIGGINS, MATTHEW THOMSON (*b.* 1888).
   Boroughmuir School. Student of Arts, 1908-12; M.A. 1912. 16th Royal Scots, Private Nov. 1914. France. Died of wounds on 7th July 1916. Pl. XXXV.

HILL, JOHN ROBERTSON (*b.* 1890).
   George Watson's College; First XV. Cadet Corps 1905-8, Cadet Sergeant. Student of Arts and Law, 1908-13; M.A. 1911; LL.B. (Distinction) 1913. Cairns Bursar and Thow Scholar. Pres. S.R.C. and Philomathic Soc. O.T.C. Infantry, Oct. 1909 to Aug. 1914, Cadet Sergeant. 3rd attached 2nd Durham Light Infantry, 2nd Lieut. Aug. 1914; Lieut. Feb. 1915. France Jan. 1915. Killed near Potijze, Belgium, on 2nd June 1915. Pl. XXXV.

PLATE XXXIV.

A. S. Harvey.

William Harrower.

J. E. Hastings.

David Heggie.

Thomas Hayhurst.

A. M. W. Hawks.

H. P. D. Helm.

Wm. Henderson.

A. H. M. Henderson.

PLATE XXXV.

R. W. Hendry.

P. G. Hendry.

J. C. Henderson-Hamilton.

H. N. Henney.

B. H. Herford.

M. T. Higgins.

C. W. Hobkinson.

R. G. Hindson.

J. R. Hill.

Roll of the Fallen

HINDSON, REGINALD GORDON (*b.* 1890).
Durban High School and Michaelhouse, Balgowan, Natal. Athletics. O.T.C. Feb. 1904 to Dec. 1907, Cadet Corporal. Student of Medicine, 1911-14. O.T.C. Artillery, Oct. 1911 to Oct. 1914, Cadet; Champion Driver. Native Rebellion in Natal, 1906. R.F.A. (S.R.), 2nd Lieut. Aug. 1914. Died in London on 13th September 1914. Pl. XXXV

HOBKINSON, CHARLES WILFRED (*b.* 1891).
United College, Bradford. Student of Arts, 1912-14. 6th York and Lancaster Regiment, 2nd Lieut. Aug. 1914. Died of wounds at Gallipoli on 23rd August 1915. Pl. XXXV.

HODGSON, ALFRED BRUCE (*b.* 1899).
Dollar Academy; First XV. O.T.C. 1916-17. Edinburgh University O.T.C. Infantry, Aug. 1917 to Jan. 1918, Cadet. Royal Air Force, Flight Cadet Jan. 1918. Died in training at 13th Canadian General Hospital, Hastings, on 23rd March 1918. Pl. XXXVI.

HOFMEYR, NICHOLAS JACOBUS (*b.* 1885).
B.A. (Cape). Student of Medicine, 1906-11; M.B., Ch.B. 1911. S.A. Medical Corps, Captain. German S.-W. and German E. Africa Campaigns, attached 2nd South African Horse. Died of dysentery at Kondoa-Waugi in 1916.

HOLMES, MATHEW (*b.* 1878).
Waitaki and Otago High Schools, N.Z. Athletics. Otago University (one year). Student of Medicine, 1897-1902. Athletics ("Blue") 1901. M.B., Ch.B. 1902; F.R.C.S.(Edin.) 1905; M.D. 1906. N.Z. Medical Corps, Major Aug. 1914; Lieut.-Colonel Dec. 1916. Samoa 1914. A.D.M.S., Egypt. Gallipoli July 1915. Sinai. No. 1 N.Z. Field Amb., France Dec. 1916. Invalided to New Zealand, Nov. 1917. A.D.M.S., Wellington, 1918. Dispatches Nov. 1914. Died of influenza at Wellington on 15th November 1918. Pl. XXXVI.

HOOPER, ALFRED OSWALD (*b.* 1878).
Epsom College; First XV. and XI. Student of Medicine, 1896-1903; M.B., Ch.B. 1903. Royal Naval Medical Service, Surgeon 1904; Staff Surgeon 1912. Killed by explosion on H.M.S. *Natal* on 30th December 1915. Pl. XXXVI.

HOPPS, HUGH JAMES (*b.* 1887).
George Watson's College; First XV. Student of Medicine, 1906-11; M.B., Ch.B. 1911. O.T.C. Artillery, Oct. 1908 to Feb. 1911, Cadet. Royal Navy, Surgeon Oct. 1913. H.M.S. *Aboukir*, Aug. 1914. Killed in action in North Sea on 22nd September 1914. Pl. XXXVI.

HORROX, HENRY M. (*b.* 1897).
George Watson's College. Student of Medicine, 1913-15. O.T.C. Artillery, Dec. 1914 to April 1915, Cadet. 24th Northumberland Fusiliers, 2nd Lieut. April 1915. France June 1916. Killed in action on the Somme on 2nd July 1916. Pl. XXXVI.

Roll of the Fallen

HOUNAM, SAMUEL WOLVES (*b.* 1896).
    Dumfries Academy. Student of Arts, 1914-15. Jardine of Tholieshope Bursar. O.T.C. Infantry, Oct. 1914 to April 1915, Cadet L/Corporal. 11th Royal Highlanders (Black Watch), 2nd Lieut. April 1915. Died on 2nd June 1918.
    Pl. XXXVI.

HOUSTON, JOHN (*b.* 1893).
    Edinburgh Institution. Student of Science, 1913-14. 3/9th Royal Scots (Highlanders), Private July 1915; Corporal April 1917. France. Wounded at Roeux on 23rd April and died at General Military Hospital, Boulogne, on 3rd May 1917.
    Pl. XXXVI.

HOUSTON, WILLIAM ROBERTSON (*b.* 1894).
    Dunfermline High School. Student of Arts, 1912-15. O.T.C. Infantry, Oct. 1914 to Jan. 1915, Cadet. 12th Royal Scots, 2nd Lieut. Jan. 1915; Acting Captain Autumn 1915; Captain 1916. France May 1915. Attached 1st Royal Scots Fusiliers. Died of wounds in France on 28th March 1916.
    Pl. XXXVI.

HOWIE, JOHN HENDERSON (*b.* 1894).
    George Heriot's School. O.T.C. 1910-13, Cadet Corporal. Student of Arts and Science, 1913-15. R.E. (Special Brigade), 3rd Battalion, Corporal July 1915. France. Died of gas poisoning on 1st September 1916 near Messines, Belgium.
    Pl. XXXVI.

HUDDLESTONE, SIDNEY CHANTLER (*b.* 1887).
    Kendal Grammar School. Student of Medicine, 1908-14; M.B., Ch.B. 1914. O.T.C. Infantry, May 1909 to June 1914, Lieut. 3rd Royal Highlanders (Black Watch (S.R.), 2nd Lieut. June 1914. France Nov. 1914. Killed at La Bassée on 25th January 1915.
    Pl. XXXVII.

HUGGAN, JAMES LAIDLAW (*b.* 1888).
    George Watson's College and Darlington Grammar School. Student of Medicine, 1905-11; M.B., Ch.B. 1911. O.T.C. Medical, March 1911 to July 1912. First XV. Edin. Univ. and London Scottish and International Rugby for Scotland. R.A.M.C., Lieut. July 1912, attached 3rd Coldstream Guards. France Aug. 1914. Battle of Mons. Dispatches Oct. 1914. Killed at the Battle of the Aisne on 16th September 1914.
    Pl. XXXVII.

HUMPHREYS, ARTHUR IDWAL (*b.* 1892).
    Nelson School, Wigton. Football and Swimming. Student of Medicine, 1910-13. O.T.C. Medical, April 1912 to Sept. 1914, Cadet. Scottish Horse, Private Sept. 1914. R.N.V.R., Sub-Lieut. Oct. 1914; Lieut. April 1915. Gallipoli Sept. 1915. Evacuation of Cape Helles, Jan. 1916. Salonika and France May 1916. Killed near Thiepval on 5th February 1917.
    Pl. XXXVII.

PLATE XXXVI.

A. B. HODGSON.

MATHEW HOLMES.

A. O. HOOPER.

H. J. HOPPS.

S. W. HOUNAM.

H. M. HORROX.

JOHN HOUSTON.

W. R. HOUSTON.

J. H. HOWIE.

PLATE XXXVII.

J. L. Huggan.

A. I. Humphreys.

S. C. Huddlestone.

G. A. Hunter.

John Hunter.

H. S. F. Hunter.

N. A. Hunter.

R. G. Hunter.

R. H. Hunter.

Roll of the Fallen

HUNTER, GEORGE ARNOLD (*b.* 1895).
George Watson's College; First XV. O.T.C. 1908-12. Student of Medicine, 1912-14. "A" XV. Scottish Horse (Field Ambulance), Private Sept. 1914; 2nd Lieut. July 1915; Lieut. Feb. 1917. Egypt Feb. 1916; Palestine. Imperial Camel Corps (M.G. Coy.). Died at Port Said on 3rd August 1917. Pl. XXXVII.

HUNTER, HUGH SWINERTON FORSYTH (*b.* 1896).
Boroughmuir School; First XV. Student of Science. O.T.C. Infantry, Nov. 1914 to March 1915, Cadet. 3rd and 1st King's Own Scottish Borderers, 2nd Lieut. March 1915. Gallipoli Oct. 1915. France. Killed in action at Beaumont Hamel on 29th April 1916. Pl. XXXVII.

HUNTER, JOHN (*b.* 1897).
Broxburn School and Bathgate Academy. Student of Arts, 1915-16. 23rd Machine-Gun Coy., Private July 1916; L/Corporal Oct. 1916. France. Killed at Passchendaele on 26th February 1918. Pl. XXXVII.

HUNTER, NORMAN ARCHBOLD (*b.* 1895).
Berwick Grammar School; Cricket. Student of Arts, 1912-15. R.A.M.C., Private Oct. 1915; Officer Cadet Dec. 1916. 26th Northumberland Fusiliers, 2nd Lieut. May 1917. France June 1917. Killed near St Quentin on 3rd September 1917. Pl. XXXVII.

HUNTER, ROBERT GIBSON (*b.* 1892).
Morrison's Academy, Crieff, and Edinburgh Academy. O.T.C. 1908-10. Student of Arts and Law, 1910-15; M.A. 1913. O.T.C. Infantry, Oct. 1910 to Feb. 1915, Cadet Coy. Sergeant-Major. 7th Argyll and Sutherland Highlanders, 2nd Lieut. Feb. 1915; Lieut. 1916. France July 1915. Killed at Roeux on 23rd April 1917. Pl. XXXVII.

HUNTER, ROBERT HOW (*b.* 1889).
Berwick Grammar School. Student of Arts, 1905-8; M.A. 1908. 21st King's Royal Rifle Corps, Private Jan. 1916. Killed in action in France on 15th September 1916. Pl. XXXVII.

HUNTER, WILLIAM ALEXANDER DOBSON (*b.* 1897).
George Watson's College. O.T.C. 1912-15, Lieut. Student of Arts, 1914-15. 3rd attached 8th Royal Highlanders (Black Watch), 9th Division, 2nd Lieut. July 1915; Lieut., Acting Captain. France Nov. 1916. 7th Seaforth Highlanders. Wounded near Arras in Jan. and in July 1917. Liaison Officer 1918. Killed near Ledeghem, Flanders, on 1st October 1918. Pl. XXXVIII.

HUSBAND, GEORGE STAUNTON (*b.* 1880).
Jamaica High School. Student of Medicine, 1898-1904; M.B., Ch.B. 1904. Indian Medical Service, Captain. D.S.O. Killed in action on 6th March 1917.

Roll of the Fallen

HUSBAND, JOSEPH SIM (*b.* 1888).
    Grove Academy, Broughty Ferry. M.A. (Hons. Engl.) 1913. 10th Gordon Highlanders, Private Nov. 1914; Sergeant, Dec. 1914; 2nd Lieut. Feb. 1915; Lieut. Sept. 1915; Captain Dec. 1915; Adjutant June 1916; Acting Major March 1918; Major April 1918. M.G.C. France. Dispatches (Loos) Sept. 1915, Jan. 1916 and April 1918. Wounded on 10th and died on 11th April 1918.   Pl. XXXVIII.

HUSBAND, PETER ROSS (*b.* 1886).
    Dundee High School. Student of Arts, 1903-8; M.A. 1908. Probationer U.F. Church. Inns of Court O.T.C., Private Dec. 1915. 1st Royal Highlanders (Black Watch), 2nd Lieut. 1916. Killed in France on 26th September 1916.   Pl. XXXVIII.

HUTCHISON, THOMAS (*b.* 1893).
    Monkton School and Ayr Academy; Dux. M.A. (Glasg.) 1913. Student of Divinity, 1913-15. O.T.C. Infantry, Oct. 1914 to Jan. 1915, Cadet. 11th Highland Light Infantry, 2nd Lieut. Jan. 1915; Bombing Officer. Killed in action on 20th May 1916.   Pl. XXXVIII.

HUTCHISON, THOMAS WALTER (*b.* 1886).
    Fettes College. Student of Law, 1907-8. Chartered Accountant, 1911. 10th Royal Scots, 2nd Lieut. 1906; Lieut. 1908; Captain 1909. Died at Edinburgh as result of an accident on 22nd November 1915.   Pl. XXXVIII.

HUTCHISON, WILLIAM MURRAY (*b.* 1893).
    Liverpool Institute. O.T.C. four years, Cadet Col.-Sergeant. Edinburgh University O.T.C. Infantry, Oct. 1912 to Aug. 1914, Cadet. 3rd attached 1st Liverpool Regiment, 2nd Lieut. Aug. 1914; Lieut. 1915; Captain 1916. France March 1915. M.C. Mentioned in Dispatches, May and Sept. 1915. Died of wounds in France on 27th April 1916.   Pl. XXXVIII.

HUTTON, WALTER FORBES (*b.* 1896).
    Dunfermline High School. Student of Science, 1913-15. O.T.C. Infantry, April to Aug. 1915, Cadet. 8th Royal Highlanders (Black Watch), 2nd Lieut. Aug. 1915. France June 1916. Killed in action on 16th July 1916. Pl. XXXVIII.

HYSLOP, JAMES (*b.* 1856).
    Student of Medicine; M.B., C.M. 1879. South African Medical Corps, Lieut.-Col.; Colonel and D.D.M.S. D.S.O. Died on service.

ILES, CHARLES COCHRANE (*b.* 1886).
    Dunedin High School and Otago University, N.Z. Student of Medicine, 1905-10; M.B., Ch.B. 1910; M.D. 1912; D.T.M. (Liverpool) 1911; D.P.H. (Dublin) 1913. R.A.M.C. (S.R.), Lieut. Aug. 1914. France Nov. 1914. Died of wounds near Estaires on 19th December 1914.   Pl. XXXVIII.

PLATE XXXVIII.

W. A. D. Hunter.

P. R. Husband.

J. S. Husband.

Thomas Hutchison.

Wm. M. Hutchison.

T. W. Hutchison.

R. S. M. Inch.

W. F. Hutton.

C. C. Iles.

PLATE XXXIX.

J. R. Ireland.

Elsie M. Inglis.

M. P. Inglis.

E. W. Irvine.

T. W. Irvine.

R. C. Irvine.

D. T. Jack.

R. N. Jervis.

J. W. Jarvis.

Roll of the Fallen

INCH, ROBERT STUART MARK (*b.* 1896).
George Watson's College. Edinburgh University O.T.C. Medical, Nov. 1914, Cadet. Norfolk Regiment, 2nd Lieut.; Lieut. Oct. 1917. France 1916 and Sept. 1917. M.C. Oct. 1916. Wounded Oct. 1916. Killed at Poelcapelle near Ypres on 22nd October 1917. Pl. XXXVIII.

INGLIS, ELSIE MAUD (*b.* 1864).
Charlotte Square School, Edinburgh. Student of Medicine; M.B., C.M. 1899; L.R.C.P. & S. (Edin.) and L.F.P.S. (Glasg.) 1892. Scottish Women's Hospitals, Founder. Serbian Orders of the White Eagle V. with Swords, April 1916, and of St Sava III.; Russian Order of St George. Died on 26th November 1917. Pl. XXXIX.

INGLIS, MAURICE PATERSON (*b.* 1891).
George Watson's College. Student of Medicine, 1909-15; M.B., Ch.B. 1914. O.T.C. Medical, April 1910 to May 1913, Cadet. R.A.M.C. (S.R.), Lieut. May 1913. Mobilised Nov. 1914. France Feb. 1915. Captain 1915. Dispatches. Killed at the Battle of the Somme on 17th September 1916. Pl. XXXIX.

IRELAND, JAMES REGINALD (*b.* 1897).
Daniel Stewart's College; First XV. and XI. 1st Highland Cadet Battn., 1912-14. Student of Science, 1914-15. O.T.C. Engineers, Jan. to July 1915, Cadet. 3rd Argyll and Sutherland Highlanders (S.R.), 2nd Lieut. July 1915. France. Killed at the Battle of the Somme on 29th October 1916. Pl. XXXIX.

IRELAND, JOHN THOMAS CRAIG (*b.* 1872).
Daniel Stewart's College. Student of Arts and Divinity; M.A. 1891. Minister, U.F. Church of Scotland. Chaplain, South African Campaign, 1900-1. Chaplain, 4th Class, 1915. France Aug. 1915. Salonika. Killed through the torpedoing of ship on 4th May 1917.

IRVINE, EDWARD WHITE (*b.* 1897).
Aberdeen Grammar School. Student of Medicine, Aberdeen Univ. and O.T.C. Medical, 1915-16. Edinburgh University O.T.C. Artillery, Aug. 1916 to Jan. 1917, Cadet; Officer Cadet Jan. 1917. R.F.A., 259th Brigade, 2nd Lieut. June 1917. Killed in action on 27th March 1918. Pl. XXXIX.

IRVINE, ROBERT CHARLES (*b.* 1885).
Queen's College, Belfast. Student of Medicine, 1907-13; M.B., Ch.B. 1913. R.A.M.C., Lieut. Oct. 1914; Captain Oct. 1915; Major Jan. 1918. Mesopotamia. Attached Indian Medical Service. Invalided home June 1916. France, 63rd Field Ambulance. Dispatches Nov. 1918. Died of influenza at Le Tréport on 10th November 1918. Pl. XXXIX.

Roll of the Fallen

IRVINE, THOMAS WALTER (*b.* 1865).
    Edinburgh Academy; First XV. and International for five years. Student of Medicine, 1883-7; M.B., C.M. 1887; F.R.C.S. and D.P.H. (Dublin) 1906. Indian Medical Service, July 1891. China 1900. Persian Frontier 1903-5. Lieut.-Col. July 1911. Chief Medical Officer for N.W.F.P. Kaisar-i-Hind, 1st Class, 1911. Died at Peshawar on 26th January 1919.   Pl. XXXIX.

JACK, DAVID TAIT (*b.* 1896).
    George Watson's College. Student of Medicine, 1914-15. 16th Royal Scots, L/Corporal 1915. France Jan. 1916. Killed in action on 29th June 1916.
        Pl. XXXIX.

JARVIS, JAMES WARDEN (*b.* 1891).
    Forfar Academy. M.A. (St Andrews) 1913. Hockey "Blue." O.T.C. Infantry, 1909-13. Student of Law, 1913-15. 7th King's Own Scottish Borderers, 2nd Lieut. Nov. 1914; Lieut. July 1915. France. Wounded at Battle of Loos on 25th and died on 26th September 1915.   Pl. XXXIX.

JASSINOWSKY, ABRAHAM (*b.* 1889).
    Student of Medicine, 1906-11; M.B., Ch.B. 1911. South African Medical Corps, Captain. German East Africa, 1916. Invalided to South Africa. Died at Windhuk in October 1918.

JENKINS, ROBERT HENRY CHARLES (*b.* 1883).
    Inverness College and Fettes College. Student of Law, 1905-7. 5th Canadian Infantry, Private Aug. 1914. 8th City of London Regiment (Post Office Rifles), 2nd Lieut. 1915. Died of wounds received in action in France 1916.

JENNINGS, FREDERICK SINCLAIR WILLS (*b.* 1882).
    St Paul's School. Student of Arts, 1902-3. 23rd Western Mounted Rifles, 1st Canadian Division, Private. France. Killed in action in Flanders on 6th July 1916.

JERVIS, ROBERT NORRIE (*b.* 1889).
    Peebles High School. Student of Science, 1909-12; B.Sc. 1912. O.T.C. Engineers, March 1910 to April 1914, Cadet Sergeant. R.E., 2nd Lieut. 1914; Lieut. 1915. France Sept. 1915. Killed at Laventie on 5th January 1916.   Pl. XXXIX.

JOHNS, FREDERICK NOEL (*b.* 1888).
    Wanganui School and Victoria College, N.Z. Student of Medicine, 1907-14; M.B., Ch.B. 1913. O.T.C. Artillery, May 1909 to Jan. 1913, Cadet. N.Z. Medical Corps, Captain April 1915; Major July 1918. Egypt, Gallipoli, and France. M.C. Jan. 1918. Killed in action on 25th August 1918.   Pl. XL.

JOHNSON, FREDERICK MILLER (*b.* 1863).
    Student of Medicine; M.B., C.M. 1886; M.D. 1888. Australian Army Medical Corps (6th Field Ambulance) Australian Imperial Force, Major. Gallipoli. Killed in action in the "Lone Pine" trenches on 29th November 1915.   Pl. XL.

PLATE XL.

R. C. JOHNSON.

F. N. JOHNS.

F. M. JOHNSON.

J. T. JOHNSTONE.

W. S. JOHNSTON.

G. W. JONES.

J. L. KELLY.

JOHN KELLIE.

JAMES KEMP.

PLATE XLI.

J. E. Kennedy.

M. A. Ker.

Alex. Kennedy.

J. B. Kincaid.

G. S. Kerr.

A. D. Kincaid.

A. D. C. King.

J. C. Kinmont.

R. F. Kilpatrick.

Roll of the Fallen

JOHNSON, RICHARD COLLING (*b.* 1894).
> Darlington Grammar School. Student of Science, 1912-15. O.T.C. Infantry, Oct. to Dec. 1914, Cadet. 13th Durham Light Infantry, 2nd Lieut. R.E. (Special Brigade), Lieut. Killed in action on 31st July 1917. Pl. XL.

JOHNSTON, WILLIAM SAVILE (*b.* 1893).
> Edinburgh Academy. O.T.C. 1909-11. Edinburgh University O.T.C. Infantry, Jan. 1913 to Aug. 1914, Cadet. 9th Royal Scots, Private Aug. 1914. 7th Argyll and Sutherland Highlanders, 2nd Lieut. Oct. 1914; Lieut. 1916. France. Wounded at Ypres in May 1915. Died of wounds in German hands at Inchy-en-Artois on 23rd March 1918. Pl. XL.

JOHNSTONE, JAMES TAIT (*b.* 1889).
> George Watson's College. Student of Science, 1910-14; B.Sc. 1914. O.T.C. Engineers, Oct. 1912 to Sept. 1914, Cadet L/Corporal. King's Own Scottish Borderers, 2nd Lieut. Sept. 1914; Border Regiment, Lieut. 1915. Gallipoli, Suvla Bay, Egypt, and France. Killed at Thiepval, the Somme, on 29th September 1916. Pl. XL.

JOLLY, JOHN SPENCER (*b.* 1889).
> Daniel Stewart's College; Dux. Student of Arts, 1906-10; M.A. (Hons. Classics) 1910. O.T.C. Infantry, May 1909 to May 1911, Cadet. 16th Royal Scots, Private; Sergeant. Killed in action in France on 1st July 1916.

JONES, GEORGE WILLIAM (*b.* 1879).
> Morgan Academy, Dundee. Student of Arts, Science, Law, and Divinity, 1897-1903; Cobb Scholar; M.A. 1903; B.Sc.; LL.B. R.N.V.R., Sub-Lieut. Royal Air Force, Lieut. and Meteorological Officer; Staff Captain. Died of pneumonia in London on 4th November 1918. Pl. XL.

KEITH, GEORGE ELPHISTONE (*b.* 1864).
> Royal High School; Athletics. Student of Medicine, 1882-7; M.B., C.M. 1887. Red Cross, M.O., 15th Detachment City of London. R.A.M.C., Captain July 1915. Died of influenza at 62nd General Hospital, Italy, on 6th December 1918.

KELLIE, JOHN (*b.* 1883).
> Kilmarnock Academy. Student of Arts and Divinity, 1900-4; M.A. 1904; B.D. Chaplain, attached 6th Cameron Highlanders, 15th Division, May 1915. Dispatches 1916-17. Killed in action on 31st July 1917. Pl. XL.

KELLY, JOHN LAWSON (*b.* 1894).
> Hurstpierpoint School. O.T.C. for three years, Cadet Sergeant. Edinburgh University O.T.C. Infantry, Sept. to Nov. 1915, Cadet. R.E., Lieut. M.C. Killed in action in France on 4th November 1918. Pl. XL.

KEMP, JAMES (*b.* 1893).
> George Watson's College. Student of Law, 1913-14. 4th Royal Scots, mobilised Aug. 1914, Private; L/Corporal Nov. 1915; Coy. Q.M.S. Egypt and Palestine Jan. 1916. Killed in action at Gaza on 19th April 1917. Pl. XL.

Roll of the Fallen

KEMP, JAMES OGILVIE (*b.* 1865).
    Student of Law, 1888-1890 and 1894-5; M.A.; LL.B.; Advocate, 1889. Q.R.V.B., 5th Royal Scots, 1898, Captain. Rejoined Oct. 1914. Died on 12th December 1917.

KENNEDY, ALEXANDER (*b.* 1893).
    Daniel Stewart's College; First XV. Student of Medicine, 1910-14. 15th Royal Scots, Private Oct. 1914; Sergeant. 11th Royal Scots, 2nd Lieut. 1917; Lieut.; Captain Oct. 1917. France. M.C. and Dispatches Oct. 1917. Wounded. Killed near Albert on 26th March 1918.   Pl. XLI.

KENNEDY, JOHN EDWIN (*b.* 1890).
    Royal Academy, Inverness. Hockey. M.A. (St Andrews) 1913. Student of Law, Edinburgh University, 1913-15. 13th Royal Scots, Private Sept. 1914. 8th Seaforth Highlanders, 2nd Lieut. Sept. 1914; Lieut. Dec. 1914. France. Killed at Loos on 25th September 1915.   Pl. XLI.

KER, MALCOLM ALBERT (*b.* 1862).
    George Watson's College. Student of Medicine, 1878-84; M.B., C.M. 1884; Resident, R. I., Edinburgh. Indian Medical Service, Lieut.-Col. Hospital Ship *Loyalty*, Aug. 1914. Invalided home Dec. 1914. Died in London on 24th February 1915.   Pl. XLI.

KERR, GEORGE STANLEY (*b.* 1897).
    Student of Medicine, 1914-16. O.T.C. Infantry, May to Nov. 1915, Cadet. 5th and 13th Royal Scots, Private. France Jan. 1916. Severely wounded at Battle of the Ancre, Nov. 1916. Killed in action in France on 22nd August 1917. Pl. XLI.

KILPATRICK, ROBERT FYFE (*b.* 1893).
    George Watson's College; First XV. Student of Law, 1910-15. Chartered Accountant, 1915. Argyll and Sutherland Highlanders, Private July 1915. France 1916. Wounded at the Battle of the Somme and died at Rouen on 25th September 1916.   Pl. XLI.

KINCAID, ANDREW DUNCAN (*b.* 1898).
    Berwickshire High School, Duns. Student of Medicine, 1915-16. O.T.C. Infantry, Oct. 1915 to Jan. 1917, Cadet; Officer Cadet. 8th Royal Highlanders (Black Watch), 2nd Lieut. May 1917. France Aug. 1917. Wounded and missing, presumed killed, at Equancourt near Cambrai on 22nd March 1918.   Pl. XLI.

KINCAID, JAMES BROWN (*b.* 1890).
    Berwickshire High School, Duns. Student of Arts, 1907-11; M.A. (Hons. Engl.) 1911. Athletics. 6th Royal Scots, 1907-14. 13th Royal Scots, 2nd Lieut. Sept. 1914; Lieut. 1916. France 1915. Killed in action at Guémappe near Arras on 23rd April 1917.   Pl. XLI.

KING, ALEXANDER DUNCAN CAMPBELL (*b.* 1886).
    Edinburgh Academy; First XV. Student of Arts, 1904-5. 18th Hussars, Lieut. 1914. Died of gas poisoning at Hooge, Flanders, on 24th May 1915.   Pl. XLI.

Roll of the Fallen

KINMONT, JOHN COLLIE (*b.* 1895).
    Merchiston Castle; Athletics. O.T.C. 1908-12. Student of Law, 1912-14. O.T.C. Infantry, Oct. 1912 to Feb. 1914, Cadet L/Corporal. 1st and 3rd Cameron Highlanders, 2nd Lieut. Nov. 1913; Lieut. April 1915; Captain April 1916. France Jan. 1915. Wounded at Bethune, La Bassée, Feb. 1915. Adjutant, School of Musketry, Edinburgh. A.D.C. to G.O.C. East Coast Defences (two years). Tank Corps, March 1917. France July 1917. Killed at Gouzeaucourt on 18th November 1917.   Pl. XLI.

KIRK, JAMES (*b.* 1873).
    Dunfermline High School. M.A. (St Andrews). Student of Divinity 1898-1901. Minister, Church of Scotland; Chaplain, 2nd Seaforth Highlanders and 7th Argyll and Sutherland Highlanders. France 1915-18. Dispatches April 1916. M.C. June 1917. Wounded at Fampoux on the Scarpe 27th March and died at Wimereux on 1st April 1918.   Pl. XLII.

KIRKLAND, WILLIAM HARRISON CAMERON (*b.* 1884).
    Ayr Academy. Student of Arts and Law, 1901-4; M.A. 1904; LL.B. 1907; Advocate, 1908. O.T.C. Infantry, Sept. to Oct. 1914, Cadet. 7th Cameron Highlanders, 44th Highland Brigade, 15th Division, 2nd Lieut. Aug. 1914; Lieut. Sept. 1914; Captain Oct. 1914. France. Killed at the Battle of Loos on 25th September 1915.   Pl. XLII.

KIRKPATRICK, ROBERT B. (See p. 116.)

KITCHENER, THE RIGHT HON. EARL KITCHENER OF KHARTOUM.
    LL.D. 1898. Lord Rector, 1914-16. Field-Marshal. Secretary of State for War. K.G., K.P., G.C.B., O.M., G.C.M.G., G.C.S.I., G.C.I.E. Drowned by sinking of H.M.S. *Hampshire* on 5th June 1916.   Pl. I.

KUNY, SIMON ALEXANDER (*b.* 1892).
    Grey College and University, Bloemfontein. Student of Medicine, 1910-15; M.B., Ch.B. 1915. O.T.C. Infantry, May 1911 to July 1915, Cadet Coy. Sergeant-Major. R.A.M.C., Lieut. July 1915; Captain July 1916. France. Died of influenza at Cape Town on 17th October 1918.   Pl. XLII.

KYDD, JOHN WILLIAM ALBERT (*b.* 1898).
    Llanelly Bounty School. O.T.C. 1914-15. Edinburgh University O.T.C. Infantry, Oct. 1916 to March 1917, Cadet; Officer Cadet. 3rd attached 19th Lancashire Fusiliers, 2nd Lieut. Aug. 1917. France. Killed at Ypres on 26th March 1918.   Pl. XLII.

LAIDLAW, JOHN LESLIE (*b.* 1894).
    Kelso High School and Merchiston Castle. Student of Medicine, 1912-14. O.T.C. Infantry, Oct. 1913 to Oct. 1914, Cadet. 10th Argyll and Sutherland Highlanders, 2nd Lieut. Oct. 1914. France Feb. 1916. Wounded at Longueval on the 16th and 17th and died of wounds on 20th July 1916.   Pl. XLII.

Roll of the Fallen

LAING, GEORGE (*b.* 1893).
    East Linton and Dunbar Schools. Student of Arts, 1912-15. Royal Scots, Private Feb. 1915. Scottish Rifles (Cameronians), 2nd Lieut. Sept. 1915. Killed in action on 10th April 1917.   Pl. XLII.

LAING, JAMES McDOUGALL (*b.* 1894).
    Nairn Academy and Allan Glen's School, Glasgow. Student of Science, 1912-14. O.T.C. Engineers, April to Oct. 1914, Cadet. 25th Battn. Machine-Gun Corps, 2nd Lieut. Oct. 1914; Lieut. Dec. 1915. Reported killed in action on 23rd March 1918.   Pl. XLII.

LAMB, JOHN McNAIR (*b.* 1899).
    George Watson's College; First XV. and XI. O.T.C. 1915-16, Cadet Sergeant. Student of Arts, 1916-17. O.T.C. Artillery, Oct. 1916 to Dec. 1917, Cadet Sergeant; Officer Cadet Dec. 1917. R.F.A., 82nd Brigade, 2nd Lieut. Aug. 1918. France. Killed in action on 4th November 1918.   Pl. XLII.

LANDELLS, THOMAS BEACH (*b.* 1895).
    Boroughmuir School. Student of Arts, 1912-14. 15th Royal Scots, Signalling Sergeant Sept. 1914. Killed in action in France on 1st July 1916.   Pl. XLII.

LASCELLES, ARTHUR MOORE, *V.C.* (See p. 754.)

LATTA, ALEXANDER JAMES JOPP (*b.* 1895).
    Edinburgh Academy. Student of Arts, 1913-15. O.T.C. Artillery, Dec. 1914 to April 1915, Cadet. R.F.A., 2nd Lieut. April 1915. France June 1915. Killed in action on 5th August 1916.   Pl. XLIII.

LATTA, ROBERT WILLIAM CAMPBELL (*b.* 1887).
    Edinburgh Academy. Student of Arts and Law, 1907-8. Inns of Court O.T.C., Private Feb. 1916; Officer Cadet Nov. 1916. 2nd Seaforth Highlanders, 2nd Lieut. March 1917; Brigade Intelligence Officer, July 1917. France May 1917. Wounded on 4th and died at 14th General Hospital on 22nd October 1917.   Pl. XLIII.

LAW, JOHN DOUGLAS (*b.* 1890).
    Boroughmuir and Broughton Schools. Student of Arts and Science, 1909-16; M.A., B.Sc. 1916. 2nd Royal Scots Fusiliers, Private June 1916. France. Killed at Battle of Arras near Chérisy on 23rd April 1917.   Pl. XLIII.

LAWRENCE, EDWARD WILLIAM (*b.* 1888).
    Christ's College, Brecon; First XI. Student of Medicine, 1905-10; M.B., Ch.B. 1910. R.A.M.C., Lieut. Nov. 1914; Captain. Attached 10th Welsh Regiment. Killed in action on 10th July 1916.   Pl. XLIII.

LAWRENCE, HENRY RUTHVEN. (See p. 116.)

LAWSON, DAVID (*b.* 1881).
    Leven School. Student of Arts; M.A. 1907. Schoolmaster. 16th Royal Scots, Private Dec. 1914; Sergeant. France. Missing, presumed killed at the Battle of the Somme on 1st July 1916.   Pl. XLIII.

PLATE XLII.

JAMES KIRK.   W. H. C. KIRKLAND.   S. A. KUNY.

J. L. LAIDLAW.   GEORGE LAING.   J. W. A. KYDD.

T. B. LANDELLS.   J. M. LAMB.   J. McD. LAING.

PLATE XLIII.

J. D. LAW.   A. J. J. LATTA.   R. W. C. LATTA.

E. W. LAWRENCE.   DAVID LAWSON.   J. L. LAWSON.

G. M. LEVACK.   JOHN LECKIE.   J. W. LAWSON.

Roll of the Fallen

LAWSON, JOHN LAWSON (*b.* 1882).
Edinburgh Academy. Student of Science, 1900-1. 2nd Seaforth Highlanders, Private Aug. 1914; 2nd Lieut. Oct. 1915. Battalion Machine-Gun Officer. France. Killed in action on 14th October 1916. Pl. XLIII.

LAWSON, JOHN WILSON (*b.* 1888).
Dunning School and Perth Academy. Student of Law, 1908-10. O.T.C. May to Nov. 1915, Cadet. Scot Maxim Cycle Corps, Private Nov. 1914. 11th Royal Highlanders (Black Watch), 2nd Lieut. May 1915. Machine-Gun Corps, 41st Divisional Brigade, Lieut.; Captain 1916. M.C. Jan. 1918. France. Killed in action near Sapignies on 24th March 1918. Pl. XLIII.

LECKIE, JOHN (*b.* 1891).
George Watson's College; Athletics. Student of Arts and Science, 1913-15. O.T.C. Engineers, Dec. 1914 to July 1915. 10th South Staffordshire Regiment, 2nd Lieut. July 1915. Machine-Gun Corps, 56th Battn., Jan. 1916; Lieut. Nov. 1916; Captain Feb. 1918; Major March 1918. France July 1916 with 56th Division. The Somme, Arras, third Battle of Ypres, and first Cambrai. M.C. June 1918. Dispatches May 1917. Wounded four times. Died of wounds received near Bullecourt on 29th August 1918. Pl. XLIII.

LEVACK, GEORGE MACLEOD (*b.* 1891).
Broughton School. Student of Medicine, 1909-14; M.B., Ch.B. 1914. R.A.M.C., Captain, attached Oxford and Bucks Light Infantry. Killed in action on 7th October 1916. Pl. XLIII.

LEWIS, CHARLES WILLIAMS (*b.* 1880).
South African College, Cape Town; B.A. (Science), (Cape University). Student of Medicine, 1899-1904 and 1910-15; M.B., Ch.B. 1914. Royal Navy, H.M.S. *Queen Mary*, Surgeon. Killed in the Battle of Jutland on 31st May 1916.
Pl. XLIV.

LIDDLE, WILLIAM (*b.* 1887).
Edinburgh Academy; First XV. Student of Arts and Law, 1905-11; M.A. 1909. Writer to the Signet, 1912. Queen's Edinburgh Mounted Rifles. 9th Royal Scots, 2nd Lieut. 1910; Lieut. 1913; Captain 1915. O.C. Signals, 17th Corps, R.A., and 17th Corps Signalling School. France Feb. 1915. Second Battle of Ypres and the Somme in 1916. Died of pneumonia on 27th September 1918. Pl. XLIV.

LINDSAY, DAVID PATON (*b.* 1883).
Longridge School. Student of Medicine, 1907-12; M.B., Ch.B. 1912. R.A.M.C., Lieut. May 1917; Captain May 1918. East Africa, May 1917. Died at Dar-es-Salaam, East Africa, on 2nd December 1918. Pl. XLIV.

LINKLATER, WILLIAM IRVINE (*b.* 1898).
George Watson's College; University Bursar. O.T.C. Edinburgh University O.T.C. Artillery, Aug. 1916 to Feb. 1917, Cadet; Officer Cadet Feb. 1917. R.F.A., 2nd Lieut. Aug. 1917. France Sept. 1917. Killed at Martinsart on 5th April 1918. Pl. XLIV.

Roll of the Fallen

LINTON, JOHN KEDDIE (*b.* 1893).
    Portobello School. Student of Science, 1910-12. 2nd Otago Infantry Regiment, Private April 1916. 2nd Anzac Corps. France. Killed in action in Flanders, on 12th October 1917.   Pl. XLIV.

LINZELL, STANLEY JAMES (*b.* 1888).
    The College, Bishop's Stortford, Herts. Student of Medicine, 1906-12; M.B., Ch.B. 1912. Pres. Royal Med. Soc. R.A.M.C., Lieut. Jan. 1914; Captain March 1915. France 1914. Attached R.E., 2nd Bridging Train. D.A.D.M.S., 32nd Division, Sept. 1916. Croix de Guerre March 1917; M.C. April 1917. Wounded Feb. 1915 and March 1917. Killed in action on 2nd April 1917.   Pl. XLIV.

LODGE, RICHARD CUTHBERT (*b.* 1894).
    Merchiston Castle. Student of Arts and Science, 1913-14. 4th Royal Scots, Private till Dec. 1914. 16th Royal Scots, 2nd Lieut. Dec. 1914; Lieut. 1915. France April 1916. Killed in action near Hargicourt on 27th August 1917.   Pl. XLIV.

LOGIE, ALEXANDER GRAHAM SPEIRS (*b.* 1866).
    Dirleton School and Edinburgh Institution. Student of Medicine, 1882-7; M.B., C.M. 1887. R.A.M.C., Lieut. April 1915; Captain. Highland Mounted Brigade Field Ambulance, Egypt Nov. 1915 to July 1916. 1st Northern General Hospital, Newcastle, Jan. 1917, where he died of pneumonia on 1st February 1919.   Pl. XLIV.

LORIMER, JAMES BANNERMAN (*b.* 1879).
    Edinburgh Academy; First XV. Student of Arts and Law, 1896-9; M.A. 1899. Writer to the Signet, 1903. Pres., Dialectic and Speculative Societies. Univ. Battery, E.C.A.V., 1896-9, Bombardier. Queen's Edin. Mtd. Rifles, 1900. 9th Royal Scots, Corporal Aug. 1914. 8th Cameron Highlanders, Lieut. Dec. 1914; Captain Feb. 1915. France Aug. 1916, attached 5th Cameron Highlanders. Killed at Roeux near Arras on 3rd May 1917.   Pl. XLIV.

LOTHIAN, NORMAN BRUCE (*b.* 1889).
    George Watson's College; First XV. and Athletics. Cadet Corps 1905-8. Student of Arts, 1908-12; M.A. (Hons. Engl.) 1912. Pres., Diagnostic Society. O.T.C. Infantry, Dec. 1909 to Feb. 1913, Cadet. 15th and 48th King's Canadian Highlanders, Private Sept. 1914. France 1915. Died of wounds received at Ypres on 21st May 1915.   Pl. XLV.

LOW, ALEXANDER PETRIE.
    Student of Medicine; M.B., C.M. 1896. R.A.M.C., Captain, attached 7th Seaforth Highlanders. Killed in action on 14th July 1916.

LOW, JOHN JACKSON (*b.* 1894).
    Perth Academy. Student of Science, 1912-15. Donald Fraser Bursar. R.E. (Special Brigade), Corporal July 1915; 2nd Lieut. Aug. 1916. France 1915. M.M. July 1916 and M.C. Aug. 1916. Killed at Ypres on 3rd December 1917.   Pl. XLV.

PLATE XLIV.

 D. P. LINDSAY.

 WM. LIDDLE.

 C. W. LEWIS.

 J. K. LINTON.

 WM. I. LINKLATER.

 J. B. LORIMER.

 A. G. S. LOGIE.

 S. J. LINZELL.

 R. C. LODGE.

PLATE XLV.

 N. B. LOTHIAN.

 J. J. LOW.

 GEORGE LOWRIE.

 WM. LOWSON.

 H. T. LUKYN-WILLIAMS.

 N. C. LUCAS.

 G. H. LUNAN.

 ROBERT LUSK.

 J. J. LYBURN.

Roll of the Fallen

LOWRIE, GEORGE (*b.* 1895).
   Boroughmuir School. Student of Arts, 1913-15. 8th, 1st and 4/5th Royal Highlanders (Black Watch), Private July 1915. France Dec. 1915 to July 1916, and Dec. 1917 till March 1918. Wounded at the Somme July 1916. Killed in action in France on 24th March 1918. Pl. XLV.

LOWSON, WILLIAM (*b.* 1884).
   George Watson's College. Student of Arts and Law, 1902-9; M.A. 1905; LL.B. 1908. Vans Dunlop Scholar. Advocate, 1908. 5th and 16th Royal Scots, Private Nov. 1914; 2nd Lieut. April 1915. France. Wounded near Beaumont Hamel. Died of wounds on 17th November 1916. Pl. XLV.

LUCAS, NORMAN CAREY (*b.* 1893).
   Pietermaritzburg School and University College. Student of Arts and Science, 1911-15; M.A. 1913; B.Sc. 1914. Carnegie "Research" Scholar. Athletics. O.T.C. Infantry, Jan. to March 1915, Cadet. Scottish Rifles, attached Connaught Rangers and 6th Brigade Royal Irish Rifles, 2nd Lieut. 1915; Captain. Gallipoli and Serbia 1915. Macedonia 1916. Died of wounds at Lahana, Macedonia, on 2nd November 1916. Pl. XLV.

LUKYN-WILLIAMS, HERBERT TEMPLE (*b.* 1886).
   Monkton Combe School. Student of Medicine; M.B., Ch.B. 1911. R.A.M.C., Lieut. Feb. 1915; Captain Feb. 1916. France. Died of wounds received at Méricourt-on-Somme on 26th March 1918. Pl. XLV.

LUNAN, GEORGE HAROLD (*b.* 1891).
   Daniel Stewart's College. Student of Medicine, 1908-13; M.B., Ch.B. 1913. O.T.C. Artillery 1908-13, Cadet Corporal. R.A.M.C., Lieut., attached 9th Lancers Aug. 1914. France 1914. Killed at Wieltze, Belgium, on 13th May 1915. Pl. XLV.

LUSK, ROBERT (*b.* 1891).
   Knox Institute, Haddington. Student of Arts, 1909-12; M.A. 1912. 4th Royal Scots, Private Nov. 1915. Killed at Gaza, Palestine, on 19th April 1917. Pl. XLV.

LYBURN, JOHN JARDINE (*b.* 1894).
   Glasgow High School and George Watson's College. Student of Science, 1912-13. 5th Dragoon Guards, Private Sept. 1914. R.F.A., 2nd Lieut. Aug. 1915. Salonika Jan. 1916. Died of dysentery at Salonika on 13th October 1916. Pl. XLV.

LYELL, DAVID (*b.* 1888).
   Merchiston Castle. Cadet Corps 1902-7; Cadet Corporal. B.A. (Oxford). Student of Law, 1911-14; LL.B. 1914. Advocate. 7th Royal Scots, 2nd Lieut. Aug. 1914. Killed in action at Gallipoli on 12th July 1915. Pl. XLVI.

LYON, ROBERT (*b.* 1891).
   Aberdeen Grammar School. M.A. (Hons. Econs.) (Aberdeen) 1912. Student of Law, 1913-14; LL.B. (Distinction) 1914. 4th Gordon Highlanders (Aberdeen Univ. Coy.) four years, Sergeant. 5th Gordon Highlanders, Lieut. Sept. 1914; Acting Captain. France. Killed near High Wood on the Somme on 30th July 1916. Pl. XLVI.

Roll of the Fallen

LYON, WALTER SCOTT STUART (*b.* 1886).
    Haileybury. Cadet Battalion 1902-5. B.A. (Oxford). Student of Law, 1909-12; LL.B. 1912. Advocate. 9th Royal Scots, April 1910, Lieut. Feb. 1913. Staff Captain, Lothian Brigade, 1914-15. France 1915. Author of "Easter at Ypres 1915, and other Poems." Killed at Ypres on 8th May 1915.   Pl. XLVI.

MACALISTER, GEORGE HOWDEN (*b.* 1891).
    George Watson's College. Student of Arts, 1910-14; M.A. (Hons. Phil.) 1914. 15th Royal Scots, Private Sept. 1914. 3/5th Royal Scots Fusiliers, attached 78th Machine-Gun Coy., 2nd Lieut. July 1915. Salonika July 1916. Missing, presumed killed on Salonika Front on 24th August 1916.   Pl. XLVI.

MACAULAY, MAXWELL STANLEY (*b.* 1887).
    Daniel Stewart's College; First XV. Student of Science, 1903-7. Assoc. I.M.E. Lothians and Border Horse, Private 1916; 2nd Lieut. Dec. 1916. Salonika. G.H.Q., Egyptian Expeditionary Force. Killed in action in Palestine on 7th May 1918.   Pl. XLVI.

McBAIN, JOHN MORTIMER (*b.* 1895).
    Aberdeen Grammar School; Dux. Edinburgh University O.T.C. Artillery, July to Aug. 1915, Cadet. R.F.A. attached 231st Brigade, 2nd Lieut. Aug. 1915. France. Died of wounds in German Field Hospital at Vraucourt, France, on 9th July 1916.   Pl. XLVI.

McCALLUM, ROBERT PAXTON FORSYTH (*b.* 1897).
    Gordon's College, Aderdeen, and Daniel Stewart's College. Edinburgh University O.T.C. Infantry, May to Sept. 1916, Cadet. R.F.C., Cadet Sept. 1916; Flight Cadet Dec. 1917. Transferred to R.N.V.R. Accidentally killed while flying in the South of England on 8th October 1918.   Pl. XLVI.

McCASKIE, ROY WHITE (*b.* 1890).
    Harris Academy, Dundee. Student of Science, 1911-14; B.Sc. 1914. R.F.A., Gunner Jan. 1915 1/6th Seaforth Highlanders, 2nd Lieut. July 1915; Lieut. 1917. France. M.C. Sept. 1917; Bar to M.C. July 1918. Died of wounds received near Rheims on 5th August 1918.   Pl. XLVI.

McCAW, HUGH JOHN (*b.* 1885).
    Dunedin High School. Student of Medicine, 1905-11; M.B., Ch.B. 1911; F.R.C.S. (Edin.) Royal Navy, Surgeon. Lambeth Infirmary, Resident Surgeon. Died there of pneumonia in November 1918.   Pl. XLVI.

McCLINTOCK, LAWSON TAIT.
    Shrewsbury. Boating. Student of Medicine; M.B., Ch.B. 1901. Medical Officer, Loddon and Hendenham Red Cross Hospital, 1915-18, and 172nd and 342nd Brigade, R.F.A., 1916-18. R.A.M.C. (V.), Captain May 1918. Mention March 1919. Died of pneumonia on 11th November 1918.   Pl. XLVII.

PLATE XLVI.

DAVID LYELL.

ROBERT LYON.

W. S. S. LYON.

J. M. McBAIN.

G. H. MACALISTER.

M. S. MACAULAY.

R. P. F. McCALLUM.

H. J. McCAW.

R. W. McCASKIE.

PLATE XLVII.

PRIMROSE McCONNELL.

L. T. McCLINTOCK.

WM. McCONAGHY.

JOHN MACDIARMID.

J. F. McCREDIE.

A. B. McCRAE.

M. D. MACDONALD.

MALCOLM MACDONALD.
(A. & S. Highlanders.)

J. M. MACDONALD.

Roll of the Fallen

M'CONAGHY, WILLIAM (*b.* 1881).
 United Services College, Westward Ho; First XV. Student of Medicine, 1899-1904; M.B., Ch.B. 1904. R.A.M.C., Lieut. 1905; Captain 1909; Major; Lieut.-Colonel. France Aug. 1914. Severely wounded Aug. 1914. Egypt and Arabia. Dispatches. D.S.O. 1918; Order of the Nile 1918. Died at Tor, Arabia, on 4th July 1918. Pl. XLVII.

McCONNELL, PRIMROSE (*b.* 1890).
 Loughton School. Student of Science, 1911-14; B.Sc. 1914, Steven Scholar. R.F.A., 101st Brigade, Gunner Sept. 1914; 2nd Lieut. Nov. 1914; Lieut. Feb. 1916; Acting Captain Nov. 1917; Captain Feb. 1918. Macedonia. Dispatches Oct. 1917 and Nov. 1918. M.C. June 1918. Killed in action on Salonika Front on 18th September 1918. Pl. XLVII.

McCORMACK, JOHN SIDES DAVIES.
 Student of Medicine; L.R.C.P. & S. (Edin.); L.F.P.S. (Glasg.) 1894. Royal Navy, H.M.S. *Black Prince*, Surgeon. Killed in action at Battle of Jutland on 31st May 1916.

McCRAE, ANDREW BOWIE (*b.* 1886).
 High School, Dundee; Football. Student of Arts and Law, 1909-11; M.A. LL.B. 1911; Law Agent. 2nd Lovat Scouts, Private Oct. 1914; Sergeant. Died of wounds at Gallipoli on 17th November 1915. Pl. XLVII.

McCREDIE, JOHN FORREST (*b.* 1896).
 High School, Stranraer; Swimming. Student of Medicine, 1914-15. Inns of Court O.T.C., Oct. 1915, Cadet; Cadet Corporal 1916. Machine-Gun Corps, 2nd Lieut. Nov. 1916. France. Missing, presumed killed at Villers-Guislain, Cambrai, on 30th November 1917. Pl. XLVII.

MACDIARMID, JOHN (*b.* 1885).
 George Watson's College. Student of Medicine, 1902-7; M.B., Ch.B. 1907. N.Z. Medical Corps, Captain 1916. Died of appendicitis at Wellington, N.Z., on 18th March 1917. Pl. XLVII.

MACDONALD, JOHN MELLIS (*b.* 1892).
 Fettes College. O.T.C. Student of Arts, 1911-14. O.T.C. Infantry, Oct. 1911 to June 1913, Cadet; June 1913 to Aug. 1914, Lieut. 1st Scottish Rifles (Cameronians), 2nd Lieut. Aug. 1914; Lieut.; Captain. France Oct. 1914, attached Royal Scots Fusiliers. First Battle of Ypres. France 1915 with 1st Scottish Rifles. Killed at High Wood on the Somme on 20th July 1916. Pl. XLVII.

MACDONALD, MALCOLM (*b.* 1893).
 George Watson's College; First XV. Student of Medicine, 1913-14. 10th Royal Highlanders (Black Watch), 2nd Lieut.; Lieut. Killed in action on the Salonika Front on 10th October 1916.

Roll of the Fallen

MACDONALD, MALCOLM (b. 1897).
    Carlisle Grammar School. Student of Medicine, 1915-16. Argyll and Sutherland Highlanders, Private. Killed in action on 13th October 1916.   Pl. XLVII.

MACDONALD, MURDOCH DONALD (b. 1888).
    Aird School, Stornoway, and Provincial Training College, Glasgow. Student of Arts, 1913-15. O.T.C. Infantry, Oct. to Dec. 1914, Cadet. 9th Seaforth Highlanders, 2nd Lieut. Dec. 1914. Killed in action on 19th July 1916.   Pl. XLVII.

MACDONALD, RODERICK OSWALD CORDEROY (b. 1893).
    Royal High School. Student of Arts, 1911-13. O.T.C. Artillery, 1911 to Sept. 1914, Cadet Bombardier. R.F.A. (S.R.), 2nd Lieut. Sept. 1914; Lieut. Dec. 1916. R.F.C., Observer, March 1917; Captain July 1918. Gallipoli, France, and Egypt. M.C. at the Battle of the Somme Aug. 1916. Dispatches June 1917. Killed in flying accident at Dover on 10th August 1918.   Pl. XLVIII.

MACDONALD BROWN, IAN (b. 1888).
    St Paul's School, London; Athletics. O.T.C. two years. B.A. (Science Tripos), (Camb.); M.A. 1913. Student of Medicine; M.R.C.S. (Eng.) and L.R.C.P. (Lond.) 1914. R.A.M.C., Lieut. Aug. 1914; Captain Sept. 1915. Gallipoli 1915-16. France, attached R.F.A., Sept. 1916. Killed in action near Ypres on 15th November 1916.   Pl. XLVIII.

McELNEY, ROBERT GERALD (b. 1892).
    Campbell College, Belfast. O.T.C. 1908-10, Cadet Corporal. Student of Medicine, 1910-11. B.A., M.B., Ch.B. (Belfast). R.A.M.C. (S.R.), Lieut. 1913; Captain 1917. France, 25th and 51st Divisions. M.C. at Battle of the Somme, Oct. 1916. Killed in action near Grevillers on 21st March 1918.   Pl. XLVIII.

McEWAN, GEORGE CAMERON (b. 1896).
    George Watson's College; First XV. Student of Arts, 1914-16. O.T.C. Infantry, Sept. 1914 to Nov. 1915, Cadet Sergeant. 10th attached 7th Seaforth Highlanders, 2nd Lieut. Nov. 1915. France Aug. 1916. Killed in action on 9th April 1917.   Pl. XLVIII.

McEWAN, JAMES ARCHIBALD (b. 1891).
    Royal High School; Athletics. Student of Arts, 1911-16. Treasurer, Philomathic Society. Machine-Gun Corps, Signaller Feb. 1916. France. Missing, presumed killed, on 21st March 1918.   Pl. XLVIII.

McEWEN, DAVID CAMPBELL (b. 1885).
    Edinburgh Academy and Radley College. Student of Law, 1905-8. Rowing. Writer to the Signet, 1910. 3/9th Royal Scots, 2nd Lieut. Dec. 1915. France Aug. 1916; Somme and Beaumont Hamel. Wounded at Vimy Ridge, Battle of Arras, on 9th and died at Aubigny on 10th April 1917.   Pl. XLVIII.

PLATE XLVIII.

R. O. C. MACDONALD.

I. MACDONALD BROWN.

R. G. McELNEY.

D. C. McEWEN.

J. A. McEWAN.

G. C. McEWAN.

IAN MACFARLANE.

C. J. B. McGEORGE.

W. R. K. MACGILLIVRAY.

PLATE XLIX.

J. G. MACINDOE.

R. A. M. MACGREGOR.

E. J. H. MACILDOWIE.

JOHN MCINTOSH.

R. R. MCINTOSH.

D. J. MACIVER.

W. R. B. MCJANNET.

KENNETH MCIVER.

J. N. MCIVER.

Roll of the Fallen

MACFARLANE, ALEXANDER NELSON (*b.* 1870).
   Royal High School. Student of Arts, 1887-91; M.A. 1891. South African Infantry, Private. Killed in action in German East Africa in July 1916.

MACFARLANE, IAN (*b.* 1888).
   George Watson's College. Student of Medicine, 1905-11; M.B., Ch.B. 1911. O.T.C. Infantry, May 1909 to Aug. 1911, Cadet. Medical Missionary, Nazareth. R.A.M.C., Lieut. April 1915; Captain April 1916. France and Egypt. Died of typhus at Kantara, Egypt, on 18th July 1917.   Pl. XLVIII.

McGEORGE, CHARLES JAMES BERTRAM (*b.* 1897).
   Dumfries Academy. Student of Medicine, 1915-17. O.T.C. Infantry, Oct. 1915 to July 1916, Cadet. 2nd Honourable Artillery Company, Private Feb. 1917. Killed in action in France on 7th October 1917.   Pl. XLVIII.

MacGILLIVRAY, WILLIAM R. K. (*b.* 1896).
   Royal Academy, Inverness; Football. Student of Medicine, 1914-17. 1st Scottish Rifles (Cameronians), Private Aug. 1916. Died of wounds on 1st February 1917.   Pl. XLVIII.

MACGREGOR, RALPH A. MONTGOMERIE (*b.* 1897).
   Tollington School, London. Student of Arts, 1915-16. O.T.C. Artillery, Feb. to July 1916, Cadet; Officer Cadet July 1916. R.G.A., 2nd Lieut. Oct. 1916; Lieut. April 1918. France, wounded. Killed in action on 26th September 1918.   Pl. XLIX.

MacILDOWIE, EDWARD JOHN HOWARD (*b.* 1891).
   Fettes College. Student of Arts, 1908-12; M.A. (Hons. Classics) 1912; B.D. (Glasg.). 9th Highland Light Infantry, 2nd Lieut. France July 1916. Killed at the Battle of the Somme on 1st November 1916.   Pl. XLIX.

MACINDOE, JAMES GRAY (*b.* 1869).
   George Watson's College. Student of Medicine, 1887-92; M.B., C.M. 1892. 6th Devonshire Regiment, Captain 1900. Transferred to R.A.M.C.; Major Sept. 1915. Invalided out of the Army in Sept. and died on 5th October 1916.   Pl. XLIX.

McINTOSH, JOHN (*b.* 1893).
   Hillhead High School, Glasgow. Edinburgh University O.T.C. Artillery, June to Dec. 1916; Cadet Bombardier; Officer Cadet Dec. 1916. R.G.A., North Scottish, attached 217th Siege Battery, 2nd Lieut. Feb. 1917. France. Killed at Vieille Chapelle on 9th April 1918.   Pl. XLIX.

McINTOSH, ROBERT RAE (*b.* 1888).
   Dollar Institution. Student of Arts, 1905-9, and Law, 1913-14; M.A. 1908. President, Diagnostic Society. Editor, *The Student*. 3rd and 1st Cameron Highlanders, 2nd Lieut. Jan. 1914; Lieut. France. Killed in action on 24th April 1915.   Pl. XLIX.

Roll of the Fallen

MACINTYRE, PAT. B. (*b.* 1885).
    Inverness and Edinburgh Institutions. Student of Science, 1902. Seaforth Highlanders, Captain. Brigade Transport Officer. Mobilised Aug. 1914. France. Dispatches Sept. 1916 and April 1917. Killed at Ypres on 3rd August 1917.
    Pl. XCIII.

MACIVER, DONALD JOHN (*b.* 1891).
    Nicolson Institute, Stornoway. Student of Arts, 1912-13. O.T.C. Infantry, Jan. to April 1915, Cadet. 4th Cameron Highlanders, 2nd Lieut. April 1915. Died of wounds on 14th October 1915.
    Pl. XLIX.

McIVER, JAMES NOBLE (*b.* 1894).
    Elgin Academy. Student of Arts, 1912-15; M.A. 1915. O.T.C. Infantry, Jan. to April 1915, Cadet. R.A.M.C., Private April 1915. 8th Royal Scots, 2nd Lieut. 1916. France. Attached 9th Gordon Highlanders, Jan. 1917. Killed in action at Ypres on 25th August 1917.
    Pl. XLIX.

McIVER, KENNETH (*b.* 1882).
    Aberdeen Grammar School. Student of Arts, 1901-4; M.A. 1904. Seaforth Highlanders, Private Oct. 1914; Sergeant. 8th Cameron Highlanders, Captain. France 1917. Killed in action on 27th March 1918.
    Pl. XLIX.

McJANNET, WILLIAM ROBERT BENNY (*b.* 1886).
    Glenalmond. B.A. (Oxford). Student of Law, 1907-10; LL.B. 1910. Writer to the Signet, 1910. 7th and 10th Seaforth Highlanders, Private Nov. 1914; Captain Jan. 1915. France June 1916. Killed in action on 15th July 1916.
    Pl. XLIX.

MACKAY, ALEXANDER KINNISON (*b.* 1894).
    Ayr Academy. Student of Arts, 1912-15. 15th Royal Scots, Private Oct. 1914. 13th attached 15th Highland Light Infantry, 2nd Lieut. July 1915. France Feb. 1916. Killed in action on 13th March 1916.
    Pl. L.

MACKAY, ARNOLD LANGLEY (*b.* 1891).
    Fettes College; First XV. Student of Arts, 1910-13; M.A. 1913. Schoolmaster. Royal Fusiliers (Public Schools Battn.), Private Sept. 1914. Royal Scots Fusiliers, 2nd Lieut. May 1915. Foreign service May 1916. Died of wounds on 31st October 1916.

MACKAY, IAN (*b.* 1883).
    Inverness College and Edinburgh Academy; First XI. Student of Law, 1904-6. Law Agent, 1907. 4th and 6th Cameron Highlanders, Lieut. March 1913; Captain Aug. 1915; Major Feb. 1918. France 1914-16 with 7th Division at Neuve Chapelle, Festubert, Givenchy, Aubers Ridge and Loos. France 1917-18. Dispatches April 1918. Wounded March 1918. Killed at Arras on 28th March 1918.
    Pl. L.

PLATE L.

J. A. C. Mackay.

Ian Mackay.

A. K. Mackay.

Alastair MacKinnon.

P. F. MacKenna.

N. N. Mackay.

T. S. Mackie.

G. A. Mackenzie.

James Mackenzie.

PLATE LI.

A. C. MacKenzie.

John MacKenzie.
(Royal Garrison Artillery.)

John Mackenzie.
(S.R. and R.F.C.)

D. F. Mackenzie.

J. A. MacKenzie.

John Mackenzie.
(S.R. and Northd. Fus.)

Kenneth Mackenzie.

Wm. McKenzie.

J. B. McKenzie.

Roll of the Fallen

MACKAY, JAMES ALASTAIR CULBARD (*b.* 1891).
Fettes College. Student of Law, 1913-14. 6th Seaforth Highlanders, Private 1908; Sergeant 1913; 2nd Lieut. Sept. 1914; Lieut. March 1915; Captain May 1915. France. M.C. May 1916. Died of wounds on 22nd July 1916.
Pl. L.

MACKAY, JOHN. (See p. 116.)

MACKAY, NORMAN NICOLSON (*b.* 1886).
Glasgow Academy. Student of Arts, 1910-12. 2/6th Seaforth Highlanders, Private March 1916. Wounded on 20th Oct. and died at Glasgow on 25th November 1916.
Pl. L.

MacKENNA, PETER FRASER (*b.* 1862).
Dumbarton Academy. Student of Law; LL.B. 1888. Procurator Fiscal. 3/5th Royal Scots Fusiliers, Major April 1915. O.C. Depot. Died on 26th November 1918.
Pl. L.

MACKENZIE, ALICK CAMPBELL (*b.* 1889).
George Heriot's School. Student of Arts and Science, 1907-11; M.A. 1911; B.Sc. 1912. Australian Forces (Infantry), Sergeant June 1916. France Oct. 1917. Killed in action in France on 5th April 1918.
Pl. LI.

MACKENZIE, DAVID FERGUSON (*b.* 1869).
George Watson's College; First XV. Student of Law, 1895-7. Solicitor. 4th Cameron Highlanders, 2nd Lieut. 1905; Lieut.; Captain Aug. 1914. France, Neuve Chapelle. Killed at Battle of Festubert in May 1915.
Pl. LI.

MACKENZIE, GEORGE ARTHUR (*b.* 1891).
Tain Royal Academy and Fettes College. Student of Arts and Medicine, 1908-12; M.A. (Hons. Classics) 1912. O.T.C. Artillery, Jan. 1909 to Feb. 1912, Cadet. 3rd, 8th and 11th Gordon Highlanders, Private Nov. 1914; Corporal; Sergeant; 2nd Lieut. Jan. 1915. France May 1915. Killed at the Battle of Loos near Haisnes on 25th September 1915.
Pl. L.

McKENZIE, JAMES (*b.* 1892).
Wallace Hall Academy, Dumfries. Student of Arts, 1910-14; M.A. (Hons. Mor. Phil.) 1914. Vans Dunlop Scholar and Lanfine Bursar. Cambridge University O.T.C. Oct. to Nov. 1914. 10th and 8th Seaforth Highlanders, 2nd Lieut. Nov. 1914. France Oct. 1915. Killed in action on 30th October 1915.
Pl. L.

MACKENZIE, JOHN (*b.* 1886).
Swiney and Lybster Schools; Athletics. Student of Arts, 1904-7; M.A. 1907. 13th Scottish Rifles, 2nd Lieut. 1915; Lieut. May 1916. 8th Northumberland Fusiliers. Gallipoli, Egypt, and France. Killed at the Battle of the Somme on 26th September 1916.
Pl. LI.

Roll of the Fallen

MACKENZIE, JOHN (*b.* 1891).
  Greenock Academy. Student of Arts and Science, 1907-10. O.T.C. Artillery, Jan. 1911 to June 1914, Cadet. 6th Cameron Highlanders, Private Nov. 1914. 4th Scottish Rifles, 2nd Lieut. Jan. 1916. Transferred to R.F.C., July 1916. Missing, presumed killed in action, December 1917.   Pl. LI.

MACKENZIE, JOHN (*b.* 1893).
  Miller Institution, Thurso. Student of Arts, 1911-15; M.A. (Hons. Maths. and Nat. Phil.) 1915. O.T.C. Artillery, Jan. to July 1916, Cadet Bombardier; Officer Cadet July 1916. R.G.A. (S.R.), 11th Siege Battery, 2nd Lieut. Oct. 1916. France Nov. 1916. Killed in action on 28th October 1917.   Pl. LI.

MACKENZIE, JOHN ALEXANDER (*b.* 1893).
  George Watson's College. Student of Medicine, 1911-16; M.B., Ch.B. 1916. O.T.C. Medical, Oct. 1914, Cadet. R.A.M.C., Lieut. Aug. 1916; Captain March 1917. France Sept. 1916. M.C. April 1918. Died of wounds in France on 10th April 1918.   Pl. LI.

McKENZIE, JOHN BANNERMAN (*b.* 1893).
  Boroughmuir School; First XV. Student of Arts, 1911-14. 6th Royal Scots, Private 1911. 1/4th Royal Scots, L/Corporal; Corporal April 1915. Wounded. Killed in action in Gallipoli on 28th June 1915.   Pl. LI.

MACKENZIE, KENNETH (*b.* 1882).
  Fettes College; Balliol College, Oxford. Student of Law, 1905-9. Writer to the Signet, 1909. 7th and 9th Royal Scots, Lieut. Oct. 1914; Captain 1915. France. Albert Medal. Killed at Heninel near Arras on 27th August 1918.   Pl. LI.

MACKENZIE, LYNEDOCH ARCHIBALD (*b.* 1885).
  Loretto. Student of Science, 1903-9; B.Sc. 1909. A.M.I.C.E. Hockey International. Q.R.V.B., Royal Scots. R.E., 1st Field Coy., E. Lancs., 2nd Lieut. 1912; Captain June 1915. Gallipoli. Died of wounds on 19th October 1915.

McKENZIE, WILLIAM (*b.* 1896).
  Dumfries Academy. Student of Arts, 1914-16. 15th Argyll and Sutherland Highlanders, Private Nov. 1915. Killed at the Battle of the Somme on 12th October 1916.   Pl. LI.

MACKIE, THOMSON SINCLAIR (*b.* 1886).
  Inverness High School. Student of Arts and Divinity, 1906-14; M.A. (Hons. Econ. Sc.) 1910. 15th Royal Scots, Private Sept. 1914. 3rd North Staffordshire Regiment, Lieut. May 1915. Killed in action on 18th November 1916.   Pl. L.

MACKINNON, ALASTAIR (*b.* 1895).
  Fettes College; First XV. and XI. O.T.C. 1912-14, Cadet L/Corporal. Student of Arts, 1914-15. O.T.C. Infantry, Oct. to Dec. 1914, Cadet. 8th Argyll and Sutherland Highlanders, attached Machine-Gun Corps, 2nd Lieut. Nov. 1914; Lieut. France Aug. 1915. Killed at the Battle of the Somme on 14th October 1916.   Pl. L.

Roll of the Fallen

MACKINNON, LACHLAN (*b.* 1891).
  Tobermory and Kingussie Schools. Student of Arts and Medicine, 1909-15; M.A. 1915. 8th Cameron Highlanders, Lieut. Killed in action in June 1916.

MACKINTOSH, JOHN (*b.* 1891).
  Aberdeen Grammar School; First XV. M.A., Aberdeen. Student of Law, 1912-1914; LL.B. 1914. 4th Gordon Highlanders 1910-13. 6th Seaforth Highlanders, 2nd Lieut. Oct. 1914; Lieut. March 1915; Captain July 1916. France June 1917. Dispatches Jan. and June 1918. Wounded at Flesquières near Cambrai Nov. 1917. Killed at St Imoges near Epernay on 23rd July 1918. Pl. LII.

MACKNIGHT, DUNDAS SIMPSON (*b.* 1875).
  Whitburn School. M.B., Ch.B. 1900. South African Campaign; Surgeon 1900. Royal Navy, Surgeon Feb. 1915; H.M. Ships *Whitby Abbey*, *Ajax*, and *Britannia*. Gallipoli, Mediterranean, North Sea, and Atlantic. Killed by the torpedoing of H.M.S. *Britannia* off Gibraltar on 9th November 1918. Pl. LII.

MACLAGAN WEDDERBURN, ROBERT HAMILTON (*b.* 1893).
  George Watson's College. Swimming. O.T.C. 1908-11, Cadet L/Corporal. Student of Arts, 1911-14; M.A. 1914. O.T.C. Infantry, Oct. 1911 to Aug. 1914, Cadet Corporal. 3rd attached 1st Scottish Rifles, 2nd Lieut. Aug. 1914. France 1914. Killed near Bois Grenier, Armentières, on 3rd February 1915. Pl. LII.

McLAREN, ARTHUR DUNCAN (*b.* 1885).
  Brighton House, Oldham. Student of Medicine, 1912-14. 15th Royal Scots, Private Dec. 1914. France. Killed in action near Arras on 9th April 1917.
  Pl. LII.

MACLAREN, JOHN FRANCIS (*b.* 1893).
  Boroughmuir School. Student of Arts, 1912-14. O.T.C. Infantry, Feb. to Aug. 1914, Cadet. 4th Cameron Highlanders, 2nd Lieut. Aug. 1914; Captain Aug. 1915. France. Killed in action at Loos on 28th September 1915. Pl. LII.

McLAREN, THOMAS JAMES (*b.* 1895).
  Dollar Institution. Student of Arts, 1913-15. O.T.C. Artillery, Oct. 1914 to March 1915, Cadet. R.F.A. (S.R.), 2nd Lieut. March 1915. France. Killed near Brabant Farm, Brielen, Ypres, on 26th January 1916. Pl. LII.

McLEAN, RAYMOND ALASTAIR (*b.* 1893).
  Brighton Grammar School. Student of Arts and Divinity, 1911-16; M.A. (Hons. Ment. Phil.) 1915. Vans Dunlop Scholar and MacLean Bursar. O.T.C. Infantry, Feb. 1913 to Jan. 1916, Cadet. 3rd and 6th Seaforth Highlanders, 2nd Lieut. Killed in action on 13th November 1916. Pl. LII.

McLEAN, ROBERT (*b.* 1889).
  Nairn Academy. Student of Science, 1910-13; B.Sc. 1913. O.T.C. Engineers, 1910 to Dec. 1913, Cadet Sergeant. Engineer, N. Nigeria. R.E., Guards Division, 2nd Lieut. Aug. 1915. France Oct. 1915. Killed at Ypres on 11th July 1916. Pl. LII.

Roll of the Fallen

McLEAN, ROBERT DRYSDALE (*b.* 1898).
George Heriot's School. O.T.C. 1912-15, Cadet L/Corporal. Edinburgh University O.T.C. Artillery, June 1916 to Feb. 1917, Cadet Bombardier; Officer Cadet Feb. 1917. R.F.A. and Royal Flying Corps, 2nd Lieut. June 1917. France July 1917. Killed near the Ypres-Poperinghe Road on 26th October 1917.   Pl. LII.

MACLENNAN, RODERICK (*b.* 1890).
Royal Academy, Inverness. Student of Law, 1910-13. Apprentice Chartered Accountant. 9th Royal Scots, L/Corporal Aug. 1914. France. Died of wounds near Ypres on 9th May 1915.   Pl. LIII.

McLEOD, DOUGLAS KEITH (*b.* 1898).
St Paul's School, Darjeeling, and George Watson's College. Edinburgh University O.T.C. Artillery, Jan. to June 1917, Cadet; Officer Cadet June 1917. R.F.A., 2nd Lieut. Dec. 1917. France Jan. 1918. Wounded near Bohain on 18th and died at Rouen on 21st October 1918.

MACLEOD, ION KEITH-FALCONER (*b.* 1888).
George Watson's College; First XI. Student of Medicine, 1908-14; M.B., Ch.B. 1914. Resident, Edinburgh Infirmary. 5th Gordon Highlanders, 1908-12. R.A.M.C., Lieut. Nov. 1915; Captain Nov. 1916. France 1915 to 1918 with the 75th Field Ambulance. Killed at Reninghelst on 27th April 1918.   Pl. LIII.

MACLEOD, VICTOR CHARLES AUGUSTUS (*b.* 1895).
George Heriot's School. O.T.C. 1911-13. Edinburgh University O.T.C. Infantry, Dec. 1913 to Feb. 1915, Cadet. 10th Scottish Rifles, 2nd Lieut. March 1915; Lieut. July 1917. Egypt Jan. 1916. Wounded May 1917. Killed in action near Gaza, Palestine, on 18th July 1917.   Pl. LIII.

MACMILLAN, CAMERON (*b.* 1880).
Edinburgh University O.T.C. Infantry, Sept. 1914 to Dec. 1915, Cadet. 10th attached 8th Seaforth Highlanders, 2nd Lieut. May 1916. Wounded 1916. Killed in action on 22nd August 1917.

McMURRAY, JOHN (*b.* 1873).
Ewart High School, Newton Stewart; Dux. Student of Law. Galloway Rifles and 1st Queen's Edinburgh. Royal Scots, Private Dec. 1914; Coy. Q.M.S., Feb. 1915; 2nd Lieut. May 1915; Lieut.; Captain. France. Killed at Passchendaele 12th October 1917.   Pl. LIII.

MACNAB, ALEXANDER (*b.* 1898).
Merchiston Castle. O.T.C. 1912-16, Cadet Corporal. Edinburgh University O.T.C. Artillery, Oct. 1916 to March 1917, Cadet; Officer Cadet March 1917. R.F.A. (S.R.), 186th Brigade, 2nd Lieut. June 1917. Gassed at Passchendaele Ridge Nov. 1917. Killed near Cambrai on 24th October 1918.   Pl. LIII.

PLATE LII.

R. H. Maclagan-Wedderburn.

D. S. MacKnight.

John Mackintosh.

T. J. McLaren.

R. D. McLean.

R. A. McLean.

J. F. MacLaren.

A. D. McLaren.

Robert McLean.

PLATE LIII.

I. K.-F. MacLeod.

Roderick Maclennan.

V. C. A. MacLeod.

Angus Macnab.

John McMurray.

Alex. Macnab.

Robert McNae.

A. D. McPhee.

J. P. McNicol.

Roll of the Fallen

MACNAB, ANGUS (*b.* 1875).
   High School, Invercargill. B.A., B.Sc. (Otago, N.Z.). Student of Medicine, 1895-1901; M.B., Ch.B. 1901; F.R.C.S. (Edin.). South African Campaign, 1901. R.A.M.C., attached London Scottish, Captain 1911. France 1914. Killed at Messines on 1st November 1914. Pl. LIII.

McNAE, ROBERT (*b.* 1884).
   Dumfries Academy. Student of Law, 1909-11. Chartered Accountant, 1911. 2nd Transvaal Scottish, Private 1914. Liverpool Regiment, 2nd Lieut.; Captain. German South-West Africa. France. Dispatches, German South-West Africa. M.C. (Battle of Guillemont) 9th Aug. 1916. Killed near Ypres on 10th October 1916. Pl. LIII.

McNICOL, JAMES PERCIVAL (*b.* 1897).
   Glasgow Academy. Edinburgh University O.T.C. Infantry, April to Aug. 1916, Cadet; Officer Cadet Aug. 1916. 4th and 10th Argyll and Sutherland Highlanders, 2nd Lieut. Nov. 1916; Lieut. Feb. 1918. France Jan. 1918. Died of wounds on 20th June 1918. Pl. LIII.

McPHAIL, PETER JOHN STEWART (*b.* 1888).
   Merchiston Castle. B.A. (Oxford) 1911. Student of Law, 1911-15. Writer to the Signet. O.T.C. Artillery, Aug. to Nov. 1915, Cadet. R.G.A., 2nd Lieut. Nov. 1915; Lieut. 1917. France Jan. 1917. Wounded March 1918. Died of pneumonia at Winchester in November 1918.

McPHEE, ARTHUR DAVID (*b.* 1895).
   Broughton School. Student of Science, 1914-15. O.T.C. Engineers, Oct. 1914 to July 1915, Cadet. Cameron Highlanders, 2nd Lieut. June 1915; Captain 1917. France 1916 to May 1918. M.C. (the Somme) 1916. Died on 8th October 1918. Pl. LIII.

MACPHERSON, DONALD (*b.* 1886).
   George Heriot's School. Student of Science, 1907-12; B.Sc. 1912; Steven and Vans Dunlop Scholar; Pres. Agric. Soc. O.T.C. Artillery, Dec. 1915 to July 1916, Cadet. Scottish Horse, 2nd Lieut. Aug. 1916. Transferred to R.F.A., Sept. 1917. France. Died in Seafield Hospital, Leith, on 11th November 1917, of wounds received in Flanders. Pl. LIV.

MACPHERSON, HUGH BANNERMAN (*b.* 1881).
   Kingussie School. Student of Law. Chartered Accountant, 1912. Hon. Artillery Coy., Private 1914. R.F.A., Officer Cadet May 1916; 2nd Lieut. Sept. 1916; Lieut. May 1918. France. M.C. March 1918. Wounded Ypres 1915. Killed at Demicourt on 27th September 1918. Pl. LIV.

Roll of the Fallen

MACPHERSON, IAN DONALD (*b.* 1892).
George Heriot's School. O.T.C. 1909-11, Cadet Corporal. Student of Science, 1911-14; B.Sc. 1914. O.T.C. Artillery, Oct. 1911 to Dec. 1914, Cadet. Assistant Conservator of Forests, Nigeria, 1915. West African Frontier Force, Lieut. 1917. Died at Edinburgh of pneumonia on 30th March 1918. Pl. LIV.

MACPHERSON, JOHN COOK (*b.* 1886).
Elgin Academy. 3rd Vol. Battn. Seaforth Highlanders, 1902-5, Private. M.A.; LL.B. (Aberdeen). Student of Law, 1910-11. 9th Royal Scots, Private Sept. 1914. 1st attached 3rd and 11th Gordon Highlanders, 2nd Lieut. March 1915. France, Aug. 1915. Killed at Hooge near Ypres on 25th September 1915. Pl. LIV.

MACPHERSON, ROBERT DUNCAN MEARNS (*b.* 1885).
George Watson's College. 4th Seaforths (Vol.), Private 1902-3. Student of Arts and Medicine, 1903-11; M.B., Ch.B. 1911. Diploma of Tropical Medicine, 1914. Athletics. O.T.C. Infantry, 1904-6 and 1909-12, Cadet Sergeant. R.A.M.C., Lieut. Aug. to Nov. 1914. 7th Seaforth Highlanders, 2nd Lieut. (combatant) Dec. 1914. France. Killed at Loos on 25th September 1915. Pl. LIV.

McPHERSON, WILLIAM (*b.* 1895).
Helmsdale School. Student of Arts, 1914-15. O.T.C. Artillery, March to Aug. 1915, Cadet. R.F.A., 2nd Lieut. Aug. 1915; Lieut. Oct. 1915. Egypt Dec. 1915. Salonika and Balkans, Nov. 1916. Killed in action in Macedonia on 8th May 1917. Pl. LIV.

MACRAE, ALEXANDER WILLIAM URQUHART (*b.* 1885).
Edinburgh Academy; B.A. (Oxford) 1906. Mounted Infantry, 1903-6. Student of Law, 1906-9; LL.B. 1909. Writer to the Signet, 1909. 1st Queen's Edinburgh Rifles, 2nd Lieut. 1907. 5th Royal Scots, Lieut. 1910; Captain 1912. Gallipoli April 1915, 29th Division. Egypt and France, 1915 to 1918. Temp. Major April 1916. Wounded twice in Gallipoli and twice in France. Killed at Parvillers, the Somme, on 11th August 1918. Pl. LIV.

MACRAE, JOSEPH NIXON (*b.* 1899).
Biggar High School. Student of Medicine, 1916-17. O.T.C. Infantry, Jan. to Aug. 1917, Cadet; Officer Cadet Aug. 1917. 3rd Border Regiment, 2nd Lieut. Dec. 1917. France Jan. 1918. Killed in a night raid near Ypres on 18th February 1918. Pl. LIV.

MACRAE, KENNETH MATHESON (*b.* 1890).
B.A. (Oxford). Student of Arts, 1907-10; M.A. 1910. O.T.C. Artillery, Oct. 1908 to March 1910, Cadet. R.F.A. (S.R.), 2nd Lieut. March 1910. France Dec. 1914, 28th Brigade, R.F.A. M.C. June 1918. Twice Mentioned in Dispatches. Killed in action near Courtrai on 1st November 1918.

PLATE LIV.

H. B. MACPHERSON.   DONALD MACPHERSON.   I. D. MACPHERSON.

WM. MCPHERSON.   R. D. M. MACPHERSON.   J. C. MACPHERSON.

P. C. MACRAE.   J. N. MACRAE.   A. W. U. MACRAE.

PLATE LV.

NORMAN McRURY.   J. W. McVICKER.   H. H. MACROSTY.

J. A. MAIN.   ALAN MAIR.   W. D. MAIR.

W. A. MALCOLM.   J. A. MARSDEN.   W. J. MANSON.

Roll of the Fallen

MACRAE, PATRICK CAMERON (*b.* 1889).
Dalwhinnie and Kingussie Schools. Student of Arts and Medicine, 1907-15; M.A. 1910; M.B., Ch.B. 1915. O.T.C. Infantry, Oct. 1909 to Oct. 1914, Cadet; Medical, 1914-15. President Celtic Society. R.A.M.C., 50th Field Amb., Lieut. 1915; Captain. Attached 80th and 116th Brigades, R.F.A. France 1915; Salonika 1916. Invalided home Aug. 1916 and died at Dalwhinnie in March 1917. Pl. LIV.

MACROSTY, HENRY HUGH (*b.* 1894).
Christ's College, Blackheath; First XV. Student of Medicine, 1912-14. O.T.C. Artillery, Feb. 1913 to Sept. 1914, Cadet. R.F.A., 53rd Brigade, 9th Division, 2nd Lieut. Sept. 1914; Lieut. Sept. 1915. France. Dispatches April 1916. Killed at Ypres on 19th December 1915. Pl. LV.

McRURY, NORMAN (*b.* 1890).
George Watson's College. Edinburgh University O.T.C. Infantry, Nov. 1909 to Oct. 1914, Cadet Pipe-Major. 11th Royal Highlanders (Black Watch), 2nd Lieut. Oct. 1914; Lieut. Feb. 1915. Attached King's Own Scottish Borderers. Gallipoli May 1915. Killed in action there on 4th June 1915. Pl. LV.

McVICKER, JOHN WILLIAM (*b.* 1897).
Coleraine Academical Institution; First XV. and Hockey. Student of Medicine, 1913-15. O.T.C. Medical, Feb. to Sept. 1914, Cadet. North Irish Horse Regiment. 13th Liverpool Regiment, Lieut. Oct. 1914. France 1915. Killed in action at the Somme on 14th July 1916. Pl. LV.

MAIN, JOHN ALEXANDER (*b.* 1881).
Linlithgow Academy. A.M.I.C.E. Edinburgh University O.T.C. Artillery, Feb. to April 1916, Cadet. R.E., 278th Railway Coy., Lieut. 1916. M.C. (posthumous). Killed in action in Flanders on 27th March 1918. Pl. LV.

MAIR, ALAN (*b.* 1897).
Bonnington School, Leith. Zoology Laboratory Attendant. 8/10th Gordon Highlanders, Private July 1916. France Dec. 1916. Died of wounds at Etaples on 29th April 1917. Pl. LV.

MAIR, WALTER DAVID (*b.* 1885).
West Ham School. Student of Arts, 1906-11; M.A. 1911. Schoolmaster. 4th Royal Scots, Private Sept. 1914. Died of wounds at Gallipoli on 14th July 1915. Pl. LV.

MALCOLM, WILLIAM ABERDEIN (*b.* 1861).
Dundee Institution. Student of Medicine, 1877-83; M.B., C.M. 1883. R.A.M.C. 1901; Major Oct. 1914. Gallipoli. Attached 1/11th London Regiment. Died of dysentery at Malta on 3rd October 1915. Pl. LV.

Roll of the Fallen

MANSON, WILLIAM JAMES (*b.* 1894).
    Boroughmuir School. Student of Medicine, 1912-14. 5th Royal Scots, Private. Wounded at the Dardanelles. Killed in action at Gallipoli in June 1915.   Pl. LV.

MARKS, HORACE OWEN (*b.* 1889).
    Mudgee Grammar School, N.S.W. Student of Medicine, 1913-15. O.T.C. Artillery, Oct. 1914 to Jan. 1915, Cadet. R.F.A., 2nd Lieut. Nov. 1914; Lieut. France. Killed near Albert on 29th October 1916.

MARSDEN, JAMES ALFRED (*b.* 1892).
    Royal High School; First XV. and XI. Student of Science, 1911-14; B.Sc. (Distinction) 1914. O.T.C. Engineers, Nov. 1911 to Oct. 1914, Cadet. R.E., Lowland Division, 2nd Lieut. Oct. 1914; Lieut. May 1915; Captain April 1916. France Dec. 1914. Dispatches June 1916. Killed in action in France on 21st April 1918.   Pl. LV.

MARSHALL, JOHN (*b.* 1887).
    Berwick Grammar School; First XV. and XI. Student of Medicine, 1903-8; M.B., Ch.B. (Hons.) 1908. M'Cosh Scholar. House Surgeon, Beaufort War Hospital, Bristol, July 1915 to Feb. 1917. R.A.M.C., Lieut. March 1917. Lost at sea on 15th April 1917.   Pl. LVI.

MARSHALL, MATTHEW BAXTER (*b.* 1896).
    Bathgate Academy. Student of Arts, 1915-16. A.S.C. (M.T.), Private Nov. 1915. Died of wounds on 6th April 1917.   Pl. LVI.

MARTIN, ARTHUR ANDERSON (*b.* 1876).
    Lawrence High School, N.Z. Student of Medicine, 1894-1900; M.B., Ch.B. (Hons.) 1900; M.D.; F.R.C.S. (Edin.) 1903. Carlisle and Grierson Scholar. South African Campaign, 1901-2. R.A.M.C., Captain Aug. 1914. N.Z. Medical Corps, Major Feb. 1916. France 1914-15 and 1916. The Marne and Aisne. 15th Field Ambulance; N.Z. 3rd Field Ambulance. Dispatches Jan. 1915 and 1916 (the Somme). Wounded at Flers and died at Amiens on 17th September 1916.   Pl. LVI.

MARTIN, JOHN (*b.* 1888).
    George Watson's and Malvern Colleges; First XV. and XI. Student of Law, 1912-14. O.T.C. Infantry, Aug. 1914, Cadet. 8th Gordon Highlanders, 2nd Lieut. Aug. 1914; Lieut.; Captain; M.C. Foreign service 1915. Killed in action on 9th April 1917.   Pl. LVI.

MARTIN, ROSS (*b.* 1898).
    George Watson's College. Y.M.C.A., Rouen, 1916. Edinburgh University O.T.C. Artillery, Jan. to April 1917, Cadet. Medically rejected, R.F.C. in 1917. Tank Corps, 2nd Lieut. 1917. Killed in action in France August 1918.   Pl. LVI.

PLATE LVI.

A. A. Martin.

M. B. Marshall.

John Marshall.

Ross Martin.

G. H. Matheson.

John Martin.

G. G. Mathewson.

J. K. Mathewson.

J. M. Matheson.

PLATE LVII.

Andrew Mathison.

B. C. Matthews.

John Maxwell.

Wellwood Maxwell.

J. J. Maybin.

C. G. C. Meister.

E. A. Meldrum.

S. G. Mellis-Smith.

J. D. L. Melrose.

Roll of the Fallen

MATHESON, GEORGE HUGH (*b.* 1893).
  Royal High School; First XV. Student of Arts and Science, 1910-15; M.A. (Hons. Maths.); B.Sc. 1915. 14th Argyll and Sutherland Highlanders, Private July 1915. Border Regiment, 2nd Lieut. Aug. 1917. Killed in action on 3rd December 1917. Pl. LVI.

MATHESON, JAMES McDONALD (*b.* 1888).
  Edinburgh Institution; Dux; First XV. Student of Medicine, 1905-8. O.T.C. Infantry, May 1909 to June 1912, Cadet L/Corporal. M.B., Ch.B. (Glasg.) 1916. R.N.V.R., Surgeon-Probationer, Oct. 1915 to April 1916, H.M.S. *Lurcher*. R.A.M.C., Lieut. 1916; Captain 1917. Mesopotamia, 21st Indian General Hospital, 1916-17. France 1917. Attached 17th Middlesex Regiment. Killed in action on 30th November 1917. Pl. LVI.

MATHEWSON, GEORGE GILLESPIE (*b.* 1895).
  Dunfermline High School. Student of Science, 1913-14. O.T.C. Engineers, Aug. 1914 to Jan. 1916, Cadet. R.E., Lieut. Jan. 1916. France Sept. 1916. Dispatches April 1918. Killed at Rouvroy near St Quentin on 27th March 1918. Pl. LVI.

MATHEWSON, JAMES KENNETH (*b.* 1897).
  Dunfermline High School. Edinburgh University O.T.C. Artillery, April to Oct. 1916, Cadet; Officer Cadet Oct. 1916. R.F.A., 2nd Lieut. May 1917. France Aug. 1917. Flanders April 1918. Wounded Sept. 1917. Killed at "Salvation Corner," Ypres, on 14th September 1918. Pl. LVI.

MATHISON, ANDREW (*b.* 1893).
  Boroughmuir School. Student of Arts, 1911-15; M.A. 1915. 9th Royal Scots, Private June 1915; L/Corporal Dec. 1916. France, 52nd Division, Oct. 1916. Died of wounds received at Arras in May 1917. Pl. LVII.

MATTHEWS, BERTRAM CASH (*b.* 1891).
  Ilminster Grammar School. Edinburgh University O.T.C. Infantry, Oct. 1912 to Aug. 1914, Cadet. 11th Royal Scots, 2nd Lieut. Aug. 1914; Lieut. Killed in action on 24th March 1917. Pl. LVII.

MAXWELL, JOHN (*b.* 1889).
  Cheltenham. Student of Law, 1910-12. 5th Royal Scots Fusiliers, 2nd Lieut. Gallipoli. Killed in action at the Dardanelles on 12th July 1915. Pl. LVII.

MAXWELL, WELLWOOD (*b.* 1890).
  Cargilfield and Rugby. Student of Law, 1912-14. R.F.A. (T.), 1st Lowland Brigade, 2nd Lieut. (five years). Artists' Rifles, 1915. 20th London Regiment, 2nd Lieut. Oct. 1915. France March 1916. Died of wounds at High Wood, near Flers on the Somme, on 16th September 1916. Pl. LVII.

Roll of the Fallen

MAYBIN, JAMES JOHNSTONE (*b.* 1887).
Ayr Academy; First XV. and XI. Student of Arts, 1905-10; M.A. (Hons. Classics) 1910. First XV. Schoolmaster. 9th, 14th and 11th Royal Scots, Private Aug. 1914; Lieut. Nov. 1914; Captain July 1916. France 1915. Battle of Loos. Killed at the Somme on 14th July 1916.   Pl. LVII.

MEISTER, CHARLES GUSTAVE CLARK (*b.* 1883).
George Watson's College. Student of Arts, 1907-10; M.A. 1910. Minister, Episcopal Church of Scotland. Chaplain, attached 7th Seaforths and 10th Argyll and Sutherland Highlanders, Nov. 1915. France Nov. 1915. Dispatches 1916. M.C. 1917. Killed in action on 18th April 1918.   Pl. LVII.

MELDRUM, ERNEST ALEXANDER (*b.* 1892).
George Watson's College. O.T.C. 1906-9, Cadet L/Corporal. Edinburgh University O.T.C. Infantry, Oct. 1909 to Feb. 1912, Cadet L/Corporal. Surma Valley Light Horse, Assam. 2/8th Gurkha Rifles, 2nd Lieut. Nov. 1914. France May 1915. Killed in action in France on 25th September 1915.   Pl. LVII.

MELLIS-SMITH, SAMUEL GRANT (*b.* 1886).
Fettes College; First XV. Student of Arts, 1905-9; M.A. 1909. O.T.C. Infantry, Oct. 1908 to Aug. 1909, Cadet Sergeant. Indian Army Reserve of Officers. 4th Gurkha Rifles, 2nd Lieut. 1914; Lieut. 1916. France, Gallipoli, Egypt, and Mesopotamia. Killed near Kut on 11th February 1917.   Pl. LVII.

MELROSE, JAMES DOUGLAS LEITCH (*b.* 1884).
George Watson's College. Student of Law, 1904-8. Writer to the Signet, 1909. R.G.A. (T.) Forth, 2nd Lieut. April 1913; Lieut. Aug. 1914; Captain June 1916; Major March 1917. France Aug. 1916. Wounded at Kemmel Hill and died at Boeschèpe near Ypres on 25th April 1918.   Pl. LVII.

MELVILLE, HARRY GEORGE (*b.* 1869).
Edinburgh Collegiate School. Student of Medicine, 1884-90; M.B., C.M. 1890; M.D. 1906; F.R.C.S. (Edin.) 1900. Indian Medical Service, Lieut. 1892; Lieut.-Colonel 1912; Temp. Colonel Aug. 1918. Waziristan, 1894-5; Punjab Frontier and Tirah, 1897-8. Mesopotamia Exp. Force, 1916-18. C.I.E. Dispatches Aug. 1918 and Feb. 1919. Died at Baghdad on 7th December 1918.   Pl. LVIII.

MENZIES, ARTHUR JOHN ALEXANDER (*b.* 1886).
Edinburgh Academy. Student of Arts and Medicine, 1905-12; M.A. 1908; M.B., Ch.B. 1912. O.T.C. Artillery, Oct. 1908 to Dec. 1909, Cadet. R.A.M.C., Lieut. Jan. 1914; Captain March 1915; D.A.D.M.S., May 1917; Lieut.-Col. Feb. 1918. France Oct. 1914 with 3rd Cavalry Division, attached 1st Royal Dragoons. Twice Mentioned in Dispatches. D.S.O. Oct. 1915 (Battle of Loos). Killed in action in France on 9th August 1918.   Pl. LVIII.

PLATE LVIII.

G. R. MILL.

H. G. MELVILLE.

A. J. A. MENZIES.

J. R. MIDDLETON.

G. H. MIDDLETON.

A. S. MIDDLETON.

J. D. MILL.

GEORGE MILLAR.

G. I. MILLAR.

PLATE LIX.

A. I. Miller.

H. W. W. Miller.

James Millar.

J. E. B. Miller.

Maurice Miller.

A. E. Millson.

Eric Milroy.

J. R. Milne.

J. W. Milne.

Roll of the Fallen

MIDDLETON, ALEXANDER SAMUEL (*b.* 1890).
  Natal and Edinburgh Academies. Student of Science, 1909-10. O.T.C. Engineers, May 1910 to May 1911. Scottish Horse, Private Sept. 1914; L/Corporal. 3rd attached 1st Cameron Highlanders, 2nd Lieut. March 1915. France 1915. Died on 30th September 1915 at Rouen of wounds received at the Battle of Loos. Pl. LVIII.

MIDDLETON, GEORGE HILTON (*b.* 1893).
  Natal and Edinburgh Academies. Student of Medicine, 1911-14 and 1916-18; M.B., Ch.B. 1918. O.T.C. Artillery, Oct. 1912 to Aug. 1914, Cadet Bombardier. R.F.A., 2nd Lowland Brigade, 2nd Lieut. Aug. 1914; Lieut. 1915. R.A.M.C., Lieut. Nov. 1918. France 1915-16. Russia 1919. Killed in action in Northern Russia on 10th August 1919. Pl. LVIII.

MIDDLETON, JAMES RUSSELL (*b.* 1883).
  Natal and Edinburgh Academies. Student of Science, 1905-6. Lord Strathcona's Horse, Trooper Aug. 1914; L/Corporal. 7th Cameron Highlanders, 2nd Lieut. 1915. R.F.C., Flight Lieut. 1916. France. Forced landing in German lines. Severely wounded; died in Mülheim am Ruhr Hospital on 21st June 1917. Pl. LVIII.

MILL, GEORGE ROBERTSON (*b.* 1880).
  Arbroath High School. Student of Medicine, 1896-1901; M.B., Ch.B. 1901; M.D. 1905. R.N.V.R., Surgeon April 1909; Staff Surgeon April 1917. Hospital Ships *Carisbrooke Castle*, *Rewa*, at Dardanelles from June to evacuation 1915, and *Patrol* 1916. Died on 11th February 1918. Pl. LVIII.

MILL, JAMES DRYSDALE (*b.* 1895).
  Moray House and Broughton Schools. Student of Arts, 1913-14. A.S.C., Feb. 1913; mobilised Aug. 1914. 3rd King's Own Scottish Borderers, 2nd Lieut. April 1915. Killed at Cape Helles on 15th October 1915. Pl. LVIII.

MILLAR, GEORGE (*b.* 1872).
  Student of Divinity, 1890-4. Minister U.F. Church of Scotland. Chaplain, Orkney R.G.A.; Captain 1914-17. Attached No. 13 General Hospital and No. 7 Stationary Hospital, Boulogne, April to Aug. 1917. Died at Boulogne on 26th August 1917. Pl. LVIII.

MILLAR, GEORGE INGLIS (*b.* 1895).
  George Watson's College. Student of Law, 1914-16. O.T.C. Artillery, Dec. 1915 to June 1916, Cadet; Officer Cadet June 1916. R.F.A., 86th Brigade, 2nd Lieut. Sept. 1916. France Jan. 1917. Killed at Arras on 8th April 1917. Pl. LVIII.

MILLAR, JAMES (*b.* 1891).
  Trinity Academy, Leith. Student of Arts, 1907-11; M.A. 1911. Schoolmaster. 9th Royal Scots. 9th Royal Highlanders (Black Watch), 2nd Lieut. Jan. 1915. France. Killed in action at Loos on 25th September 1915. Pl. LIX.

Roll of the Fallen

MILLER, ARCHIBALD INGRAM (b. 1882).
George Watson's College, and Leys School, Cambridge. Student of Medicine, 1900-5; M.B., Ch.B. 1905. R.A.M.C., Lieut. Sept. 1916. Killed in action on 11th March 1917. Pl. LIX.

MILLER, HENRY WILLIAM WATSON (b. 1896).
Edinburgh Academy. O.T.C. 1911-14. Student of Science, 1913-14. O.T.C. Engineers, April to Oct. 1914, Cadet. 10th and 6th Royal Highlanders (Black Watch), Private Oct. 1914; 2nd Lieut. Aug. 1915. France. Killed in action at the Somme on 31st July 1916. Pl. LIX.

MILLER, JOSEPH EWING BRUCE (b. 1895).
Rossall; Shooting. O.T.C. 1909-12, Cadet Sergeant. Student of Medicine, 1912-14. O.T.C. Artillery, Oct. 1913 to Aug. 1914, Cadet. 5th attached 1st Royal Irish Rifles, 2nd Lieut. Aug. 1914; Lieut. Jan. 1915. France March 1915. Wounded at Festubert on 9th and died on 24th May 1915. Pl. LIX.

MILLER, MAURICE (b. 1880).
George Heriot's School. Student of Law, 1899-1901. 16th Royal Scots, Private May 1915; 2nd Lieut. Sept. 1915. Egypt Jan. 1916. Invalided home and died at Edinburgh on 5th August 1917. Pl. LIX.

MILLSON, ALVAN EWEN (b. 1892).
Haileybury. O.T.C. 1908-10. Student of Arts, 1910-14. Inns of Court O.T.C. Oct. 1914. 4th and 6th Royal Fusiliers, 2nd Lieut. Feb. 1915; Captain. Gallipoli Sept. 1915. Invalided home Nov. 1915. France Aug. 1916. Dispatches Dec. 1917. Killed at Arras on 9th April 1917. Pl. LIX.

MILNE, JAMES ROBERTSON (b. 1890).
George Heriot's School; Athletics. Student of Law, 1910-12. Chartered Accountant, 1913. 4th Royal Scots, Private Sept. 1914. 7th King's Own Scottish Borderers, 2nd Lieut. Dec. 1914; Captain Oct. 1915; Staff Captain Aug. 1918. France July 1915. Dispatches Jan. 1919. Died at Rouen on 30th October 1918. Pl. LIX.

MILNE, JAMES WILLIAM (b. 1870).
Larchfield Academy, Helensburgh. Student of Arts, 1885-8. Military College, Sandhurst; Sword of Honour. 82nd Punjabis, Major; Lieut.-Col. 1916. France 1914-15. Mesopotamia 1917-18. Wounded at Festubert. Dispatches May 1918. C.I.E. 1919. Died of heat-stroke in the Afghan War on 21st June 1919. Pl. LIX.

MILROY, ERIC (b. 1887).
George Watson's College; First XV. Cadet Corps 1903-6, Cadet Sergeant. Student of Arts, 1906-10; M.A. 1910. Chartered Accountant, 1914. Scottish Rugby International. 9th Royal Scots, Private Aug. 1914. 11th and 8th Royal Highlanders (Black Watch), 2nd Lieut. Sept. 1914; Lieut. July 1916. France Oct. 1915. Killed at Delville Wood in November 1916. Pl. LIX.

Roll of the Fallen

MITCHELL, ANDREW NEILL (*b.* 1891).
Merchiston Castle; Athletics. Student of Arts, 1910-14. O.T.C. Infantry, Dec. 1911 to Sept. 1914, Cadet Corporal. Marathon Medal. 4th and 5th Royal Scots Fusiliers, Private Sept. 1914; Lieut. Killed at Gallipoli on 30th December 1915. Pl. LX.

MITCHELL, JAMES THOMSON RANKIN (*b.* 1888).
Airdrie and Edinburgh Academies; First XV. and XI. B.A. (Oxford) 1910. First XV. and London Scottish. Student of Law, 1910-13. Writer to the Signet, 1913. 11th Argyll and Sutherland Highlanders, 2nd Lieut. Sept. 1914; Captain 1915. 13th Royal Scots, Major July 1916. 11th Argyll and Sutherland Highlanders, Lieut.-Col. 1917. France June 1915. Dispatches. D.S.O. 1916. Croix de Guerre (France) 1918. Wounded at Arras on 28th March and died at Queen Alexandra Hospital, London, on 1st April 1918. Pl. LX.

MITCHELL, JOHN HALLIBURTON (*b.* 1890).
Cargilfield and Fettes College. Student of Science, 1910-14. O.T.C. Infantry, March 1909 to Aug. 1914, Cadet Coy. Sergeant-Major. 7th and 17th Royal Scots, Lieut. Sept. 1914. Gallipoli 1915. Captain and Adjutant 1916. France 1916 and 1917. Died of wounds on 26th October 1917.

MITCHELL, NORMAN RAMSAY (*b.* 1893).
George Watson's College. Student of Law, 1912-13. 3rd Royal Scots (S.R.), 2nd Lieut. March 1915. Lieut. Aug. 1916. Attached Royal Air Force, April 1917; Pilot Oct. 1917. Wounded at Battle of Loos, 1915. Killed through aeroplane collision on 6th June 1918. Pl. LX.

MITTON, HAROLD (*b.* 1894).
Gill College High School, Somerset East, S. Africa. O.T.C. 1908-10, Cadet. Student of Science, 1913-14. O.T.C. Artillery Oct. 1913 to Nov. 1914, Cadet. R.F.A., attached Royal Flying Corps, Aug. 1914; 2nd Lieut. Oct. 1914; Lieut. 1916. Dispatches 1917. Killed in action on 29th July 1917.

MOIR, ARCHIBALD GIFFORD (*b.* 1890).
Edinburgh Academy and Fettes College; First XV. and XI. Student of Law, 1911-13. Law Agent. 7th Argyll and Sutherland Highlanders, Lieut. Dispatches 1915. Killed in action near Ypres on 25th April 1915.

MONTGOMERY, ROBERT (*b.* 1888).
Campbeltown Grammar School. Student of Medicine, 1907-13; M.B., Ch.B. 1913. R.A.M.C., Lieut. July 1913; Captain March 1915. France 1914. Attached to 1st Gloucester Regiment. Dispatches April 1916. Killed at Loos on 26th September 1915. Pl. LX.

MOODIE, RALPH WILSON (*b.* 1892).
Dingwall Academy. Student of Law, 1913-14. Seaforth Highlanders. 9th Royal Scots, Private Aug. 1914. 6th Gordon Highlanders, Captain. France. Died of wounds on 16th May 1917. Pl. LX.

Roll of the Fallen

MOON, GEORGE BASSETT (*b.* 1885).
    Derby School; First XI. Cadet Corps, 1902-3. Birmingham University; Athletics. Student of Medicine; L.R.C.P. & S. (Edin.); L.F.P.S. (Glasg.) 1909. Royal Navy, Nov. 1914; Surgeon Jan. 1915, H.M.S. *Lion*. Killed at the Battle of Jutland on 31st May 1916.

MOORHEAD, ARTHUR HENRY (*b.* 1872).
    George Heriot's School; First XV. Student of Medicine, 1889-93; M.B., C.M. 1893. I.M.S. 1894. Lieut.-Col. 1914; Brevet Col. 1915; and A.D.M.S. Colonel, Waziristan, Chitral. Tochi Valley and third China Campaigns. France. 2nd Indian Cavalry Division. Dispatches 1915. Invalided home Dec. 1915 and died at Batheaston, Somerset, on 29th February 1916.

MOORHEAD, GEORGE OLIVER (*b.* 1866).
    St Stanislaus College, Tullamore, Ireland. Student of Medicine, 1883-8. Q.E.R., 1884-8. 10th Dismounted Rifles, S. Africa. Lieut.-Col., N. Transvaal Mounted Rifles. Nyasaland Contingent, South African Imperial Forces. South African Rebellion and German West African Campaign. Killed in action in May 1916.

MORE, ERIC ROY (*b.* 1898).
    George Watson's College. Edinburgh University O.T.C. Infantry, Nov. 1916 to May 1917, Cadet; Officer Cadet May 1917. 3rd attached 2nd Gordon Highlanders, 2nd Lieut. Sept. 1917. France and Italy. Killed in action in Italy on 27th October 1918.   Pl. LX.

MORGAN, JAMES WHITE (*b.* 1892).
    Royal High School;. Athletics. Student of Law, 1912-14. 9th Royal Scots, Private Oct. 1915; Corporal. 16th Lancashire Fusiliers, 2nd Lieut. Sept. 1917. France. Died of wounds received at the Battle of Amiens on 10th August 1918.   Pl. LX.

MORISON, ARCHIBALD ALEXANDER (*b.* 1887).
    George Watson's College; First XV. Student of Medicine, 1904-10. M.B., Ch.B. 1910. Royal Navy, Surgeon, H.M.S. *Indefatigable*. Killed in action at the Battle of Jutland on 31st May 1916.   Pl. LX.

MORRIS, HUGH (*b.* 1885).
    Diocesan College, Rondebosch. B.A. (Hons.) (Cape). Student of Medicine, 1906-11. O.T.C. Infantry, Nov. 1908 to July 1910, Cadet. 3rd Scottish Rifles (S.R.), 2nd Lieut. 1914; Lieut. Feb. 1915. Died of wounds in France on 14th July 1915.

MORRIS, JOHN (*b.* 1870).
    Ruabon Grammar School. Student of Medicine; M.B., Ch.B. 1904. F.R.C.S. (Edin.) 1909. R.A.M.C., Lieut. 1912; Captain 1915; Major 1918. France Nov. 1914. Attached 6th Cheshire Regiment. Field Ambulance. M.C. Jan. 1917. Killed in action on 7th October 1918.   Pl. LX.

PLATE LX.

J. T. R. Mitchell.

N. R. Mitchell.

A. N. Mitchell.

R. W. Moodie.

E. R. More.

Robert Montgomery.

John Morris.

A. A. Morison.

J. W. Morgan.

PLATE LXI.

#

ALEX. MORRISON.   S. H. MORRIS.   J. A. MORRISON.

J. T. MORRISON.   J. S. MORRISON.   HUGH MOSMAN.

JOHN MUIR.   A. C. MUIR.   G. V. MUIR.

Roll of the Fallen

MORRIS, SYDNEY HERBERT (*b.* 1875).
   Grammar School, Market Harborough. Student of Medicine, 1894-9; M.B., Ch.B. 1899. R.A.M.C., Captain. Died on 11th January 1918. Pl. LXI.

MORRISON, ALEXANDER (*b.* 1886).
   George Watson's College; First XV. Cadet Corps, Commissioned Officer. Student of Arts, 1906-8. 5th Cameron Highlanders, 2nd Lieut. Sept. 1914; Lieut.; Captain. Flanders May 1915. Killed at Hohenzollern Redoubt on 25th September 1915. Pl. LXI.

MORRISON, JOHN ALEXANDER (*b.* 1882).
   George Watson's College; First XV. and XI. Student of Law, 1905-6. R.G.A. Gunner. France. Killed near Amiens on 30th May 1918. Pl. LXI.

MORRISON, JOHN STEWART (*b.* 1892).
   George Heriot's School. O.T.C. 1909-12, Cadet Sergeant-Major. Student of Science, 1912-14. O.T.C. Engineers, April 1913 to Aug. 1914, Cadet L/Corporal. R.E. (Dispatch Rider) Aug. 1914, Sergeant-Major. France 1914-15. Battles of Mons, Marne, Aisne, first and second Ypres and Loos. D.C.M. Dispatches (Langemark and Gheluvelt). Died of gas poisoning at Loos on 26th September 1915. Pl. LXI.

MORRISON, JOHN TAIT (*b.* 1891).
   Carrick Academy, Maybole. Student of Law, 1914-15. R.F.A., Gunner Jan. 1916. Killed in action at Zillebeke near Ypres on 20th July 1917. Pl. LXI.

MORRISON, WILLIAM (*b.* 1886).
   Milne's Institution, Fochabers. Student of Medicine, 1904-9. M.B., Ch.B. 1909. R.A.M.C., Captain 1915. France 1915. M.C. Died of wounds and gas poisoning on 23rd October 1917.

MOSMAN, HUGH (*b.* 1861).
   Edinburgh Academy. Student of Law, 1878-81. Writer to the Signet, 1885. Yorkshire Regiment, 24th Prov. Battn., 2nd Lieut. 1914. Died at Cramlington, Northumberland, on 12th February 1916. Pl. LXI.

MOWAT, ALEXANDER (*b.* 1895).
   Miller Institution, Thurso. Student of Arts, 1913-14. 6th attached 4th Royal Scots (T.), Private 1914. Gallipoli. Killed in action on 28th June 1915. Pl. XCIII.

MUIR, ANDREW CHRISTISON M. (*b.* 1896).
   George Heriot's School. Student of Arts, 1914-15. 9th Royal Scots, Private Nov. 1914. 1st, 3rd, and 9th King's Own Scottish Borderers, 2nd Lieut. Feb. 1915. France Jan. 1915; Dardanelles Aug. 1915. Killed in action at Gallipoli on 27th October 1915. Pl. LXI.

Roll of the Fallen

MUIR, GEORGE VICTOR (*b.* 1901).
    George Watson's College. Edinburgh University O.T.C. Infantry, Oct. 1917 to Jan. 1918, Cadet. Royal Air Force, Officer Cadet Jan. 1918; 2nd Lieut. Oct. 1918. Killed in an aeroplane accident in the South of England on 18th October 1918.   Pl. LXI.

MUIR, JOHN (*b.* 1882).
    Student of Law, 1904-6. 11th and 5th Canadian Rifles, Private Aug. 1914; Acting Sergeant. France. Killed at Festubert on 24th May 1915.   Pl. LXI.

MUKERJI, KALYAN KUMAR (*b.* 1883).
    L.M.S. University, Calcutta, 1906. Student of Medicine. I.M.S. 1910, attached 8th Rajputs, 1914, Captain. Mesopotamia. M.C. Oct. 1916. Taken prisoner at Kut-el-Amara and died of typhus at Ras-el-Ain in Asia Minor in May 1917.

MUNRO, ALEXANDER (*b.* 1893).
    Kingussie School. Student of Arts, 1912-15. 1/2nd Lovat Scouts, Private Sept. 1914. Scottish Rifles, 2nd Lieut. Dec. 1915. Gallipoli Sept. to Dec. 1915; France Aug. 1916. Died of wounds at Rouen on 5th November 1916.   Pl. LXII.

MUNRO, CHARLES (*b.* 1887).
    Leith Walk and Broughton Schools. Student of Arts, 1906-9; M.A. 1909. 2nd Seaforth Highlanders, Private Nov. 1915. Died of wounds in France on 17th January 1918.   Pl. LXII.

MUNRO, DONALD GEORGE (*b.* 1895).
    Wick High School. Student of Medicine, 1914-15. O.T.C. Artillery, Dec. 1914 to May 1915, Cadet. 14th Argyll and Sutherland Highlanders, Private May 1915; Sergeant Nov. 1915. France 1915. Killed near Loos on 6th September 1916.   Pl. LXII.

MUNRO, H. F.
    Student at Edinburgh University. Seaforth Highlanders, Captain. Killed in action in September 1915.

MUNRO, JOHN (*b.* 1883).
    Royal Academy, Inverness. Student of Law, 1902-3. Barrister and Solicitor, Saskatoon. 105th Regiment Saskatoon Fusiliers, 2nd Lieut. June 1915. 65th and 44th Canadian Infantry, Adjutant. France. Wounded Nov. 1916. Killed at Vimy Ridge on 10th April 1917.   Pl. LXII.

MUNRO, JOHN SUTHERLAND (*b.* 1892).
    Dornoch School. Student of Medicine, 1909-16; M.B., Ch.B. 1916. O.T.C. Medical, Feb. to Dec. 1916, Cadet. R.A.M.C., Lieut. Dec. 1916; 102nd Field Ambulance. Mesopotamia. Died at Baghdad on 16th July 1917.   Pl. LXII.

PLATE LXII.

CHARLES MUNRO.

D. G. MUNRO.

ALEX. MUNRO.

J. S. MUNRO.

JOHN MUNRO.

T. M. MUNRO.

R. McD. MURRAY.

P. H. MURRAY.

J. R. MURRAY.

PLATE LXIII

J. S. Ness.

Thomas Nelson.

R. F. T. Newbery.

G. S. A. Nicholson.

David Nicol.

Andrew Nicol.

David Nicoll.

G. M. Nicol.

F. W. Niesche.

Roll of the Fallen

MUNRO, THOMAS MACKAY (*b.* 1890).
 Tain Royal Academy. Student of Arts, 1910-14; M.A. 1913. Schoolmaster. O.T.C. Infantry, Oct. 1910 to Dec. 1913, Cadet. 5th and 7th Seaforth Highlanders, Private Aug. 1914; 2nd Lieut. March 1915. Killed in action in France on 25th September 1915. Pl. LXII.

MURRAY, JOHN ROBERTSON (*b.* 1879).
 Elgin Academy. Student of Law, 1903-4. 9th Seaforth Highlanders, Lieut. June 1916. Died of wounds on 18th September 1917. Pl. LXII.

MURRAY, PETER HERBERT (*b.* 1896).
 Morgan Academy, Dundee; Dux. Student of Arts, 1914-16. Y.M.C.A. (Summer Vacations), 1915-16. 10th and 1st Seaforth Highlanders, Private Oct. 1916; Corporal. Died of wounds received at Tekrit, Mesopotamia, on 9th November 1917. Pl. LXII.

MURRAY, ROBERT McDIARMID (*b.* 1894).
 George Watson's College. O.T.C. 1909-11, Cadet L/Corporal. Student of Law, 1911. O.T.C. Artillery, Jan. 1912-14, Cadet. R.G.A., 2nd Lieut. Nov. 1914; Lieut. Feb. 1916. France. M.C. Feb. 1916. Died of wounds near Ypres on 25th February 1916. Pl. LXII.

MYLNE, JAMES GRAHAM (*b.* 1887).
 Edinburgh Academy. B.A. (Oxford). Student of Law, 1909-10. Writer to the Signet, 1913. 2/8th attached 1/4th Royal Scots, 2nd Lieut. May 1915; Lieut. Palestine 1917; France 1918. Killed at Queant near Bapaume on 2nd September 1918.

NEIL, ROBERT DONALD (*b.* 1896).
 Royal High School. Student of Science, 1914-15. 15th Royal Scots, Private Sept. 1914. 5th Royal Scots Fusiliers, 2nd Lieut. 1915. Egypt Jan. 1916. France March 1916. Killed in action in France on 26th October 1916. Pl. XCIII.

NEILL, WILLIAM PROUDFOOT (*b.* 1873).
 Daniel Stewart's College. Student of Law. Solicitor, 1896. Royal Scots, Lieut. Died in France on 24th December 1916.

NELSON, THOMAS (*b.* 1859).
 Perth Academy. Student of Medicine; M.B., C.M. 1880; M.D. 1886. St John's Ambulance Brigade, Assistant Commissioner, No. 3 District. Died on 4th March 1918. Pl. LXIII.

NESS, JAMES SHARP (*b.* 1896).
 Tain Royal Academy and Robert Gordon's College, Aberdeen. Student of Science, 1913-15. 1/7th Gordon Highlanders, Private Oct. 1915. Killed in action in France on 16th September 1917. Pl. LXIII.

Roll of the Fallen

NEWBERY, RICHARD FENTON THEODORE (*b.* 1891).
    Lycée, Nice, and Tonbridge School, Kent. Student of Medicine, 1909-15; M.B., Ch.B. 1915. O.T.C. Infantry, Oct. 1910 to Nov. 1913, Cadet. President, Philomathic Society. Resident, Royal Infirmary 1915. R.A.M.C., Lieut. Oct. 1915. France March 1916. Attached 6th Northamptonshires, May 1916. Killed at Trones Wood on 14th July 1916.   Pl. LXIII.

NICHOLSON, GEOFFREY SHIELD ALEC (*b.* 1894).
    Merchiston Castle. Student of Arts, 1912-15. O.T.C. Infantry, Oct. 1914 to Jan. 1916, Cadet. Aero Club Pilot Certificate at Hendon, Nov. 1915. Royal Highlanders (Black Watch), 2nd Lieut. Jan. 1916. R.F.C., Feb. 1917; Pilot May 1917. Mortally wounded at third Battle of Ypres on 21st and died on 22nd August 1917.   Pl. LXIII.

NICOL, ANDREW (*b.* 1893).
    Falkirk High School; First XI. Student of Arts, 1911-14. Royal Scots, Private Sept. 1914. King's Own Scottish Borderers, 2nd Lieut. Feb. 1915. Dispatches June 1916. Killed in action on 22nd May 1916.   Pl. LXIII.

NICOL, DAVID (*b.* 1897).
    Kelvinside Academy, Glasgow, and Edinburgh Academy. O.T.C. 1911-14, Cadet. Student of Medicine, 1914-15. O.T.C. Infantry, Oct. 1914 to July 1915, Cadet. 12th Argyll and Sutherland Highlanders, 2nd Lieut. July 1915; Lieut. July 1917; Acting Captain Sept. 1917. France June 1916. Killed in Bourlon Wood on 25th November 1917.   Pl. LXIII.

NICOL, GEORGE M. (*b.* 1887).
    Boroughmuir School. Student of Arts, 1912-14. 9th Scottish Rifles, 2nd Lieut. Aug. 1914; Lieut. June 1915. Killed at Loos on 25th September 1915.   Pl. LXIII.

NICOLL, DAVID (*b.* 1884).
    George Watson's College; Athletics. Student of Arts and Law, 1902-10; M.A. 1907; LL.B. 1910. No. 4 Coy. Q.R.V.B. Royal Scots, 1906-9, Private; London Scottish, Private, March 1916. France July 1916. Killed at Leuze Wood near Combles on 10th September 1916.   Pl. LXIII.

NIESCHE, FREDERICK WILLIAM (*b.* 1858).
    Leschen and Niehus School, Adelaide. Student of Medicine, 1876-80; M.B., C.M. 1880; M.D. 1886. M.D. (Adelaide) 1889. Australian Military Forces, Hon. Major, 1910. No. 7, Australian General Hospital, Keswick, England, 1915-17. Died at Adelaide on 13th October 1918.   Pl. LXIII.

NISBET, JOHN (*b.* 1891).
    Broughton School. Student of Arts, 1910-14; M.A. (Hons. Engl.) 1914. 9th, 14th, 3rd, and 2nd Royal Scots, Private Aug. 1914; 2nd Lieut. Nov. 1914. France Feb. 1915. Killed in action on 25th April 1915.   Pl. LXIV.

Roll of the Fallen

NISBET, POLLOK SINCLAIR (*b.* 1889).
    George Watson's College. Student of Law, 1908-12. Chartered Accountant, 1912. O.T.C. Infantry, March 1909 to July 1912, Cadet L/Corporal. 2nd Canadian Infantry, 26th Machine-Gun Corps, Lieut. 1915. Killed in action on 2nd June 1916.   Pl. LXIV.

NOBLE, JAMES DICKSON (*b.* 1869).
    Royal High School. Student of Medicine, 1888-93; M.B., C.M. 1893. R.A.M.C., Captain. Accidentally killed at Aberdeen on 12th October 1914.   Pl. LXIV.

NORTON, HENRY HALL (*b.* 1888).
    George Heriot's School. Student of Arts, 1907-12; M.A. (Hons. Hist.) 1911. Headingley Wesleyan College, Leeds, 1912-13. Minister of Wesleyan Church. R.A.M.C., Private Jan. 1915. Wounded at evacuation of Gallipoli and died at Alexandria on 27th January 1916.   Pl. LXIV.

ORME, JOHN McCALLUM (*b.* 1891).
    George Watson's College; Cadet Corps 1907-8. Student of Arts and Medicine, 1908-15; M.A. 1911; M.B., Ch.B. 1915. O.T.C. Infantry, Oct. 1908 to May 1914, Cadet. R.A.M.C. (S.R.), Captain July 1914. Attached 7th Battn. The Buffs, East Kent Regiment, Aug. 1915. M.C. 1916. Died as result of an accident on 3rd April 1917.   Pl. LXIV.

ORME, WILLIAM (*b.* 1888).
    Portree School. Student of Arts and Science, 1909-11. 15th Royal Scots, Private Sept. 1914; L/Corporal. France. Wounded at Arras on 28th April, taken prisoner, and died of wounds at Merseburg on 18th May 1917.   Pl. XCIII.

O'SULLIVAN, JOHN ANDREW HAMILTON (*b.* 1895).
    George Watson's College; First XV.; Shooting VIII. O.T.C. 1910-13, Cadet Colour-Sergeant. Student of Science, 1913-14. O.T.C. Infantry, Oct. 1913 to Sept. 1914, Cadet. 13th Highland Light Infantry, 2nd Lieut. Aug. 1914; Lieut. Dec. 1914. Attached 5th Royal Scots, Gallipoli. Killed in action there on 28th June 1915.   Pl. LXIV.

PAGAN, GEORGE HAIR (*b.* 1892).
    Merchiston Castle. Student of Arts, 1910-11. 1/7th Royal Highlanders (Black Watch), Lieut. Sept. 1914. France. 51st (Highland) Division. Killed at High Wood, the Somme, on 31st July 1916.   Pl. LXIV.

PAISLEY, THOMAS (*b.* 1885).
    High School, Brechin. Student of Law, 1905-7. Royal Scots, Private Sept. 1914. 10th Scottish Rifles, 2nd Lieut. Jan 1915. Killed in action on 25th September 1915.   Pl. LXIV.

Roll of the Fallen

PALMER, HUGH SALISBURY (*b.* 1888).
    Gresham School, Holt; Cadet Corps 1902-6, Cadet Corporal. Student of Medicine, 1906-14; M.B., Ch.B. 1914. R.A.M.C., Lieut. Nov. 1914; Captain May 1915. Attached 2nd London Rifle Brigade. 2/2nd Home Counties Field Ambulance. Dispatches Dec. 1917. Died of wounds on 25th April 1918.   Pl. LXIV.

PARK, FREDERICK ANDREW KETCHEN (*b.* 1896).
    Kendal and Manchester Grammar Schools. Student of Medicine, 1914-16. 5th Royal Lancs. Regiment, Private Jan. 1916; Officer Cadet. 137th Machine-Gun Corps, 2nd Lieut. Oct. 1916; Lieut. April 1918. France March 1917. Killed in action on 3rd October 1918.   Pl. LXV.

PATERSON, JOHN McLELLAN STEWART (*b.* 1890).
    Robert Gordon's College, Aberdeen. Student of Arts, 1909-13; M.A. (Hons. Engl.) 1913. President, Diagnostic Society. O.T.C. Infantry, Dec. 1909-13, Cadet. 4th Gordon Highlanders, Private Oct. 1914. France. Killed in action in Belgium on 23rd April 1915.

PATERSON, NORMAN KEITH (*b.* 1892).
    George Watson's College. Student of Arts, 1910-14; M.A. (Hons. Econ. Sc.) 1914. Vans Dunlop Scholar. O.T.C. Artillery, Dec. 1914 to Feb. 1915, Cadet. R.F.A. (S.R.), 2nd Lieut. Feb. 1915; Lieut. May 1916. France 1915. Killed in action on 28th June 1916.   Pl. LXV.

PATERSON, ROBERT SANDERSON (*b.* 1893).
    Royal High School and Fettes College; First XV. and XI. O.T.C. 1910-12. Student of Arts, 1912-13. O.T.C. Artillery, 1912 to Aug. 1914, Cadet. R.F.A. (S.R.), 62nd Battery, 2nd Lieut. Aug. 1914. R.H.A. ("Chestnut Troop"). France. Killed at the Battle of Neuve Chapelle on 11th March 1915.   Pl. LXV.

PATERSON, ROBERT WALKER (*b.* 1894).
    Perth Academy. Student of Arts, 1912-16. Royal Scots, Private March 1916. 2nd Sherwood Foresters, 2nd Lieut. Feb. 1917. Dispatches Dec. 1917. M.C. (posthumous). Killed in action in March 1918.   Pl. LXV.

PATERSON, WILLIAM CHARLES DAWSON (*b.* 1896).
    Royal High School. Heriot Bursar. Edinburgh University O.T.C. Infantry Aug. 1914, Cadet. 6th Royal Scots, attached 5th Liverpool Regiment, 2nd Lieut. Aug. 1915. France. Killed at Gueudecourt, Somme, on 25th September 1916.   Pl. LXV.

PATRICK, FRANCIS ALEXANDER (*b.* 1892).
    George Watson's College. Student of Arts and Science, 1909-14. O.T.C. Artillery, Nov. 1909 to Feb. 1911, Cadet. 9th Royal Scots, Private Sept. 1914. France 1915. Killed in action at Ypres on 12th April 1915.   Pl. LXV.

PLATE LXIV.

JOHN NISBET.

J. D. NOBLE.

P. S. NISBET.

J. A. H. O'SULLIVAN.

J. McC. ORME.

H. H. NORTON.

H. S. PALMER.

G. H. PAGAN.

THOMAS PAISLEY.

PLATE LXV.

N. K. Paterson.

R. S. Paterson.

F. A. K. Park.

W. C. D. Paterson.

R. W. Paterson.

F. A. Patrick.

J. B. Patrick.

M. G. Patten.

David Patton.

Roll of the Fallen

PATRICK, JOHN BONTHRONE (*b.* 1895).
    Hawick School. Student of Arts, 1913-14. O.T.C. Infantry, May 1913 to Oct. 1914, Cadet. 1/4th King's Own Scottish Borderers, 2nd Lieut. Oct. 1914. Missing, presumed killed at Gallipoli, on 12th July 1915.   Pl. LXV.

PATTEN, MURRAY GLADSTONE (*b.* 1888).
    Ormond College, Melbourne. Student of Arts, 1913-15. O.T.C. Infantry, Sept. 1914 to Feb. 1915, Cadet Sergeant. 9th Northumberland Fusiliers, Lieut. Feb. 1915; Captain. Foreign service 1915. M.C. 1917. Wounded. Killed in action on 14th April 1918.   Pl. LXV.

PATTERSON, DOUGLAS DAVID JOHN (*b.* 1898).
    Aberdeen Grammar School. Edinburgh University O.T.C. Infantry, May to Sept. 1916, Cadet; Officer Cadet Sept. 1916. 7th Seaforth Highlanders, 2nd Lieut. Jan. 1917. France April 1917. Killed at Wytschaete on 16th April 1918.

PATTISON, PETERSWALD (*b.* 1876).
    Edinburgh Academy. Student of Medicine, 1893-1901; M.B., Ch.B. 1901. D.P.H., R.C.P. & S. (Edin.) 1910. R.A.M.C., Lieut. Nov. 1914; Captain. Attached King's Own Yorkshire Light Infantry. Flanders. Invalided home in July 1915 and died at London on 22nd February 1916.

PATTON, DAVID (*b.* 1882).
    Strathbungo School, Glasgow. University O.T.C. Infantry, March 1916 to May 1917, Cadet. 8th attached 2nd Scottish Rifles, 2nd Lieut. May 1917. Died of wounds on 11th February 1918.   Pl. LXV.

PENDER, HAMISH GRANGER GEILS (*b.* 1892).
    Edinburgh Academy; Athletics. O.T.C. 1908-10. Student of Science, 1911-14. Secretary, Engineering Society. O.T.C. Engineers, April 1912 to Oct. 1914, Cadet Sergeant. 2nd Gordon Highlanders, 2nd Lieut. Oct. 1914. Killed at Battle of Neuve Chapelle on 11th or 13th March 1915.   Pl. LXVI.

PENNYCOOK, ALEXANDER (*b.* 1896).
    Dunbar School. Student of Arts, 1914-16. 3/8th and 12th Royal Scots, Private Nov. 1915; Signaller; L/Corporal. France Aug. 1916, 9th Division. Arras, Ypres, 1917. Taken prisoner on 25th April at Kemmel Hill and died of pneumonia at Saaralben, Germany, on 16th October 1918.   Pl. LXVI.

PHILIP, ANDREW (*b.* 1865).
    Kirkcaldy High School. Student of Medicine, 1888-93; M.B., C.M. 1893; M.D., D.P.H. R.A.M.C., Lieut.-Surgeon. Died at Hull as the result of an accident on 30th May 1915.   Pl. LXVI.

Roll of the Fallen

PHILIPS, ABRAHAM ZADOK (*b.* 1881).
    Burgerschool, Amsterdam. Student of Medicine, 1904-10; M.B., Ch.B. 1910; M.D. 1913; D.P.H. (Lond.) 1914; F.R.C.S. (Edin.) 1915. Hospitals in Dunkirk and London, April to July 1915. R.A.M.C., Lieut. July 1915; Captain 1916. France. 56th Field Ambulance. Wounded and gassed on 23rd and died of gas poisoning on 24th October 1917.   Pl. LXVI.

PHORSON, DOUGLAS STUART (*b.* 1889).
    Houghton-le-Spring Grammar School. Student of Medicine, 1906-8. 3rd and 18th Durham Light Infantry, 2nd Lieut. May 1915; Captain July 1916. France June 1916. Killed at Hebuterne on 16th December 1916.   Pl. LXVI.

PINKERTON, JOHN (*b.* 1882).
    Daniel Stewart's College. Vans Dunlop Scholar. Student of Arts and Divinity, 1901-5; M.A. (Hons. Classics) 1905; B.D. 1908; B.A. (Hons. Semitic Lang.) (Camb.) Minister, Church of Scotland. 1st Royal Scots, L/Corporal. Salonika. Killed in action near Struma on 1st October 1916.   Pl. LXVI.

PIRIE, GEORGE STEPHEN (*b.* 1888).
    St Andrew's College, Grahamstown, and Merchiston Castle. Student of Medicine, 1908-14; M.B., Ch.B. 1914. O.T.C. Medical, Oct. 1914-15, Cadet. R.A.M.C., Lieut.; Captain Jan. 1915. Gallipoli, 29th Division, 1915; France Dec. 1915. Twice Mentioned in Dispatches. Wounded Sept. 1915. Killed in action on 24th July 1917.   Pl. LXVI.

PLUNKETT, HAVELOCK A. T. (*b.* 1896).
    St Paul's School, Darjeeling. O.T.C. Cadet Sergeant. University O.T.C. Infantry, April to Aug. 1914, Cadet. Military College, Sandhurst, 1914. 3rd and 2nd Royal Highlanders (Black Watch), 2nd Lieut. Dec. 1914. France March 1915. Lieut. May 1915. Indian Exp. Force, Mesopotamia, Dec. 1915. Killed at Sheikh Said on 7th January 1916.   Pl. LXVI.

POLLOCK, JOHN DUNBAR (*b.* 1876).
    Church of Scotland Normal School, Edinburgh. Student of Law, 1897-9. Solicitor. 4th Royal Scots, 2nd Lieut. 1906; Lieut. 1909; Captain 1911. Killed in action at the Dardanelles on 28th June 1915.

POOL, JOHN NEWLANDS (*b.* 1894).
    Dumfries Academy. Student of Arts, 1914-16. Lennie Bursar. 3rd King's Own Scottish Borderers, Private Feb. 1916. 1st Cameronians (Scottish Rifles). Killed in action in France on 16th April 1917.   Pl. LXVI.

PORTER, WILLIAM GUTHRIE (*b.* 1878).
    Edinburgh Academy; First XV. Student of Science and Medicine, 1894-1902; B.Sc. 1898; M.B., Ch.B. 1902; F.R.C.S. (Edin.). R.A.M.C., Corporal 1900-2. South African Campaign, 1902. Surgeon-Lieut. 1907; Captain 1914; Major 1916. Attached R.G.A. (Vol.), Midlothian Battery, later R.F.A. (T.), 1st Lowland Brigade. France Autumn 1915. Wounded April 1917. D.S.O. June 1917. Killed in action on 8th June 1917.   Pl. LXVII.

PLATE LXVI.

Andrew Philip.

Alex. Pennycook.

H. G. G. Pender.

A. Z. Philips.

D. S. Phorson.

John Pinkerton.

J. N. Pool.

H. A. T. Plunkett.

G. S. Pirie.

PLATE LXVII.

 W. G. Porter.
 G. B. L. Price.
 E. F. T. Price.

 O. D. Price.
 John Prosser.
 A. S. Pringle.

 Samuel Rae.
 J. C. Rae.
 G. B. Ramsay.

Roll of the Fallen

PRICE, EDMUND FREDERICK TANNEY (b. 1862).
   Mussoorie School, India. Student of Medicine, 1879-84; M.B., C.M. 1884. Lecturer to Scottish Women's First Aid Corps. 1st Battn. City of Edinburgh Volunteer Regiment, Private. Died on parade on 27th October 1917. Pl. LXVII.

PRICE, GEORGE BERNARD LOCKING (b. 1896).
   Daniel Stewart's College; First XI. 1st Highland Cadet Battn. Student of Medicine, 1914-15. 16th Royal Scots, Private 1915; Gordon Highlanders, 2nd Lieut. March 1917. France June 1916. Wounded at the Somme in July 1916. Killed at Ypres on 22nd August 1917. Pl. LXVII.

PRICE, OWEN DOUGLAS (b. 1892).
   George Watson's College; First XV. Cadet Corps 1905-10, Cadet Sergeant. Student of Medicine, 1910-15; M.B., Ch.B. 1915. R.A.M.C. (S.R.), Lieut. July 1915; Captain 1916. Med. Exp. Force, 1915-16. West Africa, 1916-17. France 1917 and 1918, 55th Division. Died at Edinburgh on 10th December 1918 of influenza contracted in France. Pl. LXVII.

PRINGLE, ARTHUR STANLEY (b. 1877).
   Edinburgh Academy; First XV. B.A. (Camb.). Student of Law, 1899-1902; LL.B. 1902. Advocate, 1902. Q.R.V.B., No. 4 Coy., 2nd Lieut. O.T.C. Infantry, Captain and O.C. April 1908 to July 1910. 10th Scottish Rifles, Captain. France. Wounded at Hill 70, Loos, on 25th and died on 26th September 1915. Pl. LXVII.

PROSSER, JOHN (b. 1889).
   Edinburgh Academy; First XV. Student of Arts and Law, 1907-15; M.A. 1910; LL.B. (Distinction) 1912. Grierson Bursar, Thow, and Vans Dunlop Scholar. Writer to the Signet, 1913. 4th, 2/4th, 2/5th and 8th Royal Highlanders (Black Watch), 2nd Lieut. Dec. 1914; Acting Lieut. Sept. 1915; Lieut. June 1916; Acting Captain and Adjutant 1916. Flanders July 1918. Killed in action on 28th September 1918. Pl. LXVII.

PROUDFOOT, HAROLD HEAFFORD (b. 1889).
   Loughborough Grammar School. Student of Medicine, 1906-11; M.B., Ch.B. 1911. Resident, R.I.E. R.A.M.C., Lieut. May 1915; Captain May 1916. Attached R.F.A. Killed in action in September 1916.

PRYCE, ARTHUR MEURIG (b. 1878).
   Clifton. University College, Aberystwith. Student of Medicine, 1897-1903; M.B., Ch.B. 1903; M.D. R.A.M.C., Lieut.; Captain. Died of pneumonia at Calais in October 1916.

RAE, JOHN CAIRNS (b. 1892).
   George Heriot's School and Edinburgh Institution. Student of Science, 1910-14; B.Sc. 1914. O.T.C. Artillery, Oct. 1910 to June 1914, Cadet. R.F.A., 88th Brigade, Lieut. Feb. 1915; Captain Nov. 1915; Acting Major. France July 1915. M.C. (posthumous). Dispatches. Killed near Arras on 10th April 1917. Pl. LXVII.

Roll of the Fallen

RAE, SAMUEL (b. 1889).
    Kirkcudbright Academy. Student of Arts, 1907-14; M.A. (Hons. Hist.) 1912. 15th Royal Scots, Private Sept. 1914. France. Killed in action on 1st July 1916.   Pl. LXVII.

RAMSAY, GEORGE BENNETT (b. 1893).
    Daniel Stewart's College. Student of Science, 1911-14. O.T.C. Engineers, March 1912 to Oct. 1914, Cadet. R.E., Lowland Division, attached 29th Division, 2nd Lieut. Gallipoli April 1915. Dispatches. Wounded April and July 1915. Died of typhoid on Hospital Ship *Galeka* on 27th August 1915.   Pl. LXVII.

RATTRAY, DAVID (b. 1891).
    Student of Law, 1913-15. Solicitor. R.F.A., Gunner; 2nd Lieut. Died of wounds on 21st September 1918.   Pl. LXVIII.

RAWSON, ARTHUR (b. 1890).
    Royal High School; Athletics. Student of Science, 1908-14; B.Sc. 1914. Lothians and Border Horse, Private 1908. Mobilised Aug. 1914. Scottish Horse. 13th Royal Highlanders (Black Watch), 2nd Lieut. Nov. 1914; Captain and Adjutant. Gallipoli, Egypt, and Salonika. Dispatches July 1917 and Jan. 1919. Killed in action on 6th October 1918.   Pl. LXVIII.

REID, ALEXANDER (b. 1886).
    Sedbergh; First XV. and XI. O.T.C., Cadet Sergeant. Student of Law, 1900-2. Chartered Accountant, 1910. 9th Q.V. Rifles, County of London Regiment, Rifleman Aug. 1914; 2nd Lieut. Sept. 1915. France Oct. 1914. Killed at Zillebeke near Ypres on 15th February 1917.   Pl. LXVIII.

REID, ARTHUR STANLEY (b. 1885).
    Kirkcaldy High School; Athletics. Cadet Corps 1900-3, Cadet Sergeant. Student of Arts, 1903-7; M.A. (Hons. Classics) 1907. 15th Royal Scots, Private Oct. 1914; Sergeant Dec. 1915. France 1915. Killed in action near Albert on 1st July 1916.   Pl. LXVIII.

REID, DONALD (b. 1897).
    George Watson's College. Student of Medicine, 1915-16. O.T.C. Infantry, May to Dec. 1916, Cadet. 4th Highland Light Infantry, 2nd Lieut. Killed in action on 17th August 1917.   Pl. LXVIII.

REID, GEORGE (b. 1890).
    Forfar Academy. Student of Arts, 1908-11; M.A. 1911; L.C.P. O.T.C. Artillery, 1908-11. Schoolmaster. R.F.A., 11th D.A.C., 2nd Lieut. Aug. 1914; Lieut. France and Italy. Wounded at Vimy Ridge July 1916. Killed in action on 25th August 1918.   Pl. LXVIII.

REID, MATTHEW COLVILLE (b. 1894).
    Alloa Academy. Student of Arts, 1912-14. 15th Royal Scots, Private Oct. 1914; L/Corporal 1915. Killed in action in France on 22nd May 1916.   Pl. LXVIII.

PLATE LXVIII.

Alex. Reid.

David Rattray.

Arthur Rawson.

George Reid.

A. S. Reid.

Donald Reid.

W. D. Reid.

M. C. Reid.

H. H. L. Richards.

PLATE LXIX.

Robert Richardson.

W. R. Ridley.

John Ritchie.

R. J. W. Ritchie.

W. S. Ritchie.

W. H. Ritchie.

Alex. B. Robertson.

A. Burns Robertson.

Alex. Robertson.

Roll of the Fallen

REID, WILLIAM DOUGLAS (*b.* 1887).
Marlborough High School, Blenheim, N.Z. M.B., Ch.B. 1910. R.A.M.C., Captain. France Nov. 1914. 1st Welsh Fusiliers. 21st Manchester Regiment. The Somme. M.C. (Munich Trench) Jan. 1917. Wounded at the Battle of the Ancre Dec. 1916 and Jan. 1917. Killed near Ypres on 5th October 1917. Pl. LXVIII.

RENDELL, HERBERT (*b.* 1859).
Student of Medicine; M.B., C.M. 1882. 1st Newfoundland Regiment, Captain and Adjutant. France. Dispatches 1918. M.C. 1918. Killed in action in October 1918.

RENTON, FRANCIS WALLACE HOME (*b.* 1887).
Cargilfield and Sedbergh; First XV. Student of Medicine, 1908-10. 8th Border Regiment, 2nd Lieut. Dec. 1914; Lieut. 1915. France Sept. 1915. Killed near Albert on 30th August 1916.

RENTON, JAMES CRAWFORD. (See p. 116.)

RICHARDS, HUBERT HENRY LYSTER (*b.* 1892).
Marlborough College. O.T.C. Student of Medicine, 1912-14. 9th Hampshire Regiment, Private Aug. 1914. 5th Connaught Rangers, 2nd Lieut. Dispatches Dec. 1915. Killed at Kosterina, Serbia, on 7th December 1915. Pl. LXVIII.

RICHARDSON, ARTHUR ARCHIBOLD (*b.* 1891).
North Berwick High School. Student of Law, 1912-14. 9th Royal Scots, Private Aug. 1914. Argyll and Sutherland Highlanders, 2nd Lieut. Killed at the Battle of Loos on 25th September 1915.

RICHARDSON, MARTIN JAMES (*b.* 1866).
Durham School. Student of Medicine, 1883-9; M.B., C.M. 1889. R.A.M.C., Lieut. Killed in action on 3rd November 1914.

RICHARDSON, ROBERT (*b.* 1893).
Peebles High School. Student of Arts, 1913-15. 4th and 12th Royal Scots, Private Dec. 1915; L/Corporal Jan. 1917; Officer Cadet April 1917; 2nd Lieut. July 1917. France April 1918. Wounded 19th and died on 26th July 1918 near St Omer. Pl. LXIX.

RIDLEY, WILLIAM ROBERT (*b.* 1881).
Daniel Stewart's College. Student of Medicine, 1900-10; M.B., Ch.B. 1910. Serbian Medical Service, Major Aug. 1914. Field and Reserve Military Hospitals, Serbia. Serbian Red Cross Diploma and Decoration. Died at Kragujevatz about 2nd November 1914. Pl. LXIX.

RITCHIE, JOHN (*b.* 1891).
Perth Academy. Student of Law, 1912-13. Chartered Accountant, 1915. 30th Royal Fusiliers ("Sportsman's Reserve"), Private Jan. 1915. 3/6th Royal Highlanders (Black Watch). Machine-Gun Corps, 2nd Lieut. June 1915; Lieut. June 1916. Salonika. Killed on the Doïran Front on 25th April 1917. Pl. LXIX.

Roll of the Fallen

RITCHIE, RICHARD JAMES WALLACE (*b.* 1896).
George Watson's College. Student of Medicine, 1913-14. Scottish Horse Ambulance. Highland Light Infantry, Aug. 1914; Captain Feb. 1917. Killed in action on 20th May 1918.   Pl. LXIX.

RITCHIE, WILLIAM (*b.* 1874).
Perth Academy. Student of Medicine, 1890-9; M.B., Ch.B. 1899. R.A.M.C., attached Highland Light Infantry, Captain. Killed in action in April 1916.

RITCHIE, WILLIAM HAMILTON (*b.* 1896).
Trinity Academy, Leith. Student of Science, 1913-15. R.E. (Special Brigade), Corporal July 1915. France July 1915. Killed in action on 27th February 1917.   Pl. LXIX.

RITCHIE, WILLIAM SMAIL (*b.* 1876).
Daniel Stewart's College. Student of Law. Solicitor, 1901. 5th Argyll and Sutherland Highlanders, Private Feb. 1916; 2nd Lieut. Feb. 1918. Egypt Oct. 1917; Palestine and France. Killed in action in France on 29th July 1918.   Pl. LXIX.

ROBERTSON, ALEXANDER (*b.* 1882).
George Watson's College. Student of Arts, 1900-4; M.A. (Hons. Hist.) 1904. B. Litt. (Oxford) 1913. Lecturer in History, Sheffield University. 12th Yorks and Lancs. Regiment, Private Sept. 1914; Corporal. France. Killed in action at Serre, France, on 1st July 1916.   Pl. LXIX.

ROBERTSON, ALEXANDER BRASH (*b.* 1878).
Gillespie's School. Student of Arts, 1899-1901 and 1910-12; M.A. 1901; (Hons. Engl., 1911). Schoolmaster. 2/4th Royal Highlanders (Black Watch), Private Nov. 1916. Cameron Highlanders. 2/1st Scottish Horse. Drowned by the torpedoing of S.S. *Leinster* on 10th October 1918.   Pl. LXIX.

ROBERTSON, ALEXANDER WALKER (*b.* 1877).
Glenalmond and Aberdeen University. Student of Law. Solicitor. 2nd Gordon Highlanders, South African Campaign, 1900-1. 9th Argyll and Sutherland Highlanders, Captain 1915. France 1915. Killed in action on 17th August 1916.

ROBERTSON, ANGUS BURNS (*b.* 1886).
Allahabad College, India. Student of Medicine, 1905-11; M.B., Ch.B. 1911. Allahabad and Edinburgh Volunteer Rifle Corps, 1903-7. R.A.M.C., Captain May 1917. 7th Mounted Brigade, Field Ambulance, Egypt and Palestine. Died of pneumonia following influenza at Dundee on 8th November 1918.   Pl. LXIX.

ROBERTSON, CHARLES (*b.* 1879).
Perth Academy and Daniel Stewart's College. Student of Arts; M.A. 1900. Minister, Church of Scotland. Chaplain Nov. 1915. M.C. (posthumous). Died of wounds at Salonika on 3rd October 1918.   Pl. LXX.

PLATE LXX.

 D. W. Robertson.
 Charles Robertson.
 L. F. Robertson.

 W. H. Robertson-Durham.
 G. S. Rodger.
 M. F. Rodger.

 A. N. Rogers.
 J. F. Ronaldson-Lyell.
 R. C. Rogers.

PLATE LXXI.

A. A. Ross.   A. B. Ross.   William Rose.

J. A. Ross.   F. McF. Ross.   G. A. Ross.

J. G. Ross.   T. S. Ross.   Peter Ross.

Roll of the Fallen

ROBERTSON, DAVID WALKER (b. 1887).
    Royal High School. L.D.S. 1911. University O.T.C. Artillery, March to May 1916, Cadet. R.A.M.C., Lieut. June 1916; Captain July 1917. India Sept. 1916 to Nov. 1918. 2nd Division, Rawal Pindi; Dental Surgeon. Died of appendicitis at Edinburgh on 18th February 1919.   Pl. LXX.

ROBERTSON, IAN GORDON (b. 1897).
    Christ's Hospital. Student of Arts. Gordon Highlanders, 2nd Lieut. 1915. Foreign service 1916. Killed in action on 13th November 1916.

ROBERTSON, JOHN BREWIS (b. 1892).
    George Watson's College. University O.T.C. Infantry, Sept. 1914 to Feb. 1915, Cadet Sergeant. 9th Royal Highlanders (Black Watch), 2nd Lieut. Feb. 1915; Captain June 1916. Wounded at the Somme on 7th and died on 17th September 1916.

ROBERTSON, LENNOX FRASER (b. 1883).
    George Watson's College. Student of Arts, 1900-3; M.A. 1903. 29th Vancouver Battn. (2nd C.E.F.), Private; L/Corporal; Sergeant. France Oct. 1915. Wounded at the Somme on 10th and died at Aberdeen on 19th September 1916.   Pl. LXX.

ROBERTSON-DURHAM, WILLIAM HUGH (b. 1889).
    Edinburgh Academy. Student of Law, 1907-12. Writer to the Signet, 1912. 10th Scottish Rifles, Lieut. Aug. 1914; Captain March 1915. France July 1915. Killed in action at Loos on 25th September 1915.   Pl. LXX.

RODGER, GEORGE SWAN (b. 1895).
    Broughton School. Student of Science, 1914-15. O.T.C. Engineers, Oct. 1914 to April 1915, Cadet. 9th Leicester Regiment, 2nd Lieut. April 1915. Killed in action on 9th January 1917.   Pl. LXX.

RODGER, MATHEW FREER (b. 1885).
    Larchfield, Helensburgh, and Merchiston Castle; First XV. Rogerson Scholar. B.A. (Oxford). Student of Law, 1908-11; LL.B. 1911. Writer to the Signet, 1911. O.T.C. Infantry, Sept. 1914. 2nd, 3rd, and 4th Scottish Rifles, 2nd Lieut. Sept. 1914; Lieut. March 1915. France May 1915. Killed near Le Transloy, the Somme, on 23rd October 1916.   Pl. LXX.

ROGERS, ARTHUR NORMAN (b. 1889).
    Wyggeston School, Leicester. Student of Law, 1912-14. O.T.C. Infantry, April 1912 to Sept. 1914, Cadet. 7th Royal Scots (T.), 2nd Lieut. Sept. 1914; Lieut.; Captain Aug. 1916. Gallipoli, Egypt, and Palestine. Killed at Neby Samwil near Jerusalem on 24th November 1917.   Pl. LXX.

Roll of the Fallen

ROGERS, ROBERT CARMICHAEL (*b.* 1890).
 Perth Academy. Student of Arts and Medicine, 1907-15; M.A. 1910; M.B., Ch.B. 1914. Resident, R.I.E. R.A.M.C., attached R.G.A., Lieut. Dec. 1916; Captain Dec. 1917. France. Wounded Oct. 1917. Died of wounds at 14th General Hospital, France, on 2nd August 1918. Pl. LXX.

RONALDSON-LYELL, JAMES FRANCIS (*b.* 1894).
 Loretto and George Watson's College. Student of Arts and Law, 1913-16. 3rd Royal Scots, 2nd Lieut. Dec. 1915. France, Intelligence Officer. Accidentally killed in France on 26th November 1917. Pl. LXX.

ROSE, WILLIAM (*b.* 1884).
 George Watson's College. Student of Arts and Medicine, 1903-7; M.A. 1907. 4th Royal Scots, Private Aug. 1914. 10th Highland Light Infantry, Lieut. Feb. 1915. France 1915. Twice wounded. Killed at Monchy on 11th April 1917. Pl. LXXI.

ROSS, ALEXANDER AITKEN (*b.* 1861).
 George Watson's College. Student of Medicine, 1888-93; M.B., C.M. 1893. R.A.M.C., Lieut.-Col. O.C. 3rd Lowland Field Ambulance from 1908. Dardanelles. Invalided to Malta Oct. 1915. Died at London in November 1915. Pl. LXXI.

ROSS, ANDREW BEACONSFIELD (*b.* 1878).
 Tain Royal Academy and Inverness College. Student of Arts and Medicine, 1895-1902; M.A. 1898; M.B., Ch.B. 1902; M.D. 1906. Vans Dunlop Scholar (Arts) 1898. President, Royal Medical Society. 2nd Royal Irish Rifles, Lieut. Aug. 1916. Killed near Ypres on 6th August 1917. Pl. LXXI.

ROSS, FINDLAY McFADYEN (*b.* 1893).
 George Watson's College; First XV. Cadet Corps 1906-12, Cadet L/Corporal. Student of Science, 1912-14. O.T.C. Engineers, April 1913 to Sept. 1914, Cadet. 9th Royal Scots, Private Oct. 1914; L/Corporal June 1915; Lieut. Sept. 1917; Acting Captain. France Feb. 1915. M.C. Sept. 1916. Wounded June 1915 and Sept. 1916. Killed near Soissons on 1st August 1918. Pl. LXXI.

ROSS, GEORGE ALEXANDER (*b.* 1870).
 Student of Arts, 1894-6; M.A. 1896. Schoolmaster. 1/4th Royal Scots, Captain. Killed in action at the Dardanelles on 28th June 1915. Pl. LXXI.

ROSS, JAMES ANDREW (*b.* 1882).
 Buckhaven School. Student of Arts, 1904-9; M.A. 1909. 9th Highland Light Infantry, Private Sept. 1914. 4th Seaforth Highlanders, 2nd Lieut. March 1915; Lieut. Nov. 1915. Killed in action in France on 26th July 1916. Pl. LXXI.

Roll of the Fallen

ROSS, JAMES GRAHAM (*b.* 1888).
    Glenalmond. Student of Arts and Law, 1905-8; M.A. 1908; LL.B. 1911. 5th Battn. 2nd Infantry Brigade, Canadians, Private Aug. 1914. 10th and 7th Seaforth Highlanders, 2nd Lieut. France. Killed near Péronne on 30th December 1917.   Pl. LXXI.

ROSS, JAMES HECTOR (*b.* 1887).
    Royal High School. Student of Law, 1908-13. Solicitor. O.T.C. Infantry, March 1909 to Dec. 1912, Cadet. 8th Seaforth Highlanders, Private 1915; 2nd Lieut. 1916; Lieut. Foreign service 1915. Wounded Aug. 1916. Killed in action on 23rd April 1917.

ROSS, PETER (*b.* 1877).
    Thurso F.C. School. Student of Arts and Science, 1897-1903; M.A. (Hons. Maths. and Nat. Phil.) 1903; B.Sc. 1904. Schoolmaster. 16th Royal Scots, 2nd Lieut. Dec. 1914; Lieut. Feb. 1915; Captain May 1916. France. Killed near La Boisselle, the Somme, on 1st July 1916.   Pl. LXXI.

ROSS, THOMAS STEWART (*b.* 1899).
    Fettes; First XV. and XI. O.T.C., Cadet Corporal. University O.T.C. Infantry, July 1917, Cadet. 3rd Cameron Highlanders, 2nd Lieut. June 1918. France. Wounded on 4th and died on 13th November 1918 at Bohain.   Pl. LXXI.

ROUSE, A. RITCHIE (*b.* 1897).
    Daniel Stewart's College and George Heriot's School. University O.T.C. Artillery, Nov. 1915 to June 1916, Cadet. R.F.A., Officer Cadet June 1916; 2nd Lieut. Nov. 1916; Lieut. France 1918. Killed at Hamelincourt near Arras on 31st August 1918.   Pl. LXXII.

ROUT, WILLIAM OWEN NELSON (*b.* 1892).
    Waitaki School, N.Z. Student of Medicine, 1912-14. O.T.C. Medical, April to Aug. 1914. 10th Highland Light Infantry, Lieut. France. Killed in action in November 1915.

RUDDOCK, EDWARD OLIVER (*b.* 1892).
    Napier High School and University College, N.Z. Athletics. Student of Medicine, 1913-14. N.Z. Exp. Force (Field Engineers), Sapper 1914. Gallipoli. Died of appendicitis at Alexandria on 11th May 1915.   Pl. LXXII.

RULE, HUGH MACLEAN (*b.* 1891).
    Falkirk School; Athletics. Student of Arts, 1909-12; M.A. 1912. R.A.M.C., Private Sept. 1914; Corporal Feb. 1915. 2nd Argyll and Sutherland Highlanders, attached Royal Highlanders (Black Watch), June 1916. France. Killed in action on 14th July 1916.   Pl. LXXII.

Roll of the Fallen

RUNDLE, CUBITT SINDALL (*b.* 1854).
    Crediton Grammar School, and Medical School, Exeter; Athletics. Student of Medicine, 1872-7; M.B., C.M. 1877. Indian Medical Service, Surgeon-Lieut. March 1880; Lieut.-Col. Burmah Campaign, 1885-6. M.O., Prisoners of War Camp, Blanches Banques, Jersey, Nov. 1915, where he died on 11th November 1916.   Pl. LXXII.

RUSSELL, WILLIAM BLACK (*b.* 1892).
    Daniel Stewart's College. Student of Law, 1912-14. 4th, 5th, and 14th Royal Scots, Private 1909; 2nd Lieut. Nov. 1914; Lieut. Jan. 1915. Dispatches Sept. 1915. Killed in action at Gallipoli on 19th June 1915.   Pl. LXXII.

SANDEMAN, ALBERT FITZROY (*b.* 1884).
    Edinburgh Institution. Student of Law, 1914-15. O.T.C. Infantry, Nov. to Dec. 1914, Cadet. 9th and 11th Border Regiment, 2nd Lieut. Jan. 1915; Lieut. and Captain 1917. France 1915. Wounded near Albert 1915. Salonika 1916. Killed in action on 2nd December 1917.   Pl. LXXII.

SANDERS, ARCHIBALD MORTON (*b.* 1898).
    Student of Medicine. King's Own Scottish Borderers, 2nd Lieut. Died of wounds on 9th April 1917.

SANDERSON, FREDERICK BORTHWICK (*b.* 1889).
    Edinburgh Academy; Charterhouse. B.A. (Camb.). Student of Medicine, 1911-14. O.T.C. Artillery, Feb. 1913 to Sept. 1914, Cadet. R.F.A., 1st Lowland Brigade, 2nd Lieut. Sept. 1914; Lieut. France Spring 1916. Wounded on 4th and died at Rouen on 10th August 1916.   Pl. LXXII.

SANSON, WALTER EDWIN HAMMOND (*b.* 1897).
    Rossall; First XV. O.T.C. 1911-14, Cadet Corporal. Student of Medicine, 1914-15. O.T.C. Infantry, Oct. to Dec. 1914, Cadet. 9th King's Own Royal Lancaster Regiment, 2nd Lieut. Oct. 1914. France. Killed at Guillemont on 16th August 1916.   Pl. LXXII.

SCARTH, JAMES CHARLES (*b.* 1895).
    Kirkwall Burgh School. Student of Science, 1914-15. O.T.C. Engineers, Oct. 1914 to June 1915, Cadet. 10th attached 7th Seaforth Highlanders, 2nd Lieut. May 1915. France. Killed at Longueval on 14th July 1916.   Pl. LXXII.

SCHAFER, THOMAS SYDNEY HERMANN (*b.* 1891).
    Cargilfield and Edinburgh Academy. O.T.C. 1908-9. Student of Science, 1908-9. O.T.C. Infantry, June 1909 to Jan. 1911, Cadet L/Corporal. B.A. (Camb.) 1913. Australian Voluntary Hospital, France, Corporal Aug. 1914. 13th Northumberland Fusiliers, 2nd Lieut. Dec. 1914. Twice wounded at Hill 70 and killed at Loos on 26th September 1915.   Pl. LXXIII.

PLATE LXXII.

A. R. ROUSE.

H. M. RULE.

E. O. RUDDOCK.

A. F. SANDEMAN.

C. S. RUNDLE.

W. B. RUSSELL.

F. B. SANDERSON.

W. E. H. SANSON.

J. C. SCARTH.

PLATE LXXIII.

T. S. H. SCHAFER.   A. H. SCOTT.   D. L. SCOTLAND.

W. D. H. SCOTT.   M. B. SCOTT.   C. B. SCOTT.

J. J. SHANNON.   J. F. SELKIRK.   A. G. SCOUGAL.

Roll of the Fallen

SCOTLAND, DAVID LOTHIAN (*b.* 1895).
Viewpark School, Edinburgh. Student of Science, 1913-15. O.T.C. Engineers, Oct. 1913 to Oct. 1914, Cadet. 3rd, 14th, and 11th Royal Scots, 2nd Lieut. Oct. 1914; Lieut. July 1916. France, 9th Division, Oct. 1915 to July 1916, and April 1918. Wounded at Longueval, Somme, 1916. Flanders, Champagne, and Cambrai. Machine-Gun Corps, 21st Division, April 1918. Wounded at Chapel Hill near Heudicourt, and died at Le Tréport on 29th September 1918. Pl. LXXIII.

SCOTT, ANDREW HAMILTON (*b.* 1881).
Ayr Academy. Student of Arts and Law, 1899-1906; M.A. 1902; LL.B. 1906. Writer to the Signet, 1909. O.T.C. Infantry, Feb. to July 1916, Cadet L/Corporal; Officer Cadet July 1916. 4th attached 6th King's Own Scottish Borderers, 2nd Lieut. Nov. 1916; Lieut. Aug. 1918. France Jan. 1917. Missing, presumed killed in action on 3rd May 1917. Pl. LXXIII.

SCOTT, CHARLES BEVERS (*b.* 1883).
Detroit and Windsor (Ontario) High Schools. Student of Arts and Law, 1901-6; M.A. 1906. LL.B. (Toronto) 1911. Osgoode Rifle Corps, Private 1914-15. 166th Queen's Own Rifles of Toronto, attached 54th British Columbia Regiment, Lieut. Jan. 1916; Captain. France Dec. 1916. Vimy Ridge. Killed near Lens on 26th June 1917. Pl. LXXIII.

SCOTT, MUNRO BRIGGS (*b.* 1889).
Buckhaven School. Student of Arts and Science, 1907-14; M.A. 1910; B.Sc. Botanical Expert at Kew Gardens. Royal Scots, Lieut. France. Killed at Arras on 12th April 1917. Pl. LXXIII.

SCOTT, WILLIAM DUNCAN HEWETT (*b.* 1892).
Dollar Academy; Dux; First XV. Cadet Corps 1906-9, Col.-Sergeant. Student of Arts and Divinity, 1909-14; M.A. 1912. O.T.C. Artillery, Oct. 1909 to Nov. 1911, Cadet. Lothians and Border Horse, Private Sept. 1914. 4th Gordon Highlanders, Private; L/Corporal. France. Killed near Kemmel, Belgium, on 17th March 1915. Pl. LXXIII.

SCOUGAL, ALEC GRAHAM (*b.* 1888).
George Watson's College and Glasgow Academy. Student of Arts, 1906-10; M.A. (Hons. Classics) 1910. Schoolmaster. 4th, 15th, and 17th Royal Scots, Private Oct. 1914; Lieut.; Captain and Adjutant; Lieut.-Col. France. M.C. Feb. 1917. Wounded Aug. 1916. Killed near Ypres on 18th September 1918. Pl. LXXIII.

SELKIRK, JAMES FREDERICK (*b.* 1878).
George Watson's College. Student of Medicine; M.B., Ch.B. 1900; M.D. 1904. Royal Naval Reserve (Booth Line), M.O. Aug. 1914. Died in July 1917. Pl. LXXIII.

Roll of the Fallen

SENTER, JOHN WATT (*b.* 1879).
    Kildrummy School. Student of Medicine and Science, 1904-10; M.B., Ch.B. 1910; B.Sc. 1912. South African Campaign, 1900. R.A.M.C., Lieut. June 1917. Died of wounds on 9th June 1918.

SETON, MILES CHARLES CARISTON (*b.* 1885).
    Royal High School and Edinburgh Academy. Student of Medicine, 1891-1900; M.B., Ch.B. 1900. Australian Army Medical Corps, Major. Died at London on 13th January 1919.

SHANNON, JOHN JAMES (*b.* 1879).
    High School, Dumfries. Student of Medicine, 1911-16; M.B., Ch.B. 1916. O.T.C. Medical, Nov. 1914 to April 1916, Cadet. R.A.M.C., 2nd Lieut. April 1916; Captain. Attached Berkshire Yeomanry; Hon. Artillery Coy. and Lincolnshire Yeomanry. Egypt May 1916; Alexandria, Palestine. Killed near Jerusalem on 29th November 1917.   Pl. LXXIII.

SHARP, JOHN GORDON (*b.* 1863).
    Student of Medicine; M.B., C.M. 1891; M.D. 1896. R.A.M.C., Lieut. Oct. 1915. Tyne Garrison. Died in October 1917.   Pl. LXXIV.

SHAW, JOHN DONALD (*b.* 1887).
    George Watson's College. Student of Law, 1909-12. Writer to the Signet, 1911. 3/9th and 13th Royal Scots, Private Sept. 1915; 2nd Lieut. Dec. 1915; Lieut. Sept. 1917. France 1916. Killed in action on 26th July 1918.   Pl. LXXIV.

SHAW, ROBERT DYKES SOMERVILLE (*b.* 1894).
    Merchiston Castle; First XV. O.T.C. 1907-12, Cadet Corporal. University O.T.C. Infantry, Sept. to Nov. 1914, Cadet. 7th and 10th Seaforth Highlanders, 2nd Lieut. Nov. 1914; Lieut. and Captain Oct. 1916. France Oct. 1915. Wounded April 1917. Killed in action on 23rd March 1918.   Pl. LXXIV.

SHAW, WILLIAM VAUGHAN (*b.* 1889).
    George Watson's College and Dollar Academy. Student of Science, 1909-10. 2nd Scots Guards, Private Aug. 1914. Flanders Nov. 1914. Killed in action in France on 18th December 1914.   Pl. LXXIV.

SHENNAN, JOHN ERIC (*b.* 1887).
    Edinburgh Academy; First XI. Student of Law, 1908-9. Chartered Accountant, 1912. South African Defence Force. A.S.C., 2nd Lieut. Nov. 1914; Lieut.; Captain 1917. South African Rebellion, German South-West and German East Africa; 1st E.A. Exp. Force, Tonga. Died at Johannesburg of malaria on 25th November 1918.   Pl. LXXIV.

SHIRLAW, NINIAN FREDERICK (*b.* 1895).
    George Heriot's School. Student of Arts, 1914-15. O.T.C. Infantry, Jan. to June 1915, Cadet. 8th and 14th Argyll and Sutherland Highlanders, Private July 1915; Corporal. France July 1916. Killed in action on 16th May 1917.   Pl. LXXIV.

PLATE LXXIV.

J. G. Sharp.

J. D. Shaw.

R. D. S. Shaw.

N. F. Shirlaw.

W. V. Shaw.

J. E. Shennan.

D. T. Simpson.

G. D. Simpson.

H. J. Simpson.

PLATE LXXV.

J. C. SIMPSON.

D. W. SINCLAIR.

P. S. SLADE-KING.

J. B. SMALL.

FRANK SINGLETON.

H. A. SMALL.

C. E. H. SMITH.

W. E. A. SMALL.

JOHN SMALL.

Roll of the Fallen

SIMPSON, DUGALD THOMAS (*b.* 1899).
    Royal Academy, Inverness. Student of Science, 1916-17. 1/7th Royal Highlanders (Black Watch), Private April 1917. France. Missing, presumed killed between 9th and 15th April 1918.   Pl. LXXIV.

SIMPSON, GEORGE DUDDINGSTON (*b.* 1885).
    Daniel Stewart's College. Student of Arts; M.A. 1906. 5th and 4th Royal Scots, Private Nov. 1914; L/Corporal; 2nd Lieut. March 1917. France April 1917. Killed near Ypres on 22nd October 1917.   Pl. LXXIV.

SIMPSON, HAROLD JAMES (*b.* 1892).
    Falkirk High School. Student of Arts, 1911-13. 4th Royal Scots. 43rd Canadian Cameron Highlanders, Private Dec. 1914. France 1915. Died of wounds at Ypres on 15th May 1916.   Pl. LXXIV.

SIMPSON, JAMES CHRISTIAN (*b.* 1886).
    George Watson's College and Royal High School. M.A. (Camb.); M.B., C.M. 1887; M.D. 1895. R.A.M.C., Captain March 1915. 1st Eastern General Hospital. Died on 27th June 1919.   Pl. LXXV.

SINCLAIR, DAVID W. (*b.* 1896).
    Annan Academy. Student of Medicine, 1913-18; M.B., Ch.B. 1918. O.T.C. Medical, Feb. 1916 to July 1918, Cadet L/Corporal. R.A.M.C., attached 11th Royal Scots, Lieut. Aug. 1918. Died of wounds near Courtrai, Belgium, on 22nd October 1918.   Pl. LXXV.

SINGLETON, FRANK (*b.* 1894).
    Student of Arts, 1913-16. O.T.C. Infantry, Dec. 1914 to Nov. 1915, Cadet. R.A.M.C., Private, 1st Welsh Field Ambulance, Sierra Leone Detachment. Died at Freetown, West Africa, on 11th September 1918.   Pl. LXXV.

SLADE-KING, PHILIP SLADE (*b.* 1890).
    King's College, Taunton. Student of Science, 1907-13; B.Sc. 1913. O.T.C. Infantry, Feb. 1910 to Oct. 1912 and Sept. to Oct. 1914, Cadet. Lovat Scouts, Private Oct. 1914. A.S.C., 2nd Lieut. Oct. 1914; Lieut. 1915. 1st Norfolk Regiment, 2nd Lieut. Nov. 1915; Lieut. Nov. 1917. France Nov. 1914; Mesopotamia Nov. 1916. Intelligence and Political Officer. Wounded Jan. 1916. Died at Minjuna in Mesopotamia on 13th May 1918.   Pl. LXXV.

SMALL, HUGH ALEXANDER (*b.* 1891).
    Methodist College, Belfast, and Trinity College, Dublin. Student of Divinity, 1914-15. O.T.C. Oct. 1914 to Jan. 1915. 16th and 20th King's Liverpool Regiment, 2nd Lieut. Jan. 1915. M.C. May 1916. France. Killed at Trones Wood, Battle of the Somme, on 11th July 1916.   Pl. LXXV.

Roll of the Fallen

SMALL, JAMES BRUCE (*b.* 1896).
    Lasswade School. Student of Science, 1915-16. O.T.C. Engineers, Oct. 1915 to June 1916, Cadet. R.E., Pioneer June 1916. Rifle Brigade, 2nd Lieut. Sept. 1917. R.F.C., 2nd Lieut. Oct. 1917; Lieut. April 1918; Pilot Instructor May 1918. France July 1916 and July 1918. Killed in action in France on 2nd August 1918.   Pl. LXXV.

SMALL, JOHN (*b.* 1887).
    Dundee High School. M.A. (St Andrews) 1906; Student of Arts and Law, 1906-9; LL.B. 1909. Advocate, 1913. 15th Royal Scots, Private Aug. 1914. 9th Royal Highlanders (Black Watch), Lieut. 1915. France. Killed near Vermelles, Battle of Loos, on 29th April 1916.   Pl. LXXV.

SMALL, WILLIAM ERNEST ALEXANDER (*b.* 1891).
    Royal High School. Student of Science, 1908-10. Royal Horse Guards ("The Blues") Trooper Dec. 1914; L/Corporal March 1915. France. Killed at Vermelles, Battle of Loos, on 26th September 1915.   Pl. LXXV.

SMITH, CHARLES EDGAR HOLTON (*b.* 1884).
    Chigwell School; Athletics. Student of Medicine, 1906-9. L.R.C.P. & S. (Edin.); L.R.F.P.S. (Glasg.) 1911. O.T.C. Medical, 1907-8. Italian Turkish War, Surgeon 1912. R.A.M.C., Lieut. Nov. 1914; Captain Nov. 1915. Serbia 1915; Malta July 1915; France 1916. Attached 10/11th Highland Light Infantry. Order of St Sava (5th Class), 1915. Killed at Martinpuich on 16th September 1916.   Pl. LXXV.

SMITH, GEORGE BUCHANAN (*b.* 1890).
    Glasgow Academy; First XV. Cadet Corps 1907. M.A. (Hons. Hist.) (Glasg.) 1912. O.T.C. (Glasgow) 1909-13, Cadet Sergeant. LL.B. (Aberdeen) 1914. Student of Law, 1913-14. 1st, 2nd, and 3rd Gordon Highlanders, 2nd Lieut. Aug. 1914. France. Twice wounded, Kemmel and Wytschaete, Dec. 1914. Killed near Vermelles, Battle of Loos, on 25th September 1915.   Pl. LXXVI.

SMITH, GEORGE PRINGLE (*b.* 1892).
    Linlithgow Academy. Student of Arts and Science, 1910-14; M.A. (Hons. Maths.); B.Sc. (Distinction, Maths. and Nat. Phil.) 1914. 1st, 6th, and 11th Royal Scots, Private Aug. 1914; 2nd Lieut. Jan. 1915; Lieut. France Oct. 1915. Killed in action in April 1917.   Pl. LXXVI.

SMITH, HARRY GORDON (*b.* 1898).
    Perth Academy, and St Bees, Cumberland. Student of Arts, 1915-16. O.T.C. Infantry, Oct. 1915-16, Cadet Sergeant; Officer Cadet Oct. 1916. 4th Argyll and Sutherland Highlanders, 2nd Lieut. Jan. 1917. Killed near Lake Doïran, Macedonia, on 13th March 1918.   Pl. LXXVI.

PLATE LXXVI.

H. Gordon Smith.

G. B. Smith.

G. P. Smith.

H. Graham Smith.

J. M. Smith.

J. R. D. Smith.

S. F. Smith.

N. McN. Smith.

W. W. Smith.

PLATE LXXVII.

Roll of the Fallen

SMITH, HARRY GRAHAM (*b.* 1862).
Edinburgh Academy. Student of Medicine, 1878. L.R.C.S. (Edin.) 1883; L.R.C.P. (Edin.) 1884; L.D.S. (Edin.) H.M.S. Transport *Panoras*, M.O. Aug. 1914. R.A.M.C., Lieut. Dec. 1915; Captain Dec. 1916. Lost at Sea on Hospital Ship *Salta* on 11th April 1917. Pl. LXXVI.

SMITH, IAN STUART (*b.* 1895).
Alnwick Grammar and Kelso High Schools. Student of Law, 1915-16. R.G.A., 38th Welsh Heavy Battery, Gunner. Died of wounds on 1st July 1917.

SMITH, JAMES MONTAGUE (*b.* 1892).
George Watson's College. O.T.C. 1906-10, Cadet Col.-Sergeant. Student of Medicine, 1910-14. Thomson Scholar, 1910. O.T.C. Medical, Nov. 1910 to June 1911, Cadet. 5th Royal Scots, 2nd Lieut. 1911; Lieut. 1912. Mobilised Aug. 1914. Machine-Gun Officer and Acting Adjutant. Gallipoli March 1915. Wounded on 1st and died on 2nd May 1915. Pl. LXXVI.

SMITH, JOHN RANKIN DONALD (*b.* 1886).
Royal High School; First XV. Student of Arts, 1904-7; M.A. 1907. Minister of United Free Church, Ayr. Inns of Court O.T.C., Private Dec. 1915. 2nd Royal Scots Fusiliers, 2nd Lieut. 1916. France Oct. 1916. Killed in action on 31st July 1917. Pl. LXXVI.

SMITH, NORMAN McNEILL (*b.* 1895).
Merchiston Castle. University O.T.C. Infantry, Oct. 1914, Cadet. 21st Northumberland Fusiliers (2nd Tyneside Scottish), 2nd Lieut. March 1915. Killed at the Battle of the Somme on 1st July 1916. Pl. LXXVI.

SMITH, SIDNEY FRASER (*b.* 1895).
Stirling High School; First XV. Student of Arts, 1914-16. O.T.C. Artillery, Dec. 1915 to April 1916, Cadet; Officer Cadet April 1916. R.F.A., 256th Brigade, 2nd Lieut. Aug. 1916; Lieut. France Jan. 1917. Port-le-Grande, Arras, and Ypres. Wounded July and died at Ypres on 3rd September 1917. Pl. LXXVI.

SMITH, WILLIAM WATSON (*b.* 1891).
Maggieknockater School, Banffshire. Student of Law, 1914-15. O.T.C. Infantry, June to Sept. 1915, Cadet. Gordon Highlanders, 2nd Lieut. Sept. 1915. France. Died of wounds at No. 2 Red Cross Hospital, Rouen, on 18th October 1916. Pl. LXXVI.

SOMERVAIL, WILLIAM FULTON (*b.* 1890).
Loretto. Student of Science, 1911-14. 3rd and 2nd Scottish Rifles, 2nd Lieut. Aug. 1914; Lieut. March 1915; Captain June 1915; Lieut.-Col. Aug. 1917; Brigade Major Jan. 1918. France; Neuve Chapelle and Ypres. M.C. and D.S.O. Dispatches May 1915, Nov. 1917 and Nov. 1918. Twice wounded. Killed in action on 4th October 1918. Pl. LXXVII.

Roll of the Fallen

SPENCE, DAVID STEWART (*b.* 1892).
    Stromness School. Student of Arts and Science, 1912-15; M.A. 1914. O.T.C. Artillery, Oct. 1914 to March 1915, Cadet. R.F.A. (S.R.), 66th Brigade, 13th Division, 2nd Lieut. March 1915. Gallipoli. Killed at Helles on 13th December 1915.   Pl. LXXVII.

SPENCE, JOHN DICK WHITE (*b.* 1883).
    George Heriot's School. Student of Law, 1903-5. Chartered Accountant, 1907. Royal Highlanders (Black Watch), Private Nov. 1915. Killed in action in France on 31st August 1916.

SPOOR, HERBERT MATHER (*b.* 1872).
    Kingswood School, Bath. Student of Medicine, 1902-8; M.B., Ch.B. 1908. R.A.M.C., attached R.G.A., Lieut. April 1915; Captain. M.C. 1917. France. Killed at Ypres on 13th December 1917.   Pl. LXXVII.

SPROTT, DOUGLAS ANDREW (*b.* 1893).
    Appleby and Bedford Grammar Schools. O.T.C. 1909-11. Student of Medicine, 1911-14. O.T.C. Infantry, May 1912 to Oct. 1914, Cadet Corporal. 4th Border Regiment, Aug. 1914. Machine-Gun Corps, 2nd Lieut. Oct. 1914; Lieut. Feb. 1916; Captain May 1917. Burmah 1914; Mesopotamia 1917. Died at Bagdad on 4th January 1918.   Pl. LXXVII.

STALKER, DANIEL (*b.* 1890).
    Dundee High School. Student of Arts, 1908-14; M.A. (Hons. Classics) 1913. O.T.C. Artillery, Oct. 1908 to April 1912, Cadet. Surrey Rifles, Private Aug. 1914. R.F.A., Lieut. Oct. 1914; Acting Captain Aug. 1917. France. Wounded Sept. 1916. Died of wounds at Yentelle near Amiens on 12th April 1918.   Pl. LXXVII.

STANFORD, JAMES VESEY (*b.* 1893).
    Rugby. O.T.C. University O.T.C. Infantry, Aug. 1914, Cadet. 8th Seaforth Highlanders, 2nd Lieut. Killed.

STEEL, ARTHUR ROBERT
    Student of Medicine. L.R.C.P. & S. (Edin.) 1885. Royal Navy, Surgeon. Lost at sea on 28th February 1917.

STEELE, ROBERT BALFOUR (*b.* 1886).
    George Watson's College; Dux; First XV. Student of Arts, 1904-9; M.A. (Hons. Maths.) 1909. Student, Cambridge University. Calcutta Light Horse, 1914. I.A.R.O. 11th Lancers, 2nd Lieut. Aug. 1916; attached R.F.C. 1917. Egypt. Died of wounds in German prison on 22nd October 1917.   Pl. LXXVII.

Roll of the Fallen

STEVENS, NORMAN WALTER (*b.* 1887).
    Norwich Grammar School; First XI. Student of Medicine, 1905-10; M.B., Ch.B. 1910. First XV. R.A.M.C., Lieut. 1912; Captain 1914; Brevet Major 1917. France Aug. 1914. Injured at Mons; invalided home. France 1915. Wounded 1917. Dispatches 1917. Bombay Aug. 1918. Died of typhoid fever and pneumonia at Bombay on 27th July 1919.   Pl. LXXVII.

STEVENSON, JOHN SCOTT (*b.* 1896).
    George Watson's College. O.T.C., Cadet Sergeant. Student of Science, 1913-14. O.T.C. Engineers, Oct. 1913 to Oct. 1914, Cadet. 8th Royal Scots, 51st Division, 2nd Lieut. Oct. 1914. R.E., 9th Division, Lieut. Dec. 1917. France 1915 and 1918. Invalided home autumn 1916. Gassed and wounded near Ypres on 4th and died at Casualty Clearing Station on 8th October 1918.   Pl. LXXVII.

STEWART, ALEXANDER CHARLES (*b.* 1886).
    George Watson's College; Dux. Student of Arts, 1903-7; M.A. (Hons. Classics) 1907. London Scottish, Private Sept. 1914. Inns of Court O.T.C. Army Cyclist Corps, Captain. France April 1916. Wounded and missing, presumed killed near Bailleul on 12th April 1918.   Pl. LXXVII.

STEWART, ALEXANDER VIVIAN (*b.* 1895).
    Ewart High School and Boroughmuir School; First XV. Student of Medicine, 1913-14. O.T.C. Infantry, Oct. 1913 to Sept. 1914, Cadet. 9th Royal Scots, Private Sept. 1914. 4th Gordon Highlanders, 2nd Lieut. Dec. 1916. France, the Somme, and Ypres. Killed at the Battle of Arras on 23rd April 1917.
    Pl. LXXVIII.

STEWART, CHARLES EDWARD (*b.* 1887).
    Edinburgh Academy. B.A. (Oxford). Student of Law, 1908-11. Writer to the Signet, 1912. 15th Royal Scots, Private Sept. 1914. 10th Durham Light Infantry Lieut. Oct. 1914; Captain Sept. 1916. France Aug. 1915; the Somme. M.C. (posthumous). Wounded at the Battle of Arras and died at 43rd Casualty Clearing Station near Arras on 10th April 1917.   Pl. LXXVIII.

STEWART, FRANCIS WILLIAM (*b.* 1893).
    Premnay School. Student of Science, 1913-14. O.T.C. Engineers, April 1914 to Sept. 1915, Cadet. Merchant Service, S.S. *Norwegian*, 4th Engineer. Lost at sea owing to ship being mined off the Irish Coast on 13th March 1917.   Pl. LXXVIII.

STEWART, FREDERIC ARNOLD (*b.* 1893).
    Edinburgh Academy; Athletics. Student of Science, 1910-14. C.D.A. 15th Royal Scots, Private Sept. 1914. 10th Durham Light Infantry, Lieut. Oct. 1914. France Aug. 1915. Battle of Ypres. Wounded twice near Flers, Somme, on 16th September 1916 and died the same day.   Pl. LXXVIII.

Roll of the Fallen

STEWART, JAMES AITCHISON (*b.* 1890).
Edinburgh Institution and Edinburgh Academy. Student of Medicine, 1907-11. O.T.C. Artillery, Oct. 1908 to Nov. 1910, Cadet. 7th Royal Scots, Lieut. 1911 to May 1914. King's Own Scottish Borderers, 2nd Lieut. Aug. 1914. R.F.C., Lieut. 1915. France. M.C. Died of wounds at Havre on 11th October 1916. Pl. LXXVIII.

STEWART, JAMES FLEMING (*b.* 1894).
Premnay School and Fettes College. Student of Medicine, 1912-14. O.T.C. Artillery, Oct. 1912 to Dec. 1914, Cadet. R.E. (Special Brigade), Corporal Aug. 1914. France. Died of gas poisoning on 28th June 1916. Pl. LXXVIII.

STEWART, JOHN JAMES ERSKINE BROWN (*b.* 1885).
Edinburgh Academy and Malvern College. B.A. (Oxford). Student of Law, 1911-14; LL.B. 1914. O.T.C. Infantry, Sept. 1914, Cadet. 8th Seaforth Highlanders, 2nd Lieut. Sept. 1914. Resigned owing to defective eyesight. 18th Royal Fusiliers (Public Schools Battalion), Private Jan. 1915. 7th attached 12th Royal Scots, 2nd Lieut. Aug. 1916. France Nov. 1915. Wounded on 9th April and died at Le Touquet on 12th June 1917. Pl. LXXVIII.

STEWART, JOHN KENNEDY (*b.* 1896).
Daniel Stewart's College. Student of Arts, 1914-15. 16th and 4th Royal Scots, Private Dec. 1914; 2nd Lieut. March 1917. France Jan. to July 1917. Egypt and Palestine Aug. to Nov. 1917. Died of wounds on 4th November 1917.

STEWART, JOHN WALCOT (*b.* 1885).
Edinburgh Academy. Student of Law, 1904-8. Writer to the Signet, 1909. Lothians and Border Horse, Private Aug. 1914. 16th Royal Scots, 2nd Lieut. April 1915; Lieut. July 1917. France Jan. 1916. M.C. Feb. 1916. Wounded Feb. 1916. Killed at La Croiselle near Cambrai on 21st March 1918. Pl. LXXVIII.

STEWART, MUNGO (*b.* 1893).
Perth Academy; Athletics. Student of Arts and Science, 1911-14. O.T.C. Artillery, Oct. 1912 to Aug. 1914, Cadet. R.F.A., 55th Brigade, 2nd Lieut. Aug. 1914; Lieut. Oct. 1915. France, Egypt, India, and Mesopotamia. Dispatches April 1917. Wounded at the Battle of Loos. Died of wounds at Relief of Kut, Mesopotamia, on 7th February 1917. Pl. LXXIX.

STEWART, NATHANIEL WILLIAM (*b.* 1891).
Ewart High School and Boroughmuir School; Athletics. Student of Arts, Medicine and Science, 1910-14. O.T.C. Infantry, Nov. 1910 to Aug. 1914, Cadet L/Corporal. 7th Royal Scots, attached R.F.C., 2nd Lieut. Aug. 1914; Lieut. Sept. 1914. Gallipoli Aug. 1916. Egypt. Killed while directing fire of H.M.S. *Fox* off Chermwej on Red Sea on 23rd January 1917. Pl. LXXVIII.

PLATE LXXVIII.

J. J. E. B. Stewart.

A. V. Stewart.

N. W. Stewart.

J. W. Stewart.

F. A. Stewart.

C. E. Stewart.

F. W. Stewart.

J. F. Stewart.

J. A. Stewart.

PLATE LXXIX.

Mungo Stewart.

Thomas Stewart.

Robert Stewart.

H. W. Strathairn.

J. B. Strang.

A. C. Struthers.

W. M. Sturrock.

J. G. Sutherland.

A. E. Sutherland.

Roll of the Fallen

STEWART, ROBERT (*b.* 1891).
Dunfermline High School. Student of Arts, 1909-12; M.A. 1912. Schoolmaster. 8th Royal Scots (College Coy.), Private Sept. 1914. King's Own Scottish Borderers, 2nd Lieut.; Lieut. May 1915. France. Killed in action on 1st July 1916. Pl. LXXIX.

STEWART, THOMAS (*b.* 1891).
George Heriot's School. Student of Arts, 1915-16. 8th Royal Scots, Major. France 1914. Dispatches. M.C. and Bar. Killed in action on 12th September 1917. Pl. LXXIX.

STOKES, MAURICE ARTHUR.
M.A. 1912. Schoolmaster. R.A.M.C., Private June to Dec. 1918. Died of influenza on 31st March 1919.

STRANG, JAMES BUCHANAN (*b.* 1889).
Ardrishaig School. Student of Arts and Divinity, 1908-14; M.A. 1912. O.T.C. Infantry, March 1910 to July 1913, Cadet. 17th Lancashire Fusiliers, 2nd Lieut. Sept. 1915. Killed in action in France on 30th July 1916. Pl. LXXIX.

STRATHAIRN, HUBERT WILLIAM (*b.* 1883).
Morrison's Academy, Crieff. Student of Arts, 1900-5; M.A. 1905. B.A. (Oxford). Schoolmaster. 6th Royal Highlanders (Black Watch), 2nd Lieut. Aug. 1915. Wounded at Beaumont Hamel, the Somme, and died at Varennes on 16th November 1916. Pl. LXXIX.

STRUTHERS, ANDREW CRAIG (*b.* 1895).
Boroughmuir School. Student of Arts, 1913-15. O.T.C. Infantry, Oct. 1914 to June 1915, Cadet L/Corporal. 10th and 12th Scottish Rifles (Cameronians), 2nd Lieut. May 1915. France May 1916. Killed near Contalmaison (Battle of the Somme) on 14th September 1916. Pl. LXXIX.

STUART, JOHN (*b.* 1898).
Haileybury. O.T.C. University O.T.C. Infantry, Nov. 1916 to April 1917, Cadet. 3rd, 9th, and 4/5th Royal Highlanders (Black Watch), 2nd Lieut. France Dec. 1917. Killed at the Battle of Buzancy on 28th July 1918.

STUART, WILLIAM GRANT SPRUELL (*b.* 1889).
George Watson's College; School Captain. Cadet Corps, Cadet Sergeant. Student of Arts, 1908-14; M.A. (Hons. Classics) 1914. O.T.C. Artillery, March 1910 to Feb. 1911, Cadet. Scottish Horse, Private 1914. 7th Cameron Highlanders, 2nd Lieut. 1914; Lieut.; Captain Sept. 1915. France. Battles of Loos, Somme, and Ancre. M.C. Dec. 1916. Wounded Sept. 1915. Killed at Arras on 23rd April 1917.

Roll of the Fallen

STURROCK, WILLIAM MALCOLM (*b.* 1860).
Madras Academy, St Andrews. Student of Medicine, 1877-83; M.B., C.M. 1883. R.A.M.C., 1st South Midland Field Ambulance, Lieut.-Col. Died at Birmingham on 21st November 1918.   Pl. LXXIX.

SUTHERLAND, ANDERSON (*b.* 1894).
Merchiston Castle; Athletics. Student of Science, 1913-14. R.F.A., 2nd Lieut. Sept. 1914; Major. M.C. Aug. 1917. Dispatches Nov. 1918. Wounded on 28th Oct. and died in November 1918.

SUTHERLAND, ANDREW ERNEST (*b.* 1892).
Broughton School, Edinburgh. University O.T.C. Artillery, April 1913 to Aug. 1914, Cadet. R.F.A., 67th Brigade, 2nd Lieut. Aug. 1914; Lieut. Killed in action in Macedonia on 3rd October 1916.   Pl. LXXIX.

SUTHERLAND, JOHN GEORGE (*b.* 1889).
Galashiels Academy. Student of Medicine 1909-14. O.T.C. Infantry, Nov. 1911 to Sept. 1914, Cadet Corporal. 11th Highland Light Infantry, 2nd Lieut. Aug. 1914. France May 1915. Wounded on 10th and died on 11th August 1915 in France.   Pl. LXXIX.

SUTHERLAND, JOHN MACINTYRE (*b.* 1879).
Fettes College. Student of Arts, 1898-1902; M.A. (Hons. Classics) 1902. Schoolmaster. 9th Royal Scots, 2nd Lieut. Jan. 1916. France Aug. 1916. Killed near Roeux on 23rd April 1917.   Pl. LXXX.

SWAN, GEORGE HARRY (*b.* 1895).
George Watson's College. Student of Science, 1913-14. 1st Royal Scots Fusiliers, 2nd Lieut. Oct. 1914. France. Killed near Bazentin-le-Grand on 14th July 1916.   Pl. LXXX.

SYMINGTON, WILLIAM (*b.* 1865).
Edinburgh Institution. Student of Medicine; M.B., C.M. 1886. 4th Border Regiment, Surgeon-Major, July 1891. Mobilised Aug. 1914. Died at Brampton, Cumberland, on 3rd September 1916.   Pl. LXXX.

SYMONS, FRANK ALBERT (*b.* 1869).
Dalhousie College, Nova Scotia. Student of Medicine, 1887-91; M.B., C.M. 1891. R.A.M.C., Lieut. 1893; Major Oct. 1904; Lieut.-Col. 1915; Temp. Colonel Nov. 1915. South African Campaign, 1899-1902. France 1914. Mons, Marne, and Aisne. Thrice mentioned in Dispatches. D.S.O. Feb. 1915; C.M.G. Jan. 1917. Killed in action on 30th April 1917.   Pl. LXXX.

TAGGART, HENRY RAWSON (*b.* 1898).
Glasgow Academy. O.T.C. 1915-16. University O.T.C. Infantry, Sept. 1916 to April 1917, Cadet L/Corporal; Officer Cadet April 1917. 3rd Argyll and Sutherland Highlanders, 2nd Lieut. Aug. 1917. 1st Royal Highlanders (Black Watch). France May 1918. Killed near Hohenzollern Redoubt on 24th July 1918.   Pl. LXXX.

PLATE LXXX.

J. M. SUTHERLAND.   WM. SYMINGTON.   G. H. SWAN.

F. A. SYMONS.   H. R. TAGGART.   A. S. TAYLOR.

H. Y. C. TAYLOR.   S. G. TAYLOR.   W. C. TAYLOR.

PLATE LXXXI.

A. S. TENNANT.   B. C. TENNENT.   W. F. TEMPLETON.

C. C. THORBURN.   J. C. THAANUM.   F. G. THATCHER.

A. W. THOMSON.   A. G. THOMSON.   A. A. THOMSON.

Roll of the Fallen

TAYLOR, ALFRED SQUIRE (*b.* 1889).
  Campbell College, Belfast. Student of Medicine, 1907-14; M.B., Ch.B. 1914. President, University Union. First XV. O.T.C. Medical, June 1910 to Nov. 1912, Cadet. R.A.M.C., Lieut. Oct. 1914; Captain; attached Highland Light Infantry. Killed in action on 31st July 1917. Pl. LXXX.

TAYLOR, HENRY YOUNG CAMERON (*b.* 1872).
  Daniel Stewart's College. Student of Medicine, 1891-6; M.B., C.M. 1896; F.R.C.S. (Edin.) 1905. French Red Cross, Dunkirk, 1914. R.A.M.C., Captain 1915. Hampstead Military Hospital. Hospital Ship *Britannia* and Netley Hospital. Died at Netley on 25th August 1917. Pl. LXXX.

TAYLOR, STANLEY GORDON (*b.* 1896).
  Edinburgh Academy; Football and Shooting. O.T.C. 1911-14. Student of Arts, 1914-15. O.T.C. Artillery, Aug. 1914 to May 1915, Cadet Bombardier. R.F.A. (S.R.), 38th Brigade, 2nd Lieut. May 1915. France Sept. 1915. 6th Division. Ypres and the Somme. Killed at Ginchy on 21st October 1916. Pl. LXXX.

TAYLOR, WILLIAM CURRIE (*b.* 1895).
  Leith Academy. Student of Arts and Science, 1911-15; M.A.; B.Sc. 1918. President, Chemical Society. O.T.C. Artillery, Oct. 1914 to July 1915, Cadet Bombardier. R.F.A. (S.R.), 2nd Lieut. July 1915; Lieut. May 1916; Captain Nov. 1917. Died of pneumonia at Leith on 7th November 1918. Pl. LXXX.

TEMPLEMAN, CHARLES (*b.* 1858).
  Dundee High School. M.B., C.M. 1879; M.D. 1890; B.Sc. (P.H.) 1892; D.Sc. (P.H.) 1894. Lecturer on Medical Jurisprudence and Public Health, St Andrews University. R.A.M.C., Captain. Died at Dundee on 20th January 1918.

TEMPLETON, WILLIAM FOWLER (*b.* 1889).
  George Heriot's School; First XV. Student of Arts, 1907-11; M.A. (Hons. Engl.) 1911. 4th Royal Scots Fusiliers, Lieut. Oct. 1914; Captain June 1915. Egypt and Palestine Jan. 1916 to April 1918. France 1918. Wounded April and Nov. 1917. Killed at Cambrai on 1st October 1918. Pl. LXXXI.

TENNANT, ALEXANDER SMITH (*b.* 1888).
  Broughton School, Edinburgh. Student of Arts and Science, 1909-14; M.A., B.Sc. 1913. Schoolmaster. 16th Royal Scots, Private Nov. 1914. 12th Scottish Rifles, 2nd Lieut. April 1915. 9th Lancashire Fusiliers, Lieut. Dec. 1916. Gallipoli, Egypt, and France. Dispatches (Givenchy) 1916 and (Poelcapelle) 1917. Wounded Aug. 1917. Killed at Beauchamp Ridge on 27th September 1918. Pl. LXXXI.

TENNENT, BERNARD CHARLES (*b.* 1882).
  Port Chalmers High School, New Zealand. Student of Medicine, 1904-10; M.B., Ch.B. 1910; M.D. 1913. Athletics. Duchess of Sutherland's Hospital, Dunkirk. R.A.M.C., Lieut. Jan. 1915; Captain 1916; Major May 1918. M.C. and Bar. Wounded June 1917. Killed in action on 22nd August 1918. Pl. LXXXI.

Roll of the Fallen

THAANUM, JAMES CONRAD (*b.* 1888).
Wallasey Grammar School. Student of Arts and Science, 1909-14; M.A. 1912. R.G.A., 2nd Lieut. Oct. 1914. Died of wounds on 20th August 1915. Pl. LXXXI.

THATCHER, FRANCIS GEOFFREY (*b.* 1890).
Edinburgh Academy. Student of Medicine, 1907-13; M.B., Ch.B. 1913. O.T.C., Infantry Oct. 1908 to Dec. 1913, Cadet Col.-Sergeant. R.A.M.C., attached 2nd Royal West Surrey Regiment, Lieut. July 1914; Captain March 1915; Acting Major Feb. 1918. Hospital Ships *Emeraldes* and *Grantully Castle*. France 1914 and 1917. No. 13 General Hospital, 25th and 136th Field Ambulances. D.A.D.M.S. (40th Division), May 1917. M.C. 1918. Wounded at first Battle of Ypres in Oct. 1914 and again on 30th May and died on 1st June 1918. Pl. LXXXI.

THOMSON, ALAN GRAHAM (*b.* 1882).
Edinburgh Academy; Dux 1900; First XV. and XI. B.A. (Hons.) (Oxford). Student of Law, 1904-7. Writer to the Signet, 1907. 2nd and 7th Royal Scots, 2nd Lieut. July 1915; Lieut.; Captain. France Oct. 1916. Killed at Zonnebeke near Ypres on 26th September 1917. Pl. LXXXI.

THOMSON, ALEXANDER ANDERSON (*b.* 1895).
Aberdeen Grammar School. Student of Medicine, 1913-16. O.T.C. Medical, May to Nov. 1915, Cadet. 4th Gordon Highlanders, Private Nov. 1915. France. Killed in action at Arras on 9th April 1917. Pl. LXXXI.

THOMSON, ANDREW WILLIAM (*b.* 1896).
Merchiston Castle. O.T.C. 1910-14, Cadet L/Corporal. Student of Arts, 1914-15. Public Schools Battn. 4th Royal Fusiliers, Private Nov. 1914. 9th North Stafford Regiment, 2nd Lieut. Dec. 1914. France July 1915. Killed near Monchy-le-Preux, Arras, on 30th May 1917. Pl. LXXXI.

THOMSON, CHARLES (*b.* 1891).
Campbell College, Belfast. Student of Law, 1911-15. Chartered Accountant, 1915. 9th Royal Scots, Private Nov. 1915; L/Sergeant May 1916. France. Killed in action on 23rd April 1917. Pl. LXXXII.

THOMSON, ERIC JAMES (*b.* 1893).
Edinburgh Academy. O.T.C. 1909-11. Student of Law, 1913-14. 7th Royal Scots, 2nd Lieut. April 1914; Lieut. Aug. 1914. Gallipoli. Killed in action at the Dardanelles on 28th June 1915. Pl. LXXXII.

THOMSON, FRANCIS WISHART (*b.* 1891).
Edinburgh Academy and Oxford University. Student of Arts and Law, 1909-10. 7th Royal Scots, Lieut. Killed in action on 28th June 1915.

PLATE LXXXII.

F. Wyville Thomson.

Charles Thomson.

E. J. Thomson.

Haldane Thomson.

J. H. Thomson.

J. S. Thomson.

S. J. K. Thomson.

J. W. Thomson.

William Thomson.

PLATE LXXXIII.

G. M. Thornton.

L. I. L. Thornton.

A. L. Thornley.

W. L. Tod.

Thomas Todrick.

Daniel Torrance.

J. J. Tough.

John Tulloch.

S. N. Toulmin.

Roll of the Fallen

THOMSON, FRANK WYVILLE (b. 1860).
  Edinburgh Collegiate School. Student of Arts and Medicine, 1877-86; M.A. 1880; M.B., C.M. 1886; D.P.H., R.C.P.S. (Edin.) 1892; D.T.M. (Liverpool). Indian Medical Service. Retired. R.A.M.C., O.C. 2nd Scottish General Hospital, 1908-11. Tay Defences, Lieut.-Col., Aug. 1914 to Dec. 1917. Died at Linlithgow on 27th May 1918. Pl. LXXXII.

THOMSON, HALDANE (b. 1890).
  Daniel Stewart's College; First XV. Student of Science, 1908-12; B.Sc. (Distinction) 1912. 1851 Exhibitioner, Industrial Bursar. O.T.C. Engineers, 1910-13, Cadet Corporal. Lothians and Border Horse for two years. 12th Scottish Rifles, 2nd Lieut. Aug. 1914; Lieut. 1st King's Own Scottish Borderers, 1915. Gallipoli. Missing, presumed killed on 4th June 1915. Pl. LXXXII.

THOMSON, JOHN HARVEY (b. 1898).
  Edinburgh Academy. University O.T.C. Artillery, Aug. 1916 to May 1917, Cadet; Officer Cadet May 1917. 5th Argyll and Sutherland Highlanders, Private Oct. 1917. R.A.F., Cadet Dec. 1917; 2nd Lieut. (Observer) July 1918. France; Marne, and Somme. Killed near Thulin on 9th October 1918. Pl. LXXXII.

THOMSON, JOHN SNADDON (b. 1891).
  Alloa Academy. Student of Arts, 1909-13; M.A. 1913. 2nd Gordon Highlanders, Private. France. Killed at Passchendaele on 4th October 1917. Pl. LXXXII.

THOMSON, JOHN WILLIAM (b. 1892).
  George Watson's College. Student of Arts and Science, 1910-14; M.A. (Hons. Maths.) 1914; B.Sc. (Special Distinction, Maths. and Nat. Phil.). O.T.C. Artillery, Nov. 1915 to Jan. 1916, Cadet. R.G.A., 2nd Lieut. Jan. 1916; Lieut. Attached R.E., 5th Field Survey Battn. (Sound Ranging). France Dec. 1917. Died of pneumonia at Glasgow on 4th February 1919. Pl. LXXXII.

THOMSON, SYDNEY JAMES KERR (b. 1888).
  Loretto. Student of Science, 1906-10; B.Sc. 1910. Public Schools Battn. Royal Fusiliers, Private Sept. 1914. 1st and 3rd Royal Scots Fusiliers, 2nd Lieut. Feb. 1915. France June 1915. Machine-Gun Officer. Dispatches Nov. 1915. Wounded at Sanctuary Wood, Hooge, on 25th Sept. and died at Wimereux on 12th October 1915. Pl. LXXXII.

THOMSON, WILLIAM (b. 1895).
  George Watson's College. Student of Law, 1912-14. 4th Royal Scots, Private Aug. 1914. Killed in action at the Dardanelles on 28th June 1915. Pl. LXXXII.

THORBURN, CHRISTOPHER COWAN (b. 1894).
  Boroughmuir School. Student of Law, 1914-15. O.T.C. Infantry, Sept. 1914 to Jan. 1916, Cadet Sergeant. 11th attached 1st Gordon Highlanders, 2nd Lieut. Jan. 1916; Lieut. March 1917. France. Killed at Infantry Hill, Arras, on 14th June 1917. Pl. LXXXI.

Roll of the Fallen

THORNLEY, ARTHUR LINCOLN (b. 1884).
Bolton High School, and Epworth College, Rhyl. Student of Medicine; M.B., Ch.B. 1907. R.A.M.C., Lieut. Died on service in April 1916. Pl. LXXXIII.

THORNTON, GEORGE MUIR (b. 1882).
Merchiston Castle. B.A. (Oxford). Student of Law, 1904-8; LL.B. (Distinction) 1907. Advocate, 1910. 10th and 8th Seaforth Highlanders, Lieut. Nov. 1914; Captain Jan. 1916. Killed in action in Flanders on 22nd August 1917.
Pl. LXXXIII.

THORNTON, LESLIE IRVINE LUMSDEN (b. 1889).
Haileybury. Student of Arts and Law, 1907-10; M.A. 1910; LL.B. Malayan Contingent, Private Nov. 1914. 16th Cavalry (Indian Army), Lieut. Dec. 1914. India Dec. 1914. Persia, Battle of Shaiba, Feb. 1915. Dispatches Aug. and Sept. 1915. Killed in action near Bushire on 9th September 1915. Pl. LXXXIII.

TOD, WILLIAM LENNOX (b. 1887).
Edinburgh Academy. Student of Science, 1905-13. O.T.C. Engineers, Jan. 1910 to Dec. 1911, Cadet Sergeant. A.M.I.C.E. 1912. 15th Royal Scots, 2nd Lieut. Oct. 1914; Lieut. 1915; Captain 1916. France Jan. 1916. Wounded at Vimy Ridge on 9th and died at Camiers on 29th April 1917. Pl. LXXXIII.

TODRICK, THOMAS (b. 1880).
Student of Law, 1900-4. Writer to the Signet, 1904. 8th Royal Scots, Captain. Mobilised Aug. 1914. France Nov. 1914. Dispatches. Killed in action in Northern France on 15th December 1914. Pl. LXXXIII.

TORRANCE, DANIEL (b. 1899).
Stranraer Academy and High School. Student of Arts, 1916-17. Royal Marine Light Infantry, Private April 1917. France, 63rd Naval Division. Killed at the breaking of Hindenburg Line on 2nd September 1918. Pl. LXXXIII.

TOUGH, JOHN JAMES (b. 1888).
Student of Medicine, 1905-10; M.B., Ch.B. 1910. R.A.M.C., Lieut. May 1917; Captain May 1918. India, Italy, and France. Killed in action in France on 6th October 1918. Pl. LXXXIII.

TOULMIN, STEWART NEWNHAM (b. 1892).
Wei-hai-wei School, China. Student of Medicine, 1910-15. O.T.C. Medical, May 1911 to Nov. 1914, Cadet Corporal. Royal Navy, Surgeon-Probationer, Dec. 1914. Surgeon, H.M. Ships *Duke of Cornwall* and *Endymion*. Killed in action on 1st August 1917. Pl. LXXXIII.

TULLOCH, JOHN (b. 1894).
Perth Academy. Student of Medicine, 1912-16. 9th Royal Scots, Private March 1916. France Aug. 1916. Killed at Martinpuich, Somme, on 15th September 1915. Pl. LXXXIII.

Roll of the Fallen

TULLOCH, WILLIAM (*b.* 1891).
    Student of Arts, 1909-13; M.A. (Hons. Engl.) 1913. Machine-Gun Corps, 2nd Lieut. Sept. 1914. France. Killed at the Battle of the Somme on 20th July 1916.   Pl. LXXXIV.

TURNBULL, ALFRED EDWARD (*b.* 1881).
    Blairlodge School. Student of Medicine, 1901-7; M.B., Ch.B. 1907. Resident, Royal Infirmary, 1908-9. Royal Naval Reserve, Jan. 1912. Surgeon Aug. 1914, H.M.S. *Cressy*. Killed in action through sinking of *Cressy* on 22nd September 1914.   Pl. LXXXIV.

TYTLER, JAMES HALL (*b.* 1889).
    Kingussie School (Medallist). Student of Arts and Divinity, 1908-14; M.A. 1911. 3/9th Durham Light Infantry, 2nd Lieut. France. Wounded at High Wood, the Somme, on 15th and died on 16th September 1916.   Pl. XCIV.

UNDERWOOD, GEORGE MILNE (*b.* 1897).
    Merchiston Castle; O.T.C. 1912-15. Student of Medicine, 1914-16. O.T.C. Artillery, May 1915 to Jan. 1916, Cadet. Inns of Court O.T.C., Jan. 1916. R.F.C., 2nd Lieut. July 1916. Killed in action on 6th March 1917.   Pl. LXXXIV.

USHER, JOHN MILNE (*b.* 1885).
    Merchiston Castle; First XV. Student of Law, 1905-8. Chartered Accountant, 1908. 9th Gordon Highlanders, 2nd Lieut. France July 1915. Killed in action in September 1915.   Pl. LXXXIV.

VALLANCE, WILLIAM FLEMING MONCRIEFF (*b.* 1898).
    George Heriot's School. Student of Arts, 1916-17. U.F. Church Bursar. Highland Light Infantry, Private April 1917. 12th Royal Scots, L/Corporal. France March 1918. Taken prisoner in April and died at Hautmont Hospital on 19th August 1918.   Pl. LXXXIV.

VARNDELL, CHARLES HENRY ESSEX (*b.* 1893).
    Farnham Grammar School; O.T.C. 1906-11, Cadet Sergeant. Student of Arts and Science, 1911-15; M.A. 1914; B.Sc. 1915. O.T.C. Infantry, Nov. 1911 to Aug. 1914, Cadet. 6th Royal West Surrey Regiment, 2nd Lieut. Aug. 1914; Lieut. March 1916. France June 1915. Killed in action on 13th March 1916.   Pl. LXXXIV.

VASSIE, RICHARD (*b.* 1894).
    Fettes College. Student of Medicine, 1910-14. O.T.C. Infantry, Sept. 1914, Cadet. Scottish Horse, Private Sept. 1914. 12th Cheshire Regiment, 2nd Lieut. Sept. 1914; Lieut. Jan. 1915; Acting Captain. France Sept. 1915. Invalided home Oct. 1915. Died at Lanark on 13th April 1918.   Pl. LXXXIV.

Roll of the Fallen

VENABLES, JOSEPH KENDRICK (*b.* 1882).
　　High School, Christchurch, New Zealand. Student of Medicine, 1909-14. L.R.C.P. & S. (Edin.), L.R.F.P.S. (Glasg.) 1914. N.Z. Medical Corps, Captain Nov. 1915, attached 4th Field Ambulance. France. M.C. Messines June 1917. Died of wounds at a Casualty Clearing Station in France on 9th May 1918. Pl. LXXXIV.

VERTEUIL, FERNAND LOUIS J. M. de (*b.* 1879).
　　St Mary's College, Trinidad. Student of Medicine, 1898-1905; M.B., Ch.B. 1905; M.D. 1908. Royal Navy, Surgeon-Lieut., H.M.S. *Good Hope*. Killed in action off Coronel on 1st November 1914. Pl. XCIV.

VICKERS, ROBERT (*b.* 1889).
　　George Watson's College. Student of Arts and Science, 1907-12; M.A. (Hons. Maths. and Nat. Phil.) 1911; B.Sc. 1912. Bruce of Grangehill Scholar. R.F.A., 325th Brigade, Gunner June 1915; Sergeant; Sergeant-Major; 2nd Lieut. France May 1917. Died of wounds on 10th December 1917. Pl. LXXXIV.

VIVERS, JOHN (*b.* 1890).
　　Annan Academy, Dux; First XV. Student of Arts, 1906-10; M.A. (Hons. Hist.) 1910. Schoolmaster. 1/5th Royal Scots Fusiliers (T.), 1913; Captain. Gallipoli May 1915. Killed in action at the Dardanelles on 27th October 1915. Pl. LXXXV.

WADDELL, JAMES HAMILTON (*b.* 1893).
　　Normal and Broughton Schools, Edinburgh. Student of Arts and Science, 1912-15. 11th Royal Scots, Private April 1915; 2nd Lieut. Dec. 1916. Wounded and missing, presumed killed in action on 5th June 1917. Pl. LXXXV.

WADE, GRAHAME HARDIE (*b.* 1873).
　　Royal High School; First XV. Student of Law, 1892. Solicitor, 1907. 7th and 1st Argyll and Sutherland Highlanders, 1900 to 1911, Captain. Mobilised Aug. 1914. France April 1915. Killed at St Julien near Ypres on 25th April 1915.
Pl. XCIV.

WAITE, JOSEPH THORP (*b.* 1870).
　　Bootham School, York, and Manchester University. Student of Medicine, 1894-5. L.R.C.P. & S. (Edin.) and L.F.P.S. (Glasg.) 1896. 5th East Kent Regiment (Buffs), Lieut. Aug. 1914. India 1914; Persian Gulf 1915; Mesopotamia Nov. 1915. Killed at the Battle of Kut, Mesopotamia, on 21st January 1916. Pl. LXXXV.

WALKER, ARTHUR DIGHT (*b.* 1885).
　　B.A. (Sydney). Minister of Wentworth Parish, N.S.W. Student of Divinity, 1912-14. Tennis "Blue." 13th Royal Scots, Private, 1914. 4th and 19th Manchester Regiment, 2nd Lieut. May 1915. France Sept. 1916. Died of wounds on 18th October 1916. Pl. LXXXV.

PLATE LXXXIV.

Wm. Tulloch.   A. E. Turnbull.   G. M. Underwood.

W. F. M. Vallance.   C. H. E. Varndell.   J. M. Usher.

Richard Vassie.   J. K. Venables.   Robert Vickers.

PLATE LXXXV.

J. T. Waite.   J. H. Waddell.   John Vivers.

Gideon Walker.   A. D. Walker.   Robert Walker.

Wm. Walker.   C. A. P. Wallace.   Andrew Wallace.

Roll of the Fallen

WALKER, GIDEON (b. 1890).
  Daniel Stewart's College. Student of Medicine, 1907-14; M.B., Ch.B. 1912. R.A.M.C., Lieut. Sept. 1914; Captain Sept. 1916; attached 2nd Scots Guards. France Dec. 1914. Somme 1916; Bourlon Wood and La Fontaine. M.C. Sept. 1916 and Bar Oct. 1917. Killed near Royaulcourt on 27th November 1917. Pl. LXXXV.

WALKER, ROBERT (b. 1893).
  Fremantle School, and Scotch College, Claremont, W.A. First XI. Australian Government Scholar and Exhibitioner; Vans Dunlop Scholar; Student of Medicine, 1912-15. O.T.C. Infantry, Oct. 1914 to July 1915, Cadet. R.N.V.R., Surgeon-Probationer, July 1915, H.M.S. *Shark*. Killed at the Battle of Jutland on 31st May 1916. Pl. LXXXV.

WALKER, WILLIAM (b. 1878).
  Edinburgh Academy. Student of Arts, 1896-1900; M.A. 1900. O.T.C. Infantry, Oct. 1914 to Jan. 1915, Cadet. Highland Light Infantry, 2nd Lieut. 1915. King's Own Yorkshire Light Infantry, Captain Aug. 1915. France 1915. Killed in action on 1st July 1916. Pl. LXXXV.

WALLACE, ANDREW (b. 1875).
  George Heriot's School. Student of Medicine, 1891-6; M.B., C.M. 1896. 4th King's Own Scottish Borderers, Captain 1903. France. Gallipoli. Killed in action at the Dardanelles on 12th July 1915. Pl. LXXXV.

WALLACE, CHARLES ARTHUR PHIN (b. 1898).
  Daniel Stewart's College; First XV. and XI. 1st Highland Cadet Battn. University O.T.C. Infantry, May to Dec. 1916, Cadet; Officer Cadet Dec. 1916. 3rd King's Own Scottish Borderers, 2nd Lieut. May 1917. France May 1917; 9th Division. Killed in action on 23rd March 1918. Pl. LXXXV.

WALLACE, JOHN EWING (b. 1899).
  Glasgow High School. O.T.C. 1914-16, Cadet Sergeant. University O.T.C. Infantry, Nov. 1916 to Aug. 1917, Cadet. Royal Air Force, Aug. 1917, 2nd Lieut. April 1918. France. Killed in an air fight near Brise Bridge, by Marchelpot, on 9th August 1918. Pl. LXXXVI.

WALLACE, ROBERT NEILSON (b. 1881).
  Bilton Grange, Harrogate. Student of Medicine, 1901-7; M.B., Ch.B. 1907. R.A.M.C., attached 6th Royal Scots, Lieut. March 1910. Mobilised Aug. 1914; Captain Oct. 1914. 50th Stationary Hospital, Colchester. Died of pneumonia following influenza on 5th July 1918. Pl. LXXXVI.

WALLACE, WILLIAM (b. 1882).
  George Watson's College. Student of Arts, 1900-12; M.A. 1912. Schoolmaster. 9th Royal Scots, Private Aug. 1914. Royal Scots Fusiliers, 2nd Lieut. May 1915. Machine-Gun Corps. France. Wounded April 1915. Killed at Thiepval on 29th September 1916. Pl. LXXXVI.

Roll of the Fallen

WARD, JOHN SCOTT (*b.* 1885).
    Student of Medicine, 1906-7. L.R.C.P. & S. (Edin.); L.F.P.S. (Glasg.) 1907. Royal Navy, Surgeon. Lost at sea on 24th November 1916.

WATSON, ALASTAIR FISHER (*b.* 1892).
    George Watson's College; O.T.C., Cadet Corporal. Student of Science, 1910-14; B.Sc. 1914. O.T.C. Artillery, Jan. 1911 to Nov. 1913, Cadet. Lothians and Border Horse, Private 1913; Officer Cadet. 9th Royal Highlanders (Black Watch), 2nd Lieut. June 1916. France Sept. 1915 and Jan. 1917. Wounded Aug. 1916. Killed at Arras on 23rd April 1917.   Pl. LXXXVI.

WATSON, DAVID GALLOWAY (*b.* 1889).
    Royal High School; Dux. Student of Arts and Medicine, 1906-13; M.A. 1909; M.B., Ch.B. 1913. Resident, Royal Infirmary. R.A.M.C., Lieut. Aug. 1914; 2nd Bedfords; No. 5 General Hospital; No. 13 Stationary Hospital. France; Neuve Chapelle. Dispatches Nov. 1914 and Jan. 1916. Wounded at Festubert on 17th May and died at Le Touquet on 5th June 1915.   Pl. LXXXVII.

WATSON, DONALD MILLER (*b.* 1883).
    Morrison's Academy, Crieff. Student of Arts, 1901-6; M.A. (Hons. Classics) 1906. 1/5th Royal Scots, Private Sept. 1914; Sergeant Dec. 1914. Gallipoli. Killed in action at the Dardanelles in June 1915.   Pl. LXXXVI.

WATSON, FRANK FAIRWEATHER (*b.* 1893).
    Kirkcaldy High School; Athletics. O.T.C. 1909-12, Cadet Sergeant. Student of Arts, 1912-14. 4th and 14th Royal Scots, Private March 1914; 2nd Lieut.; Lieut. March 1915; Acting Captain. France. Killed near Albert on 5th August 1916.   Pl. LXXXVI.

WATSON, JAMES HENRY DIGBY (*b.* 1890).
    Edinburgh Academy, and King's School, Canterbury; Edinburgh Academicals First XV. International 1914. Student of Medicine, 1907-13; M.B., Ch.B. 1913. Royal Navy, Surgeon Aug. 1914, H.M.S. *Hawke*. Killed in action in the North Sea on 16th October 1914.   Pl. LXXXVII.

WATSON, JOHN DAVID MONCUR (*b.* 1891).
    Boroughmuir School. Student of Arts and Science, 1909-14; M.A. (Hons. Maths.) 1914; B.Sc. 1914. 9th Royal Scots, Private 1908. Mobilised Aug. 1914; L/Corporal. Died at Edinburgh on 19th February 1915.   Pl. LXXXVI.

WATSON, JOHN DOUGLAS (*b.* 1887).
    Kelso High School. Student of Arts and Law, 1904-12; M.A. 1908; LL.B. 1912. Writer to the Signet, 1912. 9th Gordon Highlanders, Machine-Gun Section, Private Sept.; Corporal Oct.; Sergeant Nov. 1914. France July 1915. Killed at St Auguste, Loos, on 25th September 1915.   Pl. LXXXVII.

PLATE LXXXVI.

J. E. Wallace.

R. N. Wallace.

Wm. Wallace.

F. F. Watson.

B. H. Watt.

C. C. Watt.

D. M. Watson.

J. D. M. Watson.

A. F. Watson.

PLATE LXXXVII.

D. G. Watson.

J. H. D. Watson.

J. D. Watson.

J. H. Watson.

N. J. Watson.

Thomas Watson.

W. N. Watson.

W. D. Watson.

W. G. D. Watson.

Roll of the Fallen

WATSON, JOHN HYNDMAN (*b.* 1886).
Campbell College, Belfast; First XV. and XI. Student of Medicine, 1908-12. O.T.C. Medical, April 1908 to Nov. 1912, Cadet Corporal. 15th Royal Scots, Dec. 1914; Sergeant 1915. France; Battle of the Somme, 1916. Wounded at Arras 1917. Killed near Armentières on 9th April 1918. Pl. LXXXVII.

WATSON, JOHN MITCHELL (*b.* 1890).
Berwickshire High School, Duns. Student of Law, 1910-14. Chartered Accountant. 4th Royal Scots, L/Corporal; Corporal. 1st King's Own Scottish Borderers, 2nd Lieut. Jan. 1915; Lieut.; Captain and Adjutant. Killed in action in Palestine on 13th November 1917.

WATSON, NORMAN BLYTH (*b.* 1893).
Student of Law, 1912-14. 1/4th Royal Scots, Private 1911. Mobilised Aug. 1914. Gallipoli. Wounded June 1915. Died at Malta on 16th August 1915.

WATSON, NORMAN JOHN (*b.* 1897).
George Watson's College; First XV. and XI. Student of Medicine, 1915-16. O.T.C. Artillery, May 1915 to March 1916, Cadet; Officer Cadet March 1916. R.F.A., C/246th Brigade, West Riding Division, 2nd Lieut. Dec. 1916. France; the Somme. Wounded in June, gassed in July 1917. Killed at Ridge Wood near Ypres on 28th May 1918. Pl. LXXXVII.

WATSON, THOMAS (*b.* 1891).
Daniel Stewart's College. Student of Law, 1909-10. Chartered Accountant, 1913. 4th Royal Scots, Private. Mobilised Aug. 1914. Dardanelles May 1915. Killed in action at Gallipoli on 28th June 1915. Pl. LXXXVII.

WATSON, WILLIAM DAVIDSON (*b.* 1892).
Peebles High School. Student of Arts, 1912-14. 5th Cameron Highlanders (Lochiel's), L/Sergeant Aug. 1914. France March 1915. Killed at the Battle of Loos on 25th September 1915. Pl. LXXXVII.

WATSON, WILLIAM GEORGE DOUGLAS (*b.* 1881).
Edinburgh Academy; First XI. Student of Law, 1903-5. Solicitor, 1907. King's Own Scottish Borderers, Lieut. Mobilised Aug. 1914. Captain. Gallipoli May 1915; Egypt; Sinai Peninsula, and Palestine. Killed near Gaza on 19th April 1917. Pl. LXXXVII.

WATSON, WILLIAM NORMAN (*b.* 1889).
Dingwall Academy. Student of Medicine, 1907-14; M.B., Ch.B. 1913. O.T.C. Infantry, Oct. 1909 to April 1913, Cadet. R.A.M.C., Lieut. Dec. 1914; Captain April 1916; attached 6th King's Own Scottish Borderers. France. M.C. at Loos, Sept. 1915. Dispatches. Died of wounds on 29th May 1916. Pl. LXXXVII.

WATT, BASIL HARRY (*b.* 1882).
Elgin Academy. Student of Arts and Medicine, 1898-1904; M.A. 1901. President of Union, 1903-4. R.A.M.C., 6th London Field Ambulance, Private Aug. 1914. 7th Cameron Highlanders, 2nd Lieut. May 1915. France. Killed at the Battle of Loos on 25th September 1915. Pl. LXXXVI.

Roll of the Fallen

WATT, CHARLES CECIL (*b.* 1895).
  Berwickshire High School, Duns. Student of Arts, 1913-15. O.T.C. Infantry, Nov. 1913 to June 1915, Cadet. Argyll and Sutherland Highlanders, Private June 1915. King's Own Scottish Borderers, 2nd Lieut. Jan. 1916. France Oct. 1916. Killed in action in France on 8th May 1917.   Pl. LXXXVI.

WEDDERBURN-MAXWELL, JAMES (*b.* 1899).
  Charterhouse; O.T.C. 1914-15. University O.T.C. Infantry, March to Oct. 1917, Cadet; Officer Cadet Oct. 1917. 3rd and 6th King's Own Scottish Borderers, 2nd Lieut. March 1918. France Aug. 1918. Wounded near Passchendaele and killed at Ledeghem Station on 1st October 1918.   Pl. LXXXVIII.

WEDDERSPOON, JACK HENRY BUTCHER (*b.* 1896).
  George Watson's College. Student of Arts, 1913-15. O.T.C. Artillery, Sept. 1914 to Jan. 1915, Cadet. R.F.A., 52nd Lowland Brigade, attached R.F.C., 2nd Lieut. Jan. 1915; Pilot and Observer. Asia Minor, Palestine, Jeddah, Aden, and France. Killed near Tournai on 6th April 1917.   Pl. LXXXVIII.

WEIR, ROBERT (*b.* 1886).
  George Watson's College. Student of Arts, 1905-7. Schoolmaster. 8th Royal Scots, Col.-Sergeant. Mobilised Aug. 1914. Lieut. Jan. 1915. France. Dispatches Nov. 1916. Killed in action on 16th November 1916.   Pl. LXXXVIII.

WEIR, WILLIAM SCOTT (*b.* 1880).
  George Watson's College. Student of Law, 1899-1903. Law Agent, 1903. 16th Royal Scots, Private Nov. 1914. France Jan. 1916. Killed at the Battle of the Somme on 1st July 1916.   Pl. LXXXVIII.

WELCH, DAVID (*b.* 1881).
  Montrose Academy. Student of Law, 1901-3. 16th Royal Scots, Private Nov. 1914. Died at Craigleith Hospital on 17th February 1915.   Pl. LXXXVIII.

WELPLY, HENRY DONALD (*b.* 1890).
  Wesley College, Dublin. Student of Medicine, 1909-14; M.B., Ch.B. 1914. R.A.M.C., Lieut. May 1915; Captain May 1916. Egypt 1916. Contracted dysentery in Egypt. Died of pneumonia in Australia on 11th March 1919.
  Pl. LXXXVIII.

WELSH, THOMAS CAIRNS (*b.* 1885).
  George Watson's College. Student of Medicine, 1904-10. 1/5th King's Own Scottish Borderers, Captain. Killed in action at the Dardanelles on 12th July 1915.

WELSH, TOM (*b.* 1884).
  Merchiston Castle; Cadet Corps 1899-1903; First XV. Student of Medicine, 1903-10; M.B., Ch.B. 1910. South African Medical Corps, Captain Nov. 1914. German S.-W. African Campaign and De Wet Rebellion, 1914-15. France 1915. M.C. Dec. 1916. Dispatches 5th and 11th Jan. 1917. Killed at Arras on 13th April 1917.   Pl. LXXXVIII.

PLATE LXXXVIII.

Robert Weir.

J. H. B. Wedderspoon.

J. Wedderburn-Maxwell.

W. S. Weir.

David Welch.

H. D. Welply.

Tom Welsh.

Algernon Westlake.

James Westwood.

PLATE LXXXIX.

 ALEX. WHITE.

 G. A. WHITE.

 R. R. WHEATLEY.

 J. P. R. WHITE.

 W. K. WHITE.

 T. J. WHITE.

 J. W. WHITELAW.

 C. B. WHITTAKER.

 D. J. WHITTON.

Roll of the Fallen

WESTLAKE, ALGERNON (*b.* 1859).
    Owens College, Manchester. Student of Medicine; M.B., C.M. 1884. R.A.M.C., Major Sept. 1916. 4th Northern General Hospital. Died on 25th May 1918.   Pl. LXXXVIII.

WESTWOOD, JAMES (*b.* 1889).
    George Heriot's and Broughton Schools, Edinburgh. Student of Arts, 1909-12; M.A. 1912. 9th Royal Scots, Private Sept. 1914; L/Corporal. France Feb. 1915 and June 1917. Wounded July 1916. R.G.A., 2nd Lieut. April 1917. Killed in action in France on 25th June 1917.   Pl. LXXXVIII.

WHEATLEY, RALPH RUTHVEN (*b.* 1892).
    Royal High School; First XV. Student of Law, 1910-11. O.T.C. Infantry, March 1909, Cadet. King's Royal Rifle Corps, 2nd Lieut. Aug. 1914. Wounded March 1918. Died at Colinton on 16th February 1919.   Pl. LXXXIX.

WHITE, ALEXANDER (*b.* 1882).
    Edinburgh Academy; Gym. VIII. Student of Arts and Law; M.A. 1903; LL.B. 1905. Writer to the Signet, 1906. Q.E.R.V.B., 1901, 2nd Lieut. 1905. 5th Royal Scots, Captain 1912. Mobilised Aug. 1914. Major June 1915. Gallipoli July 1915. Suvla Bay. Died of wounds on Hospital Ship *Arcadia* on 9th September 1915.   Pl. LXXXIX.

WHITE, GEORGE ANDERSON (*b.* 1887).
    George Watson's College. Student of Law, 1909-10. Law Agent. O.T.C. Infantry, May to Nov. 1916, Cadet. Officer Cadet Nov. 1916. 3rd attached 1st Royal Scots Fusiliers, 2nd Lieut. March 1917. France May 1917. Wounded at Hill 40, Sept. 1917. Wounded near Monchy-le-Preux on 28th and died on 30th March 1918.   Pl. LXXXIX.

WHITE, JOHN PEREGRINE ROBERTSON (*b.* 1861).
    Dr Bryce's School, Edinburgh. Student of Arts and Law, 1877-81; M.A. 1881; LL.B. Advocate, Aberdeen 1885. R.F.A., 1st Highland Brigade, Captain (retired); Captain June 1915. O.C. Depot. Died on 7th October 1916.   Pl. LXXXIX.

WHITE, THOMAS JAMES (*b.* 1894).
    Clifton Bank, St Andrews. Student of Medicine, 1912-14. O.T.C. Artillery, Oct. 1912 to Oct. 1914, Cadet. R.F.A., 2nd Lieut. Aug. 1914; Lieut. Sept. 1914. Foreign service 1915. M.C. Aug. 1917. Killed in action on 20th November 1917.   Pl. LXXXIX.

WHITE, WILLIAM KENNETH (*b.* 1893).
    Edinburgh Academy; First XV. and XI. O.T.C. 1908-11, Cadet Sergeant. Student of Arts and Law, 1911-12. 4th attached 2nd Scottish Rifles (S.R.), 2nd Lieut. 1915; Liaison Officer. France Nov. 1916. Killed in action near Ypres on 31st July 1917.   Pl. LXXXIX.

Roll of the Fallen

WHITELAW, JAMES WEIR (*b.* 1896).
George Watson's College. Student of Science, 1914-15. O.T.C. Infantry, Oct. 1915 to Jan. 1916, Cadet. 11th, 9th and 2nd Royal Scots Fusiliers, 2nd Lieut. Jan. 1916. France Sept. 1916. Missing, believed killed in action on 11th April 1917. Pl. LXXXIX.

WHITTAKER, CHARLES BROWN (*b.* 1890).
George Watson's College. Student of Arts, 1908-12; M.A. 1912. Schoolmaster. 2nd, 3rd, 6th and 12th Royal Scots, Private Aug. 1914; 2nd Lieut. Jan. 1915; Lieut. Jan. 1916. France June 1915 and April 1916. Dispatches Jan. 1916. Wounded at Hooge Sept. 1915. Killed at Guillemont, Battle of the Somme, on 22nd July 1916. Pl. LXXXIX.

WHITTON, DAVID JOHN (*b.* 1896).
Kirkcaldy High School; O.T.C. 1914-15. Student of Medicine, 1915-17. Resident, Royal Infirmary, Edinburgh. O.T.C. Medical, Nov. 1916 to Aug. 1917, Cadet. R.N.V.R., Surgeon-Probationer Aug. 1917. Killed in action on H.M.S. *Cullist*, Dundalk Bay, on 11th February 1918. Pl. LXXXIX.

WHYTE, CAMPBELL DRUMMOND.
Royal High School. Student of Science. Royal Fusiliers, Private Aug. 1914; 2nd Lieut. July 1916. Killed in action on 13th July 1916.

WIGHT, WILLIAM STEWART BALMAIN (*b.* 1898).
Dunbar School. Edinburgh University O.T.C. Infantry, Oct. 1915 to Jan. 1916. Cadet. 3rd Royal Scots, 2nd Lieut. 1916. Killed in action on 9th April 1917. Pl. XC.

WILKES, REGINALD ALEXANDER CLARK (*b.* 1885).
George Watson's College. Student of Medicine, 1903-8. 14th Canadian Infantry, 1st Contingent, Private Aug. 1914. Killed in action in France on 21st May 1915. Pl. XC.

WILLIAMS, CYRIL (*b.* 1896).
Perth Academy, and Royal High School, Edinburgh. University O.T.C. Infantry, Oct. 1911 to Jan. 1914, Cadet. Royal Military College, Sandhurst, Jan. 1914. 2nd Highland Light Infantry, 2nd Lieut. Sept. 1914; Lieut. March 1915. R.F.C., March 1916. France. Wounded at Festubert in May 1915. Missing, believed killed in air fight on 30th July 1916. Pl. XC.

WILLIAMS, JAMES ALFRED (*b.* 1897).
Foyle College, Londonderry; Swimming. Student of Medicine, 1914-15. 16th Royal Scots, Private May 1915. Royal Irish Rifles, 2nd Lieut. July 1915. France. Killed in action at Ginchy on 6th September 1916. Pl. XC.

PLATE XC.

R. A. C. Wilkes.

Cyril Williams.

W. S. B. Wight.

John Wilson.

Marion E. Wilson.

G. H. Williamson.

J. D. Wilson.

J. A. Williams.

R. A. Wilson.

PLATE XCI.

R. F. WILSON.

THOMAS WILSON.
(9th H.L.I.)

T. G. WILSON.

PERCY WISE.

L. C. WISE.

P. B. WOOD.

JAMES WOODS.

W. D. WOODROW.

R. E. WOOD.

Roll of the Fallen

WILLIAMSON, GEORGE HAMILTON (b. 1889).
 King William's College, Isle of Man; First XV. Student of Arts, 1907-11; M.A. (Hons. Classics) 1911. O.T.C. Infantry, Nov. 1908 to Oct. 1911, Cadet. 7th and 15th King's Royal Rifle Corps, 2nd Lieut. Dec. 1914; Lieut. March 1915; Captain May 1916. France. Dispatches June 1916. M.C. Oct. 1916. Died of wounds received at the Battle of Arras on 12th April 1917. Pl. XC.

WILSON, JOHN (b. 1886).
 George Watson's College. Student of Medicine, 1903-9; M.B., Ch.B. 1909. R.A.M.C., Lieut. April 1915; Captain; attached 10th Duke of Wellington's West Riding Regiment. France Aug. 1915. Killed in action in France on 9th March 1916. Pl. XC.

WILSON, JOHN DYKES (b. 1886).
 Tillicoultry School. Student of Arts and Medicine, 1903-9; M.A. 1906; M.B., Ch.B. 1909. McCosh Bursar, 1909. O.T.C. Medical, Feb. to Sept. 1909, Cadet Corporal. Indian Medical Service, 1912; Captain Sept. 1915. Invalided home from India and died on 16th February 1916. Pl. XC.

WILSON, MARIAN ELIZABETH (b. 1881).
 Notting Hill High School, London, and École Vinet, Lausanne. Student of Medicine, 1900-6; M.B., Ch.B. 1906. Scottish Women's Hospital, Royaumont, France, M.O. Nov. 1915. Médaille des Épidémies en vermeil. Died of appendicitis at St Martin, Vesubie, France, on 1st August 1917. Pl. XC.

WILSON, ROBERT ARMSTRONG (b. 1882).
 George Watson's College. Student of Medicine, 1903-11. R.F.A., Lieut. Aug. 1914; Captain Aug. 1915. France. Killed in action at Bethune on 18th October 1915. Pl. XC.

WILSON, ROBERT FORSYTH (b. 1888).
 George Watson's College. Student of Arts and Divinity, 1908-15; M.A. 1911; B.D. 1915. Licentiate, Church of Scotland. 1st and 6th Gordon Highlanders, 2nd Lieut. France. Killed at Beaumont Hamel on 13th November 1916. Pl. XCI.

WILSON, THOMAS (b. 1891).
 Royal High School. Student of Science, 1907-8. R.E. (Special Brigade), Corporal, R.F.A., 2nd Lieut. Killed in action in 1918.

WILSON, THOMAS (b. 1897).
 Boroughmuir School; Dux. Student of Arts, 1915-16. 9th Highland Light Infantry (Glasgow Highlanders), Private Oct. 1916. 15th Royal Scots. France June 1917. Wounded and taken prisoner at Ypres on 22nd Oct. 1917. Died of wounds at Ghent on 4th January 1918. Pl. XCI.

WILSON, THOMAS GILLIES (b. 1879).
 Possil School, Glasgow. Student of Arts, 1910-12; M.A. 1912. 13th Royal Scots, Private June 1915; Corporal. Missing, presumed killed in action on 28th June 1916. Pl. XCI.

Roll of the Fallen

WISE, LANCELOT CHARLES (*b.* 1894).
: Charterhouse. Student of Science, 1913-14. King Edward's Horse, Trooper 1914. North Irish Horse, 2nd Lieut. 1915. Indian Army, 3rd Skinner's Horse, Lieut. 1917. France 1915. Died at Rawal Pindi, India, May 1917. Pl. XCI.

WISE, PERCY (*b.* 1888).
: Manchester Grammar School. Student of Arts, 1914-15. R.A.M.C., Private Oct. 1915. France and Italy 1915. The Somme 1916. Killed in action on 1st February 1918. Pl. XCI.

WOOD, PETER BROWN (*b.* 1892).
: Fordyce Academy. Student of Law, 1913-14. 4th Royal Scots, Private May 1913. Mobilised Aug. 1914. Army Audit Staff, Lieut. March 1916. Wounded at Gallipoli in June 1915. Missing, now presumed killed in Egypt on 25th September 1916. Pl. XCI.

WOOD, RUSSELL ELIOTT (*b.* 1855).
: Edinburgh Academy; First XV. Student of Medicine, 1871-7; M.B., C.M. 1877; F.R.C.S. (Edin.) 1886. Zulu War 1879. Lanark Yeomanry, Surgeon 1881. R.A.M.C. (T.)., Lieut.-Col. Died on 8th February 1917. Pl. XCI.

WOODROW, WILLIAM DAVIDSON (*b.* 1883).
: Markinch School. Student of Law, 1911-13. 4th Royal Scots; mobilised Aug. 1914; Sergeant Aug. 1914; Coy. Sergeant-Major 1915; 2nd Lieut. Oct. 1916. Gallipoli, Palestine and France. Killed in action on 23rd April 1917. Pl. XCI.

WOODS, JAMES (*b.* 1877).
: Royal Academy, Belfast, and Sullivan School, Holywood. Student of Medicine, 1896-1901; M.B., Ch.B. 1901. Indian Medical Service, Major. Killed in action on 9th May 1915. Pl. XCI.

WYLES, WILLIAM W. (*b.* 1895).
: Buckhaven School. Student of Arts, 1914-15. O.T.C. Artillery, May to Oct. 1915, Cadet. R.F.A., Gunner Oct. 1915. Killed in action on 27th May 1916. Pl. XCII.

YOUNG, ANDREW (*b.* 1888).
: George Watson's College. Student of Arts, 1905-9; M.A. (Hons. Classics) 1909. Schoolmaster. R.A.M.C., 2nd London Division, Private Jan. 1915. 3rd Scottish Rifles, attached 13th Royal Scots, 2nd Lieut. Sept. 1916. France 1916. Killed in action on 26th December 1916. Pl. XCII.

YOUNG, NORMAN MITCHELL (*b.* 1890).
: Edinburgh Academy; Athletics. Student of Law, 1911-13. 9th and 1st Royal Scots, Private; 2nd Lieut. Dec. 1913; Lieut. India Dec. 1913. France Dec. 1914. Dispatches June 1915. Killed in action near Ypres on 23rd April 1915. Pl. XCII.

PLATE XCII.

W. W. Wyles.   N. M. Young.   Andrew Young.

W. S. Young.   W. A. Young.   I. Bayley Balfour.

C. A. C. Bentley.   W. H. Calvert.   W. R. Center.

PLATE XCIII.

C. E. Cumming.

John Ferguson.
(Gordon Highlanders.)

D. W. Gray.

A. L. Harley.

A. C. Hartley.

Alex. Mowat.

P. B. Macintyre.

R. D. Neil.

William Orme.

Roll of the Fallen

YOUNG, WILLIAM ALEXANDER (*b.* 1893).
  Edinburgh Institution. Student of Law, 1912-14. 9th Royal Scots, Private Aug. 1914. 2nd and 3rd Royal Highlanders (Black Watch), 2nd Lieut. Sept. 1915; Captain. France Feb. 1915. Mesopotamia Nov. 1915; Egypt and Palestine 1918. Twice mentioned in Dispatches. M.C. Aug. 1917. Wounded in Palestine on 8th and died on 10th June 1918.   Pl. XCII.

YOUNG, WILLIAM STEELE (*b.* 1893).
  George Watson's College; First XV. O.T.C. Cadet Colour-Sergeant. Student of Science, 1913-14. O.T.C. Engineers, Oct. 1913 to Sept. 1914, Cadet. R.E., 2nd Lieut. Sept. 1914; Lieut. June 1917. Gallipoli, attached 2/1st Cheshire Regiment, R.E. Suvla Bay. Egypt, 412th Coy. R.E., 52nd (Lowland) Division. Killed in action at third Battle of Gaza on 2nd November 1917.   Pl. XCII.

ANDERSON, JOHN GEORGE.
  M.B., Ch.B. 1914. R.A.M.C. (T.), Lieut.; Captain May 1915. Attached 3rd Highland Field Ambulance. M.C. Killed in action on 21st March 1918.

BALFOUR, ISAAC BAYLEY (*b.* 1889).
  Winchester; First XI. University O.T.C. Infantry, Sept. to Nov. 1914, Cadet. 14th Royal Scots, 2nd Lieut. Nov. 1914; Lieut. Attached 1st King's Own Scottish Borderers. Killed in action at the Dardanelles on 28th June 1915.
          Pl. XCII.

COX, PERCY (*b.* 1896).
  Dunfermline High School. Student of Arts, 1915-16. R.G.A., Signaller Nov. 1915. France Nov. 1916. Wounded at the Somme on 19th and died on 20th January 1917.   Pl. XCIV.

DONALDSON, SAMUEL RITCHIE (*b.* 1890).
  Kirkwall Burgh School. M.A. 1912; B.Sc. 1913. 7th Seaforth Highlanders, Private. France Jan. 1917. Killed at Kemmel Hill near Ypres on 16th April 1918.

FRASER, DONALD REGINALD (*b.* 1884).
  Blairlodge School, Polmont; First XI. Cadet Corps, Corporal. Student of Law, 1906-8. 5th Cameron Highlanders, Sergeant Sept. 1914. Killed in action in September 1915.   Pl. XCIV.

HARLEY, ALLAN LANGLANDS (*b.* 1899).
  Strathallan School, Bridge of Allan; First XV. and XI. Student of Medicine, 1916-17. 1/4th Seaforth Highlanders, Private July 1917; L/Corporal Oct. 1917. France April 1918. Wounded at La Bassée on the 9th and taken prisoner on 11th April 1918. Died of wounds at Seclin on 8th May 1918.   Pl. XCIII.

Roll of the Fallen

HARTE, JOSEPH FRANCIS (*b.* 1895).
    St Joseph's College, Dumfries. Student of Medicine, 1913-15. O.T.C. Infantry, May to July 1915, Cadet. R.A.M.C. (T.), Scottish Horse Brigade Field Ambulance, Private Aug. 1914. 5th Royal Scots, 2nd Lieut. Jan. 1917. Killed in action near Arras on 5th June 1917.   Pl. XCIV.

KIRKPATRICK, ROBERT B. (*b.* 1898).
    Boroughmuir School. Laboratory Assistant in Bacteriology. Royal Scots Fusiliers, Private May 1916; Corporal; Officer Cadet Sept. 1917. Duke of Cornwall's Light Infantry, 2nd Lieut. Feb. 1918. France May 1918. Killed in action on 23rd June 1918.   Pl. XCIV.

LAWRENCE, HENRY RUTHVEN (*b.* 1883).
    St Andrew's College, Grahamstown, South Africa. O.T.C. 1896-1900, Cadet. M.B., Ch.B. 1908; M.D. 1910; F.R.C.S. (Edin.) 1912. South African Medical Corps, Captain Sept. 1914; Acting Major Oct. 1918. German South-West Africa, 1914-15; South African Expeditionary Force, 1915-18; South African General Hospital; 4th South African Infantry; South African Field Ambulance. Dispatches April 1918. M.C. Oct. 1918. Wounded 10th November and died of influenza and pneumonia on 14th December 1918.   Pl. XCIV.

MACKAY, JOHN (*b.* 1892).
    Miller Institution, Thurso. Student of Arts, 1912-14. 4th Royal Scots (T.), Private Sept. 1914. Killed at the Dardanelles on 28th June 1915.

RENTON, JAMES CRAWFORD.
    M.B., Ch.B. 1873; M.D. 1882. R.A.M.C. (T.), Lieut.-Col. 1908. 4th Scottish General Hospital. Died in October 1919.

The following Cadets died while in Training for Military Service :—

CRAIK, DAVID (*b.* 1898).
    Royal High School. University O.T.C. Artillery, May to Sept. 1916, Cadet. Died as the result of an accident on 23rd September 1916.

KERR, WILLIAM PURVIS (*b.* 1899).
    George Watson's College and Daniel Stewart's. University O.T.C. Infantry, Dec. 1917 to June 1918, Cadet. Died on 8th June 1918.

RITCHIE, CHARLES ANDREW (*b.* 1897).
    George Watson's College. O.T.C. Corporal. Student of Medicine, 1914-15. O.T.C. Artillery, Sept. 1914 to Feb. 1915, Cadet. Died as the result of an accident on 6th February 1915.

PLATE XCIV.

P. H. S. Bezuidenhout.

Percy Cox.

J. F. Harte.

H. R. Lawrence.

D. R. Fraser.

R. B. Kirkpatrick.

J. H. Tytler.

G. H. Wade.

F. L. de Verteuil.

RECORD OF WAR SERVICE

ABERNETHY, CHARLES LAWRENCE.
　　Anderson Institute, Lerwick. M.A. 1913; M.A. (Hons. Maths.) and B.Sc. 1914. O.T.C. Infantry, Jan. 1910 to May 1913, Cadet. R.E. (Special Brigade), Pioneer. Research Chemist, Royal Arsenal, Woolwich, April 1917 to June 1919.

ABLETT, EDWARD HUTCHINSON.
　　St Bees School, Cumberland; First XV. and XI. Student of Medicine, 1912-16 and 1918-19. O.T.C. Artillery, Cadet Oct. 1914; Cadet Bombardier Oct. 1914; Cadet B.Q.M.S. Nov. 1914; 2nd Lieut. July 1915; Lieut. Nov. 1916.

ACHESON, JOHNSTON HAMILTON.
　　Rossal; First XI. M.B., C.M. 1887; D.P.H. (Camb.) 1910. Royal Navy, Fleet Surgeon, retired 1904. Admiralty Surgeon and Agent at Dover, 1912-19.

ADAM, GEORGE.
　　M.A., M.D. (Aberdeen). Student of Medicine, 1916. Certif. Tropical Medicine (Edin.). S.A.M.C., Captain 1915. R.A.M.C., Captain 1917.

ADAM, GEORGE.
　　Stonelaw School, Rutherglen. University O.T.C. Infantry, Feb. to April 1917, Cadet. 1/5th Royal Scots, Private April 1914. Royal Air Force, Cadet. Gallipoli.

ADAM, GEORGE MIN.
　　Brechin High School. M.B., Ch.B. 1912. O.T.C. Infantry, Feb. 1909 to July 1910, Cadet. 5th Royal Highlanders (Black Watch), 2nd Lieut.; Lieut. R.A.M.C., Lieut.; Captain. Peshawar, India. M.C.

ADAM, JAMES NEILSON.
　　Mill Hill School. O.T.C. 1911-13, Cadet Corporal. Student of Medicine, 1918. 19th Royal Fusiliers, Private Sept. 1914; 3rd Royal Highlanders (Black Watch), 2nd Lieut. May 1915; Lieut. July 1917. France. M.C. July 1918.

ADAM, JAMES ROBERTSON.
　　M.B., Ch.B. 1909; D.P.H., R.C.P.S. (Edin.) 1913. O.T.C. Infantry, Oct. 1908 to March 1910, Cadet Sergeant. Highland Light Infantry, Lieut. Royal Navy; R.N.D. and R.N.A.S., Surgeon. Royal Air Force, Captain.

Record of War Service

ADAM, JOHN FRASER.
Royal High School. M.A. 1909. 2/9th Royal Scots, Private March 1915. 7th and 6th Argyll and Sutherland Highlanders, 2nd Lieut. Oct. 1915; Lieut. July 1917. France Oct. 1916 and April 1918 to March 1919. Italy Dec. 1917.

ADAM, WILLIAM GEORGE.
Blairgowrie High School. M.A. 1913. R.E., 76th Field Coy., Sapper Jan. 1915. France Aug. 1915 and May 1917. R.G.A., 161st Siege Battery, 2nd Lieut. March 1917; Lieut. Sept. 1918; Acting Captain Feb. 1919; Acting Education Officer, 4th Corps Troops. Dispatches April 1918 and March 1919. Chevalier Crown of Roumania.

ADAMS, DAN. VERE MAXWELL.
M.B., Ch.B. 1898. South African Campaign, 1900. R.A.M.C. (R. of O.), Lieut.; Captain. Mobilised 1914. France 1915. Salonika. Wounded. Dispatches (Salonika) 1918.

ADAMS, EDWARD JOSCELINE PERCY.
Malvern College. Cadet Corps 1900-2. Student of Science, 1918-19. 2nd Rhodesian Regiment, 2nd Lieut. 1915; Lieut. 1918. 3rd Royal Warwickshire Regiment (S.R.)

ADAMS, GEORGE JOSEPH.
M.B., Ch.B. 1907; M.D. 1920; F.R.C.S. N.Z. Medical Corps, Lieut.; Captain.

ADAMS, HAROLD LLEWELLYN.
Daniel Stewart's College. Student of Science, 1918-19. R.F.A. (T.), 1/1st Lowland Brigade, Signaller, March 1914. France. Wounded.

ADAMS, HERBERT FREDERICK WILFRED.
Merchiston Castle; First XV. O.T.C., Cadet Sergeant. M.B., Ch.B. 1912. R.A.M.C., Lieut. Aug. 1914. Captain Aug. 1915. Attached Coldstream Guards; 1st Gloucesters; 12th Rifle Brigade; 20th Machine-Gun Battn. France. Gallipoli. Wounded Dec. 1914. Invalided from Mudros Dec. 1915.

ADAMS, THOMAS ALEXANDER.
Coleraine Academical Institution. M.B., Ch.B. 1910; D.P.H. (Belfast). R.A.M.C., Lieut. Dec. 1917; Captain 1918.

ADAMSON, ALEXANDER.
Dunfermline High School. M.A. 1908. 2/1st Highland Cyclist Battn., Private Nov. 1915; L/Corporal Sept. 1916. Tank Corps, March 1918; Officer Cadet July 1918; 2nd Lieut. Feb. 1919.

ADAMSON, ALF. FAIRGRIEVE.
Harris Academy, Dundee. M.B., Ch.B. 1912. O.T.C. Infantry, Nov. 1908 to May 1912, Cadet. Royal Navy, Surgeon Sept. 1914.

Record of War Service

ADAMSON, ROBERT.
Madras College, St Andrews, and Royal High School. M.A. 1886. Minister, U.F. Church of Scotland. Chaplain, 4th Class; attached Ammunition Column, 2nd Lowland Brigade, R.F.A., 1912. Fife and Forfar Yeomanry; 56th Training Brigade.

ADAMSON, THOMAS.
Royal High School. B.D. 1876; D.D. (Glasg.). Examiner for B.D. (Edinburgh University) 1875-81. Chaplain 1896. Colonel; attached 3rd Scottish General Hospital, Glasgow. T.D. Mention.

ADCOCK, ERNEST WILLIAM.
M.B., Ch.B. 1913. R.A.M.C., attached 6th Yorkshire Regiment, Lieut.; Captain.

ADDINSELL, AUGUSTUS WHITEHORN.
M.B., C.M. (Hons.) 1883; M.R.C.P. (Lond.) 1899. R.A.M.C., attached 2nd Cavalry Division, Captain Sept. 1914. France 1915.

ADDIS, THOMAS.
George Watson's College. M.B., Ch.B. 1905; M.D.; M.R.C.P. Assoc. Prof. of Medicine, Stanford University. American Army.

ADDIS, WILLIAM ROBERT.
George Watson's College. M.B., Ch.B. 1913. R.A.M.C., Lieut. Aug. 1914; Captain Aug. 1915. M.C. Nov. 1917.

ADDISON, WILLIAM.
George Watson's College. M.A. (Glasg.) 1915. Student of Divinity, 1918. 2nd Cameron Highlanders, Corporal Nov. 1915.

ADDISON-SCOTT, DUNCAN GORDON.
Loretto; First XV. and XI. M.B., Ch.B. 1903. Royal Navy, 1904; Staff Surgeon, 1912. H.M.S. *Ringdove*, 1914; H.M. Monitor *Earl of Peterborough*, 1915; Surgeon-Commander 1917. R.N. Sick Quarters, Torpoint, 1917-18.

ADDISON-SMITH, CHILTON LIND.
Craigmount School, Edinburgh; First XV. and XI. Student of Law. Writer to the Signet, 1899. Edinburgh University; First XV. 3rd and 10th Seaforth Highlanders, 2nd Lieut. May 1896. South African Campaign, 1899-1901. Lieut.-Col. Dec. 1914 and O.C. 6th Somerset Light Infantry, 1915; 6th Canadian Infantry Brigade; 8th Bedfords; 2nd Sherwood Foresters. O.C. 19th Labour Group, Headquarters. France Dec. 1915 to Dec. 1916. Dispatches Nov. 1918. O.B.E. (Military) Jan. 1919. Order of Wen-Hu, China.

ADIE, WILLIAM JOHN.
M.B., Ch.B. 1911; M.R.C.P. (Lond.). O.T.C. Artillery, 1908-10. R.A.M.C., Lieut.; Captain 1917; Major Jan. 1918. Attached 1st Northamptonshire and 1st Leicestershire Regiments. No. 7 General Hospital, St Omer. France, 1914-18. Dispatches 1917.

Record of War Service

ADSHEAD, GEOFFREY PALMER.
Marlborough. M.B., Ch.B. 1906. Royal Navy, Surgeon 1907; Staff Surgeon 1914; Surgeon-Commander Nov. 1918. Somaliland 1908-9; Persian Gulf 1912-13; East Indies; Egypt; Dardanelles; Adriatic 1914-18. S.M.O., H.M.S. *Ocean*, sunk in action at Dardanelles March 1915.

AFFLECK, JAMES ORMISTON.
B.Sc. 1907. Royal Engineers, 2nd Lieut.; Captain Jan. 1917; Acting Major June 1918.

AICKIN, ROLAND THOMAS GRAVES.
Auckland College and Grammar School, New Zealand. M.B., Ch.B. 1903; M.D. 1904; D.P.H. Demonstrator in Physiology. Demonstrator in Anatomy, Liverpool University and King's College, London. R.A.M.C., Lieut. July 1916; Captain July 1917.

AIKEN, DAVID.
Foyle College, Londonderry. M.B., Ch.B. 1909; F.R.C.S. (Edin.). Australian Army Medical Corps, Captain May 1918.

AIKMAN, ALEXANDER.
Daniel Stewart's College. Student of Law. Chartered Accountant, 1912. Honourable Artillery Coy., Aug. 1914. Army Pay Dept. Lieut. Jan. 1915; Captain Oct. 1917; Major Oct. 1918.

AIKMAN, CEDRIC WILLIAM.
Merchiston Castle. O.T.C. 1906-9, Cadet; M.B., Ch.B. 1914. O.T.C. Infantry, June 1909-13, Cadet L/Corporal. R.A.M.C., Lieut. April 1916; Captain April 1917.

AIKMAN, JAMES HISLOP.
Daniel Stewart's College. M.A. 1902; M.B., Ch.B. 1906; D.P.H. (Camb.) 1909. No. 4 Coy. Q.R.V.B. Royal Scots, 1899-1904, Private. R.A.M.C. (T.), Lieut. Oct. 1914; Captain Aug. 1915. Wounded April 1916. Dispatches. M.C. Jan. 1916.

AIKMAN-SMITH, ANDREW HENRY DOUGLAS.
Edinburgh Academy and Loretto. O.T.C. 1911-13. Student of Law, 1918. R.N.A.S., Sub-Lieut. Feb. 1915. Gallipoli. Invalided out.

AIKMAN-SMITH, GAVIN JAMES.
Loretto and Sedbergh. O.T.C. 1913-15. University O.T.C. Artillery, May 1916 to Jan. 1917, Cadet Corporal. 19th Fire Command R.G.A., 2nd Lieut. May 1917; Lieut. Oct. 1918.

AITCHISON, JAMES ALEXANDER.
George Heriot's School. Student of Medicine, 1918. R.A.M.C., Private Aug. 1915. 6th Royal Scots, 2nd Lieut. Jan. 1916. R.G.A. 20th (Forth) Fire Command, Lieut. Oct. 1916 to April 1919.

Record of War Service

AITCHISON, RICHARD SCOTT.
   Student of Law. Chartered Accountant, 1878. A.S.C. (T.), Highland Division Train, 2nd Lieut.; Lieut.

AITCHISON, RICHARD SCOTT (JUNR.).
   George Watson's College. O.T.C. 1912-16. University O.T.C. Infantry, Oct. 1916, Cadet. Royal Scots, Private Oct. 1917; Officer Cadet, 4th Royal Scots, 2nd Lieut. March 1918. France Oct. 1918 to Feb. 1919.

AITCHISON, ROBERT CHALMERS.
   George Heriot's School. M.B., Ch.B. 1914. O.T.C. Medical, April 1910 to June 1912, Cadet. R.A.M.C. (S.R.), July 1912; Lieut; Captain Feb. 1918; Acting Major Feb. 1919.

AITCHISON, WILLIAM.
   North Berwick High School. Student of Arts, 1912-15; M.A. 1920. O.T.C. Artillery, Oct. 1914 to Dec. 1915, Cadet. R.F.A. (S.R.), 2nd Lieut. Dec. 1915; Lieut. July 1917. Trench Mortar Officer. Royal Air Force, Pilot. France March 1916. Twice wounded. M.C. (Messines Ridge) May 1917.

AITKEN, JAMES.
   George Heriot's School. M.A. 1913; M.B., Ch.B. 1917. O.T.C. Infantry, Jan. 1911 to April 1914; and Medical, Feb. 1916 to April 1917, Cadet. R.A.M.C. (S.R.), Lieut. May 1917; Captain May 1918.

AITKEN, JAMES.
   George Watson's College; First XV. O.T.C. 1916-17. Student of Medicine, 1918. R.F.C. and Royal Air Force, Cadet Aug. 1917; 2nd Lieut. Dec. 1917 to Feb. 1919.

AITKEN, JAMES DAVIDSON.
   George Watson's College. M.A. 1911. O.T.C. Infantry, June 1909-11, Cadet. Ceylon Police, 1914 to March 1917. 3rd Rifle Brigade, 2nd Lieut. Oct. 1917. France April 1918. Wounded Aug. 1918.

AITKEN, JAMES T.
   Student of Law, 1913-14. 1/5th Royal Scots, Machine-Gun Section, Private.

AITKEN, ROBERT.
   Daniel Stewart's College. M.B., Ch.B. 1911; M.D. 1915; M.R.C.P. (Edin.). Royal Navy, Surgeon-Lieut.

AITKEN, ROBERT.
   George Watson's College. M.A. 1906. Inns of Court O.T.C., Private; 2nd Lieut. 1915; Lieut. 1917. War Office, Military Intelligence Staff, Sept. 1917. France. Twice wounded.

Record of War Service

AITKEN, ROBERT SYDNEY.
George Watson's College. Cadet Corps 1905-6. Student of Law, 1911-12; Solicitor. O.T.C. Artillery, Aug. 1914 to Jan. 1915, Cadet. R.F.A. (T.), 2nd Lieut. Jan. 1915; Lieut. June 1916. Egypt and Palestine Feb. 1916 to March 1919. Wounded at second Battle of Gaza, April 1917.

ALBERT, EDWARD.
M.A. 1909. Schoolmaster. Royal Air Force, 2nd Lieut.

ALCOCK, STANLEY CHARLES.
Derby School; First XV. and XI. O.T.C. 1910-15, Cadet Sergeant. Student of Medicine, 1915-16 and 1918-19. O.T.C. Infantry, Feb. to March 1916, Cadet. 4th and 2nd Argyll and Sutherland Highlanders, Private March 1916; 2nd Lieut. July 1916; Lieut. Jan. 1918. France 1917.

ALCORN, ALEXANDER THOMSON.
Bathgate Academy. M.A. 1909. Schoolmaster. R.F.A., 1st Lowland Brigade, June 1915; Bombardier Sept. 1915. 325th, 179th, and 169th Army, F.A. Brigade. France. Wounded at Cambrai 1917.

ALDRIDGE, ARTHUR RUSSELL.
Spring Hill School, Southampton. M.B., C.M. 1885; D.P.H. (Eng.) 1892. R.A.M.C., Lieut. 1886; Lieut.-Col. (Retired). Tibet 1904; Gallipoli 1915; Egypt 1916; Salonika 1916-17. Dispatches, Gallipoli 1915, Salonika 1916 and 1917. C.S.I. 1911; C.M.G. 1917; C.B. 1918; Médaille d'Or des Épidémies 1917; Order of Redeemer (Greece), 3rd Class Commander, 1918.

ALDRIDGE, NORMAN ELLIOTT.
Spring Hill School, Southampton. M.B., C.M. 1884; L.R.C.P. & S. (Edin.) 1888; D.P.H.; R.C.P.S. (Edin.) 1890. R.A.M.C. (T.) 1908. Mobilised Dec. 1914, Major. Attached H.Q., Southern Command, 1918-19. Radiologist.

ALEXANDER, ARCHIBALD.
George Heriot's School. M.A. 1896; B.D. 1899. Minister, U.F. Church of Scotland. Chaplain, 4th Class, France, Oct. 1915 to April 1917. 1st V.B. Royal Scots Fusiliers, May 1918. Hon. C.F. Dec. 1918.

ALEXANDER, DAVID CARNEGIE.
M.B., Ch.B. 1905. R.A.M.C., Lieut.; Captain. M.C. Dispatches.

ALEXANDER, EDWARD MURRAY-MAYNE.
Harrow. Volunteers 1901-2. Student of Law, 1905-9. Writer to the Signet, 1910. 7th Seaforth Highlanders, Lieut. Nov. 1914; Captain Dec. 1914. France May 1916 and Oct. 1917. Wounded at the Somme July 1916, and Wytschaete April 1918.

ALEXANDER, GEORGE FORBES.
High School, Dundee. M.B., C.M. 1883. Assistant in Physiology, 1884-6. R.A.M.C., April 1887; Major July 1899 (Retired). Mobilised Aug. 1914. Eye Specialist.

Record of War Service

ALEXANDER, GEORGE HAROLD PETRIE.
George Watson's College. O.T.C. 1914-17. Student of Medicine, 1918. 2nd King's Own Scottish Borderers, Private Sept. 1917; L/Corporal April 1918; Corporal Aug. 1918.

ALEXANDER, GEORGE JAMES.
George Watson's College; First XV. and XI. Student of Medicine, 1912-14 and 1918-19. O.T.C. Artillery, Oct. 1913 to Sept. 1914, Cadet. R.G.A., 2nd Lieut. Sept. 1914; Lieut. March 1916; Captain June 1917. France Aug. 1915 to Aug. 1918. Wounded Oct. 1916. Dispatches May 1917. M.C. Nov. 1917.

ALEXANDER, HENRY SCOTT ANDERSON.
M.B., Ch.B. 1914. R.A.M.C., Lieut.; Captain.

ALEXANDER, JAMES TURNBULL.
Edinburgh Academy. Shooting. O.T.C. 1914-16. University O.T.C. Artillery, 1917 Cadet. Tank Corps, Officer Cadet Jan. 1918; 2nd Lieut. Oct. 1918.

ALEXANDER, JOHN.
Daniel Stewart's College. M.A. 1902; M.B., Ch.B. 1906; D.P.H.; D.T.M. and H. 1911. R.A.M.C., 53rd Field Ambulance, Lieut. Nov. 1914; Captain 1915; Major 1918. Dispatches Jan. and June 1918 and Jan. 1919.

ALEXANDER, JOHN BUDGE.
M.A. 1904; M.B., Ch.B. (Hons.) 1907. R.A.M.C., Lieut.; Captain.

ALEXANDER, JOHN CHARLES.
Glasgow Academy; First XV. and XI. University O.T.C. Artillery, May to Nov. 1915. R.G.A. (T.), 2nd Lieut. Nov. 1915; Lieut. June 1916.

ALEXANDER, RICHARD CHARLES.
George Watson's College. M.A. 1904; M.B., Ch.B. 1908; F.R.C.S. (Edin.) 1911. Assistant in Surgery. R.A.M.C., Lieut. June 1916. France 1916. Captain June 1917; Major Jan. 1918. Dispatches Nov. 1917 and March 1919.

ALEXANDER, ROBERT HARPER.
Edinburgh Academy; First XV. O.T.C. 1908-9, Cadet; M.B., Ch.B. 1914. R.A.M.C., Lieut. Aug. 1914; Captain Aug. 1915; Acting Major June 1919. France. M.C. June 1918.

ALEXANDER, STUART MAXWELL.
George Heriot's School. Student of Medicine, 1914-15 and 1917-19. O.T.C. Infantry, Oct. 1914 to June 1915, and Medical Unit, April 1918 to Feb. 1919, Cadet. 16th Royal Scots, Corporal May 1915.

ALEXANDER, THOMAS HOOD WILSON.
Perth Academy. M.B., Ch.B. 1900; F.R.C.S. (Edin.). Red Cross, Morayshire, 1914-15. R.A.M.C., 1st Scottish General Hospital, Captain Jan. 1915; Major Nov. 1917.

Record of War Service

ALEXANDER, WILLIAM ALISTER.
George Watson's College. Cadet Corps 1905-7. M.B., Ch.B. 1912. O.T.C. Infantry, 1909-13, Cadet Sergeant. R.A.M.C., Lieut. 1915; Captain April 1916. Malta; N.-W. Frontier, India; Egypt; France.

ALEXANDER, WILLIAM GREIG.
Daniel Stewart's College. M.A. 1902. Minister, U.F. Church of Scotland. Army Chaplain, 4th Class, 1917. France and Black Sea.

ALISON, ARTHUR JAMES.
Rugby. B.A. (Oxford) 1893. Student of Law, 1893-5; LL.B. 1896. Advocate. Army Recruiting Staff, Lieut. April 1917. Ministry of National Service.

ALISON, WILLIAM INGLIS.
Kirkcaldy High School. Student of Arts and Law, 1912-14. 4th and 15th Royal Scots, Private Sept. 1914. 12th Scottish Rifles, Lieut. Bombing Instructor, France.

ALLAN, ANDREW PURVIS.
Kirkcaldy High School. Student of Science, 1910-12 and 1918-19. 2/1st Fife and Forfar Yeomanry, Sergeant Sept. 1914. R.F.A. (S.R.), 2nd Lieut. April 1917. Wounded July 1917. Lieut. Oct. 1918.

ALLAN, CHARLES FALCONER.
George Heriot's School. M.A. 1904. 7th Royal Scots, Private Dec. 1914; 2nd Lieut. Oct. 1915; Lieut. July 1917.

ALLAN, DAVID ANDREW.
Royal High School; First XV. and XI. University O.T.C. Infantry, May to Oct. 1917, Cadet. Royal Air Force (Naval), Cadet Oct. 1917; 2nd Lieut. Sept. 1918; Flight Lieut. Nov. 1918. H.M.S. *Furious*, Fleet Observer and Pilot.

ALLAN, DOUGLAS ALEXANDER.
George Watson's College. Student of Science, 1915-16 and 1919. H.M. Factory, Craigleith; Nitration Chemist, 1916-18. R.F.A., Signaller 1918-19.

ALLAN, ERNEST.
George Heriot's School; First XI. M.B., Ch.B. 1913. R.A.M.C., Lieut. April 1915; Captain April 1916. Dundee War Hospital, March 1919.

ALLAN, FRANCIS HALLIDAY.
George Watson's College. O.T.C. 1908-12, Cadet Sergeant. Student of Science, 1912-14 and 1919. O.T.C. Artillery, Oct. 1912 to Nov. 1914, Cadet. 5th Seaforth Highlanders, 2nd Lieut. Nov. 1914; Lieut. July 1915; Captain June 1916. Transferred R.E. (T.) Feb. 1918. France 1915-19; Festubert 1915, Beaumont Hamel 1916, Arras 1917, Ypres 1918.

ALLAN, FRANCIS JOHN.
Dumfries Academy and Royal Naval School, New Cross; First XV. Cadet Corps, 2nd Officer. M.B., C.M. 1880; M.D. 1883; D.P.H. (Camb.) 1887. R.A.M.C. (T.), Captain Sept. 1914. Acting Sanitary Supervisor.

Record of War Service

ALLAN, GEORGE GRANT.
  George Watson's College; First XV. and XI. O.T.C. 1908-11, Cadet. Student of Medicine, 1912-17; M.B., Ch.B. 1917. 4th Royal Scots, 1911; Lieut. and Machine-Gun Officer, 1914. R.A.M.C., Captain 1918. Egypt and Palestine.

ALLAN, GEORGE STEWART.
  Student of Science, 1913-15. O.T.C. Infantry, Feb. to April 1915, Cadet. 2nd Border Regiment, 2nd Lieut. Machine-Gun Corps, Lieut. Feb. 1916.

ALLAN, HARRY.
  George Heriot's School. Student of Medicine, 1918. 10th Seaforth Highlanders, Private June 1916. 2nd Cameron Highlanders, Jan. 1917. 2nd Northamptonshire Regiment, 2nd Lieut. Jan. 1918. Salonika Jan. to July 1917. France April 1918 to Jan. 1919.

ALLAN, JAMES.
  Student of Arts, 1913-15 and 1918-19. R.A.M.C. (T.), Private June 1915; Sergeant Jan. 1916. 3rd Lowland Field Ambulance, attached 56th Field Ambulance. Gassed March 1918.

ALLAN, JOHN EDWIN.
  M.B., Ch.B. 1911. O.T.C. Artillery, June 1909 to Feb. 1912, Cadet. R.A.M.C., Lieut. Oct. 1914; Captain April 1915. 18th Field Ambulance, France.

ALLAN, JOHN FINLAY.
  George Watson's College. M.B., Ch.B. 1901. R.A.M.C., Lieut. Sept. 1917; Captain Sept. 1918.

ALLAN, JOHN GIBSON.
  B.Sc. 1910. Student of Medicine, 1913-17; M.B., Ch.B. 1917. Anatomy Staff, 1916-17. R.A.M.C., Lieut. Aug 1917; Captain Aug. 1918. France.

ALLAN, LINDSAY GORDON.
  Scotch College, West Australia. Student of Medicine, 1912-17; M.B., Ch.B. 1917. Athletics. O.T.C. Infantry, Oct. 1914 to Feb. 1915, Cadet. R.N.V.R., Surgeon-Probationer, March to Nov. 1915. R.A.M.C., Lieut. Aug. 1917 to Dec. 1918.

ALLAN, PETER.
  George Heriot's School. M.B., Ch.B. 1910; M.D. 1920; D.P.H. No. 4 Coy. Q.R.V.B. Royal Scots, 1906-9, Private. R.A.M.C., Lieut. 1915; Captain Feb. 1918.

ALLAN, ROBERT MARSHALL.
  M.B., Ch.B. (Hons.) 1910; M.D. 1914. R.A.M.C., Captain. M.C.

ALLAN, WILLIAM.
  Miller Institution, Thurso. Student of Arts, 1914-16; M.A. 1920. R.G.A., Gunner Oct. 1916; Signaller Feb. 1917; 2nd Lieut. Dec. 1917 to May 1919.

Record of War Service

ALLAN, WILLIAM NIMMO.
    George Watson's College. O.T.C. 1911-14, Cadet Sergeant. Student of Science, 1918-19. O.T.C. Engineers, Sept. 1914, Cadet. 9th Gordon Highlanders (Pioneers), 2nd Lieut. Sept. 1914; Lieut. Oct. 1916; Captain Dec. 1917 to Jan. 1919. M.C. Aug. 1917.

ALLARDICE, FRANK.
    Forfar Academy. Student of Medicine, 1918. R.A.M.C., Private June 1917.

ALLEN, CHARLES HENRY.
    M.B., Ch.B. 1900; F.R.C.S. R.A.M.C. (T.) 1908; Captain 1912. Military Hospital, Alexandria, Egypt. Palestine. Dispatches 1917. Order of the Nile (4th Class), 1918. O.B.E. 1919.

ALLEN, RUBEN WATT.
    M.A. 1906. R.F.A., Captain; Major.

ALLEN, SAMUEL.
    Leith Academy. Student of Science, 1913-15 and 1919; B.Sc. 1920. R.E. (Special Brigade), Corporal July 1915. R.G.A., 91st Siege Battery, 2nd Lieut. May 1917; Lieut. Nov. 1918. France. Wounded June 1918.

ALLISON, A. J. T.
    George Watson's College. Student of Medicine, 1913-14. R.A.M.C., Private Sept. 1914; Corporal Dec. 1914. Attached A.S.C.; 2nd Indian Cavalry Division and H.Q. 5th Cavalry Division. France Nov. 1914 to May 1918.

ALLISON, JAMES.
    Lanark Grammar School. M.B., Ch.B. 1898. R.A.M.C., Lieut. Dec. 1914; Captain Dec. 1915.

ALLISON, JOHN.
    Royal High School. M.B., C.M. 1886; M.D. 1895; F.R.C.S. (Edin.); D.P.H. (London). Medical Staff Corps, 1898; R.A.M.C. (T.), Major 1909; Lieut.-Col. Sept. 1918. Attached North Hants. Yeomanry (T.), 8th Division, 1914-15. S.M.O. Kettering 1915-16. President, Recruiting Medical Board 1917-18 and S.M.O. Prisoners of War Camp, Canterbury, 1918-19.

ALLISON, JOHN.
    Merchiston Castle. O.T.C. 1908-11. Student of Medicine, 1911-17; M.B., Ch.B. 1917. O.T.C. Medical, Jan. 1915 to April 1917, Cadet Sergeant. R.A.M.C. (S.R.), Lieut. May 1917; Captain May 1918. India.

ALLISON, ROBERT DUNLOP REID.
    Irvine Academy. M.B., C.M. 1889; M.D. 1892. R.A.M.C., Lieut. Aug. 1916. Chairman of Recruiting Medical Board; Ministry of Pensions and Area D.C.M.S.

Record of War Service

ALLISON, THOMAS BISSET.
George Watson's College and Glenalmond. Cadet Corps 1896-8. Student of Law. Chartered Accountant, 1906. Surrey Yeomanry (T.), Private Sept. 1914. 9th Royal Highlanders (Black Watch), 2nd Lieut. Jan. 1916; Lieut. 1917. France; Ypres, Somme, and Arras. M.C.

ALLSOP, CHRISTOPHER EDWARD.
Carlisle Grammar School. Student of Music. No. 4 Coy. Q.R.V.B. Royal Scots, Private. Dollar Academy O.T.C., 2nd Lieut. Dec. 1914.

ALLSOPP, ROBERT JAMES.
George Heriot's School. M.B., Ch.B. 1909. No. 4 Coy. Q.R.V.B. Royal Scots, 1899-1904, Private. R.A.M.C., Lieut. May 1915; Captain May 1916. Med. Exp. Force.

ALMOND, CHARLES STANLEY.
Clifton College. Cadet Corps 1906-8. Student of Science, 1918. 5th West Yorkshire Regiment, 2nd Lieut. Oct. 1914; Lieut. April 1915. Wounded. Invalided out Dec. 1918.

ALPORT, ARTHUR CECIL.
South African College, Cape Town. M.B., Ch.B. 1905; M.D. 1919. S.A.M.C., Captain March 1914. R.A.M.C., Captain Dec. 1915; Major 1916. Rebellion in Transvaal and Free State, 1914. German South-West Campaign, 1915. Salonika Oct. 1916. France Aug. 1919.

ALSTON, JAMES MAXWELL.
George Watson's College. O.T.C. 1915-17. Student of Medicine, 1918-19. O.T.C. Infantry, Jan. to June 1918, Cadet Corporal. Royal Air Force, June 1918, Flight Cadet Oct. 1918 to Feb. 1919.

ALVASH, W.
R.F.A., 2nd Lieut.

AMES, FRANCIS W.
English High School, Boston. Student of Medicine, 1916. 2nd Battn. Scots Guards, Private March 1917. M.M. Sept. 1917.

AMES, WILLIAM MELVILLE.
High School, Dundee. Student of Arts and Science, 1913-15 and 1918-20; M.A. 1917; B.Sc. 1920. O.T.C. Infantry, April to Sept. 1915, Cadet. 4th Royal Highlanders (Black Watch), 2nd Lieut. Sept. 1915; Lieut. June 1917 to Dec. 1918. Attached 6th South Staffordshire Regiment. Wounded June 1917.

AMESS, JOHN.
Perth Academy. M.A. 1907. Machine-Gun Corps, 40th Coy., Private July 1917. Military Accounts Dept., Poona, India, Dec. 1918 to April 1919.

ANAND, HIRASINGH.
M.B., Ch.B. 1913. Indian Medical Service, Lieut.

Record of War Service

ANDERSON, ABNER GALLIE.
: George Watson's College. Student of Medicine, 1911-16; M.B., Ch.B. 1916. O.T.C. Medical, Oct. 1912 to Sept. 1914, and Nov. 1915 to Oct. 1916, Cadet Staff Sergeant. R.A.M.C. (T.), Field Ambulance, Scottish Horse, Private 1914. R.A.M.C. (S.R.), Lieut. Oct. 1916; Captain Nov. 1917; Major. Mesopotamia 1916-20. Dispatches.

ANDERSON, ALEXANDER.
: Olivers Mount School, Scarborough. Student of Science, 1897-8. A.R.S.M. No. 4 Coy. Q.R.V.B. Royal Scots, 1897-1900, Private. R.G.A., 2nd Lieut. Dec. 1914; Lieut. Dec. 1915; Captain Feb. 1918. South African Campaign, 1900-1. 51st Siege Battery Aug. 1915 (Sound Ranging); attached R.E. Aug. 1916. 475th Siege Battery Sept. 1917; attached R.N. Jan. 1918 to June 1919. O.B.E. (Military) June 1919.

ANDERSON, ALEXANDER JAMES.
: Royal High School. M.B., C.M. 1891; M.D. 1918. R.A.M.C., Captain Jan. 1916. France. Invalided home July 1917.

ANDERSON, ALFORD WILLIAM.
: Madras College, St Andrews. M.B., C.M. 1891; M.D. 1909. Medical Psychology Certificate, Great Britain and Ireland, 1892. R.A.M.C. (T.), 1894, Major; Lieut.-Col. March 1896. 2/1st Lowland Field Ambulance 1915. T.D. 1917.

ANDERSON, ANDREW BLAIR.
: Repton. O.T.C. 1912-14. University O.T.C. Infantry, May to Nov. 1917, Cadet. A.S.C., Motor Transport, Private Nov. 1917; Corporal Feb. 1918. Italy.

ANDERSON, ANDREW MELVILLE.
: Daniel Stewart's College. M.A. 1897. Schoolmaster's Diploma. Minister, Church of Scotland. Nyasaland Volunteer Reserve, Private Aug. 1914.

ANDERSON, CHARLES.
: Edinburgh Academy; First XV. and XI. Student of Law, 1905-10. Writer to the Signet, 1910. 1st Lovat Scouts, Private Sept. 1914; Corporal Oct. 1914; 15th Royal Scots, 2nd Lieut. Jan. 1915; Lieut. March 1915; Captain Dec. 1916. Major Nov. 1917. France Jan. 1916 to Feb. 1919. M.C. Dec. 1916; D.S.O. April 1918. Dispatches Nov. 1918.

ANDERSON, CHARLES BEVAN CAREW.
: Medical Student, 1911-16; M.B., Ch.B. 1916. O.T.C. Medical, Oct. 1911 to Sept. 1914, Cadet Corporal. R.A.M.C. (S.R.), Lieut. July 1916; Captain July 1917.

ANDERSON, CHARLES HENRY WILLIAM GATACRE.
: George Heriot's School. O.T.C. 1913-14, Cadet. Student of Science, 1919. O.T.C. Artillery, Sept. 1917 to Aug. 1918, Cadet Corporal; Acting B.Q.M.S. Officer Cadet Sept. 1918. R.G.A., 2nd Lieut. April 1919.

Record of War Service

ANDERSON, CHARLES IAN.
Edinburgh Academy. Student of Arts, 1913-15 and 1919; M.A. 1919. O.T.C. Artillery, Jan. to Sept. 1916, Cadet; Officer Cadet Sept. 1916. R.G.A. (T.), North Scottish, 2nd Lieut. Dec. 1916; Lieut. June 1918. 498th Siege Battery, France, March 1918 to Jan. 1919.

ANDERSON, DAVID.
George Heriot's School. Student of Law, 1913. Lothians and Border Horse. Mobilised Aug. 1914. Scottish Horse, attached King's Liverpool Regiment, 2nd Lieut. July 1915; Lieut. July 1917. Royal Air Force. Salonika.

ANDERSON, DAVID CHALMERS.
Royal High School; First XV. and XI. Student of Arts, 1918. 3rd Royal Highlanders (Black Watch), Private June 1916; L/Corporal May 1917; Corporal Jan. 1918. Attached 3rd and 51st Gordon Highlanders.

ANDERSON, DAVID IRVING.
M.B., Ch.B. 1904. R.A.M.C., Captain 1915; Major. Salonika, two years. Military Hospital, Liverpool, 1918. Dispatches June 1918 and 1919. O.B.E. (Military) Jan. 1919.

ANDERSON, DAVID TEMPLETON.
Bathgate Academy. Student of Medicine, 1915 and 1919. O.T.C. Medical, Nov. 1915 to March 1916, Cadet. 11th Royal Highlanders (Black Watch), Private March 1916; L/Corporal Oct. 1916; Officer Cadet. 16th Royal Scots, 2nd Lieut. May 1917; Lieut. Nov. 1918 to April 1919. France, July 1917 to April 1918. Wounded, Bac St Maur, April 1918.

ANDERSON, DONALD KENNEDY.
Milne's Institution, Fochabers. M.A. 1912. 4th Royal Scots, Sergeant. Mobilised Aug. 1914. 11th South Lancashire Regiment (Pioneers), 2nd Lieut. France.

ANDERSON, DUGALD NAIRNE.
M.B., C.M. 1896. Indian Medical Service, Captain; Major (retired).

ANDERSON, DUNCAN.
M'Laren High School, Callander. Student of Law, 1913-14. Chartered Accountant, 1915. O.T.C. Artillery, Nov. 1915 to April 1916, Cadet. R.F.A., 3/4th Lowland Brigade, Gunner 1915; 2nd Lieut. March 1917; Lieut. Sept. 1918; Adjutant April 1919. Egypt, Palestine, and Syria.

ANDERSON, ERIC WILLIAM VERDEN.
Dunchurch Hall, Rugby, and Leeds University. University O.T.C. Artillery, Aug. 1917 to April 1918, Cadet. R.F.A., Officer Cadet April 1918.

ANDERSON, ERNEST MASSON.
B.Sc. 1897; M.A. 1898. Highland Light Infantry, Private March 1916. R.E., Sapper.

Record of War Service

ANDERSON, EWING GLEN.
George Watson's College. O.T.C. 1914-16. Student of Medicine, 1916-17 and 1918-19. O.T.C. Artillery, April to Nov. 1917, Cadet. R.F.A., Officer Cadet Nov. 1917; 2nd Lieut. May 1918.

ANDERSON, FREDERICK.
Edinburgh Collegiate School. M.B., C.M. 1897; D.P.H. R.A.M.C., Lieut. Oct. 1918; Sanitary Officer, Italy.

ANDERSON, FREDERICK ALEXANDER.
Stranraer High School. Student of Medicine, 1910-15. M.B., Ch.B. 1915. R.A.M.C., Lieut. Oct. 1915; Captain Oct. 1916. M.C. Sept. 1916.

ANDERSON, GEORGE CRANSTON.
Dundee High School; Athletics. M.B., Ch.B. 1904; M.D. 1909. Anglo-French Red Cross, 1915. R.A.M.C., Lieut. June 1917; Captain June 1918. Egyptian Expeditionary Force, 69th General Hospital, Nov. 1917 to March 1919.

ANDERSON, GUSTAVE ALEXANDER MELVILLE.
M.B., Ch.B. 1913. Royal Navy. H.M.S. *Pioneer*, Surgeon-Lieut. April 1914. H.M.A.S. *Encounter* and *Australia*, Oct. 1916 to March 1917. Australia and German East Africa.

ANDERSON, HAMISH MORTON.
M.B., Ch.B. 1908. R.A.M.C., Lieut. Aug. 1914; Captain Aug. 1915; Acting Major. France and Belgium, Aug. 1914 to Feb. 1919. No. 3 General Hospital. 61st Casualty Clearing Station and 2nd Canadian Casualty Clearing Station, France.

ANDERSON, HENRY VANS.
Edinburgh Academy; First XI. O.T.C. 1911-14. Student of Medicine, 1915-16. O.T.C. Artillery, Oct. 1916 to July 1917, Cadet; Officer Cadet July 1917. R.G.A., 141st Heavy Battery, 2nd Lieut. Jan. 1918. France.

ANDERSON, HOPE PITCAIRN.
George Heriot's School. Student of Arts and Medicine, 1913-16 and 1918-19. M.A. 1919. O.T.C. Artillery, Oct. 1914 to Jan. 1916, Cadet. R.G.A., 2nd Lieut. Jan. 1916; Lieut. July 1917. Attached Royal Air Force. France.

ANDERSON, IAN.
George Watson's College. Student of Arts and Law, 1905-10. Royal Scots; Major.

ANDERSON, IAN ROSS.
George Heriot's School; First XV. O.T.C. 1913-18, Cadet C.S.M. Student of Medicine, 1918. Officer Cadet Sept. 1918. King's Royal Rifles, 2nd Lieut. March 1919.

Record of War Service

ANDERSON, JAMES.
M.A. (Hons. Classics) 1901. 14th and 19th Highland Light Infantry, Private Feb. 1916; 2nd Lieut. France 1916.

ANDERSON, JAMES.
Royal High School. M.A. 1887; M.B., C.M. 1891. B. Hy. (Durham) 1898. R.A.M.C. (T.), attached Northern Cyclist Battn., Lieut. Jan. 1914; Captain April 1915; Acting Major Dec. 1918. France, April 1915 to April 1919; Field Ambulance and No. 8 Stationary Hospital.

ANDERSON, JAMES C.
George Heriot's School. Student of Law, 1912-14. R.G.A., 70th and 337th Siege Batteries, March 1915; 2nd Lieut. Jan. 1917; Lieut. July 1918. Royal Air Force, 10th Squadron (Observer), Dec. 1917 to March 1919. France.

ANDERSON, JAMES MACMILLAN.
Edinburgh Academy; First XI. O.T.C. 1908-10. Student of Medicine, 1910-15; M.B., Ch.B. (Hons.) 1915. R.A.M.C., Lieut. Sept. 1915; Captain Sept. 1916. M.O., 18th Royal Fusiliers; 1/4th West Riding Regiment and Detention Barracks, Woking.

ANDERSON, JAMES PARKER.
M.A. 1908. 4th Seaforth Highlanders, 2nd Lieut.

ANDERSON, JAMES ROBERTSON.
Milne's Institution, Fochabers. Student of Arts and Medicine; M.B., Ch.B. 1898. No. 4 Coy. Q.R.V.B., Royal Scots, Private. R.A.M.C. (T.), Lieut. Oct. 1916; Captain Oct. 1917; Acting Major Nov. 1918. Salonika, Malta, and O.C. 58th Scottish General Hospital, France. La Médaille d'Honneur en Argent, 1918.

ANDERSON, JOHN.
M.B., Ch.B. 1899. Indian Medical Service, Captain; Major Jan. 1916. C.I.E.

ANDERSON, JOHN ALLAN.
George Watson's College. M.B., Ch.B. 1903; D.T.M. 1909; D.P.H. 1914. Vol. Medical Staff Corps, 1899-1904, Q.M.S. R.A.M.C., Lieut. July 1905; Captain Jan. 1909; Major Oct. 1915; Acting Lieut.-Col. Jan. 1918; Brevet Lieut.-Col. Jan. 1919. France Aug. to Nov. 1914; Salonika June 1917 to April 1919. Dispatches Jan. and Aug. 1917 and Jan. 1919.

ANDERSON, JOHN NORRIE.
Nicolson Institute, Stornoway. M.A. 1912. O.T.C. Artillery, Oct. 1908 to April 1913, Cadet Bombardier. R.F.A., 2nd Lieut. Oct. 1914; Acting Captain May 1917; Major April 1918. Croix de Guerre, June 1918.

ANDERSON, JOHN WILLIAM.
M.B., C.M. 1894; M.D. N.Z. Medical Corps, Captain May 1916.

Record of War Service

ANDERSON, LEWIS.
Elgin Academy. M.B., Ch.B. 1902. R.A.M.C., Lieut. 1914; Captain Oct. 1915; Acting Major March 1918. D.A.D.M.S. 1918. Attached 10th King's Royal Rifles; 11th Border Regiment; 32nd Division and 5th Army Corps. D.S.O. July 1917; M.C. Nov. 1918; Croix de Guerre Aug. 1918. Dispatches.

ANDERSON, MALCOLM BUCHAN.
Edinburgh Academy; Athletics. Edinburgh University O.T.C. Artillery, Nov. 1915 to June 1916, Cadet; Officer Cadet June 1916. A.S.C., 2nd Lieut. Oct. 1916; Lieut. Nov. 1918. France, Salonika, and South Russia.

ANDERSON, MARK LOUDEN.
Alva Academy. Student of Science, 1912-14 and 1918-19; B.Sc. 1919. 7th Argyll and Sutherland Highlanders, Private Aug. 1914. 11th Royal Highlanders (Black Watch), 2nd Lieut. July 1915. Machine-Gun Corps, 1916; Lieut. Feb. 1917. M.C. Dec. 1918.

ANDERSON, NOEL MAURICE.
Student of Medicine, 1913-15. O.T.C. Infantry, Oct. to Nov. 1914, Cadet. King's Own Yorkshire Light Infantry, 2nd Lieut. Leicestershire Regiment, Lieut. July 1917. India.

ANDERSON, NORMAN GEORGE WHYTE.
Newport School. Student of Arts, 1918. R.N.V.R., attached Royal Naval Division, Signalman Sept. 1914 to Feb. 1919.

ANDERSON, ROBERT CHARLES.
Diocesan School, Naini Tal, India. First XI. Cadet Corps, 1895-9, Corporal. B.Sc. 1906. Junior Assistant, Chemistry. R.E. (Special Brigade), March 1916; L/Corporal. Meteorological Section, 5th Army Corps, France.

ANDERSON, ROBERT JOHN.
George Heriot's School; First XV. and XI. O.T.C. 1912-16, C.S.M. Student of Science, 1918-19. O.T.C. Infantry, Dec. 1916 to May 1917, Cadet; Officer Cadet May 1917. 1st King's Royal Rifle Corps, 2nd Lieut. Aug. 1917. Wounded at Cambrai Oct. 1918. M.C. Aug. 1918.

ANDERSON, ROBERT PRINGLE.
Edinburgh Institution. B.Sc. 1911; M.B., Ch.B. 1913. R.A.M.C. (T.), Lieut. March 1915; Captain Nov. 1915; Acting Major and D.A.D.M.S., Feb. 1919. M.C. June 1918.

ANDERSON, ROBERT YUILL.
George Watson's College. M.B., C.M. 1894. R.A.M.C. (T.), mobilised Aug. 1914 to Jan. 1919; Temporary Major Dec. 1914; Major March 1916. 305th and 312th Field Ambulances; 216th and 192nd Brigades. Mentions Jan. and Sept. 1917.

Record of War Service

ANDERSON, RUPERT GEORGE.
   Loretto. O.T.C. 1914-17. Student of Medicine, 1918-19. O.T.C. Infantry, Jan. to Sept. 1918, Cadet; Officer Cadet Sept. 1918.

ANDERSON, THOMAS.
   Student of Law, 1913-15 and 1917-18. 9th Royal Scots, Private Oct. 1915.

ANDERSON, THOMAS.
   Leven School. University O.T.C. Infantry, 1917-18, Cadet; Officer Cadet, July 1918. 7th Royal Highlanders (Black Watch), 2nd Lieut. March 1919.

ANDERSON, THOMAS.
   Student of Arts, 1912-15; M.A. 1915. 15th Argyll and Sutherland Highlanders, Private.

ANDERSON, THOMAS JAMES.
   George Heriot's School. B.Sc. 1905. East African Veterinary Corps, Captain. Entomologist to the Forces. East African Campaign, 1915-17.

ANDERSON, THOMAS MACMILLAN.
   Edinburgh Academy; First XV. and XI. M.B., Ch.B. 1912; M.D. 1914. R.A.M.C., Lieut. Oct. 1915; Captain Oct. 1916. War Hospital, Warrington, 1915; Embarkation Medical Officer, Havre, July 1917-19.

ANDERSON, WILLIAM.
   Tain Royal Academy. Student of Medicine, 1916. O.T.C. Artillery, Oct. 1916 to May 1917, Cadet. R.G.A., Officer Cadet May 1917; 2nd Lieut. Sept. 1917.

ANDERSON, WILLIAM.
   M.A. 1912. Chaplain. Mauritius.

ANDERSON, WILLIAM.
   Kingussie School. Student of Arts and Medicine, 1910-15 and 1918-19; M.A. 1915. O.T.C. Infantry, May 1911 to Oct. 1914, Cadet. 6th Royal Scots, Private Oct. 1914. 7th Cameron Highlanders, 2nd Lieut. Feb. 1915; Lieut. March 1917. Attached Royal Air Force. France 1914. Wounded at Bois Grenier Dec. 1914, and at Hulluch Oct. 1915. Prisoner of War, Germany, March 1917 to Jan. 1919. M.C. Oct. 1915.

ANDERSON, WILLIAM.
   George Watson's College. M.B., Ch.B. 1905. R.A.M.C., Lieut. April 1916. Invalided out April 1917.

ANDERSON, WILLIAM LOWE. (See p. 747.)

ANDREW, ALEXANDER KEITH.
   Royal High School. Edinburgh University O.T.C. Artillery, Aug. 1914 to Jan. 1916, Cadet Sergeant. R.F.A. (S.R.), 2nd Lieut. Feb. 1916; Lieut. July 1917. France and Italy. Wounded Sept. 1916 and July 1917. Dispatches Dec. 1917. M.C. June 1918.

Record of War Service

ANDREW, ALFRED HERBERT TRESHAM.
   Bedford and St Edward's; First XV. and XI. M.B., Ch.B. 1910. No. 4 Coy. Q.R.V.B. Royal Scots, Private 1903-7. R.A.M.C. (T.), Lieut. Oct. 1914; Captain April 1915. 88th Field Ambulance, 29th Division, Med. Exp. Force.

ANDREW, ROBERT.
   Linlithgow Academy. Student of Medicine, 1908-13 and 1916-17. M.B., Ch.B. 1917. O.T.C. Infantry, 1909-13, Cadet L/Corporal. 9th Royal Highlanders (Black Watch), 2nd Lieut. Sept. 1914; Lieut. June 1915; R.A.M.C., Lieut. Aug. 1917; Captain Aug. 1918. France 1915. East Africa 1917-19. Wounded at Loos Sept. 1915.

ANDREW, THOMAS FARQUHARSON.
   Royal High School; First XV. and XI. Student of Medicine, 1913-14 and 1917-19. Lothians and Border Horse, Private Sept. 1914. 11th and 1/4th Royal Highlanders (Black Watch), 2nd Lieut. May 1915; Lieut. Nov. 1916. France Nov. 1915 to Nov. 1917. M.C. July 1916 and Bar Aug. 1917.

ANDREWS, H. R.
   Student of Law, 1894-5. Hants. Carbineers, Trooper. South African Campaign, 1899-1901. 14th West Yorkshire Regiment, Lieut. 1914.

ANDREWS, JAMES BROWN.
   Dollar Academy. Cadet Corps 1902-8, Corporal. Student of Law, 1911-12. 4th Royal Scots, Private Aug. 1914; 2nd Lieut. Feb. 1915; Lieut. Nov. 1916; Acting Captain Oct. 1917. R.A.S.C. (Special Duty), Egyptian Camel Transport Corps, March 1917. Egypt July 1915 to July 1919.

ANDREWS, JOHN ALBAN.
   M.B., Ch.B. 1912; M.R.C.S. and L.R.C.P. (London) 1912. Anatomy Staff, 1914. R.A.M.C., Captain; Major. M.C.

ANDREWS, WILLIAM J.
   Student of Arts, 1912-14. 4th Royal Scots (T.), Private.

ANGUS, A. W.
   Student of Law, 1909-11. Chartered Accountant, 1913. Scottish Rugby International. 9th Royal Scots, Private 1914; 10th Gordon Highlanders; King's Own Scottish Borderers, Captain; Lieut.-Col. D.S.O. Three times mentioned in Dispatches.

ANGUS, THOMAS CURR.
   Royal High School; First XV. and XI. Student of Arts, 1918-19. O.T.C. Infantry, Jan. to May 1915, Cadet. Royal Scots Fusiliers, 2nd Lieut. May 1915. R.E. (Signals), Nov. 1915 to April 1919; Lieut. July 1917. East Africa 1916. Dispatches Oct. 1917.

Record of War Service

ANGUS, WALTER CHALMERS SMITH.
Student of Arts and Medicine, 1911-15. M.A. 1914. 2/4th Border Regiment (S.R.), 2nd Lieut.; Lieut. June 1916; Captain. India 1915. Mesopotamia Aug. 1916 to March 1919.

ANNAN, JOHN LAING.
M.B., Ch.B. 1907; M.D. 1916. R.A.M.C., Lieut. Jan. 1915. Rejoined May 1918; Captain. Bacteriologist and Pathologist. France 1915, 1916, and 1919.

ANTHONY, JOHN.
Boroughmuir School. Student of Science, 1910-15. O.T.C. Infantry, 1915, Cadet. 5th Royal Welsh Fusiliers, 2nd Lieut. Oct. 1915; Lieut. July 1917; Acting Captain Aug. 1917. Attached 7th Royal Warwicks. Egypt. M.C. Oct. 1917.

ANTHONY, RICHARD WILLIAM.
M.B., C.M. 1897; F.R.C.S. (Edin.) 1909. Indian Medical Service, Major; Lieut.-Col. Jan. 1918.

APEDAILE, J. LEONARD.
Student of Law, 1904-6. Chartered Accountant, 1909. Montreal Heavy Artillery, Lieut.

APPLEYARD, CECIL STEELE.
Student of Medicine, 1914-16 and 1918-19. O.T.C. Infantry 1915, and Medical April 1918-19, Cadet. 6th Cameron Highlanders, Private Jan. 1916; L/Corporal March 1916; Corporal April 1917. France. Wounded July 1917.

APTHOMAS, GARTH.
M.B., Ch.B. 1912. Resident M.O., Nellhane Military Hospital, Manchester, 1916. R.A.M.C., Lieut. June 1918.

APTHORP, HUGH LLEWELLYN.
Haileybury. M.B., C.M. 1897; M.D. 1900. R.A.M.C., Lieut. Dec. 1914; Captain Dec. 1915.

ARBUCKLE, HENRY ERNEST.
High School, Durban. M.B., Ch.B. 1900; M.D. 1908; F.R.C.S. (Edin.); D.P.H. (Camb.). West African Medical Service. M.O., 3rd Scottish General Hospital, Glasgow, May to July 1916. Special List, Captain May 1917. Nyasaland Field Force. Dispatches Jan. 1919.

ARCHIBALD, DAVID.
Forfar Academy. Student of Science, 1910-12. R.F.A., Gunner Dec. 1915. R.G.A., 2nd Lieut. June 1918.

ARCHIBALD, JAMES.
North Canongate. M.A. 1889. Schoolmaster. 1st Vol. Battn. Royal Scots, Private Nov. 1914.

Record of War Service

ARCHIBALD, ROBERT.
Dollar Institution. M.A. (Glasg.). LL.B. 1907. R.G.A., Gunner Jan. 1917; Acting Bombardier 1918.

ARCHIBALD, ROBERT GEORGE.
Dollar Academy; First XV. and XI. M.B., Ch.B. 1902; M.D. 1919. First XV. R.A.M.C., Jan. 1906, Captain 1909; Major 1919. Attached Egyptian Army. D.S.O. 1918. Dispatches, Katfia 1908; Dardanelles 1915; Darfur 1916; Sudan 1919.

ARGO, ARCHIBALD.
Aberdeen Grammar School. Student of Law, 1919. O.T.C. Artillery, Jan. to May 1917, Cadet. R.F.A. (S.R.), Officer Cadet July 1917; 2nd Lieut. Feb. 1918 to March 1919. France April 1918. Invalided home Aug. 1918.

ARKWRIGHT, EUSTACE.
Bradfield. M.B., C.M. 1896. Royal Navy, Surgeon Jan. 1897; Staff Surgeon 1905; Fleet Surgeon 1913; Surgeon-Commander 1919.

ARMISTEAD, WILLIAM HENRY.
Ramsey Grammar School, Isle of Man. M.B., Ch.B. 1913. O.T.C. Artillery, 1905 to June 1910, Cadet Sergeant. R.A.M.C. (T.), Lieut. Oct. 1914; Captain April 1915.

ARMOUR, THEODORE ROBERT WILLIAM.
George Watson's College. M.B., Ch.B. (Hons.) 1897; F.R.C.S. (Edin.) 1910. R.A.M.C. (T.), Captain July 1908; Acting Major March 1918. Attached 1st Western Hospital.

ARMSTRONG, EDMOND A.
Morrison's Academy, Crieff. O.T.C. 1915-16, Cadet. Student of Arts, 1916-17 and 1919. O.T.C. Artillery, Oct. 1916 to Nov. 1917, Cadet; Officer Cadet Oct. 1917. R.F.A., B/98th Brigade, 2nd Lieut. May 1918. Salonika.

ARMSTRONG, FERGUS.
Abergele School. M.B., Ch.B. 1909; M.D. and F.R.C.S. (Edin.) 1913. O.T.C. Medical, April 1908-10, Cadet Corporal. R.A.M.C., Lieut. Sept. 1914; Captain March 1915. Welsh War Hospital. Serbian Army, Major 1915. Lady Paget's and Queen of Roumania's Hospitals, 1916-18. Taken prisoner of war at Skoplje Oct. 1915. Officer of Order of Star of Roumania, July 1917.

ARMSTRONG, JOHN SCAIFE.
Student of Medicine, 1910-15; M.B., Ch.B. 1915. O.T.C. Medical, Oct. 1914 to Aug. 1915, Cadet. R.A.M.C. (S.R.), Lieut. Aug. 1915; Captain Feb. 1916.

ARMSTRONG, LAURENCE ROBERT.
George Watson's College. B.Sc. 1913. O.T.C. Engineers, Jan. 1910 to July 1913, Cadet. R.E., 2nd Lieut.; Lieut. July 1915.

Record of War Service

ARNOLD, JOHN IRWIN.
L.R.C.P. & S. (Edin.); L.R.F.P.S. (Glasg.) 1912. R.A.M.C., Lieut.; Captain June 1916. Mediterranean Expeditionary Force.

ARNOLD-SIMMERS, WILLIAM.
Dundee High School; Athletics. M.A. (St Andrews) 1887. 1st Fife Vol. Artillery. M.B., C.M. 1890. Canadian Mounted Rifles, Cavalry Division, Trooper, 1914-16. Royal Navy Transports, Surgeon 1916 to 1919.

ARNOTT, DAVID.
Dunfermline High School. Student of Medicine, 1917-19. O.T.C. Artillery, Aug. 1917 to June 1918, Cadet. R.G.A., Officer Cadet; 2nd Lieut. Feb. 1919.

ARNOTT, ROBERT JAMES.
Dumfries Academy. M.A. 1904. Secretary, S.R.C. 1903-4. Canadian War Records Office, London, Private Feb. 1917.

ARNOTT, STANLEY.
Durham School; First XV. M.B., Ch.B. 1913. First XV. O.T.C. Artillery, Jan. 1911 to March 1914, Cadet. R.A.M.C., Captain Aug. 1914. 1st Cavalry Field Ambulance, France. 31st General Hospital, Egypt. E.A.M.C., Sudan, Bimbashi, 1917.

ARTHUR, JAMES.
M.B., Ch.B. 1902; M.D. 1911. University Battery, E.C.A.V., 1898-1903, B.Q.S.M. R.A.M.C., May 1912; Captain April 1915; Major Nov. 1915. Military Hospital, Kingston-on-Thames. 2/2nd East Anglian Field Ambulance, 1915.

ARTHUR, JOHN FELSTED STUART.
Student of Law, 1914-15. Chartered Accountant, 1918. R.F.A., 2nd Lieut.; Lieut. June 1916.

ASH, HERBERT MINGAYE.
Student of Law, 1912-14. O.T.C. Infantry, Oct. to Nov. 1914, Cadet. A.S.C., 2nd Lieut.; Lieut. July 1917.

ASH, ROBERT VACY CLIFFORD.
Pietermaritzburg College, Natal. First XI.; Cricket and Football. M.B., Ch.B. 1901; D.P.H.; R.C.P.S. (Edin.) 1903. R.A.M.C. (T.), Lieut. June 1915; Captain Dec. 1915; Major Jan. 1918. Attached 2/4th Royal Highlanders (Black Watch). 60th Field Ambulance, Adjutant. France July 1917 to June 1919. M.C. Nov. 1917.

ASHKENNY, ARMLY.
Trent College, Notts, and D.C.M.S., Cheltenham. Athletics. M.B., Ch.B. 1903; B.Sc. (P.H.) 1909. University Battery, E.C.A.V., Gunner. R.A.M.C., Lieut. Jan. 1918. France.

ASHRUFF, MOHOMED.
M.B., Ch.B. 1902. Hyderabad Military Medical Department, 1903; Major March 1915. M.O., 1st Hyderabad Imperial Service, Lancers. Egypt Oct. 1914. Invalided Feb. 1916. Depot, Imperial Service Troops, June 1916. Dispatches.

Record of War Service

ASHTON, BASIL CEDRIC.
    M.B., Ch.B. 1914. Indian Medical Service, Lieut. Jan. 1917; Med. Exp. Force.

ASHWORTH, JOSIAH WALTER ROBERT.
    Boroughmuir School. Student of Law, 1915. 8th Royal Highlanders (Black Watch), Private April 1916. Invalided Jan. 1919.

ATKINSON, ALBERT ALEXANDER.
    Foyle College, Londonderry. M.B., Ch.B. 1911. Prosector, Anatomy. O.T.C. Medical, Nov. 1908-12, Cadet Corporal. R.A.M.C. (S.R.), Lieut. Aug. 1914; Captain April 1915. Royal Air Force Medical Service, Major Oct. 1918. Dispatches June 1916.

ATKINSON, CHRISTOPHER.
    M.B., Ch.B. 1914. O.T.C. Medical, Oct. 1909 to April 1913, Cadet. R.A.M.C. (S.R.), Lieut. Aug. 1914; Captain April 1915.

ATKINSON, GEORGE ARMSTRONG.
    Royal Grammar School, Newcastle. M.B., C.M. 1882; M.D. 1887. Assistant, Materia Medica, 1883-7. Royal Navy, Acting Admiralty Surgeon and Examiner of Recruits, April 1915.

ATKINSON, JOHN JAMES.
    Daniel Stewart's College. Student of Arts, 1900-3. 5th and 6th Royal Scots (T.), Lieut.; Captain Aug. 1915.

ATKINSON, MONTAGUE PARKER.
    Forest School; First XI; Football. Student of Medicine, 1918-19. Worcestershire Regiment, Lieut. July 1917; Captain Sept. 1917.

ATKINSON, SYDNEY.
    Leith Academy. Edinburgh University O.T.C. Artillery, Oct. to Dec. 1915, Cadet. R.F.A. (S.R.), 2nd Lieut. Jan. 1916; Lieut. July 1917; Acting Captain Jan. 1918.

AUDITTO, GEORGE.
    Student of Science, 1912-14. Indian Field Ambulance.

AULD, CHARLES G.
    Ackworth School, near Pontefract. First XI.; Cricket and Football. Student of Medicine, 1915-16 and 1918. R.N.V.R., H.M.S. *Cameleon*, Surgeon-Probationer, Oct. 1917.

AULD, THOMAS McNEILL.
    Edinburgh University O.T.C. Infantry, Oct. 1915, Cadet. Royal Naval Transport, Wireless Officer, June 1917 to Nov. 1918. Mediterranean, Indian Ocean, and North Atlantic.

Record of War Service

AULD, WILLIAM ARTHUR HOPKINSON.
 Boroughmuir School. M.A. 1911. R.A.M.C., Private July 1915; Sergeant March 1916 to April 1917.

AUSTIN, FREDERICK CECIL KYLE.
 Foyle College, Londonderry; First XV. M.B., Ch.B. 1913. R.A.M.C., Temp. Lieut. Aug. 1914; Temp. Captain Aug. 1915; Lieut. Jan. 1917; Captain Feb. 1918. France 1914. Persia.

AUSTIN, WILLIAM ALFRED MARTIN.
 Student of Arts, 1912-15; M.A. 1915. 13th Argyll and Sutherland Highlanders, 2nd Lieut. May 1915; Staff Lieut. March 1917. Air Ministry, 1918; Labour, 1919.

AVERILL, LESLIE CECIL LLOYD.
 Christ's College, Christchurch, N.Z. First XI. Student of Medicine, 1918. 4th N.Z. Rifle Brigade, 2nd Lieut. Dec. 1916. France. Wounded Aug. 1918. M.C. (Bapaume) Aug. 1918.

AYMER, CHARLES ALASTAIR.
 Grammar School, Aberdeen, and Aberdeen University. O.T.C. Medical, Oct. 1915 to June 1916. Edinburgh University O.T.C. Artillery, Oct. 1916 to March 1917, Cadet; Officer Cadet April 1917. R.G.A., 2nd Lieut. July 1917.

BABINGTON, HAROLD HUBERT.
 Foyle College, Londonderry. Student of Medicine; L.R.C.P. & S. (Edin.) and L.R.F.P.S. (Glasg.) 1907. University Battery, E.C.A.V., and R.A.M.C., 1902-7, Private. Royal Navy, Surgeon Nov. 1907; Surgeon Lieut.-Commander Nov. 1915.

BABINGTON, JAMES WILLIAM HERBERT.
 M.B., Ch.B. 1904; M.D. 1912. Indian Medical Service, Captain; Major March 1916.

BABINGTON, MARCUS HILL.
 Student of Medicine; L.R.C.P. & S. (Edin.) 1898. R.A.M.C., Major; Lieut.-Col. March 1915. D.S.O.

BABONAU, ALEXANDER FREDERICK.
 M.B., Ch.B. 1906. Indian Medical Service, Captain Feb. 1910.

BADENOCH, ALFRED.
 Student of Medicine, 1912-15 and 1917-19; M.B., Ch.B. 1919. O.T.C. Artillery, Oct. 1912 to June 1915, Cadet Sergeant. R.G.A. (T.) Highland (Fife), 2nd Lieut. June 1915; Acting Lieut. and Adjutant March 1917; Lieut. June 1917. France Nov. 1915; Somme, Arras, and Ypres.

Record of War Service

BADGER, CHARLES WILLIAM.
George Heriot's School; First XV. O.T.C. 1909-10, Cadet Sergeant. Student of Science and Medicine, 1912-15 and 1917-19. O.T.C. Engineers, Nov. 1914 to Aug. 1915, Cadet L/Corporal. Royal Scots and R.G.A. (S.R.), 2nd Lieut.

BADGER, ROBERT.
George Heriot's School; Athletics. O.T.C. 1909-10, Cadet Sergeant. Student of Science, 1913-14. 9th Royal Scots, Private Sept. 1914. R.E., Aug. 1915; Sergeant-Major Jan. 1916. Royal Air Force, May 1918; Flight Cadet Nov. 1918; 2nd Lieut. March 1919.

BADGEROW, GEORGE WASHINGTON.
M.B., Ch.B. (Toronto) 1901; M.D. (Toronto) 1909; F.R.C.S. (Edin.) 1910; L.R.C.P. (London); M.R.C.S. (Eng.). Canadian Army Medical Corps, Hon. Lieut.-Col. July 1917. Consulting Surgeon for Diseases of the Throat, Nose and Ear, London Area. C.M.G. Dispatches July 1918.

BADRE, AHMAD.
Khedival School, Cairo, and Engineering College, Gezah. Student of Arts and Science, 1907-14 and 1919. Royal Scots, Private June 1917; Highland Cyclist Battn. (Black Watch); R.E. (Field Survey Battn.), Sapper. France 1918.

BAËZA, JOSHUA ISADORE.
Harrison College, Barbados. M.B., Ch.B. 1913; F.R.C.S. (Edin.). West African Medical Staff, Lieut. Nov. 1914. R.A.M.C., Captain Aug. 1917. Gold Coast. Dispatches Dec. 1915.

BAHARKHANY, SYED SHAHJAHAN.
Student of Arts, 1912-16. Indian Field Ambulance, Oct. 1914. Royal Victoria Hospital, Netley.

BAHREE, DHANI RAM.
Student of Arts and Science, 1911-16; M.A. 1915; B.Sc. (Civil Engineering) M.R.San.I. Indian Contingent, Indian Expeditionary Force (Interpreter), Dec. 1914.

BAIKIE, HUGH MACANDREW.
George Watson's College. Cadet Corps. B.Sc. 1909. A.M.I.C.E. O.T.C. Artillery, Oct. 1908 to Feb. 1911, Cadet Bombardier. Engineers I.A.R.O., attached 2nd Q.V.O. Sappers and Miners, 2nd Lieut. March 1916; Lieut. March 1917. Mesopotamian Expeditionary Force, Dec. 1916 to May 1919.

BAILDON, FRANCIS JOSEPH.
Brewood Grammar School. M.B., C.M. 1881. R.A.M.C., attached 8th Lancashire Volunteer Regiment, Lieut. April 1917.

BAILLIE, THOMAS CLEGHORN.
George Heriot's School; First XV. M.A., B.Sc. 1893; D.Sc. 1899. R.G.A., Lieut. Dec. 1914; Captain May 1916. Ceylon Jan. 1915 to Feb. 1919.

Record of War Service

BAIN, ARCHIBALD WALLACE WILLIAMSON.
George Heriot's School. Student of Arts and Science; M.A. (Hons. Maths.) 1910. R.H.A., Gunner Feb. 1917; Officer Cadet May 1917. R.F.A., 2nd Lieut. Dec. 1917; Temp. Lieut. Nov. 1918. Research Department, Woolwich Arsenal, Nov. 1918. France Jan. 1918.

BAIN, DANIEL.
Gateshead School. M.A. 1910. Schoolmaster. 6th Royal Scots (T.), 1903, Sergeant; 2nd Lieut. and Lieut. 1915; Captain 1916 to July 1919. M.C. Twice mentioned in Dispatches.

BAIN, DAVID.
Sharp's Institution, Perth. B.Sc. 1906; D.Sc. 1912. Demonstrator in Chemistry. Lothians and Border Horse (T.), L/Corporal Aug. 1914; Sergeant. Released for Munition Work (Chemist) Oct. 1915.

BAIN, FRANCIS OLIVER.
Kilmarnock Academy. O.T.C. 1908-10, Cadet L/Corporal. Student of Science, Forestry, 1912-14; B.Sc. 1919. O.T.C. Artillery, Oct. 1913-14 Cadet. R.F.A., 17th Brigade, 29th Division, 2nd Lieut. Aug. 1914; Lieut. Oct. 1916. Gallipoli 1915; Egypt 1916; France 1916-17. Dispatches May 1917.

BAIN, JAMES.
Cromarty School. Student of Arts and Science, 1910-14; M.A. 1913. Schoolmaster. 4th Seaforth Highlanders (T.), 2nd Lieut. Aug. 1915; Lieut. July 1917. Machine-Gun Corps, July 1916. R.E. (Signals), July 1918. M.C. 1917. France.

BAINBRIDGE, CHARLES FREDERICK.
M.B., Ch.B. 1906; B.Sc. Royal Navy, Surgeon 1908; Surgeon Lieut.-Commander Aug. 1918. North Sea 1914 and 1916-17; Gallipoli 1915.

BAIRD, ARCHIBALD WILLIAM.
George Watson's College. O.T.C. 1910-12. Student of Science, 1913. Royal Army Veterinary Corps, Private Aug. 1914; L/Corporal Jan. 1915; Corporal March 1915; Sergeant April 1915; Staff Sergeant April 1916. Gallipoli May 1915 to Jan. 1916; Egypt and Palestine Jan. 1916 to Jan. 1919. Dispatches 1915 and 1916.

BAIRD, HARVEY.
George Watson's College. M.B., Ch.B. 1900; M.D. 1904. R.A.M.C., Lieut. June 1917; Captain June 1918. Specialist in Mental Diseases.

BAIRD, JOSEPH HAROLD.
Student of Medicine, 1909-15; M.B., Ch.B. 1914. O.T.C. Infantry, May 1909 to March 1913, Cadet Sergeant. R.A.M.C. (S.R.), Lieut. Nov. 1913; Captain July 1915; Acting Major Aug. 1918 to March 1919. Persia. Dispatches Dec. 1915.

BAIRD, RALPH GLENN.
M.A. 1910. Schoolmaster. R.E. (Scottish Signal Service), Sapper Sept. 1914 Corporal 1915; Sergeant 1916; C.S.M. 1917.

Record of War Service

BAIRD, W. J. STIRLING.
George Watson's College. Student of Science, 1911-15. O.T.C. Artillery, Sept. 1914 to Jan. 1915, Cadet. R.F.A., 2nd Lieut. Oct. 1914; Lieut. March 1916; Captain Oct. 1916. M.C. March 1918.

BAKER, ARCHIBALD DONALD. (See p. 747.)

BA-KET, MAUNG.
M.B., C.M. 1900; B.Sc. (P.H.) 1901. Indian Medical Service, Captain; Major Sept. 1914.

BALCK, CHARLES AUGUSTUS JOHN ALBERT.
M.B., Ch.B. 1899. R.A.M.C., Captain; Major March 1914.

BALD, WILLIAM.
Student of Arts. 12th Scottish Rifles, Lieut.

BALDIE, ALEXANDER.
Grey Institute, Port Elizabeth, Cape Colony. M.B., Ch.B. 1912. R.A.M.C., Lieut. Aug. 1914; Captain Aug. 1915 to March 1919. France 1914. Médaille de l'Assistance Publique (French) Nov. 1917.

BALDWIN, ARTHUR WILLIAM.
George Watson's College. Student of Law, 1913-14. R.G.A., 156th Heavy Battery, Gunner Aug. 1914; 2nd Lieut. Oct. 1914; Lieut. June 1916.

BALFOUR, ANDREW.
George Watson's College; First XV. M.B., C.M. 1894; M.D. 1898; B.Sc. (P.H.) 1900; F.R.C.P. (Edin.); D.P.H. (Camb.). R.A.M.C., Lieut.-Col. July 1915. Member, Advisory Medical Committee. Mediterranean 1915-16; Mesopotamia 1916-17. East Africa 1917-18. C.M.G. 1912; C.B. Jan. 1918.

BALFOUR, THE RIGHT HON. ARTHUR JAMES.
Eton. Chancellor, Edinburgh University from 1891. O.M.; M.P.; D.C.L.; LL.D.; F.R.S. First Lord of Admiralty, May 1915 to Dec. 1916. Secretary of State for Foreign Affairs, Dec. 1916. Head of British Mission to America, 1917. Member of Peace Conference, Paris, 1919.

BALFOUR, HARRY HYNDMAN.
George Watson's College. M.B., C.M. 1895. South African Medical Corps, Lieut.-Col. 1909. P.M.O., Transvaal. Mobilised Sept. 1914. German South-West Africa, A.D.M.S. Invalided to Scotland, March 1915. Exp. Force of South Africa, Civil Surgeon, July 1916. M.B.E. Jan. 1918; O.B.E. June 1919. Dispatches twice.

BALFOUR, THE HON. JAMES MONCRIEFF.
Edinburgh Academy and Cheltenham College. B.A. (Oxford). Student of Law, 1901-3. Writer to the Signet, 1904. Scottish Horse (T.), 2nd Lieut. Aug. 1914; Captain Oct. 1914. Staff Captain 1915. G.H.Q., France, 1916-17. War Office, 1917. Assistant Secretary, Ministry of National Service, 1917-18. O.B.E. (Military) 1919.

Record of War Service

BALFOUR, JOHN HUTTON.
Student of Medicine, 1918. 14th Argyll and Sutherland Highlanders, Lieut. 6th King's Own Scottish Borderers.

BALFOUR, THOMAS HENRY.
Royal High School; Athletics. M.B., Ch.B. 1909; D.P.H. (Edin.) 1911. R.A.M.C., 19th Infantry Brigade, Lieut. July 1912; Captain March 1915; Acting Major May 1918; Brevet Major June 1919. Attached 2nd Argyll and Sutherland Highlanders. D.A.D.M.S. 12th Division, and XVth Corps, France. M.O., R.E., 6th Division, Field Ambulance. India. M.C. Feb. 1915. Dispatches Feb. 1915, Jan. 1917, and July 1919. Died at Quetta on 16th March 1920.

BALFOUR, WILLIAM LESLIE.
Daniel Stewart's College. Student of Medicine, 1914-16 and 1918-19. O.T.C. Medical, Oct. 1918 to Feb. 1919. R.N.V.R., Surgeon-Probationer, Oct. 1916-18.

BALFOUR-KINNEAR, GEORGE WILLIAM.
Edinburgh Academy. Student of Arts and Law. M.A. 1900. Writer to the Signet. Emeritus Professor, Amherst College, Mass. U.S.A. 48th, 37th, and 95th Canadian Highlanders, Private March 1915; Corporal 1915; Sergeant; Lieut. Nov. 1915. Invalided out August 1917.

BALFOUR-MELVILLE, EVAN WHYTE MELVILLE.
Charterhouse. B.A. (Oxford). Student of Arts. Assistant in History since 1911. Special List (Recruiting Duties), Lieut. June 1917. 1st Grade Official, Ministry of National Service.

BALKIN, ISRAEL JACOB.
High School, Oudtshoorn, Cape Colony. Cadet Corps 1904-7, Sergeant. M.B., Ch.B. 1913. O.T.C. Artillery, 1909, Cadet. R.A.M.C., Lieut. Jan. 1916.

BALL, GEORGE FALCONER.
Sedbergh; First XV. and XI. O.T.C. 1909-12, Cadet Corporal. Student of Science, 1912-14 and 1918-20. 7th Northumberland Fusiliers, 2nd Lieut. Aug. 1914; Lieut. June 1915; Captain June 1916. M.C. and Dispatches Jan. 1916.

BALLANTINE, ALEXANDER STUART.
Edinburgh Academy. Student of Medicine, 1908-10 and 1916-19. O.T.C. Infantry, May 1910-11, Cadet. 1st Monmouthshire Regiment (T.), Rifleman Sept. 1914. Discharged medically unfit 16th Aug. 1915.

BALLANTINE, ARTHUR JAMES.
M.B., Ch.B. 1912; F.R.C.S. (Edin.) 1914. O.T.C. Artillery, Nov. 1908 to Feb. 1912, Cadet. R.A.M.C., Captain. Attached 4th South African Horse, East African Expeditionary Force.

BALLANTINE, JAMES.
Edinburgh Academy. Edinburgh University O.T.C. Artillery, Feb. to July 1916, Cadet. R.G.A. (T.), North Scottish, 2nd Lieut. Dec. 1916; Lieut. June 1918. Mention Aug. 1919.

Record of War Service

BALLANTINE, JOHN.
> M.A. 1905. R.F.A., Lieut. Aug. 1918.

BALLANTYNE, CHARLES S.
> Student of Arts, 1915-16. 3rd Scottish Rifles, Private.

BALLENY, WILLIAM.
> Student of Arts, 1913-14. O.T.C. Infantry, Oct. 1913 to Sept. 1914, Cadet. 2nd Gordon Highlanders, 2nd Lieut.; Lieut. Sept. 1916.

BALSILLIE, GEORGE.
> Daniel Stewart's College. Student of Medicine, 1913-17; M.B., Ch.B. 1917. O.T.C. Medical, Nov. 1915 to Dec. 1917. Royal Navy, Surgeon-Lieut. Dec. 1917.

BAMFORD, R. B.
> Student. 8th Worcestershire Regiment, 2nd Lieut.

BANKART, ARTHUR REGINALD.
> M.B., C.M. 1892; D.P.H. (London). Royal Navy, Surgeon 1895; Surgeon-Commander. Hon. Physician to H.M. King Edward VII. 1905 and H.M. King George V. 1910. H.M.S. *Agincourt* Aug. 1914 to Jan. 1917. S.M.O., Gosport, Feb. 1917. C.V.O. Jutland Battle, May 1916. Dispatches.

BANKS, ANNIE FALCONER.
> High School, Stranraer. M.A. 1909. Q.M.A.A.C.; Assistant Administrator, Sept. 1917; Deputy Administrator in charge of Patrols 1917.

BANKS, GEORGE SMITH.
> George Watson's College. M.B., Ch.B. 1905; D.P.H. R.A.M.C., Lieut. July 1917; Captain 1918.

BANKS, JAMES NOËL.
> Kirkcaldy High School; First XV. O.T.C. 1911-18, Cadet Sergeant. Student of Medicine, 1918. Royal Air Force, Probationary Flight Officer, Royal Navy, March 1918; 2nd Lieut. Royal Air Force, April 1918.

BANKS, THOMAS WATSON.
> George Watson's College. O.T.C. 1914-16. Student of Medicine, 1919-20. O.T.C. Infantry, Feb. to April 1917, Cadet. Royal Air Force, Cadet April 1917; 2nd Lieut. Aug. 1917; Lieut. April 1918 to Sept. 1919. Egypt, Macedonia, and South Russia.

BANKS, THOMAS WILSON.
> Hamilton Place School, Edinburgh. M.B., C.M. 1891. R.A.M.C. (T.), Captain 1896; Major. Attached 8th Highland Light Infantry. Palestine and Egypt.

BANNERMAN, A. W.
> George Heriot's School. Student of Arts, 1913-15 and 1920. 4th Royal Scots (T.), Private May 1915; 2nd Lieut. June 1917; Lieut. Dec. 1917.

Record of War Service

BANNERMAN, JAMES.
Elgin Academy. Student of Medicine, 1914; L.R.C.P. & S. (Edin.); L.R.F.P. & S. (Glasg.) 1915. O.T.C. Medical, May 1911-15. R.A.M.C. (T.), Lieut. Sept. 1915; Captain March 1916 to Oct. 1919.

BANNERMAN, ROBERT GEORGE.
George Watson's College. Student of Arts and Medicine, 1909-15. Vans Dunlop Scholar. M.A. 1910; M.B., Ch.B. 1914; M.D. 1919. O.T.C. Medical, Jan. 1910 to Sept. 1914, Cadet Sergeant. R.A.M.C. (S.R.), Lieut. Aug. 1914; Captain May 1915.

BANNERMAN, WILLIAM.
M.B., C.M. 1894. R.A.M.C., Lieut. Nov. 1915; Captain Nov. 1916. Royal Air Force Medical Service, Captain Oct. 1918; Flight Lieut.

BANNERMAN, WILLIAM BURNEY.
Edinburgh Academy; First XV. M.B., C.M. 1881; M.D. 1889; B.Sc. 1896; D.Sc. 1909. Indian Medical Service, Lieut. 1883; Major-General (retired). Burmese Campaign, 1886-9. Surgeon-General, Government of Madras, 1911-18. C.S.I. 1911. K.H.P. 1913.

BAPTIE, THOMAS.
Tranent School. M.A. 1908. Schoolmaster. 3rd Royal Scots, Private June 1917; L/Corporal; Corporal; 2nd Lieut. Jan. 1919.

BARBEAU, LOUIS GABRIEL.
Royal College, Mauritius. M.B., C.M. 1891; D.P.H. (London). Mauritius Volunteer Force, Private June 1915; 2nd Lieut. Feb. 1917.

BARBOUR, GEORGE BROWN.
Merchiston Castle. Cadet Corps 1903-6. B.A. (Cambridge); M.A. (Hons. Classics) 1911. Friends' Ambulance, Belgium (Dresser), 1914-15. 1st British Ambulance, Italy, 1915-17. R.F.A., 2nd Lieut. July 1917 to Jan. 1919.

BARCLAY, ALEXANDER.
Coupar Angus School. M.A. 1902; B.D. 1906. Senior President, Theological Society. Minister, Church of Scotland. Hon. Chaplain, 1st Lanarkshire Volunteer Regiment, March 1917.

BARCLAY, HUGH BROMFIELD.
George Watson's College. Student of Arts and Science, 1913-14. O.T.C. Artillery, Oct. 1913 to Jan. 1915, Cadet. R.F.A., 42nd (E. Lancs.) Division, 2nd Lieut. Aug. 1915; Lieut. June 1916; Acting Captain March 1918; Captain. Egypt till Oct. 1915; Gallipoli Oct. 1915 to Jan. 1916; Sinai 1916-17; France 1917-19. M.C. July 1917. Twice wounded.

Record of War Service

BARCLAY, WILLIAM.
George Heriot's School. M.B., Ch.B. 1913. O.T.C. Medical, Jan. 1909 to Aug. 1914, Cadet Staff Sergeant. R.A.M.C. (S.R.), Lieut. Aug. 1914; Captain April 1915; Acting Major Jan. 1918. France. M.C. Aug. 1916. Dispatches Jan. 1919.

BARCLAY, WILLIAM ANDREW.
Perth Academy. Student of Arts, 1912-16 and 1918-19; M.A. 1916. O.T.C. Artillery, Nov. 1915 to Sept. 1916, Cadet; Officer Cadet Sept. 1916. R.G.A., 136th Siege Battery, Lieut. June 1918.

BARCLAY, WILLIAM JOHN.
Auckland College and Grammar School, New Zealand. B.A. (N.Z.) 1893; M.B., Ch.B. 1899; M.D. and F.R.C.S. (Edin.) 1903. N.Z. Medical Corps, Hospital Ship *Maheno*, Captain Jan. 1916.

BARCROFT, DAVID MALCOMSON.
Leys School, Cambridge. M.B., Ch.B. 1907; M.D. 1912. R.A.M.C., Lieut. 1918. Italy.

BARDSWELL, NOEL DEAN.
Sherborne. M.B., C.M. 1895; M.D. 1899; F.R.C.P. (Lond.); M.R.C.P. (Edin.). Rowing "Blue" 1893-5. R.A.M.C., Captain Sept. 1915; Major Dec. 1915. Mediterranean Exp. Force. Malta, Sicily, Hospital Ship *Britannic*, and France Oct. 1915 to Dec. 1916. M.V.O. 1915.

BARKER, ALEXANDER.
Perth Academy. Student of Law, 1912-14. Solicitor. R.G.A., Bombardier Sept. 1915; 2nd Lieut. Jan. 1917; Captain and Adjutant Feb. 1918 to July 1919. Croix de Guerre (French).

BARKER, FRANK.
George Heriot's School. Student of Science, 1914-15. O.T.C. Artillery, Nov. 1914 to Jan. 1915; Cadet. R.F.A. (S.R.), 2nd Lieut. Jan. 1915; Lieut. June 1917. India, Mesopotamia, France, and Palestine.

BARKER, THOMAS L.
George Watson's College. O.T.C. 1910-13, Cadet Sergeant. Student of Arts and Science, 1912-14. 4th Royal Scots (T.), 2nd Lieut. Dec. 1912; Lieut. Sept. 1914; Captain June 1915. Indian Army, Lieut. May 1916; Captain May 1919. Gallipoli 1915; Egypt and Palestine 1916 and 1917; India 1917-18; Palestine and Syria 1918 and 1919. Dispatches (Gaza) June 1917.

BARKLEY, JAMES.
Academical Institution, Coleraine. Student of Medicine; L.R.C.P. & S. (Edin.); L.F.P.S. (Glasg.) 1899. R.A.M.C. (T.), Lieut. 1900; Major; Lieut.-Col. Aug. 1915. 83rd Field Ambulance and 26th General Hospital, Etaples. Wounded near Ypres 1917. Dispatches Jan. 1918. D.S.O. 1919.

Record of War Service

BARKLEY, JAMES MORGAN.
George Watson's College. M.B., Ch.B. 1905. R.A.M.C., Lieut. Dec. 1914; Captain Dec. 1915. Egyptian Exp. Force, 1915 to July 1918.

BARKLEY, THOMAS YUILLE.
Dunfermline High School. Student of Medicine, 1910-15; M.B., Ch.B. 1915. O.T.C. Infantry, 1911-14; Medical, 1914-15, Cadet Sergeant. R.A.M.C. (S.R.), Lieut. July 1915; Captain Jan. 1916; Acting Major Jan. 1918; Acting Lieut.-Col. 27th Casualty Clearing Station, Dec. 1918 to July 1919. Dispatches June and Dec. 1918. O.B.E. (Military) Jan. 1919.

BARLOW, JOHN.
M.B., Ch.B. 1875; M.D. 1879; F.R.C.S. (Eng.). Examiner in Clinical Surgery. R.A.M.C. (T.), 1908; Lieut.-Col. Mobilised Nov. 1915. 4th Scottish General Hospital.

BARLOW, PHILIP.
Leys School, Cambridge. O.T.C. 1907-11, Cadet L/Corporal. Student of Medicine, 1912-14 and 1917-20; M.B., Ch.B. 1920. R.A.M.C. (T.), Scottish Horse Field Ambulance, Bugler, Sept. 1914. Royal Navy, Surgeon-Probationer, June 1915 to Dec. 1917.

BARNARDO, FREDERICK ADOLPHUS FLEMING.
George Watson's College. M.A. 1894; M.B., Ch.B. 1899; M.D.; F.R.C.S. (Edin.) 1912. South African Campaign, 1899-1902. Indian Medical Service, Lieut. 1902; Major 1912; Brevet Lieut.-Col. Jan. 1917; Colonel May 1918. Somaliland 1904. C.I.E. June 1918; C.B.E. June 1919.

BARNETSON, ROBERT BALFOUR.
M.B., Ch.B. 1904; M.D. 1918. R.A.M.C. (T.), Lieut.; Captain.

BARNETT, GEORGE SHUTTLEWORTH.
Student of Medicine, 1911-15 and 1917-20; M.B., Ch.B. 1920. O.T.C. Medical, Oct. 1914, Cadet. R.N.V.R., Surgeon-Probationer, Nov. 1914.

BARNETT, LOUIS EDWARD.
Wellington College, N.Z. First XV. and XI. M.B., C.M. (Hons.) 1888; L.R.C.P. (Lond.) 1889; F.R.C.S. (Eng.) 1890. Professor of Surgery, University of Otago. R.A.M.C., Lieut. and Captain May 1915. N.Z. Medical Corps, Major Aug. 1915; Lieut.-Col. Aug. 1916; Consulting Surgeon to N.Z. Forces. Dispatches 1916. C.M.G. 1918.

BARNFATHER, RONALD BELL.
Sedbergh. First XV. O.T.C. 1908-12. Student of Medicine, 1913-14. O.T.C. Artillery, Oct. 1912 to Aug. 1914, Cadet. 5th Border Regiment (T.), 2nd Lieut. Aug. 1914; Lieut. 1916; Captain June 1916.

BARNIE, WILLIAM EDWARD.
Student of Arts, 1913-15. 16th Royal Scots, Private. R.E. (Special Brigade), Corporal. France. M.M. 1917.

Record of War Service

BARR, THOMAS URE.
Fettes. University O.T.C. Artillery, July 1917 to Feb. 1918, Cadet Bombardier; Officer Cadet Feb. 1918. R.G.A., 541st Siege Battery, 2nd Lieut. Aug. 1918.

BARR, WILLIAM.
Knox Institute, Haddington. Student of Arts and Science, 1909-14; M.A. 1912; B.Sc. 1914. R.E. (Special Brigade), Corporal 1915; Sergeant.

BARRIE, WILLIAM TURNBULL.
M.B., C.M. 1880. R.A.M.C. (T.), Captain Oct. 1894. Attached 4th King's Own Scottish Borderers. T.D.

BARRINGTON-WARD, LANCELOT EDWARD.
Bromsgrove and Westminster. M.B., Ch.B. 1908; F.R.C.S. (Edin. and Eng.). Anatomy Staff, 1910. Surgeon, Serbia Relief Fund Hospital, Uskub, 1915. Surgeon, King George Hospital, 1915-19. Hon. Lieut.-Col. Serbian Army. Order of St Sava (4th Class).

BARRINGTON-WARD, VICTOR MICHAEL.
Westminster. Cadet Corps. B.Sc. 1907. Queen's Edinburgh Mounted Rifles. 5th Sherwood Foresters; 11th South Lancs. Regiment (Pioneers), Captain Oct. 1914; R.E. (Railway Troops), Major June 1915; Brevet Lieut.-Col. June 1918; Lieut.-Col. Jan. 1919. D.S.O. Oct. 1916. Dispatches Oct. 1916, Jan. and Dec. 1917 and May 1918. Croix de Guerre with Palms 1918.

BARRON, DAVID CUTHBERT.
Leven School. Student of Science and Medicine, 1910-13; B.Sc. and M.B., Ch.B. 1913; M.D. 1920. McCosh Travelling Scholar, 1912-14. O.T.C. Medical, 1910-14, Cadet Sergeant. R.A.M.C. (S.R.), Lieut. Aug. 1914; Captain April 1915; Major April 1916; Acting Lieut.-Col. Aug. 1916. No. 54 Field Ambulance. Dispatches Jan. 1917.

BARRON, RODERICK.
M.A. 1900. 15th Highland Light Infantry, L/Corporal Feb. 1916. 6th North Staffordshire Regiment, 2nd Lieut. Aug. 1917; Acting Captain Oct. 1918. M.C.

BARRS, ALFRED GEORGE.
Leicester Grammar School. M.B., C.M. 1875; M.D. 1882; F.R.C.P. (Lond.). R.A.M.C. (T.), 2nd Northern General Hospital, Leeds. Lieut.-Col. Aug. 1914.

BARRY, GERALD HUGH.
Mount St Mary's College, Chesterfield. Student of Medicine, 1911-14 and 1915-16; M.B., Ch.B. 1916. O.T.C. Medical, Nov. 1912 to Oct. 1914, Cadet. Scottish Horse, Private Aug. 1914. 13th Lancashire Fusiliers, 2nd Lieut. Oct. 1914; Lieut. Dec. 1914. R.A.M.C., Captain April 1917. Gallipoli. German East Africa July 1917. Wounded Aug. 1915.

Record of War Service

BARTHOLOMEW, GEORGE GALEN.
George Watson's College. M.B., Ch.B. 1905; L.R.C.P. & S. (Edin.); L.R.F.P.S. (Glasg.), 1904. R.A.M.C., Lieut. Feb. 1915; Captain Feb. to Oct. 1916. France 1915-16; the Somme, 36th Field Ambulance. M.C. July 1916.

BARTHOLOMEW, JOHN.
Merchiston Castle. Cadet Corps 1903-7. Student of Arts, 1910-14; M.A. 1919; Running "Blue." O.T.C. Infantry, Oct. 1911 to Aug. 1914, Cadet Sergeant. 3rd Gordon Highlanders (S.R.), 2nd Lieut. Aug. 1914; Captain April 1915. War Office, Intelligence and General Staff; Tank Corps; Staff Captain. France Oct. 1914. Ypres. Wounded, Somme (Delville Wood), July 1916. M.C. June 1915; Dispatches Jan. and June 1915 and Jan. 1916.

BARTMANN, N. H.
Student. Scottish Horse (T.), Private; 9th Royal Highlanders (Black Watch), Lieut. Dec. 1917.

BARTON, EDWYN BRACE.
Trent College. M.B., Ch.B. 1912. O.T.C. Infantry, 1909-11, Cadet L/Corporal. R.A.M.C., Lieut. Oct. 1914; Captain Oct. 1915; Acting Major Jan. 1919.

BARTY, JOHN B.
Edinburgh Academy; First XV. Student of Law. Chartered Accountant, 1912. R.F.A. (City of Aberdeen) (T.), 2nd Lieut. April 1915; Lieut. June 1916. France.

BASHFORD, ERNEST FRANCIS.
George Heriot's School. M.B., Ch.B. 1899. R.A.M.C., Captain July 1915. Mediterranean Exp. Force Aug. 1915. France Jan. 1916. 26th General Hospital and Bacteriologist, Surgical Observation Hut. The Rhine Aug. 1919. Dispatches March 1919. O.B.E. (Military) June 1919.

BASHFORD, R. J. LINDSAY.
Bedford. Student of Arts, 1898-9. Senior President, S.R.C. Army Ordnance Corps, Lieut.; Captain Oct. 1917.

BASSIN, NOEL MATTHEWS.
George Heriot's School. B.Sc. 1913. A.M.I.C.E. O.T.C. Engineers, Oct. 1910 to Sept. 1914, Cadet Corporal. R.E. (T.), (City of Dundee Fortress), 2nd Lieut. Sept. 1914; Lieut. Aug. 1915; Captain March 1917. R.E., Dundee Field Coy.

BASSIN, THEODORE A.
George Heriot's School; First XV. Student of Law. Chartered Accountant, 1914. Lothians and Border Horse, Private 1908-11. R.F.A., Lowland Brigade, Gunner Nov. 1915; Sergeant June 1916; 2nd Lieut. Feb. 1917; Lieut. Aug. 1918. 256th Brigade, R.F.A., 51st Highland Division. Wounded March 1918.

Record of War Service

BATCHELOR, RALPH CAMPBELL LINDSAY.
: Dundee High School. M.A. 1908; M.B., Ch.B. (Hons.) 1914. Assistant to Professor of Midwifery. O.T.C. Medical, 1915, Cadet. R.A.M.C., Lieut. Oct. 1915; Captain March 1917. H.M. Hospital Ship *Britannic*. 36th Field Ambulance, France; 7th Norfolks; 41st Training Reserve; 2/1st Lothians and Border Horse; 74th and 59th General Hospitals.

BATEMAN, JAMES K.
: Selkirk High School. Student of Science, 1918. R.F.A., 1st Lowland Brigade, Driver June 1915.

BATESON, JOHN FRANCIS.
: Harrow. M.B., C.M. 1881; M.R.C.S. (Eng.) 1884. R.A.M.C., 1885-1900. South African Campaign, 1899-1902. Surgeon Lieut.-Col. May 1905; Brevet Col. June 1918. Coldstream Guards, 1900-19.

BATRA, GIRDHARI LAL.
: Government and Forman Christian College, Lahore. M.B., Ch.B. 1908; D.P.H. (Durham) 1910. Indian Medical Service, Lieut. Dec. 1914 to May 1916. Special Plague M.O.

BATSON, RICHARD ERSTINE.
: Harrison College, Barbados. First XI. O.T.C. one year. Student of Medicine, 1912-14 and 1918-20; M.B., Ch.B. 1920. O.T.C. Infantry 1914, Cadet. R.N.V.R., Auxiliary Cruiser *Bayano*, Surgeon-Probationer, Dec. 1914; T.B.D. *Lawford*; Mine-sweeper *Dahlia*.

BAUER, EMIL WILLIAM.
: Edinburgh Institution. Cadet Battn. University O.T.C. Artillery, Sept. 1916 to Aug. 1917, Cadet. R.F.A. (S.R.), Officer Cadet Aug. 1917; 2nd Lieut. Sept. 1918; Lieut. Oct. 1919. France and Belgium.

BAXTER, CHARLES BOTTERILL.
: Rossall. Cadet Corps 1899-1902. M.B., Ch.B. 1907; M.R.C.S. (Eng.) and L.R.C.P. (Lond.) 1908; F.R.C.S. (Edin.) 1913. No. 4 Coy. Q.R.V.B. Royal Scots, May 1903 to Feb. 1907, Private. R.A.M.C. (T.), Lieut. July 1907; Captain Dec. 1911; Acting Major Jan. 1918; Major July 1919. 56th and 1/1st Casualty Clearing Stations. O.B.E. (Military) Jan. 1919.

BAXTER, DAVID LEISHMAN.
: Greenock School. Student of Medicine, 1911-17; M.B., Ch.B. 1916. O.T.C. Medical, Oct. to Dec. 1914, Cadet. R.N.V.R., Surgeon-Probationer, Dec. 1914 to July 1915; Surgeon Jan. 1917. Attached Royal Naval Division, Surgeon-Lieut. May 1917 to June 1919. France. Wounded Sept. 1918. M.C. Sept. 1918.

BAYNE, WALLACE RUTHERFORD.
: Wellington College. M.B., Ch.B. 1911; L.M. (Dublin). R.A.M.C., Lieut. Aug. 1917; Captain Aug. 1918. German East Africa and France.

Record of War Service

BEALE, JOHN.
Student of Medicine, 1917-18. O.T.C. Infantry, 1917-18, Cadet. Officer Cadet May 1918. Argyll and Sutherland Highlanders, 2nd Lieut. Jan. 1919.

BEALE, MAY A. B.
Ministers' Daughters' College. M.A. (Hons. Engl.) 1912. Schoolmistress. Q.M.A.A.C., attached Recruiting Staff, Scotland. Unit Administrator Dec. 1917.

BEARD, EDGAR.
Student of Science, 1911-14; B.Sc. 1914. O.T.C. Infantry, Sept. 1914 to June 1915, Cadet. R.E. (Special Brigade), Corporal July 1915. France July 1915.

BEATON, FRANK DUNCAN MURCHISON.
Glasgow High School; First XV. Student of Medicine, 1914-15, and 1918-19. O.T.C. Infantry, May 1915, and Medical Unit, June 1918, Cadet. Argyll and Sutherland Highlanders, July 1915. R.E. Royal Air Force, Cadet.

BEATON, GEORGE MACKIE.
Daniel Stewart's College; First XV. and XI. University O.T.C. Infantry, Oct. 1915 to Jan. 1916, Cadet. 14th and 17th Highland Light Infantry; 97th and 120th T.M.B., 2nd Lieut. Jan. 1916; Lieut. March 1917; Captain May 1918. France 1916. Wounded. M.C.

BEATSON, D. H.
Student of Science. 9th Border Regiment, 2nd Lieut. Aug. 1917. Three times wounded.

BEATSON, Sir GEORGE THOMAS.
King William's College, Isle of Man. First XI. B.A. (Camb.) 1870; L.R.C.S. (Edin.) 1874; M.B., C.M. 1874; M.D. 1878. Volunteer and Territorial Force, 1879-1912. A.D.M.S., Lowland Division, 1908-12. Chairman, Executive Scottish Branch, B.R.C.S. R.A.M.C. (T.), Colonel. D.L., County of City of Glasgow. K.C.B.; K.B.E. Officer of Legion of Honour.

BEATSON, ROBERT.
Merchiston Castle. Student of Law, 1910-13. Australian Contingent, L/Corporal. Gallipoli. Wounded and Invalided out.

BEATSON-BELL, JOHN.
Edinburgh Academy. M.A. 1886. Q.E.R. Indian Army, Feb. 1888, Lieut.-Col. Feb. 1914. France, Indian Exp. Force, Sept. 1914 to Jan. 1916. Dispatches June 1915.

BEATTIE, ALFRED JORDAN.
Rugby. Cadet Corps 1893-6, Cadet Sergeant. M.B., Ch.B. 1905. B.R.C.S. Nov. 1914. R.A.M.C., Lieut. Sept. 1918; Captain Oct. 1919. Mesopotamia.

Record of War Service

BEATTIE, JAMES MARTIN.
Training College, Dunedin, and Otago University, New Zealand. M.A. (N.Z.) 1889; M.B., C.M. 1894; M.D. 1901. Professor, Bacteriology, Liverpool University. R.A.M.C. (T.), 1911; Major June 1915. 1st Western General Hospital, Liverpool.

BEATTIE, JOHN MENZIES.
George Watson's College. M.A. (Hons. Classics) 1913. Schoolmaster. O.T.C. Infantry, 1908-14, Cadet Sergeant. 9th Royal Scots, Private Aug. 1914; 10th and 13th Argyll and Sutherland Highlanders, 2nd Lieut. Nov. 1915; Lieut. July 1917. France 1915-18; St Eloi, Ypres, Arras, Somme, Passchendaele. Wounded April 1915 and April 1917. M.C. 1917.

BEATTY, EARL DAVID.
H.M.S. *Britannia*. Lord Rector, Edinburgh University, 1917. LL.D. 1920. Royal Navy, Jan. 1884. Nile Expedition, 1896-8; China 1899. H.M.S. *Queen Elizabeth*, Admiral; Admiral of the Fleet, April 1919. G.C.B.; O.M.; G.C.V.O.; D.S.O. Legion of Honour.

BEATTY, MARTIN CECIL.
S.A. Institute, Belfast. M.B., Ch.B. 1900; D.P.H.; R.C.P.S.I. 1903. R.A.M.C. 1901, Captain; Major March 1913. Dispatches.

BECKERLEG, VIVIAN COLENSO.
Maritzburg College, Natal. Student of Medicine, 1913-15 and 1917-20. O.T.C. Infantry, Oct. 1914 to March 1915, Cadet. 6th Duke of Cornwall's Light Infantry, 2nd Lieut. France May to Oct. 1916. Wounded at Arras Oct. 1916. M.C.

BEDFORD, SIR CHARLES HENRY.
Edinburgh Institution. M.B., C.M. 1887; B.Sc. 1889; M.D. and D.Sc. 1892; Hon. LL.D. (St Andrews) 1913. Indian Medical Service, Lieut.-Col. (retired) 1889. S.M.O. Cromarty Defences, 1915. Deputy Chief Commissioner of Medical Services. Ministry of National Service and Commissioner for London.

BEDINGFIELD, HARRY.
Royal Academy, Inverness. M.B., Ch.B. 1911. R.A.M.C., Lieut. Jan. 1913; Captain March 1915. Attached Inniskilling Fusiliers; 5th Field Ambulance; 73rd General Hospital. France. D.S.O. Dispatches.

BEECH, JAMES.
George Watson's College. University O.T.C. Infantry, 1916-17, Cadet Sergeant. Royal Scots, Private Aug. 1917; Border Regiment, 2nd Lieut. Nov. 1917; Sherwood Foresters. France 1918.

BEESLY, LEWIS.
University College School, London. Student of Medicine, 1897-1901; L.R.C.P. & S. (Edin.); L.F.P.S. (Glasg.) 1903; F.R.C.S. (Edin.) 1905. Demonstrator in Anatomy, 1913. R.A.M.C. (T.), Lieut. 1909; Captain 1913; Major 1919. Surgical Specialist, 2nd Scottish General Hospital.

Record of War Service

BEGG, ROBERT CAMPBELL.
 Otago High School, Dunedin. M.A. (N.Z.) 1906; M.Sc. (N.Z.) 1907; M.R.C.S. (Eng.); L.R.C.P. (Lond.) 1911; M.B., Ch.B. 1912. No. 4 Coy. Q.R.V.B., Royal Scots, 1908, Private. B.R.C.S. Oct. 1914; R.A.M.C., Lieut. Jan. 1915; Captain. Mesopotamia. Dispatches Nov. 1917. M.C. Jan. 1918.

BEGG, ROGNVALD BARTLET.
 University O.T.C. Infantry, Feb. 1917, Cadet. King's Royal Rifle Corps, 2nd Lieut. Nov. 1917; Lieut. April 1919. France.

BELFORD, FREDERICK JAMES.
 George Heriot's School. M.A. 1909. L.C.P. Schoolmaster. 10th Royal Scots, Private Dec. 1915. France. Wounded at Ypres Aug. 1917.

BELFORD, JOHN RHIND.
 M.A. 1912. Schoolmaster. Lothians and Border Horse, Private; attached 17th Royal Scots. France.

BELFORD, WALTER CHEYNE.
 M.A. 1909. O.T.C. Artillery, Oct. 1909 to June 1912, Cadet. Australian Imperial Force; 11th Battn. West Australians, Lieut.; Captain. Dispatches Jan. 1917.

BELFRAGE, ANDREW TAIT.
 Edinburgh Institution; First XV. and XI. Student of Science, 1905-11. University Coy., 9th Vol. Highlanders, Royal Scots, Oct. 1904 to Nov. 1907. R.E., 2nd Lieut. Feb. 1915; Lieut. May 1916; Acting Captain Feb. 1917 to March 1917. France Feb. 1916. Invalided out Dec. 1918.

BELL, AGNES MAY.
 George Watson's Ladies' College. M.A. 1912; Teacher's Diploma (Camb.). Q.M.A.A.C., Sept. 1917; Assistant Administrator, Oct. 1917; Deputy Administrator, Nov. 1917.

BELL, ALEXANDER EDWARD.
 Ayr Academy. O.T.C. 1913-16, Cadet Corporal; University O.T.C. Artillery, July 1917 to Feb. 1918, Cadet; Officer Cadet March 1918. R.F.A., 175th Army Brigade, 2nd Lieut. Aug. 1918. France.

BELL, ARCHIBALD. (See p. 747.)

BELL, DAVID.
 Langholm Academy. M.A. 1910. R.E. (Dispatch Rider), Corporal July 1915. Italy, France, and Germany.

BELL, DAVID JOHN ROSS.
 High School, Dundee; First XV. University O.T.C. Artillery, April to May 1916, Cadet; 3rd Battn. Tank Corps, May 1916; 2nd Lieut. Jan. 1918; Lieut. July 1919. Disabled Aug. 1918. Invalided out Oct. 1919.

Record of War Service

BELL, DELVINE.
　M.B., Ch.B. 1911. First XI. O.T.C. Infantry, May 1909 to Jan. 1912, Cadet L/Corporal. R.A.M.C., Lieut. Oct. 1914; Captain April 1918; Temp. Major Aug. 1918 to March 1919. M.C. Dispatches Jan. and Oct. 1916.

BELL, DOUGLAS.
　George Watson's College. M.B., Ch.B. 1904; D.P.H., R.C.P.S. (Edin.) 1907. Royal Navy, H.M.S. *King George V.*, Surgeon, Aug. 1915 to Dec. 1918; Sanitary M.O., H.M.S. *Pembroke* (Chatham Barracks). Jutland Battle May 1916.

BELL, EDWIN ARCHIBALD.
　Daniel Stewart's College. Student of Arts and Science, 1910-14 and 1918-19; B.Sc. (Agric.) 1914; M.A. 1918; B.Sc. (Forestry) 1919. O.T.C. Engineers, Oct. 1910 to Sept. 1914, Cadet; R.G.A. (T.), Lowland Heavy Battery, 2nd Lieut. Sept. 1914; Lieut. July 1915; Captain Aug. 1917; Staff Captain, R.A., April 1918. France.

BELL, FRANCIS GORDON.
　M.B., Ch.B. 1910; M.D. 1913; F.R.C.S. (Eng.) 1913; Anatomy Staff, 1911. R.A.M.C., Lieut.; Captain March 1916; Acting Major Jan. 1918. M.C.

BELL, GEORGE JAMES HAMILTON.
　Edinburgh Academy and Blairlodge; First XV. M.B., C.M. 1882. Indian Medical Service, April 1886; Colonel June 1915. Burma 1887-9; Lushai, 1889. Inspector-General of Civil Hospitals, Bihar and Orissa. C.I.E. 1914.

BELL, HUGH WINDSOR.
　M.B., Ch.B. 1914. Canadian Army Medical Corps, Captain.

BELL, JAMES GORDON.
　Dunfermline High School. Student of Medicine, 1909-14; M.B., Ch.B. 1914; L.R.C.P. & S. (Edin.); L.R.F.P.S. (Glasg.) 1914. R.A.M.C., Lieut. Dec. 1915; Captain Dec. 1916. M.C.

BELL, JAMES HORST BRUNNEMAN.
　Bell Baxter School, Cupar. Student of Arts and Science, 1913-15 and 1918; M.A. (Hons. Maths. and Nat. Phil.) 1916; B.Sc. 1918; A.I.C. 1919. O.T.C. Infantry, Nov. 1913, Cadet. 31st Middlesex Regiment, Private Feb. to April 1917. Chemist, Explosives Factories, 1916-18.

BELL, JAMES KER.
　Student of Science, 1913-15. N.D.A. (Hons.). Royal Army Veterinary Corps, Private Nov. 1915. Invalided out Feb. 1917. Chief Executive Officer, County Durham Food Production Campaign.

BELL, JAMES LOGIE.
　Marlborough. Student of Science, 1911-14; B.Sc. 1920. 1st City of London Yeomanry (T.), (Motor Cyclist Section), L/Corporal Aug. 1914. Royal Air Force, Lieut. France. Gallipoli 1915. Wounded.

Record of War Service

BELL, JOHN DOUGLAS.
Kilmarnock and Ayr Academies; First XV. O.T.C. 1908-15, Cadet Sergeant. University O.T.C. Artillery, July to Nov. 1915, Cadet Corporal. R.F.A. (S.R.), 30th Division, 2nd Lieut. Nov. 1915; 2nd Lieut. (Regulars) Aug. 1916; Lieut. Feb. 1918. France Jan. 1916 to April 1918. M.C. June 1918.

BELL, JOHN GRENVILLE.
M.B., Ch.B. 1899; D.P.H. (Liverpool). R.A.M.C., 1903; Major Oct. 1914; Temp. Lieut.-Col. June 1915; Brevet Lieut.-Col. Jan. 1919. D.S.O. Jan. 1916.

BELL, JOHN HENRY.
M.B., Ch.B. 1909. R.A.M.C., Captain. 14th Field Ambulance, 5th Division, France 1914. Wounded Feb. 1915.

BELL, JOHN HENRY MONTGOMERIE.
George Watson's College. M.B., Ch.B. 1901; M.D. 1907; F.R.C.S. (Edin.) 1907. Canadian Army Medical Corps, Captain, 1915; Major Dec. 1917. France Feb. 1915 to Aug. 1917. Vimy Ridge.

BELL, JOSEPH.
George Watson's College; First XV. Student of Law, 1895-7. Chartered Accountant. 179th Battn. (Cameron Highlanders) Canadian Exp. Force, Lieut. Nov. 1915; Captain and Q.M. May 1916; reverted Lieut. Dec. 1917; Acting Captain July 1918; Captain Feb. 1919. Staff, General Auditor, Canadian Service, Dec. 1917.

BELL, LEWIS HAY IRVING.
Edinburgh Academy. M.B., Ch.B. 1904. University Battery, E.C.A.V., 1897-1900, Gunner. R.A.M.C., Lieut. Nov. 1914; Captain Nov. 1915. France May 1915 to June 1917; Italy 1918.

BELL, ROBERT.
Broughton School, Edinburgh. 16th Royal Scots, Private 1914. University O.T.C. Infantry, Dec. 1917 to July 1918, Cadet Corporal; Officer Cadet 1918. Royal Scots, 2nd Lieut. 1919.

BELL, ROBERT DUNCAN.
George Heriot's School. M.A. 1899; B.Sc. 1902. Poona Volunteer Rifles, Private 1909; transferred to Simla Rifles, I.D.F., April 1917. Indian Munitions Board, March 1917. C.I.E. June 1919.

BELL, THOMAS CARMICHAEL.
Mercer's School, London. First XI. Student of Arts and Science; B.Sc. 1912. A.S.C., 2nd Lieut. Aug. 1914; 4th Bedfordshire Regiment, Lieut. Jan. 1915; Captain Jan. 1915; Staff Captain March 1918. Egypt and Gallipoli 1915; France 1916-19; Somme, Arras, Ypres, Lens, and Mons. O.B.E. (Military) June 1919.

BELL, VERNON. (See p. 747.)

Record of War Service

BELL, WHITEFORD JAMES EDWARD.
    M.B., Ch.B. 1905. R.A.M.C., Major July 1918; Acting Lieut.-Col. D.S.O.

BELL, WILLIAM.
    Edinburgh Academy. O.T.C. 1914-16. University O.T.C. Artillery, Aug. 1916 to Feb. 1917, Cadet Bombardier. R.F.A., 102nd Brigade; Officer Cadet Feb. 1917; 2nd Lieut. July 1917; Lieut. 1918; Acting Adjutant 1919.

BELL, WILLIAM FREDERICK.
    Edinburgh Collegiate School. Student of Arts and Divinity; M.A. 1884. Minister, U.F. Church. Perthshire Vol. Regiment, Private Sept. 1916.

BELL, WILLIAM IVOR.
    George Watson's College. Cadet Corps 1905-8. B.Sc. 1914. President, Engineering Society. O.T.C. Engineers, 1912-14, Cadet Sergeant. R.E. (S.R.), 19th Division, Signal Coy., 2nd Lieut. Aug. 1914; Captain, Acting Major, Jan. 1918; 5th Corps and 35th Division, Jan. 1917 to May 1919. Festubert, Somme, Passchendaele, Ypres. M.C. Jan. 1917; Croix de Guerre (Belgium) Jan. 1919. Dispatches Jan. 1917 and Jan. 1919.

BENNEE, ARCHIBALD JOHN.
    Royal High School. M.B., Ch.B. 1911. R.A.M.C., Lieut. May 1916; Captain May 1917. France 1917-19. Invalided out Oct. 1919.

BENNET, JOHN.
    George Heriot's School. Student of Medicine, 1911-16; M.B., Ch.B. 1916. O.T.C. Infantry, 1912-15; Medical, 1915-16, Cadet. R.A.M.C., Lieut. July 1916; Captain Jan. 1917. Military Bacteriological Laboratory, Egypt.

BENNET-CLARK, THOMAS WILFRED.
    Edinburgh Academy. M.A. 1907; LL.B. 1910. 9th (T.) and 11th Royal Scots, 2nd Lieut. 1911; Lieut. 1913; Acting Captain April 1915; Captain June 1916. France Feb. 1915 to March 1919; Ypres 1915, Somme 1916, Arras 1917, and Soissons 1918. The Rhine March 1919. Gassed July 1916.

BENNETT, AGNES ELIZABETH LLOYD.
    Cheltenham College, and High School, Sydney, N.S.W. B.Sc. (Australia); M.B., C.M. 1900; M.D. 1911. N.Z. Medical Corps, N.Z. Exp. Force, Egypt; Captain May 1915. Scottish Women's Hospital, Macedonia, 1916-17. R.A.M.C., Netley Welsh Hospital, 1918-19. Order of St Sava (3rd Class), and Royal Red Cross of Serbia 1917.

BENNETT, HUGH.
    M.B., C.M. 1891. Indian Medical Service, Major; Lieut.-Col. July 1913.

BENNETT, JOHN WESLEY.
    Wesley College, Dublin. First XV. and XI. Student of Medicine, 1909-13; M.B., Ch.B. 1914. Rugby and Cricket "Blue." R.A.M.C. (T.), Lieut. Nov. 1915; Captain Nov. 1916. France 1916; Mesopotamia 1917; India 1919.

Record of War Service

BENNETT, ROBERT BROWN.
George Watson's College. Student of Arts and Science, 1913-15, and 1918-20; M.A. (Hons. Maths.) 1920. O.T.C. Infantry, Oct. 1913 to Nov. 1915, Cadet Sergeant. 8th Royal Highlanders (Black Watch), 2nd Lieut. Nov. 1915; Lieut. July 1917. France. Wounded at Longueval July 1916.

BENNETT, WILLIAM.
M.B., C.M. 1898. R.A.M.C. 1900; Major 1912; Lieut.-Col. 1917. South African Campaign, 1899-1902. Somaliland, 1903-4. France. Dispatches 1916, 1917, and 1918. D.S.O. 1916; Croix de Guerre (French) 1918; O.B.E. 1919.

BENNETT, W. GORDON.
Central School, Leeds. B.Sc. (Hons.) (Leeds) 1913; M.Sc.; A.I.C. University O.T.C. Artillery, Oct. 1914 to March 1915, Cadet. Assistant in Chemistry. R.F.A. (S.R.), 6th "B" Res. Brigade, 2nd Lieut. March 1915; Lieut. Feb. 1917; Acting Captain March 1918; 46th Brigade, R.F.A., 14th Division. France. Dispatches April 1918. M.C. Sept. 1918.

BENNETT, WILLIAM HENRY HENDER.
Oaklands, Mittagong, N.S.W. First XV. and XI. Sydney University. Football "Blue." M.B., C.M. 1890. Cricket "Blue." R.A.M.C. (T.), Lieut. Oct. 1914; Captain April 1915. Attached 2/4th King's Own Yorkshire Light Infantry; 12th South Staffords; 52nd Labour Group, Headquarters. Royal Air Force, Captain April 1918. France Jan. 1917 to Dec. 1918.

BENNING, W. S.
Student of Medicine. 11th Scottish Rifles, 2nd Lieut.

BENSON, HENRY PORTER D'ARCY.
Melbourne Grammar School, Australia. M.B., C.M. 1892; M.D., M.R.C.P. and F.R.C.S. (Edin.) 1896. R.A.M.C., Lieut. May 1915; Captain May 1916. Curragh Military Hospital, Surgeon, July 1915 to Jan. 1917.

BENSON, JOSEPH MITCHELL.
Rossall. M.B., Ch.B. 1900. Northern Province, Nigeria, Medical Corps; attached R.E. (T.), M.O.; Surgeon-Captain 1909; R.A.M.C. (T.), Captain 1916. France Jan. 1917 to Aug. 1918.

BENSON, WALTER TYRRELL.
B.Sc. (St Andrews). Student of Medicine, 1913-18; M.B., Ch.B. 1918. O.T.C. Medical, Feb. 1916 to April 1918, Cadet Corporal. R.N.V.R., H.M.S. *Norman*, Surgeon-Probationer May to Dec. 1916. Royal Navy, Surgeon-Lieut. July 1918.

BENTLEY, JAMES.
M.B., Ch.B. 1904. Australian Army Medical Corps, Captain Nov. 1914; Major Nov. 1916; attached 3rd Light Horse, Australian Imperial Force. Dardanelles. Twice mentioned in Dispatches. M.C.

Record of War Service

BERRIE, ALEXANDER ROBERT.
M.B., Ch.B. 1904. R.A.M.C. (T.), Lieut. April 1917; Captain April 1918. Salonika June 1917 to Feb. 1919. The Black Sea Feb. to Oct. 1919.

BERRY, Sir GEORGE ANDREAS.
Marlborough. M.B., C.M. 1876; F.R.C.S. (Edin.); LL.D. Member of University Court. R.A.M.C. (T.), Major and Ophthalmic Surgeon, 1908. 2nd Scottish General Hospital.

BERRY, JOHN PARTON.
"The College," Harrogate. M.B., Ch.B. 1907. Royal Navy, Surgeon, Nov. 1909. H.M.S. *Agincourt*, 1915; Surgeon-Lieut.-Commander, 1918-19. Dispatches. H.M.S. *Alcantara*, Feb. 1916.

BERRY, JOSEPH AUSTIN.
St Joseph's College, Dumfries. O.T.C. 1914-17, 2nd Lieut. University O.T.C. Artillery, 1917, Cadet; Officer Cadet Dec. 1917. R.F.A., 2nd Lieut. Aug. 1918.

BERRY, PREM NATH.
Student of Medicine, 1910-15; M.B., Ch.B. 1914. Indian Medical Service, Lieut. Nov. 1914.

BERRY, RICHARD JAMES ARTHUR.
M.B., C.M. 1891; M.D. 1894; M.D. (Melbourne); F.R.C.S. (Edin.). Australian Army Medical Corps, Major 1915. Registrar, No. 5 Australian General Hospital.

BERRY-HART, J. H. B.
Merchiston Castle; First XV. O.T.C. 1900-5, Cadet L/Corporal. Student of Medicine, 1907-11. O.T.C. Artillery, June 1908 to Nov. 1912, Cadet Farrier Corporal. 40th Pathans, Indian Army, 2nd Lieut. Jan. 1915; Lieut. Jan. 1916; Acting Captain Jan. 1918; Captain to July 1919; 20th and 2/33rd Punjabis. France 1915; British East Africa 1916; Mesopotamia 1917.

BERTRAM, DAVID CRAIG.
Royal High School. Student of Science, 1918-19. O.T.C. Infantry, 1918, Cadet Sergeant; Officer Cadet. 4th Seaforth Highlanders, 2nd Lieut. March 1919.

BERTRAM, DAVID MINTO.
George Watson's College; First XV. O.T.C. 1912-17, Cadet Sergeant. Student of Medicine, 1918-19. O.T.C. Artillery, Feb. to Dec. 1917, Cadet Corporal; Officer Cadet Dec. 1917. R.F.A. (T.), 2nd Lieut. June 1918. France. Somme Offensive 1918. Wounded Aug. 1918.

BETHELL, STANLEY EWART.
Student of Medicine, 1909-14; M.B., Ch.B. 1914. R.A.M.C., Lieut. Feb. 1916; Captain Feb. 1917.

Record of War Service

BETHUNE, CHARLES MURDOCH.
Royal Academy, Inverness; First XI. Student of Medicine, 1918. Royal Air Force, Cadet May 1918; Flight Cadet Oct. 1918 to Feb. 1919.

BETT, MALCOLM JAMES.
Student of Medicine, 1916-17 and 1918-19. O.T.C. Infantry, Nov. 1916 to April 1917, Cadet. 6th, 2nd, and 5th Royal Highlanders (Black Watch), 2nd Lieut. May 1917; Lieut. Egypt Jan. 1918. France June 1918 to Jan. 1919.

BEVERIDGE, ALEXANDER.
George Watson's College. Student of Medicine, 1914 and 1919. O.T.C. Artillery, 1914, Cadet. R.G.A., 2nd Lieut. Jan. 1915; Lieut. July 1917 to Jan. 1919. India July 1915; Mesopotamia, Kut Relief Force, Dec. 1915 to June 1916. Invalided home June 1916.

BEVERIDGE, GORDON.
Edinburgh Academy; First XV. Student of Medicine, 1909-14; L.R.C.P. & S. (Edin.) 1919. O.T.C. Artillery, Oct. 1908 to Aug. 1914, Lieut. R.F.A. (S.R.), 2nd Lieut. Aug. 1914; Lieut. June 1915; Captain Aug. 1915; Major Sept. 1916. France Oct. 1914 to March 1918. M.C. Jan. 1917.

BEVERIDGE, HENRY ERSKINE.
Abbotsholme, Derbyshire. Student of Science, 1901-2. A.S.C., 2nd Lieut. May 1915; Lieut. Oct. 1915. Salonika Jan. 1916. Invalided out May 1918.

BEVERIDGE, JAMES.
Dunfermline High School. M.A. 1887. Schoolmaster. 6th V.B. Royal Scots, Private Jan. 1917; 2nd Lieut. Jan. 1918; Lieut. July 1918.

BEVERIDGE, JOHN ALEXANDER.
Edinburgh Academy. O.T.C. 1913-16. Student of Science, 1918. O.T.C. Infantry, 1917-18, Cadet. Royal Air Force, Officer Cadet Feb. 1918.

BEVERIDGE, PETER ADAMSON.
Pathhead School. M.A. (Hons. Phil.) 1907. Schoolmaster. 137th Canadian Infantry, 2nd Lieut. Dec. 1915; Lieut. Jan. 1916; Captain March 1916; Major Aug. 1916. France 1917 to April 1919.

BEVERIDGE, ROBERT.
Student of Law, 1915-17. A.S.C. (M.T.), Private; Corporal 1916; 2nd Lieut.; Captain Nov. 1916. France. M.C. Dispatches.

BEVERIDGE, ROBERT.
George Heriot's School. Student of Law, 1915-17. R.G.A., 185th Siege Battery, Gunner April 1917; Bombardier July 1917. France. Gassed Jan. 1918. Wounded June 1918.

Record of War Service

BEVERIDGE, THOMAS LORIMER.
Ayr Academy. Student of Arts, 1889-92. Chaplain, 2nd Class, 6th Corps Headquarters, May 1915; Deputy Assistant Principal Chaplain, Jan. 1918; Assistant Principal Chaplain, Royal Air Force, June 1919. France. Mention March 1919.

BEVERIDGE, WILFRED WILLIAM OGILVY.
Kensington School. M.B., C.M. 1887; D.P.H. (Camb.) 1904. Army Medical Service, Colonel and A.D.M.S.; Brigadier-General Nov. 1919. Director of Hygiene, War Office. South African Campaign, 1899-1902. D.S.O. France Aug. 1914 to May 1919. Chevalier de la Légion d'Honneur, April 1918. C.B.; C.B.E. Order of St Stanislaus (Russia). Four times mentioned in Dispatches.

BHATIA, A. S.
Student of Arts, 1913-15. Indian Field Ambulance.

BIDEN, WILLIAM MERVYN.
Epsom College. Cadet Corps 1900-2. M.B., Ch.B. 1910. R.A.M.C. (S.R.), Lieut. March 1910; Captain Sept. 1913; Acting Major Sept. 1919. 17th Field Ambulance, 6th Division. France Sept. 1914 to Aug. 1917; Italy June 1918 to March 1919. Wounded Feb. 1916. Dispatches 1916. M.C. April 1917.

BIDIE, GEORGE.
Oxford Military College. Cadet 1881-4, Under Officer. M.B., C.M. 1908; M.D. 1912; M.R.C.P. (London); F.R.C.S. (Edin.). Rowing "Blue." Indian Medical Service, 1893; Lieut.-Col. 1913. 26th K.G.O. Light Cavalry, and 2nd Q.V.O. Sappers and Miners. O.C. Indian Troops Hospital, Bangalore.

BIGGAM, ALEXANDER GORDON.
George Watson's College. M.B., Ch.B. 1911. University Coy., 9th Royal Scots (Highlanders). R.A.M.C., Lieut.; Captain March 1915; Acting Lieut.-Col. 1919. France Nov. 1914, Lahore Division; India 1917; Waziristan 1919. Wounded at La Bassée, March 1915.

BIGGAM, JAMES.
Stranraer High School. M.B., Ch.B. 1914. O.T.C. Artillery, 1908-14, Cadet Sergeant. R.A.M.C., Lieut. Oct. 1914; Captain Oct. 1915; Acting Major June 1917. D.A.D.M.S., 3rd Cavalry Division. France and The Rhine Oct. 1914 to Sept. 1919. Dispatches June 1917 and May 1918. M.C. Nov. 1918; Bar to M.C. Jan. 1919.

BIGGAM, THOMAS.
Stranraer Academy. M.B., Ch.B. 1897. R.A.M.C. 1900; Major Jan. 1912; Lieut.-Col. March 1918. South African Campaign; China 1900; France 1914.

Record of War Service

BIGNOLD, CHARLES ALFRED.
Ayr Academy. M.A. 1905; M.B., Ch.B. 1909; B.Sc. 1911. O.T.C. Medical, April 1909 to Jan. 1911, Cadet. R.A.M.C., Captain Sept. 1914; Major June 1918. 11th Field Ambulance, France, Aug. 1914 to Jan. 1915. India June 1916. M.O. Enteric Depôt, Wellington, Oct. 1917. D.A.D.M.S., Poona Division, June 1918 to Feb. 1919.

BIGNOLD, HERBERT ARTHUR.
Royal High School. Student of Science, 1913-15 and 1918-20. O.T.C. Engineers, 1914-15, Cadet. Royal Air Force; Gordon Highlanders.

BIGNOLD, MARY FLORENCE.
Ayr Academy. M.B., Ch.B. 1907. Scottish Women's Hospitals, Serbia, Assistant Physician, April to Oct. 1915; St John's Military Hospital, Malta; Civil Surgeon 1916. Attached R.A.M.C., Medical Officer, Aug. 1916.

BILTON, LEWIS LEONARD.
Edinburgh Academy; First XV. Student of Law, 1898-1904. Writer to the Signet, 1904. No. 4 Coy. Q.R.V.B. Royal Scots, 1899, L/Corporal. A.S.C. (Lowland Mounted Brigade), Captain Sept. 1914; Major 1915; Lieut.-Col. 1916. 17th Royal Scots; 8th Worcestershire Regiment (T.) C.M.G. and Croix de Guerre (Belgium) 1918. Twice mentioned in Dispatches.

BINKS, HORACE BURCHAM.
Student of Medicine, 1909-14; M.B., Ch.B. 1914. O.T.C. Infantry, Feb. 1910 to Oct. 1912, Cadet. R.A.M.C., Lieut. March 1915; Captain March 1916; attached 6th Loyal North Lancashire Regiment. Gallipoli June to Nov. 1915; Mesopotamia June 1916 to April 1919; India April to Oct. 1919.

BINNIE, JOHN JAMES ROUSE.
Airdrie Academy. Student of Medicine, 1913-16 and 1918-19; M.B., Ch.B. 1919. O.T.C. Artillery, Oct. 1914 to March 1916, Cadet. R.N.V.R., Surgeon-Probationer, March 1916.

BINNS, JAMES BRANGWYN.
King Edward VI. School, Birmingham and City of London School. Student of Arts, 1910-14; M.A. 1914. 16th Middlesex Regiment, Private Sept. 1914. 9th Royal Berkshire Regiment, 2nd Lieut. March 1915. Invalided out June 1915.

BIRCH, DE BURGH.
Manilla Hall, Clifton, Bristol, and Bristol Medical School. M.B., C.M. 1877; M.D. 1880. Assistant to Professor of Medicine, 1877-1880. No. 4 Coy. Q.R.V.B. Royal Scots, Private. R.A.M.C. (T.), Lieut.-Col. Feb. 1908; Colonel A.M.S. April 1908. A.D.M.S. Jan. 1915. France Jan. 1917. V.D. 1908. Dispatches Dec. 1916 and Dec. 1917. C.B. (Civil) 1909.

Record of War Service

BIRD, JOHN TURNBULL.
Hutton School, Berwickshire. Student of Arts and Divinity; M.A. 1881. Chaplain 1891; 1st Class, July 1913; Assistant Principal Chaplain, Jan. 1917. Rouen 1916. Dispatches Oct. 1914 and Jan. 1917. C.M.G. Jan. 1917.

BIRD, WILLIAM.
Student of Medicine, 1909-14; M.B., Ch.B. 1914. O.T.C. Medical, April 1909 to June 1913, Cadet Corporal. R.A.M.C., Lieut. Sept. 1914; Captain April 1915.

BIRNIE, ARTHUR.
George Heriot's School. M.A. 1912. Lecturer in Economic History, Aberdeen University. R.A.M.C., Private Aug. 1915; L/Corporal Sept. 1915; Sergeant Nov. 1915. Attached 102nd Field Ambulance.

BIRRELL, EDWIN THOMAS FAIRWEATHER.
Trinity College, Glenalmond. Cadet Corps 1886-90, L/Corporal. M.B., C.M. 1895. R.A.M.C., Lieut. July 1896; Lieut.-Col. March 1915; Colonel Dec. 1917. D.A.D.M.S.; A.D.M.S. and D.D.M.S. Balkan War, 1912-13, as Commissioner B.R.C.S. for Bulgaria. France 1914-19. Dispatches Oct. 1914, June 1915, Jan. and Dec. 1916, Nov. 1917, Jan. 1918 and Jan. 1919. C.M.G. 1915; C.B. 1917. Serbian White Eagle; Greek Order of Redeemer; Greek Military Merit.

BIRRELL, JOHN HAMILTON.
Gillespie's School, Edinburgh. M.A. 1902. R.G.A., Gunner April 1917; L/Bombardier May 1918. France and The Rhine 1917 to Jan. 1919.

BISHOP, RICHARD THOMAS WALLIS.
Student of Science, 1915-16. O.T.C. Artillery, May 1916 to Feb. 1917, Cadet. R.F.A., 2nd Lieut. July 1917; 350th Army Brigade, France.

BISSET, WALTER.
George Watson's College. M.A. 1905; B.Sc., M.B., Ch.B. 1909. O.T.C. Medical, 1908, Cadet Staff Sergeant. R.A.M.C., Captain Jan. 1911; Acting Lieut.-Col. June 1919. Lahore British General Hospital; No. 8 British and No. 6 Combined Field Ambulances. France 1914-15; Mesopotamia 1916-18; Afghanistan May to Aug. 1919. M.C. Aug. 1918.

BISSET-SMITH, RAYMOND.
Ashton-under-Lyne School. M.A. 1911; M.B., Ch.B. 1917. O.T.C. Infantry, 1908-11; Medical, 1912-14 and 1915-17, Cadet. R.A.M.C. (S.R.), Lieut. May 1917; Captain May 1918. East African Carrier Corps.

BLACK, EDWARD HAMILTON.
Boston Grammar School, Lincs. First XV. and XI. M.B., Ch.B. 1906; D.P.H. (Camb.) 1914. R.A.M.C., Lieut. June 1915; Captain June 1916. France Jan. 1918 to Feb. 1919.

BLACK, FRANCIS GEORGE HAMILTON ROLLO.
M.B., Ch.B. 1907. Royal Navy, Surgeon; Staff Surgeon Nov. 1916.

Record of War Service

BLACK, JAMES.
M.B., Ch.B. 1908; M.D. 1911. R.A.M.C., Lieut. Aug. 1918.

BLACK, JOHN DANIEL McLEOD.
M.A. 1900. Schoolmaster. 4th Cameron Highlanders, Aug. 1914; 2nd Lieut. Oct. 1914; Lieut. June 1916; Captain July 1918. France. Wounded. Lewis Gun and Musketry Instructor, Y.O.T.C., Ripon.

BLACK, JOHN GRAHAM.
Royal High School; Athletics. Student of Arts, 1914-15. O.T.C. Infantry, 1914-15, Cadet. 5th Cameron Highlanders, 2nd Lieut. June 1915; Lieut.

BLACK, JOHN MURRAY.
George Watson's College. O.T.C. 1914-15. Student of Medicine, 1915-17. O.T.C. Infantry, 1917, and Medical, April 1918-19, Cadet; Officer Cadet Jan. 1918.

BLACK, NORMAN.
King William's College, Isle of Man. M.B., Ch.B. 1905. R.A.M.C., Lieut. Jan. 1915; Captain April 1915; Major Jan. 1917; attached 11th Argyll and Sutherland Highlanders. S.M.O. Straits Settlements, Jan. 1917-19. M.C. June 1915. O.B.E. (Military) July 1919.

BLACK, ROBERT.
Ayr Academy. Student of Law, 1910-12. R.F.A. (T.), 1st Lowland Brigade, Gunner Aug. 1914. 5th Royal Scots, 2nd Lieut. March 1915; Temp. Lieut. Jan. 1916; Lieut. (Subst.) July 1916; Acting Captain Nov. 1917 to May 1918. France with R.E. (Special Brigade).

BLACK, ROBERT BARCLAY.
M.B., Ch.B. 1897. R.A.M.C., Major (Subst.) Aug. 1912 (retired). D.A.D.M.S. D.S.O. Dispatches.

BLACK, THOMAS WILSON.
Edinburgh Academy and Clayesmore School, Winchester. Student of Law, 1911-14. Lothians and Border Horse (T.), Private April 1913. R.G.A., 1/1st Lowland Heavy Battery, 2nd Lieut. March 1915; Lieut. June 1916. France July 1916 to May 1917.

BLACKADDER, WILLIAM.
High School, Dundee. B.Sc. 1897. No. 4 Coy. Q.R.V.B. Royal Scots, 1894-7, Private. R.G.A., 2nd Lieut. Dec. 1915. R.E., 2nd Lieut. May 1917; Lieut. Nov. 1919. Dispatches July 1919.

BLACKLAY, OLIVER HENRY.
M.B., Ch.B. 1910; M.D. (Gold Medal) 1913; F.R.C.S. (Edin.). R.A.M.C. (T.), Lieut. Aug. 1914; Captain April 1915. 3rd Field Ambulance, East Lancs. Division. Cairo Military Hospital, Dec. 1916. Wounded at Dardanelles July 1915.

Record of War Service

BLACKLEDGE, WILLIAM THOMAS.
L.R.C.P. & S. 1889; M.B., C.M. 1893. R.A.M.C. (T.), 1900; Major; Acting Lieut.-Col. March 1915. President, Medical Board, Mersey Defences, 1917-19.

BLACKLEY, A. ERNEST.
Lanark School. Student of Medicine, 1914-16 and 1918-20. O.T.C. Medical, Dec. 1915 to April 1917, Cadet. R.N.V.R., Surgeon-Sub-Lieut., March 1917. Mine-sweepers, Destroyers, "Q" Ships.

BLACKLOCK, BREADALBANE.
M.B., Ch.B. 1902; M.D. R.A.M.C., Lieut. July 1918; attached 83rd General Hospital, Boulogne.

BLACKWELL, THOMAS CHARLES.
Rugby. M.B., Ch.B. 1903; M.D. 1907. Royal Navy, Surgeon, Aug. 1914.

BLACKWOOD, ROBERT CECIL.
Edinburgh Academy; First XV. B.Sc. 1910. O.T.C. Artillery, 1908-13, Cadet Corporal. 3rd Royal Scots, 2nd Lieut. Aug. 1914; Lieut.; Captain 1916; Acting Major June 1919. Wounded Sept. 1915. M.C. 1915. Dispatches.

BLACKWOOD, WILLIAM.
Lincoln Grammar School. M.B., Ch.B. 1902. University Battery, E.C.A.V., 1897-1901, Corporal. R.A.M.C. (T.), Lieut. June 1908; Captain July 1912; Acting Major Oct. 1915; Acting Lieut.-Col. April 1917; attached 25th Field Ambulance and 2/1st Wessex Field Ambulance, France. Dispatches May 1915, June and Dec. 1918. D.S.O. June 1918 and Bar to D.S.O. Sept. 1919.

BLACKWOOD, WILLIAM THORBURN.
Edinburgh Academy; First XI. M.A. 1904; LL.B. and Writer to the Signet, 1917. Inns of Court O.T.C., Dec. 1915. 8th Royal Scots (T.), 2nd Lieut. Dec. 1916; Lieut. June 1918; Acting Captain June 1918; Acting Major Jan. 1919. France Feb. 1917 to April 1918. M.C. 1918.

BLADES, DANIEL PATTERSON.
Berwickshire High School, Duns. M.A. 1913; LL.B. 1914. Advocate. Senior President, S.R.C. and Diagnostic Society. O.T.C. Infantry, 1915-16, Cadet Sergeant; Officer Cadet July 1916. 3rd and 6th Cameron Highlanders, 2nd Lieut. Nov. 1916. France Jan. to Nov. 1917. Invalided out April 1918.

BLAIR, ALEXANDER STEVENSON.
Loretto, and Brasenose College, Oxford; First XV. and XI. B.A. (Oxford) 1886; Student of Law, 1886-9. Writer to the Signet, 1889. 9th Royal Scots, 1900; Lieut.-Col. and O.C. 1912-16. Mobilised Aug. 1914. France Feb. 1915 to Dec. 1917. C.M.G. Dispatches 1916 and 1917. T.D. 1918.

Record of War Service

BLAIR, ARCHIBALD.
Merchiston Castle. Cadet Corps 1896-7. B.A. (Camb.) 1900; Student of Law, 1900-3. Writer to the Signet, 1904. 8th Royal Scots (T.), 2nd Lieut. Sept. 1914; Lieut. June 1915. Wounded May 1915. Invalided out Dec. 1916. Recommissioned, Royal Air Force, Lieut. May 1917. France.

BLAIR, DOUGLAS PANTON.
Sharp's School, Perth. M.B., Ch.B. 1906; D.P.H. R.A.M.C. (T.), Lieut. June 1916; Captain June 1917.

BLAIR, GEORGE.
Kirkcaldy High School. M.B., Ch.B. 1905; F.R.C.S. (Edin.). R.A.M.C., Lieut. Sept. 1915; Captain March 1918.

BLAIR, GRAHAM.
George Heriot's School. O.T.C. 1915-17, Cadet L/Corporal. Edinburgh University O.T.C. Artillery, Aug. 1917 to March 1918, Cadet; Officer Cadet March 1918. R.G.A., 2nd Lieut. Oct. 1918 to Sept. 1919.

BLAIR, HUGH ALEXANDER.
Edinburgh Academy and Sedbergh. Student of Law, 1908-9. Chartered Accountant, 1912. Q.E. Mounted Rifles. R.F.A. (T.), 1st Lowland Brigade, Lieut.; Captain June 1916; Acting Major Aug. 1917. India.

BLAIR, JAMES RICHARD.
Daniel Stewart's College; First XV. M.A. (Hons. Classics) 1912. O.T.C. Infantry, 1909-14, Cadet Sergeant. 10th Middlesex Regiment, 2nd Lieut. March 1915; Lieut. 1917. 30th Lancers (Indian Cavalry), Captain 1918. India.

BLAIR, JOHN MONCRIEFF.
George Watson's College. O.T.C. 1912-14, Cadet. Student of Medicine, 1914-15 and 1918-19. O.T.C. Infantry, 1914-15, and Medical, 1918-19, Cadet. R.E. (Special Brigade), Private July 1915; Corporal Aug. 1915 to Dec. 1918.

BLAIR, RALPH.
Merchiston Castle; First XV. Cadet Corps 1904-5. Student of Law. Chartered Accountant, 1911. R.E. (T.), 2nd Lieut.; Lieut. June 1916; Captain. France 1915; Salonika and Near East 1915-20. Dispatches Oct. 1917.

BLAIR, ROBERT BERTRAM.
Kirkcaldy High School. M.B., Ch.B. 1911; F.R.C.S. (Edin.) 1914. O.T.C. Artillery, 1907-12, Cadet Corporal. R.A.M.C., Lieut. Oct. 1914; Captain Oct. 1915; Acting Major May 1918. 59th Casualty Clearing Station, France.

BLAIR, THOMAS.
Edinburgh Academy. O.T.C. 1910-12. Student of Science, 1912-14. O.T.C. Engineers, Nov. 1912 to Oct. 1914, Cadet. 10th Royal Scots (Cyclists), 2nd Lieut. Oct. 1914; Lieut. Sept. 1915; Captain March 1916; attached 5/6th Royal Scots, France. Gassed April 1918.

Record of War Service

BLAIR, WILLIAM ROBERT.
 Alloa Academy. Student of Arts and Law, 1911-15; M.A. 1912; LL.B. 1915. O.T.C. Infantry, 1914-15, Cadet. 7th Argyll and Sutherland Highlanders (T.), 2nd Lieut. Feb. 1915; Lieut. June 1916; Acting Captain June 1918. France 1917-18. Wounded and Gassed. M.C. Nov. 1917.

BLANCHARD, HENRY HUBBARD.
 Student of Divinity, 1918-19. 85th Battn. Nova Scotia Highlanders, Canadian Exp. Force, Private March 1916. France. M.M. April 1917.

BLANCHARD, ROBERT JOHNSTONE.
 M.B., C.M. 1877. Canadian Army Medical Corps, June 1915, Lieut.-Col. and O.C. 3rd Casualty Clearing Station. Dispatches.

BLISS, DOUGLAS PERCY.
 George Watson's College; First XV. O.T.C. 1915-17. Student of Arts, 1918-19, O.T.C. Artillery, Jan. to April 1918, Cadet. 4th Highland Light Infantry, Private April 1918; L/Corporal Aug. 1918.

BLISS, ROGER PERCY.
 George Watson's College. Student of Medicine, 1916-17 and 1918-19. O.T.C. Medical, May 1918-20, Cadet. 9th King's Own Scottish Borderers (S.R.), Private April 1917; 2nd Lieut. Royal Air Force.

BLOCKLEY, JOHN PHILLIPS.
 Rossall. Cadet Corps 1902-5. M.B., Ch.B. 1912. O.T.C. Artillery, Oct. 1908 to Jan. 1913, Cadet Sergeant. R.A.M.C., Lieut. Jan. 1915; Captain Jan. 1916.

BLOOM, ARTHUR.
 M.B., Ch.B. 1911. O.T.C. Infantry, Jan. 1909 to June 1912, Cadet L/Corporal. R.A.M.C., Lieut.; Captain March 1916. Red Cross Hospital, France. M.C.

BLUMER, CHARLES ERIC MILNES.
 Marlborough. O.T.C. 1913-16, Cadet Corporal. Student of Medicine, 1916. Sherwood Foresters, Private May 1917. North Staffordshire Regiment, 2nd Lieut. Aug. 1918.

BLUNDELL, HIGHT.
 Royal Grammar School, Giggleswick. Athletics. M.B., C.M. 1891; M.D. 1898. R.A.M.C., Lieut. May 1915; Captain May 1916.

BLYTH, HENRY.
 Royal High School. M.B., Ch.B. 1908; D.P.H. R.A.M.C., Lieut. Sept. 1916; Captain Sept. 1917.

BLYTH, HERBERT MACDONALD.
 Merchiston Castle. Student of Law, 1915-16. Chartered Accountant, 1919. 3rd King's Own Scottish Borderers, Private Jan. 1916; 2nd Lieut. March 1917; Lieut. Sept. 1918. Egypt and Palestine June 1917; France July 1918. Wounded Aug. 1918.

Record of War Service

BLYTH, JAMES.
George Heriot's School. M.A. 1910. Motor Machine-Gun Corps (Signal Section), Private March 1915. Tank Corps. France. Wounded May 1917. Discharged June 1918.

BOAG, JOHN HAMILTON.
M.B., Ch.B. 1912; D.P.H., R.C.P.S. (Edin.) 1914. O.T.C. Artillery, 1908-12, Cadet. R.A.M.C., Lieut.; Captain Aug. 1918. India. M.C. Dispatches.

BOAL, JACKSON GRAHAME.
Campbell College, Belfast; First XV. and XI. M.B., Ch.B. 1910. O.T.C. Medical, April 1908 to Nov. 1912, Cadet L/Corporal. Royal Navy, Surgeon-Lieut.-Commander Oct. 1912.

BODINGTON, PERCIVAL JAMES.
Haileybury. M.B., Ch.B. 1899. Royal Horse Guards, Surgeon-Captain, Nov. 1900. South African Campaign, 1900.

BOINVILLE, VIVIAN CHASTEL DE.
Haileybury. M.B., Ch.B. 1901; M.D. 1906. R.A.M.C. (T.), Captain 1908; attached 57th General Hospital, France.

BOMFORD, DOUGLAS R.
Wycliffe College, Gloucester. Student of Medicine, 1913-14. 2/8th Worcestershire Regiment (T.), 2nd Lieut. Sept. 1914; Captain Jan. 1917. Wounded Oct. 1916 and April 1917. Invalided out.

BOMFORD, LESLIE RAYMOND.
Student of Medicine, 1914-15. O.T.C. Infantry, May to July 1915, Cadet. 8th Worcestershire Regiment, 2nd Lieut. July 1915; Lieut. July 1917; Acting Captain Aug. 1918. M.C. May 1918 and Bar to M.C. Aug. 1918; D.S.O. Nov. 1918. Twice mentioned in Dispatches.

BONALLO, JAMES.
B.D. 1871. Chaplain, Highland Mounted Brigade, Sept. 1914. Lovat Scouts. Scottish Churches Huts in France. Dispatches 1918.

BONAR, JOHN MITCHELL.
Bradford Grammar School; First XV. Student of Medicine, 1914-15 and 1918-19. A.S.C. (M.T.), Private Sept. 1915; L/Corporal May 1916; 2nd Lieut. March 1917. Invalided out April 1918.

BONAR, THOMSON.
Taunton School. O.T.C. 1913-14. Student of Medicine, 1914-15 and 1919. 16th Royal Scots, Private Dec. 1914. R.E., Corporal June 1915 to March 1919.

BOND, FREDERICK FIELDING.
Commercial Academy, Accrington. M.B., C.M. 1884; M.D. 1886; D.P.H. (Lond.) 1889. No. 4 Coy. Q.R.V.B., Private. R.A.M.C., Captain Sept. 1914 to Jan. 1915. West African Royal Mail, Surgeon, 1917-18.

Record of War Service

BOND, JOHN HENRY RICHARD.
United Services College, Westward Ho. First XI.; Football. M.B., C.M. 1882. Winnipeg University O.T.C., Feb. 1915-16, Captain. Winnipeg Infantry Reserve Militia. Canadian Army Medical Corps, Captain June 1917.

BOND, REGINALD ST GEORGE SMALLBRIDGE.
M.B., C.M. 1894; F.R.C.S. (Edin.) 1897; D.P.H. (Lond.) 1916; M.R.C.P. (Lond.) 1919. Royal Navy, May 1898, Surgeon-Commander May 1914. H.M.S. *Commonwealth*, April 1914 to July 1916. R.N. Hospital, Plymouth, July 1916 to Dec. 1918; Naval Health Officer, Devonport, Dec. 1918.

BONE, BERTRAM MAYHEW.
Royal Grammar School, Lancaster; First XV. M.B., C.M. 1897; F.R.C.S. (Edin.) 1906. R.A.M.C., Lieut. Nov. 1914; Captain Nov. 1915. H.M. Hospital Ship *Dunluce Castle*. Egypt. 1st Border Regiment. Cape Helles and Suvla Bay. Invalided out Jan. 1916.

BONE, HUGH.
Ayr Academy. M.A. (Hons. Classics) 1914. O.T.C. Infantry, Oct. to Dec. 1914. 16th Royal Scots, Private Dec. 1914. France. Wounded July 1916. Invalided out Dec. 1916.

BONE, JAMES HOUSTON.
Royal High School. University O.T.C. Infantry, June 1917 to Jan. 1918, Cadet. Royal Air Force, Flight Cadet Jan. 1918.

BONNAR, J. CALDERWOOD.
George Watson's College. Student of Arts and Law, 1910-14. Advocate, 1914. 4th Royal Dublin Fusiliers (S.R.), 2nd Lieut. Nov. 1914; Lieut. Jan. 1916; Captain June 1917.

BONNELL, EMRYCE ANTHONY.
St David's County School, Pembrokeshire. Student of Arts, 1915-16. R.A.M.C., Welsh Field Ambulance, Private Nov. 1915. 34th Ambulance Train, France.

BOOG-WATSON, WILLIAM NAIRN.
Merchiston Castle and George Watson's College. Student of Medicine, 1915-16 and 1918-19. O.T.C. Artillery Aug. to Dec. 1914, and Medical, Oct. 1915 to Oct. 1916, Cadet. Royal Military College, Jan. to March 1915. R.G.A., Gunner July 1916; 2nd Lieut. Dec. 1917. France.

BOOTH, HERBERT.
Ellesmere College, Shropshire. Athletics. Cadet Corps 1900-4, Cadet Corporal. Student of Medicine, 1913-14; Pharmaceutical Chemist. R.A.M.C., No. 9 General Hospital, Private Aug. 1914; Sergeant Nov. 1914; Officer Cadet March 1916. 10th and 1st Loyal North Lancashire Regiment, 2nd Lieut. Nov. 1916; Lieut. April 1917; Acting Captain Aug. 1917. France 1914-18. Dispatches Dec. 1917.

Record of War Service

BOOTH, JOHN COOPER.
 Bedford Grammar School. M.B., Ch.B. 1912. Australian Army Medical Corps, Captain April 1916.

BOOTHBY, ROBERT JOHN GRAHAM.
 Eton. O.T.C. 1915-18, Cadet L/Corporal. Student of Arts, 1918. Scots Guards, Officer Cadet May 1918; 2nd Lieut. Feb. 1919.

BORROWMAN, CHARLES GORDON.
 George Watson's College. O.T.C. 1907-9. M.A. 1912. O.T.C. Infantry, Oct. 1909 to July 1911, Cadet Corporal. 2/4th Gurkha Rifles, 2nd Lieut. Jan. 1912; Lieut. April 1914; Captain Jan. 1916. India 1914-16 and 1919; Mesopotamia 1916-17.

BORTHWICK, GEORGE ARTHUR.
 George Watson's College. M.B., Ch.B. 1913; D.T.M. & H. 1914; D.P.H. 1920. Barrister-at-Law, Gray's Inn. R.A.M.C., Lieut. Feb. 1915; Captain Feb. 1916. 12th Field Ambulance, 4th Division. France. Invalided out July 1916.

BORTHWICK, JOHN.
 George Heriot's School. Anatomy Department, University. R.F.A. (T.), 1st Lowland Brigade, Driver 1909; Acting Bombardier Oct. 1914; Bombardier Jan. 1915.

BORTHWICK, THOMAS.
 M.B., Ch.B. 1881; M.D. 1891. Australian Army Medical Corps, Major Aug. 1915. No. 7 Australian General Hospital, Bacteriologist.

BORWICK, GEORGE.
 Leith Academy. M.A. 1913. Schoolmaster. 9th Royal Scots (T.), March 1909; 2nd Lieut. Feb. 1915; Temp. Lieut. July 1915; Temp. Captain Oct. 1915; Lieut. July 1916. France. M.C. April 1917.

BOSE, SATIS.
 M.B., C.M. 1897. Indian Medical Service, June 1901; Major Dec. 1912. Mobilised Aug. 1915. Mesopotamia. Besieged in Kut and taken Prisoner. India.

BOSTOCK, JOHN SOUTHEY.
 Lancing; First XI., Cricket and Football. M.B., Ch.B. 1900. R.A.M.C., Jan. 1901; Major Oct. 1912; Brevet Lieut.-Col. June 1915; Brevet Col. Jan. 1918. Dispatches June 1915 and Feb. 1917.

BOSTON, RALPH BURN.
 Student of Medicine, 1910-15; M.B., Ch.B. 1915. O.T.C. Medical, Nov. 1914-15, Cadet. Royal Navy, Surgeon April 1915. H.M.S. *Mars*.

Record of War Service

BOSWELL, DUDLEY WILLIAM.
Norwich Grammar School. M.B., Ch.B. 1904; M.D. 1907; D.P.H. (Camb.) 1918. R.A.M.C. (T.), Lieut. 1909, Captain 1912; Acting Major April 1915; Brevet Major June 1917; Acting Lieut.-Col. Dec. 1917. 2nd East Anglian Brigade, Gallipoli; 302nd and 154th Field Ambulances and 84th Casualty Clearing Station, North Russia. Syven Force.

BOW, JOHN SUTHERLAND.
Stirling High School. Student of Medicine, 1912-17; M.B., Ch.B. (Hons.) 1917. Anatomy Staff, 1916-17. O.T.C. Infantry, Oct. 1914 to Dec. 1915, Cadet L/Corporal; and Medical, Dec. 1915 to July 1917, Cadet Corporal. R.A.M.C. (S.R.), Lieut. Aug. 1917; Captain Aug. 1918. Mesopotamia.

BOWDEN, TOM ROSE.
Shrewsbury. O.T.C. 1911-15, Cadet L/Corporal. Student of Medicine, 1918. R.G.A., 2nd Lieut. Dec. 1915; Lieut. June 1917; Acting Captain Sept. 1918. France Dec. 1916 to Jan. 1919. 220th Siege Battery.

BOWEN-REES, RICHARD ERIC.
Eltham College, Kent; First XV. and XI. Student of Medicine, 1914-15 and 1918-19. Inns of Court O.T.C., Private July 1915. 1/5th Royal Welsh Fusiliers, 2nd Lieut. Dec. 1915; Lieut. July 1917. Egypt and Palestine June 1916 to Feb. 1919. M.C. Oct. 1918. Dispatches Jan. 1919.

BOWERBANK, FREDERICK THOMPSON.
M.B., Ch.B. 1904; M.D. 1917. N.Z. Medical Corps, April 1915; Temp. Major Jan. 1916; Major March 1918. No. 1 N.Z. General Hospital. Dispatches March 1916, Aug. 1917, March and Dec. 1918, and March 1919. O.B.E. May 1919.

BOWERS, GEORGE PERCY FARMAR.
George Heriot's School. O.T.C. 1909-15, Cadet Sergeant. Student of Medicine, 1915. R.E. (Special Brigade), Corporal Feb. 1916. 5th Northumberland Fusiliers, 2nd Lieut. Feb. 1919. France April 1916 to Dec. 1918.

BOWES, JOHN.
Bolton Grammar School. M.B., C.M. 1882; M.D. 1887. R.A.M.C., Lieut. April 1915; Captain April 1916; Major April 1917. Registrar, Military Hospital, Kinmel Park, 1916-18. Dispatches 1916.

BOWIE, JOHN DARLING.
George Watson's College; First XV. and XI. M.B., Ch.B. 1906. R.A.M.C., Lieut.; Captain Jan. 1914; Acting Lieut.-Col. Aug. 1916; Brevet Major June 1919. Indian Hospital, Brighton, and Field Ambulance. France June 1915 to April 1919. Three times mentioned in Dispatches. D.S.O. Sept. 1916.

Record of War Service

BOWIE, JOHN MACAULAY.
George Watson's College. M.B., Ch.B. 1898; M.D. 1901; M.R.C.P. 1902, and F.R.C.S. (Edin.) 1903. R.A.M.C. (T.) 1906, Captain 1910; Major 1918. France, M.O., 9th Royal Scots, 1915. Wounded at second Battle of Ypres 1915. Malta 1917; Salonika 1917-18. Croix de Guerre. Dispatches Jan. 1916.

BOWMAN, ROBERT McMILLAN.
Bangor School, County Down. Student of Medicine, 1912-17; M.B., Ch.B. 1917. O.T.C. Medical, Feb. 1916 to April 1917, Cadet. Royal Navy, Surgeon-Lieut. April 1917 to March 1919.

BOWSER, PHILIP RANDOLPH.
Loretto. O.T.C. 1911-14. Student of Medicine, 1914-15. O.T.C. Artillery, Oct. 1914 to Aug. 1915, Cadet. Royal Military Academy, Woolwich, Aug. 1915, R.G.A., 2nd Lieut. Feb. 1916; Lieut. Aug. 1917.

BOYACK, RUSSELL.
Daniel Stewart's College. Student of Law, 1914-15. Lothians and Border Horse (T.), Private Dec. 1914. R.G.A., Lieut. June 1915; Captain May 1918. France. Dispatches March 1919.

BOYD, ALLAN STUART.
Edinburgh Academy. M.B., C.M. 1893; M.D. 1912. South African Campaign, 1900-2. South African Medical Corps, Captain 1916; Major June 1917.

BOYD, EDWARD.
Edinburgh Academy; First XI. Student of Law, 1888-9; Chartered Accountant, 1891. R.N.V.R., Lieut. Jan. 1915.

BOYD, FRANCIS DARBY.
Edinburgh Academy; First XV. and Shooting VIII. M.B., C.M. 1888; M.D. 1893; F.R.C.P. (Edin.) 1892. Professor of Clinical Medicine. Army Medical Service, Major; Lieut.-Col. 1917; Colonel 1918. 2nd Scottish General and Bangour Hospitals. 58th General Hospital, France, 1917. Egyptian Exp. Force, G.H.Q., Palestine. C.M.G. 1901; C.B. and Dispatches 1919.

BOYD, JAMES ROBERTS.
M.B., Ch.B. 1911; M.D. 1914. R.A.M.C., Captain Oct. 1915 to Oct. 1916. N.Z. Medical Corps, 1916-18. Palestine. Invalided to New Zealand Aug. 1918. M.C. July 1916.

BOYD, JOHN.
M.A. 1876. Sheriff-Substitute. R.G.A., Forth Brigade, 1877. Rejoined Nov. 1914, Captain and Musketry Staff Officer, London Scottish; Queen's Westminster Rifles; 5th Brigade, 2nd London Division; West Riding Division and Northumbrian Brigade.

BOYD, JOHN CAMPBELL.
M.B., Ch.B. 1906; M.D. 1912. R.A.M.C., Lieut. Sept. 1915; Captain Sept. 1916. Dispatches May 1917.

Record of War Service

BOYD, THOMAS JAMIESON LAYCOCK STIRLING.
Edinburgh Academy. M.A. (Oxford). Student of Science, 1905-9. R.N.V.R., Paymaster Sub-Lieut., Dec. 1914. Royal Air Force, Wireless Section, Lieut.; attached H.Q., France, March 1918 to April 1919.

BOYD, WILLIAM.
George Watson's College. O.T.C. Oct. 1913 to July 1915. Student of Medicine, 1915-16 and 1918-19. O.T.C. Artillery, May 1916-17, Cadet Sergeant. R.F.A., Officer Cadet May 1917; 2nd Lieut. Oct. 1917. D/307th Brigade. France.

BOYD, WILLIAM HENRY STUART.
Bo'ness Academy. Student of Medicine, 1914-16 and 1917-19. 5th Royal Scots, Private; Machine-Gun Corps, 2nd Lieut.

BOYDEN, PERCY HAMILTON.
George Watson's College and King Edward VI. School, Birmingham. M.B., C.M. 1890; M.D. 1899. Royal Navy, H.M.S. *Excellent*, Surgeon-Commander, 1907. Inter-allied Sanitary Commission, 1916-19. Commander of Military Order of Avis (Portuguese) 1917.

BOYES, WILLIAM PURVES.
George Watson's College. M.A. 1903. Minister of U.F. Church, 1907. Chaplain, 2nd Royal Scots Fusiliers; Captain May 1916. France 1916-18.

BOYLE, HENRY ALOYSIUS.
M.B., Ch.B. 1913. R.A.M.C., Lieut. Feb. 1916; Captain Feb. 1917. Russia, Army of Black Sea.

BRADLEY, FREDERICK HOYSTED.
M.B., Ch.B. 1906. R.A.M.C., Captain. D.S.O. M.C.

BRADLEY, RICHARD JAMES.
M.B., Ch.B. 1901. Indian Medical Service, Major July 1913.

BRAID, FREDERIC LUNAN.
Gordon's College, Aberdeen. C.D.A. (Aberdeen). University O.T.C. Artillery, Dec. 1915 to Feb. 1916, Cadet. 3rd Gordon Highlanders, Private Aug. 1916. Attached 2nd Royal Scots; 2nd London Regiment (Royal Fusiliers); 2nd Royal Fusiliers. Wounded Sept. 1917 and invalided out.

BRAMWELL, ARCHIBALD CAMPBELL.
Fettes. O.T.C. 1914-17, Cadet. Student of Science, 1919. O.T.C. Artillery, Sept 1917 to April 1918, Cadet. Cavalry, Officer Cadet April 1918.

BRAMWELL, BYROM STANLEY.
Cheltenham. B.A. (Cantab.); LL.B. 1902. Advocate. R.F.A. (T.), 1st Lowland Brigade, Lieut.; Captain June 1916. Royal Artillery, 52nd Division, Staff Captain. Gallipoli and France.

Record of War Service

BRAMWELL, EDWIN.
    Cheltenham. M.B., C.M. 1896; M.D. 1919; F.R.C.P. (Edin.) 1903; F.R.C.P. (Lond.) 1907. Physician, R.I.E.; Lecturer on Clinical Medicine. R.A.M.C. (T.), Captain 1898. 2nd Scottish General, Edinburgh War, and Royal Victoria Hospitals.

BRAMWELL, HERBERT.
    Cheltenham. M.B., Ch.B. 1884; M.D. 1888; F.R.C.S. (Edin.) 1897. Navy Admiralty Surgeon, North Shields, 1886-1906. R.A.M.C. (T.), Lieut.-Col. May 1912. Attached Gloucester Hussars, Aug. 1914. Devonport, Taunton, and Tidworth Military Hospitals, March 1915 to Nov. 1918. Mention Aug. 1917.

BRAMWELL, HUGH RANSOM.
    University and High Schools, Nottingham. M.B., C.M. 1884; M.R.C.S. (Eng.) 1886. Assistant to Professor of Clinical Medicine. R.A.M.C., Captain June 1915.

BRANCH, EDMUND RALPH.
    George Watson's College; First XI. M.B., Ch.B. 1898; D.T.M. and H. Edinburgh Vol. Medical Service Coy. 1893-8, Sergeant. R.A.M.C., Lieut. Sept. 1916; Captain Sept. 1917; Acting Major March 1918. Leith and Edinburgh War Hospitals. Prisoners of War Hospital, Stobs.

BRAND, GEORGE BELL.
    George Watson's College. M.B., Ch.B. 1902. R.A.M.C. (T.), Lieut. Lowland Division, A.S.C., May 1911; Captain Nov. 1914. Aurist to 70th and 27th General Hospitals, and 45th Indian General Hospital, Cairo, 1918. Dispatches, Salonika, Dec. 1916.

BRANDER, GEORGE LAING.
    Royal High School. M.A. 1900; B.D. Minister of U.F. Church, 1906. 11th Royal Scots, 2nd Lieut. Sept. 1914; Lieut. Feb. 1915. Wounded and taken Prisoner of War.

BRANDER, WILLIAM BROWNE.
    George Watson's College; Athletics. M.A. (Hons. Classics) 1903. Indian Defence Force, Captain Sept. 1914. C.B.E. (Civil).

BRANFORD, FREDERICK VICTOR.
    Student of Arts, 1912-15 and 1916-17; M.A. 1916. Royal Air Force, 2nd Lieut. July 1916; Captain Jan. 1918. Interned in Holland after being shot down on Dutch-Belgium Frontier, 1917.

BRANFORD, JOHN FREDERICK KYTCHEN.
    Daniel Stewart's College. M.A. 1890. Clergyman, Church of England. Chaplain to Army Forces, 4th Class, 1916.

BRASH, JAMES COUPER.
    George Watson's College. M.A. 1906; B.Sc. 1908; M.B., Ch.B. 1910. Senior President, S.R.C., 1909-10. Leeds University O.T.C. Infantry, 1911-13, Cadet Sergeant. R.A.M.C. (S.R.), Lieut. April 1914; Captain April 1915; Acting Major Jan. 1918. France 1914-19. M.C. April 1916.

Record of War Service

BRASSEY, LAWRENCE PERCIVAL.
: M.B., Ch.B. 1900. Indian Medical Service, Major Dec. 1912; attached 91st Punjabis. Dispatches.

BRAYNE, WILLIAM FREDERICK.
: Derby; First XV. Cadet Corps 1890-4; Lieut. B.A. (Camb.) 1897; M.B., Ch.B. 1903. Indian Medical Service, Lieut. Jan. 1904; Captain Jan. 1907; Major July 1915. East Africa 1914-15; Mesopotamia 1918; Afghan War 1919.

BRAYSHAW, HAROLD CURRIE.
: St John's College, Johannesburg. First XI. Student of Medicine, 1916-18; M.B., Ch.B. 1918. 1st Battn. Cape Town Highlanders, Corporal Aug. 1914 to Dec. 1915.

BREBNER, ALICK.
: George Watson's College. B.Sc. 1905. Biliar Light Horse, Lieut. 1915. India. C.I.E. 1920.

BREBNER, CHARLES STUART.
: Darlington Grammar School. M.B., C.M. 1898; M.D. 1904; D.P.H. (Camb.) 1903. R.A.M.C. (T.), 1908; Temp. Major 1914; Acting Lieut.-Col. Aug. 1916 to Dec. 1918. O.C. 2/1st London Field Ambulance, 1914. Overseas Feb. 1916 to Dec. 1918. D.S.O. 1918. Dispatches Jan. 1917 and Jan. 1918.

BREBNER, GEORGE GUSTAV RADLOFF.
: M.A. 1903. 5th Mounted Brigade, South Africa; Lieut. 1915. German South-West Africa.

BREEKS, CHARLES WILKINSON.
: Rugby and Oxford. M.B., C.M. 1898; D.P.H. (Cantab.) 1902. South African Medical Corps, Lieut. Feb. 1915; Captain 1916.

BREMNER, ALEXANDER.
: M.B., Ch.B. 1913; D.T.M. & H. 1919. O.T.C. Infantry, Oct. 1909-12, Cadet. R.A.M.C., Lieut. Sept. 1914; Captain Sept. 1915; attached 2nd Royal Dublin Fusiliers; 17th Northumberland Fusiliers; 31st Field Ambulance and 7th Royal Munster Fusiliers. Salonika. M.C. June 1916. Dispatches July 1916.

BREMNER, DUGALD CHARLES.
: Craigmount House. M.B., C.M. 1892. R.A.M.C. (T.), Lieut. Oct. 1914; Captain June 1915; Major Feb. 1919; attached 8th Royal Scots (T.).

BREMNER, FREDERICK RUSSELL.
: Madras Academy, St Andrews. M.A. (St Andrews) 1888; M.B., C.M. 1903; M.D. 1919; L.R.C.P. & S. (Edin.) 1903. R.A.M.C. (T.), Lieut. Oct. 1908; Captain 1909; Major Aug. 1914.

BREMNER, THOMAS PENNINGTON.
: Eastbourne College. Student of Medicine. 1st King's Liverpool Regiment, 2nd Lieut. Sept. 1914; Lieut. Nov. 1914. Prisoner of War in Germany Aug. 1916 to Nov. 1918.

Record of War Service

BRESLIN, JOHN DUNLOP.
George Watson's College. M.A. 1907. Schoolmaster. College Coy., 6th Royal Scots, 1904-9, Sergeant. 17th Highland Light Infantry, 2nd Lieut. Dec. 1915; Lieut. July 1917. Wounded April 1917 and invalided out on 3rd April 1918.

BREWIS, ROBERT R.
Edinburgh Academy. Student of Law, 1909-10. Chartered Accountant, 1913. Lancashire Fusiliers, Private Oct. 1914; 2nd Lieut. Jan. 1915; Lieut. June 1916; Acting Captain April 1918. M.C. March 1918.

BREWIS, THOMAS.
Edinburgh Institution. Student of Medicine, 1914-15 and 1917-19. O.T.C. Medical, April 1918 to Jan. 1919, Cadet. R.E., City of Edinburgh (T.), Sapper.

BRIDGES, JAMES WHITESIDE.
M.B., C.M. 1888. Canadian Army Medical Corps, Lieut.-Col. 2nd General Hospital, France. Canadian Exp. Force, 1914. C.B.E.

BRIGGS, ARCHIBALD SMITH.
High School, Dundee. University O.T.C. Artillery, March to Sept. 1916, Cadet; Officer Cadet Oct. 1916. R.G.A., 2nd Lieut. France 1917.

BRIGGS, HUGH FRANCIS.
Dollar Academy. M.B., Ch.B. 1907. Royal Navy, Surgeon-Lieut. May 1909; Surgeon-Lieut.-Commander May 1917.

BRIMS, DONALD.
Student of Medicine, 1918. R.F.A., Gunner Dec. 1916; L/Corporal Nov. 1917. 8th Lincolnshire Regiment and 21st Labour Group H.Q. France 1917-18.

BRINDLE, EDWARD HERBERT.
Daniel Stewart's College. Cadet Corps 1912-14. Student of Medicine, 1918. 12th Royal Scots, Private Nov. 1916; 2nd Lieut. March 1919.

BRITTON, THOMAS CONN.
Strabane Academy. Student of Medicine, 1907-15; M.B., Ch.B. 1914. R.A.M.C. (T.), Lieut. Nov. 1914; Captain May 1915; Acting Major March 1918.

BROAD, BENJAMIN WILLIAM.
Monmouth. M.B., C.M. 1894. R.A.M.C. (T.), Dec. 1908; Major. 3rd West General Hospital, Cardiff.

BROADWOOD, CHARLES STEWART.
George Heriot's School; First XV. and XI. Student of Arts, 1918-19. O.T.C. Infantry, Aug. to Oct. 1915, Cadet. 14th Royal Scots, 2nd Lieut. Oct. 1915; Lieut. July 1917; attached R.E. (Signals).

Record of War Service

BROADWOOD, ROBERT GRANT.
George Heriot's School; First XV. and XI. Student of Arts and Medicine, 1913-15 and 1918-19; B.Sc. 1919. O.T.C. Artillery, Nov. 1914-15, Cadet. R.G.A., 2nd Lieut. Dec. 1915; Lieut. France. Wounded. M.C. March 1917.

BROATCH, GEORGE THOMAS.
M.B., C.M. 1883. Royal Navy, 1886; Fleet Surgeon Aug. 1902; Surgeon-Captain May 1916; attached R.N. Barracks, Portsmouth; H.M.S. *Royal Sovereign* and R.N. Hospital, Malta. C.B.E. Jan. 1919. Officer of the Legion of Honour (France) March 1919.

BRODIE, PETER MARTIN.
George Watson's College. O.T.C. Student of Medicine, 1911-14 and 1917-19; M.B., Ch.B. 1919. O.T.C. Medical, Aug. to Sept. 1914, Cadet. R.A.M.C. (T.); Scottish Horse Brigade Field Ambulance, Private. 6th Seaforth Highlanders, 2nd Lieut. Sept. 1915 to July 1917.

BROGDEN, GEORGE ALEXANDER.
B.A. (Camb.) 1889; M.B., Ch.B. 1899; M.D. 1904. R.A.M.C. (T.), Captain. 4th Leicestershire Regiment.

BROMLEY, WILLIAM JOHN DALE.
Royal Grammar School, Lancaster; First XV. and XI. M.B., Ch.B. 1899. Queen Mary's Military Hospital, Whalley, 1916-17. R.A.M.C., Captain July 1917; Acting Major April to May 1919.

BROOK, ALEXANDER BARNETT.
Invergordon Academy. Student of Medicine, 1908-14; M.B., Ch.B. 1914. 4th Seaforth Highlanders, 1908; Lieut. Aug. 1914. R.A.M.C., Lieut. May 1915; Captain May 1916. France. Wounded at Neuve Chapelle March 1915. Dispatches Aug. 1919.

BROOKE-PECHELL, Sir AUGUSTUS ALEXANDER (Bart.).
Hanley-on-Thames Grammar School. M.B., C.M. 1881. R.A.M.C., Lieut.-Col. (retired). Burma Campaign, 1885-7. War Office, Dec. 1914 to April 1919.

BROOKHOUSE, HERBERT.
Repton. Student of Science, 1901-2. 13th Manchester Regiment, 2nd Lieut. Feb. 1915; Captain and R.T.O. 1917. Mesopotamia.

BROOKS, CHARLES MONTAGUE.
Durham; First XV. O.T.C. 1914-16. University O.T.C. Artillery, 1917-18, Cadet; Officer Cadet Feb. 1918. Tank Corps, 2nd Battn., 2nd Lieut. Oct. 1919.

BROOKSBANK, BERTRAM.
Keighly Grammar School. Student of Arts, 1910-15; M.A. 1914. University Diploma in Education, 1915. H.A.C., Private Jan. 1916. Wounded. Invalided out Jan. 1919.

Record of War Service

BROOME, HAROLD HOLKER.
 M.B., Ch.B. 1898; M.R.C.S., L.R.C.P. (Lond.) 1901; F.R.C.S. (Eng.) 1913. Professor of Anatomy, Lahore Medical College. Indian Medical Service, Major July 1914. N.-W. Frontier, Mohmand Front 1915; Mesopotamia 1916; German East Africa 1917.

BROTHERSTON, GEORGE.
 George Watson's College. M.A. 1910. Schoolmaster. O.T.C. Infantry, 1908-12, Cadet Sergeant. 5th Royal Scots Fusiliers, 2nd Lieut. Nov. 1913; Lieut. Aug. 1914; Captain Aug. 1915. Gallipoli 1915; Sinai 1916; Palestine 1917; France 1918. Twice Wounded. Invalided out July 1919.

BROUGH, DANIEL.
 M.B., C.M. 1896; M.R.C.S., L.R.C.P. (Lond.) 1901; D.P.H. (Camb.) 1903. R.A.M.C., Lieut. Jan. 1915; Captain Jan. 1916. Sanitary Officer and D.A.D.M.S.

BROUGH, THOMAS.
 Glasgow Academy. O.T.C. 1910-13. University O.T.C. Artillery, May to Nov. 1916, Cadet Bombardier; Officer Cadet Nov. 1916. R.F.A. (S.R.), 2nd Lieut. March 1917; Lieut. Sept. 1918; Staff Captain April 1919. France May 1917; The Rhine April 1919. Wounded at Nine Wood Nov. 1917.

BROUN, JAMES CRAWFORD CALDWELL.
 M.A. 1880; LL.B. Advocate, 1886. Sheriff-Substitute of Ayr. 7th Gordon Highlanders (T.), Shetland Coy., Major June 1905.

BROWN, ALEXANDER.
 George Watson's College. University O.T.C. Infantry, Aug 1915, Cadet. 6th Royal Scots, 2nd Lieut. Oct. 1915; Lieut. July 1917. France.

BROWN, ALEXANDER MORRIS.
 George Watson's College. M.A. 1887; LL.B. (Distinction) 1893; D.C.L. (Heidelberg) 1892. First XV. 16th and 1st Saskatchewan Regiment, 2nd Lieut. July 1916; Lieut. Nov. 1916 to Nov. 1918. Overseas May 1917 to Oct. 1918.

BROWN, ALEXANDER SMITH.
 George Watson's College. Student of Law, 1909-12. Chartered Accountant, 1914. 9th Royal Scots (T.), Private July 1914; L/Corporal; Corporal; Sergeant; Regt. Q.M.S. France Feb. 1915 to Dec. 1918.

BROWN, ANDREW CASSELS.
 Fettes; First XV. M.B., Ch.B. 1898; M.D. 1902. R.A.M.C., Lieut. Oct. 1915; Captain July 1918. Mudros Oct. 1915; Alexandria Feb. 1916; H.M.S. *Princess Elizabeth* Jan. 1918. Wallasey Military Hospital, 1918-19.

BROWN, AUBREY GARDNER.
 George Watson's College and Christ's Hospital. M.A. 1906; M.B., Ch.B. 1911. University Battery, E.C.A.V., 1904-6; O.T.C. Medical, 1906-10, Cadet. R.A.M.C., Lieut. Feb. 1913; Captain March 1915.

Record of War Service

BROWN, CECIL CARRON.
Alloa Academy; First XI. Student of Medicine, 1914-19; M.B., Ch.B. 1919. O.T.C. Medical, 1916-17, Cadet. R.N.V.R., Surgeon-Probationer, March 1917.

BROWN, CHARLES MARSHALL.
Royal High School; First XV. Student of Arts and Law, 1911-14; M.A. 1912; LL.B. 1914. Advocate. O.T.C. Infantry, Sept. to Oct. 1914, Cadet L/Corporal. Royal Fusiliers (Sportsman's Battn.), Private Oct. 1914. 3rd and 1st Gordon Highlanders, 2nd Lieut. Nov. 1914; Lieut. July 1915; Captain July 1917. France. Wounded at Hooge Sept. 1915, and at Passchendaele Sept. 1917.

BROWN, CHARLES ROLLAND.
Falkirk High School. University O.T.C. Infantry, Dec. 1913 to Aug. 1914, Cadet. 6th Royal Highlanders (Black Watch), 2nd Lieut. Aug. 1914; Lieut. Nov. 1916. Attached Machine-Gun Corps. M.C. Aug. 1917.

BROWN, COLIN EDNIE.
Student of Science, 1913-14. Scottish Horse (T.), Private.

BROWN, CYRIL WILLIAM GILLINGHAM. (See p. 747.)

BROWN, DAVID.
High School, Dalkeith. M.A. (Hons.) 1916. 3rd Royal Scots. Attached Durham Light Infantry, 2nd Lieut. Jan. 1917; Lieut. July 1918. India, Mesopotamia, and Persia.

BROWN, DAVID JACK.
George Heriot's School. Student of Law, 1913-14. R.N.V.R. Aug. 1914. Assistant-Paymaster March 1917; Paymaster-Lieut. March to July 1919.

BROWN, DOUGLAS L.
Berwickshire High School. Student of Medicine, 1916 and 1918-19. O.T.C. Artillery, 1917-18, and Medical, 1918-19, Cadet. R.F.A., Gunner July 1917.

BROWN, ERIC BARLOW.
Leys School, Cambridge; First XV. O.T.C. 1908-12, Cadet Colour-Sergeant. Cambridge University O.T.C. 1912-13. Student of Medicine, 1912-14 and 1916-19; M.B., Ch.B. 1918. O.T.C. Infantry, May 1913 to Sept. 1914, Cadet. 3rd and 2nd Loyal North Lancashire Regiment, 2nd Lieut. Aug. 1914; Lieut.; Captain Aug. 1915. East Africa 1914-16.

BROWN, FRANCIS LEONARD.
Edinburgh Academy. M.A. 1885; M.D. 1890. R.A.M.C., Lieut. Sept. 1915; Captain Sept. 1916-17.

BROWN, FRANCIS ROBERT.
George Watson's College; Rugby Football. M.B., Ch.B. 1913. R.A.M.C., Lieut. May 1915; Captain May 1916; Acting Major May 1918. 28th General Hospital and 27th Casualty Clearing Station, Salonika and the Black Sea. O.B.E. and Dispatches June 1919.

Record of War Service

BROWN, FRANK ALEXANDER.
George Watson's College. Student of Science, 1918. 9th Royal Scots, Private March 1917; L/Corporal 1918.

BROWN, FREDERICK GEORGE HARMAN.
Student of Medicine, 1913-14 and 1918-20; M.B., Ch.B. 1920. O.T.C. Infantry, Sept. 1914 to March 1915, Cadet. Royal Navy, Surgeon-Probationer, April 1916 to Sept. 1917. H.M.S. *Oracle* and H.M.S. *Ariel*. Battle of Jutland.

BROWN, GAVIN STIELL.
Royal High School. M.B., Ch.B. 1909. R.A.M.C., Lieut. Aug. 1914; Captain Aug. 1915; Acting Major Nov. 1918. 13th General Hospital, Boulogne. M.C. Nov. 1918.

BROWN, GEORGE.
Royal High School. Student of Arts, 1910-15; M.A. 1915. Lecturer in Greek and Philosophy, Amherst College, Mass. O.T.C. Infantry, Oct. 1910 to July 1915, Cadet Corporal. 4th Gordon Highlanders, 2nd Lieut. July 1915; Temp. Lieut. March 1916; Acting Captain March 1917-18; Lieut. July 1917. R.E., Signal Service, March 1918 to Sept. 1919.

BROWN, GEORGE EVERARD.
Merchiston Castle and Durham School. O.T.C. 1915-17. University O.T.C. Artillery, Nov. 1917 to April 1918, Cadet. Royal Air Force, April 1918; Cadet May 1918; Flight Cadet Nov. 1918.

BROWN, GEORGE HERBERT JAMES.
Bishop Cotton's School and College, India. M.B., Ch.B. 1899. No. 4 Coy. Q.R.V.B. Royal Scots, 1895-9, Corporal. R.A.M.C., Lieut. Jan. 1903; Captain July 1906; Major Sept. 1914; Acting Lieut.-Col. July 1915 to Nov. 1917. Attached 7th Division; 23rd Field Ambulance, and 26th General Hospital. France Oct. 1914 to Jan. 1919. Bacteriologist. D.S.O. Dispatches Jan. 1916.

BROWN, GIFFORD HOSEASON.
Student of Science, 1913-14. O.T.C. Infantry, April to Sept. 1914, Cadet. 3rd Border Regiment (S.R.), 2nd Lieut. Aug. 1914.

BROWN, HARRY GAMBLE.
George Heriot's School. Student of Arts, 1911-14; M.A. 1919. 6th Royal Scots, Private Sept. 1914. Machine-Gun Corps (Motor), 2nd Lieut. Dec. 1914; Lieut. Nov. 1915; Acting Captain Dec. 1916. France Jan. 1916-18; India Feb. 1918.

BROWN, HENRY GREY.
George Watson's College. M.B., C.M. 1896; M.D. 1901. R.A.M.C., Lieut. Aug. 1916; Captain Aug. 1917. 43rd General Hospital, Salonika.

BROWN, HENRY HILTON.
Royal High School; First XV. M.B., Ch.B. 1911; D.P.H. (Edin.) 1914. O.T.C. Medical, 1905-11, Cadet. R.A.M.C. (S.R.), Lieut. Mobilised Aug. 1914; Captain Oct. 1915; Acting Major Jan. 1918. France 1914. Italian Medal for Asiago Plateau.

Record of War Service

BROWN, HENRY REYNOLDS.
 M.A. 1890; M.B., C.M. 1894; M.D. 1901. British Red Cross Hospital, Dinard, 1914-15. R.A.M.C., Lieut. March 1915; Captain March 1916-17. Essex R.A.S.C., M.T. (V.), Lieut. Nov. 1917.

BROWN, JAMES.
 Galashiels Academy. Student of Arts, 1912-15 and 1918-19; M.A. (Hons. Classics) 1916. Non-Combatant Corps, Private July 1916 to Jan 1919.

BROWN, JAMES.
 Dalkeith High School. Student of Arts, 1904-7. O.T.C. Infantry, Feb. to May 1916, Cadet; Officer Cadet May 1916. 4th, 6th, and 9th Seaforth Highlanders, 2nd Lieut. Sept. 1916; Lieut. March 1918. France. Twice Wounded.

BROWN, JAMES.
 Lasswade School. Student of Arts and Divinity, 1914-18; M.A. 1918. O.T.C. Infantry, May 1917 to June 1918, Cadet. 15th Scottish Rifles, Private June 1918. Attached 21st, 1st, and 3rd Highland Light Infantry.

BROWN, JAMES.
 Student. 7th Cameron Highlanders, Captain.

BROWN, JAMES.
 Fraserburgh Academy; First XI. Student of Medicine, 1918. 1st Gordon Highlanders, Private Sept. 1914; Sergeant Feb. 1915; 2nd Lieut. Sept. 1915; Lieut. 1916. Trench Mortar Battery. France 1914. Wounded at the Somme 1916.

BROWN, JAMES ALEXANDER.
 Ayr Academy. O.T.C. 1910-15. University O.T.C. Artillery, Sept. 1916 to April 1917, Cadet Bombardier; Officer Cadet April 1917. R.F.A., 2nd Lieut. Sept. 1917. 83rd Brigade, France. Wounded and Prisoner of War, March to Dec. 1918. Invalided out.

BROWN, JAMES COWIE.
 Alloa Academy; First XI. M.A. (Glasg.). Student of Law, 1911-15; LL.B. 1914. O.T.C. Engineers, Dec. 1914 to June 1915, Cadet. R.E. (T.), City of Edinburgh Fortress, 2nd Lieut. June 1915; Lieut. June 1916. Attached Sound Ranging Section, France.

BROWN, JAMES CRICHTON.
 George Heriot's School. Student of Law. Chartered Accountant, 1915. Canadian Artillery, Montreal Heavy Brigade, Private Aug. 1914. Transferred 125th Coy., Canadian Forestry Corps, Sergeant Aug. 1919. Overseas for two years.

BROWN, JAMES EDWARD MYLES.
 M.B., Ch.B. 1903. R.A.M.C., South African Campaign, 1900, Private; Lieut. 1914; Captain. No. 1 Ambulance, 1st Division, France. India.

Record of War Service

BROWN, JAMES GODFREY LYON.
George Watson's College. Student of Medicine, 1910-14 and 1917-19; M.B., Ch.B. 1919. President, S.R.C. O.T.C. Artillery, Oct. 1910 to Aug. 1914, Cadet Bombardier. R.F.A., 2nd Lieut. Aug. 1914; Lieut. Sept. 1915. Attached R.H.A., 1st Indian Cavalry Division. R.F.C. and Royal Air Force; Flight Lieut. June 1916; Flight Commander Dec. 1916. France 1915. Wounded at Neuve Chapelle.

BROWN, JOHN FALCONER.
Auckland Grammar School, New Zealand. M.B., Ch.B. 1910; M.D. 1915. N.Z. Medical Corps, Captain May 1915; Major Sept. 1917. N.Z. Division.

BROWN, KENNETH ROBERT.
Leys School, Cambridge. O.T.C. 1911-13. Student of Medicine, 1919-20. O.T.C. Artillery, June to Dec. 1916, Cadet. R.G.A., Officer Cadet Dec. 1916; 2nd Lieut. April 1917; Lieut.; Brigade Signal Officer. France 1917-19. M.C. June 1919.

BROWN, NORMAN MACDOWELL.
George Watson's College. Student of Medicine, 1915-16. O.T.C. Infantry, 1915-16, Cadet. R.E., Special Brigade (Pioneer), May 1916. France 1916-19. Vimy Ridge, Lens, and Dixmude. Wounded June 1916.

BROWN, PETER GORDON.
Royal High School. M.A. 1903. F.I.A. R.N.R., Assistant-Paymaster, July 1915; Paymaster-Lieut. July 1917. Secretary to Flag Captain, Rosyth, April 1916-19.

BROWN, ROBERT ANDREW.
Knox Institute, Haddington. M.A. 1903. Schoolmaster. 1/10th Royal Scots (T.), 2nd Lieut. Jan. 1914; Lieut. 1915; Captain June 1916.

BROWN, STAIR DICKSON.
Lasswade School. Student of Arts and Law, 1915-17 and 1918-19; M.A. 1919. O.T.C. Infantry, Oct. 1916 to June 1917, Cadet; Officer Cadet June 1917. 5th and 8th Rifle Brigade, 2nd Lieut. June 1917 to Dec. 1918. France.

BROWN, THOMAS ANDREW PETRIE.
M.A. 1906. Schoolmaster. "H" (College) Coy., 6th V.B. Royal Scots, 1902-10, Sergeant. R.E., 180th Coy., Corporal July 1915. France Aug. 1915 to Oct. 1916, and Oct. 1917 to July 1918. Wounded Oct. 1916.

BROWN, THOMAS ARNOLD.
George Watson's College; Dux. Student of Arts and Science, 1911-15; M.A. and B.Sc. 1915. O.T.C. Artillery, Aug. 1915 to March 1916, Cadet. R.G.A., Officer Cadet March 1916; 2nd Lieut.; Lieut. March 1918. Gibraltar 1917-19.

BROWN, THOMAS BARLOW.
George Heriot's School. Student of Law, 1913-14. 15th Royal Scots, Private Sept. 1914. France. Twice Wounded.

Record of War Service

BROWN, THOMAS GRAHAM.
Edinburgh Academy. B.Sc. 1903; D.Sc. 1914; M.B., Ch.B. 1906; M.D. 1912. Lecturer in Experimental Physiology, University of Manchester. R.A.M.C., Lieut. March 1915; Captain March 1916. Salonika 1916-19.

BROWN, WALTER HEWITSON.
Daniel Stewart's College. Student of Medicine, 1910-11. O.T.C. Medical, Oct. 1910 to Sept. 1914, Cadet Sergeant. R.A.M.C. (T.), attached Scottish Horse Brigade Field Ambulance, Q.M.S. Sept. 1914; Sergeant-Major March 1915. 3rd Highland Field Ambulance. A.S.C. (T.), Lieut. July 1915; Captain March 1919. 23rd and 64th Highland Division Train, and 21st M.T. Reception Park.

BROWN, WILLIAM.
M.B., Ch.B. 1901. Vol. Medical Staff Corps, 1895-1901. R.A.M.C. (T.), 1912; Lieut.-Col. May 1917. Scottish Horse Brigade Field Ambulance, Egyptian Exp. Force, Palestine. Dispatches 1919. O.B.E. 1919.

BROWN, WILLIAM ARMOUR.
B.Sc. (Glasg.) 1895; M.B., Ch.B. 1903. R.A.M.C., Lieut.; Captain March 1917.

BROWN, WILLIAM THOMSON.
George Watson's College. M.B., Ch.B. 1913. O.T.C. Artillery, Oct. 1910 to Jan. 1914, Cadet Bombardier. R.A.M.C. (T.), Captain Dec. 1916. Scottish Horse Brigade Field Ambulance. M.C.

BROWN, WILLIAM WELSH.
High School, Falkirk. Student of Medicine, 1911-14 and 1916-17; M.B., Ch.B. 1917. O.T.C. Artillery, Oct. 1913 to Aug. 1914, Cadet. R.F.A., 2nd Lieut. Aug. 1914; Lieut.; Captain. R.A.M.C. India.

BROWNE, BERNARD SCORE.
M.B., Ch.B. 1908. R.A.M.C., Lieut. M.C.

BROWNE, LESLIE AITCHISON.
Merchiston Castle. B.Sc. 1913. No. 4 University Coy., McGill University, Montreal. Princess Patricia's Canadian Light Infantry, Private Sept. 1915. France. Wounded at Ypres June 1916. Explosives Chemist, Jan. 1917 to June 1918.

BROWNLEE, ARTHUR OXLAND INNES.
Student of Medicine, 1910-14 and 1917-18; M.B., Ch.B. 1917. O.T.C. Artillery, Oct. 1910 to Aug. 1914, Cadet Corporal. R.F.A. (Meerut Division), 2nd Lieut. Aug. 1914; Lieut. June 1915. South African Medical Corps, Captain April 1918. France 1914. Wounded 1915.

BROWNLEE, CHARLES.
Umtata School, South Africa. Student of Medicine, 1913-14 and 1918-19. Lothians and Border Horse (T.), Private Aug. 1914. King's Own Yorkshire Light Infantry, 2nd Lieut. June 1917. Attached Royal Air Force (Observer), Dec. 1917. France Sept. 1915, Aug. 1917, March to June 1918; Salonika Dec. 1915 to Nov. 1916.

Record of War Service

BROWNLEE, CHARLES ABERCROMBIE ERIC INNES.
Dale College, South Africa. Cadet Corps 1901-6; Lieut. Student of Medicine, 1908-14 and 1915-16; M.B., Ch.B. 1916. O.T.C. Artillery, Feb. 1909 to Aug. 1914, Cadet Corporal. R.F.A., 2nd Lieut. Aug. 1914; Lieut. Sept. 1915. R.A.M.C., Lieut. July 1916; Captain Dec. 1916 to March 1919. France Feb. to Sept. 1915; India Oct. 1917 to Dec. 1918.

BROWNLEE, JAMES.
Daniel Stewart's College. M.B., Ch.B. 1901; M.D. 1904. R.A.M.C., Lieut. Sept. 1916.

BROWNLEE, JAMES ALEXANDER.
Boroughmuir School. Student of Arts and Science, 1915-16 and 1918-19. Royal Navy, H.M. T.B.D. *Narwhal*, Ord. Seaman, April 1916.

BROWNLEE, J. I.
M.B., C.M. Cape Medical Corps, Major.

BROWNLIE, CLAUDE B.
George Watson's College. Student of Medicine, 1912-14 and 1917-19. O.T.C. Medical, Oct. 1912 to Aug. 1914, Cadet. 10th Argyll and Sutherland Highlanders, 2nd Lieut. Aug. 1914; Lieut. June 1915; Acting Captain Nov. 1916. France 1915-16; Festubert and Loos. Wounded.

BROWNLIE, JAMES RUTHERFORD.
Stranraer High School. Student of Law, 1907-9; Law Agent, 1910. 7th Royal Scots Fusiliers, Private Oct. 1914. 9th Border Regiment (Pioneers), 2nd Lieut. Dec. 1914; Lieut. July 1917; Captain and Adjutant April 1918. M.C. May 1917. Croix de Guerre with Palms, May 1919.

BRUCE, ALEXANDER ERIC.
Aberdeen Grammar School. University O.T.C. Artillery, May to Nov. 1916, Cadet Bombardier; Officer Cadet Nov. 1916. R.G.A., 322nd Siege Battery, 2nd Lieut. Feb. 1917; Lieut. Sept. 1918 to Jan. 1919. Wounded Sept. 1918.

BRUCE, ALEXANDER NINIAN.
George Watson's College. B.Sc. 1904; M.B., Ch.B. and D.Sc. 1909; M.D. 1911. Lecturer, Physiology of the Nervous System. R.A.M.C., Captain April 1916; Lieut.-Col. July 1918. Crookston and Dunblane War Hospitals.

BRUCE, BENJAMIN BAIN.
Miller Institution, Thurso. M.A. 1903. Schoolmaster. R.G.A., 102nd and 64th Coys., Gunner Dec. 1915; L/Bombardier March 1918.

BRUCE, CHARLES DAVID.
Dollar Academy. O.T.C. 1913-17. Student of Medicine, 1919. O.T.C. Artillery, 1917-18, Cadet; Officer Cadet Feb. 1918. R.G.A., 2nd Lieut. Aug. 1918.

Record of War Service

BRUCE, SIR DAVID.
Stirling High School. M.B., C.M. 1881; F.R.S. 1899; D.Sc. (Hon. Dublin); LL.D. (Glasgow and Liverpool); F.R.C.P. (Lond.); Corr. Institut de France. R.A.M.C. 1883. South African Campaign, 1899-1902. Lieut.-Col.; Major-General; Surgeon-General 1912. Chairman, W.O., Pathological, Tetanus and Trench Fever Committees. C.B. 1905; Knighted 1908; K.C.B. 1918. Retired May 1919.

BRUCE, DAVID.
Perth Academy. Student of Law, 1918. 11th King's Liverpool Regiment, Private May 1916. Wounded and invalided out.

BRUCE, DOUGLAS W.
Banff Academy. M.A. (Aberdeen). Student of Divinity, 1907-10; Minister, Church of Scotland. Football "Blue." 4th Gordon Highlanders, Lieut. Jan. 1916. Wounded March 1918.

BRUCE, GEORGE ROBERT.
Dunfermline High School. M.A. (St Andrews) 1906; M.B., Ch.B. 1910; M.D. 1914; D.P.H. (Camb.) 1913. R.A.M.C. (S.R.), Lieut. Oct. 1914; Captain April 1915; Major Nov. 1917. Sanitary Officer, Malta, Nov. 1917. Dispatches March 1918. O.B.E. (Military) June 1919.

BRUCE, JAMES.
Dundee High School. Student of Law, 1911-14. 4th Royal Highlanders (Black Watch), 2nd Lieut. Nov. 1914; Lieut. June 1918. Egyptian Exp. Force.

BRUCE, JAMES.
Student of Law, 1898-1903. Writer to the Signet, 1904. A.S.C. (T.), Captain April 1909. Mobilised Aug. 1914; Major June 1916. 1/1st Lowland Mounted Brigade, T. and S. Column. Dardanelles Sept. 1915; Egypt Jan. 1916; Italy Dec. 1917 to Jan. 1919. Dispatches (Italy) 6th and 18th Jan. 1919.

BRUCE, JAMES.
George Watson's College. Student of Law, 1881-4. Solicitor before the Supreme Courts and Notary Public, 1900. Q.E.R., 1882-4, Private. 4th Royal Scots, 2nd Lieut. July 1915; Lieut. July 1916 to Aug. 1917. Royal Defence Corps.

BRUCE, JAMES WHITSON KEMP.
M.B., Ch.B. 1913. Royal Navy, Surgeon Aug. 1914. H.M.S. *Edgar*.

BRUCE, JOHN.
Kelso High School. M.B., C.M. 1890. Q.E.R. 1883-8, Private. R.A.M.C. (T.), Captain Jan. 1915; Major Feb. 1915; Lieut.-Col. Jan. 1917. Attached 2/1st East Lancashire Field Ambulance, July 1915 to June 1919. 29th Casualty Clearing Station, Bonn. France; third Ypres, Nieuport, Passchendaele, Somme, and Courtrai. Dispatches March 1918 and Aug. 1919. O.B.E. (Military) June 1919. T.D. Aug. 1919.

Record of War Service

BRUCE, LEWIS CAMPBELL
Edinburgh Academy. M.B., Ch.B. 1889; M.D. 1894; M.R.C.P. (Edin.) 1896; F.R.C.P. (Edin.) 1901. R.A.M.C. (T.), Lieut. Sept. 1914; Captain Aug. 1915; Acting Major Jan. 1917; Acting Lieut.-Col. Jan. 1918. Attached Scottish Horse. O.C. Murthly War Hospital, Jan. 1917 to March 1919. M.C. and Dispatches, Gallipoli, Nov. 1915.

BRUCE, MATTHEW.
M.B., C.M. 1885. R.A.M.C. (V.), Major Jan. 1918. 3rd Northumberland Field Ambulance.

BRUCE, ROBERT.
Student of Science, 1915-16. O.T.C. Infantry, Feb. to Sept. 1916, Cadet. 9th Royal Scots (T.), L/Corporal.

BRUCE, ROBERT.
Perth Academy. Student of Science, 1918-19. R.G.A., Gunner.

BRUCE, ROBERT TENNANT.
M.B., C.M. 1894; M.D. 1903. R.A.M.C. (T.), Lieut.; Captain May 1915. Attached 2nd Highland Field Ambulance.

BRUCE, WILLIAM.
Edinburgh Academy. M.B., Ch.B. 1911. Q.R.V.B. Royal Scots, Bugler. N.Z. Medical Corps, Captain April 1915; Major July 1918; Lieut.-Col. April 1920. Egypt, France. Dispatches. O.B.E. 1919.

BRUCE, WILLIAM.
Royal High School; First XV. M.A. (Hons. Classics) 1909. Schoolmaster. 9th Royal Scots, Private May 1916; L/Corporal Aug. 1917.

BRUCE, WILLIAM PHIN DODDS.
George Watson's College. Student of Arts, 1918. 52nd Gordon Highlanders. Private June 1918.

BRUCE-LOW, EDWARD.
Merchiston Castle and George Watson's College. Student of Medicine, 1918. 9th Royal Scots (T.), Private June 1915. Machine-Gun Corps. France 1916.

BRUMMITT, ELLIOTT ARTHUR.
Prince Alfred College, Adelaide. M.B., Ch.B. 1908. Australian Army Medical Corps, Captain May 1915; Major Aug. 1917. 11th Australian Field Ambulance. Mediterranean Exp. Force 1915. Egypt 1916; France Aug. 1917 to Dec. 1919. Dispatches April 1918.

BRUNT, EDGAR HAROLD.
St Paul's School. M.B., Ch.B. 1898. R.A.M.C. (T.), Major March 1916. Attached 5th North Staffordshire Regiment; 43rd and 37th Casualty Clearing Stations.

Record of War Service

BRUNTON, GEORGE LLEWELLYN.
Daniel Stewart's College. M.B., Ch.B. 1903; M.D. 1913. R.A.M.C., Lieut. Dec. 1914; Captain Dec. 1915. France May 1915 to Nov. 1918.

BRUNTON, GEORGE McQUEEN.
Dunfermline High School and Daniel Stewart's College. M.B., Ch.B. 1903. R.A.M.C. (T.), Lieut. April 1917; Captain April 1918. Egypt.

BRUNTON, ROBERT STANLEY.
George Watson's College. Student of Medicine, 1905-7 and 1913-15. O.T.C. Medical, 1915-16, Cadet. R.N.V.R., Surgeon Sub-Lieut. April 1918.

BRUNTON, WILLIAM DAVID.
Perth Academy. Student of Medicine, 1912-17; M.B., Ch.B. 1917. O.T.C. Infantry, 1914-15; Medical, 1915-17, Cadet. Royal Navy, Surgeon-Lieut. July 1917. Attached 3rd Royal Marine Battn., Mediterranean.

BRYCE, GEORGE.
George Heriot's School; First XV. Student of Science, 1903-6 and 1910; B.Sc. 1906. Ceylon Planters' Rifle Corps; Ceylon Riots, May and June 1915. R.A.M.C. (T.), Sanitary Service, Lieut. March 1917; Captain April 1918.

BRYCE, JAMES.
George Heriot's School; First XV. and XI. O.T.C. 1910-11, Cadet Colour-Sergeant. Student of Science, 1911-14; B.Sc. 1914. Royal Army Veterinary Corps, Private Jan. 1915; Corporal Feb. 1915; Sergeant Oct. 1915; Regt. Sergeant-Major, Feb. 1917. Attached G.H.Q., Egyptian Exp. Force. Dispatches Sept. 1916. Meritorious Service Medal Jan. 1919.

BRYCE, WILLIAM HENDERSON.
Edinburgh Collegiate School; First XV. and XI. M.B., Ch.B. 1894. Q.R.V.B. Royal Scots, nine years. R.A.M.C. (T.), Major Oct. 1916.

BRYDON, ROBERT SOMERVILLE.
George Heriot's School. O.T.C. 1909-10. Student of Arts, 1910-15; M.A. (Hons. Hist.) 1914. R.G.A., Gunner Feb. 1916.

BRYDONE, JAMES.
George Watson's College. Student of Medicine, 1917-18. O.T.C. Infantry, Feb. to April 1917, Cadet. R.F.C., 2nd Mechanic, May 1917; 2nd Lieut. July 1917; Lieut. April 1918. France; first Cambrai, Passchendaele. Wounded and Prisoner of War, Dec. 1917-18.

BRYDONE, THOMAS.
Moffat Academy. M.A. 1906; B.Sc. 1910. Neil Arnott Scholar, 1908. Demonstrator (Nat. Phil. and Maths.), 1908-10. 4th, 6th, and 13th Royal Scots (T.), Private 1903; 2nd Lieut. 1912; Lieut. Nov. 1914; Temp. Captain May 1916; Captain April 1917. France. Wounded at Monchy-le-Preux, Arras, April 1917. Invalided out Nov. 1918. Dispatches April 1917.

Record of War Service

BRYSON, LEONARD HORNER.
 Blairlodge. M.B., C.M. 1889; M.D.; M.R.C.S. (Eng.) and L.R.C.P. (Lond.) 1893. R.A.M.C., Lieut. June 1915; Captain June 1916 to Nov. 1918.

BUCHAN, DAVID CAMPBELL.
 Daniel Stewart's College. Student of Arts and Science, 1916-17 and 1918-19; M.A. 1920. T.N.T. Factory, Craigleith, Chemist. Royal Air Force, Cadet July 1917; 2nd Lieut.

BUCHAN, HENRY FRANCIS W.
 Edinburgh Academy. Student of Law, 1913. O.T.C. Infantry, Jan. 1912, Cadet. R.F.A. (T.), 1st Lowland Brigade, 2nd Lieut.; Lieut.; Captain June 1916.

BUCHAN, WILLIAM TAYLOR.
 Alloa Academy. M.A. (St Andrews) 1910; M.B., Ch.B. 1914. R.A.M.C., Lieut. May 1915; Captain May 1916. Alexandria, Egypt. Dispatches 1919.

BUCHANAN, DOUGLAS.
 George Watson's College. O.T.C. 1911-15. Student of Science, 1916. Royal Army Veterinary Corps (Dresser Squad), Private Oct. 1916.

BUCHANAN, GEORGE.
 Student of Medicine, 1913-18; M.B., Ch.B. 1918. O.T.C. Medical, 1915, Cadet. R.N.V.R., H.M.S. *Morning Star*, Surgeon-Probationer, Nov. 1915.

BUCHANAN, HENRY MEREDITH.
 M.B., Ch.B. 1911. N.Z. Medical Corps, Captain; Major Sept. 1916. Attached Otago Mounted Rifles.

BUCHANAN, JOHN.
 George Watson's College. O.T.C. 1914-16. Student of Arts, 1918-19. 2nd Royal Scots, Private Aug. 1916; L/Corporal April 1917. 469th H.S.E. Coy. Labour Corps.

BUCHANAN, JOHN CECIL RANKIN.
 Daniel Stewart's College; First XV. Cadet Battn. 1912-15, Sergeant. Student of Medicine, 1914-15. O.T.C. Infantry, May to July 1915, Cadet L/Corporal. 8th Royal Highlanders (Black Watch), 2nd Lieut. July 1915; Lieut. July 1917. France, Mesopotamia, and Palestine. Wounded in France Aug. 1916. Dispatches Jan. 1917.

BUCHANAN, JOHN VASSIE.
 Langholm Academy. M.B., Ch.B. 1913. O.T.C. Artillery, June 1909-12, Cadet. R.A.M.C., Lieut. March 1915; Captain March 1916. 21st and 27th General Hospitals, 1916-17, and Aden Field Force, 1918-19.

BUCHANAN, ROBERT.
 George Watson's College. M.B., Ch.B. 1904. R.A.M.C., Lieut. April 1917; Acting Major June 1918. 19th Stationary Hospital, East Africa.

Record of War Service

BUCHANAN, ROBERT DICK.
George Watson's College. M.B., C.M. 1889; M.D. 1901. R.A.M.C., Lieut. Oct. 1915; Captain Oct. 1916. 6th General Hospital, Rouen.

BUCHANAN, ROBERT WILSON.
Daniel Stewart's College. M.A. 1896; B.Sc. 1899; M.B., Ch.B. 1901. R.A.M.C., Lieut. April 1915; Captain Dec. 1915. Mediterranean and British Exp. Forces.

BUCHANAN, WALTER JAMES.
Rangoon High School. M.B., C.M. 1896; M.D. 1909. Moulmein Vol. Rifles, Sept. 1917.

BUCHER, DAVID ERIC.
Edinburgh Academy. O.T.C. 1914-15. Student of Science, 1918. 3rd Gordon Highlanders (S.R.), Private March 1916; L/Corporal May 1916; Corporal Dec. 1916; 2nd Lieut. April 1917; Lieut. Nov. 1918.

BUCKLEY, HUGH CLIVE.
M.B., Ch.B. 1904. Indian Medical Service, Captain; Major Aug. 1916.

BUCKNER, JOHN.
M.B., Ch.B; L.R.C.P. & S. (Edin.) 1902; L.F.P.S. (Glasg.) 1902. R.A.M.C. (T.), Captain Oct. 1911; attached 1st Welsh Field Ambulance.

BUDGE, DAVID.
Dunbar School. Student of Arts, 1918-19. R.N.V.R., H.M.S. *Cyclops*, Signalman, May 1916.

BUDLER, ARTHUR HAROLD DE WET.
Student of Medicine, 1911-17; M.B., Ch.B. 1916. O.T.C. Artillery, Dec. 1914 to March 1915, Cadet. 25th Royal Fusiliers, Private. South African Medical Corps, Captain Feb. 1917.

BUIST, ARTHUR WILLIAM TREMINHEERE.
M.B., C.M. 1888. Indian Medical Service, Lieut.-Col. 1911. No. 13 Combined Field Ambulance, Rawal Pindi, 1915.

BUIST, DAVID STIRLING.
Perth Academy. M.B., Ch.B. 1907. R.A.M.C., attached Egyptian Army, Lieut. Aug. 1908; Captain Feb. 1913. Mudros 1915; Mongalla and Darfur 1916; Nyima 1917-18. Dispatches (Mongalla) 1916 and (Nyima) 1917. Order of the Nile (4th Class).

BUIST, HERBERT JOHN MARTIN.
George Watson's College. M.B., C.M. 1890. R.A.M.C., Lieut. 1891; Lieut.-Col. 1913; Col. 1917. Malakand 1897; Tirah 1897-8; South Africa 1899-1902. D.S.O. 1901; C.M.G. 1918; Legion of Honour, Croix de Guerre (France) and Serbian Order of St Sava 1917. Dispatches (German S.-W. Africa) Aug. 1915; (Salonika) Nov. 1917 and Jan. 1919.

Record of War Service

BUIST, JOHN MARTIN.
　M.B., C.M. 1893; D.P.H. and Diploma Tropical Medicine (Camb.) 1904. R.A.M.C., Major Jan. 1906; Lieut.-Col.

BULLOCH, OSWALD HUNTLY.
　M.B., Ch.B. 1909. R.A.M.C., Captain Feb. 1918. 2/3rd Wessex Field Ambulance and 2/6th King's Liverpool Regiment. France.

BULLOCK, ARTHUR EDWIN.
　Warwick School; First XV. and XI. M.B., C.M. 1888. R.A.M.C. (T.), Lieut. Sept. 1914; Captain April 1915. Attached Gloucestershire Yeomanry. Dispatches. M.C.

BULLOCK, WILLIAM EWART.
　M.B., Ch.B. 1912; M.D. 1913. R.A.M.C., Lieut. Dec. 1914; Captain Dec. 1915. Dispatches 1918.

BULMAN, JOHN RODERICK.
　M.B., Ch.B. 1913. R.A.M.C. (T.), Captain. No. 2 Convalescent Depôt, Salonika.

BURGES, CYRIL PHILLIPS.
　Taunton School. O.T.C. 1913-17. Student of Medicine, 1918. R.F.A., 2nd Lieut. April 1917. France Dec. 1917 to Oct. 1918.

BURGESS, CHARLES HERBERT.
　Royal School, Dungannon. M.B., Ch.B. 1906. R.A.M.C., Lieut. Dec. 1916; Captain Dec. 1917. Dispatches Oct. 1918.

BURGESS, WILLIAM LESLIE.
　George Heriot's School. M.B., Ch.B. 1909; M.D. 1912; D.T.M. & H. 1911; D.P.H. 1914. Lecturer in Public Health, St Andrews University. R.A.M.C., Lieut. Sept. 1914; Captain April to Dec. 1915.

BURLEIGH, JOHN HENDERSON SEAFORTH.
　George Watson's College. Student of Arts and Divinity, 1911-15, 1916-17, and 1918-19; M.A. 1915. O.T.C. Infantry, Jan. 1914 to March 1915, Cadet. 2/4th King's Own Scottish Borderers, 2nd Lieut. July 1915; Lieut. May to Oct. 1916.

BURLEIGH, THOMAS HUNTLYWOOD.
　Kelso High School. Student of Arts, 1912-14 and 1918-20; M.A. 1920. R.A.M.C., Private Oct. 1914. 33rd and 44th Field Ambulances. M.M. Oct. 1918.

BURLEIGH, WALTER HENRY.
　King Edward's High School, Birmingham; First XV. and XI. O.T.C. 1909-11; Cadet Corporal. Student of Science, 1911-13. O.T.C. Engineers, 1911-13, Cadet. A.S.C. (M.T.), 2nd Lieut. Aug. 1914; Lieut. March 1915; Captain March 1917 to June 1919. France and Italy.

Record of War Service

BURN-MURDOCH, ALEXANDER.
Edinburgh Academy; First XI. B.A. 1908 and LL.B. (Camb.) 1911. Student of Arts 1905-6, and Law 1907-11. Writer to the Signet, 1911. Notary Public, 1913. 8th Royal Scots (T.), 2nd Lieut. March 1915; Lieut. June 1916. France July to Aug. 1915 and June to Oct. 1917. Invalided out Jan. 1919.

BURN-MURDOCH, HECTOR.
Merchiston Castle. Student of Law, 1903-5; B.A. and LL.B. (Camb.), and Advocate, 1905; Barrister-at-Law, 1907; Lecturer in English Law. Cameron Highlanders, Temp. Lieut. Nov. 1914; Temp. Captain Jan. 1915; Temp. Major May 1916; Captain (Reg.) Nov. 1916; Major June 1919. Attached 14th Argyll and Sutherland Highlanders; Royal Air Force and Admiralty. France, April 1916-17.

BURN-MURDOCH, THOMAS MONCK.
Collegiate School, Edinburgh. M.B., C.M. 1877; F.R.C.P. (Edin.) 1899. Lecturer on Diseases of Children. Rugby "Blue." R.A.M.C., Hon. Major Feb. 1916. Springburn and Woodside, and Dalmeny War Hospitals.

BURNE, H. WALLACE.
Edinburgh Academy. O.T.C. 1909-11. Student of Medicine, 1911-14 and 1918-19. O.T.C. Infantry, April 1913 to Aug. 1914, Cadet. R.A.M.C. (T.), 3/1st Scottish Horse Field Ambulance, Private Sept. 1914; 2nd Serbian Army Field Ambulance, Sept. to Dec. 1915. 3/1st Scottish Horse Feb. 1916; 1/6th Royal Highlanders (Black Watch), Jan. 1917.

BURNESS, EDWARD WALKER.
Royal High School. Student of Arts, 1916-17. O.T.C. Infantry, Jan. to Oct. 1917, Cadet Corporal; Officer Cadet Oct. 1917. 3rd, 9th, 6th, and 11th Royal Scots, 2nd Lieut. Feb. 1918; Lieut. Aug. 1919. France.

BURNESS, RONALD.
Edinburgh Academy; First XV. Student of Arts and Law, 1893-1900. Writer to the Signet, 1900. Lothians and Border Horse, Private Sept. 1914. 2nd Lovat Scouts, 2nd Lieut. March 1915; Lieut. June 1916. Attached 10th Cameron Highlanders. Egypt Dec. 1915; Salonika Oct. 1916; France June 1918.

BURNET, DAVID S.
Knox Institute, Haddington. Student of Law, 1907-9. 8th and 1st Royal Scots Oct. 1901; Lieut. Dec. 1914; Captain July 1915.

BURNET, EDWARD.
B.A. (Camb.); M.B., Ch.B. 1906; B.Sc. 1908. British Red Cross Society. R.A.M.C., Lieut. Sept. 1914.

BURNET, GEORGE BAIN.
Dundee High School. Student of Arts, 1912-15; M.A. 1915. O.T.C. Infantry, 1914-15, Cadet. R.A.M.C., 3/1st Lowland Field Ambulance, Private and L/Corporal 1915; Corporal 1916. R.G.A., 2nd Lieut. June 1917; Lieut. 1918. France.

Record of War Service

BURNET, GILBERT.
King William's College, Isle of Man. M.B., Ch.B. 1910. R.A.M.C., Lieut. May 1917. East Africa. M.C. July 1918.

BURNET, JAMES.
Daniel Stewart's College. Student of Arts, 1916-17. O.T.C. Artillery, Feb. to Nov. 1916, Cadet Bombardier; Officer Cadet Nov. 1916. R.F.A. (T.), 2nd Lieut. March 1917; Lieut. Sept. 1918; Acting Captain 1919. Egypt and Palestine July 1917-19.

BURNET, WILLIAM.
Knox Institute, Haddington. Student of Law, 1903-5; Law Agent and Notary Public, 1919. 8th, 7th, and 2nd Royal Scots 1900, Captain June 1916. 4th Highland Light Infantry. Mention Feb. 1918.

BURNETT, JOHN RODGER.
George Watson's College. O.T.C. 1915-17, Sergeant. Student of Science, 1917 and 1919. O.T.C. Artillery, Dec. 1917 to June 1918, Cadet Bombardier; Officer Cadet June 1918. R.H.A. and R.F.A., 2nd Lieut. March 1919.

BURNETT, ROBERT.
Aberdeen Grammar School. B.D. 1890. Minister, Church of Scotland. Chaplain, 3rd Argyll and Sutherland Highlanders, May to Nov. 1915. 3rd Vol. Battn. Royal Scots, Sergeant Jan. 1917 to June 1919. Chaplain with Egyptian Exp. Forces (4th Class), Sept. 1919.

BURNETT-SMITH, JAMES.
M.B., C.M. 1891; L.R.C.P. & S. (Edin.), and L.F.P.S. (Glasg.) 1891. R.A.M.C., Lieut. Jan. 1916; Captain May 1916. Attached 64th Division for sixteen months. Torpedoed May 1917 on way to Egypt.

BURNHAM, CECIL.
Glasgow Academy. Cadet Corps 1901-2. M.B., Ch.B. 1911; F.R.C.S. (Edin.). Demonstrator in Anatomy, 1914-15. Football "Blue." R.A.M.C., Lieut. March 1915; Captain March 1916; Acting Major Feb. 1918.

BURNIE, ROBERT McCALL.
Lockerbie Academy. Student of Medicine, 1914-19; M.B., Ch.B. 1919. Diploma of Tropical Medicine (Liverpool). O.T.C. Infantry, Oct. 1914-15, Cadet. R.N.V.R., Surgeon-Probationer, Aug. 1915. Destroyers, North Sea and Mediterranean.

BURNS, ANDREW SHAW.
Kilmarnock Academy; First XI. Student of Medicine, 1915-16 and 1917-19. O.T.C. Medical, Oct. 1917 to Feb. 1919, Cadet. R.G.A., Signaller June 1916.

BURNS, FRANCIS PETER. (See p. 748.)

BURNS, HENRY.
Royal High School. M.B., Ch.B. 1908. Royal Navy, Surgeon May 1909; Staff Surgeon May 1917; Surgeon-Lieut.-Commander 1918. H.M. Ships *Arethusa, Canterbury, Centaur, Curacoa,* and *Vernon.* O.B.E. Aug. 1919.

Record of War Service

BURNS, JAMES GOLDER.
St John's Grammar School, Hamilton. M.A. 1896; B.D. 1899. Minister, U.F. Church of Scotland. Chaplain, 4th Class 1901; 3rd Class 1911; 2nd Class 1916. Deputy Assistant Principal Chaplain, July 1917. France May 1915-19. Dispatches March 1919. T.D. June 1919.

BURNS, JAMES HENRY LAURENCE.
Musselburgh Grammar School. Student of Arts, 1918. R.A.M.C. (T.), Private Oct. 1915; Corporal Sept. 1918. 3/3rd Lowland Field Ambulance Oct. 1915, and 58th Scottish General Hospital April 1917 to Jan. 1919.

BURNS, JOHN CRAWFORD.
Teviot Grove Academy and Selkirk High School; First XV. M.B., Ch.B. 1917. O.T.C. Medical, 1915-17, Cadet Sergeant. R.A.M.C., Lieut. Aug. 1917; Captain Aug. 1918. 36th Combined Field Ambulance. Mesopotamia Sept. 1917; Southern Kurdistan 1919.

BURNS, JOHN GEORGE.
Student of Law, 1909-11. Advocate, 1911. 9th Royal Scots (T.), Lieut. June 1916; Captain. France 1915-19.

BURNS, ROBERT.
Teviot Grove Academy, Hawick. M.A. 1910. Schoolmaster. R.F.A., 1st Lowland Brigade (T.), Driver Sept. 1914. 6th Royal Scots (T.), 2nd Lieut. July 1915; Lieut. Dec. 1916. Egyptian Exp. Force. Wounded at Nebi Samwil, Palestine, Nov. 1917.

BURNS, ROBERT EDWARD.
C.B. College, Perth, West Australia. First XV. and XI. Student of Medicine, 1913-16 and 1918; M.B., Ch.B. 1918. Anatomy Staff, 1915-17. O.T.C. Infantry, Nov. 1914 to March 1916, Cadet. Royal Air Force Medical Service, Lieut. Oct. 1918. Mediterranean Exp. Force.

BURNS, THOMAS ALEXANDER.
Dundee High School. Student of Science, 1913-14. O.T.C. Engineers, Oct. 1913 to Nov. 1914, Cadet. R.G.A. (North Scottish) (T.), Gunner Sept. 1914; 2nd Lieut. Feb. 1915; Lieut. June 1916; Acting Captain July 1917. Gallipoli, Egypt and France.

BURNS, WILLIAM.
Teviot Grove Academy, Hawick. Student of Law, 1906-8. 6th Royal Scots (T.), 2nd Lieut. 1912; Captain Sept. 1916. 2/4th Royal Scots, Adjutant Aug. 1916-17. Overseas Nov. to Dec. 1917 and Sept. 1918-19.

BURNS, WILLIAM.
Montrose Academy. Student of Science, 1904-7; B.Sc. 1907; D.Sc. 1914. 35th Poona Battn., Indian Defence Force, Captain April 1917; 114th Mahrattas, Lieut. Oct. 1917 to Jan. 1919. School of Musketry (Indian), Poona.

Record of War Service

BURNS, WILLIAM JAMES.
Ayr Academy. O.T.C. 1912-17, Cadet Sergeant. Student of Medicine, 1918. Royal Air Force, 2nd Lieut. July 1917, 94th Squadron.

BURNS, WILLIAM KEDSLIE.
North Berwick High School. Student of Law, 1917. O.T.C. Infantry, March to Oct. 1917, Cadet; Officer Cadet Oct. 1917. 1st Cameron Highlanders, 2nd Lieut. Feb. 1918. France.

BURNS, WILLIAM ROSE.
Brechin High School. Student of Arts, 1891. South African Scottish, Private. Overseas Exp. Force.

BURR, JOHN.
Dundee High School. Student of Arts and Divinity, 1887-94; M.A. 1891. Minister, Church of Scotland. Chaplain 4th Class, Oct. 1915. 157th Brigade. 52nd Division, Mediterranean and Egyptian Exp. Force.

BURR, WILLIAM SIMPSON.
Bo'ness Academy. Student of Medicine, 1916-19. O.T.C. Artillery, 1917-18, Gunner; Medical, 1918-19, Cadet. R.F.A., Officer Cadet.

BURROW, JOSEPH LE FLEMING COY.
M.B., Ch.B. 1910; M.R.C.P. (Lond.) 1913. R.A.M.C. (T.), Captain Aug. 1914. 33rd Mounted Brigade Field Ambulance, Egypt, 1915-16; in charge of Medical Division, Military Hospital, Cairo; 2nd Northern General Hospital.

BURT, LEONARD ANDERSON PEARCE.
M.B., Ch.B. 1909. R.A.M.C., Lieut.; Captain (retired). Attached 7th Duke of Cornwall's Light Infantry.

BURT, THOMAS DUNCANSON.
George Heriot's School; First XV. and XI. O.T.C. 1910-14, Cadet L/Corporal, Student of Medicine, 1918. 5th Royal Scots, Private Sept. 1914; 2nd Lieut. Jan. 1915; Lieut. July 1917. Gallipoli; France. Twice Wounded.

BURTON, THOMAS JOHN.
M.B., C.M. 1889; M.D. 1896. R.A.M.C., Lieut.

BUSCKE, GEORGE HENDERSON.
Edinburgh Academy; First XI. Student of Science, 1918-19. O.T.C. Infantry, Oct. 1914 to March 1915, Cadet L/Corporal. 21st Northumberland Fusiliers, 2nd Lieut. March 1915; Lieut. Oct. 1916. Machine-Gun Corps. Invalided out Jan. 1918.

Record of War Service

BUTCHART, HENRY JACKSON.
Aberdeen Grammar School. B.L. (Aberdeen) 1905; Student of Law, 1906-7; Law Agent. Queen's Edinburgh Mounted Rifles, 1905. 2nd Scottish Horse, 2nd Lieut. 1907; Captain 1913; Major June 1916. 2nd Reserve Regiment of Cavalry, 1915-16. Egyptian and British Exp. Forces, June 1916 to July 1919. 52nd Lowland and 74th (Yeomanry) Divisions. Dispatches Jan. and June 1918. D.S.O. June 1918. Star of Roumania (Officer Class).

BUTLER, ALAN LUMSDEN.
Warriston. Glasgow University O.T.C. 1917, Cadet. University O.T.C. Artillery, 1917-18, Cadet. R.G.A., Officer Cadet May 1918; 2nd Lieut. Feb. 1919.

BUTLER, EDWIN.
Wimbourne Grammar School. L.R.C.P. & S. (Edin.) and L.R.F.P.S. (Glasg.) 1916. O.T.C. Medical, Feb. to Oct. 1916. R.A.M.C. (S.R.), Lieut. Nov. 1916; Captain Nov. 1917; Acting Major Aug. 1918. O.C. 22nd Indian General Hospital, Nov. 1918. Mesopotamia. Dispatches June 1919.

BUTTAR, FERNIE LOUDEN.
George Watson's College. Student of Science and Medicine, 1912-15 and 1918-20. O.T.C. Infantry, Oct. 1912 to Sept. 1914, Cadet. 8th, 9th, and 4th Royal Scots (T.), Private Sept. 1914; 2nd Lieut. Dec. 1915; Lieut. July 1917. Attached R.E. (Signal Service), June 1917. 37th Division and 6th Corps. France Feb. to Dec. 1915, and Nov. 1917 to Dec. 1918. Second Battle of Ypres, Passchendaele.

BUTTER, ANDREW JAMES MOYES.
Perth Academy; First XI. Student of Arts and Medicine, 1913-15 and 1919; M.A. 1919. O.T.C. Artillery, Feb. to July 1915, Cadet. R.E. (Special Brigade), Sapper July 1915; Sergeant March 1917; 2nd Lieut. June 1917; Lieut. Dec. 1918. France two years. Wounded. M.M. April 1917.

BUYERS, GEORGE ALSTON.
Aberdeen Grammar School. Student of Law, 1911-13. 7th Gordon Highlanders, Lieut. March 1918.

BYRES, GEORGE M.
George Watson's College; First XI. Student of Law, 1909 and 1912-13. Chartered Accountant, 1914. 4th Royal Scots (T.), Private 1909; Lieut. May 1915; Captain May 1916; Adjutant March 1917. France 1916-19. Dispatches Sept. 1918-19.

CADELL, HEW FRANCIS.
Edinburgh Academy and Haileybury. Student of Law. Writer to the Signet, 1891. Lothians and Border Horse, 1888; Major March 1902. Mobilised Aug. 1914. France; attached 5th Corps Cavalry Regiment for two years. Worcestershire Yeomanry and Anzac Mounted Division, Palestine, for one year. T.D.

Record of War Service

CADELL, JOHN MACFARLANE.
Collegiate School, Edinburgh. M.B., C.M. 1884. Indian Medical Service, Oct. 1885; Lieut.-Col. (retired) 1913. R.A.M.C. (T.), Major Oct. 1914 to March 1919. Attached 10th Royal Scots. Egypt.

CADELL, LEWIS IRVING.
Collegiate School, Edinburgh. M.A. 1886. Writer to the Signet, 1889. Q.E.R. 1882-7, Corporal. National Reserve, Captain Nov. 1914. A.S.C. (M.T.), (V.), Oct. 1917; Lieut. Jan. 1918. Special Constable. Voluntary Munition Worker, 1915-16.

CADMAN, DONALD ARTHUR.
Daniel Stewart's College. Student of Medicine, 1914-19; M.B., Ch.B. 1919. O.T.C. Medical, Nov. 1915 to Oct. 1916, Cadet. R.N.V.R., A.B. Seaman, Nov. 1916; Surgeon Sub-Lieut. Jan. 1917. Dover and Harwich Patrol and Escort. Duties at Plymouth, H.M.S. *Laverock*.

CAIE, JOHN MYLES. (See p. 748.)

CAIRD, ANDREW JAMES.
Perth Academy; First XV. Student of Arts, Science, and Medicine, 1908-16; M.A. 1912; B.Sc. 1915; M.B., Ch.B. 1916. O.T.C. Medical, Nov. 1914-16, Cadet Sergeant. R.A.M.C., Lieut. July 1916; Captain July 1917. Edinburgh War Hospital.

CAIRD, FRANCIS MITCHELL.
Royal High School. M.B., C.M. 1877; F.R.C.S. (Edin.). Professor of Clinical Surgery. R.A.M.C. (T.), Lieut.-Col. April 1914. 2nd Scottish General Hospital, Consulting Surgeon. France (Colonel A.M.S.) 1916-17. Seafield War Hospital, 1917-18. Dispatches 1917.

CAIRD, KARL F.
Edinburgh Academy. Student of Medicine, 1912-15 and 1919. 11th Highland Light Infantry, 2nd Lieut. Oct. 1914; Lieut. Royal Air Force.

CAIRNIE, JOHN BRUCE.
Miller Institution, Thurso. M.A. 1911; B.Sc. 1912. O.T.C. Artillery, Oct. 1909 to Nov. 1912, Cadet. 5th Seaforth Highlanders (T.), Sept. 1914; 2nd Lieut. March 1915; Lieut. June 1917. Attached King's African Rifles, Oct. 1918.

CAIRNS, ALEXANDER GORDON.
George Watson's College; First XV. and XI. B.A. (Oxford). Student of Arts and Law, 1895-8 and 1902-5; M.A. 1898; Writer to the Signet, 1906. Lothians and Border Horse, Private Sept. 1914. R.F.A., 2nd Lieut. Feb. 1915; Lieut. Dec. 1915 Captain 32nd Brigade, 4th Division, 1915-16 and 1918. France.

Record of War Service

CAIRNS, CHARLES R.
George Watson's College. Student of Law, 1905-7; Chartered Accountant, 1910. 9th Royal Scots (T.), Private.

CAIRNS, FRANCIS DAVIDSON.
George Watson's College. M.B., Ch.B. 1911. Demonstrator in Anatomy, 1914. R.A.M.C., Lieut.; Captain Aug. 1915.

CAIRNS, GEORGE DOUGLAS.
George Watson's College. M.B., Ch.B. 1910; D.P.H. (Edin.) 1914. R.A.M.C., Lieut. March 1915; Captain March 1916. France 1915-17. Second Battle of Ypres and Festubert.

CAIRNS, JAMES DOUGLAS.
Edinburgh Academy; First XV. O.T.C. 1913-16. Student of Arts, 1918-20. 2/7th Royal Highlanders (Black Watch), Private Nov. 1916-17. R.E. (Signals), Sapper and Acting L/Corporal 1917-19.

CAIRNS, JAMES WILLIAM.
Royal High School. M.B., Ch.B. 1905; M.D. 1914; D.P.H. (Edin.) 1910. Medical Staff Corps, Vol., Private. R.A.M.C. (T.), Lieut. Nov. 1914; Captain May 1915; Major Jan. 1918. France 1914; Salonika 1915. Invalided out Feb. 1919. Dispatches June 1915.

CAIRNS, JOHN.
Duns School. Student of Arts, 1882-5. Berwickshire Rifle Vols. Nov. 1880. 4th Royal Scots (V.), Captain. 3rd West Kent Regiment (V.), Major. Assistant Principal Chaplain, Oct. 1918. V.D. O.B.E. (Military) June 1919.

CAIRNS, LAWSON MILLER.
Royal High School. M.B., C.M. 1897; M.D. 1908. R.A.M.C., Lieut. Nov. 1914; Captain Nov. 1916.

CAIRNS, RONALD McDONALD.
Workington College; First XV. and XI. Student of Medicine, 1913-16 and 1917-20; M.B., Ch.B. 1920. R.N.V.R., Surgeon-Probationer, April 1916. H.M. Ships *Pasley*, *Acheron*, *Sarpedon*, and *Seymour*.

CAITHNESS, HUGH PEACE.
Queen Elizabeth's Grammar School, Blackburn. Student of Medicine, 1909-14; M.B., Ch.B. 1914. R.A.M.C., Lieut. Feb. 1916; Captain Feb. 1917. France. Gassed, Ypres Salient, Nov. 1917.

CALDER, CLARENCE ALEXANDER.
Munro College, Jamaica; First XI., Cricket and Football. Student of Medicine, 1913-15 and 1917-20. O.T.C. Artillery, Oct. 1914 to July 1915, Cadet. Hon. Artillery Coy., R.H.A., Gunner July 1915; L/Bombardier. Egypt.

Record of War Service

CALDER, JOHN ALEXANDER.
Grove and Harris Academies, Dundee; First XI. M.A. (Hons. Hist.) 1911. O.T.C. Infantry, May 1909 to June 1912, Cadet Corporal. Inns of Court O.T.C., Private Sept. 1918 to Jan. 1919.

CALDER, WILLIAM.
Student of Arts, 1912-14. O.T.C. Infantry, Oct. 1912 to Aug. 1914, Cadet. 4th Cameron Highlanders (T.), 2nd Lieut. Aug. 1914; Captain Oct. 1917.

CALDER, WILLIAM GORDON.
George Watson's College; First XV. and XI. Student of Arts and Science, 1912-14. R.E., 49th Coy. and Special Brigade, Sept. 1914-16. 1/8th Royal Scots (T.), 2nd Lieut. Jan. 1917; Lieut. July 1918. France May 1917 to Nov. 1918; Ypres and Cambrai.

CALDER, WILLIAM JOHNSON.
Northampton Grammar School. M.B., C.M. 1878; M.D. 1899. South African Campaign, 1900-1. R.A.M.C., Captain Sept. 1916. France 1916. Invalided out Nov. 1917.

CALDWELL, JOHN STEWART.
Mid-Calder School. M.B., Ch.B. 1906. R.A.M.C., Lieut. March 1915; Captain March 1916. France April 1915 to June 1919.

CALLANDER, HUGH.
M.A. 1913. R.A.M.C., L/Corporal. Injured in torpedoing of H.M.S. *Royal Edward*.

CALLANDER, LAWRENCE DOUGAL.
M.B., Ch.B. 1910; M.D. 1920. R.A.M.C., Lieut. June 1917; Captain June 1918. 24th Indian General Hospital, Mesopotamia. Surgical Specialist at Kut.

CALLEN, JAMES ANDERSON.
George Watson's College. Student of Science, 1913-14. O.T.C. Engineers, Dec. 1913 to Oct. 1914, Cadet. R.E., Sapper Sept. 1914. 10th Scottish Rifles, 2nd Lieut. Oct. 1914; Lieut. Feb. 1915; Captain Sept. 1915. Transferred R.E. (Signal Service) Lieut. Feb. 1917; Acting Captain May 1918. France July 1915; Loos and Hill 70. Wounded March 1916. M.C. Jan. 1916; Croix de Guerre (French) Aug. 1918. Dispatches.

CALLENDER, DUNCAN McNAB.
Edinburgh Academy. M.A. 1899; M.B., Ch.B. 1902; M.D. 1919; F.R.C.S., (Edin.) 1905. R.A.M.C., Lieut. April 1915; Captain April 1916.

CALVER, DOUGLAS EDWARD.
Kilmarnock Academy; First XV. and XI. Student of Arts and Science, 1912-14, and 1919-20. O.T.C. Infantry, Feb. 1913 to Sept. 1914, Cadet. 11th Royal Scots, 2nd Lieut. Sept. 1914; Lieut. Aug. 1916. Transferred A.S.C. (M.T.), April 1917 to April 1919. Wounded Aug. 1915.

Record of War Service

CALVER, ROBERT HENRY SHERWOOD.
: Edinburgh Institution; First XV. 1st (Highland) Cadet Battn., Royal Scots, 1914-17, Sergeant. Student of Arts and Law, 1917 and 1919-20. O.T.C. Artillery, May to Sept. 1917, Cadet. Royal Navy, Sub-Lieut. Sept. 1917, attached R.N.A.S. Royal Air Force, 2nd Lieut. April 1918.

CALWELL, ANDREW FISHER.
: Epsom and Blairlodge; First XV. and XI. Cadet Corps 1897-1904, Sergeant. M.B., Ch.B. 1912. M.O., Langholm Auxiliary Hospital, 1915-18. R.A.M.C. Lieut. April 1918. M.C.

CAMERON, ALAN HAY.
: Dollar Institution. O.T.C. 1910-16, Sergeant. Student of Science, 1916-17. O.T.C. Engineers, 1916-17; Infantry, 1917, Cadet Sergeant. R.E. (Signals), Aug. 1917; 2nd Lieut. Feb. 1918. France and The Rhine.

CAMERON, ALBERT.
: M.B., C.M. 1892. R.A.M.C., Captain May 1915.

CAMERON, ALEXANDER JOHN.
: Fettes. O.T.C. 1912-16. Edinburgh University O.T.C. Artillery, Sept. 1916 to Jan. 1917, Cadet. Scottish Horse Jan. 1917. 6th Royal Highlanders (Black Watch), 2nd Lieut. June. 1918. France.

CAMERON, ALEXANDER THOMAS.
: M.A. 1904; B.Sc. 1906; F.I.C. 1918. Assistant Professor of Physiology, University of Manitoba. O.T.C., Lieut. Sept. 1915; Captain Oct. 1916. R.A.M.C. (T.), Captain April 1917 to May 1919. No. 1 Water Tank (M.T.) Coy. France April 1916-19. Dispatches June 1917.

CAMERON, ANGUS.
: M.A. 1907. Schoolmaster. 3rd Seaforth Highlanders, Lieut. Aug. 1914; Captain March 1918. France April to July 1915; Salonika May 1917 to Oct. 1918; Egypt 1920. Educational Officer, Glencorse, 1918 to Nov. 1919. Wounded France July 1915.

CAMERON, ANGUS.
: Perth Academy; First XV. and XI. Student of Medicine, 1908-14; M.B., Ch.B. 1914. O.T.C. Infantry, Oct. 1909-13, Cadet Colour-Sergeant. R.A.M.C. (T.), Lieut. Oct. 1914; Captain April 1915; Acting Major Nov. 1918. Egypt. M.C. April 1918.

CAMERON, DAVID HUGH.
: Dundee High School. Student of Science, 1917-20; B.Sc. 1920. 4th Highland Light Infantry, Private April 1918. Royal Air Force, Cadet Sept. 1918.

CAMERON, DAVID WILKIE.
: George Watson's College. B.A. (Hons., Camb.); M.A. (Hons. Maths.) 1911; B.Sc. Schoolmaster. Royal Navy, H.M.S. *Emperor of India*, Naval Instructor, Jan. 1916. Jutland Battle, May 1916.

Record of War Service

CAMERON, DONALD.
Royal Academy, Inverness. Student of Medicine, 1918. Royal Navy, Able Seaman, June 1916. H.M.A. Ships *Melbourne* and *Cornwall*.

CAMERON, DONALD BLACK.
Lasswade School. Student of Arts, 1918-19. O.T.C. Artillery, 1917-18, Cadet. R.G.A., Officer Cadet June 1918; 2nd Lieut. May 1919.

CAMERON, DONALD HUGH.
Robert Gordon's College, Aberdeen. Student of Arts and Medicine, 1913-15 and 1918-19; M.A. 1912; M.B., Ch.B. 1918. O.T.C. Medical, April to Nov. 1915, Cadet. R.N.V.R., H.M.S. *Nizam*, Surgeon-Probationer, Nov. 1915 to April 1917. Royal Navy, Surgeon-Lieut. July 1919.

CAMERON, DUGALD.
Kingussie School; First XI., Football. Student of Arts and Medicine, 1911-14 and 1918-19; M.A. 1914. O.T.C. Artillery, 1914-15, Cadet. R.F.A. (S.R.), 2nd Lieut. June 1915; Lieut. July 1917 to Jan. 1919. Salonika Oct. 1915; Serbia Nov. 1915. Wounded at Barakli-Dzuma May 1917 and invalided home July 1917. M.C. Aug. 1917.

CAMERON, DUNCAN ALEXANDER.
Stockton High School. M.B., C.M. 1898. R.A.M.C. (T.), Surgeon-Lieut. 1905; Captain 1908; Major 1914; Lieut.-Col. Oct. 1914. Durham Light Infantry; 2nd Northumbrian Field Ambulance. France 1914; Egypt 1915; Salonika 1916. President, No. 4 T.M.B., Northern Command, Nov. 1918. Dispatches June 1915.

CAMERON, DUNCAN FRASER.
George Watson's College. O.T.C. 1915-17. Student of Science, 1917 and 1918-19. O.T.C. Artillery, April 1917 to Jan. 1918, Cadet Bombardier; Officer Cadet Jan. 1918. Tank Corps, 2nd Lieut. Oct. 1918.

CAMERON, ERNEST HUGH.
George Watson's College. M.B., Ch.B. 1910; F.R.C.S. (Edin.) 1914. R.A.M.C., Lieut. Jan. 1916; Captain Jan. 1917. India.

CAMERON, EWEN.
M.B., Ch.B. 1902. Royal Navy, Staff Surgeon Feb. 1914. M.V.O.

CAMERON, GEORGE S.
Student of Science. Lothians and Border Horse (T.), Private.

CAMERON, IAN.
Greenock Academy. Student of Law, 1907-9. 4th Cameron Highlanders (T.), 2nd Lieut.

CAMERON, ISABELLA DOUGLAS.
M.B., Ch.B. 1898; M.D. 1906; D.P.H. (Camb.) 1905. Q.M.A.A.C., Medical Controller, March to Sept. 1917.

Record of War Service

CAMERON, JAMES.
M.B., C.M. 1887; M.D. 1894; M.D. (Lond.) 1910; M.R.C.P. (Edin.) 1904. Assistant, Eye Department, R.I.E. R.A.M.C., Captain Feb. 1918.

CAMERON, JAMES ALEXANDER.
Perth Academy. M.A. 1901; LL.B. 1904. Writer to the Signet, 1911. No. 4 Coy. Q.R.V.B., Royal Scots, 1899-1903. Assistant Recruiting Staff Officer, Lieut. July to Dec. 1917. Staff of Ministry of National Service to Jan. 1919.

CAMERON, JAMES BLACK.
George Watson's College; First XV. and XI. M.A. 1903; LL.B. 1905. Writer to the Signet, 1907. University Battery, E.C.A.V., 1900-4, Gunner. R.G.A. (T.), City of Edinburgh Heavy Battery, 1906; Major Dec. 1913. France, Hooge, 1915; Somme 1916; Arras 1917. D.S.O. and Dispatches June 1917.

CAMERON, JAMES WALES.
George Watson's College. M.A. (Hons. Phil.) 1907. Chaplain, 4th Class, Aug. 1916; Acting Senior Chaplain March 1919; Acting Assistant Principal Chaplain July 1919. Malta, Italy, Egypt.

CAMERON, JOHN.
Oban School. O.T.C. 1916-17. Student of Medicine, 1917-19. O.T.C. Medical April to Sept. 1918, Cadet. R.N.V.R., Midshipman.

CAMERON, JOHN.
Allan Glen's School, Glasgow. University O.T.C. Artillery, Dec. 1915 to March 1916, Cadet. Cavalry Officer Cadet Corps, March to Aug. 1916.

CAMERON, JOHN.
Edinburgh Academy. O.T.C. 1914-17, L/Corporal. Student of Arts, 1917 and 1919. O.T.C. Infantry, Oct. 1917 to March 1918, Cadet. R.N.V.R., Midshipman, April 1918. H.M.S. P39 Escort Flotilla and H.M.S. *Windsor*.

CAMERON, JOHN SPROAT TAYLOR.
Edinburgh Academy. M.A. 1888; LL.B. (Distinction) 1892; Advocate, 1893; Examiner in Law. 9th Royal Scots (T.), 2nd Lieut. 1900; Major 1912. Acting as Judge Advocate, Scottish Command, 1918-19. France 1915. T.D. 1919.

CAMERON, NEIL.
George Watson's College. M.A. 1909. Probationer, U.F. Church of Scotland. 5th Seaforth Highlanders, Private June 1915; Sergeant. 9th Royal Scots, 2nd Lieut. June 1917; Lieut. Wounded April 1918.

CAMERON, ROBERT EVAN.
Sedbergh and King William's College, I.O.M. Student of Medicine, 1908-14; M.B., Ch.B. 1914. O.T.C. Artillery, June 1909 to April 1912, Cadet. Royal Navy, Surgeon-Lieut. Aug. 1914. H.M.S. *Benbow*. Jutland May 1916. R.N. Hospital, Portland, 1916-17. Mesopotamia and China.

CAMERON, ROBERT GRIERSON.
Student of Arts, 1913-14. 4th Royal Scots (T.), Private.

Record of War Service

CAMERON, ROBERT THEODORE.
Inverness Royal Academy. M.A. 1907. Minister of U.F. Church of Scotland. Y.M.C.A. Work, France. Chaplain, 4th Class, 11th Royal Scots, Captain. May 1916-17. Recommissioned Oct. 1918.

CAMERON, RODERIC DUNCAN.
George Watson's College. Student of Medicine, 1911-16; M.B., Ch.B. 1916. O.T.C. Medical, Oct. 1912 to July 1916, Captain. R.A.M.C. (S.R.), Lieut. Sept. 1914; Acting Captain March 1916; Captain Jan. 1917; Acting Major Sept. 1919. Salonika, Struma Valley, Vardar, and Doiran. Dispatches Nov. 1917 and Nov. 1918. M.C. Jan. 1919.

CAMERON, THOMAS FORBES.
George Watson's College. M.A. 1911. O.T.C. Infantry, Oct. 1909-12, Cadet. Northumberland Fusiliers (N.E. Rly. Battn.), 2nd Lieut. Nov. 1914; Captain 1916; Acting Major 1917. France.

CAMERON, THOMAS WRIGHT MOIR.
Allan Glen's School, Glasgow. Glasgow University O.T.C. Engineers, 1912-14. Student of Science, 1918. 15th Highland Light Infantry, 2nd Lieut. Sept. 1914; Captain Nov. 1915. R.F.C. and Royal Air Force, Sept. 1916 to Jan. 1919.

CAMPBELL, ALBERT.
George Heriot's School. Student of Medicine, 1916-17. O.T.C. Artillery, Sept. 1916 to March 1917, Cadet; Officer Cadet April 1917. R.G.A., 2nd Lieut. June 1917; Lieut. Dec. 1918. France. Invalided home Oct. 1919.

CAMPBELL, ALBERT GORDON.
George Watson's College. O.T.C. 1913-16. University O.T.C. Artillery, Oct. 1916 to May 1917, Cadet; Officer Cadet May 1917. Indian Army, 93rd Burma Infantry, 2nd Lieut. Jan. 1918; Lieut. Jan. 1919. Egypt, Palestine, Damascus, and Aleppo 1918.

CAMPBELL, ALEXANDER.
Perth Academy; First XV. Student of Arts, 1910-14; M.A. (Hons. Engl.) 1914. Rangoon Vol. Rifles, March 1915. I.A.R.O., 130th K.G.O. Baluchis, 2nd Lieut. Aug. 1916; Lieut. Aug. 1917; Temp. Captain Sept. 1917 to Jan. 1918. German East Africa. M.C. July 1918.

CAMPBELL, ALEXANDER DAVID.
George Watson's College. M.B., Ch.B. 1912; D.P.H. 1913. O.T.C. Artillery, 1905-11, Cadet. R.A.M.C., Lieut. July 1916; Captain Aug. 1917. Embarkation Medical Officer, Boulogne.

CAMPBELL, ALEXANDER FRASER.
Royal High School. Student of Medicine, 1910-15; M.B., Ch.B. 1915. 4th Scottish General Hospital, C.M.P., May 1916 to Jan. 1917. R.A.M.C., Lieut. Feb. 1917; Captain Feb. 1918. Egypt May 1917.

Record of War Service

CAMPBELL, ALEXANDER JOHN.
B.A.; M.A. 1880. Chaplain 1887; 1st Class April 1908. North Scottish R.G.A. (T.), Tay Defences. V.D. Mention.

CAMPBELL, ALEXANDER JOHN.
George Watson's College. M.A. 1891; M.B., C.M. 1894; M.D. 1898. R.A.M.C., Captain April 1915-16.

CAMPBELL, ALEXANDER STEWART.
Kirkcudbright Academy. M.A. 1907. R.A.M.C., Private Oct. 1914. 16th Field Ambulance. M.M. Oct. 1918.

CAMPBELL, ALFRED WALTER.
M.B., C.M. 1889; M.D. 1892. Australian Army Medical Corps, Major 1914. 2nd Australian General Hospital.

CAMPBELL, ANDREW.
Aberdeen Grammar School; First XV. and XI. M.B., Ch.B. 1910; D.P.H. O.T.C. Artillery, 1904 to Dec. 1910, Cadet Sergeant. Indian Medical Service, Lieut. March 1917; Captain May 1918; Otologist to War Hospitals, Karachi.

CAMPBELL, ANGUS HENRY.
Dollar Academy. Student of Science and Medicine, 1913-15; B.Sc. 1915. R.A.M.C., Protozoologist, Dec. 1915.

CAMPBELL, ARCHIBALD BROWN.
George Watson's College. M.A. 1886; LL.B. and Writer to the Signet, 1889. 1st Vol. Battn. Royal Scots, Private 1914; L/Corporal; 2nd Lieut.; Lieut.; Acting Adjutant.

CAMPBELL, ARCHIBALD MARSHALL.
Hilton College, Natal. Athletics. O.T.C. 1902-12, Sergeant. University O.T.C. Artillery, Nov. 1915 to Feb. 1916, Cadet. Natal Carabiniers, Trooper Sept. 1914. German West Africa. R.F.A., Officer Cadet Feb. 1916; Lieut. July 1917. Royal Air Force.

CAMPBELL, ARTHUR.
Foyle College, Londonderry; First XV. and XI. Student of Medicine, 1913-15 and 1917-19. O.T.C. Medical, Nov. 1914 to March 1915, Cadet. 10th Border Regiment, 2nd Lieut. March 1915. Machine-Gun Corps Dec. 1915, Lieut. Oct. 1916. M.C. July 1916.

CAMPBELL, ARTHUR THOMAS.
Edinburgh Academy. O.T.C. 1910-11. Student of Law, 1912-15. O.T.C. Infantry, Jan. to April 1915, Cadet. Leicestershire Yeomanry (T.), 2nd Lieut. April 1915; Lieut. June 1916. Attached 16th and 12th Lancers. France, Feb. 1916 to Sept. 1919.

Record of War Service

CAMPBELL, CHARLES MACFIE.
George Watson's College. M.A. 1897; B.Sc. 1900; M.B., Ch.B. 1902; M.D. 1911. United States Army, Contract Surgeon Oct. to Dec. 1917 and June to July 1918. United States Army Medical Corps, Private Oct. 1918.

CAMPBELL, DAVID.
Miller Institution, Thurso. M.A. 1913. Schoolmaster. 4th and 6th Royal Scots (T.), Private 1910. Mobilised Aug. 1914. Argyll and Sutherland Highlanders 2nd Lieut. Nov. 1914. Machine-Gun Corps Feb. 1916; Lieut. July 1916; Acting Major April 1918. M.C. and Bar.

CAMPBELL, DONALD GRAHAM.
George Watson's College; First XV. M.B., C.M. 1892. President of S.R.C. 1889-90. R.A.M.C. (T.), Major May 1913. Mobilised Aug. 1914. Acting Lieut.-Col. Sept. 1918. 6th Seaforth Highlanders. No. 3 Ambulance Train; 139th Field Ambulance. France May 1915 to Dec. 1918.

CAMPBELL, DONALD HOPE.
Student of Law, 1911-13. Chartered Accountant, 1914. O.T.C. Infantry, May 1909 to Feb. 1912, Cadet. 9th Royal Scots (T.), Private Aug. 1914; L/Corporal April 1915. France 1915.

CAMPBELL, ERNEST KENNETH.
M.B., C.M. 1884; M.R.C.S. 1884; F.R.C.S. (Eng.) 1886. R.A.M.C., Lieut. Jan. 1917; Captain July 1917; Major Aug. 1919. Ophthalmist. Dispatches 1919.

CAMPBELL, FREDERICK WILLIAM.
George Watson's College. Student of Law, 1905-7. Chartered Accountant, 1913. O.T.C. Infantry, Nov. 1915 to Feb. 1916, Cadet; Officer Cadet March 1916. 4th Royal Scots, 2nd Lieut. July 1916; Lieut. Jan. 1918; Acting Captain Nov. 1917; Captain May 1918. France.

CAMPBELL, GEORGE.
Students' Representative Council Clerk. Royal Scots Greys, Private Sept. 1914. Scots Guards, Private May 1915 to March 1919. Wounded April and Sept. 1916.

CAMPBELL, GEORGE GORDON.
Pietermaritzburg College. O.T.C. 1904-11, Sergeant-Major. Student of Medicine, 1912-14 and 1919-20. O.T.C. Artillery, Oct. 1913-14, Cadet. R.F.A. 55th Brigade, 2nd Lieut. Aug. 1914; Lieut. Royal Air Force. Egypt and Gallipoli 1915-16; East Africa 1916-18. Wounded at Gallipoli.

CAMPBELL, GEORGE MacDONALD. (See p. 748.)

CAMPBELL, HUGH MARY.
Holy Cross Academy, Leith. Student of Arts, 1918. Forth R.G.A., Gunner July 1915; L/Bombardier. 108th Siege Battery.

CAMPBELL, IVOR.
Student of Medicine, 1915-16 and 1919-20. O.T.C. Infantry, Oct. 1915 to April 1916, Cadet. R.E. (Special Brigade), Private.

Record of War Service

CAMPBELL, JAMES DUNCAN.
Golspie School; First XI., Cricket and Football. Student of Arts, 1913-14. O.T.C. Artillery, Oct. 1915 to June 1916, Cadet; Officer Cadet June 1916. 2nd Lovat Scouts, 2nd Lieut. Sept. 1916; Lieut. March 1918. Attached 12th Royal Scots Fusiliers. Egypt, Palestine, and France. Dispatches.

CAMPBELL, JAMES IAN. (See p. 748.)

CAMPBELL, JOHN.
Oban School. Student of Medicine, 1912-14 and 1917-20. O.T.C. Infantry, 1913-14, Cadet. 9th Royal Highlanders (Black Watch), 2nd Lieut. Sept. 1914; Lieut. Sept. 1916; Acting Captain Nov. 1917 to April 1918. Wounded at Loos Sept. 1915.

CAMPBELL, JOHN DOUGLAS-BOSWELL.
Fettes; First XV. Student of Law, 1906-11. Writer to the Signet, 1911. R.H. and R.F.A. (S.R.), 2nd Lieut. Aug. 1914; Lieut. July 1917. Remount Depôt, Ayr, 1914-15. 6 "C" Reserve Brigade, 1917-19. R.H.A., France, 1916-17.

CAMPBELL, JOHN FORBES.
Mackie Academy, Stonehaven. L.D.S.; L.R.C.P. & S. (Edin.) and L.R.F.P.S. (Glasg.) 1917. University O.T.C. Medical, April 1915, Cadet. R.A.M.C. (S.R.), Lieut. July 1917; Captain Aug. 1918. Mesopotamia and Persia.

CAMPBELL, JOHN McPHAIL.
North Berwick High School. Student of Medicine, 1916 and 1919. O.T.C. Artillery, April to Dec. 1916, Cadet Bombardier; Officer Cadet Dec. 1916. R.G.A., 51st Siege Battery, 2nd Lieut. March 1917; Lieut. Sept. 1918.

CAMPBELL, JOHN PROFEIT.
M.B., Ch.B. 1900. 10th Royal Scots (T.), Captain.

CAMPBELL, JOHN YOUNG.
Royal Academy, Inverness. M.A. 1909. Probationer, U.F. Church of Scotland. Inns of Court O.T.C. Feb. 1916. R.G.A. (S.R.), 2nd Lieut. Aug. 1916; Lieut. Feb. 1918. Dispatches Jan. 1918.

CAMPBELL, LACHLAN GRAHAM.
North Berwick High School. Student of Arts and Medicine, 1911-14 and 1918-19; M.A. 1914. O.T.C. Artillery, Oct. 1911-14, Cadet Bombardier. R.G.A., 2nd Lieut. Oct. 1914; Lieut. April 1916; Captain April 1917; Acting Major Feb. 1918 to March 1919. M.C. Aug. 1916. Dispatches Dec. 1918.

CAMPBELL, ROBERT BROWN.
George Watson's College. M.B., C.M. 1895; M.D. and F.R.C.P. (Edin.) 1912. Royal Navy, H.M.S. *Crescent*, Surgeon-Commander May 1918.

CAMPBELL, RODERICK ALAN.
Edinburgh Academy. M.B., Ch.B. 1907; M.D. 1910. R.A.M.C., Lieut. Dec. 1914; Captain Sept. 1917. France and German East Africa.

Record of War Service

CAMPBELL, SAMUEL BURNSIDE BOYD.
Foyle College, Londonderry; First XV. and XI. M.B., Ch.B. 1912; M.R.C.P. (Edin.) 1914; F.R.C.P. (Edin.) 1919. Rugby "Blue" and Irish International. R.A.M.C., Lieut. Dec. 1914; Captain Dec. 1915; Acting Major Jan. 1918. Dispatches June 1918. M.C. Oct. 1918.

CAMPBELL, SAMUEL GEORGE.
Bishop's College, Maritzburg, Natal. M.B., C.M. 1882; M.D. 1886; F.R.C.P. & S. (Edin.); M.R.C.S. (Eng.); D.P.H. South African Campaign, Natal Medical Corps. Native Rebellion 1910. Major M.I. Durham Defence Corps, Major Nov. 1915.

CAMPBELL, THOMAS.
M.B., Ch.B. 1905. Canadian Army Medical Corps, Captain Aug. 1917. France 1915; Salonika 1916. Invalided home.

CAMPBELL, THOMAS FREDERICK.
M.B., Ch.B. 1905. R.A.M.C., Lieut. Nov. 1916. Surgical Specialist, Colaba War Hospital, Bombay.

CAMPBELL, WALTER.
Beath School, Cowdenbeath. Student of Medicine, 1917-19. O.T.C. Medical, April to Sept. 1918, Cadet. 53rd Y.S. Battn. Gordon Highlanders, Private Aug. 1918; L/Corporal Dec. 1918.

CAMPBELL, WILFRED SAMUEL HAMILTON.
M.B., Ch.B. 1913; D.P.H. R.A.M.C. (T.), Sanitary Service, Lieut. Dec. 1915; Captain June 1916.

CAMPBELL, WILLIAM.
Daniel Stewart's College. M.B., Ch.B. (Hons.) 1911; B.Sc. (P.H.) 1913. Assistant to Professors, Public Health, 1912-13, and Pathology, 1914-19. No. 4 Coy. Q.R.V.B., Royal Scots. O.T.C. Infantry, 1909-10, Cadet Corporal. R.A.M.C., Lieut. July 1915; Captain July 1916. Pathologist, Alexandria Dist. and Pellagra Commission. Gallipoli and Egypt. Dispatches 1916 and June 1919.

CAMPBELL, WILLIAM SIBBALD.
George Watson's College; First XV. M.B., C.M. 1892; M.D. 1906. R.A.M.C., Lieut. May 1915; Captain May 1916; Major (Local) 1916-18; Captain 1918.

CANDLER-HOPE, GEORGE JOHN BROWN.
M.B., C.M. 1891. R.A.M.C., Lieut. June 1915. M.O. in charge of Brompton Auxiliary Military Hospital, and 51st and 52nd Squads, Royal Air Force.

CANDLISH, ERIC ELSMORE.
Student of Medicine, 1913-14 and 1918-19. R.A.M.C. (T.). Scottish Horse Brigade Field Ambulance, Sept. 1914. R.F.A. (T.), 2nd Lieut. June 1915; Lieut. July 1917 to April 1918; Acting Captain 1917. Egypt and Palestine Aug. 1915 to Jan. 1917; France Jan. 1917 to March 1918.

Record of War Service

CANNON, JOHN WILSON.
Kendal Grammar School. M.B., Ch.B. 1913. O.T.C. Medical, Jan. 1909 to April 1914, Cadet. R.A.M.C., Lieut. Sept. 1914; Captain April 1915. 2nd Lincolnshire Regiment. France 1914; Cameroons 1915; India 1916; Mesopotamia 1916-19. Wounded Neuve Chapelle. Dispatches April 1915.

CANSFIELD, ELLISON.
Bradford Grammar School. M.B., Ch.B. 1908. R.A.M.C., Lieut. April 1918. M.O. 7th Lincolnshire Regiment, May to Aug. 1918. France. Gassed, Somme, Aug. 1918. Invalided out Feb. 1919.

CANT, ANDREW McGREGOR.
Dunfermline High School. Student of Arts, 1911-15; M.A. 1915. Highland Light Infantry, 2nd Lieut. May 1915. Machine-Gun Corps, 1916; Lieut. Jan. 1917. France July 1916 to Nov. 1918; Somme, Vimy Ridge, Arras, and St Quentin. Persia. Dispatches. M.C. March 1918.

CANT, ROBERT BREMNER.
Arbroath High School; First XI., Cricket and Football. University O.T.C. Engineers, March 1917, Cadet; Officer Cadet. R.E., 63rd Field Coy., Feb. 1917, 2nd Lieut. Nov. 1917; Lieut. May 1919. M.C. Oct. 1918.

CAPPER, DAVID SYNGE.
Royal High School. M.A. 1884. Professor of Mechanical Engineering, King's College, London. Q.E.R., Private 1882-5. London University O.T.C. (T.), 1909; Lieut.-Col. 1912. Commanded Schools of Instruction, 1914-16. 75th Royal Warwickshire Regiment, Major March 1916. France June to Nov. 1916.

CAPPER, STEWART HENBEST.
M.A. 1880. Professor of Architecture, Manchester University. 6th Manchester Regiment (T.), Captain; Brevet Major Dec. 1913; Captain July 1915; Acting Major Dec. 1915. Censor, Port Said, Alexandria, and Cairo. Dispatches (twice). T.D.

CARGILL, JAMES ALEXANDER RUSSELL.
Edinburgh Academy; First XV. M.B., Ch.B. 1908. Queen's Edinburgh Mounted Rifles, Private, two years. 9th Royal Scots (V.), Private, three years. Royal Navy, Temporary Surgeon-Lieut. Aug. 1914. Attached Royal Marine Artillery, Heavy Howitzer Brigade. H.M.S. *Vindictive*, Surgeon-Captain.

CARGIN, HERBERT MACPHERSON.
Royal School, Dungannon, Ireland; First XV. and XI. M.B., Ch.B. 1905; M.D. 1913. Special Sanitary Officer, Tees Garrison, March 1915-17. Royal Air Force Medical Service, Lieut. June 1918.

Record of War Service

CARLETON, KEITH OSBORNE.
Daniel Stewart's College. Student of Arts, 1908-15; M.A. 1915. O.T.C. Infantry, Nov. 1909 to Sept. 1914, Cadet. Indian Army (Unattached List), April 1915, Lieut. April 1916; Captain April 1919. 3rd King's Own Scottish Borderers, May to Oct 1915. 25th, 26th and 30th Punjabis, Nov. 1915 to Sept. 1918. 143rd Narsingh (Dholpur) Infantry, Sept. 1918 to May 1919. 69th Punjabis May 1919. India and Mesopotamia 1916-18.

CARLISLE, HENRY GEORGE.
Edinburgh Academy. M.B., Ch.B. 1899; M.D. 1904. Medical Research Committee, 1915. R.A.M.C., Lieut. Jan. 1916; Captain Jan. 1917. Mediterranean 1915; France 1916-18.

CARLOW, WALTER WADDELL.
Edinburgh Academy. M.A. 1905; M.B., Ch.B. 1910; F.R.C.S. (Edin.) 1912. Demonstrator of Anatomy, 1911-12 and 1914-17. Clinical (Surgical) Tutor, 1913-17 and 1919. R.A.M.C., Lieut. June 1917; Captain June 1918. Surgical Specialist, 40th Casualty Clearing Station. Salonika.

CARLYLE, ROBERT CARLYLE.
Ripon. M.B., Ch.B. 1911. 9th Royal Scots, Private 1906-9. R.A.M.C., Lieut. 1912; Captain March 1915. Attached Egyptian Army, Feb. 1917. Malta 1914-17; Sudan 1917. White Eagle (5th Class), with Swords (Serbia).

CARMENT, ANDREW GRAY.
Dollar Academy and George Watson's College. M.B., C.M. 1896; B.Sc. 1909; M.D. 1911. Zanzibar Medical Service. Naval Wounded Hospital Ship *Gascon*, Oct. 1914. British E. African Exp. Force, Jan. 1915 to July 1916. R.A.M.C. (T.), Lieut. Oct. 1916; Captain Oct. 1917 to March 1919. Russia and Macedonia 1918. Invalided home Oct. 1918. 3rd Western General Hospital, Cardiff.

CARMICHAEL, ARCHIBALD NATHANIEL SHIRLEY.
Edinburgh Academy. M.B., C.M. 1892. No. 4 Coy. Q.R.V.B., Royal Scots, 1886-92, Sergeant. R.A.M.C. (T.), Lieut. Oct. 1914; Captain April 1915; Acting Major Jan. 1918. Lovat Scouts. D.A.D.M.S., 73rd Division, Independent Force (Kent), and 23rd Army Corps.

CARMICHAEL, DONALD GORDON.
M.B., Ch.B. 1902. R.A.M.C., Major Oct. 1914. India Dec. 1915.

CARMICHAEL, EDWARD ARNOLD.
Edinburgh Academy. Student of Medicine, 1912-14 and 1917-19. O.T.C. Medical, April 1918 to Jan. 1919, Cadet L/Corporal. R.A.M.C. (T.), Private Sept. 1914. Scottish Horse Brigade Field Ambulance.

Record of War Service

CARMICHAEL, JAMES CHARLES GORDON.
United Service College, Westward Ho! M.B., Ch.B. 1902; D.P.H. (Camb.) 1912. R.A.M.C., Lieut. Jan. 1903; Captain July 1906; Major Oct. 1914; Acting Lieut.-Col. Nov. 1917. O.C. 29th Casualty Clearing Station, Oct. 1917. Malta Aug. 1914; France April 1917 and Germany Feb. 1919. Dispatches March, and Nov. 1918. O.B.E. June 1919.

CARMICHAEL, KENNETH FRANCIS.
Royal High School. Student of Science, 1918-19. O.T.C. Infantry, June 1917 to May 1918, Cadet L/Corporal; Officer Cadet May 1918.

CARMICHAEL, NORMAN SCOTT.
Edinburgh Academy. M.B., Ch.B. 1905; F.R.C.P. (Edin.) 1913. Physician to Royal Hospital for Sick Children. R.A.M.C. (T.), Lieut. July 1916; Captain July 1917; Acting Major Aug. 1918. Order of St Sava, June 1917.

CARMICHAEL, WILLIAM ROBERT CLARK.
George Watson's College. University O.T.C. Infantry, May to August 1915, Cadet. 1st and 2nd Highland Light Infantry, 2nd Lieut. Aug. 1915; Lieut. July 1917 to March 1919. Attached Royal Air Force. France, the Somme 1916. Wounded and Prisoner of War, Oct. 1916 to March 1918.

CARNON, WILLIAM.
M.A. 1908. O.T.C. Artillery, June 1915, Cadet. R.F.A. (T.), 1st Lowland Brigade, 2nd Lieut. June 1915; Lieut. Dec. 1916; Acting Captain and Adjutant May 1918. R.G.A. (T.), No. 33 Scottish Fire Command.

CARR, GEORGE JAMESON.
M.B., Ch.B. 1910. O.T.C. Medical, May 1909 to Oct. 1910, Cadet. Royal Navy, Surgeon-Lieut. Nov. 1910; Surgeon-Lieut.-Commander. Royal Marine Artillery.

CARR, JOHN CECIL.
Oliver's Mount School, Scarborough. M.B., Ch.B. 1899; M.D. 1904; M.R.C.P. (Edin.). R.A.M.C. (T.), Lieut. July 1918. O.C. No. 4 Native Labour Stationary Hospital (Chinese), Rouen.

CARROTHERS, WILLIAM ALEXANDER. (See p. 748.)

CARRUTHERS, GEORGE JAMES ROGERSON.
George Watson's College. M.B., Ch.B. 1899. R.A.M.C., Lieut. July 1916; Captain July 1917. Salonika 1916-19.

CARRUTHERS, JAMES.
Craigmount and Morelands. Student of Law, 1894-7. Writer to the Signet, 1899. Royal Artillery, Major Oct. 1914. Deputy Assistant Director of Artillery, March 1918. M.V.O.; D.S.O.

CARRUTHERS, JOHN FERGUSON.
M.B., Ch.B. 1892; M.D. 1897. R.A.M.C., Major June 1918.

Record of War Service

CARRUTHERS, PETER WALTER.
Merchiston Castle. Student of Medicine, 1906-15; M.B., Ch.B. 1914. Royal Navy, Surgeon-Lieut. Oct. 1914. H.M. Ships *Weymouth*, *Goliath*, and *Pembroke*. East and South Africa 1915; Mediterranean 1916; N. Russian Exp. Force.

CARRUTHERS, VINCENT THEODORE.
Tonbridge School. M.B., Ch.B. 1904; F.R.C.S. (Edin.) 1908. R.A.M.C., Lieut. 1907; Captain 1910; Acting Major Jan. 1918; Major Jan. 1919. France Aug. 1914 to Jan. 1919. Dispatches Nov. 1914.

CARR-WHITE, PERCY.
St Thomas's Hospital. M.B., C.M. 1889; F.R.C.S. (Edin.); D.T.M. (Liverpool). Q.E.R., 1885-9, Private. Indian Medical Service, 1890; Lieut.-Col. 1910; Colonel June 1916. Burma 1891-2. N.-W. Frontier, India, 1897-8. D.D.M.S., East Persian Force, Jan. to April 1919; A.D.M.S., Afghan War, 1919. K.H.P.

CARSON, JOSEPH THOMPSON.
Cookstown Academy; First XI. M.B., Ch.B. 1908. No. 4 Coy. Q.R.V.B., Royal Scots, 1903-7, Corporal. R.A.M.C., Lieut. Oct. 1915; Captain Oct. 1916 to Dec. 1918. 28th General Hospital, Salonika (Radiographer), Nov. 1915 to Aug. 1918. Serbian Order of St Sava (5th Class).

CARTER, DAVID.
Grantchester, Cambridge. Student of Arts, 1914-15. R.F.A., Gunner Oct. 1916; Sergeant Jan. 1919. Mesopotamia May 1917; Palestine May 1918 to Oct. 1919.

CASE, HENRY WILLIAM.
M.B., C.M. 1893. R.A.M.C. (T.), Captain June 1915. 8th Manchester Regiment.

CASSADAY, ERNEST ELGIN.
Dundee High School. M.B., Ch.B. 1903; D.P.H.; L.D.S. R.A.M.C., Lieut. July 1917; Captain July 1918. 129th Field Ambulance, 7th Division, Egypt.

CASSELS, JAMES.
Ayr Academy. Student of Arts and Science, 1910-15; M.A. (Hons. Maths.) 1914; B.Sc. Schoolmaster. Royal Navy, H.M.S. *Benbow*; H.M. Mine-sweeper *Lysander II.* (Wireless Operator), March 1916; C.P.O. April 1918; Warrant Officer Oct. 1918 to Feb. 1919.

CASSIDY, LOUIS LAWRENCE.
M.B., Ch.B. 1908; F.R.C.S. (Ireland) 1911. R.A.M.C., Lieut. Oct. 1914; Captain Oct. 1915. 30th Field Ambulance. France and Salonika.

CASSILLIS, THE RIGHT HON. THE EARL OF.
Eton. Eton College Vols. 1887-90, Private. Trinity College, Cambridge. Student of Law, 1895-7. Advocate, 1897. South African Campaign, 1900-2. 3rd, 1st and 2nd Royal Scots Fusiliers, Dec. 1914; Captain Dec. 1899; Major 1911; Rejoined Dec. 1914. Town Major of Bailleul Dec. 1915, and Lassel Dec. 1918. Dispatches July 1919.

Record of War Service

CATHCART, CHARLES WALKER.
Loretto. M.A. 1873; M.B., C.M. 1878; F.R.C.S. (Edin.) 1880; F.R.C.S. (Eng.) 1879. Demonstrator of Anatomy and Lecturer on Clinical Surgery. Q.E.R., Colour-Sergeant 1869-74. R.A.M.C. (T.), Lieut.-Col. 1908. 2nd Scottish General Hospital, 1914; Edinburgh War and Edenhall Hospitals, 1915-19. C.B.E. 1918. Hon. Associate Order of St John of Jerusalem 1918.

CATHCART, JOHN.
Ballymena Academy. M.B., Ch.B. 1910; D.P.H., R.C.S. & P. (Ireland) 1911. R.A.M.C., Lieut. March 1916; Captain March 1917.

CATTANACH, DAVID LYNEDOCH.
George Watson's College. M.A. (Hons. Classics) 1904. Minister, Church of Scotland. R.F.A., Gunner June 1916; Bombardier; Sergeant; 2nd Lieut. Dec. 1917. Mesopotamia.

CATTANACH, JAMES ALEXANDER JACKSON.
Royal High School. Student of Arts, 1911-14. O.T.C. Infantry, 1914, Cadet. 5th and 13th Royal Scots (T.), Private Sept. 1914; 2nd Lieut. 1915; Lieut. and Adjutant July 1917; Captain. Attached 8th Welsh Labour Corps; Arab Labour Corps. Gallipoli 1915; Egypt 1915-16; Mesopotamia 1916-18.

CATTANACH, JAMES GIBSON.
M.B., C.M. 1893. R.A.M.C. (T.), Captain; Lieut.-Col. July 1908. Edinburgh War Hospital.

CATTANACH, JOHN RODERICK.
George Heriot's School. M.A. 1913. Schoolmaster. 1st and 2nd Gordon Highlanders, 2nd Lieut. Dec. 1915; Lieut. July 1917.

CATTANACH, JOSEPH HARDIE.
Edinburgh Academy and George Watson's College. M.A. 1899. Minister, Church of Scotland. R.A.M.C., Private Dec. 1915. Discharged May 1916. Scottish Churches Huts, France, 1916-17.

CATTO, ROBERT.
Robert Gordon's College, Aberdeen. University O.T.C. Infantry, Feb. to July 1917, Cadet L/Corporal; Officer Cadet July 1917. 10th Sherwood Foresters, 2nd Lieut. Nov. 1917; Lieut. May 1919. 3/7th Border Regiment.

CAVAYE, ROBERT McLELLAND.
George Heriot's School. University O.T.C. Infantry, May to Oct. 1916, Cadet; Officer Cadet Oct. 1916. 1st and 2nd Cameron Highlanders, 2nd Lieut. Jan. 1917; Lieut. July 1918. Attached 2nd King's Liverpool Regiment; 1st Seaforth Highlanders. India and Mesopotamia June to Dec. 1917; Egyptian Exp. Force, 1918-19.

Record of War Service

CAVAYE, RONALD J.
Charterhouse. Student of Law, 1909. Chartered Accountant, 1913. 1st and 3rd Cameron Highlanders, Captain 1911. France Oct. to Nov. 1914 and Jan. to Sept. 1918. Wounded Nov. 1914. M.B.E. May 1919.

CAVERHILL, AUSTIN MACK.
Clifton Bank, St Andrews. M.B., Ch.B. 1902; M.D. 1916; D.T.M. (Liverpool). R.A.M.C., Lieut. March 1917; Captain March 1918; Acting Major April 1918. 52nd Field Ambulance. Dispatches March 1919.

CAVERHILL, THOMAS PEARSON.
Clifton Bank, St Andrews. M.B., Ch.B. 1903. R.A.M.C. (T.), Lieut. Nov. 1914; Captain Nov. 1915; Acting Major Jan. 1918. Lothians and Border Horse. No. 2 Casualty Clearing Station, June 1916.

CHALIHA, LAKSHMI PRASAD.
Student of Medicine, 1913-14; L.M.S.N. (Calcutta) 1895; D.P.H.; F.R.C.P. & S. (Edin.). Indian Field Ambulance.

CHALLINOR, ARTHUR BERTRAM.
University O.T.C. Artillery, April to May, 1917 Cadet. Royal Air Force and Rifle Brigade, Cadet. Taken Prisoner on 27th May 1918.

CHALMERS, ADAM.
Student of Law, 1907-11. Chartered Accountant, 1911. 6th Royal Scots (T.), 2nd Lieut.; Lieut. July 1917.

CHALMERS, JAMES.
M.A., B.Sc. 1902. Schoolmaster. 15th Royal Scots, Sergeant.

CHALMERS, THOMAS.
M.A. 1911. Schoolmaster. 9th Royal Scots, Private Sept. 1914; Officer Cadet. 4th Cameron Highlanders, 2nd Lieut. 1915; Lieut. June 1916; Captain. France. Wounded at Festubert May 1915.

CHALMERS, THOMAS EDWARD BAIN.
Edinburgh Institution. B.Sc. 1910; M.I.A.E. O.T.C. Artillery, 1904 to Jan. 1910, Cadet; transferred Engineer Unit, Cadet L/Corporal. A.S.C. (M.T.), 2nd Lieut. Aug. 1915; Lieut. Oct. 1916; Captain Oct. 1918. 12th M.A.C. Aug. 1915. Tank Corps, Jan. 1917. France Sept. 1915 to April 1919; Loos 1915, Arras, third Ypres, and Cambrai 1917. M.C. Aug. 1917.

CHALMERS, WILLIAM KENNEDY.
Student of Medicine, 1909-15; M.B., Ch.B. 1914. Royal Navy, Surgeon Jan. 1915.

CHAMBERS, JAMES.
Student of Medicine, 1911-12. O.T.C. Artillery, Oct. 1911 to Feb. 1913, Cadet, and Medical, April 1913 to Feb. 1915, Cadet. R.F.A., Captain; Acting Major. M.C.

Record of War Service

CHAMBERS, ROBERT ALEXANDER.
Perth Academy; First XI. M.B., Ch.B. 1904. No. 4 Coy. Q.R.V.B., Royal Scots, 1901-4, Private. Indian Medical Service Sept. 1906, Captain Sept. 1909; Major Sept. 1918. Mesopotamia Feb. 1916 and Nov. 1917; India March 1917 and 1919. O.B.E. (Military) Feb. 1919. Dispatches Nov. 1918.

CHAMBERS, WALTER DUNCANSON.
M.A. 1906; M.B., Ch.B. 1910; M.D. 1913. O.T.C. Artillery, Oct. 1908-9, Cadet. Royal Inniskilling Fusiliers Sept. 1914, Captain Nov. 1914. R.A.M.C., Captain June 1915. No. 8 Stationary Hospital, France. Dispatches Dec. 1916.

CHAMPENOIS, JULIEN JACQUES.
Lycée de Nevers and Paris University. M.A. 1908. B. Litt. (Oxford). Lecturer. 13th Régiment d'Infanterie (French Army), Corporal Aug. 1914; Lieut. 1915.

CHANDLER, FREDERICK CHARLES.
Student of Medicine, 1909-15; M.B., Ch.B. 1914. O.T.C. Medical, Oct. 1909 to Nov. 1911, Cadet. R.A.M.C. (T.), Lieut.; Captain April 1918; Major. 62nd Field Ambulance, France. M.C.

CHAPMAN, EDWARD SEYMOUR.
Sherbourn. Student of Medicine. M.B., Ch.B. 1901, and M.D. (Glasg.) 1905; F.R.C.S. (Edin.) R.A.M.C. (T.), Lieut. Dec. 1914; Captain Dec. 1915.

CHAPMAN, OSMUND HARRY.
Old Clee Grammar School. M.B., C.M. 1894; M.D. 1905; D.P.H. (Manchester) 1905. R.A.M.C. (T.), Oct. 1908, Major April 1916. 4th Northern General Hospital, Lincoln.

CHAPMAN, PHILIP FRANCIS.
M.B., C.M. 1894. Indian Medical Service, Major; Lieut.-Col. July 1917.

CHAPMAN, WILLIAM NOEL JAMES.
Falkirk High School. Student of Medicine, 1915-19. R.N.V.R., Surgeon Sub-Lieut. May 1918.

CHARLESWORTH, FRANCIS.
Blairlodge. M.B., C.M. 1882. R.A.M.C., Lieut. and Captain 1915; Major May 1916.

CHARNOCK, JOHN PHETHEAN.
Bolton High School. M.B., Ch.B. 1910. R.A.M.C. (S.R.), Lieut. 1910; Captain Sept. 1914; Acting Major Aug. 1918. Mesopotamia. Dispatches 1919.

CHASSEAUD, HENRY MAURICE.
M.B., C.M. 1890; M.D. 1892. R.A.M.C., Major Sept. 1915; Lieut.-Col. Nov. 1917.

CHATTERJEE, SISIR CHANDRA.
M.B., Ch.B. 1912. Indian Medical Service, Lieut. Dec. 1916. Indian Exp. Force.

Record of War Service

CHAUDHURI, MANMATHA NATH.
Krishnagar School and Presidency College, Calcutta. First XI. M.B., C.M. 1897. Indian Medical Service, 1899; Major 1911; Lieut.-Col. July 1919. Mesopotamia Aug. 1915 to May 1918. Dispatches Nov. 1916 and Nov. 1917.

CHESSOR, GEORGE CLINTON.
Fraserburgh Academy; Athletics. University O.T.C. Artillery, Jan. to June 1916, Cadet. R.F.A. (T.), 3/1st Lowland Brigade, 2nd Lieut. Aug. 1916; Lieut. Feb. 1918; Staff Captain Nov. 1918. Mesopotamia. Staff Officer to C.R.A., Fraser's Force, Kurdistan Operations, 1919.

CHEVES, ALEXANDER BRUCE.
Sutton Valence; First XV. M.B., Ch.B. 1911. R.A.M.C., Lieut. Aug. 1914; Captain Aug. 1915. Dispatches June 1916. M.C. Jan. 1917.

CHEW, WILLIAM ROGER.
M.B. (Hons.) (Cape of Good Hope). M.B., C.M. 1887. South African Medical Corps, Captain March 1915; German South West Africa. Union Central African Imperial Service Contingent, Sept. 1915. Dispatches 1915. Invalided out March 1918.

CHEYNE, SIR WILLIAM WATSON, BART., M.P.
New Grammar School, Aberdeen. M.B., C.M. 1875; F.R.C.S. (Eng.) 1879. Royal Navy, Consulting Surgeon 1914; Surgeon-General 1915; Surgeon Rear-Admiral 1918. K.C.M.G. C.B.

CHIENE, GEORGE LYALL.
Edinburgh Academy; First XV. and XI. M.B., C.M. 1897; F.R.C.S. (Edin.) 1901. South African Campaign, 1900-1. R.A.M.C. (T.), Captain July 1908; Acting Major May to Oct. 1918. 58th Scottish General Hospital, France, and 2nd Scottish General Hospital.

CHILD, ARMANDO DUMAS.
Ware College and Sevenoaks School. M.B., Ch.B. 1909; D.P.H. (Lond.). R.A.M.C., Captain Sept. 1914. 19th Casualty Clearing Station, Lahore, 1914-16, Specialist Sanitary Officer. Camiers Jan. 1916; Etaples June 1917. Dispatches May and Nov. 1918. O.B.E. (Military) Jan. 1919.

CHILDS, TOM WILLIAM JAMES.
Wellington College, New Zealand. First XV. College Rifles 1905-7, Corporal. M.B., Ch.B. 1913. O.T.C. Infantry, Jan. 1909-10, Cadet Corporal. N.Z. Army Medical Corps, Captain Jan. 1917. Egypt. Dispatches 1917.

CHILL, EDWIN ALBERT.
King's College School, London. M.B., C.M. 1883; M.D. 1886. Q.E.R., 1879-83. R.A.M.C. (T.), Captain. O.C. Clive Military Hospital, Southall. Seconded to County of London R.A.S.C. (V.). Assistant County Director, Middlesex Red Cross. O.B.E. June 1918.

Record of War Service

CHISHOLM, ALEXANDER ERNEST.
Edinburgh Academy. M.B., Ch.B. 1906; F.R.C.S. (Edin.) 1909. Anatomy Staff, 1911-14. R.A.M.C., Lieut. Sept. 1914; Captain Sept. 1915. 15th Casualty Clearing Station, France.

CHISHOLM, ALEXANDER FRASER.
M.A. 1911. O.T.C. Artillery, Oct. 1909 to Feb. 1913, Cadet. R.F.A. (S.R.) Nov. 1914; 2nd Lieut. May 1915; Lieut. July 1917. France.

CHISHOLM, COLIN CARSTAIRS.
George Watson's College. Student of Law, 1908-9. Gold Coast Regiment (Transport), Captain Aug. 1914. Surrender of Togoland.

CHISHOLM, JOHN.
Royal Academy, Inverness. M.B., Ch.B. 1905. R.A.M.C., Lieut. Dec. 1914; Captain Dec. 1915.

CHISHOLM, RODERICK.
Kingussie School. 4th Cameron Highlanders (T.), Private 1909-13. Student of Arts, 1912-14. 6th Royal Scots (T.), Private April 1914; 2nd Lieut. Nov. 1916; Lieut. May 1918; Acting Captain March 1918; Captain Nov. 1918. 7th Cameron Highlanders. Transferred Labour Corps July 1918. France.

CHODAK, HENRY ALEXIS.
Student of Medicine, 1910-14 and 1919; M.R.C.S., L.R.C.P. (Eng.) O.T.C. Infantry, Sept. to Oct. 1914, Cadet. 15th Royal Scots, Private Oct. 1914. R.A.M.C., Lieut. May 1918. M.C. Nov. 1918.

CHOYCE, CHARLES COLEY.
New Zealand Schools. B.Sc. (N.Z.) 1897; M.B., Ch.B. 1901; M.D. 1903; F.R.C.S. (Eng.) 1905. R.A.M.C., Captain April 1915; Major May 1915; Lieut.-Col. 1917; Colonel Sept. 1918. O.C. Surgical Division, 19th General Hospital, 1915-17; Consulting Surgeon, Egyptian Exp. Force, 1917-19. Dispatches 1915, 1917, and 1918. C.M.G. and C.B.E. (Military) 1919.

CHRISTIE, ARTHUR WILLIAM STARK.
Fettes. M.B., Ch.B. 1901; F.R.C.S. (Edin.) 1904. R.A.M.C., Lieut. Dec. 1914; Captain Dec. 1915; Acting Major Jan. 1918 to March 1919. Dispatches May 1918. Croix de Guerre (French) Dec. 1918.

CHRISTIE, DAVID HAMILTON.
George Watson's College. M.A. 1899. Schoolmaster. No. 6 (McGill) o/s Battery, Siege Artillery, Canadian Exp. Force, Q.M.S. May 1916. France March 1917 to Dec. 1918; Vimy Ridge, Hill 70, Passchendaele 1917; Arras, Mons, 1918. Khaki University of Canada, Jan. to July 1919.

CHRISTIE, DUNCAN.
M.A. 1912. Schoolmaster. 2/8th Royal Scots (T.), Lieut. April 1915; Captain June 1916.

Record of War Service

CHRISTIE, GRAHAM WILSON.
: Royal High School. M.B., Ch.B. 1913. O.T.C. Medical, June 1910 to July 1913, Cadet. R.A.M.C., Lieut. July 1915; Captain July 1916. 10th Royal Highlanders (Black Watch), 12th East Surrey Regiment, and 140th Field Ambulance. France Oct. 1915; The Rhine. Wounded Sept. 1918. M.C. Sept. 1918.

CHRISTIE, IAN FRANCIS.
: Edinburgh Academy. O.T.C. 1908-10. Student of Arts, 1912-13. O.T.C. Artillery, 1915-16, Cadet. 2/1st Scottish Horse, 2nd Lieut. Nov. 1916. I.A.R.O., Lieut. Nov. 1917. India 1917-18. Egypt 1918-19.

CHRISTIE, JAMES MALCOLM.
: M.B., Ch.B. 1906; F.R.C.S. (Edin.). R.A.M.C., Captain Oct. 1917.

CHRISTIE, JULIA VERONICA (*née* HENSLOW).
: M.B., Ch.B. 1913. Red Cross 1916. Auxiliary, R.A.M.C., attached Q.M.A.A.C., Nov. 1916. Monyhull Military Hospital, Birmingham. Medical Controller, Q.M.A.A.C., Birmingham and Midlands, Sept. 1917. Brocton and Rafety Camps. Stafford, March 1919. W.R.A.F. Hostels.

CHRISTIE, R. M.
: Student of Science. 13th Highland Light Infantry, Captain.

CHRISTIE, WILLIAM ALEXANDER KYNOCH.
: George Heriot's School. B.Sc. 1902. Indian Army, 12th Cavalry, 2nd Lieut.; Lieut. April 1916. Attached Royal Engineers. India June 1915.

CHRISTIE, WILLIAM FRANCIS.
: George Watson's College. M.B., Ch.B. 1909. O.T.C. Artillery, Nov. 1905-8, Cadet. R.A.M.C., Lieut. 1912; Captain March 1915; D.A.D.M.S. and Acting Major May 1918; Brevet-Major 1919. Singapore Sept. 1915. Twice Mentioned in Dispatches.

CHRISTIE, WILLIAM LESLIE.
: Edinburgh Academy. M.A. 1903; LL.B. 1906. Writer to the Signet, 1907, and Notary Public. R.G.A., 17th Siege Battery, 2nd Lieut. Nov. 1914; Lieut. June 1916; Acting Captain March 1918; Acting Major. France Aug. 1915 and May 1916.

CHRISTIE, WILLIAM MELVILLE.
: Dollar Academy. Student of Medicine, 1910-15; M.B., Ch.B. 1915. O.T.C. Infantry, May 1911 to Nov. 1914, Cadet. British Red Cross Society, France (Dresser), Nov. 1914. R.A.M.C., Lieut. Oct. 1915; Captain March 1917. Prisoner of War March to Dec. 1918.

CHRISTY, CUTHBERT.
: Oliver's Mount School, Scarborough. M.B., C.M. 1893. Mackenzie Bursaries in Anatomy. Assistant Demonstrator in Pathology. 2nd Battn. West African Field Force, Northern Nigeria, 1898-1900. R.A.M.C. (T.), Major Nov. 1916. East African Exp. Force 1917; Mesopotamia 1918.

Record of War Service

CHRYSTAL, JOHN MURRAY.
: Student of Science, 1912-14. O.T.C. Engineers, Nov. 1912 to Oct. 1914, Cadet Sergeant. R.E., 2nd Lieut. Oct. 1914.

CHURCH, DUNCAN MACDONALD COCHRANE.
: Loretto. M.B., Ch.B., 1904. Indian Medical Service, Feb. 1906, Major. Attached 7th Hariana Lancers, Indian Exp. Force. N.-W.F.P., India; Mesopotamia and Palestine. Wounded in Mesopotamia April 1915.

CHURCHILL, EDWARD ARCHIBALD HICKLING.
: Clifton College; First XV. O.T.C. 1906-8. Student of Science, 1910-14; B.Sc. 1914. Boxing "Blue." 5th Somerset Light Infantry (T.), 2nd Lieut. Aug. 1914; Captain June 1916; Acting Major 1918. Attached Indian Army. Mohmand Campaign, N.-W. Frontier, and Aden. O.C. 33rd Division, Signal Coy., Sappers and Miners. Baluchistan Field Force 1919.

CLARK, ALEXANDER FRASER MACDONALD.
: M.A. 1901; B.Sc. R.F.A., Lieut. Dec. 1914. R.E., March 1915. France June 1915. Wounded Sept. 1915.

CLARK, ALEXANDER LANDALE.
: Merchiston Castle. O.T.C. 1913-15. Student of Medicine, 1915-16 and 1918-19. 1/1st Highland Cyclist Battn. (T.), Jan. 1916; 2nd Lieut. Aug. 1916; Lieut. Feb. 1918. Invalided out Jan. 1919.

CLARK, ALLAN E. L.
: Clerk, Works' Office. 5th and 11th Royal Scots, Private July 1914; Corporal and 2nd Lieut. Aug. 1915; Lieut. March 1917; Captain April 1917. France. Wounded June 1917. Invalided out June 1919.

CLARK, ARTHUR GRUCHY.
: Student of Medicine, 1910-15; M.B., Ch.B. 1915. O.T.C. Medical, Oct. 1914 to July 1915, Cadet. R.A.M.C., Lieut. Aug. 1915; Captain Aug. 1916. 76th Field Ambulance, 8th Loyal North Lancashire Regiment and 2nd South Lancashire Regiment. Prisoner of War in Germany April to Dec. 1918. M.C.

CLARK, ARTHUR STIRLING.
: Student of Arts, 1912-14 and 1919-20. O.T.C. Artillery, Oct. 1913 to Nov. 1914, Cadet. R.G.A., 85th Siege Battery, 2nd Lieut. Oct. 1914; Acting Captain Dec. 1916; Lieut. Feb. 1917; Acting Major April 1918. France May 1916.

CLARK, COLIN FRASER MACDUFF.
: University O.T.C. Artillery, May 1917-18, Cadet Bombardier; Officer Cadet, May 1918. R.F.A., 2nd Lieut. March 1919.

CLARK, EDWARD JAMES.
: Royal Academy, Inverness. Student of Medicine, 1910-16. M.B., Ch.B. 1915. R.A.M.C., Lieut. Oct. 1915; Captain Jan. 1917. France 1916. M.C. Nov. 1917.

Record of War Service

CLARK, EDWIN.
George Heriot's School. O.T.C. 1914-16, L/Corporal. Student of Medicine, 1916-17 and 1918-19. 9th King's Own Scottish Borderers, Private April 1917. Royal Air Force, Lieut.

CLARK, ERNEST SHAW.
M.B., C.M. 1889. R.A.M.C., Major; Lieut.-Col. March 1915.

CLARK, FRANCIS WILLIAM.
Nelson School, Wigton, Cumberland; First XV. and XI. Student of Medicine, 1911-16; M.B., Ch.B. 1916. O.T.C. Infantry, May 1911-14, Cadet L/Corporal, and Medical, Nov. 1914 to April 1916, Cadet. R.A.M.C., Lieut. May 1916; Captain May 1917. M.O., 1/8th Scottish Rifles. Mesopotamia, Egypt, Palestine, and France. M.C. (Rheims) Aug. 1918.

CLARK, GEORGE PAGAN.
Kirkcaldy High School; First XV. O.T.C. 1907-9. Student of Arts, 1917, 1/1st Fife and Forfar Yeomanry (Signaller), Sept. 1914.

CLARK, GILBERT.
Rutherford College, Newcastle-on-Tyne. B.Sc. 1912. R.G.A., 2nd Lieut. Nov. 1914; Lieut. Oct. 1916; Acting Captain June 1917; Acting Major Nov. 1917; Captain Feb. 1918. Dispatches Nov. 1916.

CLARK, HERBERT ERLAND FORDYCE.
Royal High School; First XI. Student of Medicine, 1918. Lothians and Border Horse, Private, Oct. 1914. 9th Royal Scots, 2nd Lieut. September 1916; Lieut. March 1918. Attached Royal Air Force. Wounded in France Jan. 1918.

CLARK, HERBERT WILLIAM.
Royal High School. Student of Law, 1909-11. Law Agent, 1913. O.T.C. Infantry, March 1909 to July 1915, Cadet Sergeant. 4th Highland Light Infantry (S.R.), 2nd Lieut. July 1915; Lieut. July 1917. R.E. 1917. Wireless Officer, 2nd Corps. France and The Rhine.

CLARK, JAMES AITKEN.
M.B., C.M. 1886. R.A.M.C. (T.), Major. 5th Royal Scots.

CLARK, JAMES NEIL CAMPBELL.
George Watson's College; Dux. Student of Arts, 1918-19. O.T.C. Artillery, 1916-17, Cadet Bombardier; Officer Cadet Feb. 1917. R.F.A., 2nd Lieut. July 1917. 95th Brigade, 21st Division. France Oct. 1917 to July 1918. Gassed.

CLARK, JAMES THOMSON DORAN.
Student of Medicine, 1918. 4th, 9th, and 10th Scottish Rifles, 2nd Lieut. Sept. 1915; Lieut. July 1917; Captain Feb. 1918. France. 4th Tank Battn. Dec. 1916 to Jan. 1919.

Record of War Service

CLARK, JOHN.
    M.B., C.M. 1905. R.A.M.C., Captain May 1915. O.C. 28th Ambulance Train. France.

CLARK, JOHN LAIDLOW.
    Whitehaven County School; First XV. and XI. Student of Medicine, 1917-19. O.T.C. Infantry, Sept. 1917 to May 1918, Cadet L/Corporal. 4th Border Regiment, May 1918. Royal Scots, 2nd Lieut. Feb. 1919.

CLARK, KATHERINE JANE STARK.
    M.B., Ch.B. 1903; M.D. 1907; D.P.H. 1906. R.A.M.C. (Aux.); attached Q.M.A.A.C., Medical Controller, 1917. Travelling Medical Boards, 1917. President, Medical Boards, Scottish Command, 1919.

CLARK, STEPHEN FRAZER.
    George Watson's College; First XV. and XI. M.B., C.M. 1885; D.P.H. (Ireland) 1902. Army Medical Service, 1887; Lieut.-Col.; Colonel and A.D.M.S. March 1915. France 1914-15. Attached Royal Serbian Army, 1916-18. Dispatches Oct. 1914. Order of St Sava, 3rd Class (Serbia); Croix de Guerre (French); Officier de la Légion d'Honneur.

CLARK, WALTER SCOTT.
    M.A. (Hons. Classics) 1909. Oxford University O.T.C. 7th Argyll and Sutherland Highlanders, 2nd Lieut. Oct. 1915; Lieut. Feb. 1918. Attached 4th South Wales Borderers. France; Mesopotamia Jan. 1917; India.

CLARK, WILLIAM CARRIE.
    Daniel Stewart's College. Student of Arts and Divinity, 1912-15; M.A. 1912. O.T.C. Artillery, Oct. 1914 to Dec. 1914, Cadet. R.G.A., 2nd Lieut. Dec. 1914; Lieut. March 1916; Captain Nov. 1917. Commandant, Fao, Persian Gulf.

CLARK, WILLIAM MORRISON.
    Leith Academy. Student of Science, 1913-14 and 1919-20. O.T.C. Engineers, 1913-14, Cadet. 1/9th Royal Scots, Private Aug. 1914. 1st Argyll and Sutherland Highlanders, 2nd Lieut. Aug. 1915; Lieut. March 1917; Acting Captain Aug. 1918. France Feb. to Nov. 1915, and Aug. 1918; Salonika Dec. 1915 to Jan. 1917. Wounded Sept. 1916.

CLARKE, ANDREW ROBERT FAUSSET.
    Student of Medicine, 1910-15; M.B., Ch.B. 1915. R.A.M.C. (S.R.), Lieut.; Captain Jan. 1916; Acting Major Jan. 1918. Med. Exp. Force.

CLARKE, CHARLES MELVILLE.
    Edinburgh Academy. O.T.C. 1914-15. Student of Arts, 1915-16 and 1918-19. O.T.C. Infantry, Oct. 1915 to Aug. 1916, Cadet; Officer Cadet. 11th Argyll and Sutherland Highlanders, Private Aug. 1916.

Record of War Service

CLARKE, FREDERICK ORLANDO.
M.B., Ch.B. 1911; M.D. 1917. R.A.M.C., Lieut. March 1915; Captain March 1916; Acting Major Jan. 1919. M.C. Sept. 1918; Bar to M.C. Oct. 1918.

CLARKE, JAMES ALEXANDER.
Elgin Academy and Kingussie School. Student of Arts and Divinity, 1906-14; M.A. 1914. Universités de Dijon and Grenoble, Faculté de Lettres, Diplômes Supérieures. Minister, Church of Scotland. R.G.A. (S.R.), 2nd Lieut. Jan. 1916; Lieut. July 1917. Regimental Gas Officer, Inchkeith, 1917. France. Invalided home Oct. 1918.

CLARKE, JAMES HAY.
Dunfermline High School. Student of Arts and Medicine, 1914-16 and 1918-19; M.A. 1916. O.T.C. Artillery, Oct. 1914 to March 1915, Cadet. R.G.A., 359th Siege Battery, Gunner Sept. 1915; Gunnery Instructor Sept. 1916; 2nd Lieut. April 1917; Lieut. Sept. 1918.

CLARKE, ROBERT RENDEL.
Student of Science, 1915-16 and 1918-19. R.E. (Special Brigade), Sapper May 1916. France July 1916 to Dec. 1918.

CLARKE, THOMAS WILLIAM.
M.B., Ch.B. 1913. O.T.C. Medical 1910-14, Cadet Sergeant. R.A.M.C. Lieut. May 1914; Captain April 1915; Acting Major Jan. 1918. France Aug. 1914 to Nov. 1919. Wounded March 1915 and March 1918. M.C. March 1915; Bar to M.C. Feb. 1919. Twice Mentioned in Dispatches.

CLARKE, WILLIAM BRIGGS.
Harrison College, Barbados. M.B., C.M. 1893. R.A.M.C., Lieut. June 1917. Cross Channel Hospital Ship.

CLAYTON, NEVILLE MORRISON.
Gateshead School; First XI., Football. Student of Science, 1917 and 1919. O.T.C. Infantry, Jan. to Sept. 1917, Cadet. 3rd Gordon Highlanders, Private Oct. 1917. 3rd Border Regiment (S.R.), 2nd Lieut. March 1918. Wounded at Courtrai Oct. 1918 and invalided out.

CLEEVES, FREDERICK ROBERT.
Welshpool Grammar School. University O.T.C. Infantry, Dec. 1916 to June 1917, Cadet L/Corporal; Officer Cadet June 1917. 6th King's Royal Rifle Corps, 2nd Lieut. Sept. 1917; Lieut. March 1919. France Nov. 1917. Dispatches July 1919.

CLEGHORN, ALFRED MAXWELL.
Dundee High School; First XV. Student of Science, 1911-14; B.Sc. 1914. O.T.C. Engineers, Oct. 1911-14, Cadet. R.E., City of Dundee Fortress (T.), Sapper Sept. 1914; Sergeant 1915; Lieut. May 1915; Acting Captain Dec. 1917 to July 1919. 205th Field Coy. France Jan. 1916 to July 1919. Dispatches Dec. 1917 and June 1918. Croix de Guerre (Belgium) April 1918. M.C. June 1919.

Record of War Service

CLEGHORN, JOHN SMITH.
Dundee High School. B.Sc. 1911. A.M.I.C.E. R.E., 2nd Lieut. Sept. 1915; Lieut. June 1916. 1/2nd and 401st Highland Field Coy. (T.). Resident Engineer, Turnberry Aerodrome. France, 51st Division, 1916 and 1917.

CLELAND, ALEXANDER.
Daniel Stewart's College. Student of Medicine, 1911-16; M.B., Ch.B. 1916. O.T.C. Medical, Nov. 1915 to April 1916, Cadet. R.A.M.C., Lieut. July 1916; Captain July 1917. Italy.

CLEMENTS, JOHN BURTON.
Liverpool Institute. Student of Science, 1918-19. 1/10th King's Liverpool Scottish, Aug. 1914; Lieut. July 1917. Dispatches May 1917.

CLEMENTS, THOMAS EDWIN.
George Watson's College; First XV. and XI. Student of Science, 1911-15; B.Sc. 1919. R.F.A., 2nd Lieut. April 1915; Lieut. June 1916. 1st Lowland Brigade (T.). India, Mesopotamia, Palestine, and France. M.C. Jan. 1919.

CLEPHANE, WALTER JAMES.
George Watson's College. O.T.C. 1912-13. Student of Medicine, 1914-15. O.T.C. Infantry, Oct. 1914 to Jan. 1915, Cadet. R.F.A. (T.), 1st Lowland Brigade, Gunner Jan. 1915; Bombardier Sept. 1917. Invalided from Sinai Peninsula, Aug. 1916.

CLIFT, HARRY LECHMERE.
Eastbourne High School. M.B., Ch.B. 1901. R.A.M.C., Lieut. May 1917; Captain May 1918. France.

CLIVE, EDWARD A. B.
Haileybury. University O.T.C., Adjutant 1908-12. Seaforth Highlanders, 1898; Captain 1904. South African Campaign, 1898-1901. 3rd Grade Staff Officer, War Office, Aug. 1914; 2nd Grade G.S.O. Sept. 1915.

CLOW, ANDREW W. BROWN.
George Heriot's School. Student of Law, 1899-1904. Scottish Horse (T.), Private.

CLUNESS, ANDREW THOMAS.
Anderson Institute, Lerwick; Athletics. M.A. (Hons. Classics) 1913. Schoolmaster. O.T.C. Infantry, Jan. 1910 to June 1912, Cadet. 1st Cameron Highlanders, Private March 1915; L/Corporal July 1916; Corporal Dec. 1917. Machine-Gun Corps, 1916-19. Wounded at Loos, June 1916; High Wood, Sept. 1916; near Ypres, Aug. 1917; and Offoy near Ham, March 1918. M.M. Aug. 1917.

CLYDE, JAMES LATHAM McDIARMID.
Edinburgh Academy. O.T.C. 1913-16, L/Corporal. University O.T.C. Artillery, 1917, Cadet; Officer Cadet March 1917. Forth R.G.A. (T.), 2nd Lieut. Sept. 1917; Lieut. March 1918.

Record of War Service

COATES, JOHN MANDALL.
Daniel Stewart's College. M.B., C.M. 1895; M.D. 1899. South African Field Force, 1900-2, Civil Surgeon. R.A.M.C., Captain May 1915. Hon. Associate, Order of St John of Jerusalem.

COATES, NORMAN.
Student of Science, 1913-14. Army Dispatch Rider. France.

COATS, HECTOR WILLIAM.
University O.T.C. Artillery, June to Sept. 1918, Cadet. R.N.V.R., Midshipman, Sept. 1918.

COATS, JOHN DUNDAS ORR. (See p. 748.)

COATS, WILLIAM ANDERSON.
Royal High School. Student of Medicine, 1909-15; M.B., Ch.B. 1914. O.T.C. Medical, Nov. 1909-11, Cadet. R.A.M.C., 62nd Field Ambulance, Lieut. Feb. 1915; Captain Feb. 1916. R.M.O., 10th Essex Regiment, 9th Leicestershire Regiment, 1916, 2/5th King's Own Yorkshire Light Infantry, 1917-18, and 8th Cornwall Regiment, 1918-19. S.M.O., Sollum, Egypt. Wounded July 1916 and Sept. 1918.

COBB, WILLIAM GRAHAME.
Rugby. M.B., Ch.B. 1907. R.A.M.C., Lieut. Sept. 1915; Captain Feb. 1918. M.O. (G.L.), attached West African Field Force, Cameroons, and Royal African Rifles. France and East Africa. D.S.O. Oct. 1918.

COCHRAN, ROBERT MICHAEL.
Dollar Academy. Cadet Corps 1902-8. Student of Law, 1911-14. R.F.A. (T.), Gunner Sept. 1910. Mobilised Sept. 1915. R.G.A., Oct. 1915 to Jan. 1919.

COCHRAN-PATRICK, NEIL JAMES KENNEDY.
Edinburgh Academy. B.A. (Camb.), LL.B. 1890. J.P. and D.L. (Ayrshire). Advocate, 1890. 2/4th Royal Scots Fusiliers (T.) Oct. 1914, Captain. Appeal Military Representative for Renfrew and Bute, March 1916 to Dec. 1918. M.B.E. Nov. 1918.

COCHRANE, ALEXANDER YOUNGER PEATTIE.
Bo'ness Academy; First XV. and XI. Student of Arts and Medicine, 1910-14 and 1918-19; M.A. 1913. R.N.V.R., Lieut. 1915. Attached Hood Battn., 63rd Royal Naval Division. Wounded and Gassed Feb. 1917.

COCHRANE, ANDREW.
Daniel Stewart's College. M.B., Ch.B. 1910. R.A.M.C., Lieut. June 1915; Captain June 1916.

COCHRANE, CHARLES WILLIAM.
Morgan Academy, Dundee. B.Sc. 1898. Volunteers 1898-1908. Territorial Force from 1908. Mobilised Aug. 1914. A.S.C., 51st Highland Division, Major and O.C. April 1915; Lieut.-Col. June 1916. Senior Mechanical Transport Officer Aug. 1917. France April 1915. Lent to American Forces, July to Dec. 1918. Dispatches Jan. 1916 and June 1918. D.S.O. June 1918. T.D. June 1919.

Record of War Service

COCHRANE, EDWARD ASHLEY.
University O.T.C. Infantry, Nov. to Dec. 1915, Cadet. 4th King's Own Scottish Borderers, Lieut. July 1917. Attached 5th Royal Warwickshire Regiment. Croce di Guerra Dec. 1918. Dispatches April 1918.

COCHRANE, WALLACE KENNETH.
George Watson's College. University O.T.C. Infantry, May to Oct. 1916, Cadet; Officer Cadet Oct. 1916. 2nd Seaforth Highlanders, 2nd Lieut. March 1917; Lieut. Sept. 1918. Attached 12th Argyll and Sutherland Highlanders, 1919. France 1917; Constantinople 1919. Wounded at Ypres Oct. 1917, and Arras Sept. 1918.

COCHRANE, WILLIAM ALEXANDER.
Daniel Stewart's College. Student of Medicine, 1910-15; M.B., Ch.B. (Hons.) 1915. O.T.C. Medical, May 1911 to March 1915, Cadet. R.A.M.C. (T.), Lieut. Dec. 1915; Captain Dec. 1916. M.O., 9th Leicestershire Regiment, 1916. Orthopædic Surgeon, Edinburgh War Hospital, 1917.

COCHRANE, WILLIAM T.
Ayr Academy. Student of Arts, 1909-11. 9th Royal Scots (T.), Private. 5th Royal Scots Fusiliers, 2nd Lieut. Aug. 1915; Lieut. July 1918; Temp. Captain Jan. 1919. Egypt. Dispatches March 1918.

COCKS, HORACE.
M.B., C.M. 1882. Demonstrator of Pathology, 1883. Q.E.R. 1879-83, Private. R.A.M.C., 1886, Lieut.-Col. (Retired). Mobilised Jan. 1916. S.M.O., Cardiff, to Nov. 1917. Transferred to National Service as D.C.M.S. to March 1919.

COETZEE, CORNELIUS HERMANUS HUBERTUS.
Student of Medicine, 1910-15. M.B., Ch.B. 1915. O.T.C. Artillery, Nov. 1912 to Oct. 1914, Cadet Bombardier. R.F.A., 2nd Lieut. Aug. 1914.

COGHLAN, EDWARD FRANCIS.
M.B., Ch.B. 1911; M.D. 1914; M.R.C.S. (Eng.), and L.R.C.P. (Lond.) 1899. R.A.M.C.

COGHLAN, GERALD SPENCER.
Ratcliffe College, Leicester. L.R.C.P. & S. (Edin.), and L.F.P.S. (Glasg.) 1901. No. 4 Coy. Q.E.R.V.B., Royal Scots, 1897-1900, Private. South African Medical Corps. Boer War, 1901-2. Lieut. June 1915; Captain June 1917. Med. Exp. Force.

COHEN, ASHER.
M.B., Ch.B. 1912. South African Medical Corps, Captain April 1916.

COLEMAN, ALBERT.
M.B., C.M. 1887. Indian Medical Service, Lieut.-Col. Feb. 1915.

COLES, WILLIAM EDWARD KYTE.
Berkhamsted. Cadet Corps, 1906-8. Student of Medicine, 1909-12. L.M.S.S.A. (Lond.) 1914. O.T.C. Infantry, May 1909-10, and Medical June 1910 to March 1912, Cadet. R.A.M.C., Lieut. Sept. 1914; Captain Sept. 1915.

Record of War Service

COLLIE, JAMES.
Brechin High School. Student of Arts, 1911-15. R.F.A. (T.), Gunner Aug. 1915; Sergeant June 1916; 2nd Lieut. April 1917; Lieut. Oct. 1918. No. 13 Mountain Battery, R.G.A.

COLLIE, LESLIE.
Brechin High School. Student of Science, 1916-17 and 1918-19. R.E., Sapper April 1917. Attached Field Survey Coy.

COLLIER, DAVID ERIC.
George Heriot's School. Student of Arts and Science, 1914-15. R.E. (Special Coy.), Corporal July 1915. R.G.A. (S.R.), 2nd Lieut. May 1917; Lieut. Nov. 1918. 214th Siege Battery. M.C. May 1918.

COLLIER, HOWARD EBENEZER.
Reading School; Athletics. Cadet Corps 1903-7, Sergeant. M.B., Ch.B. 1914. R.A.M.C., Lieut. May 1915; Captain May 1916. 1st Gloucestershire Regiment and 2nd King's Royal Rifle Corps. Med. Exp. Force. M.C. July 1919.

COLLIER, J. W. P.
George Watson's College; O.T.C. 1909-13, Sergeant. Student of Medicine, 1918-19. O.T.C. Artillery, Aug. 1914 to Jan. 1915, Cadet Bombardier. R.G.A., 2nd Lieut. Sept. 1914; Lieut. 1915. France April 1915 to Dec. 1916.

COLLINSON, ARTHUR GORE.
Daniel Stewart's College. Student of Arts and Science, 1909-13. M.A. (Hons. Classics) 1913. O.T.C. Infantry, April 1910 to Oct. 1914, Cadet. 6th Royal Highlanders (Black Watch), Private Oct. 1914 to Jan. 1917. 2nd and 11th Royal Scots Fusiliers to Sept. 1917. France.

COLLINSON, WALTER JULIUS.
Elizabeth College, Guernsey. M.B., Ch.B. 1899; D.T.M. (Liverpool). Indian Medical Service, Sept. 1902; Major March 1914. No. 6 Indian General Hospital, Cairo, Sept. to Dec. 1914. Attached No. 5 Indian General Hospital, Alexandria, Dec. 1914 to June 1916.

COLMAN, HORACE CRAKANTHORP.
Bishop's Stortford College; First XI. M.B., C.M. 1896; M.D. 1900. R.A.M.C. (T.), Jan. 1900; Captain April 1907; Major Aug. 1914. T.D. 1919.

COLOMBOS, DEMETRIUS.
Lyceum, Malta. Student of Medicine, 1911-16. M.B., Ch.B. 1916. R.A.M.C. (S.R.), Lieut. Aug. 1916; Captain Feb. 1917; Acting Major and Registrar. Constantinople.

COLWELL, ERIC RICHARD.
Trowbridge High School and Chester-le-Street School. First XI. Student of Science, 1918. Durham University O.T.C. Infantry, Feb. to April 1917, Cadet L/Corporal. 1/5th York and Lancaster Regiment, Private Oct. 1916; 2nd Lieut. Aug. 1917; Lieut. March 1919. Wounded April 1918.

Record of War Service

COMBE, ARTHUR CHARLES.
Edinburgh Academy and Loretto. Student of Law, 1909-11. R.F.A. (T.), 1st Lowland Brigade, Lieut.; Captain June 1916. 1/4th Wessex Brigade, India, Dec. 1914. 55th Brigade, Mesopotamia, Sept. 1916; Poona Nov. 1918.

COMRIE, JOHN DIXON.
George Watson's College. M.A. 1894; B.Sc. 1897; M.B., Ch.B. 1899; M.D. 1910. Lecturer on History of Medicine and Clinical Medicine. R.A.M.C., Dec. 1904; Major July 1909; Acting Lieut.-Col. May 1918; Lieut.-Col., May 1919. 73rd General Hospital, France. North Russian Force, Consulting Physician, 1919.

COMRIE, THOMAS.
University O.T.C. Infantry, Nov. 1915 to Jan. 1916, Cadet. 7th Gordon Highlanders, 2nd Lieut. Jan. 1916; Lieut. March 1917. 51st Division, France. Royal Air Force, July 1918. Egypt and Palestine.

CONDER, ARCHIBALD FRANCIS REIGNIER.
Edinburgh Academy. M.B., Ch.B. 1902; M.D. 1904. University Battery, E.C.A.V., 1897-1902, Gunner. Auxiliary R.C. Hospital, 1914-17. R.A.M.C., Lieut. May 1917; Captain May 1918. 109th Field Ambulance, 36th (Ulster) Division; 10th Corps, Sept. 1918. M.C. Dec. 1918.

CONDIE, HARRY HUTCHISON.
Buckhaven School. Student of Medicine, 1916. R.E. (Special Coy.), Pioneer April 1917.

CONDIE, ROBERT M. (See p. 748.)

CONNELL, ALEXANDER.
M.A. 1886; B.D. 1890. Presbyterian Minister. Chaplain, 10th King's Liverpool Regiment (Liverpool Scottish) (T.), April 1908. Major 1919.

CONNELL, CHARLES GIBSON.
Edinburgh Institution. Student of Law, 1917-19. O.T.C. Artillery, March to Nov. 1917, Cadet Corporal; Officer Cadet Nov. 1917. R.F.A., 2nd Lieut. May 1918. Salonika Aug. 1918 to Feb. 1919.

CONNELL, ERNEST H.
Merchiston Castle; First XI. Student of Medicine, 1913-15 and 1917-19. O.T.C. Corporal. R.A.M.C., Private May 1915. Attached Indian Medical Service, 6th Meerut Division. Mesopotamia Jan. 1916 to March 1917.

CONNELL, J. C. W.
University O.T.C., Adjutant July 1913 to Aug. 1914. 2nd King's Own Scottish Borderers, Captain; Major Dec. 1914; Lieut.-Col. France 1914. D.S.O. Dispatches.

CONNELL, ROBERT MACNAUGHTON.
George Watson's College. Student of Arts, 1912-14. 9th Royal Scots, Private Sept. 1914. R.G.A. (T.), 2nd Lieut. March 1915; Lieut. June 1916; Acting Captain Jan. 1918. France. Wounded at Kemmel, April 1918. M.C. Jan. 1919.

Record of War Service

CONNOLLY, JAMES HARRIS.
M.B., Ch.B. 1902; M.D. 1906; F.R.C.S. (Eng.). R.A.M.C., Captain Dec. 1915. Surgical Specialist, 2/2nd London Casualty Clearing Station, France, 1917.

CONNOR, JOHN.
Pathology Department. 2nd Highland Light Infantry, Aug. 1905. Mobilised Aug. 1914, Private; Corporal March 1916; Acting Sergeant Oct. 1916. France 1914.

CONSIDINE, HUGH HERBERT.
Merchiston Castle; First XV. Cadet Corps 1902-5, Sergeant. B.A. (Camb.). Student of Law, 1909-12. Writer to the Signet, 1912. R.G.A. (S.R.), 2nd Lieut. Nov. 1915; Lieut. June 1917. France March 1916 to Sept. 1917; Beaumont Hamel, Oct. 1916; Arras, Bullecourt, third Ypres, Vimy Ridge, and Monchy, 1917. Attached Board of Trade, Timber Supply Department, Jan. 1918 to March 1919.

CONSTABLE, ANDREW HENDERSON BRIGGS.
Dollar Academy. M.A. 1884; LL.B. 1887. King's Counsel, Sheriff of Caithness, Orkney, and Zetland, 1908. General Service Recruiting, Captain, March 1916.

COOK, ADRIAN HENRY.
Rugby. B.A. (Oxford). Student of Law, 1910-11. O.T.C. Infantry, Sept. to Oct. 1914, Cadet. 11th Argyll and Sutherland Highlanders, 2nd Lieut. Sept. 1914; Lieut. Nov. 1914; Captain March 1916. France. Dispatches June 1916 and March 1919.

COOK, ALAN GIBB.
Royal High School. First XV. and XI. M.B., Ch.B. 1904. R.A.M.C., Lieut. July 1915; Captain July 1916; Acting Major April 1918. 11th Middlesex Regiment, and 36th Field Ambulance. M.C.

COOK, DUNCAN.
Otago High School, New Zealand; First XV. Cadet Corps 1905-7. Student of Medicine, 1912-17 and 1919-20; M.B., Ch.B. 1917; M.D. 1920; M.R.C.P. Feb. 1920. Demonstrator in Anatomy. O.T.C. Medical, March 1915-17, Cadet Corporal. Royal Navy, Surgeon-Lieut., April 1918. Mine-sweeping Service.

COOK, FREDERICK SQUIRES.
St Paul's, Cambridge. B.Sc. 1894. 5th Seaforth Highlanders, Captain Feb. 1916. Mobilised Aug. 1914.

COOK, HENRY PATTULLO.
Edinburgh Academy. M.B., Ch.B. 1905; F.R.C.S. (Edin.) 1911. Indian Medical Service, Feb. 1906; Captain Feb. 1909; Major Aug. 1917. India.

COOK, JAMES ALEXANDER LUMSDEN.
Marist Brothers' College, Johannesburg. Student of Medicine, 1913-18; M.B., Ch.B. 1918. O.T.C. Artillery, Oct. 1914 to Feb. 1916, Cadet. R.N.V.R., Surgeon-Probationer, Feb. 1916; Royal Navy, Surgeon-Lieut., July 1918 to Aug. 1919.

Record of War Service

COOK, JOHN.
    M.R.C.S. (Eng.) 1861; L.S.A. (Lond.) 1863; M.D. 1865; M.R.C.P. (Lond.) 1871. R.A.M.C., Lieut.-Col.

COOK, JOHN BURTON.
    Dunfermline High School. M.B., Ch.B. 1913. R.A.M.C., Lieut. June 1917; Captain June 1918.

COOKE-TAYLOR, CHARLES RALPH.
    Fettes. B.A. (Oxford) 1906. Barrister at Law. Student of Medicine, 1917. O.T.C. Medical, Oct. 1917 to July 1918, Cadet. Serbian Relief Fund. Serbian Army Jan. 1915, Hon. Lieut. June 1915.

COOKSON, HENRY ANSTEY.
    Clifton College. M.B., Ch.B. 1910; F.R.C.S. (Edin.); D.P.H. (Camb. with Distinction). Anatomy Staff, 1913. Hockey and Cricket "Blue." Hockey International. R.A.M.C. (T.), Lieut. June 1915; Captain July 1915; Major April 1917. 1/6th London Field Ambulance. 12th and 55th General Hospitals. France, Dec. 1915 to Jan. 1919.

COOPER, CHARLES GORDON TOWERS.
    Charterhouse. O.T.C. 1908-12, Sergeant. Student of Science, 1912-14. R.E. (T.), City of Edinburgh Fortress, 2nd Lieut. Nov. 1913; Lieut. Dec. 1914. 400th Highland Field Coy. M.C. Oct. 1918.

COOPER, DANIEL STIRLING.
    Ballymoney, Ireland. M.B., Ch.B. 1912. R.A.M.C., Lieut. Sept. 1914; Captain Sept. 1915.

COOPER, DUNCAN GORDON.
    M.B., Ch.B. 1908. Indian Medical Service, Captain July 1912.

COOPER, JAMES MURRAY.
    George Watson's College. Student of Arts and Law, 1912-15 and 1919; M.A. 1914; LL.B. and Writer to the Signet, 1919. Forth R.G.A. (T.), 2nd Lieut. April 1915; Lieut. June 1916; Captain July 1917. France Dec. 1916 to Oct. 1917; Somme, Arras, and Nieuport. Gassed and Invalided home Sept. 1917.

COOPER, WILLIAM.
    Broughton School, Edinburgh. Student of Arts, 1913-16; M.A. 1916 (Hons. Maths. and Nat. Phil.) and B.Sc. 1920. R.N.V.R., Wireless Telegraphist, Feb. 1916; Sub-Lieut. Feb. 1918; Acting Lieut. Sept. 1918; Lieut. Feb. 1919.

COOPER, WILLIAM.
    Kirkwall Burgh School. Student of Arts, 1913-15. O.T.C. Infantry, Jan. to May 1915, Cadet. 9th Royal Scots (T.), Private April 1915; Acting Sergeant Aug. 1918. France. Wounded at Arras April 1917, and Loos Sept. 1918.

Record of War Service

COOPER, WILLIAM RICHARD.
Holt Horne School, Cheshunt, Herts; First XI. M.A. (Hons. Hist.) 1907. Schoolmaster's Diploma. George Watson's College O.T.C., 2nd Lieut. 1911; Lieut. 1912. 4th Royal Scots (T.), Captain 1914; Acting Major Dec. 1915; Major July 1917. Gallipoli and Egypt. H.Q., No. 1 Corps, France. Dispatches Sept. 1916.

COPELAND, ROBERT JAMES.
M.B., C.M. 1886. Army Medical Service, July 1887; Lieut.-Col. Jan. 1912; Colonel March 1915. France Aug. 1914 to March 1919. Dispatches.

COPEMAN, DONALD ALFRED.
George Watson's College. O.T.C. 1916-18, Cadet Sergeant. Student of Science, 1918. Royal Air Force, Cadet Aug. 1918.

COPLAND, JAMES ALEXANDER.
University O.T.C. Artillery, Dec. 1915 to Sept. 1916, Cadet; Officer Cadet Sept. 1916. North Scottish R.G.A. (T.), 2nd Lieut. Nov. 1916; Acting Lieut. Feb. 1917; Lieut. May 1918; Acting Captain Jan. 1919.

CORBETT, CHARLES HENRY.
King Edward VI. School, Bath; First XI. O.T.C. Colour-Sergeant. M.B., Ch.B. 1907; M.D. 1915. R.A.M.C., Lieut. June 1915; Captain June 1916; Acting Major Jan. 1918.

CORBETT, PERCY BARNARD.
King Edward VI. School, Bath; First XI., Cricket and Football. O.T.C. 1907-10. Student of Medicine, 1910-16; M.B., Ch.B. 1915. O.T.C. Medical, Nov. 1914 to April 1915, Cadet. B.R.C.S., Surgical Dresser. Meerut Division, Casualty Clearing Station, France, 1914. R.A.M.C. (S.R.), Lieut. March 1915; Captain April 1916; Acting Major Jan. 1918. Prisoner of War March to Dec. 1918.

CORE, WILLIAM.
George Watson's College. M.A. 1901; M.B., Ch.B. 1906. R.A.M.C., Lieut. Sept. 1915; Captain Sept. 1916. 1st Garrison Battn., Sherwood Foresters. Suvla Bay 1915; Imbros 1915 and 1916; Egypt 1916-18.

CORKILL, HAROLD KEITH.
Wellington College, N.Z. O.T.C. 1911-15, C.S.M. Student of Medicine, 1916-17 and 1918-19. N.Z. Medical Corps, Jan. to March 1916. R.F.A. (S.R.), April 1917; 2nd Lieut. Oct. 1917. France Dec. 1917 to Feb. 1919. Wounded at Ypres April 1918.

CORKILL, THOMAS FREDERICK.
Wellington College, N.Z. O.T.C. 1907-10, Lieut. Student of Medicine, 1911-15; M.B., Ch.B. 1915; M.D. 1920. O.T.C. Medical, 1912-14, Cadet L/Corporal. R.A.M.C. (S.R.), Lieut. Sept. 1914; Captain June 1916; Acting Major Jan. 1918. France, 139th Field Ambulance, Dec. 1915 to March 1919. Wounded March 1918. Dispatches June 1917. Order of Leopold of Belgium Aug. 1917; M.C. Sept. 1917; Belgian Croix de Guerre Feb. 1918; Bar to M.C. Dec. 1918.

Record of War Service

CORMACK, ALEXANDER.
> Ayr Academy. M.A. 1906; LL.B. 2/5th Royal Scots Fusiliers, 2nd Lieut. Nov. 1915; Lieut. July 1917; Temp. Captain Sept. 1918 to April 1919. Divisional Education Officer, 64th, 67th, and 71st Divisions.

CORMACK, B. WILLIAM.
> Ayr Academy. Student of Law, 1896-7. Hong Kong Port Artillery, Gunner 1915.

CORMACK, DAVID.
> George Watson's College. M.A. 1904; LL.B. and Writer to the Signet, 1908. Notary Public. R.F.A., 2nd Lieut. Dec. 1915; Lieut. May 1918 to March 1919. Attached 93rd Brigade. France Feb. 1917 to Jan. 1919.

CORMACK, DOUGLAS JOHN.
> Elgin Academy. Student of Law. O.T.C. Artillery, March to Aug. 1916, Cadet Corporal; Officer Cadet Sept. 1916. R.G.A. (T.), 2nd Lieut. Dec. 1916; Lieut. June 1918.

CORMACK, FREDERICK EUNSON.
> George Heriot's School. B.Sc. 1912. Surma Valley Light Horse, Trooper. I.A.R.O., 2nd Lieut.

CORMACK, HARRY SLATER.
> Royal High School. M.B., Ch.B. 1908; F.R.C.S. (Edin.). Indian Medical Service, Lieut.; Captain July 1914. Dispatches. M.C.

CORMACK, JAMES.
> Pulteneytown Academy, Wick. Student of Law, 1906-8. Solicitor and Barrister-at-Law, Manitoba. 5th Seaforth Highlanders, April 1915; 2nd Lieut. Oct. 1915; Lieut. May 1918.

CORMACK, ROBERT PAIRMAN.
> George Watson's College. Cadet Corps 1905-8, Corporal. M.B., Ch.B. 1914. O.T.C. Infantry, March 1909-11, and Medical, 1911-12, Cadet. R.A.M.C. (S.R.), 1912; Captain July 1915; Captain (Regulars) Jan. 1917. Egypt, German East Africa, and India. Dispatches March 1918.

CORMACK, WALTER GEORGE.
> Fettes. O.T.C. 1914-16. University O.T.C. Artillery, 1917-18, Cadet Bombardier; Officer Cadet June 1918. R.H.A. and R.F.A., 2nd Lieut. March 1919.

CORMACK, WILLIAM PETRIE.
> Royal Academy, Tain. M.B., Ch.B. 1900. Australian Army Medical Corps, Captain 1915. No. 15 Australian General Hospital, Adelaide, and at Camp for Civilian Forces, Gawler, South Australia.

CORNER, CHARLES LEWIS.
> George Watson's College. University O.T.C. Infantry, Jan. to June 1917, Cadet Sergeant; Officer Cadet June 1917. 2nd Rifle Brigade, 2nd Lieut. Oct. 1917. France. Wounded at Second Battle of the Somme, Aug. 1918. Invalided out.

Record of War Service

CORNER, SAMUEL GORDON.
Royal Academy, Inverness. M.A. 1902; M.B., Ch.B. 1906; M.D. 1910. No. 4 Coy. Q.R.V.B., Royal Scots, Colour-Sergeant. South African Campaign, 1900-1. R.A.M.C., Lieut. 1917; Captain July 1918. East African Exp. Force.

CORRIE, JAMES.
Edinburgh Academy; First XV. Student of Science, 1919. O.T.C. Artillery 1917, Cadet Corporal; Officer Cadet Sept. 1917. R.F.A. (S.R.), 156th Brigade, 2nd Lieut. March 1918. Midland Division, Ammunition Column. The Rhine, April to July 1919.

CORRY, MATTHEW.
National School, Letterkenny. M.B., C.M. 1896; M.D. 1911. Indian Medical Service, Major July 1911.

CORSTORPHINE, EDWARD ELLICE.
Merchiston Castle. O.T.C. 1913-17. University O.T.C. Infantry, 1917-18, Cadet; Officer Cadet. 3rd Argyll and Sutherland Highlanders, 2nd Lieut. Oct. 1918.

COSSAR, CHARLES.
M.A. 1893. R.F.A. (T.), 1st Lowland Brigade, Captain.

COTTERILL, Sir JOSEPH MONTAGU.
Brighton College; First XI. M.B., C.M. 1875; F.R.C.S. (Edin.) 1878. Lecturer and Examiner on Clinical Surgery. R.A.M.C. (T.), Lieut.-Col. July 1908. Mobilised Aug. 1914. 2nd Scottish General Hospital. C.M.G. 1917. Dispatches July 1917. Knight Bachelor 1919.

COTTON, GEORGE MORTON.
Edinburgh Institution. Student of Law. Chartered Accountant, 1907. 4th Royal Scots Fusiliers, Private; 2nd Lieut. March 1917.

COTTON, WILLIAM.
Royal High School. M.A. 1880; M.B., C.M. 1883; D.P.H. (Camb.) 1889; M.D. 1896. R.A.M.C. (T.), Captain April 1915. 2nd Southern General Hospital, France; in charge of X-Rays for three years.

COULING, ARTHUR VIVIAN.
George Watson's College. O.T.C. Student of Science, 1910-11. O.T.C. Engineers, 1910-11, Cadet. Royal Horse Guards ("The Blues"), Private Aug. 1914; 2nd Lieut. Oct. 1915; Lieut. July 1917. 14th West Yorkshire Regiment; 19th Hussars; R.E., Field Survey Battn., Jan. 1918.

COULL, GEORGE CHARLES.
Daniel Stewart's College. Student of Science, 1912-14 and 1919-20; B.Sc. 1920. O.T.C. Artillery, 1910-14, Cadet Bombardier. Scottish Horse, 2nd Lieut. Aug. 1914. R.F.A. (T.), 2nd Highland Brigade; Lieut. June 1916; Acting Captain March 1918; Captain and Acting Major Jan. 1919. France May 1915. Army of the Rhine, Nov. 1918 to Aug. 1919.

Record of War Service

COULL, ROBERT.
Daniel Stewart's College. Student of Science, 1909-14; B.Sc. 1919. O.T.C. Infantry, Nov. 1909-14, Cadet Sergeant. 6th Royal Scots (T.), 2nd Lieut.; Lieut. Nov. 1915. Attached R.E. (Signal Service), Aug. 1917. France.

COULLIE, ALEXANDER GLOVER.
Royal High School. M.B., Ch.B. 1904; F.R.C.S. (Edin.) 1907. Indian Medical Service, July 1907; Captain July 1910; Major Jan. 1919; Acting Lieut.-Col. April 1918. Egypt, Palestine and Syria, Nov. 1914. O.C. 15th (I.S.) Cavalry Brigade Field Ambulance, April 1918. Dispatches Jan. 1919.

COULLIE, JAMES ARTHUR.
Fettes. Student of Arts and Divinity; M.A. (Hons. Classics) 1906. Minister, Church of Scotland. No. 4 Coy. Q.R.V.B., Royal Scots, 1902-5. Y.M.C.A. in France 1916. Army Chaplain Jan. 1917.

COULSON, THOMAS EDMUND.
Charterhouse. M.B., Ch.B. 1904; M.D. 1909; F.R.C.S. (Edin.) 1908. R.A.M.C. (T.), Temp. Lieut. Aug. 1918; Acting Major Sept. 1918; Temp. Captain Aug. 1919. 86th General Hospital, Syren, North Russian Exp. Force.

COULTER, WILLIAM.
King's College, Goulburn, N.S.W. First XV. Royal (Dick) Veterinary College O.T.C. Student of Science, 1918. 2nd Scottish Horse, Aug. 1914, Corporal. Dispatches (Gallipoli). D.C.M. June 1916.

COULTHARD, JOSEPH JEFFERSON.
St Bees, Cumberland. O.T.C. 1912-14, Corporal. Student of Medicine, 1915-16 and 1918-19. O.T.C. Artillery, March to June 1916, Cadet. R.F.A., 78th Brigade, 2nd Lieut. Sept. 1916; Lieut. March 1918. France Nov. 1916. Invalided Oct. 1917. R.A., G.H.Q., July 1918 to Jan. 1919. Invalided out Feb. 1919.

COUPER, DANIEL ROSS.
James Gillespie's School. Student of Law, 1895-6. 9th Royal Scots (T.). Q.M.S.

COUPER, JOHN SINCLAIR.
Arnold House School, Blackpool. Student of Medicine, 1915-16 and 1918-19. A.S.C., Private July 1916. Dispatch Rider, 1916-19.

COUPER, WILLIAM DICK.
George Watson's College. Student of Medicine, 1918. 9th Royal Scots, Private Oct. 1915; L/Corporal June 1916; Officer Cadet April 1918; 2nd Lieut. Feb. 1919. France. Three times Wounded.

COURT, ALEXANDER COSGRAVE.
M.B., Ch.B. 1908; M.D. 1913. President, Dialectic Society. R.A.M.C. (S.R.), Lieut. 1910; Captain Dec. 1913. Mobilised Aug. 1914. M.C. 1917.

Record of War Service

COURTNEY, BERTRAM JOSEPH.
King William's College, I.O.M.; First XV. M.B., Ch.B. 1899; M.D. 1903; West African Medical Service, Captain Dec. 1914; Major Aug. 1918. Attached King's African Rifles, June 1917. Cameroons, 1915. S.M.O., Nyassa Rhodesia Force, May to Nov. 1918. Dispatches Dec. 1918 and May 1919 (East Africa).

COUSLAND, KENNETH HARRINGTON.
George Watson's College; First XV. Student of Arts, 1913-14. O.T.C. Artillery, Oct. 1913-14, Cadet. R.F.A. (T.), 1st Lowland Brigade, 2nd Lieut. Aug. 1914; Lieut. June 1915; Captain Oct. 1915; Major April 1918. 179th Brigade, France, March 1916 to June 1919. Wounded April and Oct. 1918. M.C. July 1918. Dispatches (twice) Oct. 1918. Croix de Guerre June 1919.

COUTIE, ALEXANDER.
George Heriot's School. O.T.C. 1913-15, Sergeant. Student of Science, 1915-17 and 1918-20; B.Sc. 1920. R.E. (Special Brigade), Sapper Aug. 1916. 9th Scottish Rifles, Private. Labour Corps.

COUTTS, ALFRED.
M.A. 1884; B.D. 1888. Minister, United Free Church of Scotland. Chaplain, 77th Infantry Brigade; Captain Oct. 1914.

COUTTS, DONALD GORDON.
Edinburgh Academy. O.T.C. 1912-14. Student of Medicine, 1914-15 and 1918-20. O.T.C. Artillery, 1914-15, Cadet. 3rd Seaforth Highlanders, 2nd Lieut. June 1915; Lieut. May 1917. Signal Service, R.E., July 1918.

COUTTS, FREDERICK THOM KYDD.
Kimberley High School, South Africa. First XI., Football. Student of Law, 1906-9. Chartered Accountant, 1910. 1st Transvaal Scottish, Lieut. Aug. 1914. South West Africa 1914-15.

COUTTS, WALDEMAR.
Student of Medicine, 1912-15. 3rd Seaforth Highlanders, 2nd Lieut.

COUTTS, WILLIAM ALEXANDER.
Junior Clerk of Senatus. R.A.M.C. (T.), Private Dec. 1914; Sergeant March 1917. 2/3rd Lowland Field Ambulance. Dispatches March 1919.

COUTTS, WILLIAM BARRON.
Kirkcaldy High School. M.A. 1909; B.Sc. 1912. O.T.C. Artillery, 1915, Cadet. R.G.A. (S.R.), 2nd Lieut. Dec. 1915; Lieut. July 1917. Instructor, Ordnance Column. Gibraltar March 1916 to Aug. 1917; Woolwich 1917-18.

COVENTRY, CHARLES JAMES.
University O.T.C. Infantry, May to Sept. 1915, Cadet. Cameron Highlanders, 2nd Lieut. Sept. 1915; Lieut. July 1917 to Jan. 1919.

COWAN, AGNES MARSHALL.
M.B. Ch.B. 1906. R.A.M.C., attached Q.M.A.A.C., Medical Officer, May 1918. Assistant Medical Officer, H.M. Factory, Gretna, April 1917-18.

Record of War Service

COWAN, ALISTER FORBES.
Merchiston Castle. O.T.C. 1901-3. M.B., Ch.B. 1912. R.A.M.C., Lieut. Aug. 1914. Rejoined May 1917. Captain Nov. 1917. France.

COWAN, ANDREW.
Dumfries Academy; First XI. Student of Medicine, 1916. O.T.C. Artillery, 1917, Cadet Corporal; Officer Cadet Aug. 1917. R.F.A., 45th Battery, 2nd Lieut. Jan. 1918. France Feb. 1918 to June 1919. Wounded July 1918. M.C. Dec. 1918.

COWAN, CHARLES EMELIUS LOWTHER.
M.A. 1892. President, Dialectic Society, 1891. No. 4 Coy. Q.R.V.B., Royal Scots, 1889-92, L/Corporal. Chaplain, Royal Navy, 1897; R.M.S. *Carisbrook Castle*, 1914; R.N. Barracks, Devonport; H.M.S. *Canada;* R.N. Barracks, Portsmouth, 1915-17, and H.M. Dockyard Church, Devonport, 1918. Battle of Jutland May 1916.

COWAN, JOHN.
Ley's School, Cambridge. M.A. (Glasg.) 1891; LL.B. 1897. King's Counsel. R.E. (T.), Captain July 1915; Major June 1916. Mention March 1919. O.B.E. June 1919.

COWAN, JOHN MacINTYRE.
Kirkcaldy High School. M.A. 1909. Schoolmaster. R.G.A., 213th Siege Battery, Signaller, May 1917.

COWAN, JOHN MACQUEEN.
Robert Gordon's College, Aberdeen. M.A. 1913; B.Sc., 1914. Assistant to Professor of Botany. President, Dialectic Society. O.T.C. Artillery, 1910-14, Cadet Bombardier. R.G.A. (I.A.R.O.), 2nd Lieut. 1917; Lieut. India, Egypt, and Palestine, 1917-19. Dispatches.

COWAN, JOHN MUIR.
Dumfries Academy. Student of Medicine, 1916-17 and 1918-19. O.T.C. Artillery, Jan. to May 1917, Cadet. R.G.A. (T.), 2nd Lieut. Sept. 1917 to Dec. 1918.

COWAN, ROBERT McNAIR WILSON.
Central High School, Leeds. Student of Arts, 1915-16. 11th Northumberland Fusiliers, Private July 1916. France and Italy.

COWAN, RUSSELL.
George Heriot's School. Student of Science, 1918. R.E., "Z" Special Coy., Pioneer Nov. 1916.

COWAN, WILLIAM.
Perth Academy. Student of Arts, 1881-5 and 1919; M.A. 1919. President, Dialectic Society, 1887. Chaplain, 4th Class, Sept. 1915 to April 1919. Malta.

Record of War Service

COWAN, WILLIAM.
Edinburgh Academy. Student of Law, 1891-5. Writer to the Signet, 1896. University Battery E.C.A.V., Captain 1910. City of Edinburgh R.G.A. (T.), Captain Oct. 1914; Major Dec. 1916 to March 1919. Coast Defence 1915-17. France 1918.

COWARD, NOËL ANTHONY.
Blairlodge; First XV. and XI. Cadet Corps 1898-1903, Colour-Sergeant. M.B., Ch.B. 1909; M.D. 1913; D.P.H. (Oxford) 1914. R.A.M.C., Lieut. Oct. 1914; Captain Oct. 1915. Royal Lancaster Regiment, Oct. 1914-15. France July 1915 to Dec. 1918. Senior Sanitary Officer, Havre, May 1916. Dispatches July 1916 and Dec. 1918. O.B.E. (Military) Dec. 1918.

COWE, THOMAS.
George Watson's College. O.T.C. 1913-15. University O.T.C. Infantry, Oct. 1917, Cadet. 7th Royal Scots (T.), 2nd Lieut. Nov. 1917.

COWIESON, JOHN JOHNSTONE.
Normal Training College, Edinburgh. Student of Science, 1912-15. O.T.C. Artillery, 1914-15, Cadet. R.F.A. (T.), 2nd Lieut. July 1915; Lieut. June 1916. 3rd East Lancashire Brigade. Dardanelles, Egypt, France, and Sinai.

COWLING, HARRY WALTER.
King's College, Taunton; First XI. O.T.C. 1906-10, Corporal. Student of Science, 1912-15; B.Sc. 1915. O.T.C. Engineers, 1912-15, Cadet. R.E. (S.R.), 2nd Lieut. June 1915; Lieut. June 1916; Acting Captain Oct. 1917. France.

COWPER, CHARLES NEAVES.
Edinburgh Collegiate School. Student of Law, 1895-9. Writer to the Signet, 1901. 1st City of Edinburgh Vol. Regiment, Sept. 1914 to Dec. 1916. R.G.A., Gunner Dec. 1916; L/Bombardier June 1917; Corporal Jan. 1919.

COWPER, JOHN JAMES McPHAIL.
Royal High School. M.A. 1886. Chaplain 1893; 2nd Class, July 1916. South African Campaign, 1900-2. France 1915. Dispatches Jan. 1916.

COX, ALFRED BERRIDGE.
Eastbourne College; First XI. M.B., Ch.B. 1903. Royal Navy, May 1904; Staff Surgeon, May 1912; Surgeon-Commander, June 1917. H.M.S. *Lion;* Cameroons, West Africa, Feb. 1915; German East Africa, June 1915 to Aug. 1916, and Grand Fleet April 1917 to Nov. 1918. Heligoland and Dogger Bank.

COX, JOSHUA JOHN.
Edinburgh Institution. M.B., C.M. 1875; M.D. 1881; F.R.C.S. (Edin.) 1880 R.A.M.C. (T.), Major 1909. 2nd Western General Hospital, Manchester, Oct. 1914. Commissioner of Medical Services, North-West Scotland, 1917-18. Dispatches 1917. O.B.E. (Military) 1919.

Record of War Service

CRABBIE, JOHN EDWARD.
Edinburgh Academy; First XV. B.A. (Oxford). Student of Law, 1902-4. Advocate, 1905. 6th Royal Highlanders (Black Watch) (T.), Lieut. Oct. 1914; Captain June 1916. O.B.E.

CRAGG, FRANCIS WILLIAM.
Kendal Grammar School. M.B., Ch.B. 1905; M.D. No. 4 Coy. Q.R.V.B., Royal Scots, Private. Indian Medical Service, Lieut. Sept. 1906; Captain Sept. 1909; Major April 1918. Egypt Dec. 1914 to Jan. 1916. India.

CRAIG, ALEXANDER CURRIE CARRUTHERS.
George Watson's College. Student of Medicine, 1912-18; M.B., Ch.B. 1917. O.T.C. Artillery, Dec. 1914 to July 1915, Cadet. Royal Navy, Surgeon-Probationer, July 1915; Surgeon Jan. 1918.

CRAIG, ALEXANDER NELSON.
M.B., Ch.B. 1914. R.A.M.C., Lieut.

CRAIG, ARCHIBALD CAMPBELL.
Kelso High School. Cadet Corps 1904-6, Corporal. M.A. 1910. Senior President, Dialectic Society. 13th Royal Scots, Private Oct. 1914; 2nd Lieut. Dec. 1914; Lieut. July 1917. Intelligence Corps, Oct. 1917 to Aug. 1919. France. M.C. June 1919.

CRAIG, ARCHIBALD HAY.
George Watson's College. Student of Law, 1907-9. Chartered Accountant, 1910. London Scottish, Private 1914; 13th Royal Scots, 1915; Captain 1917; Major May 1918. France 1914-18. Wounded Oct. 1914 and July 1918. D.S.O.; M.C. Twice Mentioned in Dispatches.

CRAIG, ARTHUR.
Student of Medicine, 1910-15. L.D.S. (Edin.) 1914; L.R.C.P. & S. (Edin.), and L.R.F.P.S. (Glasg.) 1915. O.T.C. Medical, Nov. 1914 to May 1915, Cadet. Royal Navy, Surgeon-Lieut., May 1915. H.M.S. *Warspite*.

CRAIG, DAVID DOUGALL HEPBURN.
Edinburgh Institution; First XV. Cadet Corps 1915-17. Student of Medicine, 1919. O.T.C. Artillery, 1917, Cadet. Royal Air Force, Officer Cadet Nov. 1917; 2nd Lieut. Nov. 1918 to April 1919.

CRAIG, DAVID DUNCAN.
M.A., B.Sc. (St Andrews). M.B., Ch.B. 1908. R.A.M.C., Lieut. Aug. 1914; Captain Aug. 1915. 2nd East Lancashire Regiment. France Nov. 1914. M.C. Dispatches.

CRAIG, EFFIE MARION DOUGLAS.
Teviot Grove Academy, Hawick. M.B., Ch.B. 1912. R.A.M.C., Sept. 1916. Malta and Salonika.

Record of War Service

CRAIG, GEORGE.
: George Watson's College. M.B., C.M. 1890. South African Campaign, 1900-1. N.Z. Medical Corps, 1900; Major March 1915; Lieut.-Col. Oct. 1917. Gallipoli 1915; Achi Baba and Suvla Bay; France, Messines and Somme. Twice wounded. Dispatches April 1915, 1917, and Oct. 1918. D.S.O.

CRAIG, JAMES.
: George Watson's College. Student of Law, 1883-5. Chartered Accountant, 1886. Notary Public, 1896. 7th Argyll and Sutherland Highlanders, 2nd Lieut. 1887; Lieut.-Col. 1906 and O.C. Sept. 1906 to April 1915. France, Messines 1914-15; Somme 1917-18. T.D. Dispatches Feb. 1917 and 1919.

CRAIG, JOHN GIBSON.
: Royal High School. M.B., Ch.B. 1905; F.R.C.S. (Edin.) 1908. R.A.M.C., Lieut. Dec. 1915; Captain Dec. 1916. Surgical Specialist. O.B.E. June 1919.

CRAIG, JOHN RICHARD.
: Kelso High School. M.A. 1904. O.T.C. Infantry, Jan. to April 1915, Cadet. 14th and 17th Royal Scots, 2nd Lieut. March 1915; Lieut. July 1917; Captain Oct. 1917; Bombing Instructor Jan. to Dec. 1916. Wounded Sept. 1918.

CRAIG, JOHN WILLIAM.
: Castle Douglas Academy and St Andrews University. M.B., C.M. 1893. Royal Navy, May 1896. South African War, 1899-1902. Surgeon-Commander 1919.

CRAIG, NICHOLAS SMITH.
: Ley's School, Cambridge. O.T.C. 1912-15, L/Corporal. Student of Medicine, 1915-16 and 1918-19. O.T.C. Infantry, May to Dec. 1916, Cadet. 3rd, 10th, and 5/6th Royal Scots, Private Dec. 1916; Officer Cadet Dec. 1916; 2nd Lieut. March 1917. France Aug. 1917 to April 1918. M.C. March 1918.

CRAIG, THEODORE.
: George Watson's College. M.B., Ch.B. 1907; F.R.S.M. (Lond.). Deputy Surgeon to Admiralty, Blyth Submarine Station, 1915-17. R.A.M.C., Lieut. April 1917; Captain April 1918. O.C., No. 2 Clearing Station Hospital, Kilossa, German East Africa, 1917-18. Mental Specialist, Devonport Military Hospital.

CRAIG, WALTER JAMES FAIRLIE.
: Morgan Academy, Dundee. Student of Medicine, 1911-16; M.B., Ch.B. 1916. O.T.C. Medical, 1912-14, Cadet Sergeant. R.A.M.C. (S.R.), Lieut. Sept. 1914; Captain Jan. 1917. R.A.M.C. (Regulars), April 1919; Captain Jan. 1920. Salonika 1916-17; Palestine 1917-18; France and India 1918-19.

CRAIG, WILLIAM.
: Prior School, Lifford. M.B., Ch.B. 1898. R.A.M.C., Lieut.; Captain Nov. 1916.

CRAIG, WILLIAM BANNERMAN.
: M.A. 1889; M.B., C.M. 1894. Australian Army Medical Corps, Major. D.S.O.

Record of War Service

CRAIG, WILLIAM CARRUTHERS.
George Watson's College. Student of Medicine, 1910-16; M.B., Ch.B. 1916. O.T.C. Medical, 1914-16, Cadet. R.A.M.C., Lieut. Jan. 1917; Captain Jan. 1918.

CRAIG, W. M.
George Watson's College. Student of Law, 1910-12. Chartered Accountant, 1913. Lothians and Border Horse (T.), Private Aug. 1914; Sergeant. R.F.A., 2nd Lieut. Feb. 1917; Lieut. Aug. 1918. France and Italy Sept. 1915 to June 1918.

CRAIG, WILLIAM PITCAIRN.
M.A. 1902. Minister, Church of Scotland. Chaplain, July 1915, 106th Infantry Brigade and 26th General Hospital.

CRAIG-BROWN, ERNEST.
Merchiston Castle. Cadet Corps 1886-7. Student of Science, 1887-8. West Indian Regiment, 1895; Lieut. Aug. 1897. Sierra Leone Rising, 1898. Wounded. Cameron Highlanders, Captain Dec. 1899; Major Sept. 1914; Brevet Lieut.-Col. June 1917. South African Campaign, 1900-2. D.S.O. Feb. 1915. Dispatches Feb. and June 1915, Jan. 1916, June 1917 and June 1918. Montenegrin Order of Danilo (4th Class), Oct. 1916.

CRAMB, DOUGLAS ROBERT.
George Watson's College. O.T.C. 1912-15, Pipe-Major. Student of Medicine, 1915 and 1918-19. Anatomy Staff, 1919. O.T.C. Infantry, 1915-17, Cadet Sergeant. 6th and 9th Rifle Brigade, 2nd Lieut. France Nov. 1917 to Aug. 1918.

CRAN, DISNEY HERBERT DUSCH.
Royal High School. M.B., Ch.B. 1911; M.D. 1919. B.R.C.S. Nov. 1915, and R.A.M.C., Lieut. March 1916; Captain March 1917. No. 11 Stationary Hospital, Rouen. Pathologist, Nov. 1915 to Feb. 1919.

CRAN, NORMAN DUDLEY.
Fettes. O.T.C. 1911-15, L/Corporal. Student of Medicine, 1915. O.T.C. Artillery, May to Dec. 1915, Cadet. R.F.A. (T.), 2nd Lieut. Dec. 1915; Regulars, Sept. 1916; Lieut. March 1918. Wounded. Invalided out April 1919.

CRAN, PETER McLELLAN.
George Watson's College. B.Sc. 1909. A.M.I.C.E. R.E. (S.R.), 2nd Lieut. Jan. 1910; Lieut. Aug. 1914; Captain June 1917. Dispatches Feb. 1917. O.B.E. (Military) June 1919.

CRANSTON, Sir ROBERT.
Member of University Court. Lord Provost of Edinburgh, 1903. Artillery Tay Defences, 1864. Queen's Rifle Brigade, Lieut. 1870; Captain; Major; Colonel; Brig.-General. 15th, 16th and 17th Royal Scots. K.C.V.O.; C.B.; C.B.E.; V.D.; Officer Legion of Honour (French); Knight of St Olaf (Norway).

CRAVEN, RICHARD.
Mount St Mary's, Eckington, Chesterfield. M.B., C.M. 1898. R.A.M.C., Lieut. July 1915; Captain July 1916. R.F.A., 39th Division.

Record of War Service

CRAWFORD, DIROM GREY.
Cheltenham. M.B., C.M. 1881. First XV. Indian Medical Service, Oct. 1881; Lieut.-Col. 1901. Retired Dec. 1911. Rejoined Nov. 1914 to March 1919. H.M. Hospital Ship *Syria*, Nov. 1914. Brighton Indian Hospital, Dec. 1914-15.

CRAWFORD, EDWARD JAMES.
Ballymena Academy. First XV. Student of Medicine, 1918. Belfast University O.T.C. Infantry, Oct. 1914 to March 1915, Cadet. Royal Naval Division Armoured Cars Squadron, Petty Officer Nov. 1915. R.F.A. and R.G.A., 2nd Lieut. Nov. 1918. Russian St George Medal March 1917.

CRAWFORD, GAVIN ALEXANDER.
George Watson's College. University O.T.C. Infantry, April 1915, Cadet L/Corporal. Indian Army, 2nd Lieut. Dec. 1915; Lieut. Sept. 1917. 2/102nd King Edward's Own Grenadiers. France and India.

CRAWFORD, GILBERT MALCOLM.
George Watson's College. Student of Law, 1892-3. Solicitor before the Supreme Courts, 1897. President, Scots Law Society, 1899. Cameronians (Scottish Rifles), 2nd Lieut. April 1915. Royal Irish Fusiliers, Lieut. April 1916; Royal Dublin Fusiliers, Captain Aug. 1917. France. M.C. Oct. 1918.

CRAWFORD, JAMES.
Greenock Academy; Athletics. Student of Medicine, 1918. 1st Cameron Highlanders, Private March 1916; 2nd Lieut. June 1917; Lieut. Dec. 1918. 7th Tank Battalion.

CRAWFORD, JAMES MUIR.
M.B., C.M. 1888; L.R.C.P. & S. (Edin.) and L.F.P.S. (Glasg.) 1888. Indian Medical Service, 1891; Lieut.-Col. Jan. 1911. Indian General Hospital. 1914. O.B.E.

CRAWFORD, JOHN ANDREW.
George Watson's College. M.B., Ch.B. 1916. O.T.C. Medical, Nov. 1914 to April 1916, Cadet Sergeant. R.A.M.C. (S.R.), Lieut. April 1916; Captain Oct. 1916. Mesopotamia.

CRAWFORD, JOHN HAMILTON.
Duffus School, Elginshire. Student of Medicine, 1913-18; M.B., Ch.B. 1918. Anatomy Staff, 1919. O.T.C. Artillery, Oct. 1914 to Dec. 1915, Cadet. R.N.V.R. Surgeon-Probationer, Dec. 1915-16. Royal Navy, Surgeon-Lieut., Aug. 1918, H.M.S. *Dartmouth*.

CRAWFORD, JOHN RALSTON.
Crieff Academy. University O.T.C. Artillery, May 1916 to Feb. 1917, Cadet. R.F.A. and A.S.C., Recruiting Staff, Officer Cadet Feb. 1917.

Record of War Service

CRAWFORD, ROBERT CAMPBELL.
Loretto; First XV. O.T.C. 1909-10, Cadet Corporal. Student of Medicine, 1910-16; M.B., Ch.B. 1916. O.T.C. Medical, Nov. 1914-16, Cadet. Resident House Physician, R.I.E. Rugby "Blue." R.A.M.C. (T.), Lieut. July 1916; Captain July 1917. Med. Exp. Force, Aug. 1916. Invalided home Dec. 1918.

CRAWFORD, THOMAS JOHNSTONE.
George Heriot's School. O.T.C. 1913-15. University O.T.C. Artillery, 1916-17, Cadet Bombardier; Officer Cadet Sept. 1917. R.F.A. (S.R.), 2nd Lieut. March 1918; Lieut. Sept. to Nov. 1919. France and The Rhine.

CRAWFORD, WILLIAM.
M.A. 1911; B.D. Minister, Church of Scotland. O.T.C. Infantry, March 1910 to April 1913, Cadet. Chaplain 4th Class, May 1915. M.C.

CRAWFORD, WILLIAM SCOTT.
Cheltenham; First XV. Student of Medicine, 1903-8. 4th and 10th Royal Scots (T.), Private Aug. 1914; 2nd Lieut. Feb. 1915; Temp. Lieut. Aug. 1915; Temp. Captain June 1916. Lanarkshire Yeomanry, Lieut. Dec. 1917.

CREASER, FREDERICK GEORGE.
Drogheda Grammar School. Student of Medicine, 1914-15 and 1918-19. O.T.C. Artillery, Oct. 1914 to May 1915, Cadet. 14th Argyll and Sutherland Highlanders Corporal May 1915; Sergeant July 1915. R.F.A., 2nd Lieut. June 1917; Lieut. Dec. 1918. R.E. M.C. Dec. 1918. Dispatches Jan. 1919.

CRERAR, ALASTAIR HENRY.
Edinburgh Academy, and Bootham School, York. Student of Law, 1915 and 1919. O.T.C. Infantry, Oct. 1915 to Jan. 1916, Cadet. 9th and 2nd Royal Scots Fusiliers, 2nd Lieut. Jan. 1916; Lieut. July 1917. Royal Air Force, Pilot. Wounded Oct. 1916.

CRERAR, DONALD BAYNE.
Morrison's Academy, Crieff. M.B., C.M. 1893. R.A.M.C., Lieut. June 1915; Captain June 1916 to March 1919. Military Hospital, Stransall Camp, York. M.O., War Hospital, Bradford.

CRERAR, GEORGE DUNCAN.
George Watson's College. O.T.C. 1917. Student of Science, 1917 and 1919. O.T.C. Artillery, 1917-18, Cadet Corporal; Officer Cadet July 1918. R.G.A., 2nd Lieut. May 1919.

CREW, FRANK ALBERT ELEY.
King Edward VI. School, Birmingham. M.B., Ch.B. 1912. O.T.C. Medical, Nov. 1908 to April 1913, Cadet Staff Sergeant. 6th Devonshire Regiment, Captain June 1916; Major Aug. 1917. Employed with R.A.M.C., 3rd Field Ambulance, France. India 1915.

Record of War Service

CRICHTON, CRAWFORD SMITH.
Arbroath High School. M.B., Ch.B. 1903; M.D. 1910. R.A.M.C., Lieut. April 1915; Captain April 1916; Major 1917. O.C. Surrey R.A.M.C. (V.).

CRICHTON, DAVID CUTHBERT COLLINGWOOD.
Edinburgh Academy. O.T.C. 1915. University O.T.C. Artillery, 1915-17, Cadet. R.A.S.C. (M.T.), Private Jan. 1918; 2nd Lieut. April 1918; Lieut. Oct. 1919. Attached Indian M.T., Waziristan Field Force.

CRICHTON, DAVID MACQUORN-RANKINE.
George Heriot's School. M.B., C.M. 1894; B.Sc. (P.H.) 1899. R.A.M.C., Lieut. Aug 1915; Captain Aug. 1916. Nasrieh 1915-16. Imperial School of Instruction, Egypt, 1917-18, and Kasr-et-Nild Staff. G.H.Q., 2nd Échelon, Egyptian Exp. Force, 1918-19.

CRICHTON, JAMES SMITH.
Linlithgow Academy. M.B., Ch.B. 1914. R.A.M.C., Lieut. April 1917; Captain April 1918. Invalided out Feb. 1919.

CRICHTON, THOMAS SMITH.
Arbroath High School; Athletics. M.A. 1905. Minister, U.F. Church of Scotland. 16th Royal Scots, Private Feb. 1915. 20th, 24th, and 2nd Northumberland Fusiliers, 2nd Lieut. May 1915; Lieut. July 1917.

CRICHTON, WILLIAM PALMERSTON.
Boroughmuir. MA. 1913. Schoolmaster. 6th King's Own Scottish Borderers, Q.M.S.

CRIDLAND, EDWARD CARTER.
M.B., C.M. 1888. Royal Navy, H.M.S. *President V.*, Surgeon-Commander.

CRIPPS, FRANCIS ROY.
George Watson's College. Student of Medicine, 1912-17; M.B., Ch.B. 1916; L.M. (Dublin). O.T.C. Medical, Nov. 1914-15, Cadet. R.N.V.R., Surgeon-Probationer, April 1915. Royal Navy, Surgeon, Jan. 1917-20. Harwich Destroyer Flotilla 1915. Mine-sweepers and Grand Fleet 1917. Lent Royal Air Force, British Ægean Force, 1918.

CRISP, THOMAS.
Tenterfield, New South Wales. Student of Medicine, 1911-16 and 1917-18; M.B., Ch.B. 1916; M.D. O.T.C. Artillery, Oct. 1912-14, Cadet Bombardier. R.F.A. (S.R.), 2nd Lieut. Aug. 1914. R.A.M.C. (S.R.), Lieut. 1916; Captain April 1917. France.

CRITCHLEY, LEOPOLD OCTAVIUS.
St Drostone's College, Aberlour. M.A. 1896; B.Sc. Minister, Episcopal Church of Scotland. Chaplain 1915. 157th Brigade, 52nd Division. G.H.Q., Dardanelles. Hon. Chaplain 1918.

Record of War Service

CROCKET, JAMES.
M.A. 1887; B.Sc. 1891. Minister, U.F. Church of Scotland. 1st Haddingtonshire Vols., Private Aug. 1915.

CROCKETT, THOMAS.
Royal High School; First XV. M.A. (Hons. Engl.) 1905. Schoolmaster. Rugby "Blue." 6th Royal Highlanders (Black Watch) (T.), 2nd Lieut. Sept. 1914; Lieut. Dec. 1914; Captain July 1915; Major Feb. 1918. Attached Machine-Gun Corps.

CROLE, GERARD BRUCE. (See p. 748.)

CROLIUS, JOHN ROBERT.
Hong Kong. Student of Medicine, 1911-14. L.M.S.S.A. (Lond.) 1915. O.T.C. Medical, 1912-14, Cadet Corporal. R.A.M.C., Lieut. Aug. 1914; Captain Sept. 1915; Acting Major and D.A.D.M.S., 3rd Corps, Nov. 1918. 62nd and 54th Field Ambulances. Médaille des Épidémies 1920.

CROLL, ANDREW.
Dundee School. M.B., C.M. 1893; M.D. 1899; F.R.C.S. (Edin.) 1911; F.A.C.S. (America) 1914. Canadian Army Medical Corps, Lieut. 1914; Captain 1915; Major 1916; Lieut.-Col. 1917. Chief Surgeon, No. 2 Canadian General Hospital, France, and Military Hospital, Halifax, Canada. Dispatches Oct. 1916.

CROMARTY, ROBERT.
Leith Academy. Student of Arts, 1912-16. M.A. (Hons. Engl.) 1916. Schoolmaster. 2/4th Seaforth Highlanders, Private Nov. 1916; Hon. Sergeant May 1917; L/Corporal March 1918. 2/3rd County of London Yeomanry.

CROMBIE, JAMES MOIR.
George Watson's College. Cadet Corps 1905-9, L/Corporal. Student of Medicine, 1918-20. 9th Royal Scots, Private Aug. 1914. R.G.A., 60th Brigade, 2nd Lieut. March 1915; Lieut. June 1916. France, June 1916 to Jan. 1919.

CROMBIE, JOHN FRANK.
Clifton Bank, St Andrews; First XV. M.B., C.M. 1891; M.D. 1906; D.P.H., (Edin.) 1897. R.A.M.C. (T.) 1896; Major 1910; Acting Lieut.-Col. Dec. 1916. Attached 8th Royal Scots. No. 139 Field Ambulance, and No. 12 Stationary Service. France. Order of St John of Jerusalem 1916. Dispatches June 1917, Jan. and Dec. 1918. D.S.O. Jan. 1918; T.D.; Médaille des Épidémies Jan. 1919.

CROMBIE, ROBERT OGILVIE.
Daniel Stewart's College. Student of Science, 1918. Royal Navy, H.M.T. *Teviot* (Wireless Operator).

CROMIE, GEORGE.
Student of Medicine, 1908-14; M.B., Ch.B. 1913. O.T.C. Infantry, Jan. 1909 to July 1915, Cadet; 2nd Lieut.

Record of War Service

CROOKS, THOMAS.
 Hawick High School. Student of Arts, 1914-15. R.E., 189th Coy., Corporal Aug. 1915; Special Brigade 1916-19. France 1915-19. Wounded Dec. 1916.

CROSBIE, KENNETH CHRISTOPHER.
 Epsom College; First XV. and XI. Hockey. Student of Medicine, 1910-14 and 1916-18; M.B., Ch.B. 1918. O.T.C. Artillery, 1909-14, Cadet. R.F.A., 2nd Lieut. Aug. 1914; Lieut. May 1916; Captain Oct. 1916. M.C. Oct. 1916.

CROSS, ROBERT.
 M.B., C.M. 1895. R.A.M.C. (T.), Captain Sept. 1908. 10th Royal Scots. M.O. in charge of Troops at Linlithgow.

CROW, DOUGLAS ARTHUR.
 Fort William School. M.B., Ch.B. 1911. R.A.M.C., Lieut. March 1916; Captain March 1918.

CROW, WILLIAM JAMES.
 Daniel Stewart's College. M.B., Ch.B. 1901; M.D. 1917. R.A.M.C., Lieut. July 1916; Captain July 1917. Salonika July 1916 to March 1918; France June to Dec. 1918.

CROWDEN, HARRY GRAHAM.
 George Watson's College; First XI. M.A. 1912. Schoolmaster. 9th and 13th Royal Scots, Private; L/Corporal 1914; 2nd Lieut. Jan. 1915; Lieut. France 1915 and 1916; Loos and Somme. Wounded Sept. 1915.

CRUICKSHANK, ALEXANDER JOHNSTON.
 Robert Gordon's College, Aberdeen. University O.T.C. Artillery, 1917-18, Cadet; Officer Cadet May 1918. R.G.A., 2nd Lieut. Oct. 1918.

CRUICKSHANK, JAMES ALEXANDER.
 Haileybury. M.B., Ch.B. 1905; M.D. 1914. Indian Medical Service, Captain Feb. 1910; Major Aug. 1918. M.C. Aug. 1916.

CRUICKSHANK, JOHN C.
 George Watson's College. O.T.C. 1913-16, L/Corporal. Student of Medicine, 1916-17 and 1918-20. O.T.C. Medical, May 1918 to Feb. 1919, Cadet. Gordon Highlanders, Private.

CRUICKSHANKS, GEORGE.
 George Watson's College. Student of Arts, 1903-5. University Battery, E.C.A.V., Gunner, 1903-5. 11th and 1st Scottish Rifles, Lieut.; Captain Nov. 1914.

CULBERTSON, ROBERT.
 George Watson's College. M.A. (Hons. Classics) 1911. Schoolmaster. 2/1st Lothians and Border Horse (T.), Private Nov. 1915. 9th Cyclist Brigade (Signal Section), L/Corporal Dec. 1916. R.E. (Signals), R.A. H.Q., Sapper April 1918. France 1918-19.

Record of War Service

CULLEN, KENNETH DOUGLAS.
Edinburgh Academy. M.A. 1911; LL.B. 1913. R.E., 49th Coy., Sapper Sept. 1914; 2nd Lieut. Dec. 1914; Lieut. May 1915; Acting Captain Nov. 1916. City of Edinburgh Fortress, R.E.

CULLEN, WILLIAM BARBOUR ALEXANDER KENNEDY.
M.B., Ch.B. 1903; M.D. 1906. Indian Medical Service, Captain 1915; Major 2/2nd Ghurkha Rifles.

CULLEN, WILLIAM DOUGLAS LAING.
Edinburgh Academy; First XV. O.T.C. 1910-13. Student of Medicine, 1913-14. O.T.C. Artillery, 1913-14, Cadet. Lothians and Border Horse (T.), Private Sept. 1914. R.G.A. (Lowland), Lieut. France, Salonika, and Aden.

CUMMING, ARTHUR GORDON.
Miller Institution, Thurso. Student of Medicine, 1913-16 and 1917-19. O.T.C. Medical, Jan. 1915 to March 1916, Cadet. 1/5th and 6th Seaforth Highlanders, Private April 1916; L/Corporal Nov. 1916; 2nd Lieut. Aug. to Dec. 1917. France Aug. 1916 to March 1917.

CUMMING, GEORGE GORDON.
M.B., Ch.B. 1903. South African Medical Corps, Captain.

CUMMING, HERBERT GRANT.
Grantown Grammar School. M.A. 1908; B.Sc. Australian Imperial Forces, 46th Battn., Private Nov. 1916; Corporal Oct. 1917; 2nd Lieut. Oct. 1918; Lieut. Feb. 1919. M.M. Oct. 1917.

CUNNINGHAM, ANDREW.
Perth Academy. B.Sc. 1911. Lecturer in Bacteriology, Edinburgh, and East of Scotland Agricultural College. O.T.C. Artillery, Nov. 1915 to March 1916, Cadet; Officer Cadet March 1916. Scottish Horse, 2nd Lieut. Aug. 1916. R.F.A. (T.), 2nd Lieut. July 1917; Lieut. Jan. 1919. France.

CUNNINGHAM, BARBARA MARTIN.
M.B., Ch.B. 1901; M.D. 1909; D.P.H. (Camb.) 1910. R.A.M.C., British Military Hospital, Limoges, France, and Imtarfa, Malta, Aug. 1916. 61st and 42nd General Hospitals, Salonika, 1917-18. O.B.E. June 1917. Dispatches (Salonika) Sept. 1917.

CUNNINGHAM, DONALD ALEC.
George Watson's College. Student of Medicine, 1913-14 and 1918-19. O.T.C. Medical, Feb. 1916, Cadet. R.N.V.R., Surgeon-Probationer.

CUNNINGHAM, FRANCIS WILLIAM MURRAY.
Fettes. M.B., Ch.B. 1907; M.D. 1909. R.A.M.C., Captain July 1912; Lieut.-Col. Feb. 1917. Attached Indian Contingent, 1914-15. France 1916-19. Dispatches Jan. 1916. D.S.O. June 1918.

Record of War Service

CUNNINGHAM, JOHN BAIRD.
M.B., Ch.B. 1913. R.A.M.C., Lieut. Jan. 1916; Captain Jan. 1917 to Feb. 1919. France March 1916 to Oct. 1917, and Italy Oct. 1917 to Feb. 1919.

CUNNINGHAM, JOHN FODEN.
M.A. 1914. 1st Seaforth Highlanders, Corporal.

CUNNINGHAM, LESLIE BENNET CRAIGIE.
Sedbergh. Student of Science, 1913-14. O.T.C. Engineers, 1913 to Sept. 1914, Cadet. 9th King's Own Scottish Borderers, 2nd Lieut.; Lieut. May 1916. Attached R.E. (Signal Service), July 1915. France.

CUNNINGHAM, RICHARD GRAHAM.
Galashiels High School. M.B., Ch.B. 1906. R.A.M.C., Lieut. 1917. 49th General Hospital, Salonika.

CUNNINGHAM, ROBERT JEFFREY.
Edinburgh Academy. M.A. 1887; LL.B. 1892. No. 4 Coy. Q.R.V.B., Royal Scots, 1885-90. 1st and 5th King's Own Scottish Borderers, 1898. South African Campaign, 1900. Captain 1906. Mobilised Aug. 1914. O.C. Regimental Depôt, Dumfries, April 1915 to Oct. 1919. T.D.

CUNNINGHAM, ROBERT YOUNG.
M.A. 1887. 8th Argyll and Sutherland Highlanders, 2nd Lieut. 1889; Captain 1895; Major Oct. 1914. Training Troops, Dunoon and Stobs, 1914-15. Officer, Leith Docks, 1915-16. Depôt, Randalstown, Ireland, Feb. to Oct. 1916.

CUNNISON, DAVID KEITH.
George Watson's College. M.A. 1901; LL.B. 1904. Calcutta Scottish (Infantry), Lieut.; Captain.

CUNNISON, THOMAS JOHN.
George Watson's College. M.A., B.Sc. 1910. Schoolmaster. O.T.C. Artillery, 1907-11, Cadet Sergeant. R.F.A. (T.), 2nd Lieut. 1911. Mobilised Sept. 1914; Lieut. March 1915; Captain Jan. 1917. Gallipoli 1915; France 1916-18; Somme 1916, Arras, Ypres, Cambrai 1917. Dispatches May 1917. M.C. Jan. 1918; Croix de Guerre (Belgian) Sept. 1918.

CURR, THOMAS.
Daniel Stewart's College. University O.T.C. Infantry, Aug. to Sept. 1915, Cadet. 9th Argyll and Sutherland Highlanders 2nd Lieut. Oct. 1915; Lieut. Sept. 1917; Captain July 1918. R.E., Aug. 1917. O.C. Printing Coy., R.E., G.H.Q., France, July 1918. Italy.

CURR, THOMAS SIMPSON.
Edinburgh Institution; First XV. and XI. 1st Highland Cadet Battn., 1912-17; Cadet 2nd Lieut. Student of Science, 1917-19. 2/28th London (Artists' Rifles) O.T.C., Private Oct. 1918.

Record of War Service

CURRELL, JAMES ALEXANDER.
M.B., Ch.B. 1906. R.A.M.C., Lieut. May 1917; Captain May 1918; Acting Major Dec. 1918.

CURRIE, DUNCAN WILLIAM.
Bowmore School, Islay. M.B., C.M. 1876; M.D. (Glasg.) 1890; D.P.H. (Camb.) 1886; B.Sc. (P.H. Edin.) 1892. R.A.M.C. (T.), Lieut.-Col. (Retired) 1910. Rejoined Aug. 1914. Examiner of Recruits. Pensions Board, Stirling. Armsbrae Auxiliary Hospital. V.D.

CURRIE, JOHN RONALD.
Ayr Academy. M.A. 1891; M.A. (Oxford); M.B., Ch.B. 1898; M.D. (Glasg.) 1910; D.P.H. (Birmingham) 1904. R.A.M.C., Captain March 1916. Portsmouth, Taranto, Peath, and Dunkirk.

CURRIE, ROBERT.
Night Watchman, Edinburgh University. 3rd Dragoon Guards, Trooper Oct. 1914; Corporal Jan. 1918; Sergeant Aug. 1918. A.S.C., Nov. 1917 to April 1919. Died on 29th August 1920.

CUSHNY, ALEXANDER OGILVY.
Student of Law, 1912-14. 7th Royal Scots (T.), Captain June 1915; Staff Captain Aug. 1916. M.C. April 1918.

CUTHBERT, ANDREW HUME.
Royal High School. Student of Arts and Medicine, 1900-3 and 1918-19. M.A. 1903. O.T.C. Medical, Nov. 1918 to Feb. 1919, Cadet. R.A.M.C., Scottish Horse Field Ambulance, Sergeant Sept. 1914; Staff Sergeant July 1915.

CUTHBERT, DAVID ANDREW ROLLO.
Perth Academy; First XV. Student of Law, 1914-15. O.T.C. Infantry, June to Sept. 1915, Cadet. 4th King's Own Scottish Borderers (T.), 2nd Lieut. Sept. 1915; Lieut. July 1917. Attached 1st Highland Light Infantry. Egypt Jan. 1916 to March 1918. France Oct. 1918 to Feb. 1919. M.C. Nov. 1917.

CUTHBERT, GEORGE.
Perth Academy, and Moray House, Edinburgh. Student of Arts, 1913-16 and 1919. M.A. (Hons. Mental Phil.) 1919. R.N.V.R., Chief Petty Officer, Sept. 1916 to 1919.

CUTHBERT, JAMES ARTHUR.
Alloa Academy; First XI. Student of Medicine, 1918. R.N.V.R., Signalman June 1916; Midshipman Dec. 1916; Sub.-Lieut. May 1918 to Jan. 1919. H.M.T.B. Destroyers *Peyton* and *Trojan*, Grand Fleet.

CUTHBERT, JAMES HARVEY.
M.B., Ch.B., 1912. R.A.M.C., Lieut.; Captain June 1916.

CUTHBERT, JAMES MACKIE.
M.B., Ch.B. 1898. R.A.M.C., Major Oct. 1910. 9th Hospital Corps.

Record of War Service

CUTHBERT, JOHN.
    Harris Academy, Dundee. M.A. 1909. Schoolmaster. R.F.A., Gunner Jan. 1915; 2nd Lieut. Aug. 1915; Lieut. March 1917; Acting Captain March 1918. Attached Trench Mortar Battery, March 1917. Dispatches May 1918. M.C. June 1918.

CUTHBERT, THOMAS WILKINSON.
    Edinburgh Academy. Student of Science, 1890-5. 4th Seaforth Highlanders (T.), Major. D.S.O. Dispatches.

CUTHBERT, WILLIAM JOHNSTON.
    Fettes. O.T.C. 1909-10. M.A. (Hons. Classics) 1914. O.T.C. Infantry, 1910-14, Cadet. 7th Royal Scots Fusiliers, 2nd Lieut. Nov. 1914; Lieut. July 1916. 1st (Reserve) Garrison Battn., Highland Light Infantry.

CUTHBERTSON, RONALD KERR.
    Edinburgh Academy. O.T.C. 1916-17. Student of Arts and Law, 1917-19. O.T.C. Artillery, Aug. 1917 to April 1918, Cadet Bombardier; Officer Cadet. April 1918. R.G.A., 2nd Lieut.

CUTT, JOHN.
    Kirkwall Burgh School. M.A. 1906. Schoolmaster. 1st Gordon Highlanders, Private Dec. 1914; L/Corporal May 1915; Corporal Sept. 1915; Sergeant March 1916. R.E. (Special Coy.), Sept. 1915. France. Certificate for Gallant Conduct July 1915. M.M. May 1917.

D'ABREU, VICTOR EUGENE.
    La Martiniere College, Lucknow, India. B.Sc. 1911. A.M.I.C.E. O.T.C. Engineers, Dec. 1915 to Jan. 1916, Cadet. R.E., 234th Light Railway Forward Coy., 2nd Lieut. Jan. 1916; Lieut. July 1917; Captain Aug. 1918.

DALGLEISH, JAMES.
    Trinity Academy, Leith. Student of Arts and Science, 1913-15. O.T.C. Infantry, May to Sept. 1915, Cadet. 4th Argyll and Sutherland Highlanders (S.R.), 2nd Lieut. Sept. 1915; Lieut. May 1917.

DALGLEISH, JOHN.
    Queen's College, British Guiana. First XI. M.B., Ch.B. 1901; M.D. 1909; R.A.M.C., Captain June 1917. 21st General Hospital, Alexandria, Egypt.

DALL, JOHN.
    George Heriot's School. M.A. 1909. Schoolmaster. R.A.M.C., Private June 1915; Sergeant April 1916; Lieut. Sept. 1917; Captain Sept. 1918. Attached R.E., Anti-Gas Establishment, July 1916.

DALLAS, JOHN D.
    Student of Law, 1899-1904. Advocate, 1905. 16th Royal Scots, Lieut. May 1916. 2nd King's African Rifles, July 1917.

Record of War Service

DALRYMPLE, WILLIAM.
Student of Law. Chartered Accountant. 13th Argyll and Sutherland Highlanders, 2nd Lieut.

D'ALTON, OLIVER CLEAVELAND.
Queen Elizabeth's Grammar School, Barnet, Herts. Student of Medicine, 1884-8. Q.E.R. New South Wales Irish Rifles, 2nd Lieut. 1910; Lieut.; Captain. 33rd Infantry, Commonwealth Military Forces, Aug. 1915. Assistant Censor, Aug. 1914. Invalided out Aug. 1915. Training Battn., Liverpool, N.S.W.

DALZIEL, EWEN GLENDINNING.
George Watson's College and Edinburgh Academy. O.T.C. 1913-16, Cadet Corporal. Student of Medicine, 1918-20. O.T.C. Artillery, 1916-17, Cadet Bombardier; Officer Cadet July 1917. R.F.A., 2nd Lieut. Dec. 1917. France 1918. Wounded. M.C. July 1918.

DALZIEL, ROBERT McLAUCHLAN.
Dollar Academy and Edinburgh Institution; First XV. M.B., Ch.B. 1899. Indian Medical Service, Lieut., Jan. 1901; Major July 1912. Egypt 1914-16. India.

DALZIEL, Sir THOMAS KENNEDY.
M.B., C.M. 1883; F.R.F.P. & S. (Glasg.). Late Professor of Surgery, Anderson's College, Glasgow. R.A.M.C. (T.), 1888; Lieut.-Col. 1908. 3rd Scottish General Hospital. Surgeon, R.E. Glasgow Submarine Miners.

DAMAN, THOMAS WALTER ALFRED.
M.A. (Camb.). Athletics. M.B., C.M. 1897. Rowing. Lincolnshire Vol. Regiment 1898-9, Surgeon-Lieut. R.A.M.C. (T.), Major 1908. 4th Northern General Hospital. President, Recruiting Boards, Lincoln and Leicester.

DANDIE, JAMES NAUGHTON.
George Watson's College. O.T.C. 1907-12, Cadet Sergeant. Student of Arts and Law, 1912-14 and 1918-19; M.A. 1919. O.T.C. Artillery, Oct. 1912 to Aug. 1914, Cadet. R.G.A. (T.) (Highland Fife), 2nd Lieut. Aug. 1914; Temp. Lieut. April 1915; Lieut. June 1916; Acting Captain Sept. 1917 to March 1919. France May 1915 to Jan. 1919. Dispatches May 1917. M.C. Jan. 1918.

DANGERFIELD, ARTHUR.
Edinburgh Academy. M.B., Ch.B. 1905; D.T.M. and H. 1906; F.R.C.S. (Edin.) 1910. R.A.M.C., Lieut. 1916; attached Royal Serbian Army.

DANIEL, HENRY NORMAN.
Student of Medicine, 1912-14 and 1917-19; M.B., Ch.B. 1918. O.T.C. Artillery, Nov. 1913 to Sept. 1914, Cadet. R.F.A., 2nd Lieut. Sept. 1914.

DARBYSHIRE, THOMAS H. LESLIE.
Sedbergh. Cadet Corps 1894-6. Student of Science, 1918-19. Canadian Forces, Trooper Aug. 1914. 7th Sherwood Foresters, 2nd Lieut. May 1915; Lieut. July 1916; Captain. Invalided out.

Record of War Service

DARLING, EDWIN.
 Student of Science. O.T.C. Artillery, Feb. 1913 to Oct. 1914, Cadet. R.F.A. (T.), Lieut. Oct. 1914; Captain. Attached 4th Northumbrian (Howitzer) Brigade. Prisoner of War.

DARLING, JAMES WALKER.
 Merchiston Castle. Cadet Corps 1904-6. Student of Medicine, 1908-14; M.B., Ch.B. 1914; O.T.C. Artillery, 1909-12, Cadet. R.A.M.C., Lieut. June 1915; Captain 1916. Malta 1915. M.O., 1st Scots Guards. M.C. July 1917.

DARLING, JOHN MAY.
 Royal High School; First XV. M.A. and M.B., Ch.B. 1903; F.R.C.S. (Edin.) O.T.C. Medical, 1896-1903, Cadet Staff Sergeant, and 1906-14, Captain. South African Campaign, 1900. R.A.M.C. (S.R.), Lieut. March 1906; Captain July 1908; Acting Major 1915. France Aug. 1914-15; Egypt 1915-18; Salonika 1918-19. D.S.O. Dispatches.

DARLING, THOMAS NEWMAN.
 Reading School; First XI., Cricket and Football. L.R.C.P. & S. (Edin.) and L.R.F.P.S. (Glasg.) 1905; F.R.G.S. Physician, Royal Family, Spain. R.A.M.C., Captain Oct. 1914. Director of Red Cross Hospitals in France, 1914-16. H.M. Hospital Ship *Assaye*, 1916-17. India, Egypt, East Africa, and Mesopotamia. India 1918-19.

DARLING, WALTER.
 Merchiston Castle. Student 1908. 30th Reserve Battn. Canadian Infantry, Corporal.

DARLING, WILLIAM.
 Royal High School and George Watson's College. M.A., M.B., Ch.B. 1899; F.R.C.S. 1903; D.P.H. (Edin.). 1906. O.T.C. Medical, 1894-1914, Captain. R.A.M.C. (S.R.), Captain; Acting Major. No. 28 Field Ambulance, France, Aug. 1914 to May 1919. Mons. Wounded. M.C. June 1915. Twice Mentioned in Dispatches.

DARLINGTON, WILLIAM.
 M.B., Ch.B. 1910. R.A.M.C., Lieut. Dec. 1915; Captain Dec. 1916 to March 1919. France 1916-19.

DARNLEY, JAMES.
 Galashiels Academy. Student of Law, 1913-15. R.F.C., 3rd Air Mechanic, April 1917; 2nd Air Mechanic, Nov. 1917; 1st Air Mechanic, July 1918; Corporal Dec. 1918 to July 1919.

DAUTH, DIEDERIK JOHN.
 South African College School, and University, Cape Town. First XV. Cadet Corps 1905-8, Sergeant. Student of Medicine, 1909-14; M.B., Ch.B. 1914. O.T.C. Artillery, Jan. 1910 to Nov. 1912. South African Medical Corps, 1914 to July 1915. R.A.M.C., Aug. 1915; Captain 1917. South African Medical Corps, Major Jan. 1918. H.M. Hospital Ship *Assaye*, 1916-17. Dispatches, German South-West Africa, April 1915 and July 1918.

Record of War Service

DAVID, JESUDASAN SELLYAH.
Student of Medicine, 1915; L.R.C.P. & S. (Edin.), and L.R.F.P.S. (Glasg.) 1915. Indian Medical Service, Lieut. March 1916; Captain March 1917.

DAVIDSON, ALAN MUNRO.
Dundee High School; First XV. and XI. Student of Arts and Divinity, 1911-15 and 1919; M.A. 1915. O.T.C. Artillery, 1914-15, Cadet. R.F.A. (S.R.), 2nd Lieut. Aug. 1915; Lieut. Dec. 1916; Captain Jan. 1919. M.C. April 1917.

DAVIDSON, ALEXANDER WHYTE.
Edinburgh Academy. O.T.C. 1910-15, Cadet L/Corporal. 10th Seaforth Highlanders, Private May 1916; L/Corporal Aug. 1916. 3rd attached 1st Northumberland Fusiliers, 2nd Lieut. Aug. 1917 to Jan. 1919. France and The Rhine. M.C. Oct. 1918.

DAVIDSON, ANDREW McCONNELL.
Bootham School, Yorks; Athletics. M.B., Ch.B. 1912; M.D. (Winnipeg) 1912. R.A.M.C., Lieut. June 1915; Captain Aug. 1916. Canadian Army Medical Corps, Nov. 1917 to Feb. 1919. Boulogne 1916.

DAVIDSON, A. NEVILE.
North Berwick High School. Student of Arts, 1915-17. O.T.C. Artillery, Jan. 1917 to April 1918, Cadet; Officer Cadet April 1918. R.G.A. (Anti-Aircraft), 2nd Lieut. Sept. 1918.

DAVIDSON, ANDREW RUTHERFORD.
Aylwin College, Westmorland. F.F.A. and A.I.A. University O.T.C. Artillery, May to Nov. 1916, Cadet; Officer Cadet Nov. 1916. R.G.A. (Forth), 2nd Lieut. Jan. 1917; Lieut. July 1918.

DAVIDSON, DAVID ALEXANDER GIBB.
Viewpark School, Edinburgh. Student of Science, 1915-16. O.T.C. Artillery, Nov. 1915 to Dec. 1916, Cadet Bombardier; Officer Cadet Dec. 1916. R.G.A. (S.R.), 78th Brigade, 2nd Lieut. March 1917; Lieut. Sept. 1918; Acting Captain Oct. 1918 to July 1919. France April 1917.

DAVIDSON, DONALD.
Student of Arts and Divinity, 1910-15; M.A. 1914. O.T.C. Artillery, Dec. 1914 to May 1915, Cadet. R.E., Sapper, May 1915. R.F.A., 2nd Lieut. Aug. 1915; Lieut. July 1917; Acting Captain Sept. 1917.

DAVIDSON, EDWARD SELBY.
Gresham's School, Holt, Norfolk, and La Villa, Ouchy, Lausanne. Athletics. O.T.C. 1911-12. Student of Science, 1914-15. O.T.C. Infantry, Jan. to May 1915, Cadet. 6th and 1/4th Royal Scots (T.), 2nd Lieut. May 1915; Temp. Lieut. Aug. 1916; Lieut. July 1917. Royal Air Force, April 1918. Palestine 1917-18.

Record of War Service

DAVIDSON, FRANCIS ALEXANDER.
 High School, Dundee. Student of Science, 1914-15 and 1919. R.F.A., Gunner Nov. 1915. Wounded Aug. 1918.

DAVIDSON, FRANCIS JOHN.
 M.B., Ch.B. 1908. R.A.M.C. (T.), Captain Nov. 1915. M.O., 2/9th Middlesex Regiment.

DAVIDSON, FREDERICK CHURCHILL.
 Fettes; Athletics. M.B., Ch.B. 1912. R.A.M.C., Lieut. 1913; Captain March 1915; Acting Lieut.-Col. March 1917-19. Field Ambulance, France. M.C. and Dispatches 1915.

DAVIDSON, GEORGE FORREST.
 Berwickshire High School, Duns; Athletics. Student of Science, 1915-17. R.A.M.C., Private April 1917; Corporal Oct. 1917. No. 4 Water Tank Coy. France.

DAVIDSON, HARCOURT M.
 Student of Arts. Minister, Church of Scotland. Army Chaplain.

DAVIDSON, HERBERT JOHN.
 Edinburgh Academy. Student of Medicine, 1911-16; M.B., Ch.B. 1916. O.T.C. Medical, Oct. 1915 to March 1916, Cadet. R.A.M.C., Lieut. May 1916; Captain May 1917. 2nd Field Ambulance (R.N.D.), July 1916. 7th Royal Fusiliers, April 1917. Prisoner in Germany Dec. 1917 to March 1918. Italy May 1918 to Aug. 1919. M.C.

DAVIDSON, HUGH STEVENSON.
 Edinburgh Institution. M.B., Ch.B. 1903; F.R.C.S. (Edin.) 1906; R.A.M.C., Lieut. April 1915; Captain April 1916; Acting Major Jan. 1918; Acting Lieut.-Col. Oct. 1918. O.B.E. Dispatches June 1919.

DAVIDSON, JAMES.
 Dumfries Academy. Student of Medicine, 1913-15 and 1917-20. M.B., Ch.B. 1920. O.T.C. Infantry, 1914-15, Cadet. R.N.V.R., Surgeon-Probationer, 1915. H.M.S. *Opportune*. Grand Fleet, 4th and 14th Destroyer Flotillas. Battle of Jutland, May 1916.

DAVIDSON, JAMES.
 Edinburgh Academy. M.A. 1886; M.B., C.M. 1891; M.D. 1902. No. 4 Coy. Q.R.V.B., Royal Scots, 1886-91, Sergeant. Indian Medical Service, Surgeon-Lieut. 1893; Lieut.-Col. 1913. Waziristan 1894; Chitral 1895; Sudan 1896; Tirah 1897-8; Tibet 1903-4; Abor 1911-12; H.M. Hospital Ship *Syria* 1915-17; Afghan War 1919. A.D.M.S. Kohat Area. Dispatches and D.S.O. 1912.

DAVIDSON, JOHN.
 High School, Peebles. Student of Medicine, 1914-16 and 1918-19. O.T.C. Medical, Sept. 1918 to Feb. 1919, Cadet. R.A.M.C., Private July 1916.

Record of War Service

DAVIDSON, J. D.
> Student of Science. R.A.M.C. (T.), Lieut.; Captain Jan. 1918. O.C. No. 41 Sanitary Section. France 1917.

DAVIDSON, JOHN POLSON.
> George Watson's College; First XV. M.B., Ch.B. 1912. R.A.M.C., Lieut. Oct. 1914; Captain Oct. 1915; Acting Major Jan. 1918; Acting Lieut.-Col. June to Dec. 1919. France 1915-17 and 1918; Loos 1915, Somme 1916 and 1917, Messines 1917; Italy Nov. 1917 to March 1918; The Rhine Jan. to Dec. 1919. M.C. Jan. 1917; Bar to M.C. March 1918.

DAVIDSON, JOHN RANDOLPH.
> George Watson's College. M.A. 1903; B.Sc. 1905. Lecturer in Biology, Gizeh, Egypt. Egyptian Labour Corps, 2nd Lieut. July 1916; Lieut. Sept. 1917. Inspector of Recruiting (Egypt).

DAVIDSON, LEYBURNE STANLEY PATRICK.
> Cheltenham; First XV. and XI. O.T.C. 1907-11, L/Sergeant. Student of Medicine, 1911-13 and 1918-19. Cambridge University O.T.C. Medical, 1913-14, Cadet. 6th Gordon Highlanders, 2nd Lieut. Aug. 1914; Lieut. Oct. 1914; Captain April 1915-17. France 1914. Wounded at Festubert May 1915.

DAVIDSON, MORDKO SHLIOMA.
> B.Sc. 1915. R.A.S.C. (M.T.), Corporal; 2nd Lieut. Feb. 1916; Lieut. 55th Auxiliary Petrol Coy., France.

DAVIDSON, PETER.
> M.A. 1876; M.B., C.M. 1880. R.A.M.C. (T.), Captain 1908; Major Oct. 1913.

DAVIDSON, ROBERT.
> Student of Arts. 6th Royal Scots (T.), Private.

DAVIDSON, ROBERT CECIL.
> Bell Baxter School, Cupar; First XI. Student of Arts and Law, 1914-16; M.A. 1920. O.T.C. Artillery, Oct. 1914 to April 1916, Cadet. R.F.A., 5th Reserve Brigade, Gunner April 1916; 2nd Lieut. Jan. 1917; Lieut. July 1918. 230th Brigade. France March 1917 to June 1919.

DAVIDSON, ROBERT RUSSELL.
> M.A. 1907. Minister, U.F. Church of Scotland. A.S.C. (M.T.), Private Aug. 1916. Italy.

DAVIDSON, ROGER ALASTAIR McLAREN.
> Fettes; First XI. O.T.C. 1914-18, Cadet L/Corporal. Student of Arts, 1918. Royal Highlanders (Black Watch), Officer Cadet, Sept. 1918; 2nd Lieut. May 1919.

DAVIDSON, ROGER STEWART.
> Perth Academy, and Royal High School. M.A. 1889; B.D. 1892. Minister, Church of Scotland. Chaplain, Highland Cyclist Battn. (T.), Lieut.-Col. Feb. 1894. 4th Scottish General Hospital, 1915. 64th Highland Division, 1916. Mention 1918.

Record of War Service

DAVIDSON, STANLEY.
Student of Medicine, 1916-18. 6th Gordon Highlanders, Captain. Wounded and Discharged.

DAVIDSON, THOMAS.
Edinburgh Academy and Merchiston Castle. O.T.C. 1906-10, Cadet Corporal. Student of Science, 1910-14. O.T.C. Infantry, Dec. 1911 to Feb. 1914, Cadet Sergeant. 4th Cameron Highlanders, 2nd Lieut. May 1915; Lieut. Sept. 1916; Captain Oct. 1916-19. R.F.C. May 1916. France May 1916 to June 1917. Prisoner of War in Germany June 1917 to Dec. 1918.

DAVIDSON, THOMAS.
George Watson's College. M.A. (Hons. Classics) 1900; M.B., Ch.B. 1905. R.A.M.C., Lieut. Nov. 1915; Captain Nov. 1916. Mesopotamia 1916. Invalided home 1917.

DAVIDSON, WILLIAM WATSON.
Daniel Stewart's College. Student of Law, 1919. O.T.C. Artillery, Dec. 1915 to June 1916, Cadet; Officer Cadet July 1916. R.G.A., 6th Corps, 2nd Lieut. Oct. 1916; Lieut. April 1918 to Feb. 1919. France.

DAVIE, JAMES MURRAY.
Daniel Stewart's College; Athletics. Cadet Corps 1912-14, 2nd Lieut. Student of Science, 1918. 16th Royal Scots, 2nd Lieut. Nov. 1914; Lieut. Feb. 1915; Captain July 1916. France 1915-17, 34th Division. Wounded. M.C. July 1916. Dispatches Aug. 1916.

DAVIE, JAMES PATERSON.
Bathgate Academy. Student of Arts, 1913-16; M.A. 1916. R.N.V.R., Wireless Operator, Feb. 1916; Sub-Lieut. Sept. 1917; Lieut. Sept. 1918-19.

DAVIE, PETER COUSIN. (See p. 748.)

DAVIE, ROBERT.
Broughton School, Edinburgh. M.A. 1912. 6th Royal Highlanders (Black Watch) (T.), Private Sept. 1914. 4th Royal Scots (T.), 2nd Lieut. June 1917; Lieut. Dec. 1918.

DAVIE, THOMAS MACNAUGHTON.
George Heriot's School. Student of Medicine, 1909-14; M.B., Ch.B. 1914. O.T.C. Medical, Jan. 1909 to Feb. 1914, Cadet Sergeant. R.A.M.C. (S.R.), Lieut. Aug. 1914; Captain April 1915. 4th Hussars and 5th Gordon Highlanders. M.C.; Bar to M.C. March 1918.

DAVIES, ARNOLD.
B.A. (Lond.); M.B., Ch.B. 1906; D.T.M. & H.; D.P.H. (Wales). R.A.M.C., Lieut. July 1917; Captain July 1918.

DAVIES, GLYN ALEXANDER.
Scotch College, Claremont, West Australia. Student of Medicine, 1918. Australian Army Medical Corps, Private May 1915. Officer Cadet. 34th Battn. Australian Infantry, 2nd Lieut. June 1917; Lieut. Sept. 1917. Egypt, Gallipoli, and France.

Record of War Service

DAVIES, H. NORMAN.
Darlington Grammar School; First XI. Durham University O.T.C. May to Dec. 1916. Student of Medicine, 1918. 2nd King's Own Scottish Borderers, Dec. 1916; 2nd Lieut. May 1917; Lieut. to June 1919.

DAVIES, JOHN HOWARD.
Swansea Grammar School. Student of Arts, 1915-16. R.A.M.C., Private Nov. 1915. 1st Welsh Field Ambulance and No. 7 Ambulance Train. France.

DAVIES, PHILIP LYS.
George Watson's College. M.B., Ch.B. 1912. R.A.M.C., Lieut.

DAVIES, PURSER.
Menai Bridge Grammar School, North Wales. M.B., Ch.B. 1908. Royal Navy, H.M.S. *Frasffield*, Surgeon Jan. 1915. R.A.M.C., Lieut. Dec. 1915; Captain Dec. 1916. 1/6th London Field Ambulance, 1st Indian Cavalry Division. Prisoners of War Camp, Bramley. France. M.C. Oct. 1918.

DAVIES, REGINALD WYNYARD.
Hereford Cathedral School; First XI. Cadet Corps 1900-3, C.S.M. M.B., Ch.B. 1911. R.A.M.C., Lieut. May 1915; Captain Dec. 1916. M.O., R.E., 25th Division, France, 1915; 21st Indian General Hospital, Amara, Mesopotamia, 1916; and 21st General Hospital, Alexandria, Egypt, May 1917.

DAVIES, WILLIAM HOWARD.
Darlington School. Student of Medicine, 1913-15. O.T.C. Infantry, Nov. to Dec. 1914, Cadet. 8th King's Own Scottish Borderers, 2nd Lieut. Dec. 1914. 2nd Royal Scots, Lieut. Dec. 1917. Royal Air Force.

DAVIES-JONES, CHARLES WILLIAM SAUNDERSON.
Epsom College. Student of Medicine, 1909-15; M.B., Ch.B. 1915. B.R.C.S., Boulogne (Dresser), 1914. R.A.M.C., Lieut. Aug. 1915; Captain Aug. 1916.

DAVIES-JONES, CYRIL. (See p. 748.)

DAVIN, ALFRED LUCIAN VINCENT.
Student of Medicine, 1910-16. M.B., Ch.B. 1916. O.T.C. Medical 1915-16, Cadet. R.A.M.C. (S.R.), Lieut. Oct. 1916; Captain April 1917. Mesopotamia 1917, India 1917-19.

DAVIN, LAURENCE FRANK.
Student of Medicine, 1912-13. O.T.C. Artillery, Feb. 1909 to May 1913, Cadet. 11th Royal Scots, Lieut.; Captain May 1917. Wounded May 1916. M.C.

DAVISON, ANDREW WEIR.
Bolton School. Student of Medicine, 1914-19. O.T.C. Infantry, 1915; Medical, 1915-16, Cadet. R.N.V.R., Surgeon-Probationer, Aug. 1916.

Record of War Service

DAVISON, WILLIAM HENDERSON.
Royal School, Dungannon; First XV. M.B., Ch.B. 1903; D.P.H. (Birmingham) 1908. L.M. (Rotunda) 1912. Barrister-at-Law, 1913. University Battery, E.C.A.V., 1899-1902; Gunner. R.A.M.C. (T.), Lieut. June 1915; Captain Dec. 1915; Acting Major, March 1918. 61st South Midland Division, 1915. France, D.A.D.M.S., Sanitation, Third Army, May 1916 to Nov. 1918. Dispatches Jan. 1916, Dec. 1917, and Jan. 1919. O.B.E. (Military) Jan. 1919.

DAWE, JAMES HENRY.
M.B., C.M. 1885. R.A.M.C., 1906; Captain. Invalided out. Plymouth Medical Recruiting Board, 1917-18.

DAWSON, FRANK INGLIS.
M.B., Ch.B. 1902; M.D. 1905; F.R.C.S. (Edin.) 1905. R.A.M.C., Captain April to Dec. 1918. Surgical Specialist, France.

DAWSON, PERCY FURNEAUX.
Edinburgh Academy and George Watson's College. M.A. 1900. Writer to the Signet, 1903. Medically rejected 1914-15. R.G.A., Gunner Oct. 1916; 2nd Lieut. Oct. 1917; Lieut. April 1919.

DAWSON, WILLIAM.
Kirkcaldy School. Student of Law, 1906-8. Solicitor. O.T.C. Infantry, Oct. 1915 to Jan. 1916, Cadet. 2nd and 6th Gordon Highlanders, 2nd Lieut. Jan. 1916; Lieut. March 1917; Acting Captain April 1918. 51st Division. France May to Nov. 1917 and April 1918. Wounded at Armentières April 1918.

DEA, ANDREW BUCHAN.
George Heriot's School. M.A. and B.Sc. 1911. Schoolmaster. R.E., 1st Field Survey Battn., Corporal Aug. 1915; 2nd Lieut. Sept. 1916; Lieut. March 1918.

DEANE, CHARLES GORDON.
Harrison College, Barbados. M.B., Ch.B. 1912. 8th British West Indies Regiment, Surgeon-Captain April 1917. M.C. June 1918.

DEAR, JOHN ALEXANDER.
George Watson's College. University O.T.C. Artillery, Feb. to April 1917, Cadet. Royal Air Force, Officer Cadet April 1917; Lieut. July 1917. Interned in Holland Aug. to Nov. 1918.

DEAS, GEORGE FRANCIS.
Fettes; First XV. B.A. (Oxford); LL.B. 1903. J.P. Advocate. Barrister-at-Law. 9th Royal Scots (T.), Captain Oct. 1914.

DEAS, JAMES HAY.
Hamilton Academy. Student of Arts, 1917. O.T.C. Artillery, 1917, Cadet; Officer Cadet Jan. 1918. R.F.A., 255th Brigade, 2nd Lieut. June 1918.

Record of War Service

DEAS, LEONARD JOSEPH MONTAGU.
Clifton College. Cadet Corps 1887-9. M.B., Ch.B. 1898; F.R.C.S. (Edin.) 1911. Indian Medical Service, June 1900; Major and Acting Lieut.-Col. Dec. 1911; Brevet Lieut.-Col. May 1917. 112th Indian Field Ambulance. France Nov. 1914 to Dec. 1915; Mesopotamia Jan. 1916 to April 1919, Relief of Kut and Capture of Baghdad. Dispatches Jan. 1916 and Aug. 1917. Croix de Guerre (French).

DEAS, PERCY.
Madras College, St Andrews, and Rossall. Student of Law, 1911-14. Law Agent, 1919. R.A.S.C. (T.), Lieut. May 1913. Mobilised Aug. 1914; Captain Oct. 1914; Major July 1918. Serbia, Bulgaria, Macedonia, Egypt, Palestine, and Syria, 1915-1919. O.B.E.

DEAS, ROBERT TURNBULL.
George Watson's College. Student of Medicine, 1916-19. O.T.C. Artillery, Aug. 1917 to April 1918, Cadet; Officer Cadet April 1918. R.F.A., 2nd Lieut.

DEDMAN, JOHN JOHNSTONE.
Ewart High School, Newton-Stewart. Student of Science, 1914-15. O.T.C. Engineers, Oct. 1914 to March 1915, Cadet. 10th Border Regiment, 2nd Lieut. March 1915; Lieut. Dec. 1916; Captain July 1918. 2/119th Infantry, Indian Army. Gallipoli July 1915; Egypt Dec. 1915; France Dec. 1916; India Nov. 1917.

DE LA PRYME, PERCY CHRISTOPHER.
Dover College. Student of Arts and Law, 1896-9. Senior President, S.R.C., and Ath. Club, 1899-1900. 1st XV. A.S.C., 2nd Lieut. 1900; Major 1914; Temp. Lieut.-Col. 1915; Brevet Lieut.-Col. 1919. 6th and 31st Divisional Train, Adjutant and O.C. 1914. A.D. of S. and T., 15th and 20th Corps, 1916. France, the Marne, the Aisne, Romani, Beersheba, Jerusalem, 1st and 2nd Gaza, Palestine, and Syria. Dispatches 1914, 1917, and 1918. D.S.O. 1917.

DELGADO, ALFRED ERROLL.
Potsdam College, Jamaica. M.B., Ch.B. 1912. R.A.M.C. (T.), 1st East Anglian Field Ambulance, Lieut. Oct. 1914; Captain April 1915. Dispatches June 1918.

DEMAINE, JOHN WILLIAM.
M.A. 1913. 21st West Yorkshire Regiment, Private Dec. 1915 1st Worcestershire Regiment, 2nd Lieut. June 1917; Lieut. Dec. 1918 to Jan. 1919. France June 1916 to Jan. 1917. Wounded at Passchendaele Dec. 1917.

DEMPSTER, RONALD SCOTT.
Perth Academy. Cadet Corps 1914-15, Sergeant. Student of Law, 1919. O.T.C. Artillery, March 1916 to Jan. 1917, Cadet Sergeant; Officer Cadet Feb. 1917. R.F.A., 112th Brigade, 2nd Lieut. May 1917; Lieut. Nov. 1918. France. Wounded at Ypres July 1917.

DENHAM, ARTHUR ARMSTRONG.
Student of Medicine, 1913-14 and 1918-19. O.T.C. Infantry, Oct. 1914 to Dec. 1915, Cadet. R.N.V.R., Surgeon-Probationer, Nov. 1915. H.M.S. *Marvel*.

Record of War Service

DENMAN, WALTER JAMES.
George Watson's College. Mus.Bac. 1909. A.R.C.O. 2nd Leicestershire Regiment, May 1909; Bandmaster 1913-19.

DENNING, FREDERICK ARTHUR VERE.
St Andrew's College, Dublin. Student of Medicine, 1910-14. L.R.C.P. & S. (Edin.) and L.R.F.P.S. (Glasg.) 1915. O.T.C. Infantry, May 1911 to Nov. 1913, Cadet. R.N.V.R., Surgeon-Probationer, Aug. 1914. Royal Navy, H.M.S. *Princess Royal*, Surgeon May 1915. Jutland Battle May 1916.

DENNISON, ARTHUR.
Darlington Grammar School. M.B., C.M. 1893; M.D. 1895. R.A.M.C. (Sanitary Staff), Lieut. Oct. 1915; Captain Oct. 1916. Mudros, Malta, and Macedonia, from Nov. 1915 to April 1919.

DENNLER, HANS LESLIE.
Dundee High School. Student of Arts, 1912-15 and 1919. M.A. (Hons. Classics) 1919. Treasurer S.R.C., 1914-15. O.T.C. Infantry, Jan. to July 1915, Cadet. 2/4th Gordon Highlanders, 2nd Lieut. July 1915; Lieut. Jan. 1918. Attached 1st Argyll and Sutherland Highlanders. Staff, Intelligence, Nov. 1918 to Jan. 1919.

DERHAM, THOMAS HANSON CROSSFIELD.
Preston Grammar School. M.B., C.M. 1894. R.A.M.C. (T.), Lieut. 1909; Captain 1912. M.O., Loyal North Lancashire Regiment, France. Shepherd's Bush Hospital.

DERRICK, THOMAS.
Lanark Grammar School. M.B., Ch.B. 1907. N.Z. Medical Corps, Lieut, Aug. 1917; Captain Nov. 1917.

DERRY, DOUGLAS ERITH.
M.B., Ch.B. 1903. R.A.M.C., Lieut. Nov. 1914; Captain Feb. 1916. M.C. Sept. 1917.

DEUCHARS, JAMES McGAVIN.
George Watson's College; First XV. M.B., Ch.B. 1908. R.A.M.C. (T.), Lieut. Feb. 1915; Captain Aug. 1915. 6th Royal Highlanders (Black Watch). M.O. in charge of Wemyss Castle Hospital, Fife.

DEVEREUX, ARTHUR CECIL.
M.B., Ch.B. 1903. F.R.C.S. (Eng.) 1909. No. 4 Coy. Q.R.V.B., Royal Scots, 1900-3. R.A.M.C. (T.), Lieut. 1911; Captain Aug. 1914. 2nd Welsh Field Ambulance and Casualty Clearing Station, Gallipoli, Egypt, and Palestine.

DEWAR, DAVID DEAS.
Edinburgh Academy; First XV. Student of Law, 1891. Writer to the Signet, 1897. 23rd Royal Fusiliers (1st Sportsman's Battn.), Private Oct. 1914. France Nov. 1914 to March 1916. Cambrai and Festubert.

DEWAR, FRANCIS.
Daniel Stewart's College. M.A. (Hons. Classics) 1895. I.C.S. 2/4th and 2/5th Gurkha Rifles, 2nd Lieut. May 1915; Lieut; Temp. Captain Oct. 1917.

Record of War Service

DEWAR, THOMAS FINLAYSON.
Arbroath High School. B.Sc. (P.H.) 1888; D.Sc. 1906; M.B., C.M. 1887 and M.D. (Aberd.) 1890. R.A.M.C. and A.M.S., Acting Surgeon 1888; Surgeon-Major 1901; Lieut.-Col. 1908; Temp. Colonel March 1916-19. South African Campaign, 1900-1. France. D.A.D.M.S., 51st Division. A.D.M.S., First Army, Northern Army, and 57th Division. T.D. 1908. Four times Mentioned in Dispatches. C.B. 1918.

DEWAR, WILLIAM SHAW.
Dingwall Academy. Student of Law, 1908-9. Law Agent, 1913. 4th Seaforth Highlanders, April 1914; Captain March 1915; Major Oct. 1918. Tank Corps, May to Dec. 1918. France Nov. 1914 to Jan. 1918. Dispatches March 1915 and May 1916.

DEY, KSHIRENDRA MOHAN.
Student of Medicine, 1912-18. M.B., Ch.B. 1917. Indian Field Ambulance.

DICK, ALAN MacDONALD.
St Bees Grammar School. M.B., Ch.B. 1906; M.R.C.S. 1909 and F.R.C.S. (Eng.) 1910; L.R.C.P. (Lond.) 1909. Indian Medical Service, 1909; Captain 1912; Brevet-Major, June 1918. Mesopotamian Exp. Force. Dispatches April 1918 and Feb. 1919.

DICK, GEORGE.
George Watson's College. M.B., Ch.B. 1898; B.Sc. (P.H.) 1900. R.A.M.C. (T.), Jan. 1909; Captain 1915. 1st Highland Field Ambulance. France 1915. 14th Stationary Hospital, France, 1918.

DICK, JAMES ADAM.
B.A. (Sydney) 1886. M.B., C.M. 1890; M.D. 1892; F.R.C.S. (Edin.) 1901. Australian Army Medical Corps, Lieut.-Col. May 1915; Colonel April 1918. South African Campaign, 1899-1902. 1st, 2nd, and 3rd Australian General Hospitals, and 1st Australian Casualty Clearing Station, 1915-19. Dispatches Dec. 1917 and Dec. 1918. C.M.G. Jan. 1919.

DICK, JAMES HAMILTON.
Ayr Academy; First XV. Student of Medicine, 1912-15 and 1917-20; M.B., Ch.B. 1920. R.A.M.C. (T.), Scottish Horse Brigade Field Ambulance, Private Oct. 1914. 5th Royal Scots Fusiliers, 2nd Lieut. Aug. 1915; Captain July 1917. France 1916-17. Wounded at Ypres Aug. 1917. M.C. April 1917.

DICK, JOHN.
Ayr Academy; First XV. Student of Medicine, 1910-15; M.B., Ch.B. 1915; D.P.H. 1920. O.T.C. Medical, Nov. 1914-16, Cadet Sergeant. R.A.M.C., Lieut. May 1917; Captain May 1918. Merryflats War Hospital, Glasgow, Nov. 1916 to May 1917. Attached King's African Rifles, East Africa.

Record of War Service

DICK, KENNETH SAGE.
Ayr Academy; First XV. Student of Medicine, 1913-14 and 1919-20. R.A.M.C., (T.), Scottish Horse Brigade Field Ambulance, Private Oct. 1914. 5th Royal Scots Fusiliers (T.), 2nd Lieut. Aug. 1915; Lieut. July 1917. Egypt 1916; France 1917-18. Wounded at Arras Jan. 1918.

DICK, ROBERT JAMES.
George Watson's College. Student of Arts and Medicine, 1892-8; M.B. Ch.B., 1898; M.D. 1910. R.A.M.C., Lieut. March 1917.

DICK, THOMAS.
George Heriot's School. University Battery, E.C.A.V., 1902-6, Corporal. Student of Medicine, 1902-9. H.M. D. S. *Marylebone*.

DICK, WILLIAM CHARLES.
Daniel Stewart's College. Student of Law, 1899-1900. Solicitor. O.T.C. Infantry, May to Oct. 1916, Cadet; Officer Cadet Oct. 1916. 6th King's Own Scottish Borderers, 2nd Lieut. Jan. 1917; Lieut. July 1918; Court-Martial Officer, May 1918; Assistant Staff Captain Oct. 1918. France. Mention Aug. 1918.

DICK-CLELAND, THOMAS S.
Student of Arts and Medicine, 1895-1900 and 1904-6. R.F.A., 2nd Lieut. 1900; Lieut. (Retired) 1903; Lieut. June 1917. South African Campaign, 1900-3.

DICKIE, EDGAR PRIMROSE.
Dumfries Academy. Student of Arts, 1915-16 and 1918-19. O.T.C. Infantry, 1915-16, Cadet. 1/5th and 3rd King's Own Scottish Borderers, Private Nov. 1916; 2nd Lieut. March 1917; Lieut. Sept. 1918; Captain Oct. 1918. M.C. Oct. 1918.

DICKIE, JOHN KOLBE MILNE.
Royal High School. M.B., Ch.B. 1909; M.D. 1912; F.R.C.S. (Edin.) 1913. Demonstrator in Anatomy, 1911-14. R.A.M.C., Lieut. May 1915; Captain May 1916. Ear Specialist to Second Army. France Oct. 1915 to March 1919.

DICKIN, EDWARD PERCIVAL.
Northampton Grammar School. M.B., C.M. 1893; M.D. 1899; M.R.C.S. (Eng.) 1895; L.R.C.P. (Lond.) 1895. R.A.M.C., Captain June 1915. Officer in charge of Medical Division, General Hospital, Tigné, Malta.

DICKINSON, WILLIAM HENRY.
M.B., Ch.B. 1898. Indian Medical Service, Major Jan. 1911.

DICKSON, ALEXANDER.
George Watson's College. Student of Medicine, 1914-15. O.T.C. Artillery, Oct. 1914 to May 1915, Cadet Bombardier. R.F.A. (S.R.), 2nd Lieut. May 1915; Lieut. July 1917. Royal Air Force, No. 17 Squadron, 1918. Indian Frontier 1915-16; Mesopotamia 1916-17; Egypt and Salonika 1917-19; South Russia 1919.

Record of War Service

DICKSON, ALEXANDER BRODIE HILL.
Edinburgh Academy and Glenalmond. O.T.C. 1911-14. Student of Science, 1915-16 and 1918-19. O.T.C. Engineers, Oct. 1915, Cadet. R.E. (T.), City of Edinburgh Fortress, 2nd Lieut. Oct. 1915; Lieut. June 1916. Attached Royal Air Force, June 1918.

DICKSON, CHARLES HAY.
George Heriot's School; O.T.C. 1912-14. Student of Science, 1916 and 1918-19. 10/11th Highland Light Infantry, Private June 1916. France. Wounded and taken Prisoner at Ypres July 1917 to Dec. 1918.

DICKSON, DAVID ELLIOT.
Harris Academy, Dundee. M.B., C.M. 1897; M.D. 1908; F.R.C.S. (Edin.) 1907. R.A.M.C. (T.) 1904, Captain 1908; Major Feb. 1916. 1/7th Royal Highlanders (Black Watch), and 26th General Hospital.

DICKSON, F. W.
Student of Arts. 16th Royal Scots, Private.

DICKSON, IAN DUNBAR.
Epsom College. Cadet Corps 1901-4, 2nd Lieut. M.B., Ch.B. 1909; M.D. 1912. First XV. 9th V.B. Highlanders, Royal Scots, 1904-6, Private. R.A.M.C. (S.R.), Captain Dec. 1909. France. Wounded. Dispatches 1917. M.C. 1918.

DICKSON, JAMES.
M.B., Ch.B. 1916. R.A.M.C., Captain April 1917. M.C.

DICKSON, JAMES TODD.
M.B., Ch.B. 1908. R.A.M.C., Lieut. 1st Royal Irish Regiment. France 1915; Salonika 1916.

DICKSON, JOHN RHODES.
M.B., C.M. 1889; D.P.H., R.C.P.S. (Eng.) 1899. R.A.M.C., Lieut. April 1915; Captain April 1916. Bacteriologist.

DICKSON, JOHN ROBERT.
Edinburgh Academy; First XV. and XI. B.A. (Oxford). Student of Law, 1906-9. Advocate, 1909. 3rd and 5th Cameron Highlanders, April 1915; Lieut. Nov. 1916; Captain Nov. 1918. Attached 10th Royal Scots.

DICKSON, MAURICE RHYND.
Marlborough; First XV. and XI. B.A. (Oxford). First XV. Student of Law, 1904-7; Writer to the Signet, 1907. Scottish Rugby and Cricket International. 8th Royal Scots Fusiliers, Lieut. Sept. 1915; Captain Nov. 1915; Major July 1916; Lieut.-Col. May 1918. 8th Duke of Cornwall's Light Infantry, and 12th Argyll and Sutherland Highlanders. France, Macedonia, and Bulgaria, 1915-19. D.S.O. Legion of Honour (Officier), France. Twice Mentioned in Dispatches.

Record of War Service

DICKSON, ROBERT CECIL. [Killed in India in 1919.]
    M.B., Ch.B. 1911. O.T.C. Artillery, Oct. 1908 to Feb. 1911, Cadet. R.A.M.C. (S.R.), Lieut. May 1912; Captain Aug. 1915. France Aug. 1914 to Nov. 1915.

DICKSON, RONALD GEORGE ALEXANDER.
    George Watson's College and Glenalmond. Cadet Corps 1906-9. Student of Arts and Medicine, 1909-14 and 1919. O.T.C. Infantry, 1910-14, Cadet C.S.M. 6th Royal Highlanders (Black Watch) (T.), 2nd Lieut. Nov. 1914; Lieut. July 1917; Temp. Captain Dec. 1916 to March 1917, and March to Oct. 1919. France May 1915 to Feb. 1919; The Rhine, Feb. to Aug. 1919. Wounded June 1915.

DICKSON, THOMAS BLAIR.
    George Watson's College. O.T.C. 1913-15. Student of Science, 1919. O.T.C. Artillery, Jan. to April 1917, Cadet; Officer Cadet April 1917. R.F.C., 2nd Lieut. Aug. 1917; Lieut. April 1918.

DICKSON, THOMAS GRAEME.
    Fettes. Student of Medicine, 1886-96; L.R.C.P. & S. (Edin.), and L.R.F.P.S. (Glasg.) 1896. Derbyshire County Cricket. R.A.M.C., Lieut. May 1918; Captain May 1919. Machine-Gun Corps. Military Hospital, Clipstone and Cannock Chase, and Lord Derby War Hospital, Warrington. Neurologist.

DICKSON, THOMAS HERBERT.
    George Watson's College. M.B., Ch.B. 1906. R.A.M.C., Captain Jan. 1913.

DICKSON, WALTER.
    George Watson's College. M.B., C.M. 1890; M.D. 1901. R.A.M.C., Lieut. Nov. 1915; Captain Dec. 1916. M.O., Duke of Cornwall's Light Infantry; Cambridge and Wellesley House Officers' Hospitals, Aldershot. S.M.O., A.S.C., Aldershot.

DICKSON, WILLIAM ELLIOT CARNEGIE.
    Edinburgh Academy. B.Sc. 1898; M.B., Ch.B. 1901; M.D. 1905; F.R.C.P. (Edin.) 1908. Lecturer on Pathological Bacteriology. Civil Surgeon, 1915-17. R.A.M.C., Captain July 1917 to April 1919.

DICKSON, WILLIAM FERGUSON.
    Dumfries Academy. Student of Arts, 1912-14. 1st Reserve Regiment of Cavalry, Trooper Sept. 1914. 13th Scottish Rifles, 2nd Lieut. March 1915; Lieut. July 1917; Acting Captain and Adjutant, April 1918. 5th Royal Irish Fusiliers. Suvla Sept. 1915; Serbia Oct. to Dec. 1915; Macedonia 1916-17; Palestine Oct. 1917 to April 1918; France May 1918 to June 1919. Dispatches 1919.

DICKSON, WILLIAM MUIR.
    Student of Medicine, 1909-14; M.B., Ch.B. 1914. R.A.M.C. (S.R.), Lieut. Nov. 1914; Captain May 1915.

DILL, ALFRED VINCENT.
    Marlborough. Student of Medicine, 1911-16; M.B., Ch.B. (Hons.) 1916. Anatomy Staff, 1915-16. O.T.C. Medical, Oct. 1914 to July 1916, Cadet Corporal. R.A.M.C. (T.), Lieut. July 1916; Captain July 1917.

Record of War Service

DILL, MARCUS GRAHAM.
Marlborough. M.B., Ch.B. 1905; M.D. 1909. R.A.M.C., Lieut. 1906; Captain 1909; Brevet Major Jan. 1916; Major Jan. 1918. Dispatches Jan. 1916.

DILLON, FREDERICK.
St Bede's, Manchester. M.B., Ch.B. 1909. R.A.M.C., Lieut. Sept. 1915; Captain Sept. 1916. Neurologist to Third Army, France, Dec. 1916 to Oct. 1918. Dispatches Jan. 1919.

DINGLE, EDWARD DOUGLAS.
Municipal Secondary School, Derby. Student of Medicine, 1915-16 and 1918-19. O.T.C. Medical, May 1918 to March 1919, Cadet. R.G.A. (Siege) Gunner Oct. 1916; Bombardier Dec. 1916. France May to Aug. 1917.

DINGWALL-FORDYCE, ALEXANDER.
Edinburgh Academy. M.B., Ch.B. 1898; M.D. 1904; F.R.C.P. (Edin.) 1903. Physician, Royal Hospital Sick Children. R.A.M.C., Captain Aug. 1915; Acting Major Oct. 1918.

DINWIDDIE, JAMES LINTON NORRIS.
Dumfries Academy. Student of Arts, 1914-16 and 1917-19; M.A. 1919. Munition Factory, 1915-18. City of Edinburgh R.E. (Volunteers), Corporal 1917-18.

DINWIDDIE, MELVILLE.
Dumfries Academy; First XI. Student of Arts and Divinity, 1910-14; M.A. 1914. O.T.C. Infantry, Oct. 1910 to Aug. 1914, Cadet Colour-Sergeant. 3rd and 1st Gordon Highlanders, 2nd Lieut. Aug. 1914; Captain and Adjutant April 1915; Lieut. (Regulars) Dec. 1914; Captain Jan. 1917; Staff Captain July 1916; D.A.A.G. Oct. 1917; Temp. Major (G.H.Q. Staff) Nov. 1917. France. M.C. July 1915; D.S.O. June 1917; O.B.E. June 1919. Dispatches July 1915, June 1916, June 1917, Jan. 1918, Jan. and June 1919.

DISHINGTON, ISAAC.
Glasgow Academy. O.T.C. 1913-15. University O.T.C. Artillery, 1917, Cadet Corporal; Officer Cadet Jan. 1918. R.G.A., 2nd Lieut. Aug. 1918.

DIXON, FREDERICK.
Student of Arts, 1912-15. O.T.C. Infantry, Oct. to Dec. 1914, Cadet. Royal Scots, Private Dec. 1914. 9th King's Own Yorkshire Light Infantry, 2nd Lieut. 1915.

DIXON, JAMES HERBERT.
M.B., C.M. 1895; M.D. 1908. R.A.M.C. (T.), 1904; Captain May 1908; Temp. Major May 1915; Major Nov. 1916. London Mounted Brigade Field Ambulance, 58th Division, 18th and 5th Corps. France Aug. 1914; Egypt. Staff A.M.D.S., War Office.

DIXSON, DOUGLAS HONEYMAN.
Edinburgh Academy. University O.T.C. Artillery, 1915, Cadet. R.F.A. (S.R.), 2nd Lieut. Nov. 1915; Lieut. July 1917. France. Wounded.

Record of War Service

DOBBIE, JAMES.
Bathgate Academy. Student of Arts, 1917 and 1919-20; M.A. 1920. 6th Machine-Gun Corps, April 1918.

DOBBIN, JOHN ROBSON.
Royal Academical Institute, Belfast. M.B., Ch.B. 1903. Army Medical Staff Corps, 1899-1903, Corporal. R.A.M.C., Lieut. Sept. 1915; Captain Sept. 1916.

DOBELL, CLARENCE BRIAN.
Clifton College. M.B., C.M. 1893; M.D. 1904; M.R.C.S. (Eng.) and L.R.C.P. (Lond.) 1894; F.R.C.P. (Edin.) 1918. R.A.M.C., Lieut. April 1915; Captain 1916; Major March 1917. Mention 1917.

DOBIE, DAVID ROBERTSON.
George Watson's College. M.B., C.M. 1882; M.D. 1885; F.R.C.S. (Edin.) 1902; D.P.H. (Edin.) 1906. 2nd Vol. Battn. King's Own Scottish Borderers, Lieut. 1897; Captain. R.A.M.C. (T.), Major 1909.

DOBIE, JOHN GORDON.
George Watson's College. University O.T.C. Infantry, Nov. 1915 to Oct. 1916, Cadet Sergeant; Officer Cadet Oct. 1916. 8th Seaforth Highlanders, 2nd Lieut. Jan. 1917. France 1917. Invalided out 1918.

DOBIE, WILLIAM GARDINER MURCHIE.
Dumfries Academy. Student of Arts and Law, 1911-15 and 1918-19; M.A. 1914. O.T.C. Infantry, Oct. to Dec. 1914, Cadet. 4th Cameron Highlanders (T.), 2nd Lieut. Jan. 1915; Lieut. June 1916. 1st Lovat Scouts. France March to July 1915, Nov. to Dec. 1916, and Nov. to Dec. 1917. Invalided home June 1918.

DOBIE, WILLIAM JARDINE.
George Watson's College. Student of Law, 1910-13; Thow Scholar. 1st Vol. Battn. Royal Scots, Private Aug. 1914; Corporal and Sergeant 1918.

DOBSON, JOHN GREENLAW.
George Heriot's School. Student of Science and Medicine, 1909-15 and 1918-19; B.Sc. 1913; M.B., Ch.B. 1915. B.R.C.S. (Dresser), 1914. Royal Navy, Surgeon-Lieut., April 1915. Russia. Wounded. D.S.O. Sept. 1918.

DOBSON, WILLIAM GOLDIE.
George Heriot's School; First XV. and XI. Student of Arts and Science, 1912-15 and 1918-19. O.T.C. Artillery, Oct. 1914 to Feb. 1915, Cadet. R.F.A., 1st Lowland Brigade (T.), 2nd Lieut. Jan. 1915; Lieut. July 1915; Acting Captain March 1916 to March 1919. India 1916; Mesopotamia 1917-19.

DODD, GEORGE EDWARD.
George Watson's College. M.A. 1904; B.D. 1907. Indian Ecclesiastical Establishment, 1912. Junior Chaplain, Church of Scotland, Jan. 1914. Indian Exp. Force, Egypt, 1914. France 1915 to Dec. 1916; India 1917-19.

Record of War Service

DODD, HENRY BLACK.
George Watson's College. B.Sc. 1913. O.T.C. Engineers, 1910-13, Cadet. Madras Rifles, Lieut. 1913.

DODGSON, HENRY.
Pocklington, Yorks; First XI. M.B., Ch.B. 1901. Athletics. Volunteers and Territorial Force, 1895-1911. R.A.M.C., Temp. Captain Dec. 1916; Major Dec. 1917; Lieut.-Col. 1918. France 1917 and Nov. to Dec. 1918. M.O., 2nd Worcestershire Regiment; 19th Field Ambulance, 33rd Division; 310th London Field Ambulance, March to Oct. 1918; 42nd Motor Ambulance Convoy, 22nd Corps. T.D. March 1919.

DODS, JOSEPH ESPIE.
Brisbane Grammar School. M.B., Ch.B. 1897; D.P.H., R.C.P.S.I. 1898. Medical Staff Corps, 1896-7, Sergeant. South African Campaign, 1899-1900, Queensland Defence Force, Captain 1899. Australian Army Medical Corps, Captain Oct. 1914; Major Jan. 1916; Lieut.-Col. Jan. 1917. Egypt. Wounded at Gallipoli Aug. 1915. M.C. Jan. 1916; D.S.O. Jan. 1917. Dispatches Jan. 1916 and Jan. 1917.

DODSON, HENRY REGINALD.
Royal High School; First XV. and XI. Student of Medicine, 1914-19; M.B., Ch.B. 1919. O.T.C. Infantry, Oct. 1914 to June 1916, Cadet Sergeant; and Unattached List (T.F.), 2nd Lieut. June 1916 to Nov. 1918.

DOHERTY, JOSEPH DOMINIC.
M.B., C.M. 1897; M.D. 1899. R.A.M.C., Lieut.; Captain June 1917.

DOIG, WILLIAM.
Daniel Stewart's College. M.B., C.M. 1881; M.D. 1892; D.P.H. (Dublin) 1918. R.A.M.C. (T.), Major 1912. Mobilised Nov. 1914 to March 1919. 1/4th King's Own Scottish Borderers.

DOLD, CEDRIC LEWIS.
Student of Medicine, 1908-14; M.B., Ch.B. 1914. O.T.C. Artillery, 1908 to Feb. 1914, Cadet. R.A.M.C., Lieut.; Captain Aug. 1915.

DOLONGHAN, ALEXANDER.
Annan Academy. Student of Arts, 1918. 53rd T.R. Battn. Highland Light Infantry, Private July 1918.

DON, JAMES LINDSAY.
Dundee High School. University O.T.C. Infantry, March to August 1917, Cadet; Officer Cadet Sept. 1917. R.G.A. (T.), North Scottish, 2nd Lieut. March 1918; Lieut. Sept. 1919. Attached 37th Mountain Battery, India.

Record of War Service

DONALD, ARCHIBALD.
   Craigmount House, Edinburgh. M.B., C.M. 1883; M.D. 1886; M.R.C.S. (Eng.) 1883; F.R.C.P. (Lond.) 1915. Professor of Obstetrics, University of Manchester. R.A.M.C. (T.), Lieut. July 1910; Captain Jan. 1912. Mobilised Aug. 1914. 2nd Western General Hospital, Manchester.

DONALD, ARCHIBALD DOUGLAS.
   George Watson's College and Sedbergh; First XV. B.Sc. 1911. O.T.C. Engineers, May 1909 to Sept. 1911, Cadet Corporal. 1/1st City of Edinburgh Field Coy. R.E. (T.), 2nd Lieut. May 1915; Lieut. June 1916.

DONALD, CHARLES WILLIAM.
   Kirkwall School. M.B., C.M. 1892; M.D. 1904; F.R.C.S. (Edin.) 1899. R.A.M.C., South African Campaign, 1900-1; Lieut. Feb. 1915; Captain Feb. to June 1916. Egypt Aug. 1915 to June 1916.

DONALD, DAVID.
   Student of Medicine, 1888-92. L.R.C.P. & S. (Edin.), L.F.P.S. (Glasg.) 1892; M.D. (Durham) 1908. R.A.M.C., Major 1913; Lieut.-Col. Dec. 1916. Canadian Artillery, 1914-15. Medical Boards, 1916. Hospital Ship, 1917. France 1918-19. A.D.M.S. Dispatches (three times). Order of St John of Jerusalem.

DONALD, DOUGLAS ALAN.
   Sedbergh. M.B., Ch.B. 1912. R.A.M.C., Lieut. June 1915; Captain June 1916 to April 1919. M.C. 1916.

DONALD, GEORGE HENRY.
   Albany Academy, Glasgow. M.A. 1898. Minister, Church of Scotland. Chaplain, Highland Division, Captain Feb. 1915; Major April 1918. France 1915.

DONALD, HENRY.
   Clydebank School; First XI., Football. Student of Arts, 1913-16; M.A. 1919. 3rd Royal Scots, Private Jan. 1916; L/Corporal Sept. 1916. Attached Fourth Army H.Q.

DONALD, PERCY.
   George Watson's College. B.Sc. 1912. A.M.I.C.E. O.T.C. Engineers, 1910-13, Cadet. Field Coy. Engineers, R.N. Division, Sapper Sept. 1914; 2nd Lieut. Nov. 1916. R.E., 51st Field Coy., 1917. R.E., Light Railway Forward Coy., Lieut. May 1918; Acting Captain Aug. 1918-19. Gallipoli 1915; France 1916-19. Arras, Ypres, and Cambrai.

DONALD, POLLOK.
   George Watson's College. M.B., Ch.B. 1907; D.P.H. (Vict.). R.A.M.C., Lieut. Oct. 1915; Captain Oct. 1916.

DONALDSON, CHARLES JAMES.
   Royal High School. M.A. 1905; B.D. 1908. Minister, Church of Scotland, Chaplain, 4th Class, Sept. 1915. 6th Scottish Rifles and 9th Highland Light Infantry. Invalided home Sept. 1916. Coast Watcher, Royal Navy, 1916-18.

Record of War Service

DONALDSON, HERBERT.
George Watson's College. Student of Law, 1905-7. Chartered Accountant, 1909. R.N.V.R., Ordinary Seaman, Dec. 1914. Royal Naval Division, 2nd Lieut. Nov. 1915; Lieut. Dec. 1917. Gallipoli and France. Wounded at Beaucourt (Battle of the Ancre) Nov. 1916, and Martinpuich March 1918. D.S.O. March 1918. Dispatches.

DONALDSON, JAMES.
Daniel Stewart's College. M.B., Ch.B. 1908. R.A.M.C., Lieut. May 1917; Captain May 1918. France and Italy.

DONALDSON, THOMAS.
Bo'ness Academy. Student of Arts, 1912-16. Royal Scots, Private.

DONNAN, JOHN McFARLANE.
Port William School. M.B., Ch.B. 1912. O.T.C. Medical, Jan. 1909 to Feb. 1912, Cadet. R.A.M.C., Lieut. April 1916; Captain April 1917; Acting Major March 1918. Invalided out.

DORWARD, R. STEWART.
Galashiels Academy. Student of Science, 1912-15 and 1919. O.T.C. Engineers, Nov. 1913 to Feb. 1915, Cadet L/Corporal. R.E. (T.), 2nd Lieut. Feb. 1915; Lieut. June 1916. Attached 1st Mounted Division, Signal Squadron. Mechanical (Cable) Trench Excavators. France.

DOTT, GEORGE.
Royal High School. Student of Science, 1912-14. R.G.A. (T.) (Forth), Gunner Sept. 1914. 70th Siege Battery. France March 1916 to Dec. 1918.

DOUDNEY, HUGH D.
Student of Medicine, 1903-9. King Edward's Horse, Private Aug. 1914. 12th Royal Fusiliers, Lieut. March 1916; Captain. France. Twice Wounded.

DOUGAL, ALEXANDER.
George Watson's College; First XV. Student of Law, 1911-15; M.A. 1914; LL.B. 1915. Writer to the Signet, 1919. R.G.A. (T.) (Forth), 2nd Lieut. Nov. 1915; Lieut. June 1916. Siege Battery, France, Nov. 1917.

DOUGAL, ALEXANDER TAYLOR.
Linlithgow Academy. Student of Science, 1913-14. O.T.C. Engineers, Oct. 1913 to Oct. 1914, Cadet. R.E., Dundee Fortress (T.), Sapper Sept. 1914. Officer Cadet Sept. 1916. 2nd Royal Highlanders (Black Watch), 2nd Lieut. Jan. 1917; Lieut. July 1918 to Aug. 1919. Attached Royal Air Force, Aug. 1918 to March 1919. France 1914.

DOUGAL, LAURENCE DICKSON.
University O.T.C. Infantry, March 1917, Cadet; Officer Cadet Oct. 1917. 4th Royal Scots, 2nd Lieut. Feb. 1918; Lieut. Sept. 1919. The Rhine, Nov. 1918 to Oct. 1919.

Record of War Service

DOUGALL, ROBERT.
　　Perth Academy. Student of Science, 1913-15. R.E. (T.), Sapper Jan. 1915; L/Corporal May 1915; Corporal Sept. 1916; Sergeant Jan. 1917. Attached 1/1st City of Dundee. France.

DOUGHTY, ALLAN GORDON.
　　George Watson's College. Student of Law, 1908-10. 7th Royal Highlanders (Black Watch), 2nd Lieut. Oct. 1915; Lieut. July 1917. Wounded March 1918.

DOUGHTY, WILLIAM FORREST.
　　Boroughmuir School. M.A. 1913. O.T.C. Infantry, Jan. 1911 to March 1914, Cadet. Lothians and Border Horse (T.), Private Nov. 1914. 4th King's Own Scottish Borderers, 2nd Lieut. Aug. 1917; Lieut. Feb. 1918. Palestine and France. Wounded at Cambrai Oct. 1918.

DOUGLAS, ANDREW RICHMOND.
　　M.B., Ch.B. 1902. R.A.M.C., Lieut.; Captain.

DOUGLAS, ARCHIBALD MATHESON.
　　George Watson's College. O.T.C. 1909-13, Corporal. Student of Arts, 1913-14 and 1918-20; M.A. 1920. O.T.C. Infantry, 1913-14, Cadet. 9th Royal Scots (T.), Private Sept. 1914. R.E. (Special Coy.), Corporal July 1915.

DOUGLAS, CHARLES.
　　Dumfries Academy. M.B., Ch.B. 1901. R.A.M.C. (T.), 1909; Captain Sept. 1914. Ayrshire and 18th Brigade R.H.A. Dispatches 1918.

DOUGLAS, CHARLES EDWARD.
　　Edinburgh Collegiate School. M.B., C.M. 1877; M.D. 1882; D.P.H. (Camb.) 1894; F.R.C.S. (Edin.) 1898. Q.E.R. 1873-7, Private. 1st Fife Royal Volunteers, 1884. South African Campaign, 1900-1; Hon. Captain 1901. R.A.M.C. (T.), Lieut.-Col. 1907, attached R.E. France. 51st Highland Casualty Clearing Station. 223rd Brigade, and D.A.D.M.S., 23rd Army Corps. V.D. 1902.

DOUGLAS, ERNEST J.
　　George Watson's College. Student of Science, 1916 and 1919. O.T.C. Infantry, May to Sept. 1916, Cadet; Officer Cadet Sept. 1916. Machine-Gun Corps, 2nd Lieut. March 1917; Lieut. Sept. 1918 to Jan. 1919. Attached Royal Naval Division, France.

DOUGLAS, GEORGE JAMES C.
　　George Watson's College. Student of Arts, 1911-14; M.A. 1914. O.T.C. Artillery, Oct. 1909-14, Cadet. Chaplain, 4th Class, June 1916. France.

DOUGLAS, GEORGE PURVES.
　　George Watson's College. Student of Science, 1911-14; B.Sc. 1914. O.T.C. Engineers, Feb. 1912 to Nov. 1914, Cadet. 15th Royal Scots, 2nd Lieut. Oct. 1914; Lieut. Sept. 1915. France. M.C. and Dispatches Aug. 1916.

Record of War Service

DOUGLAS, GEORGE ROBERT POYNTER.
Perth Academy. Student of Law, 1902-3. Solicitor, 1905. Volunteer Service, 1899. Highland Cyclist Battn., Captain Nov. 1914. Attached 8th Cheshire Regiment. British Military Mission, South Russia, March 1919. Dispatches 1917. M.C. June 1918.

DOUGLAS, JAMES.
George Heriot's School. Student of Law, 1902-4. Chartered Accountant, 1904. R.N.V.R., Paymaster-Lieut.-Commander 1907-10. R.N.R., Assistant Paymaster, June 1915; Paymaster-Lieut. Feb. 1919. Cape Station, South Africa.

DOUGLAS, JOHN.
George Watson's College. M.A. 1905. Minister, U.F. Church of Scotland. Y.M.C.A., France, April to Aug. 1915. Chaplain; Captain Dec. 1915 to June 1919; France. No. 2 General Hospital; 59th Casualty Clearing Station; 20th Field Ambulance; G.H.Q.; 2nd Echelon, and No. 8 Stationary Hospital. Invalided out.

DOUGLAS, JOHN PRIMROSE.
Dumfries Academy. M.B., Ch.B. 1900. R.A.M.C., Lieut. Feb. 1916; Captain Feb. 1917 to April 1919.

DOUGLAS, MACKENZIE.
George Watson's College; First XV. M.A. 1903; M.B., Ch.B. 1907; M.D. 1910. R.A.M.C., Lieut. Dec. 1914; Captain Feb. 1916. France and Salonika.

DOUGLAS, OTTO GERRARD.
Royal High School. University O.T.C. Artillery, Dec. 1916 to June 1917, Cadet; Officer Cadet June 1917. R.F.A., 91st Brigade, 2nd Lieut. Oct. 1917; Lieut. May 1919. France.

DOUGLAS, ROBERT.
George Watson's College. M.A. (Hons. Classics) 1912. 46th Punjabis (I.A.R.O.). 2nd Lieut. Aug. 1916; Lieut. Aug. 1917; Temp. Captain Nov. 1917. 49th Bengalis; Mohmand Blockade Force, 1916-17; Waziristan Field Force, 1917.

DOUGLAS, WILLIAM GEORGE.
Edinburgh Academy. Student of Science, 1912-14; C.D.A., 1919. 8th King's Own Scottish Borderers, Private Oct. 1911; 2nd Lieut. Dec. 1914; Lieut. Sept. 1915. France July 1915 to April 1916, and May to June 1918. Wounded June 1918.

DOUGLAS, WILLIAM LOW.
Falkirk High School; First XI., Cricket and Football. Student of Arts, 1912-15; M.A. (Hons. Classics) 1916. 11th Royal Scots, Private Dec. 1915; Corporal Aug. 1916; 2nd Lieut. Jan. 1917; Lieut. June 1918. France. Taken Prisoner at Gauche Wood in March 1918. M.C. Oct. 1917.

Record of War Service

DOUGLAS, WILLIAM SANDILANDS.
Edinburgh Academy. O.T.C. 1914-15. Student of Arts, 1915-16. O.T.C. Artillery, 1916-17, Cadet Corporal; Officer Cadet June 1917. R.F.A. (S.R.), 2nd Lieut. Oct. 1917; Lieut. April 1919. France. The Rhine 1919.

DOUGLAS-CRAWFORD, DOUGLAS.
Liverpool Institute. M.B., C.M. 1887; F.R.C.S. (Eng.) 1894. Lecturer in Clinical Surgery and Surgical Anatomy, University of Liverpool. R.A.M.C. (T.), Captain July 1908; Major 1917. 1st Western General Hospital, Liverpool; 14th and 57th General Hospitals. Overseas 1917.

DOUGLAS ELLIOT, ROBERT ARTHUR.
Edinburgh Institution, and Aylwin College, Arnside. Student of Science, 1913-14. Northern Bengal Mounted Rifles, Trooper Nov. 1914 to Dec. 1915. I.A.R.O., 2nd Lieut. Jan. 1916; Lieut. Jan. 1917; Captain Jan. 1920. G.H.Q., Baghdad, Mesopotamia.

DOULL, DONALD.
Wick Academy. M.A. 1904; A.R.C.Sc. (Lond.). 2nd and 5th Argyll and Sutherland Highlanders, Private June 1918. Educational Instructor, Calais.

DOVE, GEORGE.
Student of Science, 1865. A.S.C., Major. Transport Officer. Mersey Defences, Western Command.

DOVE, ROLLAND ATKINSON.
Sedbergh; First XV. and XI. M.B., C.M., L.R.C.P. & S. (Edin.) and L.F.P.S. (Glasg.) 1893; D.P.H., R.C.P.S. (Eng.) 1900. R.A.M.C. (T.), Major Aug. 1914. 5th Southern General Hospital, 1914-16; 29th Stationary Hospital, Salonika, 1916; 29th Stationary Hospital, Italy, 1917. O.C. Prisoners of War Hospital, Arguala, Italy, 1918. Italian War Medal (Battle of Asiago Plateau).

DOVEY, ARCHIBALD CAMPBELL.
Merchiston Castle and Bedford Grammar School. O.T.C. 1911-12. Student of Medicine, 1914-15 and 1918-19. O.T.C. Artillery, 1914-15, Cadet. R.F.A., 2nd Lieut. Aug. 1915; Lieut. July 1917. France March 1916 to Dec. 1918.

DOVEY, JOHN EDWARD.
Merchiston Castle and Bedford Grammar School. O.T.C. 1911-12. Student of Medicine, 1919-20. O.T.C. Artillery, Oct. 1915 to March 1916, Cadet; Officer Cadet March 1916. R.F.A., 2nd Lieut. July 1916; Lieut. Jan. 1918. France. Wounded Nov. 1916 and Gassed Aug. 1918.

DOW, ALASTAIR I.
George Heriot's School. Student of Arts, 1914-16. 11th Gordon Highlanders, 2nd Lieut.

Record of War Service

DOW, CARL WILLIAM.
Perth Academy. Student of Science, 1914-15. Army Veterinary Corps, Private March 1915; L/Corporal Dec. 1915; Corporal Oct. 1916 Invalided out July 1918.

DOW, NORMAN DAVID.
Perth Academy. B.Sc. 1911. Princess Patricia's Canadian Light Infantry, Private; Lieut. April 1917. France 1915. M.M.

DOW, ROBERT.
M.B., Ch.B. 1911. R.A.M.C., Lieut. July 1915; Captain July 1916.

DOW, THOMAS MILLER.
George Watson's College; First XV. Student of Arts, 1909-14; M.A. (Hons. Classics) 1914. Boxing (Featherweight). O.T.C. Infantry, March 1910-14, Cadet. Indian Army Reserve, 2nd Lieut. 1916; Lieut. 1917. N.-W. Frontier, India, and Mesopotamia.

DOWDEN, ARTHUR ERNEST.
Edinburgh Academy. Student of Medicine, 1913-15. O.T.C. Infantry, Sept. 1914 to Jan. 1915, Cadet. 9th Gordon Highlanders, Private and Sergeant Jan. 1915; 2nd Lieut. Aug. 1917; Acting Captain Oct. 1918; Lieut. May 1919. Divisional Intelligence Officer, Feb. to Oct. 1918. Liaison Officer, Trieste, 1919. Dispatches June and Oct. 1918.

DOWDEN, JOHN WHEELER.
Merchiston Castle; First XI. M.B., C.M. 1890; F.R.C.S. (Edin.) 1894. R.A.M.C. (T.), Captain July 1908. 2nd Scottish General Hospital.

DOWER, ALEXANDER.
George Watson's College. Student of Medicine, 1914-15 and 1917-19. Anatomy Staff, 1918-19. 14th Argyll and Sutherland Highlanders, Private.

DOWIE, GEORGE.
James Gillespie's School. Student of Science, 1895-7. R.A.M.C., Sergeant.

DOWNIE, DAVID.
Musselburgh Grammar School; First XI. Student of Arts, 1907-14; M.A. 1914. 1/10th and 7th Royal Scots, Private May 1917; L/Corporal Nov. 1917.

DOWNIE, WILLIAM.
Bo'ness School. Student of Arts, 1914-16 and 1919-20; M.A. 1920. Highland Light Infantry, Private March 1917; Corporal. 6th Queen's Own Royal West Kent Regiment, 2nd Lieut. Jan. 1918. France.

DOWNIE, WILLIAM JAMES.
Lanark School. M.A. 1913. R.A.M.C., Private Oct. 1915; Corporal March 1918. Egypt Oct. 1916 to Aug. 1919.

Record of War Service

DRAKE, LESLIE ALEXANDER.
King Edward VII. School, King's Lynn. M.B., C.M. 1902. R.A.M.C., Lieut. Jan. 1915; Captain Jan. 1916.

DRENNAN, ALEXANDER MURRAY.
Kelvinside Academy, Glasgow. M.B., Ch.B. 1906; F.R.C.P. (Edin.). Professor of Pathology, Otago University, New Zealand. R.A.M.C., Lieut. Oct. 1915. Pathologist, No. 27 General Hospital, Mudros, 1915-16, and 21st General Hospital, Alexandria, 1916.

DRENNAN, MATHEW ROBERTSON.
Ayr Academy. M.A. 1907; M.B., Ch.B. 1910; F.R.C.S. (Edin.) Demonstrator in Anatomy, 1911-13. South African Medical Corps. 7th Mounted Brigade Field Ambulance, Captain Feb. 1915.

DREVER, JOHN.
Leith Academy. Student of Arts, 1911-15; M.A. 1915. R.A.M.C., Private April 1915; Corporal Nov. 1915 to Dec. 1917.

DREVER, JOHN BARRY STEWART.
George Heriot's School. Student of Law, 1912-14. R.A.S.C., Corporal June 1915.

DREVER, WALTER SINCLAIR.
Broughton School, Edinburgh. Student of Law, 1914-15 and 1919-20. 9th Royal Scots, Private Dec. 1914; Corporal. 5th Scottish Rifles, 2nd Lieut. Dec. 1917. Invalided home May 1915. France. Wounded and Gassed May 1918.

DREW, FRANCIS CHARLES.
Diocesan College, Rondebosch, Cape. M.B., Ch.B. 1902; D.P.H. 1907. South African Medical Corps, Captain Oct. 1914. R.A.M.C., Captain July 1915. 139th Field Ambulance, 1917. South African Rebellion, 1914-15; German West Africa; Salonika 1915; France 1916-17. Invalided out 1917.

DREW, JOHN ALEXANDER.
Fettes College. B.A. (Camb.) 1902. Student of Divinity, 1902-5. Minister, Church of Scotland. 16th Royal Scots, Private Nov. 1914. 4/5th Royal Highlanders (Black Watch), Lieut. 1915; Acting Captain and Adjutant, 1918. France June 1916 to Feb. 1919.

DREYER, FREDERICK BERNARDUS.
M.B., Ch.B. 1912; M.D. 1917. R.A.M.C., Lieut. 71st Field Ambulance.

DRUMMOND, ANDREW.
Daniel Stewart's College. B.Sc. 1908. A.M.I.C.E. R.E., Officer Cadet Aug. 1916; 2nd Lieut. Oct. 1916; Lieut. April 1918-19.

DRUMMOND, GRAHAM THOMSON.
Daniel Stewart's College. M.B., Ch.B. 1904. R.A.M.C., Lieut. Aug. 1917; Captain Aug. 1918.

Record of War Service

DRUMMOND, JOHN.
Napier High School, New Zealand. First XV. and XI. Cadet Corps 1897-1902, Lieut. M.B., Ch.B. 1910; M.D. 1913; M.R.C.P. (Edin.). South African Medical Corps, Captain Sept. 1915 to April 1919. Dispatches June 1919.

DRUMMOND, JOHN WHITEHORN.
George Watson's College; O.T.C. 1914-15. Student of Arts, 1915-16 and 1918-20; M.A. 1920. O.T.C. Infantry, Oct. 1915 to June 1916, Cadet. 3rd Royal Highlanders (Black Watch), Private April 1916. Cameron Highlanders, 2nd Lieut. Sept. 1918 to Feb. 1919.

DRUMMOND, REDVERS WHITE SMITH.
Royal High School; First XI. Student of Law, 1917 and 1920. O.T.C. Infantry, Dec. 1917 to May 1918, Cadet. Royal Air Force, Cadet May 1918; Flight Cadet Oct. 1918 to Jan. 1919.

DRUMMOND, WILLIAM MILLER.
Royal High School, and St Mary's School, Melrose. Student of Law, 1908-10. Chartered Accountant, 1911. O.T.C. Infantry, Oct. 1914 to July 1915, Cadet. 3rd attached 1st Cameron Highlanders, 2nd Lieut. July 1915; Acting Captain Sept. 1916; Lieut. July 1917. 1st Infantry Brigade, Staff Captain May 1918. Wounded three times. France 1915-19. M.C. Sept. 1916; Croix de Guerre avec Palme Oct. 1918. Dispatches Nov. 1918.

DRUMMOND SHIELS, THOMAS.
University O.T.C. Infantry, Aug. to Oct. 1915, Cadet. 6th Royal Scots, 2nd Lieut. Oct. 1915; Lieut. July 1917; Captain April 1918. Attached 27th Trench Mortar Battery. France. M.C. July 1918. Croix de Guerre (Belgian) Sept. 1918. Dispatches 1919.

DRYBURGH, ALEXANDER MITCHELL.
George Heriot's School. Student of Arts, 1914-15 and 1918-19. 1st and 2nd Lovat Scouts, 2nd Lieut. June 1915. 10th Cameron Highlanders.

DRYNAN, ALEXANDER ERSKINE.
Bedford Grammar School. M.B., Ch.B. 1911. R.A.M.C., Captain Oct. 1915; Acting Major March 1918. 1/4th Lincolnshire Regiment.

DRYSDALE, MATTHEW ROBERT.
Sandymount Academical Institution. B.A. (Trinity College, Dublin). Student of Divinity, 1912-15. O.T.C. Artillery, Oct. 1914 to March 1915, Cadet. R.G.A. (T.) (Forth), 2nd Lieut. March 1915; Lieut. June 1916. Singapore Sept. 1918 to Sept. 1919.

DUDDY, HENRY MERCER.
Kirkcaldy High School. O.T.C. 1914-16. University O.T.C. Infantry, Dec. 1917 to July 1918, Cadet; Officer Cadet July to Oct. 1918. Artists' Rifles O.T.C., Oct. 1918 to Jan. 1919. R.A.S.C., Private.

Record of War Service

DUDGEON, WILLIAM CUNNINGHAM.
Edinburgh Academy; First XV. Student of Law. Writer to the Signet, 1891. 10th Royal Scots (T.), 1905-12. Rejoined as Major Sept. 1914 to Oct. 1918.

DUFF, ALEXANDER MacGREGOR.
George Watson's College; First XV. Student of Medicine, 1912-14 and 1918-19. O.T.C. Artillery, Oct. 1913-14, Cadet. R.F.A., 2nd Lieut. Oct. 1914; Lieut. Nov. 1914; Acting Captain Dec. 1914 to March 1915 and Dec. 1916 to Sept. 1918. France; Somme, Ancre, Arras, Messines, and Ypres. Dispatches Jan. 1917. M.C. Jan. 1919.

DUFF, DAVID KERR.
George Watson's College. Student of Science, 1912-14. M.Inst.C.E. O.T.C. Artillery, 1914-15, Cadet. R.F.A. and Anti-Aircraft, 2nd Lieut. May 1915; Lieut. June 1917; Acting Captain March 1918 to April 1919. France 1915-19; Somme, Arras, and Armentières. Croix de Guerre (French).

DUFF, DONALD GORDON.
Royal High School. Student of Medicine, 1911-16; M.B., Ch.B. 1916. O.T.C. Infantry, 1912-15, Medical, 1915-16, Cadet. R.A.M.C., Lieut. Aug. 1916; Captain Feb. 1917. 190th Brigade, R.F.A., France. Dispatches May 1918. M.C. June 1918.

DUFF, IAN DUNCAN.
Royal High School. M.A. 1909. Schoolmaster. 9th Royal Scots (T.), Private.

DUFF, WILLIAM RICHMOND.
George Watson's College. O.T.C. 1910-15, Cadet Officer. Student of Medicine, 1918. 17th Royal Scots, 2nd Lieut. April 1915; Lieut. March 1917; Captain and Adjutant, Jan. 1918. France; Somme 1916 and 1918, Ypres 1917. Dispatches May 1917 and June 1918.

DUFFES, ARTHUR PATERSON.
George Watson's College. M.A. 1901; LL.B. 1904. Advocate, 1910, and Barrister of the Inner Temple. O.T.C. Artillery, May to Sept. 1916. R.G.A. (T.), North Scottish, 2nd Lieut. Nov. 1916; Lieut. May 1918; Captain Dec. 1918. France, with Siege Battery. M.C. 1919.

DUFFIELD, FRANCIS ANTROBUS.
Birmingham Institute. M.B., Ch.B. 1910. Lecturer in Physiology, Sheffield University. R.A.M.C. (S.R.), Lieut. Dec. 1914; Captain July 1915. France, 2nd and 7th Divisions. 10th Mobile Laboratory.

DUGDALE, JAMES NORMAN.
Student of Medicine, 1915-16. O.T.C. Infantry, Oct. 1915 to Jan. 1916, Cadet. 18th Durham Light Infantry, 2nd Lieut. Jan. 1916; Lieut. June 1917. R.F.C., Dec. 1917. France July 1916 to April 1918. Egypt and Palestine Nov. 1918 to March 1919.

DUGUID, IAN.
Linlithgow Academy. Student of Medicine, 1918. R.N.V.R., Able Seaman.

Record of War Service

DUGUID, PETER.
Fettes. B.A. (Oxford). Oxford University Volunteers, 1903-7, Sergeant. Student of Law, 1909-14. O.T.C. Infantry, March 1909 to Aug. 1914, Cadet Sergeant. 3rd and 2nd Gordon Highlanders, 2nd Lieut. Aug. 1914; Lieut. Jan. 1915; Captain April 1915. France. Wounded at Ypres Oct. 1914 and Festubert May 1915.

DUGUID, WILLIAM.
Student of Medicine, 1908-14. M.B., Ch.B. 1913. R.A.M.C., Lieut.; Captain Aug. 1915.

DUKE, ALEXANDER LEONARD.
M.B., Ch.B. (Aberdeen) 1888; B.Sc. (P.H.) 1908. Indian Medical Service, Lieut.-Col.

DUKE, MARK.
Student of Medicine, 1915-16. O.T.C. Artillery, Oct. 1915-16, Cadet Corporal. Royal Military Academy, Woolwich, 1916-17. R.F.A., 2nd Lieut. June 1917; Lieut. Nov. 1918.

DUKES, CUTHBERT ESQUIRE.
Caterham School. Student of Medicine, 1909-14; M.B., Ch.B. 1914; M.D. 1918. O.T.C. Infantry, Nov. 1909 to Feb. 1913, Cadet. R.A.M.C., Lieut. Dec. 1914; Captain Dec. 1915; Major Feb. 1919. 3rd and 21st Casualty Clearing Stations, France 1917-19. O.B.E. (Military) and Dispatches Nov. 1918.

DUN, ROBERT CRAIG.
Loretto. M.B., C.M. 1893; B.Sc. 1896; L.R.C.P. (Lond.) 1895; F.R.C.S. (Eng.) 1902. R.A.M.C. (T.), Lieut. 1908; Captain 1912; Acting Lieut.-Col. Nov. 1917; Brevet Major Jan. 1918. Lancashire Hussars. Dispatches Jan. 1918.

DUNBAR, HENRY JOHN.
George Watson's College. M.B., Ch.B. 1902; M.D. 1905; F.R.C.S. (Edin.) 1908. R.A.M.C. (T.), 1908; Captain 1912; Acting Major April 1915. 2nd Welsh Field Ambulance, Egypt, 1916. Gallipoli, Suvla Bay; Sinai and Palestine, first and second Gaza. Dispatches 1918. O.B.E. 1919.

DUNBAR, HENRY MERRY.
B.Sc. 1915. O.T.C. Engineers, Jan. 1912 to Nov. 1914, Cadet. Egyptian Exp. Force.

DUNBAR, ROBERT TAYLOR.
Harris Academy, Dundee. Student of Arts and Science, 1907-10 and 1913-15. M.A. (Hons. Maths.) and B.Sc. (Distinction, Nat. Phil.) 1915. Schoolmaster. O.T.C. Artillery, Dec. 1914 to Aug. 1915, Cadet. R.G.A., North Scottish (T.), 2nd Lieut. Aug. 1915; Lieut. June 1916; Acting Captain May 1917. Field Survey Coy., R.E. (Sound Ranging), Dec. 1917 to Nov. 1918. France 1916-17. In Hospital Nov. 1918 to July 1919.

Record of War Service

DUNBAR, WILLIAM PATERSON.
Harris Academy, Dundee. B.Sc. 1911. A.M.I.C.E. O.T.C. Engineers, 1910-11, Cadet. Royal Fusiliers, Private Dec. 1914. Royal Highlanders (Black Watch), 2nd Lieut. April 1915; Lieut. July 1917. R.E., 1918-19.

DUNCAN, CECIL GOSMAN.
Edinburgh Academy. Student of Science, 1914-15. C.D.A. O.T.C. Artillery, Oct. 1914 to Feb. 1915, Cadet. Fife and Forfar Yeomanry (T.), Private Feb. 1915. 14th Royal Highlanders (Black Watch), 2nd Lieut. June 1915; Lieut. Oct. 1916. France. Wounded near Péronne Sept. 1918.

DUNCAN, GEORGE LAWRENCE.
George Heriot's School. M.B., Ch.B. 1907. Indian Medical Service, Captain Jan. 1913. France.

DUNCAN, GEORGE MORRISON.
George Heriot's School. University O.T.C. Infantry, March to Aug. 1916, Cadet; Officer Cadet Aug. 1916. 16th Royal Scots, 2nd Lieut. Nov. 1916; Lieut. Nov. 1917. France. Wounded. Invalided out March 1919.

DUNCAN, GEORGE SANG.
Darlington Grammar School. M.A. 1901; B.Sc. 1902. 4th Royal Scots, Private Nov. 1915. Labour Corps, 2nd Lieut. April 1917; Lieut. Oct. 1918. Egyptian Labour Corps. Egypt and Palestine. Invalided out Oct. 1918.

DUNCAN, GEORGE SIMPSON.
Forfar Academy. B.A. (Camb.); M.A. 1906; B.D. 1913. Minister, Church of Scotland. Professor of Biblical Criticism, St Andrews University. Chaplain, 4th Class, Sept. 1915-19. Attached G.H.Q., 1st Echelon, France, Captain. Twice Mentioned in Dispatches. O.B.E. (Military) Jan. 1919.

DUNCAN, GEORGE WILSON.
Merchiston Castle. O.T.C. 1908-11. Student of Medicine, 1911-12. O.T.C. Artillery, Jan. to June 1912, and Infantry, Sept. to Oct. 1914, Cadet. 8th Seaforth Highlanders, 2nd Lieut. Sept. 1914; Lieut. Feb. 1915; Captain May 1916. Dispatches June 1916. M.C. Jan. 1917.

DUNCAN, JAMES FERGUSON.
M.B., Ch.B. 1902; F.R.C.S. (Edin.). N.Z. Medical Corps, Captain Dec. 1916.

DUNCAN, JAMES OGILVIE.
Dundee High School. M.A. (St Andrews); B.L. 1907; LL.B. 1908. 4th Royal Highlanders (Black Watch) (T.), Captain Oct. 1912. Railway Traffic Officer Jan. 1917.

DUNCAN, JOHN.
Kinross School. M.B., Ch.B. 1902. South African Medical Corps, Captain Jan. 1916. 11th South African Infantry, German East Africa.

Record of War Service

DUNCAN, JOHN ALFRED ALEXANDER.
    Student of Medicine, 1912-14 and 1916-18. O.T.C. Infantry, Dec. 1912 to Oct. 1915, Cadet. 3rd Yorkshire Regiment, Lieut. M.C.

DUNCAN, JOHN DAVIDSON.
    Inverbrothock School. M.B., C.M. 1893. 5th Royal Highlanders (Black Watch), Captain. R.A.M.C. (S.R.), Captain April 1915; Acting Major March 1918.

DUNCAN, JOHN DONALD CAMPBELL.
    M.B., Ch.B. 1906. N.Z. Medical Corps, Lieut. Aug. 1914; Captain Sept. 1915. France. Wounded at the Somme Sept. 1916.

DUNCAN, LESLIE.
    Robert Gordon's College, Aberdeen. M.A. (Aberd.); Student of Divinity, 1914-16. 2nd Cameron Highlanders (S.R.), March 1916; 2nd Lieut. July 1916; Captain Jan. 1918. Special Service Officer; Kurdistan, North-West Persia, 1918-19.

DUNCAN, ROBERT.
    Macduff School. M.B., Ch.B. 1906. R.A.M.C., Lieut. June 1917; Captain June 1918.

DUNCAN, ROBERT DUNDAS.
    Edinburgh Academy. O.T.C. 1908-13, Cadet Sergeant. B.Sc. 1913. A.M.I.C.E. O.T.C. Engineers, Oct. 1910 to Feb. 1913, Cadet Corporal. Unattached List with O.T.C., Lieut. Oct. 1913. Transferred to Lowland Division, R.E. (T.), Jan. 1915; Temp. Captain July 1915; Captain June 1916. 65th Division, R.E., France. Forward Light Railway Training School, March 1918 to June 1919.

DUNCAN, THOMAS.
    George Watson's College. Student of Law, 1913-14. 10th Highland Light Infantry, 2nd Lieut. Dec. 1914; Lieut. July 1917; Captain Feb. 1918. Wounded at Loos Sept. 1915. France and India.

DUNCAN, THOMAS.
    Kinross School. M.B., C.M. 1886. Q.E.R. 1878-81, Private. R.A.M.C., Lieut. 1908; Captain 1911; Major 1914-18. 24th Field Ambulance, France, 1914-16.

DUNCAN, THOMAS SMITH.
    Kirkcaldy High School; First XV. and XI. O.T.C. 1905-12, Officer Cadet. Student of Medicine, 1912-17; M.B., Ch.B. 1917. O.T.C. Infantry, 1914-15, and Medical, 1916-17, Cadet. Royal Navy, Surgeon-Lieut., July 1917.

DUNCANSON, FRANCIS.
    George Watson's College. M.A. 1896. Schoolmaster. Royal Highlanders (Black Watch), Private March 1916. France; Somme, Ypres, and St Quentin. Wounded. M.M. Dec. 1916.

Record of War Service

DUNDAS, CHARLES.
Miller Institution, Thurso. Student of Arts, 1914-16 and 1918-20; M.A. 1920. 5th and 4th Seaforth Highlanders, Private April 1916; L/Corporal; Corporal; 2nd Lieut. Aug. 1918.

DUNDAS, JAMES.
George Watson's College. M.B., Ch.B. 1905; M.D. 1910; D.P.H., R.C.P.S. (Edin.) 1907. R.A.M.C. (T.), Lieut. 1909; Captain April 1913; Acting Major June 1918. France 1917. Dispatches Jan. 1918.

DUNDEE, CHARLES.
Royal Academical Institution, Belfast. Athletics. M.B., Ch.B. 1913; D.P.H., R.C.P. (Edin.). R.A.M.C., Lieut. April 1916; Captain April 1917. M.C.

DUNDEE, WILLIAM BOYLE HILL.
Royal Academical Institution, Belfast. M.B., Ch.B. 1913. R.A.M.C., Lieut. Sept. 1917; Captain May 1918.

DUNLOP, ALFRED JOSEPH.
George Watson's College. M.B., Ch.B. 1913. O.T.C. Medical, April 1910-13. Cadet L/Corporal. R.A.M.C., Lieut. Nov. 1915; Captain Nov. 1916; Major April 1918; Captain March 1919. M.C. June 1919.

DUNLOP, DAVID.
Student of Medicine, 1910-15; M.B., Ch.B. 1915. R.A.M.C., Lieut. Sept. 1915; Captain Sept. 1916. 30th Division, France, Nov. 1915 to Sept. 1917. India Jan. 1918.

DUNLOP, GAVIN ALEXANDER.
Merchant Taylor's. Student of Medicine, 1914 and 1919. R.A.M.C., No. 4 M.A.C., Private Sept. 1914. Scottish Rifles, 2nd Lieut. 1918. France Nov. 1914 to Nov. 1917.

DUNLOP, JAMES.
M.A. (Glasg.); LL.B. 1896. 9th Scottish Provisional Battn., Orderly Room Sergeant, 1896-1916. 9th Highland Light Infantry (T.), Aug. 1914; L/Sergeant Nov. 1914; Sergeant June 1915. Territorial Efficiency Medal.

DUNLOP, JAMES ANDERSON.
Lasswade School. Student of Science, 1918-19. 8th Royal Scots, Private Dec. 1915. 6th and 15th Highland Light Infantry, 2nd Lieut. Aug. 1917. France.

DUNLOP, JOSEPH.
George Watson's College. Student of Medicine, 1909-15; M.B., Ch.B. 1914. R.A.M.C., Lieut. July 1915; Captain July 1916. Malta and Salonika.

DUNLOP, THOMAS.
Coleraine Academical Institution. M.B., C.M. 1893; D.P.H. (Camb.). St John's Ambulance Brigade, V.A.D., and Red Cross Hospitals, Torquay, for four years. R.A.M.C., Lieut. Aug. 1916.

Record of War Service

DUNLOP, WILLIAM.
: M.B., Ch.B. 1909. O.T.C. Artillery, 1904 to July 1910, Cadet. R.A.M.C. (S.R.), Lieut. Aug. 1914; Captain April 1915; Acting Major Aug. 1918. France 1914-15; Mesopotamia Jan. 1916-19. Dispatches March and June 1918 and June 1919. O.B.E. Nov. 1918.

DUNLOP, WILLIAM FORBES.
: Lanark Grammar School. Student of Medicine, 1909-15; M.B., Ch.B. 1914. R.A.M.C., Lieut. Dec. 1914; Captain May 1916; Acting Major March 1919. Prisoner of War May to Oct. 1918. Demobilised June 1919.

DUNLOP-SMITH, SIR JAMES ROBERT.
: Royal High School; First XV. M.A. 1878. 22nd Regiment, 2nd Lieut. 1879; Lieut.-Col. 1905. India 1914-19. Political A.D.C. to Secretary of State for India, and Delegate to Peace Conference. C.I.E. 1901; K.C.S.I. 1910; K.C.V.O. 1916; Knight Commander, North Star of Sweden; Order of St John of Jerusalem.

DUNN, BERNARD VENN.
: Taunton School. M.B., Ch.B. 1913. R.A.M.C., Lieut. Aug. 1914-15. M.O., V.A.D., Leicester 13. Dispatches Jan. 1916.

DUNN, CUTHBERT LINDSAY.
: Londonderry Academy. Student of Medicine, 1892-9; L.R.C.P. & S. (Edin.); L.F.P.S. (Glasg.) 1899. Indian Medical Service, Major March 1914.

DUNN, GEORGE.
: George Watson's College. M.A., B.Sc. 1905. R.A.M.C., Private.

DUNN, JAMES CHURCHHILL.
: Clifton Bank, St Andrews, and Glasgow Academy. M.B., C.M. 1893; M.D. 1897; D.P.H. (Camb.) 1908. Imperial Yeomanry, South African Campaign, 1900-2. R.A.M.C., Lieut. Jan. 1915; Captain Jan. 1916. M.C. Aug. 1916; Bar to M.C. June 1917; D.S.O. Oct. 1917. Dispatches Jan. 1916 and Jan. 1918.

DUNN, JOHN PETRIE.
: George Watson's College. Student of Arts and Music, 1896-9. Bucher Scholar. 4th Royal Scots (T.), Private Feb. 1915; L/Corporal May 1915; 2nd Lieut. Sept. 1916; Lieut. Nov. 1917. Intelligence Corps, April 1917. France; Somme and Ypres. The Rhine, Nov. 1918 to June 1919.

DUNNETT, GEORGE VICTOR.
: Kilmarnock Academy. M.A. (Hons. Classics) 1900; B.D. 1903. Minister, Church of Scotland. Chaplain, Mediterranean Forces, Oct. 1915; 10th Division, France. Dispatches Nov. 1917 and May 1918. O.B.E. (Military) June 1918.

DUNNETT, HAMILTON DAVID FORRESTER.
: Kilmarnock Academy. M.A. 1899; B.D. 1903. Minister, Church of Scotland. Chaplain, 4th Class; Captain Oct. 1917. Egypt and Palestine. Attached 52nd Division, Artillery.

Record of War Service

DUNS, STEWART.
  Berwick High School. Student of Science, 1913-15. O.T.C. Artillery, Oct. 1914 to Feb. 1915, Cadet. R.F.A., 2nd Lieut. Feb. 1915.

DUNSE, JOHN.
  George Watson's College. Student of Science, 1918-19. Lothians and Border Horse, Private Dec. 1917. 4th King's Royal Rifles, Rifleman. Salonika 1916-18; France 1918-19. Wounded Oct. 1918.

DUPONT, JOHN MUNRO.
  M.B., Ch.B. 1901; M.D. 1905. South African Campaign, 1901-2. R.A.M.C., Captain May 1914; Temp. Major Sept. 1915. 2nd S.W. Mounted Brigade Field Ambulance. Gallipoli, Egypt, and France.

DURRAN, JOHN.
  Daniel Stewart's College. 1st Highland Cadet Battn. 1914-17, Corporal. Student of Medicine, 1917-19. O.T.C. Artillery, Sept. 1917 to July 1918, Cadet Corporal; Officer Cadet July 1918.

DURWARD, CHARLES WALTER.
  St Mary's, Melrose, and Giggleswick; First XV. Student of Medicine, 1918-19. 1/1st Highland Cyclist Battn., 2nd Lieut. March 1915; Lieut. July 1916; Captain April 1919. 16th Highland Light Infantry. Captain, Brigade Staff, Feb. to June 1917. France. Wounded at Passchendaele Dec. 1917.

DURWARD, WALTER STEWART.
  George Watson's College. Student of Medicine, 1908; L.D.S. (Edin.). O.T.C. Artillery, Oct. 1908 to Aug. 1914, 2nd Lieut. Transferred to R.F.A. (S.R.), Aug. 1914. R.H. and R.F.A. (Regulars), May 1915, Temp. Captain Aug. 1916; Lieut. July 1917. France Nov. 1914 to Sept. 1915, and March 1916 to July 1917. Twice Wounded. M.C. and Dispatches Jan. 1916.

DUSTAGIR, SYED MOHAMAD.
  Student of Arts, 1914-15. Indian Field Ambulance.

DUTT, DWYENDRA NATH.
  Student of Medicine, 1913-15. Indian Field Ambulance.

DUTT, SURENDRA NATH.
  M.A., LL.B. 1912; B.A. (Calcutta). Barrister-at-Law. Advocate. Professor, Law, Calcutta University, 1913-16. Bengal Light Horse Unit, Trooper Oct. 1917; Corporal Nov. 1918; Q.M.S. Dec. 1918.

DYER, EDMUND EUSTACE.
  M.B., C.M. 1889. R.A.M.C. (T.), Major July 1911.

DYER, ETHELBERT WILLIAM.
  Durban High School. M.B., Ch.B. 1906; D.T.M. and H. 1909; F.R.C.S. (Edin.) 1909. South African Medical Corps, Captain Jan. 1915.

Record of War Service

DYKES, ANDREW LESLIE.
Warwick School. M.B., Ch.B. 1908; M.D. 1910; D.P.H., R.C.P.S. (Eng.) 1913. Royal Naval Air Service, Surgeon, Oct. 1914. Royal Air Force. France. Italy. Dispatches Jan. 1919.

DYKES, HAROLD BALFOUR.
Dumfries Academy. Student of Medicine, 1911-14 and 1916-17; M.B., Ch.B. 1917. O.T.C. Medical, May 1912 to Sept. 1914, Cadet. Unattached List, 2nd Lieut. Sept. 1916 to Aug. 1917. 9th King's Own Scottish Borderers, 2nd Lieut. Sept. 1914; Lieut. April 1915 to May 1916. R.A.M.C., Lieut. Aug. 1917; Captain Oct. 1918. Gallipoli, Egypt, Sinai, and France, 1915-16. India and Persian Gulf 1917-19.

DYKES, SAMUEL SLIMMON.
Dumfries Academy. M.B., Ch.B. 1906. No. 4 Coy. Q.R.V.B. Royal Scots, 1902-5. R.A.M.C., Captain 1912; Major Sept. 1918. India, Mesopotamia, E. Africa, Persian Gulf, North Russia.

DYMOCK, THEDFORD.
Linlithgow Academy. B.Sc. (Lond.). University O.T.C. Artillery, Nov. 1915 to June 1916, Cadet Bombardier; Officer Cadet June 1916. R.G.A. (S.R.), 2nd Lieut. Oct. 1916; Lieut. April 1918. 202nd Heavy Battery, Palestine.

DYSON, THOMAS EDWARD.
M.B., C.M. 1883. Indian Medical Service, Colonel Jan. 1914. A.D.M.S. 1918.

EADIE, ROBERT BURNS.
Garfield, Workington. Student of Medicine, 1910-15; M.B., Ch.B. 1915. B.R.C.S., France (Dresser), Oct. to Dec. 1914. R.A.M.C., Lieut. Oct. 1915; Captain Oct. 1916. India.

EADIE, WILLIAM STEWART.
Perth Academy. Student of Law, 1913-14. Chartered Accountant. O.T.C. Infantry, Sept. 1914 to May 1915, Cadet Sergeant. 17th Royal Scots, 2nd Lieut. April 1915; Lieut. July 1915. France. Wounded at the Somme Aug. 1916 and at Epehy Sept. 1917.

EAGLES, VICTOR THOMAS WILLIAM.
Philander Smith College, Naini Tal, India. Cadet Corps 1903-8, Sergeant. Student of Medicine, 1908-12; L.R.C.P. & S. (Edin.) and L.R.F.P.S. (Glasg.) 1912. Hockey and Cricket "Blue." O.T.C. Artillery, 1909-12, Cadet. R.F.A., 2nd Lieut. Oct. 1914; Lieut. Feb. 1915. R.A.M.C., Lieut. Aug. 1915; Captain Aug. 1916. H.M. Troop Ship *Ballarat*, to India, Dec. 1915. Mesopotamia, Egypt, and India. France 1915 and 1916-17. Dispatches 1916. M.C. (Somme) Feb. 1917.

EAMES, CHARLES WILLIAM.
M.B., C.M. 1896; M.D. 1906; M.R.C.S. (Eng.), and L.R.C.P. (Lond.) 1895. R.A.M.C. (T.), Lieut. 1908; Captain 1912; Temp. Major Oct. 1914; Temp. Lieut.-Col. Sept. 1915. 2/2nd W.R.F. Ambulance, 62nd Division, Oct. 1914 to March 1919. Mention Jan. 1917. Dispatches May and Nov. 1918. D.S.O. Jan. 1919.

Record of War Service

EARLE, LESLIE MEREDITH.
M.B., C.M. 1878; M.D. 1880. R.A.M.C., Jan. 1917; Lieut. Jan. 1918; Captain Feb. 1919. Netley Hospital.

EASON, JOHN.
M.B., C.M. 1896; M.D. R.A.M.C. (T.), Captain; Major July 1908. 2nd Scottish General Hospital.

EASTON, WALTER.
Golspie School. M.A. 1913. Schoolmaster. O.T.C. Artillery, July to Nov. 1915, Cadet. R.G.A. (S.R.), 2nd Lieut. Nov. 1915; Lieut. July 1917.

EATON, ERNEST MILNE.
Glasgow School. Student of Medicine, 1914-15; M.B., Ch.B. 1906, and M.D. (Glasg.) 1915. R.A.M.C., May 1915; Lieut. July 1915; Captain Aug. 1916.

EATON, RICHARD OLIVER.
Foyle College, Londonderry. O.T.C. 1913-14. Student of Medicine, 1915-16. O.T.C. Infantry, Oct. to Nov. 1915, Cadet. 14th Argyll and Sutherland Highlanders, Private Sept. 1915; L/Corporal May 1916. 7th Royal Highlanders (Black Watch), Corporal July 1916. 1st and 3rd Royal Irish Fusiliers, 2nd Lieut. April 1917; Lieut. Oct. 1918 to July 1919. France. Four times Wounded M.C. Aug. 1918.

EBAN, ISAAC.
George Heriot's School. Student of Arts, Science and Medicine, 1908-13 and 1915-17; M.A. (Hons. Maths.) 1912; B.Sc. 3rd Scottish Rifles, Private March to Oct. 1917. Belfast University O.T.C. Medical, Oct. 1917.

EBSWORTH, KEVIN JOSEPH.
Student of Medicine, 1913-14 and 1918-19. R.A.M.C. (T.). Scottish Horse Brigade, Private.

ECKERSLEY, EDWIN.
M.B., C.M. 1884. D.P.H., R.C.P.S. (Eng.) 1907. Army Medical Service, July 1886, Colonel. Ashanti, 1895-6. South African Campaign, 1899-1902. A.D.M.S., Simla, March 1915, and A.D.M.S., 1st (Peshawar) Division, Sept. 1915 to Oct. 1918. K.H.P. Dec. 1917.

EDEN, LOUIS THOMAS.
M.B., Ch.B. 1910. R.A.M.C., Lieut. Feb. 1915; attached 9th Rifle Brigade. V.A.D. Warwick and British Red Cross.

EDEN, THOMAS WATTS.
M.B., C.M. 1888; M.D. 1891; F.R.C.S. (Edin.), F.R.C.P. (Lond.). R.A.M.C., Captain March 1915; Major Nov. 1915.

EDGAR, CHARLES SAMUEL.
Ayr Academy. M.A. (Hons. Classics) 1896; Boden Sanskrit Scholar and B.A. (Oxford) 1898. Professor of Greek, Stellenbosch University. South African Campaign, 1901-3. South African Heavy Artillery, Gunner April to Dec. 1917. Trade Intelligence Department, Dec. 1917 to March 1919.

Record of War Service

EDGAR, FRANK.
George Watson's College; First XI. Student of Arts, 1888-91. Solicitor. B.L. Barrister-at-Law, Nigeria. 6th Royal Scots, 1893; Major 1908. Nigerian Land Contingent, Aug. 1914. West African Frontier Force, Nigeria, 1915-16. T.D.

EDGAR, ROBERT DICKSON.
Moffat Academy. M.A. 1910. Schoolmaster. George Heriot's School O.T.C., Lieut. May 1914. 17th Royal Scots, Captain April 1915; Adjutant and Q.M. France.

EDINGTON, ALEXANDER.
George Watson's College. M.B., C.M. 1886; M.D. 1900; D.T.M. and H. 1906; D.P.H. (Edin.) 1906. Assistant to Professor of Surgery, 1886-1901. South African Medical Corps, Major Jan. 1916; Acting Lieut.-Col. May 1917. East Africa.

EDINGTON, ALEXANDER DANIEL.
George Watson's College. B.Sc. 1905; M.B., Ch.B. 1907. No. 4 Coy. Q.R.V.B. 1904-6, Sergeant (Machine-Gun). South African Medical Corps, Captain Feb. 1914; Adjutant Aug. 1914. Dispatches and Croix de Guerre.

EDINGTON, DAVID CAMERON.
George Watson's College. B.Sc. 1909. No. 4 Coy. Q.R.V.B. 1904-5, Corporal. South African Army Service Corps, Lieut. Aug. 1914. 5th South African Infantry. Dispatches.

EDINGTON, JAMES WILLIAM.
Student of Medicine, 1908-14; M.B., Ch.B. 1913; M.D. 1920; D.P.H. (Edin.) 1914. R.A.M.C., Lieut. June 1915; Captain July 1915. Croix de Guerre (French), 1917.

EDMOND, JOHN JAMES BALMANNO.
George Heriot's School. O.T.C. 1909-11, Cadet Sergeant. Student of Medicine, 1911-16; M.B., Ch.B. 1916. O.T.C. Medical, May 1912 to Sept. 1914, Cadet. R.A.M.C., Private Aug. 1914. R.A.M.C. (S.R.), Lieut. July 1916; Captain Jan. 1917. Salonika and France. Wounded. M.C. Nov. 1918.

EDMONDSON, REGINALD ARTHUR.
Sedbergh. O.T.C. 1913-17. Student of Medicine, 1916-19. O.T.C. Artillery, 1917-18, Cadet; Officer Cadet Feb. 1918. R.F.A., 15th Reserve Battery, 2nd Lieut.

EDMUNDS, GARNET W.
Student of Law. Chartered Accountant, 1903. Army Pay Corps, Lieut.

EDWARDS, ALEXANDER HENRY.
M.B., C.M. 1896; F.R.C.S. (Edin.) 1902. R.A.M.C., Captain July 1908. 3rd Scottish General Hospital.

Record of War Service

EDWARDS, COSMO GRANT NIVEN.
George Watson's College and Fettes. Student of Medicine, 1913-14. O.T.C. Infantry, 1914, Cadet. 11th Highland Light Infantry, 2nd Lieut. May 1916; Lieut. March 1917. India.

EDWARDS, EBAN HENRY.
St Mark's College, London. M.B., C.M. 1880. B.R.C.S. St John's Ambulance. France April to Aug. 1915. Y.M.C.A., France Aug. 1917 to Feb. 1918. R.A.M.C., Lieut. April 1918; Captain April 1919. Chinese Base Hospital, France.

EDWARDS, GEORGE JEHU.
George Heriot's School. Student of Arts and Divinity, 1907-14; M.A. 1910. President, S.R.C. Licentiate, Church of Scotland. Chaplain, 4th Class; Captain Sept. 1914. Portsmouth.

EDWARDS, HERBERT JOHN.
Aberdeen Grammar School. University O.T.C. Infantry, 1917-18, Cadet L/Corporal; Officer Cadet June 1918. Gordon Highlanders, 2nd Lieut. Feb. 1919.

EDWARDS, JAMES H.
Student of Science. 8th Royal Scots (T.), Lieut.

EDWARDS, JOHN CLIFTON SPENCER.
University School, Rochester. Student of Medicine, 1918. 2/1st Essex Yeomanry, Private March 1917. 1st Essex Regiment.

EDWARDS, PETER WILLIAMS.
County School and University College, Aberystwyth; Athletics. Student of Medicine, 1910-16. M.B., Ch.B. 1915. O.T.C. Medical, 1912-14, Cadet. R.A.M.C. (S.R.), Lieut. Aug. 1914-15. O.T.C., Captain March 1916. France 1915. Wounded July 1917, and invalided out Oct. 1918. Dispatches Dec. 1916.

EDWARDS, ROBERT.
George Watson's College; First XV. and XI. M.B., Ch.B. 1907. R.A.M.C., Lieut. Sept. 1916; Captain Sept. 1917; Acting Major March 1918. France; Somme 1916, Arras 1917.

EGGELING, HANS FRIEDRICH.
George Watson's College. M.A. (Hons. Classics) 1902. Lecturer in German. Special Service (V.B. Royal Scots), July to Aug. 1918.

ELDER, ALEXANDER AUSTIN.
M.A. 1908. Artists' Rifles, Private Sept. 1914. 2nd Shropshire Light Infantry, 2nd Lieut. June 1915. Intelligence Officer, 28th Division, Feb. 1917 to March 1919. France Dec. 1914; Salonika Nov. 1915. Twice Mentioned in Dispatches.

ELDER, EDWARD MEDCALF.
Daniel Stewart's College; First XV. and XI. University O.T.C. Infantry, Nov. 1915, Cadet. Royal Highlanders (Black Watch), 2nd Lieut. Jan. 1916; Lieut. July 1917; Acting Captain Feb. 1919. India, Mesopotamia, Persia, and South Russia. M.C. Oct. 1919.

Record of War Service

ELDER, JAMES HISLOP.
Edinburgh Academy. O.T.C. 1910-11. Student of Science, 1911-14; B.Sc. 1914. O.T.C. Engineers, Oct. 1912 to Aug. 1914, Cadet. 8th Royal Scots (T.), 2nd Lieut. Aug. 1914; Lieut. June 1916. Machine-Gun Corps, Acting Captain. Scottish Command School of Musketry, and Machine-Gun School, Grantham. France.

ELLIOT, ANDREW.
Royal High School. M.A. 1884; M.B., C.M. 1888; M.D. 1894; D.P.H., R.C.P.S. (Eng.) 1892; M.R.C.P. (Lond.) 1902. Q.E.R. 1885-9, Private. Medical Staff Corps, Dec. 1904. R.A.M.C. (T.), Captain 1908; Temp. Major May 1915; Major Dec. 1916. South African Campaign, 1900-1. 1st City of London Field Ambulance. Imtarfa, Malta; Salonika, and France. T.D. Jan. 1919. Dispatches July 1919.

ELLIOT, JOHN STEPHEN.
Merchiston Castle. M.B., Ch.B. 1913. Royal Navy, H.M.S. *King Edward VII.*, Surgeon Oct. 1913; Acting Surgeon-Lieut.-Commander, Oct. 1918. H.M. Monitor 16, Eastern Mediterranean, 1916. Royal Air Force, 1917-18; and H.M.S. *Cleopatra*, North Sea and Baltic, 1918-19.

ELLIOT, STUART DOUGLAS.
Kirkton School. Student of Law, 1878-81. Volunteers, 1876-1905; Lieut.-Col. 6th Royal Scots (T.); Lieut.-Col. March 1915-16. 2/1st City of Edinburgh Volunteers, Major June 1917 to Feb. 1918. V.D. 1899.

ELLIOT, WILLIAM GILBERT DOUGLAS.
George Watson's College. O.T.C. 1915-16. Student of Law, 1917 and 1919. O.T.C. Infantry, May 1917 to Jan. 1918, Cadet; Officer Cadet Jan. 1918. Royal Scots, 2nd Lieut. July 1918. France and The Rhine, Oct. 1918 to May 1919.

ELLIOTT, ARTHUR CAMPBELL.
Cheltenham. Cadet Corps 1882-6. M.B., C.M. 1891. R.A.M.C., Captain July 1910. M.O., Chaseside Auxiliary Military Hospital, St Anne's-on-Sea, and 150th Brigade, R.F.A. Recruiting Office, 1914-19. O.B.E. April 1920.

ELLIOTT, GEORGE MAXWELL
St Andrew's College, Dublin. M.B., Ch.B. 1912. Hockey International. R.A.M.C., Lieut. April 1915; Captain April 1916. Gallipoli, Egypt, Sinai, Palestine and Syria.

ELLIOTT, JAMES SANDS.
Wellington College, New Zealand. Cadet Corps 1893-6, Sergeant. M.B., Ch.B. 1902; M.D. 1912. University Medical Staff Corps, 1897-1902, Corporal. R.A.M.C., South African Campaign, 1900. N.Z. Medical Corps, Captain 1910; Major 1914; Lieut.-Col. 1915. R.A.M.C., Temp. Lieut.-Col. Jan. 1916. N.Z. Hospital Ship *Maheno*. A.D.M.S., Wellington Military District, N.Z.

Record of War Service

ELLIOTT, OLIVER GILMOUR.
St Andrew's College, Dublin. M.A. 1912. Royal Scots, Private June 1916.

ELLIOTT, ROBERT.
St Andrew's College, Dublin; First XV. M.A. 1907. Minister, U.F. Church of Scotland. No. 4 Coy. Q.R.V.B., Royal Scots, 1904-7, Private. 2nd, 8th, and 4th Cameron Highlanders, Private Jan. 1916; Officer Cadet April 1916; 2nd Lieut. Aug. 1916; Lieut. Feb. 1918. 6th Machine-Gun Corps. Salonika Nov. 1916 to July 1918.

ELLIOTT, WILLIAM ERNEST LLOYD.
M.B., C.M. 1888; M.D. 1900. Q.E.R. 1883-8, Private. R.A.M.C. (T.), Lieut. Feb. 1913; Captain April 1915. Montgomeryshire Yeomanry. Recruiting Board, Ashton-under-Lyne, and Manchester.

ELLIS, EDWARD CLEVELAND.
George Watson's College. O.T.C. 1914-16. Student of Medicine, 1916-17. O.T.C. Artillery, Oct. 1916 to July 1917, Cadet Bombardier. R.F.A., Officer Cadet July 1917; 2nd Lieut. Dec. 1917. 150th Army Brigade. France June 1918; Le Cateau.

ELLIS, ROBERT SIDNEY.
School for Sons of Missionaries, Blackheath, London; First XV. and XI M.B., Ch.B. 1900. R.A.M.C., Lieut. Oct. 1915; Captain Oct. 1916 to Jan. 1919. S.M.O., Railway Construction Coys., Egyptian Labour Corps, Palestine.

ELLISTON, CHATTERTON ERIC.
Ipswich. M.B., Ch.B. 1905; M.D. 1909. R.A.M.C., Lieut. Dec. 1917; Captain Dec. 1918. 8th Yorkshire Regiment, 23rd Division, France.

ELMSLIE, ALEXANDER HARPER.
M.B., Ch.B. 1910. B.R.C.S. Surgeon Oct. 1914 to March 1915. 13th Argyll and Sutherland Highlanders, 2nd Lieut. April 1915; Lieut. March 1916. N.Z. Medical Corps, Captain July 1917.

ELSWORTH, GEORGE.
Thornton School. Student of Medicine, 1909-15; M.B., Ch.B. 1915. R.A.M.C., Lieut. Nov. 1915; Captain Nov. 1916. France and The Rhine.

ELSWORTH, RICHARD COGSWELL.
M.B., C.M. 1888; M.D. 1901; F.R.C.S. (Eng.) 1896. Demonstrator in Anatomy. R.A.M.C., Captain Dec. 1908; Major June 1915. 3rd Western General Hospital.

ELSWORTH, THOMAS GEOFFREY.
M.B., C.M. 1900; M.D. 1906. R.A.M.C., Lieut.; Captain July 1916.

EMSLIE, JOHN WATSON.
George Heriot's School. M.A. 1908. Student of Divinity, 1915-16. Minister, Church of Scotland. 2/4th Seaforth Highlanders, Private April 1918; 2nd Lieut. July 1918; Lieut. Jan. 1919. 151st Chinese Corps, Havre.

Record of War Service

ENGLISH, HENRY H.
South African College School; First XV. O.T.C. 1910-12. Student of Science, 1913-14. Army Veterinary Corps, Sergeant Sept. 1914; 2nd Lieut. Aug. 1917; Lieut. Oct. 1918. Hussars and 8th Cavalry, Indian Army; Egyptian Exp. Force, 1915-17; India.

ERSKINE, ALEXANDER RALPH.
George Watson's College; First XV. and XI. O.T.C. 1908-11, Cadet Sergeant. Student of Medicine, 1911-14 and 1916-19; M.B., Ch.B. 1919. O.T.C. Medical, 1914, Cadet. Scottish Horse, Corporal Sept. 1914. 11th Scottish Rifles, 2nd Lieut. Feb. 1915; Lieut. June 1916. France 1915-16.

ERSKINE, JAMES.
Perth Academy. Student of Arts, 1913-15. R.E., Corporal July 1915. Royal Air Force, 2nd Lieut.

ERSKINE, JAMES YOUNG.
M.A. 1915. Schoolmaster. No. 1 Wireless School, Private.

ERSKINE, WILLIAM ANDREW.
George Watson's College; First XV. O.T.C. 1914-16, Cadet Corporal. Student of Medicine, 1916. O.T.C. Artillery 1916-17, Cadet Corporal. Royal Air Force, Sept. 1917; 2nd Lieut. Jan. 1918. Italy, 34th Squadron.

ESPLIN, FRANK.
Brechin High School. Student of Arts, 1913-15 and 1917-19. 2nd Royal Scots, Private April 1915; L/Corporal Aug. 1916 to July 1917. France. Wounded at Serre Nov. 1916.

EUNSON, WILLIAM TULLOCH.
Kirkwall School. Student of Arts, 1913-17; M.A. 1917. Royal Scots, July 1917. R.A.S.C. (M.T.). France.

EVANS, DAVID GORDON.
M.B., C.M. 1883; M.D. 1888; D.P.H. (Oxford) 1911. R.A.M.C. (S.R.), Lieut. Jan. 1917.

EVANS, HARRY.
Grove Park School, Wrexham. M.B., Ch.B. 1912; M.D. 1920. O.T.C. Medical, 1909-12, Cadet. R.A.M.C. (S.R.), Lieut. 1913; Captain April 1915. France Aug. 1914 to May 1919.

EVANS, SAMUEL.
M.B., C.M. 1893; L.R.C.P. & S. (Edin.), and L.F.P.S. (Glasg.) 1888. Indian Medical Service, Lieut.-Col. July 1914.

EVANS, THOMAS RICHARD.
University College, Aberystwyth; First XI., Football. M.B., Ch.B. 1910; M.D. 1914. President, University Welsh Association. R.A.M.C., Lieut. Aug. 1917; Captain Aug. 1918. Military Hospital, Cannock Chase. R.G.A. and Royal Air Force, Catterick.

Record of War Service

EVANS, WILLIAM EDGAR.
  Merchiston Castle. B.Sc. 1905. 2/6th Royal Highlanders (Black Watch), Private Oct. 1916. R.A.M.C. (T.), 1st London Sanitary Coy., Lieut. March 1917; Captain March 1918. Mesopotamia and Persia, 46th Sanitary Section, Oct. 1917 to Feb. 1919.

EVANS, WILLIAM GLYN.
  Grove Park School, Wrexham. M.B., Ch.B. 1908; M.D. 1913; D.P.H. (Manchester) 1913. R.N.V.R., Surgeon, Sept. 1914.

EVERARD, HORACE NATHANIEL.
  M.B., C.M. 1880; M.D. 1894; L.R.C.S. 1880. R.A.M.C., Lieut. Aug. 1914; Captain Jan. 1916; Netley Hospital to April 1919.

EVERETT, WILLIAM.
  Broughton School, Edinburgh. Student of Medicine, 1912-17; M.B., Ch.B. 1917. Anatomy Staff, 1916. O.T.C. Medical, Feb. 1916 to July 1917, Cadet. R.A.M.C., Sergeant, Netley Hospital. Royal Navy, Surgeon, 1917. Mediterranean and Bermuda Royal Naval Hospital.

EWAN, EDWARD LESLIE.
  West Hartlepool School. Student of Medicine, 1913-16 and 1917-19. R.N.V.R., Surgeon-Probationer.

EWEN, JOHN SPENCE.
  Methlick School; Athletics. M.A. 1899 and B.Sc. (Aberdeen) 1905; Student of Divinity, 1911-14; B.D. 1914. Minister, Church of Scotland. Chaplain, 9th Seaforth Highlanders; Captain Dec. 1916. France. Gassed at Railway Wood Sept. 1917.

EWING, ALEXANDER JAMES.
  M.A. 1906; M.B., Ch.B. 1910. R.A.M.C., Lieut. Sept. 1914; Captain April 1915. Dispatches Jan. 1916.

EWING, ALEXANDER WILLIAM GORDON.
  Dean Close School, Cheltenham. O.T.C. 1912-13. Student of Arts, 1916-17; M.A. 1917. Glasgow University O.T.C. Infantry, Aug. 1914 to Dec. 1915, Cadet. London Scottish, Private May 1918.

EWING, BASIL GEORGE.
  Academical Institution, Coleraine; First XV. and XI. M.B., C.M. 1890. R.A.M.C. (T.), Lieut. Oct. 1915; Captain April 1916. Norfolk Regiment.

EWING, CHARLES MANSFIELD.
  George Watson's College. M.A. (Hons. Classics) 1908. Schoolmaster. 83rd Canadians (Infantry) Aug. 1915, Sergeant. 75th Canadian Infantry Battn., France.

Record of War Service

EWING, JOHN.
Royal High School; First XI. M.A. (Hons. Hist.) 1907. Lecturer in History (Colonial and Indian). 6th King's Own Scottish Borderers, April 1915; 2nd Lieut. May 1915; Lieut. Feb. 1917; Captain and Adjutant April 1917; Acting Major Oct. 1918; Brevet Major June 1919. France. M.C. Sept. 1917, and Bar to M.C. Oct. 1918; Belgian Croix de Guerre Oct. 1918. Dispatches March 1919.

EWKYN, FREDERICK BENTLEY.
Clifton College. Student of Medicine, 1908-14; M.B., Ch.B. 1914. Royal Navy, Surgeon-Lieut., Aug. 1914. Wounded Nov. 1916.

FAHMY, ERNEST CHALMERS.
School for Sons of Missionaries, Blackheath, London. Student of Medicine, 1911-14 and 1916-19; M.B., Ch.B. 1918. First XV.; International, Scotland, 1919-20. R.F.A., Gunner Oct. 1914; Sergeant March 1915. France 1915-16. Wounded April 1916.

FAILL, CHARLES JAMES CAMPBELL.
George Watson's College. Student of Medicine, 1903-4; L.R.C.P. & S. (Edin.), L.R.F.P.S. (Glasg.) 1908; M.R.C.P. (Eng.); F.R.C.P. (Edin.). O.T.C. Medical, 1904-9, Cadet. Royal Navy, Surgeon-Lieut., Aug. 1914. H.M. Ships *Queen Elizabeth* and *King Alfred.* Royal Naval Hospital, Plymouth, and H.M. Hospital Ship *Soudan.*

FAIRBAIRN, JOHN.
Queen's College, British Guiana. M.B., Ch.B. 1902; D.P.H. (Glasg.). R.A.M.C. Jan. 1904; Captain July 1907; Major July 1915; Temp. Lieut.-Col. Jan. 1916 to Feb. 1917. France, Jan. 1916 to Feb. 1917.

FAIRBAIRN, WILLIAM RONALD DODDS.
Merchiston Castle. O.T.C. 1902-7. Student of Arts and Medicine, 1907-11 and 1918-19; M.A. 1911. O.T.C. Engineers, May to Nov. 1915, Cadet. R.G.A. (T.), 2nd Lieut. Nov. 1915; Lieut. June 1916. Egypt and Palestine.

FAIRFIELD, LETITIA DENNY.
M.B., Ch.B. 1907; M.D. 1911; D.P.H., R.C.P. (Lond.), 1912. R.A.M.C., attached Q.M.A.A.C., Area Medical Controller, Oct. 1917. Royal Air Force, Hon. Lieut.-Col. July 1918.

FAIRGRIEVE, THOMAS DALGLEISH.
George Watson's College. Student of Arts, 1910-14; M.A. 1914. O.T.C. Artillery, 1914, Cadet. R.F.A., 2nd Lieut. Oct. 1914; Lieut. Jan. 1916; Acting Captain Sept. 1916; Acting Major April 1917. France 1915-17; Somme, Vimy, Messines, and Ypres; Salonika, 1918-19. Wounded Oct. 1917 and Aug. 1918. M.C. Aug. 1916.

FAIRLEY, AMY ALEXANDRA.
Collegiate School, Bournemouth. Student of Arts, 1913-16; M.A. 1916. W.R.N.S., Clerk, May 1918. Port Edgar Base.

Record of War Service

FAIRLEY, DAVID ANDREW.
　Student of Law, 1896-1900. Chartered Accountant, 1901. A.S.C., Lieut. March 1915. Attached Scottish Command H.Q.

FAIRLEY, GEORGE DONALDSON.
　George Watson's College. M.A. 1910; M.B., Ch.B. 1914. R.A.M.C., Lieut. April 1915; Captain April 1916. France 1915-18; Loos, Somme, Ancre, Hill 70, Bapaume, 1917; Arras, Kemmel, fourth Ypres, Lys, and Scheldt, 1918.

FAIRLEY, HENRY.
　Broughton School, Edinburgh. Student of Science, 1915-16 and 1918-19. Royal Navy, Able Seaman, Jan. 1917. Mediterranean. Munitions, Jan. 1916 to Jan. 1917.

FAIRLEY, JAMES HENRY BARRIE. (See p. 748.)

FAIRLEY, ROBERT REID.
　Boroughmuir School. Student of Arts and Science, 1915-16 and 1918-19. O.T.C. Artillery, Nov. 1915 to Aug. 1916, Cadet; Officer Cadet Aug. 1916. R.G.A., 2nd Lieut. Nov. 1916; Lieut. May 1918.

FAIRLEY, WILLIAM.
　Boroughmuir School; First XI. Student of Arts, 1918. Royal Navy, H.M.S. *Ganges II.*, Ordinary Seaman, Aug. 1917; Able Seaman April 1918.

FAIRLEY, WILLIAM.
　Edinburgh Academy. O.T.C., 1908-10. Student of Law, 1912-15. R.F.A. (T.), 2nd Lieut. June 1915; Lieut. June 1916. 1st Northumbrian Brigade, 51st Division, France, July 1916 to July 1917 and April 1918-19. Wounded at Heninel near Arras July 1917.

FAIRWEATHER, DAVID OSWALD.
　George Watson's College. M.B., Ch.B. 1912. R.A.M.C., Lieut. June 1917; Captain June 1918. India.

FAIRWEATHER, GEORGE MONCUR.
　M.A. 1895. Minister, U.F. Church of Scotland. Chaplain, 4th Class. 9th Gordon Highlanders, Dec. 1916. Hon. Chaplain Jan. 1919. M.C. Jan. 1918.

FAIRWEATHER, JOSIAH WILLIAM CHALMERS.
　Montrose Academy. Student of Medicine, 1912-18; M.B., Ch.B. 1917. O.T.C. Artillery, 1912-15, Medical, 1915-16, Cadet. R.N.V.R., Surgeon-Probationer, April 1916-17. R.A.M.C. (S.R.), Lieut. Feb. 1918; Captain Feb. 1919. The Black Sea.

FAIRWEATHER, REGINALD M. D.
　Loretto. O.T.C., 1909-12. Student of Arts, 1914-15. 9th Royal Scots, Private Sept. 1914. 4th and 17th Highland Light Infantry, 2nd Lieut. July 1915; Lieut. April 1917. Royal Air Force, 1917-18. M.C. Sept. 1917.

Record of War Service

FALCONER, ARCHIBALD BRODIE.
    George Heriot's School; First XV. Student of Law, 1908-10. 5th and 8th Royal Scots, Private Sept. 1914; Sergeant Dec. 1914; 2nd Lieut. Feb. 1915; Lieut. June 1915; Captain and Adjutant Dec. 1915. M.C. Jan. 1919.

FALCONER, DALLAS SCOTT.
    Student of Science and Medicine, 1909-15; B.Sc. 1913; M.B., Ch.B. 1915. O.T.C. Infantry, June 1909 to April 1913, Cadet. Royal Navy, Temp. Surgeon.

FALCONER, GERALD SCOTT.
    Edinburgh Academy; First XI. M.A. 1905. Minister, U.F. Church of Scotland. Scottish Churches Hut, Hesdin, France, March to Aug. 1917. Chaplain Nov. 1917. The Rhine April to Aug. 1919. Gordon Highlanders.

FALCONER, JAMES ALEXANDER.
    Inverness High School. Student of Law, 1907-9. Chartered Accountant, 1909. Lothians and Border Horse (T.), Private Dec. 1912. Highland Light Infantry, 2nd Lieut. Aug. 1917. France 1915. Factory Audit and Costs Department, Ministry of Munitions, London.

FALCONER, JOHN IRELAND.
    Student of Law. M.A., LL.B. 1903. 2/9th Royal Scots (T.), Lieut. Oct. 1914; Temp. Captain and Adjutant March 1915; Captain June 1916; Temp. Major July 1916. France 1918-19.

FALCONER, KEITH DOUGLAS.
    M.B., Ch.B. 1913. R.A.M.C., Lieut. Nov. 1914; Captain Nov. 1915. France Sept. 1915-19. M.C. June 1918.

FALCONER, ROBERT.
    George Watson's College. M.A. 1903; LL.B. 1908. 7th Gordon Highlanders, Oct. 1909; Lieut.; Captain June 1915.

FARIE, GILBERT JOHN.
    Stirling High School. M.B., Ch.B. 1903. R.A.M.C., Lieut. Oct. 1916; Captain Oct. 1917. Hon. M.O. Surrey Red Cross V.A.D., and Hon. Surgeon, Wimbledon Auxiliary War Hospital. M.C. June 1919.

FARMER, WILLIAM SYDNEY.
    Stirling High School. Student of Law, 1902-3. Law Agent, 1909. O.T.C. Infantry, Dec. 1914 to Feb. 1915, Cadet. 10th Royal Scots, 2nd Lieut. Feb. 1915; Lieut. June 1916. 10th Cheshire Regiment, Adjutant. Dispatches Nov. 1917. M.C. July 1918.

FARQUHAR, HENRY.
    Aberdeen Grammar School. B.D. 1882. Acting Chaplain June 1910; Chaplain Aug. 1914. Naval Forces (Presbyterian), Dover, Aug. 1914 to Sept. 1917. Belton Park, Grantham, and Rugely Camps. M.B.E. June 1919.

Record of War Service

FARQUHAR, JAMES.
Fettes. O.T.C., 1911-13. Student of Arts, 1913-15. O.T.C. Infantry, Dec. 1914 to Oct. 1915, Cadet. R.G.A. (Lowland City of Edinburgh), Gunner Oct. 1915. 1/1st Warwick Heavy Battery.

FARQUHARSON, DAVID.
Musselburgh Grammar School; Dux. Student of Medicine, 1915-16 and 1918-19. O.T.C. Artillery, Nov. 1915 to June 1916, Cadet. 10th Royal Highlanders (Black Watch), Private July 1916; L/Corporal. Salonika and France.

FARQUHARSON, DAVID ANDERSON.
M.B., C.M. 1894. Professor of Physiology, Royal (Dick) Veterinary College. R.A.M.C., Lieut.; Captain May 1919. India.

FARQUHARSON, DONALD PETER McLAREN.
Morrison's Academy, Crieff. M.B., C.M. 1890; D.P.H. (Manchester), 1909. R.A.M.C. (T.); Rejoined as Captain Feb. 1915; Major June 1918. 4th Cameron Highlanders. Sanitary Officer, France, and Sanitary Adviser, Irish Command.

FARQUHARSON, J. C. L.
Student. 1st London Scottish (T.). Wounded.

FARRELL, ALFRED EDMOND.
Dunfermline High School. Student of Arts and Science, 1912-15 and 1918-20. M.A. 1915. O.T.C. Infantry, Oct. 1913 to April 1916, Cadet. R.F.A., 337th Brigade, Driver, April 1917; 2nd Lieut. May 1918. Mesopotamia.

FASSON, FRANCIS HAMILTON.
Merchiston Castle; First XV. and XI. Cadet Corps 1891-6, Sergeant. B.A. (Camb.). Student of Law. First XV., Edinburgh and Cambridge Universities; International, Scotland, 1900-2; Hockey International, 1904-6. Writer to the Signet, 1904. 2nd Scottish Horse (T.), 2nd Lieut. Aug. 1914; Lieut.; Captain June 1916; Adjutant. Remount Service, Salonika, 1918. Gallipoli and Egypt. Twice Mentioned in Dispatches.

FASSON, ROBERT ROBERTSON.
Merchiston Castle. M.B., Ch.B. 1899; M.D. 1912; D.P.H. (Camb.) 1911. Royal Navy, Surgeon 1900; Staff Surgeon 1908; Major (R.A.F.M.S.) 1917; Surgeon-Commander (R.N.) Nov. 1918. H.M. Ships *Powerful, Chester*, and *Inflexible*.

FAULKNER, HUGH.
Clifton. Cadet Corps 1889-92. M.B., Ch.B. 1899; M.D. 1903. Medical Staff Corps, 1895-9, Sergeant. R.A.M.C., Lieut. Dec. 1914; Captain Dec. 1915; Acting Major 1916; Acting Lieut.-Col. 1916. S.M.O., G.H.Q. 2nd Echelon. Dispatches Jan. 1917.

FAULKNER, SYDNEY BOYD.
M.B., Ch.B. 1907. R.A.M.C., Lieut.

Record of War Service

FAWCETT, ALAN WORDSWORTH.
Clifton. O.T.C. 1912-14. Student of Medicine, 1915-16. Demonstrator in Anatomy, Bristol University. O.T.C. Infantry, 1915-16, Cadet. Royal Navy, Surgeon-Probationer, April 1916. H.M. T.B.D. *Tigress*, Mudros, Dardanelles.

FAYRER, Sir JOSEPH (Bart.).
Rugby. M.A. (Camb.) 1885; F.R.C.S. (Edin.) 1887; M.D. (St Andrews) 1889. Superintendent, R.I.E. R.A.M.C., 1886; Lieut.-Col. July 1906. Retired 1911. R.A.M.C. (T.). O.C. 2nd Scottish General Hospital, 1912. Mobilised Aug. 1914 to Feb. 1919. Knight of Grace, Order of St John of Jerusalem, 1912. Mention 1916. C.B.E. (Military) Jan. 1919.

FELL, ALFRED NOLAN.
Nelson College, New Zealand. First XV. and XI. Cadet Corps 1892-6, Sergeant. M.B., Ch.B. 1902; M.D. 1905. Rugby "Blue" and International, Scotland, 1901-3. R.A.M.C., Lieut. Jan. 1918; Captain Jan. 1919. 21st Stationary Hospital, Salonika.

FELLOWS, FREDERICK McFARLANE.
M.B., C.M. 1892; F.R.C.S. (Edin.) R.A.M.C., Lieut. July 1918.

FENELON, KEVIN GERARD.
Merchiston Castle. Student of Arts and Science, 1915-17. O.T.C. Infantry, Nov. 1915 to Aug. 1917, Cadet L/Corporal; Officer Cadet Aug. 1917. R.E., 2nd Lieut. Feb. 1918; Temp. Captain April 1919. The Rhine.

FENN, ROBERT MATTHEW.
Mount Redford School, Exeter. M.B., C.M. 1890. R.A.M.C., Lieut. Sept. 1916; Captain Sept. 1917; Major March 1918 to July 1919. Berrington War Hospital, Shrewsbury.

FENTON, HENRY FELIX.
M.B., Ch.B. 1905. 1st King's Own Yorkshire Light Infantry, Captain. R.A.M.C., Lieut. Aug. 1916; Captain Aug. 1917.

FENTON, JAMES STEVENSON.
Dundee High School. M.A. (Hons. Classics) 1912. Colonial Service. West African Contingent. Inland Water Transport, R.E., 2nd Lieut. Jan. 1917; Lieut. July 1918. Mesopotamia.

FENTON, JOHN CHARLES.
George Watson's College. M.A. 1900; LL.B. 1902; Advocate, 1904. 23rd Royal Fusiliers, Private Dec. 1914; L/Corporal; L/Sergeant; 2nd Lieut. May 1915; Lieut. Oct. 1915. France 1915-16; Somme. Wounded at Delville Wood July 1916. Appeal Military Representative, Ross and Sutherland, 1917. H.Q., Ministry of National Service, 1918.

Record of War Service

FENTON, NIGEL MACPHIE.
  Dundee High School. Student of Medicine, 1915-16. O.T.C. Infantry, Feb. to July 1915, Cadet. R.G.A., 37th Indian Mountain Battery, Aug. 1915; Lieut. Dec. 1917. India.

FENWICK, HAROLD HENDERSON.
  George Watson's College. Student of Science, 1909-14. 3rd Signal Coy. R.E., Motor Dispatch Rider Aug. 1914; Sergeant Dispatch Rider 1917. France 1914-19.

FENWICK, STANLEY.
  George Watson's College. Student of Medicine, 1909-14; M.B., Ch.B. 1914. R.A.M.C., Lieut. Oct. 1914; Captain Oct. 1915; Major April 1918 to April 1920. France Nov. 1914, the Rhine, and Persia. M.C. Oct. 1918.

FERGUSON, ALEXANDER EDWARD.
  Royal High School; First XV. Student of Science, 1915-17. O.T.C. Infantry, Feb. 1916 to March 1917, Cadet. 3rd King's Own Scottish Borderers, Private March 1917. Machine-Gun Corps, 2nd Lieut. Sept. 1917. Wounded April 1918.

FERGUSON, ANDREW JAMES.
  George Watson's College. Student of Arts and Medicine, 1905-14; M.A. 1911; M.B., Ch.B. 1914. President, Union and S.R.C. R.A.M.C., Lieut. Sept. 1915; Captain June 1918; Acting Major March 1919. 112th Field Ambulance. Reserve Household Battn., Jan. to Dec. 1917. France.

FERGUSON, DUNCAN LAMONT. (See p. 749.)

FERGUSON, HARRY S.
  George Watson's College. Student of Law, 1911-14. Writer to the Signet, 1914. Highland Cyclist Battn., Private 1908; 2nd Lieut. April 1913; Lieut. Nov. 1914; Captain April 1915.

FERGUSON, HENRY TAYLOR.
  George Watson's College. Student of Arts, 1914-16 and 1918-19. 11th Royal Scots, Private. R.G.A., Gunner.

FERGUSON, JAMES HAIG.
  Collegiate School, Edinburgh. M.B., C.M. 1884; M.D. 1890; F.R.C.P. 1889; & S. (Edin.) 1902; M.R.C.S. (Eng.) 1884. Lecturer in Clinical Gynæcology. 1/1st City of Edinburgh Volunteer Regiment, Private Dec. 1914.

FERGUSON, JOHN ALEXANDER.
  Daniel Stewart's College; First XV. and XI. M.A. 1901; B.A. (Oxford). Oxford University Volunteers, 1899-1902, Sergeant. 5th Punjab Light Horse Volunteers, Trooper 1911. Indian Defence Force, 2nd Lieut. April 1917; Captain Oct. 1918. O.B.E. Jan. 1919.

FERGUSON, JOHN CAMERON.
  Alyth School. M.A. 1909. Schoolmaster. R.G.A., 536th Battery, Gunner Aug. 1917; L/Bombardier (Signaller).

Record of War Service

FERGUSON, JOHN JAMES HARROWER.
Brechin High School. M.B., Ch.B. 1906. President, S.R.C. R.A.M.C., Lieut. June 1915; Captain June 1916. France, 9th Division; first Somme, Arras, Nieuport, Ypres; Italy, 41st Division, 1917-18; Somme March to April 1918; Ypres to Oct. 1918. M.C. and Bar May 1918.

FERGUSON, KARL VICTOR MACDONALD.
George Watson's College. Student of Arts and Science, 1916-17 and 1918-19. O.T.C. Artillery, Dec. 1916 to Oct. 1917, Cadet. R.F.A., Gunner Oct. 1918.

FERGUSON, KENNETH C.
Student of Medicine, 1911-14. O.T.C. Artillery, Oct. 1912 to May 1914, Cadet Bombardier. 4th Argyll and Sutherland Highlanders, 2nd Lieut. Aug. 1914; Lieut. Oct. 1916; Captain Feb. 1918. Dardanelles, Egypt, and Cyprus.

FERGUSON, THOMAS LOWE.
Daniel Stewart's College. Student of Law, 1913-14. Lothians and Border Horse, Private. Mobilised Aug. 1914. 4th Royal Scots (T.), 2nd Lieut. Feb. 1915; Lieut. Sept. 1915; Captain May 1916 to March 1919.

FERGUSON, WILLIAM HAIG.
Edinburgh Academy. B.A. (Camb.) 1913. Student of Medicine, 1911-16; M.B., Ch.B. 1916. O.T.C. Medical, May 1915 to March 1916, Cadet L/Corporal. R.A.M.C. (Regulars), Lieut. April 1916; Captain Nov. 1916. Wounded Oct. 1918. M.C. Sept. 1918. Dispatches Oct. 1918. Bar to M.C. March 1919.

FERGUSON, WILLIAM PIKE.
George Watson's College. M.A. 1903; B.Sc. 1905; M.B., Ch.B. 1907; M.D. 1911. R.A.M.C. (T.), Lieut. Sept. 1914; Temp. Captain Feb. 1915; Captain April 1915; Acting Major Jan. 1918 to March 1919. 3rd East Lancashire Field Ambulance. France; Nieuport, Passchendaele, and Somme. M.C. June 1919.

FERGUSON, WILLIAM ALEXANDER MACLEOD.
Student of Arts, 1911-14. Royal Fusiliers, Public Schools Battn., Private.

FERGUSSON, ADAM WIGHTMAN.
Langholm School. M.A. 1890; B.D. 1893. Minister, Church of Scotland, Chaplain, 4th Royal Highlanders (Black Watch); Captain May 1912. Craigleith Military Hospital, 1915.

FERGUSSON, DAVID REGINALD.
Ayr Academy; First XV. O.T.C. 1911-15, Pipe-Major. University O.T.C. Infantry, May 1917 to Jan. 1918, Cadet Sergeant; Officer Cadet. 3rd and 1st Royal Scots Fusiliers, 2nd Lieut. June 1918. France Aug. 1918.

FERGUSSON, DONALD CAMERON.
B.Sc. 1913. Lecturer in Forestry. O.T.C. Artillery, Dec. 1914 to July 1915, Cadet. R.F.A., 2nd Lieut. July 1915; Lieut. July 1917. R.H.A. France. Wounded April 1918. Dispatches April 1918. M.C. Aug. 1918.

Record of War Service

FERGUSSON, DONALD FERGUS.
   Stirling High School. Student of Arts, 1912. R.A.M.C., Private Oct. 1914. 11th Royal Highlanders (Black Watch), 2nd Lieut. Oct. 1914. Resigned May 1915. R.G.A., 120th Heavy Battery, Gunner May 1915. France 1916-17; the Somme. Hospital May 1917. Invalided out April 1918.

FERGUSSON, DUNCAN.
   Student of Medicine, 1913-18; M.B., Ch.B. 1918. O.T.C. Infantry, 1914-16; Medical, Unattached List, 2nd Lieut. 1916-18.

FERGUSSON, JAMES WIGHTMAN.
   Dundee High School. Student of Arts, 1916-17 and 1918-19. R.F.A., Gunner 1917.

FERGUSSON, VIVIAN MOFFATT.
   Burlington House, Richmond. Student of Medicine, 1896-8. University Coy. E.C.A.V., Gunner. Royal Artillery, 2nd Lieut. 1900; Lieut. 1901; Captain 1908; Major Oct. 1914; Brevet Lieut.-Col. June 1917; Acting Lieut.-Col. Aug. 1917. France Jan. 1915; Macedonia Dec. 1915; Egypt and Palestine May 1916 to Nov. 1918. D.S.O. Jan. 1916. Six times Mentioned in Dispatches.

FERLIE, ROBERT.
   George Heriot's School; First XV. and XI. Student of Science, 1910-14; B.Sc. 1914. A.I.C. R.E. (Chemist's Battn.), Sapper Nov. 1915; Motor Dispatch Rider 1916. France. Chemist, H.M. Factory, Pembry, South Wales, 1917-18.

FERMIE, ARTHUR NOEL.
   St Joseph's College, Dumfries. Student of Science, 1916-17. Army Pay Corps, Private July 1918; Corporal July 1919.

FERNEY, EDWARD MURRAY.
   George Heriot's School. Student of Medicine, 1909-14. Scottish Horse (T.), L/Corporal Sept. 1914; 2nd Lieut.; Lieut. July 1917. 13th Royal Highlanders (Black Watch).

FERREIRA, EDWIN CARL FERNANDES.
   Charterhouse. Student of Science, 1913-14. O.T.C. Infantry, Oct. 1912 to Sept. 1914, Cadet. 9th and 12th Scottish Rifles, 2nd Lieut. Aug. 1914; Lieut. Feb. 1915; Captain July 1916. 1st Seaforth Highlanders. Royal Air Force. France, Salonika, and Palestine.

FERREIRA, PHILIP DENNIS FERNANDES.
   Charterhouse. Student of Science, 1912-14. O.T.C. Infantry, 1912-14, Cadet. 9th Scottish Rifles, 2nd Lieut. Aug. 1914; Lieut. May 1916; Acting Captain July 1917. France May 1915 to Jan. 1919. Dispatches June 1919.

FERRIE, ARCHIBALD McLAREN.
   Student of Medicine 1911-16; M.B., Ch.B. 1916. O.T.C. Medical, Nov. 1914 to July 1916, Cadet. R.A.M.C., Lieut. Aug. 1916; Captain Feb. 1917; Acting Major and D.A.D.M.S. Dec. 1918. 6th East Kent Regiment (Buffs). France. M.C. Jan. 1918.

Record of War Service

FERRIER, DOUGLAS.
    Grammar School, Old Aberdeen. M.A. 1887. Minister, U.F. Church of Scotland. Chaplain, 4th Class, Feb. 1913. 6th Scottish Rifles (T.), 2nd Lowland Division and Officiating Minister, Hillpark V.A.D. Hospital.

FETHERSTON, RICHARD HERBERT JOSEPH.
    Wesley College, Melbourne. M.B., C.M. 1886; M.D. 1888; L.R.C.S. (Ireland) 1884. Australian Army Medical Corps, 1887; Lieut.-Col. Aug. 1914; Colonel Jan. 1915; Surgeon-General Jan. 1916. D.G.M.S. Australia, 1914-19. Dispatches March 1916.

FFRENCH, ERNEST GEORGE.
    M.B., Ch.B. 1898; M.D. 1906; F.R.C.S. (Edin.) 1909. R.A.M.C., Major May 1913.

FINDLATER, ALEXANDER JOHN MACDONALD.
    Royal High School. Student of Medicine, 1916-17 and 1918-19. O.T.C. Artillery, May 1917 to June 1918, Cadet. R.F.A., Officer Cadet June 1918.

FINDLATER, THOMAS CADZOW.
    Student of Medicine, 1908-14; M.B., Ch.B. 1914. R.A.M.C., Lieut. June 1915; Captain June 1916.

FINDLAY, GEORGE WILLIAM MARSHALL.
    Dean Close School, Cheltenham. O.T.C. 1908-10, L/Corporal. Student of Medicine, 1910-16; M.B., Ch.B. 1915; M.D. 1920. Royal Navy, Surgeon-Probationer, April 1915; Surgeon-Lieut. Dec. 1915. O.B.E. (Military) July 1919.

FINDLAY, JAMES LESLIE.
    Dollar Academy and George Watson's College. Student of Arts, 1888-9. L.Th. (Durham). Chaplain, 4th Class, 1901. South African Campaign, 1901-2. Chaplain, 2nd Class; Principal Chaplain, Black Sea, July 1919. France 1914. D.S.O.; Italian Military Cross. Three times Mentioned in Dispatches.

FINDLAY, JOHN.
    M.B., Ch.B. 1908; M.D. 1913; D.P.H., R.C.P.S. (Eng.) 1910. R.A.M.C., Lieut. Sept. 1917; Captain Sept. 1918. 26th Field Ambulance. M.O., 1st Worcestershire Regiment. France. Prisoner of War May 1918 (Stralsund).

FINDLAY, JOHN MERRIEVALE. (See p. 749.)

FINDLAY, RONALD STUART.
    Merchiston Castle; First XV. O.T.C. 1913-16, Cadet Corporal. Student of Commerce. O.T.C. Infantry, July 1917 to Jan. 1918, Cadet; Officer Cadet Jan. 1918. 1/5th Royal Scots Fusiliers, 2nd Lieut. June 1918. M.C.

FINLAY, GILBERT LAURIE KERR.
    Winchester. M.B., C.M. 1898. Civil Surgeon, South African Campaign, 1900-1. R.A.M.C., Lieut. Aug. 1914; Captain Aug. 1915. France 1914-17. No. 1 Medical Discharge Board, April 1918 to May 1919. Wounded April 1915. Mention.

Record of War Service

FINLAY, THOMAS MATTHEW.
Sandwick School, Shetland. M.A. 1902; B.Sc. (Distinction) 1911. Lecturer in Geology. Scottish Horse (T.), Private Sept. 1914; 2nd Lieut. March 1915; Captain Aug. 1916. France 1918. Wounded at Ledeghem Oct. 1918.

FINLAY, THOMAS YULE.
Royal High School. M.B., Ch.B. 1907; M.D. 1912. R.A.M.C., Lieut. 1916.

FINLAYSON, DONALD.
Wick School. M.A., B.Sc. 1912. 2nd and 1st Lovat Scouts (T.), Private Sept. 1914; Corporal; Sergeant; Sergeant-Major; 2nd Lieut. Dec. 1915; Lieut. July 1917. M.C. and Bar April 1918.

FINLAYSON, WILLIAM LOGIE.
M.A. 1909; B.D. 1911. Minister, Church of Scotland. R.A.M.C., Private.

FINN, WILFRID.
Hymers College. O.T.C. 1911-13. Student of Medicine, 1914. O.T.C. Infantry, June 1915, Cadet. 9th Yorkshire Regiment, 2nd Lieut. Oct. 1915; Lieut. 1917.

FIRTH, ARTHUR HARCUS.
Daniel Stewart's College. M.A. 1897; M.B. Ch.B. 1901; M.D. 1913. R.A.M.C., Lieut. Jan. 1918; Captain Jan. to May 1919.

FIRTH, EDWARD KINGSLEY ANSON.
Haileybury. O.T.C. 1914-17. Student of Medicine, 1917 and 1919. O.T.C. Infantry, May 1917 to April 1918, Cadet; Officer Cadet May 1918. Royal West Surrey Regiment, 2nd Lieut. Feb. 1919.

FISCHER, LEWIS GORDON.
M.B., C.M. 1885. Indian Medical Service, Lieut.-Col. March 1907.

FISHER, ALASTAIR MACDOUGALL.
George Watson's College. Student of Law, 1904-6. Chartered Accountant, 1908. 5th Montreal Highlanders, Lieut. Wounded.

FISHER, DAVID LEONARD.
M.B., C.M. 1897. R.A.M.C. (T.), Lieut. 1908; Captain 1910; Major Oct. 1914; Acting Lieut.-Col. Oct. 1916. 3rd Northumbrian Field Ambulance. O.C., 86th Field Ambulance, 1916-18. France 1915; Salonika 1915-18; Constantinople 1918. D.S.O. Officier Légion d'Honneur. Dispatches 1915, 1916, and 1917.

FISHER, HARRY STEEL.
Glasgow High School and George Watson's College. O.T.C. 1910-11. Student of Medicine, 1912-14 and 1918-19. O.T.C. Artillery, Oct. 1911 to July 1915, and Medical, April 1918-19, Cadet. R.E., Corporal July 1915.

FISHER, JOHN W. D.
George Heriot's School. Student of Science, 1912-14. O.T.C. Artillery, Nov. 1914 to April 1915, Cadet. R.F.A. (S.R.), 282nd Brigade, 2nd Lieut. April 1915; Lieut. June 1917; Acting Captain June 1918. Dispatches May 1918.

Record of War Service

FISHER, K. S.
Student of Arts. Machine-Gun Corps, L/Corporal.

FISHER, MATTHEW GEORGE.
M.A. 1910; LL.B. and Advocate, 1913. O.T.C. Infantry, Sept. 1914 to Jan. 1915, Cadet. 4th Border Regiment, 2nd Lieut. Jan. 1915; Lieut. July 1917. Staff Captain Aug. 1917; Brigade Major Aug. 1919. Jubbulpore Brigade, India, March 1915 to Nov. 1919.

FISHER, THOMAS.
Leith Academy. University O.T.C. Artillery, Dec. 1917 to Sept. 1918, Cadet Corporal; Officer Cadet Sept. 1918. R.F.A., 2nd Lieut. April 1919.

FITZGERALD, GORDON WILLIAM.
M.B., C.M. 1898; M.D. 1901. R.A.M.C. (T.), Major Sept. 1914; Temp. Lieut.-Col. Dec. 1917. 1st Field Ambulance, East Lancashire Division; Fusehill War Hospital.

FITZGERALD, WILLIAM ERNEST.
George Watson's College. M.B., Ch.B. 1911; D.P.H. R.A.M.C. (T.), Lieut. Sept. 1914; Captain April 1915. Attached 6th Manchesters. France 1917-18. No. 6 General Hospital, Rouen, Feb. to July 1918. Railway Engineers, No. 1 Section, July to Dec. 1918. Portland Military Hospital, 1919. Gassed at Passchendaele. M.C. July 1917.

FITZMAURICE, HENRY GODFREY.
Student of Medicine, 1918-19. O.T.C. Medical, 1914, Cadet. R.N.V.R., Surgeon-Probationer.

FITZPATRICK, OWEN.
Clongowes Wood College. Student of Medicine, 1915-20; M.B., Ch.B. 1920. O.T.C. Medical, Oct. 1915 to Feb. 1918, Cadet. Royal Navy, Surgeon Sub-Lieut. March 1918.

FITZWILLIAMS, DUNCAN CAMPBELL LLOYD.
Christ College, Brecon; First XV. O.T.C. M.B., Ch.B. 1902; M.D., Ch.M.; F.R.C.S. (Edin.) and (Lond.). Volunteer Medical Staff Corps, 1901-2, Sergeant. South African Campaign, 1900-1. R.A.M.C. (T.), Captain 1913; Major June 1918; Lieut.-Col. Oct. 1918. 1st City of London Field Ambulance. Chevalier Crown of Rumania; St Vladimir (4th Class); St Anna (2nd and 3rd Class); St Stanislaus (2nd and 3rd Class); all with Swords. Dispatches 1919.

FLECK, JAMES.
Edinburgh Academy. Student of Law, 1912-13. 4th Royal Scots (T.), Lieut.; Capt. Oct. 1916. Employed with Ministry of Labour.

FLEMING, ALEXANDER MATHERS.
Clair Hall Academy, Edinburgh. M.B., C.M. 1895. Indian Medical Service, 1898; Major July 1910; Lieut.-Col. 1918. Mesopotamia Feb. 1916 to June 1918. 22nd Combined Field Ambulance, 1917. India 1919. A.D.M.S., Deraját Division. Waziristan, Nov. 1919.

Record of War Service

FLEMING, ARCHIBALD.
  Perth Academy. M.A. 1883; D.D. Minister, Church of Scotland, Chaplain, 4th Class, Nov. 1900; 2nd Class, Nov. 1918. London Scottish.

FLEMING, ARCHIBALD NICOL.
  Fettes; First XV. and XI. M.B., C.M. 1895; F.R.C.S. (Edin.). Indian Medical Service, June 1896; Major Jan. 1908; Lieut.-Col. Jan. 1916. Tirah Campaign, N.F.W., India, 1897. France Sept. 1914; Egypt April 1918. Dispatches June 1916 and Jan. 1918. D.S.O. Jan. 1918.

FLEMING, DAVID.
  George Watson's College. Student of Arts, 1910-15; M.A. 1914. Schoolmaster. 9th Royal Scots (T.), Private Oct. 1914. 4th Seaforth Highlanders, 2nd Lieut. July 1915; Lieut. July 1917 to Jan. 1919. Attached 1/5th Argyll and Sutherland Highlanders. France and Palestine. Wounded April 1915. M.C. and Croix de Guerre avec Palme Nov. 1918.

FLEMING, DAVID PINKERTON.
  Student of Arts and Law, 1900-2. M.A. and LL.B. (Glasg). Advocate, 1902. 5th Scottish Rifles, Feb. 1915; Captain Feb. 1915; Major Oct. 1918. M.C.; Croix de Guerre (Belgian). Dispatches Feb. 1917.

FLEMING, GEORGE.
  Royal High School. M.B., C.M. 1891; M.R.C.P. (Edin.) 1895. R.A.M.C., Lieut. Sept. 1916; Captain Sept. 1917. Hospital Ship, March to April 1917. Connaught Hospital, Aldershot.

FLEMING, JOHN GAGE.
  Ampleforth School. M.B., Ch.B. 1907. R.A.M.C., Aug. 1916, Captain. 44th General Hospital.

FLEMING, ROBERT.
  Student of Law, 1893-5. S.S.C. 1899. 4th Royal Scots (T.), Capt. Sept. 1914; Major. Employed with Ministry of National Service.

FLEMING, ROBERT ALEXANDER.
  Larchfield, Helensburgh, and Craigmount, Edinburgh. M.A. 1884; M.B., C.M. 1888; M.D. 1896; F.R.C.P. (Edin.) 1892. Senior Lecturer in Clinical Medicine, R.I.E. R.A.M.C. (T.), Captain 1908. Mobilised Sept. 1914; Major March 1918. 2nd Scottish General Hospital. Salonika July 1916 to Feb. 1918.

FLEMING, SAMUEL.
  M.B., C.M. 1890; D.P.H. (Camb.). R.A.M.C., Lieut. March 1915; Captain Jan. 1916; Major March 1916; Brevet Lieut.-Col. June 1919. General Courts-Martial H.Q., Aldershot, March 1915 to Jan. 1918. D.A.D.G. and Legal Adviser, Army Medical Department, War Office, 1918-19. Mention Jan. 1917.

FLEMING, WILLIAM ARNOT.
  George Watson's College. M.A. 1900; LL.B. 1902. Advocate, 1904. 8th Royal Scots (T.), Captain Jan. 1915. Pioneers, 51st Division. France 1917-18. Wounded.

Record of War Service

FLEMINGTON, ROBERT RUSSELL.
Student of Science, 1912-14. R.G.A., Forth (T.), June 1913; Captain Oct. 1915. Indian Army Supply and Transport Corps, Captain.

FLETCHER, C. M. R.
Student of Medicine. Royal Navy, Assistant Surgeon.

FLETCHER, FRANCIS SAMUEL BROOK.
Giggleswick; First XV. M.B., Ch.B. 1910. R.A.M.C., Lieut. July 1915; Captain Feb. 1917 to April 1919.

FLETCHER, HENRY JAMES.
Tonbridge and Owens College, Manchester. M.B., C.M. 1882. R.A.M.C. (Reg.), 1885. Indian Frontier, 1891; South African Campaign, 1900-2; Lieut.-Col. May 1905. Employed 1917-18.

FLETCHER, HUGH NETHERSOLE.
Charterhouse. M.B., Ch.B. 1903; M.D. 1909; F.R.C.S. (Edin.) 1905. First XV. and XI. R.A.M.C. (T.), Captain 1911. 2nd Eastern General Hospital, Aug. 1914 to Sept. 1917. 55th General Hospital, France, Oct. 1917 to Feb. 1919.

FLETCHER, JOHN SANDISON.
Wick High School. Student of Arts, 1916-19. Gordon Highlanders (Graduate Battn.), Private.

FLETCHER, JOSEPH EDWARD.
Edward VI. School, Retford; First XI. Student of Medicine, 1914-15 and 1918-19. O.T.C. Medical, Oct. 1914 to July 1915, Cadet. R.A.M.C., Private Aug. 1915. 2/20th London Regiment, Private May 1916; L/Corporal Nov. 1916. 7th Sherwood Foresters, 2nd Lieut. Sept. to Nov. 1917.

FLETCHER, MILES HENRY ALEXANDER.
St Edward's, Oxford. O.T.C. 1909-11. Student of Medicine, 1912-14. O.T.C. Artillery, Nov. 1912 to Aug. 1914, Cadet. R.F.A., 56th Brigade, 2nd Lieut. Aug. 1914; Lieut. Jan. 1918. Royal Air Force, Oct. 1917. Cape Helles, Dardanelles 1915; Mesopotamia 1916-17; Egypt 1918.

FLETCHER, ROBERT FRANCIS GORDON.
Edinburgh Academy. University O.T.C. Artillery, 1915-16, Cadet; B.Q.M.S.; Officer Cadet Jan. 1917. R.F.A. (T.), 2nd Lieut. June 1917. Salonika.

FLETCHER, WILLIAM.
M.B., C.M. 1892. R.A.M.C., Captain July 1916. D.S.O.

FLETT, DAVID ALEXANDER.
Kirkwall Burgh School. Student of Arts, 1914-15. O.T.C. Artillery, Oct. 1914 to June 1915, Cadet. R.F.A., 2nd Lieut. June 1915; Lieut. Sept. 1916; Acting Captain.

Record of War Service

FLETT, JAMES THOMAS.
Kirkwall Burgh School. Student of Science, 1913-14 and 1918-19. O.T.C. Engineers, Jan. to Oct. 1914, Cadet. R.E., City of Dundee, Sapper Oct. 1914. R.G.A., 2nd Lieut. Nov. 1915; Lieut. July 1917; Acting Captain Dec. 1917; Acting Major March 1919.

FOGGIE, WILLIAM EDWARD.
Dundee High School. M.A. 1889; M.B., C.M. 1893; M.D. 1910. Lecturer, Diseases of Skin, St Andrews University. R.A.M.C. (T.), Feb. 1897, Lieut.-Col. May 1913. 3rd Highland Field Ambulance. D.S.O. June 1918; T.D. 1918. Dispatches April 1918. Associate, Order of St John of Jerusalem.

FOGGO, JOHN F.
George Heriot's School. Student of Science, 1917. O.T.C. Artillery, April to Nov. 1917, Cadet; Officer Cadet Nov. 1917. Royal Air Force, Flight Cadet May 1918; 2nd Lieut. July 1918. France; 205th Squadron.

FOOTE, WILLIAM.
Dunfermline High School. Student of Arts, 1909-12 and 1918-19; M.A. 1912. 4th Royal Scots, Private Sept. 1914. Wounded at Gallipoli July 1915.

FORBES, ALASTAIR GORDON.
Royal High School. M.B., Ch.B. 1912. O.T.C. Artillery, 1908-13, Cadet Farrier Sergeant. South African Medical Corps, Captain Sept. 1914 to Oct. 1919. De Beers Ambulance Corps. German S.-W. Africa; Egypt and France 1914-18. Wounded. M.C.

FORBES, ALEXANDER KEITH.
Royal High School. M.B., Ch.B. 1912. Naval Transport Service, Surgeon Aug. to Oct. 1914. R.A.M.C., Lieut. Nov. 1914; Captain Nov. 1915. France 1914. 1st Coldstream Guards. Serbian Order of St Sava (5th Class), June 1915. M.C. Sept. 1918.

FORBES, DAVID LAING.
Broughton School, Edinburgh. Student of Science, 1918. R.F.A., Gunner Sept. 1914. 255th Brigade, 51st Division.

FORBES, DONALD THOMSON.
Pitlochry School. M.A. 1911. 5th and 12th Highland Light Infantry, Private Nov. 1915; L/Corporal 1916; 2nd Lieut. March 1918. Attached Scottish Rifles. France 1918-19.

FORBES, DUNCAN.
Perth Academy. M.B., Ch.B. 1898; M.D., B.Sc. (P.H.) 1901; D.P.H. (Camb.) 1901. R.A.M.C. (T.), Sanitary Corps, Captain; Major Oct. 1915. M.B.E.

FORBES, HENRY NICOLL.
George Watson's College. M.A. (Hons. Phil.) 1912. Oxford University, 1912-14. Minister, Church of England, 1914. Chaplain, 4th Class, Nov. 1915.

Record of War Service

FORBES, JAMES.
Dunfermline High School. Student of Arts, 1913-15 and 1918-19. O.T.C. Infantry, 1914-15, Cadet. Army Gymnastic Staff, C.S.M. Instructor.

FORBES, JOHN DOUGLAS.
Ayr Academy; First XI. O.T.C. 1910-14. Student of Arts, 1916-17 and 1918-19. O.T.C. Infantry, 1916-17, Cadet L/Corporal. East Kent Regiment (Buffs), Private June 1917. Lancashire Fusiliers, 2nd Lieut. Sept. 1917 to Jan. 1919.

FORBES, JOHN RICHARD MACKENZIE.
Stobhill School. M.A. 1902; B.D. 1906. Minister, Church of Scotland. Motor Ambulance (Driver) 1915-16. Chaplain, 4th Class, Captain Aug. 1916. France; Somme, and Belgium; 34th Casualty Clearing Station, 1916-17.

FORBES, LEWIS JEX-BLAKE.
B.Sc. 1910. O.T.C. Artillery, 1908-10, Cadet; transferred to Engineers. R.G.A., 2nd Lieut. Feb. 1915. R.E., Lieut. Oct. 1915; Captain. Egypt.

FORBES, WILLIAM JOHN.
Crieff and Perth Academies. M.A. 1906; B.D. 1909. Minister, Church of Scotland. Chaplain, 4th Class, Captain May 1916. Royal Scots and R.E.

FORBES, WILLIAM SMITH.
M.B., Ch.B. 1907. O.T.C. Infantry, 1911-15, Captain and O.C. Oct. 1914 to April 1915. R.A.M.C. (T.), Captain April 1915. 1/1st London Casualty Clearing Station.

FORD, PATRICK JOHNSTON.
Edinburgh Academy. M.A. (Oxford); LL.B. 1907. Advocate 1907. M.P. 1920. 2/4th Cameron Highlanders, Lieut. Nov. 1914 to April 1915. Invalided out. Military Representative, Midlothian Tribunal, 1915-16. Temp. Hon. Lieut. Recruiting, Jan. 1917. General Staff, Scottish Command, Nov. 1918 to Jan. 1919.

FORD, STANLEY.
Bridlington Grammar School. Student of Medicine, 1910-14 and 1919-20. O.T.C. Medical, April 1918 to Feb. 1919, Cadet. R.A.M.C., Private Dec. 1914.

FORD ROBERTSON, ALEXANDER.
Edinburgh Academy. O.T.C. 1915-16. Student of Science, 1916-17. O.T.C. Artillery, April 1917-18, Cadet; Officer Cadet, April 1918. R.F.A., 2nd Lieut. Feb. 1919.

FORD ROBERTSON, WILLIAM MARSDEN.
Edinburgh Academy. O.T.C. 1915-17. Student of Medicine, 1918-19. O.T.C. Artillery, April 1917-18, Cadet; Officer Cadet April 1918. R.F.A., 2nd Lieut. Feb. 1919.

FORDYCE, ALEXANDER RUSSELL.
Daniel Stewart's College. M.B., Ch.B. 1899. R.A.M.C. (T.), Lieut. Nov. 1914; Captain June 1915. France. Wounded March 1918.

Record of War Service

FORKER, THOMAS McEWEN.
 Broughton School, Edinburgh. M.A. 1912. Schoolmaster. R.E. (Special Brigade), Corporal Sept. 1915.

FORMAN, ARTHUR.
 Merchiston Castle; First XI. Cadet Corps 1902-7, Cadet Pipe-Major. B.Sc. (Glasg.). A.M.I.C.E. University O.T.C. Engineers, 1912-13, Cadet L/Corporal. R.E., 85th Field Coy., 2nd Lieut. Sept. 1915; Lieut. May 1916; Captain April 1918; Acting Major Feb. 1919. 66th Field Coy., Dec. 1918 to Feb. 1919. Baghdad Railways, Feb. to Aug. 1919. M.C. Jan. 1918; Croix de Guerre (Salonika) Sept. 1916.

FORREST, ANDREW WALKER.
 George Watson's College. Student of Arts and Medicine, 1910-15; M.A. 1912; M.B., Ch.B. 1915; M.D. 1920. O.T.C. Infantry, 1910-13, Medical, 1914-15, Cadet. R.A.M.C., Lieut. May 1915; Captain May 1916 to April 1919. 10th Royal Hussars. France 1915-18; second Ypres, Loos 1915; Arras 1917; Cambrai 1918. Wounded March 1918.

FORREST, GAVIN ADDIE.
 Glasgow High School. M.B., Ch.B. 1901. N.Z. Medical Corps, Captain Feb. 1916.

FORREST, JAMES AQUILON.
 M.B., C.M. 1895. Royal Navy, 1898; Surgeon-Commander, 1914. H.M. Ships *Berwick*, *Lancaster*, and *Vincent*.

FORREST, JOHN VINCENT.
 M.B., C.M. 1894. Army Medical Service, July 1895; Lieut.-Col. March 1915; Colonel Dec. 1917. South African Campaign, 1899-1902. France 1914; Italy 1918. Dispatches Oct. 1914, May 1915, June 1916, June 1918, Jan. and June 1919. C.M.G. June 1916. Associate, Order of St John of Jerusalem, Dec. 1916. C.B. June 1919.

FORREST, PETER.
 Student of Arts, 1912-14. 4th Royal Scots (T.), Private.

FORREST, STEPHEN.
 George Watson's College. M.A. 1903; M.B., Ch.B. 1907; M.D. 1910. University Coy., E.C.A.V. 1902, Gunner. R.A.M.C., Lieut. 1915; Captain July 1916. Mudros 1915; Egypt 1916.

FORRESTER, ROBERT BLAIR.
 Lancaster Royal Grammar School. M.A. (Hons. Econ. Sc.) 1909. Lecturer in Economics, Manchester University, 1909-12, and Aberdeen University, 1912-19. Machine-Gun Corps (T.), Private July 1918.

FORRESTER, ROBERT CAIRNS.
 George Watson's College. O.T.C. 1913-15. Student of Medicine, 1918-19. 7th Royal Scots, 2nd Lieut. Aug. 1915; Lieut. Sept. 1916. France 1917-18; Ypres and Cambrai. Twice Wounded.

Record of War Service

FORRESTER, WILLIAM ROXBURGH.
Glasgow Academy. Student of Arts, 1912-14; M.A. (Hons. Ment. Phil.) 1914. Assistant, Moral Philosophy. 5th and 15th Royal Scots, Private Oct. 1914. 11th Gordon Highlanders, 2nd Lieut. Dec. 1914. R.F.A., 2nd Lieut. June 1915; Lieut. July 1917. France Sept. 1915; Mesopotamia Jan. 1916; Persia June 1918; India Dec. 1918. M.C. July 1918.

FORSON, MARGARET WIGHTMAN.
Perth Academy; First XI. M.A. 1912. Q.M.A.A.C., May 1917.

FORSTER, WILLIAM CHARLES HUGHAN.
M.B., C.M. 1896. Indian Medical Service, Major Jan. 1911.

FORSYTH, A. R.
Student. A.S.C. (T.), Captain Aug. 1914. Highland Mounted Brigade, Transport and Supply Column.

FORSYTH, CHARLES.
Wakefield School; First XV. and XI. M.B., Ch.B. 1898; M.D. 1908; F.R.C.S. (Edin.) 1902; D.T.M. (Liverpool). Lecturer on Midwifery, Hong-Kong University. Attached R.A.M.C., Oct. 1914. M.O. in charge of German Camp, Hong-Kong.

FORSYTH, CHARLES CALDER.
Student of Medicine, 1909; L.R.C.P. & S. (Edin.), and L.R.F.P.S. (Glasg.) 1913; L.D.S. O.T.C. Infantry, Jan. 1911 to Nov. 1913, Cadet. 8th Seaforth Highlanders, Lieut. Aug. 1914; Captain Nov. 1914. R.A.M.C., Captain July 1916; Acting Major Jan. 1918 to March 1919. France June 1915 to Jan. 1917. Dispatches 1916 and 1918. M.C. April 1918.

FORSYTH, HENRY RUSSELL.
Montrose Academy; First XV. University O.T.C. Artillery, Nov. 1915 to Jan. 1916, Cadet. R.F.A., 2nd Lieut. Jan. 1916; Lieut. July 1917.

FORSYTH, WILLIAM HENRY.
Royal High School. M.B., Ch.B. 1904; D.T.M. and H. 1910. Medical Staff Corps (V.), 1899-1902, Private. R.A.M.C., Lieut. 1906; Major July 1916; Acting Lieut.-Col. Aug. 1916. France 1914. 38th Field Ambulance and No. 15 Casualty Clearing Station. Dispatches May 1917 and Nov. 1918. D.S.O. Jan. 1919.

FORTUNE, ERNEST GEORGE.
Edinburgh Academy. M.B., C.M. 1892; F.R.C.S. (Edin.). R.A.M.C. (T.), Captain July 1908. Mobilised Aug. 1914. 3rd Scottish General Hospital.

FORTUNE, MACKENZIE.
George Watson's College. Student of Science, 1913-15. O.T.C. Infantry, May to Oct. 1915, Cadet. R.F.A. (T.), 2nd Lieut. Oct. 1915; Lieut. June 1916; Captain 1918. 1st Lowland Brigade. France Jan. 1916-19. M.C.

FOSTER, ARTHUR.
Caterham Congregational School. M.B., C.M. 1893; M.D. 1897. R.A.M.C. (T.), Captain July 1915. 5th Northern General Hospital, Leicester.

Record of War Service

FOSTER, FRANCIS GREGORY.
    Fettes. M.A. 1907; M.B., Ch.B. 1913. O.T.C. Infantry, 1909-13, Cadet Colour-Sergeant. R.A.M.C. (S.R.), Lieut. April 1913. Mobilised Aug. 1914, Captain April 1915; Acting Major Nov. 1918. France 1914. Dispatches Jan. 1917 and April 1919.

FOSTER, LANCELOT WILLIAM.
    Thanet School, Kent. Student of Medicine, 1912-16. O.T.C. Artillery, 1912-14; Cadet. Croix Rouge Française. Artists' Rifles, Private Oct. 1917. Attached 63rd Naval Division, France. Wounded and taken Prisoner near Cambrai, March 1918.

FOSTER, MALCOLM.
    Sedbergh. Student of Medicine, 1912-16; M.B., Ch.B. 1916. O.T.C. Medical, Nov. 1915 to July 1916, Cadet Corporal. R.A.M.C. (T.), Scottish Horse, Private. R.A.M.C. (S.R.), Lieut. July 1916; Captain Jan. 1917. Mesopotamia, Persia, and N.-W. Frontier, India. Dispatches Nov. 1917.

FOTHERGILL, ALAN ARMOUR.
    Edinburgh Academy. O.T.C. 1912-15, Cadet Corporal. Student of Arts, 1915-16 and 1918-19. 8th Seaforth Highlanders, Private May 1916; L/Corporal. France. Gassed 1918.

FOTHERGILL, GEORGE ALGERNON.
    Uppingham; Athletics. M.B., C.M. 1895. R.A.M.C., Lieut. Oct. 1918. 3C Reserve Brigade, R.F.A.; Connaught and Cambridge Hospitals. M.O., 1st Cavalry Brigade, and Royal Irish Rifles, Aldershot.

FOTHERGILL, REGINALD HANNAY.
    Repton. M.B., Ch.B. 1906. R.A.M.C., Lieut. Jan. 1915; Captain 1916. Wounded 1916. Dispatches Jan. 1916.

FOUCHÉ, FRANÇOIS PETRUS.
    Graaff Reinet College; First XV. and XI. Cadet Corps 1899-1903, Sergeant-Major. M.B., Ch.B. 1910. South African Medical Corps, Captain Oct. 1914 to Feb. 1915. South African Rebellion.

FOULIS, DOUGLAS AINSLIE.
    George Watson's College; First XV. M.A. 1905. 10th Scottish Rifles, Private Aug. 1914; 2nd Lieut. Dec. 1914; Major and Acting Lieut.-Col. March 1918. France. D.S.O. April 1917. Three times Mentioned in Dispatches.

FOWLER, JAMES.
    Hawick Academy. M.A. 1910; B.Sc. 1912. Science Master. O.T.C. Artillery, 1908-10, Cadet Sergeant. R.F.A. (S.R.), 2nd Lieut. March 1910. Royal Air Force (Canada), Aug. 1918.

FOWLER, JAMES STEWART.
    Edinburgh Academy. M.B., C.M. 1892; M.D. 1899. Lecturer, Diseases of Children. R.A.M.C., Captain July 1916.

Record of War Service

FOWLER, WILLIAM.
: M.A. 1895. 3rd Vol. Battn., Royal Scots (Midlothian), Private; 2nd Lieut.; Lieut.

FOWLER, WILLIAM ALEXANDER.
: Invergordon. Student of Arts, 1913-15 and 1918-19; M.A. 1919. O.T.C. Artillery, Feb. to Sept. 1915, Cadet. R.F.A., 2nd Lieut. Sept. 1915; Lieut. July 1916. Dispatches Dec. 1918.

FOX, ROBERT ALGERNON.
: Clifton. M.B., C.M. 1893. Australian Army Medical Corps, Captain May 1917.

FRAME, ROBERT.
: M.A. 1912. Schoolmaster. 12th Argyll and Sutherland Highlanders, Sergeant. Salonika.

FRANCIS, DAVID EDWARD.
: Swansea Grammar School. B.A. Student of Medicine, 1908, 1916-17 and 1918-19. O.T.C. Infantry, 1910-13, Cadet. 2nd King's Own Scottish Borderers.

FRANCIS, HUMPHREY CHILTON HOWARD.
: Haileybury. O.T.C. 1907. M.A. (Durham). Student of Arts, 1914. 9th Royal Scots, May to Aug. 1914, Private. R.A.O.C., Private Aug. 1914 to May 1915. 9th Royal Scots (T.), 2nd Lieut. July 1915 to Aug. 1916. A.O. Department, Lieut. Aug. 1916; Acting Captain Dec. 1918 to March 1919.

FRANKISH, THOMAS.
: M.B., C.M. 1889; B.Sc. (P.H.) 1894. R.F.A. (T.), Feb. 1898; Lieut.-Col. 1912. 1st East Lancashire Brigade. Mobilised Aug. 1914. Transferred to R.A.M.C. (T.), Major; Hon. Lieut.-Col. March 1915. Egypt. T.D.

FRASER, ALASTAIR NORMAN.
: Blairlodge. Cadet Corps 1896-8. M.B., Ch.B. 1904. Vol. Medical Staff Corps, 1899-1904, Q.M.S. South African Campaign, 1900-1. R.A.M.C., Lieut. 1904; Captain 1908; Major July 1915. D.A.D.M.S., Embarkation, Alexandria. Codford Training Centre and Officers' School. 20th Field Ambulance. France. Afghanistan 1919; D.A.D.M.S., N.W.F.P., India. D.S.O. June 1916. Twice Mentioned in Dispatches 1916.

FRASER, ALEXANDER.
: Royal Academy, Inverness. Student of Medicine, 1918. 3rd, 11th, and 12th Royal Scots, Private Feb. 1918. France. Twice Wounded.

FRASER, ARTHUR SMITH.
: Leith Academy. Student of Arts, 1915-16 and 1918-20; M.A. 1920. R.A.M.C. (T.), Private; May 1916, Corporal. 1st Eastern General Hospital.

FRASER, CATHERINE.
: M.B., Ch.B. 1900; D.P.H. (Camb.). Women's Hospital Corps. Attached R.A.M.C., Assistant Surgeon. Military Hospital, Endell Street, London, 1915-17. M.O., H.M. Factory, Pembrey, 1917-18. M.B.E. June 1918.

Record of War Service

FRASER, CHARLES.
M.A. 1895; M.B., Ch.B. 1900; M.D. 1904; D.P.H. (Camb.). R.A.M.C., Captain Nov. 1915. Reinforcement Camp, France.

FRASER, CHARLES LACHLAN.
Montrose Academy and Royal High School. Student of Medicine, 1877; L.R.C.P. & S. (Edin.) 1885; F.R.C.S. (Edin.) 1887; D.P.H. 1890; F.R.C.P. (Edin.) 1895. 4th Volunteer Battn. Northumberland Fusiliers, Captain 1876. R.A.M.C. (T.), Lieut.-Col. Retired May 1914. Berwick Hospital. V.D.

FRASER, DAVID DENHOLM.
George Watson's College. Student of Arts and Divinity, 1888-96; M.A. 1892, Minister, Church of Scotland. Chaplain, 4th Class, Captain July 1915.

FRASER, DONALD ALEXANDER.
Royal Academy, Inverness; First XI. Student of Medicine, 1918. R.G.A. (T.), Gunner Aug. 1914; 2nd Lieut. Feb. 1917; Lieut. Aug. 1918.

FRASER, DOUGLAS JAMES.
Student of Arts, 1910-14. O.T.C. Artillery, 1910-14, Cadet Bombardier. R.F.A., 2nd Lieut. Aug. 1914; Captain Sept. 1917; Acting Major Nov. 1917. M.C.

FRASER, DUNCAN MENZIES.
Inverness College. Student of Science, 1911-14 and 1918-19; B.Sc. 1919. O.T.C. Engineers, May 1912 to Sept. 1914, Cadet C.S.M. R.E. (S.R.), Aug. 1914; 2nd Lieut. Sept. 1914; Lieut. July 1915; Captain Nov. 1917. France Aug. 1915. Wounded July 1917. M.C. Sept. 1917.

FRASER, EDWARD MATHESON.
Student of Medicine, 1913-16 and 1918-19. R.N.V.R., Surgeon-Probationer, May 1916. H.M. Ships *Contest*, *Mansfield*, and *Simoom*. Dover Patrol and Grand Fleet.

FRASER, FRANCIS RICHARD.
Edinburgh Academy; First XV. B.A. (Camb.); M.B., Ch.B. 1910; F.R.C.S. (Edin.). Harvard University Unit, 22nd General Hospital, Aug. 1915 to May 1916. R.A.M.C., Lieut. May 1916; Captain May 1917; Acting Major Oct. 1918.

FRASER, FRANCIS WILLIAM.
Inverness College. Student of Law, 1912-14. 4th Cameron Highlanders, 2nd Lieut. Nov. 1915; Lieut. July 1917; Captain July 1918; Acting Staff-Lieut. Sept. 1918. Attached 11th Royal Welsh Fusiliers. G.H.Q., Salonika, two years.

FRASER, FRANK.
M.B., C.M. 1881; M.D. 1885; L.R.C.P. & S. (Edin.) 1881. R.A.M.C. (V.), Captain June 1915. V.A.D. Hospital, Lyglie, Kent; Penhurst Aerodrome; Prisoners of War Camp, Edenbridge.

Record of War Service

FRASER, GEORGE.
George Watson's College. M.A. 1903. Minister, U.F. Church of Scotland. 8th Highland Light Infantry, Private Feb. 1915. 5/6th Scottish Rifles, 2nd Lieut.; Lieut. March 1918. France 1918.

FRASER, GEORGE ALEXANDER.
Edinburgh Academy. M.A. 1898. Chartered Accountant, 1903. Lothians and Border Horse, Private Sept. 1914. 7/8th King's Own Scottish Borderers, 2nd Lieut. March 1915; Lieut. Nov. 1915 to Feb. 1919. France. Wounded Aug. 1916. Attached War Office, May 1917. M.B.E. June 1919.

FRASER, GEORGE HUDSON.
Student of Medicine, 1911-16; M.B. Ch.B. 1916. O.T.C. Medical, Nov. 1915 to April 1916, Cadet. R.A.M.C. (T.), Private. Scottish Horse Brigade Field Ambulance, 1914. R.A.M.C., Lieut. April 1916; Captain April 1917.

FRASER, HENRY.
Arbroath High School. B.Sc. 1906. R.F.A. (T.), 2nd Highland Brigade, 2nd Lieut. May 1908; Captain 1912; Major March 1916. France May 1915. Wounded at Hebuterne March 1918. Dispatches June 1916 and June 1917. D.S.O. June 1917.

FRASER, HUGH ERSKINE.
George Watson's College. O.T.C. 1916-17. Student of Arts, 1918-19. O.T.C. Artillery, 1917, Cadet; Officer Cadet Aug. 1917. R.F.A., 2nd Lieut. Jan. 1918. France March 1918 to Jan. 1919; Ancre. Wounded Aug. 1918.

FRASER, IAN MARTIN.
Edinburgh Academy. O.T.C. 1910-12. Student of Arts, 1912-14; M.A. 1918. O.T.C. Infantry, Oct. 1912 to Aug. 1914, Cadet L/Corporal. 1/7th Welsh Fusiliers (T.), 2nd Lieut. Sept. 1914; Lieut. Aug. 1915; Acting Captain Nov. 1915; Captain Sept. 1916; Major Feb. 1918. Attached Machine-Gun Corps, March 1916. Gallipoli, Egypt, and Palestine, July 1915 to Aug. 1917; India.

FRASER, IAN ROBERTSON.
Royal High School. B.Sc. 1913. A.M.I.C.E. O.T.C. Engineers, Dec. 1911 to April 1915, Cadet. R.E., Lowland Division, 2nd Lieut. April 1915; Lieut. June 1916; Captain Nov. 1918. Railway Operating Division, R.E., Egypt. Acting District Engineer, Palestine Military Railway.

FRASER, JAMES.
Dingwall Academy. B.Sc. (Forestry) 1912; B.Sc. (Pure Science) 1913. Assistant Forestry Department, 1913-14. Argyll and Sutherland Highlanders, Private May 1915. Seaforth Highlanders, 2nd Lieut. April 1917. R.E., Lieut. June 1917.

FRASER, JAMES ALEXANDER.
Perth Academy; First XV. Student of Arts, 1914. O.T.C. Artillery, Jan. to July 1915, Cadet. R.F.A., 2nd Lieut. July 1915; Lieut. June 1916. Signalling Officer, Artillery Brigade, June 1917 to Dec. 1918.

Record of War Service

FRASER, JAMES EVERARD.
　　Royal High School. Student of Science, 1917. O.T.C. Artillery, May to Dec. 1917, Cadet; Officer Cadet Dec. 1917. R.G.A., 238th Siege Battery, 2nd Lieut. June 1918.

FRASER, JOHN.
　　M.B., Ch.B. 1907; Ch.M. 1910; M.D. 1912. Lecturer, Diseases of Children. R.A.M.C., Lieut. Aug. 1914; Captain Sept. 1914. M.C. Dispatches Jan. 1917.

FRASER, JOHN ALEXANDER.
　　Trinity Academy, Leith. Student of Arts, 1914-15. O.T.C. Infantry, April to Sept. 1915. 9th Royal Scots Fusiliers, 2nd Lieut. Sept. 1915; Lieut. Oct. 1916; Major March 1918 to May 1919. Machine-Gun Corps, March 1916. Wounded and invalided Aug. 1918. M.C. July 1916; Bar to M.C. Oct. 1917.

FRASER, JOHN FORMAN.
　　Daniel Stewart's College. Cadet Corps 1914-16, Cadet Corporal. Student of Medicine, 1918. 2/1st Ayrshire Yeomanry, L/Corporal March 1917. R.F.A., 2nd Lieut. Nov. 1918 to Feb. 1919.

FRASER, JOHN GALLIE.
　　George Watson's College. M.B., C.M. 1893; M.R.C.P. (Lond.) 1908. 4th Seaforth Highlanders, Private for five years. North London Brigade, Captain. Attached 19th Middlesex Regiment. R.A.M.C., Lieut. 1916. 26th and 27th Durham Light Infantry.

FRASER, KENNETH.
　　Edinburgh Academy. M.B., Ch.B. 1909; M.D. 1914; D.P.H. R.A.M.C., Lieut. May 1915; Captain May 1916.

FRASER, KENNETH GRANT.
　　Student of Medicine, 1913-14. L.R.C.P. & S. (Edin.) and L.R.F.P.S. (Glasg.) 1914. R.A.M.C., Lieut. Oct. 1914; Captain Oct. 1915; Acting Major Jan. 1918; Acting Lieut.-Col. March to May 1919. Wounded Sept. 1916. Dispatches Dec. 1916. Croix de Guerre March 1917.

FRASER, MARK STEWART.
　　M.B., Ch.B. 1906; M.D. 1910; D.P.H., R.C.P.S. (Edin.) & F.R.C.S. (Edin.) 1909. R.A.M.C., Lieut. May 1915; Captain Feb. 1917.

FRASER, ROBERT.
　　George Watson's College. M.B., Ch.B. 1907. D.P.H. (Edin.). R.A.M.C., Lieut. June 1917; Captain June 1918. Mesopotamia 1917-19. Dispatches Feb. 1919.

FRASER, THOMAS.
　　Royal High School; First XV. and XI. M.B., Ch.B. 1909. R.A.M.C., Lieut. June 1917; Captain June 1918. India.

FRASER, THOMAS DUNBAR STANLEY.
　　Daniel Stewart's College. 1st Highland Cadet Battn., 1911-15. University O.T.C. Artillery, Jan. to Dec. 1917, Cadet. R.F.A., Gunner Dec. 1917.

Record of War Service

FRASER, THOMAS GRIERSON.
George Watson's College. Student of Law, 1916-17 and 1918-19. 79th Training Reserve Battn., Private. 47th Battn. Machine-Gun Corps, Corporal. France 1918.

FRASER, THOMAS HOWDEN.
George Watson's College. M.A. 1910; LL.B. 1912. Lecturer on Economics, University of Manitoba, 1912-17. 52nd District H.Q., Canadian Forestry Corps, Sergeant May 1917 to June 1919.

FRASER, WALTER CALDWELL.
George Watson's College. Student of Science, 1912-14. 15th Royal Scots, Private Sept. 1914. 9th and 6th Royal Scots Fusiliers, 2nd Lieut. Jan. 1915; Lieut. July 1917; Acting Captain July 1916. France. Wounded four times and once Gassed.

FRASER, WILLIAM JAMES.
Robert Gordon's College, Aberdeen. M.B., Ch.B. 1904; F.R.C.S. (Edin.) 1908. Indian Medical Service, Lieut. 1906; Captain 1909; Major Aug. 1917. 38th Dogras. H.M. Hospital Ship *Varela*, Sept. 1915 to Dec. 1917. Mesopotamia May 1918-19. Dispatches 1919.

FRASER, WILLIAM SMITH.
Daniel Stewart's College. University O.T.C. Artillery, 1917, Cadet; Officer Cadet Aug. 1917. R.F.A. (S.R.), 48th Brigade, 2nd Lieut. Jan. 1918.

FRENCH, JOHN.
Student of Arts and Science, 1910-14; B.Sc. 1913; M.A. 1914. East of Scotland Munitions Board. City of Edinburgh R.E. (Vol.), 2nd Lieut.

FREW, ALEXANDER.
Spiers School, Beith; First XV. and XI. M.B., Ch.B. 1900; M.D. 1908. Assistant to Professor of Anatomy. South African Campaign, 1901-2. R.A.M.C., Lieut. July 1915; Captain July 1916. 1st Newfoundland Regiment. France.

FREW, DANIEL LINKSTONE.
Bo'ness Academy. Student of Medicine, 1917-19. 52nd (Graduate Battn.), Highland Light Infantry, Private May 1918 to Feb. 1919.

FREW, DAVID BENNY.
George Heriot's School. B.Sc. 1912. A.M.I.C.E.; A.M.I.M.E. O.T.C. Engineers, 1909-12, Cadet. 4th Royal Scots, Private Sept. 1914. R.E., 2nd Lieut. Dec. 1914; Captain and Adjutant May 1915; Major Nov. 1915 to Feb. 1919. France 1916-19. Dispatches Dec. 1917. M.C. May 1918.

FREW, ROBERT.
Glasgow Academy. O.T.C. 1912-15, L/Corporal. University O.T.C. Artillery, 1917, Cadet; Officer Cadet Aug. 1917. R.G.A., 2nd Lieut. Jan. 1918.

Record of War Service

FREW, ROBERT SKEOCH.
 M.B., Ch.B. 1905; M.D. 1910; F.R.C.P. (Lond.). R.A.M.C., Lieut. May 1917; Major April to Dec. 1918.

FREYER, DERMOT JOHNSTON.
 Student of Medicine, 1908-9. London Irish Rifles, Captain Sept. 1914.

FRY, AUGUSTINE SARGOOD.
 George Watson's College. M.B., Ch.B. 1913. O.T.C. Artillery, Oct. 1908 to April 1913, Cadet. R.A.M.C., Lieut. 1915. Indian Medical Service, March 1916; Acting Captain 1916. 61st Field Ambulance, France, one year. Persia, two years.

FRY, JOHN LOWE SARGOOD.
 George Watson's College. Student of Medicine, 1916-17. O.T.C. Artillery, Jan. to April 1917, Cadet. Royal Air Force, Officer Cadet April 1917; 2nd Lieut. Aug. 1917; Lieut. April 1918 to March 1920. France, Somme, Jan. to Nov. 1918.

FULLARTON, JOHN.
 Ayr Academy. M.B., Ch.B. 1899. Royal Navy 1902; H.M.S. *Dryad*, Staff Surgeon 1910; Fleet Surgeon Feb. 1918.

FULLER, EDWARD BARNARD.
 South African College, Cape Town. First XI. Cadet Corps 1885-7, Captain. M.B., C.M. 1891; L.R.C.S. 1891 and F.R.C.S. (Edin.) 1893. South African Medical Corps, 1913. Mobilised, Major, June 1916; Lieut.-Col. June 1917. No. 2 General Hospital, Maitland, June 1916-18.

FULLER, HUGH HARCUS CAVENDISH.
 Bishop's Stortford College, Herts; First XV. and XI. M.B., Ch.B. 1912. R.A.M.C., Lieut. Nov. 1914; Captain 1915-16. Invalided home Jan. 1916. Mercantile Marine Service.

FULLER, THOMAS ARTHUR.
 South African College School, Cape Town. First XV. and XI. Cadet Corps 1904-7, Lieut. Student of Medicine, 1909-14; M.B., Ch.B. 1914. O.T.C. Artillery, Oct. 1909 to Nov. 1912, Cadet. R.A.M.C., Lieut. 1915. South African Medical Corps, Captain May 1916; Major Nov. 1918-19. Dispatches May 1919.

FULLERTON, EDWARD.
 Student of Medicine, 1910-15; M.B., Ch.B. 1915. O.T.C. Medical Oct. 1914, Cadet. R.A.M.C., Lieut. 21st (S.B.), Manchester Regiment.

FULSS, FREDERICK CHARLES JULIUS.
 M.B., C.M. 1888. South African Medical Corps, Captain Nov. 1916.

FULTON, ADAM.
 Student of Medicine, 1914-15. O.T.C. Infantry, Oct. 1914 to March 1915, Cadet. 10th Border Regiment, 2nd Lieut.; Lieut. Aug. 1915.

Record of War Service

FULTON, JOHN STRUTHERS.
Ardrossan Academy. Student of Medicine, 1914-16 and 1917-19. O.T.C. Artillery, Nov. 1915 to July 1916, Cadet; Officer Cadet July 1916. R.F.A. (S.R.), 2nd Lieut. Oct. 1916; Lieut. April 1918. France 1917; Italy 1917-18.

FULTON, ROBERT VALPY.
Otago High School, New Zealand. M.B., C.M. 1889; M.D. 1905. N.Z. Volunteers (21 years), Lieut. to Major. N.Z. Medical Corps, Lieut.-Col. Jan. 1917. District Travelling Medical Boards.

FYFE, CLEVELAND.
George Watson's College. Student of Arts, 1905-6. No. 4 Coy., Q.R.V.B. Royal Scots, 1905-6, Private. 31st Labour Group H.Q., Sept. 1914; 2nd Lieut. July 1917; Acting Captain and Adjutant April 1918. France 1917-19, Arras, Somme; The Rhine.

FYFE, WILLIAM DEY.
George Watson's College. M.A. 1906; B.D. (Aberdeen). Minister, Church of Scotland. Chaplain, 4th Class, R.G.A., Nov. 1917. France; Cambrai 1917, Amiens 1918.

FYFFE, DAVID.
Dundee High School. Student of Arts and Law, 1918. Royal Navy Armoured Car Brigade, Sept. 1914; 1st Class P.O. Dec. 1914; 2nd Lieut. Nov. 1916; Lieut. March 1918; Captain Aug. 1918. Tank Corps.

GABITES, GEORGE EDWARD.
Timaru High School, New Zealand. B.Sc. (Agriculture); M.B., C.M. 1894; F.R.C.S. (Edin.). N.Z. Medical Corps, Aug. 1917; Lieut.-Col. June 1918. Camp Commandant, N.Z. Medical Corps Training Camp, Awapuni, Palmerston North. C.B.E. June 1919.

GADGIL, BHASKAR BALWANTRAO.
Student of Medicine, 1911-16. M.B., Ch.B. 1916. Indian Medical Service, Lieut. July 1917.

GAILLETON, ALFRED THOMAS.
M.B., Ch.B. 1898. Royal Navy, Staff Surgeon; Surgeon-Commander Aug. 1917. H.M.S. *Minerva*.

GALBRAITH, HAROLD GRAHAM.
Charterhouse. O.T.C. 1909-11, Cadet Corporal. B.A. (Camb.); Student of Law, 1914 and 1919. Motor Machine-Gun Service, May 1915. R.G.A., 2nd Lieut. July 1916; Lieut. Jan. 1918-19. France 1915.

GALBRAITH, JAMES JOHN.
M.B., Ch.B. 1899; M.D. 1903. Seaforth Highlanders (A.R.O., Ross and Cromarty), Lieut. Nov. 1915.

Record of War Service

GALBRAITH, WILLIAM.
 Winchester. B.A. (Oxford). Student of Law; LL.B. and Writer to the Signet, 1888. Vol. Battn., Royal Scots, Private to Sergeant 1914-18.

GALGUT, ELIJAH LOUIS.
 M.B., Ch.B. 1915. Dresser, Edinburgh and Border Hospital, Dunkirk. South African Medical Corps, Captain Feb. 1916.

GALL, ALEXANDER BRUCE.
 Broughton School, Edinburgh. Student of Arts and Science, 1909-10, and 1919-20. R.G.A., Gunner Aug. 1914.

GALL, ARTHUR MONCRIEFFE.
 Lasswade School. Student of Science, 1916-17 and 1918-19. O.T.C. Infantry, Feb. to Sept. 1917, Cadet; Officer Cadet Sept. 1917. Hampshire Regiment, 2nd Lieut. Feb. 1918. Attached Berkshire Regiment.

GALL, DAVID MENMUIR. (See p. 749.)

GALL, JOHN.
 George Heriot's School. Student of Arts and Science, 1908-14; M.A. (Hons. Maths.), and B.Sc. 1913. R.E. (Special Brigade), Corporal July 1915. Field Survey Coy., July 1917. France.

GALLAHER, JOHN FREDERICK.
 Queen's College, Belfast. M.B., Ch.B. 1905. R.A.M.C., Lieut. Jan. 1916; Captain Jan. 1917. France.

GALLETLY, ALEXANDER.
 M.B., Ch.B. 1910. R.A.M.C., Lieut.; Captain Nov. 1915. M.C.

GALLETLY, EDWARD LEWIS.
 Merchiston Castle. M.B., Ch.B. 1909. R.A.M.C., Lieut. May 1917; Captain May 1918.

GALLIE, DAVID ALEXANDER.
 Student of Medicine, 1912-14. O.T.C. Artillery, March 1910 to April 1913, Cadet. A.S.C. (T.), Lowland Division Train, Lieut. France.

GALLOWAY, DAVID MURRAY.
 Edinburgh Academy. O.T.C. 1913-14. Student of Medicine, 1914-16. O.T.C. Infantry, Feb. to June 1916, Cadet. Cameron Highlanders, Private May 1916; L/Corporal July 1916. R.F.C., 2nd Lieut. Aug. 1917. R.A.F., Lieut. April 1918.

GALLOWAY, NORMAN PATRICK ROBERT.
 Bedford Modern School. O.T.C. 1906-12, Sergeant. Student of Medicine, 1912-17; M.B., Ch.B. 1917. O.T.C. Medical, Feb. 1913-17, Cadet. R.A.M.C. (S.R.), Lieut. Aug. 1917; Captain Aug. 1918.

GALLOWAY, ROBERT ANGUS.
 George Watson's College. Student of Science, 1914-15. O.T.C. Engineers, Oct. 1914 to July 1915, Cadet. R.E. (T.), 3/1st Lowland Field Coy., 2nd Lieut. July 1915; Lieut. June 1916; Acting Captain Nov. 1918. 409th Lowland Field Coy. France March 1916 to April 1919. Wounded. M.C. June 1919.

Record of War Service

GALLOWAY, ROBERT MENZIES.
Birkenhead Institute; First XI. Student of Medicine, 1915-19. Anatomy Staff, 1919. R.N.V.R., Surgeon-Probationer, Aug. 1917.

GALT, WILLIAM CRAIG.
Giggleswick. O.T.C. 1913-16. Student of Medicine, 1916-18 and 1919-20, R.N.A.S.B.R. Dec. 1917. R.N.V.R., Surgeon Sub-Lieut., April 1918 to Feb. 1919.

GAMBLE, CROMWELL.
St Andrew's College, Dublin. M.B., Ch.B. 1910; D.P.H. 1914. No. 4 Coy. Q.R.V.B., Royal Scots, 1904-8. O.T.C. Infantry, 1908-9, Cadet Sergeant, Medical Oct. to Nov. 1914, Cadet. R.A.M.C. (S.R.), Lieut. Nov. 1914; Captain May 1915. R.H. and R.F.A. Base Depôt, France. Dispatches Nov. 1918. Médaille des Épidémies.

GANAPATHY, CODANDA MADIAH.
M.B., Ch.B. 1911; D.P.H. (Camb.). Indian Medical Service, Temp. Lieut. Dec. 1914; Temp. Captain Dec. 1915. Hospital Ship *Lalilia*, Mediterranean, 1915-16. Egypt 1917-18; Palestine 1918-19. M.C. Oct. 1918.

GARDEN, ARTHUR WILLIAM.
Edinburgh Academy. M.A. (Oxford). Student of Law, 1906-10. Writer to the Signet, 1910. A.S.C. (T.), 2nd Lieut. Sept. 1914; Lieut. March 1915. Lowland Mounted Brigade, Transport and Supply Column. Salonika.

GARDHAM, HENRY COOPER.
Royal High School. B.Sc. 1910. A.M.I.C.E. Lecturer in Engineering Department, April to Dec. 1919. R.F.A. (T.), 1st Lowland Brigade, Lieut. June 1915; Captain April 1918. Attached R.E., India, March to Oct. 1917. Mesopotamia Oct. 1917 to March 1919.

GARDINER, PATRICK PHILIP LYON.
Stranraer High School. Student of Arts and Law, 1915-16 and 1918-19. O.T.C. Infantry, 1915-16, Cadet. 3rd and 10th Argyll and Sutherland Highlanders, 2nd Lieut.; Lieut. Feb. 1918. France Oct. 1916 to Jan. 1918. M.C. Sept. 1918.

GARDINER, WILLIAM TYLER.
Royal High School. M.B., Ch.B. 1908; F.R.C.S. (Edin.) 1911. Clinical Tutor, Ear, Nose, and Throat. R.A.M.C. (T.), Lieut. 1912; Captain April 1915; Major Jan. 1918. Attached 1st Lowland Brigade, R.F.A. Gallipoli and Egypt. M.C. June 1917. Dispatches July 1917 and March 1919.

GARDINER, WILLIAM WALLACE DUNLOP.
Daniel Stewart's College. M.A. 1908; B.D. Minister, Church of Scotland, Chaplain, Aldershot, May to Oct. 1916. France Oct. 1916.

GARDNER, FRANK HEY SOMERS.
M.B., Ch.B. 1906. R.A.M.C., Lieut.

Record of War Service

GARDNER, GEORGE GORDON WRANGLES.
George Watson's College. B.L. 1909. Law Agent. R.E., 49th Coy., L/Corporal March 1915. 7th Highland Light Infantry, 2nd Lieut. Nov. 1915. Invalided out March 1916.

GARDNER, JAMES SCOTT.
B.L. 1913. 11th West Riding Regiment, Lieut. 1915.

GARDNER, LOUIS PATRICK MACKENZIE.
George Heriot's School. M.B., Ch.B. 1905. R.A.M.C., Lieut. July 1918. East Africa.

GARDNER, THOMAS.
Bathgate Academy. M.B., Ch.B. 1908; M.D. 1910. R.A.M.C., Lieut. Oct. 1916; Captain Oct. 1917. 36th Stationary Hospital, and 1st Nigerian Regiment. German East Africa.

GARDNER, WILLIAM.
Falkirk High School. Student of Law, 1913-15. Law Agent. R.F.A. (T.), 2/2nd Ayrshire Battery, Gunner Nov. 1915; Bombardier Dec. 1915; Corporal Feb. 1918; 2nd Lieut. Oct. 1918. R.H.A., "K" Reserve Battery.

GARDNER, WILLIAM ROSS.
Falkirk School. M.B., Ch.B. 1912. O.T.C. Medical, April 1908 to Nov. 1910, Cadet Corporal. R.A.M.C. (S.R.), Lieut. Nov. 1910; Captain May 1914; Lieut.-Col. Nov. 1916. France Aug. 1914 to May 1919. 138th Field Ambulance. Wounded at second Ypres April 1915. Dispatches June 1916 and Dec. 1917. D.S.O. Dec. 1917; Bar to D.S.O. Sept. 1918; Croix de Guerre (French) Sept. 1918.

GARRETT FISHER, WILLIAM EDWARD.
M.A. 1891. 24th Royal Fusiliers (2nd Sportsman's Battn.), Private Dec. 1914. 16th Highland Light Infantry (78th T.R.B.), Lieut. March 1915; Captain April 1917. Education Officer, 32nd Division, Feb. 1919. War Office, June 1919. France and The Rhine. M.C. 1918.

GARRIGAN, GEORGE ROSS.
George Heriot's School. Student of Arts, 1910-15 and 1918-19; M.A. 1914. Minister, Scottish Episcopal Church. R.N.V.R., Sub-Lieut. 1915 to June 1918.

GARRIGAN, THOMAS R.
George Heriot's School; First XV. and XI. Student of Science, 1910-11. R.N.V.R. and R.N.A.S., Sub-Lieut. May 1916; Lieut. April 1917. Royal Air Force, Captain Aug. 1918.

GARRIOCK, JOHN.
Moray House, Edinburgh. M.A. 1900; B.Sc. 1912. 1st Banffshire Volunteer Regiment, Corporal 1916.

Record of War Service

GARSON, IAN GEORGE MELLIS.
Merchiston Castle. O.T.C. 1910-12. Student of Medicine, 1913-15. O.T.C. Infantry, Jan. to March 1915, Cadet. 6th King's Own Scottish Borderers, 2nd Lieut. March 1915; Lieut. Jan. 1917; Captain June 1919. Musketry and Machine-Gun Instructor. India, March 1916.

GARSON, JOHN GEORGE.
M.B., C.M. 1875; M.D. 1878; L.R.C.S. (Edin.) 1875. R.A.M.C., Lieut. June 1915; Captain June 1916. Prisoners of War and Neurological Hospitals, Epsom.

GARSON, PATRICK CLASON.
Merchiston Castle; First XV. and XI. O.T.C. 1912-14. Student of Medicine, 1915-16 and 1919. O.T.C. Infantry, Oct. 1915 to Jan. 1916, Cadet. Gordon Highlanders, 2nd Lieut. Feb. 1916; Lieut. July 1917. France. Gassed and Wounded in Flanders July 1917, and near Rheims July 1918.

GARVIE, JOHN.
Perth Academy. M.B., C.M. 1885. Indian Medical Service, 1887; Lieut.-Col. 1907; Colonel March 1917. Meerut War Hospital, and A.D.M.S., Allahabad and Lucknow. Inspector-General of Civil Hospitals, Assam.

GASKELL, HUGH SELWYN.
Haileybury. Cadet Corps 1895-7. M.B., Ch.B. 1906. No. 4 Coy., Q.R.V.B. Royal Scots, 1898-9, Private. South African Campaign, 1899-1901. M.O., Queen's Westminster's, 1910-13. R.A.M.C., Lieut. March 1916; Captain 1917.

GASPERINE, JOHN J.
Student of Medicine, 1911-14. R.N.V.R., Hospital Ship No. 4, Surgeon-Probationer; Surgeon July 1916.

GASSON, SYDNEY GEORGE HAYCROFT.
St Andrew's College, Grahamstown. O.T.C. 1910-14, Sergeant. Student of Medicine, 1916-19. R.N.V.R., Surgeon-Sub.-Lieut. H.M.S. *Nugent*. Belgian Coast 1918.

GAVIN, FREDERICK WILLIAM. (See p. 749.)

GAVIN, JOHN.
Edinburgh Academy. Student of Arts and Law, 1912-15; M.A. 1915. O.T.C. Infantry, Oct. 1914 to Dec. 1915, Cadet. 9th Royal Scots (T.), Private April 1916; Acting Sergeant. Ministry of National Service, July 1918.

GAVIN, WILLIAM STRACHAN.
Edinburgh Academy. O.T.C. 1908-9. Student of Law, 1913-14. 16th Royal Scots, Private Sept. 1914; 2nd Lieut. June 1915; Lieut. July 1917; Captain Feb. 1918. M.C. April 1917.

GAVINE, CONSTANCE.
Edinburgh Ladies' College. Student of Arts, 1913-17; M.A. (Hons. Mod. Lang.) 1917. Q.M.A.A.C., Clerk, May 1917.

Record of War Service

GAY, DENIS THOMPSON PRIOR.
  High School, Panchgani, India. First XI. Student of Medicine, 1913-17; M.B., Ch.B. 1917. Indian Medical Service, Lieut. July 1918; Captain Aug. 1919. Turkey in Asia.

GEDDES, SIR AUCKLAND CAMPBELL.
  George Watson's College. M.B., Ch.B. 1903; M.D. 1908. Assistant, Anatomy Department; Professor of Anatomy, McGill University. No. 4 Coy. Q.R.V.B., Royal Scots. O.T.C. Infantry, Major and O.C., 1908; Brevet Lieut.-Col. June 1916; Hon. Brigadier-General Aug. 1917. Director, Civil Recruiting. C.B. and K.C.B. 1917.

GEE, OSWALD ARNOLD.
  M.A.; M.B., C.M. 1900. R.A.M.C., Lieut.; Captain Dec. 1915.

GEIKIE, GEORGE RAMSAY.
  Merchiston Castle. Mus. Bac. 1910. R.N.V.R., Lieut. 1917. Hydrophone Service.

GEIKIE, JAMES STEWART.
  Merchiston Castle; First XV. and XI. M.B., Ch.B. 1900; M.D. 1909. Royal Navy, Surgeon Jan. 1917. H.M.S. *Agincourt*, and Royal Naval Hospital, Haslar.

GELLATLY, ROBERT.
  M.B., Ch.B. 1897. R.A.M.C., Lieut. Sept. 1917; Captain. Huddersfield War Hospital.

GELLERT, HARRY HERBERT.
  M.B., Ch.B. 1914. O.T.C. Infantry, 1909-12, Cadet L/Corporal Royal Navy, Surgeon March 1915; Surgeon-Lieut. Dec. 1918. H.M. Ships *Victory*, *Albion*, *Vivid*, *Gunner*, *Europa*, *President*, *Ark Royal*, and *Theseus II*. Royal Air Force. Mudros and Imbros July 1918; South Russia Dec. 1918 to Aug. 1919.

GEMMELL, ROBERT.
  Middlesbrough High School. University O.T.C. Infantry, 1917, Cadet; Officer Cadet Oct. 1917. Labour Corps, 2nd Lieut. Dec. 1917 to March 1919.

GEMMELL, WILLIAM ERIC.
  Clifton Bank, St Andrews; First XV. and XI. Student of Science, 1917 and 1919. O.T.C. Infantry, March to Oct. 1917, Cadet. Royal Flying Corps, Officer Cadet Oct. 1917. Royal Air Force, 22nd Wing, 2nd Lieut. France.

GEMMILL, WILLIAM.
  Spiers School; First XI. M.A. 1901; M.B., Ch.B. 1905; F.R.C.S. (Eng.) 1913. Late Demonstrator of Anatomy. R.A.M.C., Lieut. Nov. 1915; Captain Nov. 1916; Acting Major Jan. 1919. 14th General Hospital, March 1917. 83rd General Hospital, May 1918 to July 1919.

GENNEY, FREDERICK STEPHENSON.
  M.B., C.M. 1890. R.A.M.C., Major.

Record of War Service

GENTLE, WILLIAM.
George Heriot's School. B.Sc. 1903. Schoolmaster. O.T.C. Artillery, June to Sept. 1915, Cadet. R.F.A. (T.), 1st Lowland Brigade, 2nd Lieut. Sept. 1915; Lieut. June 1916. France. Wounded June 1917.

GENTLES, ROBERT.
Falkirk High School. Student of Law, 1918-19. O.T.C. Infantry, Jan. 1911; 2nd Lieut. Dec. 1914; Lieut. April 1915; Captain Nov. 1918; O.C. March 1919. University School of Instruction, April 1915. No. 9 O.C. Battn., Gailes, March 1916 to Sept. 1917.

GEOGHEGAN, JOSEPH.
George Watson's College. M.B., Ch.B. 1911; F.R.C.S. (Edin.) 1917. Colonial Medical Service, 1912-16. R.A.M.C., Lieut. 1916; Captain Oct. 1917. France 1916-17; Messines.

GEORGE, ALFRED WALTER.
M.B., C.M. 1889; M.D. 1896; M.R.C.S. (Eng.), and L.R.C.P. (Lond.) 1889. R.A.M.C., Captain July 1917.

GEORGESON, ERIK H. M.
Student of Arts and Science, 1911-12 and 1918-19. 3rd Royal Scots, 2nd Lieut.; Lieut. July 1917.

GEORGESON, FREDERICK HUGH.
M.A. 1881. Minister, U.F. Church of Scotland. Chaplain. 2/1st Lothian Infantry Brigade. 3rd and 2nd King's Own Scottish Borderers, and 53rd (Y.S.) Gordon Highlanders.

GEORGESON, HAROLD.
Student of Law, 1919. O.T.C. Infantry, June to Oct. 1916, Cadet; Officer Cadet Oct. 1916. 3rd attached 2nd Seaforth Highlanders, 2nd Lieut. April 1917; Lieut. Sept. 1918. France. M.C. March 1918.

GERRARD, JOHN SMART.
George Heriot's School. Student of Arts and Science, 1908-14; M.A. 1912; B.Sc. 1914. R.F.A. (T.), Gunner Sept. 1915; 2nd Lieut. Oct. 1915; Lieut. June 1916.

GERRICKÉ, ONEY MORTIMER.
South African College. Cadet Corps, 1895-8, Sergeant-Major. M.B., Ch.B. 1907; L.R.C.P. & S. (Edin.) and L.F.P.S. (Glasg.) 1907. President, South African Union. South African Medical Corps, Captain March 1917. Attached H.Q., Pretoria, May 1919.

GHOSH, ABANI MOHAN.
Student of Medicine, 1911-15. M.B., Ch.B. 1915; Indian Field Ambulance, Dec. 1914. Indian Medical Service, Lieut. Feb. 1916.

Record of War Service

GHOSH, PRATUL KUMAR.
Student of Medicine, 1909-16; M.B., Ch.B. 1915. Indian Field Ambulance, Lieut.

GIBB, CLARENCE WILLIAM.
Brighton Hove Grammar School, Sussex; First XI. Student of Law, 1911-13. Chartered Accountant, 1914. 9th Royal Scots (T.), Private Sept. 1914. Wounded April 1915. Invalided out July 1915.

GIBB, F. CRICHTON.
Royal High School. Student of Law, 1911-14 and 1918-19. 5th Royal Scots (T.) Private Sept. 1914. Machine-Gun Corps, 2nd Lieut. Aug. 1916; Lieut. Feb. 1918. Gallipoli April 1915; France Nov. 1916. Deputy Assistant Censor, Havre and Boulogne, Dec. 1918.

GIBB, HAMILTON ALEXANDER ROSSKEEN.
Royal High School. Student of Arts, 1912-15 and 1919; M.A. 1919. O.T.C. Artillery, Oct. 1912 to May 1916, Lieut. R.F.A. (T.), Lieut. June 1916; Acting Captain and Adjutant May 1918. School of Instruction, Artillery, 1915-16. France and Italy 1916-19. Dispatches July 1919.

GIBB, JAMES RATTRAY.
Perth Academy and Royal High School, Edinburgh. Student of Law, 1911-14. Advocate, 1915. R.N.A.S. and Royal Air Force, June 1917, Captain.

GIBB, J.
Student. Lothians and Border Horse (T.), Private.

GIBB, JOHN WALKER.
George Heriot's School. O.T.C. 1910-11. Student of Science, 1918. Lothians and Border Horse, Private Nov. 1914. 9th Royal Scots, Oct. 1916. Officer Cadet Jan. 1917. 10th Northumberland Fusiliers, 2nd Lieut. May 1917; Lieut. Nov. 1918. France.

GIBB, WALTER JAMES.
Royal High School. Student of Arts, 1910-15; M.A. 1915. O.T.C. Infantry, Feb. to July 1915, Cadet. 5th Gordon Highlanders (T.), 2nd Lieut. July 1915; Lieut. July 1917; Acting Captain Aug. 1918 to Jan. 1919. France. Wounded March and Nov. 1916.

GIBBS, FREDERICK GEORGE.
George Watson's College. Student of Medicine; L.R.C.P. & S. (Edin.); L.R.F.P.S. (Glasg.) and L.D.S. (Edin.) 1913. O.T.C. Infantry, Oct. 1910 to April 1914, Cadet. R.A.M.C., Lieut. June 1915; Captain June 1916. France Aug. 1915; Italy June 1917 to Aug. 1919.

GIBBS, OWEN STANLEY.
Loughboro' Grammar School. Student of Medicine, 1917-19. 46th Division, Cyclist Coy., Private Aug. 1914. France Feb. to May 1915, and Oct. 1915 to May 1916. Invalided out July 1916.

Record of War Service

GIBLIN, NORRIS.
    Leslie House School, Hobart, Tasmania. B.A. (Tasmania). Student of Medicine, 1911-15 and 1918-19. O.T.C. Medical, and Artillery, Dec. 1914 to July 1915, Cadet. R.F.A. (T.), 4th North Midland Brigade, 2nd Lieut. May 1915; Temp. Lieut. Feb. 1916; Lieut. June 1916; Acting Captain May 1917 to Jan. 1919. France Nov. 1915. M.C. Sept. 1918.

GIBSON, ALEXANDER.
    M.A. 1904; M.B., Ch.B. 1908. Anatomy Staff, 1910-12. R.A.M.C., Lieut. July 1915; Captain 1915. Canadian Army Medical Corps, Major. Orthopædic Surgeon, Manitoba Military Hospital.

GIBSON, ANDREW.
    Neilson School, Paisley. M.B., Ch.B. 1897; F.R.C.S. (Edin.) 1901. R.A.M.C., Lieut. Aug. 1915; Captain Dec. 1915. Hospital Ship *Grantully Castle*. Salonika 1915-16. Drumpellier Auxiliary Hospital, Coatbridge, 1914-15 and 1917-19.

GIBSON, ARTHUR KEITH.
    George Watson's College. Student of Medicine, 1911-16; M.B., Ch.B. 1916. O.T.C. Medical, Nov. 1914 to July 1916, Cadet. R.A.M.C. (S.R.), Lieut. July 1916; Captain Jan. 1917.

GIBSON, CAMERON ROBERTSON.
    Kilmarnock Academy. M.A. (Glasg.); M.B., Ch.B. 1903; D.P.H. (Liverpool and Camb.). R.A.M.C., Lieut. Aug. 1914; Captain Aug. 1915; Major Aug. 1918.

GIBSON, CHARLES JOHN.
    M.B., C.M. 1880; M.D. 1898. R.A.M.C., Lieut.

GIBSON, EDMUND VALENTINE.
    M.B., C.M. 1890; M.D. 1892. Channel Islands Militia, Surgeon-Major Nov. 1911.

GIBSON, EDWARD PENROSE FORBES.
    Madras College, St Andrews. Student of Arts, 1894-5. President and Hon. Treasurer, Diagnostic Society, 1898. University Battery, E.C.A.V., 1894-8, Bombardier. R.G.A., Bombardier May 1917. France.

GIBSON, FREDERICK PETER.
    George Watson's College. M.B., Ch.B. 1910. O.T.C. Medical, 1906-8, Cadet Sergeant. R.A.M.C., Lieut. Oct. 1914; Captain April 1915; Major Dec. 1918. France and Italy Nov. 1914 to Feb. 1919.

GIBSON, GEORGE HERBERT RAE.
    Edinburgh Academy. M.B., Ch.B. 1906; M.D. 1910; F.R.C.P. (Edin.). South Africa, 1900-1. Canadian Army Medical Corps, Captain Aug. 1914; Major Jan. 1917. M.O., 7th Canadian Infantry, Aug. 1914. 1st Canadian Division, A.D.C. to G.O.C., Oct. 1915; D.A.D.M.S. May 1916 to July 1918. 3rd Canadian Field Ambulance, July 1918. France. Croix de Guerre (French) 1916; D.S.O. 1918.

Record of War Service

GIBSON, GEORGE McKAY.
Boroughmuir School. Student of Medicine, 1918. R.A.M.C., Private and Stretcher Bearer Jan. 1916.

GIBSON, HENRY JAMES CRAIG.
Merchiston Castle. O.T.C. M.A. (Glasg.); Student of Medicine, 1909-14; M.B., Ch.B. 1914; M.D. 1920. R.A.M.C., Lieut. 1916; Captain and Adjutant May 1917.

GIBSON, HENRY WILLIAM.
Dundee Institution. M.A. (St Andrews). St Andrews University Battery. LL.B. 1891. President, Scots Law Society. Minister, Episcopal Church of Scotland. Acting Chaplain to Forces, 1906-8. 1st Argyllshire Volunteers, Private 1916; 2nd Lieut. June 1918.

GIBSON, HERBERT ROBERT BURNETT.
Edinburgh Academy. M.B., Ch.B. 1908. Indian Medical Service, Lieut. 1909; Captain 1912; Brevet Major June 1919; Acting Lieut.-Col. Sept. 1916 to June 1920. Hospital Ship, Oct. 1914 to Nov. 1915. E.I.F. Nov. 1915 to June 1917. Bushire Force, June 1917 to May 1920. Dispatches Sept. 1917.

GIBSON, HUGH CRAIGIE.
Kirkwall Burgh School. M.B., C.M. 1904. R.A.M.C., Lieut. July 1915; Captain July 1916; Acting Major Jan. 1919. Edinburgh War Hospital, Bangour; Glenalmond and Perth War Hospitals.

GIBSON, JAMES ALBERT.
Royal High School. M.B., C.M. 1889; M.D. 1897; D.P.H. (Ireland). No. 4 Coy. Q.E.R., Private. R.A.M.C. (T.), Captain Aug. 1914. Sanitary Officer, Portsmouth Garrison, March 1919.

GIBSON, JOHN.
Edinburgh Academy. O.T.C. 1914-17. University O.T.C. Artillery. Feb. to Aug. 1917, Cadet. R.F.A., Officer Cadet Aug. 1917; 2nd Lieut. Jan. 1918. Royal Air Force, March 1918; Pilot, Oct. 1918 to Jan. 1919.

GIBSON, JOHN GIBSON.
George Watson's College. M.A. and B.Sc. (Distinction) 1911. O.T.C. Artillery, 1910-12, Cadet. 19th Battn. London Regiment (T.), Private Sept. 1914; Corporal July 1915; Sergeant; 2nd Lieut. May 1916; Lieut. Nov. 1917; Acting Captain Feb. 1918. Special Brigade and Field Survey Coy., R.E. Attached General Staff (Intelligence), G.H.Q., Egypt. Wounded Aug. 1916.

GIBSON, JOHN LOCKHART.
Edinburgh Collegiate School. M.B., C.M. (Hons.) 1881; M.D. 1885 (Gold Medal); M.R.C.S. (Eng.) 1885; Assistant to Professor of Physiology, 1882-3; Demonstrator of Physiology, 1884; Resident, R.I.E.; President, Royal Medical Society. Australian Army Medical Corps, Major May 1915. 3rd Australian General Hospital, Lemnos and Abbasia. R.A.M.C. (Temp.), Ophthalmologist, Queensland.

Record of War Service

GIBSON, LAURENCE.
Fettes. M.B., Ch.B. 1906; D.P.H. (Edin.). No. 4 Coy. Q.R.V.B., Royal Scots, 1898-1906, Sergeant. Royal Navy, H.M.S. *Melton*, Sub-Lieut. June 1918. Mine-sweeping Aug. 1918-19.

GIBSON, MATTHEW JOHN.
Cookstown Academy. Student of Medicine, 1913-18. M.B., Ch.B. 1918. O.T.C. Infantry, Oct. 1914 to July 1915, Cadet. R.N.V.R., H.M. Ships *Moresby* and *Druid*, Surgeon-Probationer, Sept. 1915. R.A.M.C., Lieut. Sept. 1918 to Nov. 1919.

GIBSON, RICHARD EDWARD.
Student of Medicine, 1909-14; M.B., Ch.B. 1914. O.T.C. Artillery, 1910-13, Cadet. R.A.M.C., Lieut. Aug. 1914; Captain Feb. 1918. France 1914. No. 8 General Hospital. D.A.D.M.S. O.B.E.

GIBSON, RICHARD NORMAN.
Sedbergh and St Edward's, Oxford; Athletics. O.T.C. 1908-10. Student of Medicine, 1912-17; M.B., Ch.B. 1917. R.N.V.R., Surgeon-Probationer. Royal Navy, Surgeon Jan. 1918.

GIBSON, RONALD.
Fettes. O.T.C. 1915-17. University O.T.C. Infantry, July 1917 to Feb. 1918, Cadet L/Corporal; Officer Cadet Feb. 1918. 7th Argyll and Sutherland Highlanders (T.), 2nd Lieut. July 1918. 13th Royal Highlanders (Black Watch), Oct. 1918 to June 1919. France.

GIBSON, THOMAS.
Edinburgh Academy; First XV. O.T.C. 1911-16, Cadet Corporal. Student of Science, 1918. 7th Tank Battn., Feb. 1916, 2nd Lieut. Feb. 1917; Lieut. July 1918; Captain Oct. 1918.

GIBSON, WALTER ELLIOT SCOTT.
Dunbar School. University O.T.C. Artillery, Jan. to Nov. 1917, Cadet; Officer Cadet Nov. 1917. Forth R.G.A., 20th Field Coy., 2nd Lieut. Aug. 1918.

GIBSON, W. P. S.
Edinburgh Academy. Student of Law, 1900-2. Chartered Accountant, 1905. 7th Royal Highlanders (Black Watch), 2nd Lieut. May 1915; Lieut. July 1917; Acting Captain Sept. 1917 to Feb. 1919. France 1915.

GIFFORD, JOHN.
Edinburgh Institution. Student of Science, 1899-1902. South African Campaign, 1900-1. South African Field Forces, Major. D.A.Q.M.G. Jan. 1915. Cameronians (Scottish Rifles), 1915-16. Transferred King's Own Yorkshire Light Infantry, Captain Nov. 1915. German S.-W. Africa 1914-15. France July 1915-1919. Dispatches Aug. 1918 for German S.-W. Africa service.

Record of War Service

GILBERTSON, JOHN GREGOR.
Royal High School. M.A. 1886. Fellow of Punjab University. A.S.C. (I.A.R.O.), 2nd Lieut. April 1918. Assistant Postal and Cable Censor, Bombay, April 1918-19.

GILCHRIST, ALEXANDER.
Waid Academy, Anstruther. Student of Law. O.T.C. Infantry, May 1915 to Jan. 1916, Cadet. Highland Light Infantry, 2nd Lieut. Jan. 1916; Lieut. July 1917; Captain Oct. 1918. France. Croix de Guerre (Belgian).

GILCHRIST, ANDREW RAE.
Campbell College, Belfast. O.T.C. 1914-16, Cadet Corporal. Student of Medicine, 1916-19. O.T.C. Artillery, 1917-18; Medical, 1918-19, Cadet. R.F.A., Officer Cadet Feb. to April 1918.

GILCHRIST, EWEN GEORGE MACPHERSON.
George Heriot's School; First XI. Student of Medicine, 1909-15. M.B., Ch.B. 1915. O.T.C. Medical, Nov. 1914 to July 1915, Cadet. R.A.M.C., Lieut. July 1915; Captain July 1916. 1/3rd East Anglian Field Ambulance, Egypt.

GILCHRIST, JOHN.
Glasgow High School. M.B., C.M. 1895; M.D. 1902. R.A.M.C. (T.), Captain July 1908. Mobilised Dec. 1914. 3rd Scottish General Hospital. France. 58th General Hospital.

GILCHRIST, JOHN JAMES.
Student of Medicine, 1908-14. O.T.C. Infantry, May 1909 to July 1913, Cadet. 1st Cameron Highlanders, L/Corporal; 2nd Lieut. D.C.M.

GILCHRIST, KENNETH ALEXANDER.
M.B., Ch.B. 1911. O.T.C. Artillery, 1909 to Feb. 1911, Cadet. South African Campaign, 1900-1. South African Medical Corps, Captain March 1916; Major June 1918. German East Africa 1916. O.C. No. 1 Laboratory, Roberts Heights. M.C. and Dispatches Oct. 1916.

GILCHRIST, SAMUEL.
George Heriot's School. University O.T.C. Infantry, June to Oct. 1917, Cadet. R.F.C., Officer Cadet Oct. 1917. Royal Air Force, Lieut.

GILCHRIST, WILLIAM RITCHIE.
Waid Academy, Anstruther. Student of Law, 1909-11. Royal Scots, Private Feb. 1918; Corporal Oct 1918. M.M.

GILDARD, JAMES GRAHAM AFFLECK.
Kelvinside Academy, Glasgow; First XV. O.T.C. 1911-16, Cadet Sergeant. University O.T.C. Artillery, 1917, Cadet Corporal; Officer Cadet July 1917. R.F.A. (S.R.), 2nd Lieut. Dec. 1917; Lieut. June 1919. Dispatches (Russia) Aug. 1919.

Record of War Service

GILES, AUSTIN CHARLES.
Epsom College. M.B., Ch.B. 1913. R.A.M.C., Lieut. Feb. 1915; Captain Feb. 1916. France. Wounded at Loos Sept. 1915, and gassed at Ypres June 1917. Dispatches June 1916. M.C. June 1917.

GILL, CECIL ERNEST GASPAR.
St John's School, Leatherhead. O.T.C. 1913-15, Cadet L/Corporal. Student of Medicine, 1918. Cambridgeshire Regiment, 2nd Lieut. Oct. 1915; Lieut. July 1916. Royal Air Force. Croce di Guerra Jan. 1919.

GILL, GURDIAL SINGH.
Student of Medicine, 1913-20. Indian Field Ambulance, Nov. 1914.

GILL, HERBERT HOPE.
King William's College, Isle of Man. M.B., C.M. 1894. Royal Navy, Nov. 1895; Surgeon-Commander. H.M. Ships *Centurion*, *Prince George*, and *Bacchante*.

GILL, H. S. HOPE.
King William's College, Isle of Man. Student of Law, 1888-9. Chartered Accountant, 1889. Q.R.V.B., Royal Scots, 1889. 9th Royal Scots (T.), Captain Oct. 1914.

GILL, JOHN GALBRAITH.
Brentwood Grammar School; First XI. M.B., Ch.B. 1912. O.T.C. Artillery, 1908-12, Cadet Sergeant. R.A.M.C., Lieut. Jan. 1914; Captain April 1915; Acting Lieut.-Col. Nov. 1917 to May 1919. France Aug. 1914 to Nov. 1917. M.O., 25th Brigade, R.F.A.; 70th Field Ambulance. D.A.D.M.S., 23rd Division. Italy Nov. 1917 to May 1919. 71st Field Ambulance; 41st Combined Field Ambulance. India May 1919. Dispatches Dec. 1917. M.C. Jan. 1917. D.S.O. Jan. 1918; O.B.E. (Military) June 1919.

GILL, SYDNEY.
Chatsworth School, Carlisle. Student of Medicine, 1918. 3rd Battn. Rifle Brigade, Private Jan. 1916; 2nd Lieut. Oct. 1917.

GILLAN, JOHN ROBERT WILSON.
Edinburgh Academy. O.T.C. to 1909. B.A. (Oxford), 1912; Student of Divinity, 1913-14. O.T.C. Artillery, Oct. 1913 to Dec. 1914, Cadet B.Q.M.S. 6th Gordon Highlanders (T.), Lieut. Dec. 1914; Captain May 1915. 14th Sudanese Regiment, Major 1918. France 1915-17; Egypt, Sudan, 1918-19. Wounded near Festubert, June 1915 and April 1917.

GILLESPIE, ARCHIBALD.
M.B., Ch.B. 1902; M.D. 1906. R.A.M.C., Lieut. June 1915; Captain July 1916. 32nd Division, Ammunition Column, R.F.A., 1917.

GILLESPIE, HOPE MURRAY.
Dumfries Academy. M.B., Ch.B. 1904. R.A.M.C., Lieut. June 1916; Captain June 1917. 13th Leicestershire Regiment. France Nov. 1916. M.C. May 1918.

Record of War Service

GILLESPIE, JOHN IMRIE.
Edinburgh Academy. Student of Law, 1899-1901. Chartered Accountant, 1903. 15th Royal Scots, Private.

GILLESPIE, JOHN MARCHBANK.
George Watson's College. M.B., Ch.B. 1911. R.A.M.C., Lieut. Aug. 1914; Captain Aug. 1915. 2nd Northumberland Fusiliers. France; Ypres May 1915. Prisoner of War, May to June 1915. Malta Nov. 1915. M.C. May 1915. Dispatches July and Sept. 1915.

GILLESPIE, WILLIAM DOUGLAS.
Edinburgh Academy. O.T.C. 1913-16, Cadet L/Corporal. Student of Law, 1916 and 1919. O.T.C. Artillery, Oct. 1916 to July 1917, Cadet Bombardier; Officer Cadet July 1917. R.F.A., 2nd Lieut. Dec. 1917; Lieut. June 1919.

GILLESPIE, WILLIAM RUSSELL.
George Watson's College. M.A. 1905. 3rd attached 11th Border Regiment, 2nd Lieut.; Lieut. July 1917.

GILLIES, ALEXANDER CAMPBELL.
George Watson's College; First XV. O.T.C. 1915-18, Cadet Sergeant. Student of Science and Medicine, 1918-19. O.T.C. Artillery, March to Oct. 1918, Cadet Bombardier. R.G.A., Officer Cadet Oct. 1918.

GILLIES, ARTHUR HUNTER DENHOLM.
Fettes; First XI. B.A. (Oxford). Student of Law, 1911-15 and 1919; LL.B. 1919. 9th Royal Scots (T.), Private Oct. 1914; 2nd Lieut. March 1915; Temp. Lieut. Feb. 1916; Lieut. Aug. 1917. France Jan. 1917 to March 1918. Wounded at Arras April 1917. The Rhine, Nov. 1918 to Jan 1919.

GILLIES, JOHN.
Broughton School. Student of Medicine, 1913-14 and 1918-19. 13th Highland Light Infantry, Private Sept. 1914; 2nd Lieut. May 1915; Lieut. Feb. 1917; Captain Dec. 1917. M.C. Sept. 1917.

GILLIES, PATRICK HUNTER.
M.B., C.M. 1890; B.Sc. (P.H.) 1897. R.A.M.C., July 1915; Captain. Med. Exp. Force 1915. Transferred to Ministry of National Service and Pensions, Feb. 1918.

GILLIES, WILLIAM FORMAN.
Knox Institute, Haddington. Student of Arts and Science, 1913-15 and 1917-19; M.A. 1919 (Hons. Maths. and Nat. Phil. 1920); B.Sc. 1919. R.E. (Special Brigade), Corporal July 1915.

GILLIESON, WILLIAM PHIN.
Thurso Academy. M.A. 1901. Minister, Church of Scotland. Chaplain, 4th Class, Sept. 1915; 3rd Class Jan. 1918. Attached 2nd Ayrshire Imperial Yeomanry, 1914-15. 1st Scots Guards, Aug. 1915. Senior Chaplain, 51st Highland Division, March 1918. France. Dispatches 1918. M.C. Jan. 1919.

Record of War Service

GILLILAND, HANS.
Rossall. M.B., Ch.B. 1912. Royal Navy, Surgeon-Lieut. Dec. 1916.

GILLISON, KEITH.
Eltham College, London. Cadet Corps 1916-18, Corporal. Student of Medicine, 1918. 2nd Artists' Rifles O.T.C., Private July 1918 to Jan. 1919.

GILLMAN, HORACE ARTHUR.
George Watson's College. Student of Arts and Science, 1910-16; M.A. (Hons. Maths.) 1915; B.Sc. Schoolmaster. 2/10th (Cycle Battn.), Royal Scots, Private March 1917; L/Corporal July 1917. R.N.V.R., H.M.S. *President V.*, Sub.-Lieut. April 1918. Royal Air Force, Lieut. April 1918. Meteorological Station, Ireland.

GILLON, STAIR AGNEW.
LL.B. 1904. King's Own Scottish Borderers, Lieut. Nov. 1914; Captain Aug. 1916. Gallipoli Oct. 1915; Egypt Jan. 1916; France March 1916 to April 1917 and Oct. 1918 to Jan. 1919.

GILLON, WILLIAM.
George Watson's College; Dux. M.A., B.Sc. 1912. Schoolmaster. O.T.C. Infantry, 1910-13, Cadet. 15th Argyll and Sutherland Highlanders, Private Nov. 1915. R.N.A.S., Sub-Lieut. R.N.V.R., Lieut. June 1917. Royal Air Force, Captain.

GILMORE, THOMAS JACKSON.
Royal School, Dungannon; First XV. and XI. M.B., Ch.B. 1909. R.A.M.C., Lieut. Aug. 1915; Captain Aug. 1916. France and Salonika Sept. 1915 to March 1919.

GILMOUR, ANDREW.
Royal High School; First XI. Student of Arts, 1917-19; M.A. (Hons. Classics) 1920. 14th Argyll and Sutherland Highlanders, Private June 1915. France June 1916 to Feb. 1917. Invalided out June 1917.

GILMOUR, ANDREW.
George Watson's College. M.B., Ch.B. 1898; M.D. 1903; D.P.H., R.C.P.S. (Edin.) and F.P.S. (Glasg.) 1903; M.R.C.P. (Edin.) 1912. Vol. Medical Staff Corps 1894-8, Private. R.A.M.C., Lieut. Nov. 1914; Captain Nov. 1915.

GILMOUR, JOHN.
George Watson's College. M.B., Ch.B. 1906; F.R.C.S. (Edin.); Hon. M.A. University of Michigan, U.S.A. R.A.M.C., Lieut. 1910; Captain July 1913; D.A.D.M.S.; Brevet Major 1918. British Mission to United States, 1917. Egypt, Dardanelles, Serbia, Palestine, and East Africa. M.C. 1916.

GILMOUR, MAURICE EDWARD.
University O.T.C. Artillery, 1916, Cadet; Officer Cadet April 1916. R.F.A. (T.), 4th Lowland Brigade, 2nd Lieut. June 1917; Lieut. Dec. 1918.

Record of War Service

GILROY, ELLIOT RUSSELL.
Glenalmond. Cadet Corps 1904-5. Student of Science, 1918. 3/5th Royal Highlanders (Black Watch), 2nd Lieut. May 1915.

GILRUTH, JOHN GRANT.
Royal High School. Student of Medicine, 1912-15 and 1916-18; M.B., Ch.B. 1917. O.T.C. Artillery, Oct. 1914 to April 1915, Cadet. Royal Navy, Surgeon-Probationer, April 1915 to Sept. 1916; Surgeon Dec. 1917. H.M.S. *Sandhurst*.

GIRDWOOD, ARTHUR INGLIS.
High School, Butterworth, Transkei. M.B., Ch.B. 1908. South African Medical Corps, Captain Aug. 1914. Union Forces, German South-West Africa. R.A.M.C., Mesopotamia. Dispatches Aug. 1918.

GIRDWOOD, ROBERT LAURIE.
M.A. 1904; M.B., Ch.B. 1908. South African Medical Corps, Surgeon-Captain; Major Dec. 1915; Acting Lieut.-Col. Union Forces, German South-West Africa. D.S.O.

GIRLING, EDWIN CHARLES.
Ipswich Grammar School. M.B., Ch.B. 1906; M.D. 1915. R.A.M.C., Lieut. Oct. 1915; Captain Oct. 1916 to April 1919.

GIVEN, JAMES.
University (Maths. Department), Warder. Highland Light Infantry, Private Jan. 1915. India.

GLAISTER, THOMAS DERRICK. (See p. 749.)

GLASS, GAVIN HAMILTON.
Musselburgh Grammar School. Student of Arts, 1917-19. No. 9 Officer Cadet Battn., Cadet.

GLASSE, JOHN MORLEY.
George Watson's College. M.B., Ch.B. 1903. No. 4 Coy. Q.R.V.B., Royal Scots, and Volunteer Medical Staff Corps, 1895-1900, Private. South African Campaign, 1900-1. R.A.M.C., Lieut. Sept. 1914; Captain April 1918. Embarkation Medical Officer, Rouen, 1914-15. Mesopotamia 1917-18. Dispatches Feb. 1915.

GLEGG, CHARLES SIEVWRIGHT.
George Watson's College. M.B., C.M. 1893. Volunteer Medical Staff Corps, 1898-1903, Corporal. Civil Medical Officer, Dec. 1914-16. R.A.M.C., Lieut. June 1916; Captain June 1917. Royal Air Force Medical Service, June 1918 to March 1919.

GLEGG, WILLIAM LITTLE.
George Watson's College. M.B., Ch.B. 1912. O.T.C. Medical, April 1908-12, Cadet Corporal. R.N.A.S. (Armoured Cars), Surgeon Jan. 1915. Order of St Stanislaus (3rd Class), 1917; Chevalier of the Order of the Crown of Rumania, Dispatches (Zeebrugge) and D.S.C. 1918.

Record of War Service

GLEN, ALEXANDER ERNEST.
Glasgow Academy. University O.T.C. Infantry, 1916, Cadet; Officer Cadet Oct. 1916. 8th Cameronians (Scottish Rifles), 2nd Lieut. March 1917. 10th Scottish Rifles, France. Arras 1917. Wounded at Monchy le Preux, Nov. 1917.

GLEN, DOUGLAS JAMES.
Student of Medicine, 1909-14; M.B., Ch.B. 1914. B.R.C.S., 1914-15. R.A.M.C., Lieut. 1915; Captain Aug. 1916; Major March 1918. 2nd Scottish General Hospital. Med. Exp. Force.

GLEN, JOHN MACKENZIE.
Daniel Stewart's College. M.A. 1905; Hon. Econs. 1907. No. 4 Coy. Q.R.V.B., Royal Scots, 1905-7, Private. Inns of Court O.T.C. (T.), Sept. 1914 to July 1915, Sergeant. 5th Bedfordshire Regiment, 2nd Lieut. July 1915; Lieut. July 1917 to Dec. 1918. France. Wounded Sept. 1918.

GLENDINNING, ANDREW.
Dryfesdale School. M.A. 1908. Minister, U.F. Church of Scotland. R.A.M.C., Private March 1916. Chaplain, 4th Class, Dec. 1917.

GLENNY, DAVID JOHNSTON.
Student of Law, 1913-14. O.T.C. Infantry, 1914, Cadet. 9th Royal Highlanders (Black Watch), 2nd Lieut. July 1917; Lieut. Jan. 1918. France June 1915. Wounded Sept. 1915.

GLOVER, JAMES.
George Watson's College; First XV. Student of Medicine, 1914 and 1919. O.T.C. Artillery, 1914, Cadet. R.F.A., 2nd Lieut. Oct. 1914; Lieut. Aug. 1916. R.F.C. and Royal Air Force. Gallipoli 1915; France 1916-18. Wounded 1915.

GLOVER, JAMES ANDERSON.
Student. 3rd King's Own Scottish Borderers, Captain; Adjutant and Quartermaster. Invalided out May 1918.

GLOVER, JOHN HASTINGS.
M.B., C.M. 1893. R.A.M.C., Captain Jan. 1916. Torpedoed three times.

GLYNN, ARTHUR SAMUEL.
George Watson's College; First XV. Student of Medicine, 1909-14; M.B., Ch.B. 1914. R.A.M.C., Lieut. Aug. 1914; Captain Aug. 1915. No. 5 General Hospital, France. 1st Northumberland Fusiliers. Royal Air Force (Squadron Leader), Aug. 1919. Egypt 1919. Dispatches June 1915 and April 1916.

GOIL, DWARKA PRASAD.
Saháranpur, India. M.B., Ch.B. 1902; F.R.C.S. (Edin.) 1914. Indian Medical Service, Jan. 1903; Major July 1914. Egypt Nov. 1914 to March 1916; Persia March 1917. Invalided from Field Service, April 1918. India.

Record of War Service

GOLDIE, ARTHUR EVELYN.
St John's School, Barbados, B.W.I. M.B., Ch.B. 1900. R.A.M.C., Sept. 1915; Captain June 1917 to July 1919. Egypt March 1917; Salonika June 1918.

GOLDIE, THOMAS SMITH.
Robertson's Academy, Edinburgh. Student of Arts and Divinity, 1872-9; M.A. 1878. Minister, Church of Scotland. 1st Volunteer Battn., Royal Scots, Feb. 1917. 95th Special Service Volunteer Coy.

GOLDIE, WILLIAM.
Daniel Stewart's College; First XV. Student of Arts and Medicine, 1909-16; M.A. 1912; M.B., Ch.B. 1915. O.T.C. Infantry, May 1909 to Aug. 1914, Cadet Sergeant. 6th Royal Scots (T.), Private Aug. 1914. R.A.M.C. (T.), Lieut. July 1915; Captain May 1916; Major Jan. 1919. Dispatches July 1917. M.C. March 1918.

GOLLCHER, FREDERIK KARL.
Collegiate School, Malta. Student of Medicine, 1914-15. Artists' Rifles O.T.C., Private Oct. 1915. France. Wounded at Passchendaele Ridge.

GOMEZ, GEORGE ROBERT.
St Mary's College, Trinidad. Student of Medicine, 1918. 2/6th Devon Regiment, Private Jan. 1916 to March 1919. India and Salonika.

GONIN, EDMUND HENRI.
Brighton College. M.B., C.M. 1890; M.D. 1897. R.A.M.C. (T.), Lieut. May 1915; Captain Nov. 1915. 4th Royal Sussex Regiment (T.), 1916. France.

GOODALL, ALEXANDER.
George Watson's College. M.B., Ch.B. 1898; M.D. 1901; F.R.C.P. (Edin.) 1904. Lecturer on Clinical Medicine. Volunteer Medical Staff Corps, 1893-8, Sergeant. R.A.M.C., Major June 1917. Salonika and Italy.

GOODALL, CHARLES.
George Watson's College and Fettes. M.A. 1902; B.D. 1905. Minister, Church of Scotland. Y.M.C.A. Work, France, July to Oct. 1916. Chaplain, 4th Class, Malta, Dec. 1916-19.

GOODFELLOW, L. T.
Student. R.F.A., Lieut.

GOODSIR, JAMES T.
Student of Arts, 1912-14. 4th and 14th Royal Scots (T.), L/Corporal; 2nd Lieut. July 1916; Lieut. April 1917; Acting Captain July 1918.

GOODWIN, ERNEST WILLIAM. (See p. 749.)

GOPSILL, FRANK HAROLD.
Birmingham and London Universities O.T.C. 1909-14. Student of Commerce, 1918. West Surrey Regiment, 2nd Lieut. Aug. 1914. Invalided out June 1918.

Record of War Service

GORDON, ALEXANDER BRUCE.
: M.B., Ch.B. 1908; M.D. 1911; F.R.C.S. (Edin.) 1911. R.A.M.C., Lieut.

GORDON, ALEXANDER MacLENNAN.
: Halifax Academy, Nova Scotia. M.A. 1895; B.D. 1898. Chaplain, Hon. Captain, Sept. 1914; Hon. Major July 1916; Hon. Lieut.-Col. April 1919. 1st and 4th Canadian Divisions, France Feb. 1915. Wounded Aug. 1918. M.C. Jan. 1917; D.S.O. Dec. 1918.

GORDON, ALEXANDER STEWART.
: George Heriot's School; Athletics. M.B., Ch.B. 1904; M.D. (Hons.) 1910; D.P.H. (Edin.) 1910. Vol. Medical Staff Corps, 1898-1904, Sergeant. South African War, 1900. Royal Navy, Admiralty Surgeon. Rosyth and Forth Defences.

GORDON, ARCHIBALD ALEXANDER.
: Edinburgh Collegiate School. Student of Law, 1886-8. Chartered Accountant, 1889. Staff, Royal Naval Division, Antwerp, Aug. 1914. Army Special List; Major. Courier du Roi de Belges, Oct. 1914. France 1914. C.B.E.; M.V.O.; Commander of the Crown; Order of Leopold with Swords; Croix civique (1st Class), with Swords and Bar, 1914-15; Croix de Guerre with Palm (Belgium), Croix de Guerre with Palm (France); Order of St Anne (2nd Class), (Russia).

GORDON, ARCHIBALD TAYLOR.
: Glenluce Academy. M.A. 1907. 6th Royal Scots (T.), Private Sept. 1914; L/Corporal 1914; Sergeant 1915; 2nd Lieut. 1916; Lieut. Aug. 1917; Temp. Captain Oct. 1917. 53rd Machine-Gun Corps. Egypt and Palestine.

GORDON, CHARLES AUGUSTINE.
: St Edmund's College, Ware, Herts; First XI., Football. Student of Law, 1901-6. Writer to the Signet, 1906. 8th and 9th Royal Scots (T.), Private Feb. 1915; 2nd Lieut. July 1915; Lieut. July 1917. France Sept. 1916 to Nov. 1919. Wounded Aug. 1917.

GORDON, CHRISTOPHER.
: Repton. M.B., Ch.B. 1913. R.A.M.C., Lieut. May 1917; Captain May 1918. Invalided out June 1919.

GORDON, CLEMENTINA MARY.
: M.A. (Hons. Hist.) 1907. Secretary, S.R.C. Secretary, Rosebery R.S. Recruiting Committee, 1915-16. Q.M.A.A.C., Area and Recruiting Controller, N. and W. Commands, July 1917 to Jan. 1919. Mention Sept. 1919.

GORDON, COLIN.
: Repton. M.B., C.M. 1889. R.A.M.C., Lieut. July 1915; Captain July 1916-17.

GORDON, EDWARD SKENE.
: Beath School. Student of Medicine, 1917-20. O.T.C. Medical, April 1918 to May 1919, Cadet. Wireless Officer, H.M. Hospital Ship *Grantully Castle*, Jan. 1917; Wireless Officer, H.M.T. *Duchess of Argyle*, April 1917.

Record of War Service

GORDON, GEORGE ARTHUR.
Highgate School; First XI., Football. Cadet Corps 1897-1900. M.B., Ch.B. 1906; M.D. 1908. University Battery, E.C.A.V., 1900-5, Bombardier. R.A.M.C., Lieut. Nov. 1915.

GORDON, HAROLD.
Student of Medicine, 1911-19. O.T.C. Infantry, May to July 1915, Cadet. R.N.V.R., Surgeon-Probationer.

GORDON, HECTOR ANGUS.
Leeds Central High School. University O.T.C. Infantry, 1917-18, Cadet. 3rd Gordon Highlanders, Private July 1918. Royal Scots, 2nd Lieut. March 1919.

GORDON, HENRY WILLIAM.
Student of Law, 1915-16. Royal Scots, Private Feb. 1916. 1/7th Royal Highlanders (Black Watch). R.A.S.C. (M.T.). France.

GORDON, THE HON. HUNTLY DOUGLAS.
Student of Law. Advocate, 1885. 9th Royal Scots (T.), 2nd Lieut.; Lieut. June 1916.

GORDON, JAMES ALEXANDER.
M.B., Ch.B. 1908. No. 4 Coy. Q.R.V.B., Royal Scots, 1903-6. R.N.A.S., Surgeon Jan. 1915; No. 6 Squadron Armoured Cars. Royal Air Force Medical Service, Captain.

GORDON, JAMES WALLACE.
George Heriot's School; First XV. Student of Medicine; L.R.C.P. & S. (Edin.) 1917, L.D.S. (Edin.). O.T.C. Medical, April 1915 to Feb. 1917, Cadet. Edinburgh War Hospital, Aug. 1915 to July 1916. R.A.M.C., Lieut. Feb. 1917; Captain Feb. 1918. France and German East Africa.

GORDON, JOHN.
George Watson's College. M.A. 1883. Minister, Church of Scotland. Red Cross, 1915. Y.M.C.A., Rouen and Havre 1915; Mudros and Salonika 1916. R.G.A. (V.). (City of Aberdeen), Gunner April 1918; Lieut. May 1918.

GORDON, MARK.
Servitor. University. 13th Hussars, Farrier Sergeant. South African Campaign, 1899-1902, Scottish Horse (T.), Farrier Q.M.S. Sept. 1914. Transferred to R.F.A. Jan. 1917. Warrant Officer, June 1917 to Feb. 1919.

GORDON, PHILIP JAMES.
M.A. 1878. Indian Army 1881; Lieut.-Col. (retired). Imperial General Staff, War Office, 1914-19. General Staff Officer (2nd Grade), Jan. 1918. O.B.E. Commander of the Portuguese Order of Avis.

GORDON, WILLIAM.
George Heriot's School. B.Sc. 1911. A.M.I.Mech.E.; Lecturer in Engineering; Government Department Researches. R.F.A.(T.), unattached List, O.T.C. Artillery, 2nd Lieut. March 1917. Instructor in Map Reading, Aug. 1916 to Nov. 1918.

Record of War Service

GORDON, WILLIAM GRANT.
  Ayr Academy; First XV. O.T.C. 1913-17. Student of Commerce, 1919. O.T.C. Infantry, June 1917 to May 1918, Cadet L/Corporal. 6th Gordon Highlanders, 2nd Lieut. 1918.

GORDON, WILLIAM JOHN.
  Merchiston Castle. M.A. 1877. Writer to the Signet, 1882. R.N.R., Islands of Yell and Fetlar. R.N.V.R., Lieut. District Commander, Jan. 1915.

GORDON, WILLIAM LENNOX.
  M.B., Ch.B. 1906; M.D.; F.R.C.S. (Edin.) 1910. Anatomy Staff, 1910. South African Medical Corps, Lieut.; Captain Nov. 1914.

GORDON-HALL, FREDERICK WILLIAM GEORGE.
  M.B., C.M. 1883. R.A.M.C., Lieut. Jan. 1886; Colonel March 1915. C.B. Egyptian Dispatches 1916.

GORMAN, JOHN PATRICK.
  Student of Arts, 1912-15; M.A. 1915. O.T.C. Artillery, Oct. 1912 to April 1915, Cadet. R.G.A. (T.), 2nd Lieut. Dec. 1915; Lieut. July 1917. 1/1st Warwick Heavy Battery. France Feb. 1917; Italy Nov. 1917. Wounded, Austrian Offensive, Asiago, June 1918. Dispatches April 1918.

GORRIE, PETER.
  George Watson's College. M.B., Ch.B. 1908; M.D. 1910. No. 4 Coy. Q.R.V.B., Royal Scots, 1903-8. R.A.M.C., Lieut. May 1915.

GORRIE, ROBERT MacLAGAN.
  George Watson's College. Student of Science, 1918-20. O.T.C. Artillery, Oct. 1913-14, Cadet. 1st Scottish Horse (T.) Field Ambulance, Private Sept. 1914; 2nd Lieut. July 1915. R.F.A. Feb. 1917, Acting Lieut. July 1917; Acting Captain April 1918-19. France; Arras 1917. Dispatches March 1919.

GORRIE, WILLIAM.
  Dundee High School. M.B., Ch.B. 1897; M.D. 1911; D.P.H. 1910. R.A.M.C., Lieut. July 1917; Captain July 1918 to March 1919. 69th General Hospital, Egypt.

GOSSIP, ARTHUR JOHN.
  George Watson's College. M.A. 1894. Minister, U.F. Church of Scotland, Chaplain. 9th Highland Light Infantry (Glasgow Highlanders), Captain June 1917. France 1917-18; Ypres.

GOSSIP, JAMES.
  Inverness College. M.B., Ch.B. 1912; M.D. 1920. O.T.C. Artillery, Nov. 1908 to Dec. 1911, Cadet. R.A.M.C., Lieut. July 1913; Captain April 1915; Acting Major March 1918. Stationary Hospital, Rouen.

Record of War Service

GOSTWYCK, CECIL HUBERT GOSTWYCK.
　　Inverness College. M.B., Ch.B. 1899; F.R.C.P. (Edin.) 1914; Diploma Psych. (Durham); M.P.C. R.A.M.C., Lieut. Nov. 1915-16; Rejoined Lieut. July 1918; Captain Jan. 1919.

GOTTSCHALK, MAX.
　　Student. Scottish Horse (T.), Private.

GOUDIE, JOHN J.
　　Student. Scottish Horse (T.), Private.

GOULD, ALLAN DALGLEISH.
　　Student of Medicine, 1918. 53rd (Y.S.) Highland Light Infantry, Private.

GOULD, DAVID COLLIE.
　　Royal High School. Student of Arts, 1915. 3rd Royal Scots Fusiliers, Private Feb. 1917. 16th and 3rd Royal Scots.

GOULD, JOHN.
　　Broughton School. Student of Arts, 1912-14; M.A. 1919. 4th Royal Scots (T.), Private Aug. 1914; 2nd Lieut. April 1917; Lieut. Oct. 1918. Labour Corps; 259th A.E. Coy., Fourth Army H.Q.

GOURLAY, GEOFFRY BALFOUR.
　　Merchiston Castle; First XV. and XI. O.T.C. 1909-13, Cadet Corporal. Student of Science, 1913-14. O.T.C. Infantry, Sept. 1914, Cadet. 9th Gordon Highlanders, 2nd Lieut. Sept. 1914; Captain; Major April 1917; Acting Lieut.-Col. France. Twice Wounded. M.C. Dec. 1916; Croix de Guerre avec Palme (French) July 1918. Dispatches.

GOURLAY, WILLIAM BALFOUR.
　　Edinburgh Academy. B.A. (Camb.) 1903. Student of Medicine, 1905-10; L.R.C.P. & S. (Edin.) and L.R.F.P.S. (Glasg.) 1910; M.B., B.C. (Camb.) 1914. St Leonard's Red Cross Hospital (Edin.). R.A.M.C., Lieut. June 1915; Captain June 1916. Egypt, France, and North Russia. M.C. (North Russia) Nov. 1918.

GOW, GEORGE ALEXANDER.
　　George Heriot's School. O.T.C. 1912-16, Cadet Pipe-Major. Student of Arts, 1916-17. O.T.C. Artillery, Jan. to Oct. 1917, Cadet; Officer Cadet Oct. 1917. R.E. (Signal Service), 2nd Lieut. May 1918. The Rhine.

GOW, JOHN MILLER.
　　Perth Academy. Student of Arts and Divinity, 1909-15 and 1918-19; M.A. 1913; O.T.C. Artillery, Oct. 1914 to March 1915, Cadet. R.F.A., 2nd Lieut. March 1915; Lieut. July 1917 to Feb. 1919. M.C. June 1917. Dispatches July 1917.

Record of War Service

GOWAN, ALASTAIR AIKENHEAD.
George Watson's College; First XV. Student of Law, 1910-13. Chartered Accountant, 1913. 9th Royal Scots, 1909-13, L/Corporal. Montreal Heavy Brigade, Canadian Artillery. R.G.A. (S.R.), 2nd Lieut. Sept. 1916; Lieut. March 1918 to Jan. 1919. France Dec. 1916 to March 1918. Wounded March 1918. Dispatches April 1918.

GOWAN, ANTHONY THOMPSON.
Edinburgh Academy; First XV. Student of Medicine, 1903-9. 4th Canadian Infantry Battn., Private Aug. 1914; L/Corporal Feb. 1916. France Feb. 1915 to Sept. 1917. Twice Wounded.

GOWANS, THOMAS.
Fettes; First XV. and XI. M.B., Ch.B. 1902. Clinical Ophthalmologist, Durham University. R.A.M.C. (T.), 1908; Lieut.-Col. Aug. 1914. 1st Northern General Hospital, 1912-17 and 1918-19; 59th General Hospital, France, April 1917-18. Mention 1916.

GOWANS, WILLIAM HARVEY.
Dundee High School. M.B., Ch.B. 1906; L.D.S. (Edin.) 1906; D.P.H. (St Andrews). B.R.C. Auxiliary Hospital, Broughty Ferry, 1915-17. R.A.M.C., Lieut. June 1917; Captain June 1918. O.C. British Ophthalmic Hospital, Jerusalem, 1918-19.

GRACE, CHARLES LINDESAY PLAYFAIR.
Fettes. B.A. (Camb.). Student of Law, 1913-15. Writer to the Signet, 1919. O.T.C. Infantry, Oct. 1914 to Feb. 1915, Cadet L/Corporal. Highland Cyclist Battn., 2nd Lieut. Feb. 1915; Lieut. Feb. 1916; Captain Nov. 1916.

GRACE, RICHARD FAIRFAX.
Student of Medicine, 1914-15. 16th Royal Scots, Private.

GRACIE, ANDREW JOHN AINSLIE.
North Berwick High School. Student of Science, 1916-18. O.T.C. Artillery, Oct. 1917 to Sept. 1918, Cadet; Officer Cadet, R.E. Highland Light Infantry, Sept. 1918 to Feb. 1919.

GRACIE, DAVID SMART.
Student of Science, 1918. 16th Royal Scots, Private Dec. 1914; L/Corporal. France. Wounded and taken Prisoner at the Somme, July 1916.

GRACIE, JAMES.
Wanlockhead School. M.A. 1887; B.D. 1891. Minister, U.F. Church of Scotland. Chaplain, attached Royal Air Force, April 1918.

GRACIE, JOHN McARTHUR CAMPBELL.
Broughton School. Student of Science, 1914-15. O.T.C. Engineers, 1914-15, Cadet. 9th and 2nd Royal Scots Fusiliers, 2nd Lieut. April 1915; Lieut. July 1917. France. Wounded and taken Prisoner at Guillemont, July 1916.

Record of War Service

GRAHAM, ALASTAIR MUNRO.
　　Kirkcaldy School. O.T.C. four years. Student of Science, 1918-19. O.T.C. Infantry, Nov. 1916 to Sept. 1917, Cadet; Officer Cadet. 2nd Royal Scots, 2nd Lieut. June 1918 to April 1919. France 1918. The Rhine.

GRAHAM, DAVID CHARTERIS.
　　Student of Medicine, 1909-15. M.B., Ch.B. 1914. L.R.C.P. & S. (Edin.) and L.R.F.P.S. (Glasg.) 1914. R.A.M.C., Captain. 2nd Scottish General Hospital.

GRAHAM, DAVID JAMES.
　　George Watson's College. M.B., C.M. 1895; M.D. 1899; F.R.C.P. (Edin.) 1901. R.A.M.C. (T.), July 1908. Mobilised, Captain, Aug. 1914; Major Nov. 1914; Acting Lieut.-Col. 1917; Lieut.-Col. 1919. 58th Scottish General Hospital, France, and 2nd Scottish General Hospital, Edinburgh. Mention 1917. O.B.E. (Military).

GRAHAM, DONALD.
　　Kingussie School. M.A. 1910. O.T.C. Infantry, 1909-13, Cadet. R.N.R., Seaman Nov. 1915-16. Naval Schoolmaster, 1916; Warrant Schoolmaster, 1917-19.

GRAHAM, GILBERT MALISE.
　　M.B., Ch.B. 1911. Royal Navy, Surgeon April 1914.

GRAHAM, HAROLD.
　　Carlisle Grammar School; First XV. and XI. University O.T.C. Infantry, Aug. 1917 to May 1918, Cadet Corporal; Officer Cadet May 1918. 2/10th Royal Scots, 2nd Lieut. Feb. 1919.

GRAHAM, INGRAM ANNAN.
　　Regent Road School. M.A. 1909. 2/6th Seaforth Highlanders, Private May 1916; L/Corporal Aug. 1917. 2/1st Scottish Horse to Dec. 1918.

GRAHAM, JAMES.
　　M.B., C.M. 1897; M.D. 1915. R.A.M.C., Lieut.; Captain June 1917.

GRAHAM, JAMES.
　　M.A. 1892. No. 4 Coy. Q.R.V.B., Royal Scots, 1899-1903. 2/4th Royal Scots (T.) Private Dec. 1914; L/Corporal June 1915; Sergeant Nov. 1915.

GRAHAM, JOHN MACKENZIE.
　　Dingwall Academy. Student of Medicine, 1918. 52nd Gordon Highlanders, Private June 1918; L/Corporal Aug. to Dec. 1918.

GRAHAM, MANNERS HAMILTON NISBET.
　　Edinburgh Academy. O.T.C. 1908-9. Student of Science, 1909-12. 7th Royal Highlanders (Black Watch) (T.), 2nd Lieut. Jan. 1913; Lieut. Dec. 1914; Captain July 1915. France. Wounded Nov. 1915. Assistant Recruiting Officer, Scottish Command, July to Dec. 1917.

Record of War Service

GRAHAM, ROBERT BALFOUR.
Kelso Grammar School. Student of Arts, 1879-80; L.R.C.P. & S. (Edin.) 1884; F.R.C.S. (Edin.) 1888; D.P.H. (Edin.) 1894. Volunteer Medical Staff Corps, Acting Surgeon 1887; Lieut.-Col. 1906. R.A.M.C., Lieut.-Col. Nov. 1915 to Aug. 1918. Western Command Depôt, 1915-16. President, Recruiting Medical Board, Scotland, 1916-17. Craiglockhart War Hospital, 1917-18. V.D. 1907.

GRAHAM, SIMMON DICKSON.
M.B., C.M. 1893. R.A.M.C. (T.), Captain Dec. 1915. Gallipoli.

GRAHAM, THOMAS.
M.B., Ch.B. 1901. R.A.M.C. (T.), Lieut. Aug. 1914; Captain April 1915; Major Aug. 1918. 2nd North Midland Field Ambulance. M.C.

GRAHAM, WILLIAM THOMSON.
Perth Academy. M.B., Ch.B. 1909. R.A.M.C., Lieut. Feb. 1911; Captain July 1914. Indian Exp. Force. Mesopotamia 1914-18; Palestine 1918-19. Dispatches 1916 and 1919. O.B.E. June 1919.

GRAHAM-YOOLL, MALCOLM ANDREW.
Edinburgh Academy. O.T.C. 1912-16. Student of Medicine, 1915-17 and 1918-19. O.T.C. Artillery, April 1916 to Feb. 1917, Cadet; Officer Cadet Feb. 1917. R.F.A. (S.R.), 2nd Lieut. July 1917.

GRAHAME, MALCOLM CLAUD RUSSELL.
Westminster School. M.B., Ch.B. 1911; L.R.C.P. & S. (Edin.) and L.F.P.S. (Glasg.) 1906; D.P.H. (Edin.), and D.T.M. (Liverpool) 1913. University Battery, E.C.A.V., and O.T.C. Artillery, 1899-1912, Lieut. South African Campaign, 1900-1. R.A.M.C., Lieut. Aug. 1914; Captain Aug. 1915. Sanitary Officer.

GRAINGER STEWART, THOMAS.
Edinburgh Academy. O.T.C. 1912-14. Student of Arts and Law, 1914-15 and 1919. O.T.C. Infantry, Oct. to Dec. 1914, Cadet. 16th attached 17th Royal Scots, 2nd Lieut. Dec. 1914; Lieut. July 1917; Acting Captain and Adjutant Dec. 1918 to May 1919. France. M.C. Jan. 1917.

GRANGER, THOMAS ARTHUR.
M.B., C.M. 1892. Indian Medical Service, Lieut. July 1894. Mekran Expedition, 1898; Parachamkanis 1899. Brevet Lieut.-Col. Jan. 1914; Lieut.-Col. July 1914. Hon. Surgeon to Viceroy of India, Sept. 1914. Egypt and Gallipoli, 1915; France 1916-18. Dispatches Dec. 1917 and April 1918. C.M.G. June 1918.

GRANT, ALEXANDER.
George Watson's College. Student of Science. A.S.C., 2nd Lieut. Aug. 1914; Lieut.; Captain Nov. 1917; Acting Major March 1918. 3rd Division Ammunition Column. Twice Mentioned in Dispatches.

Record of War Service

GRANT, ALEXANDER.
Glenrinnes School. M.A. 1898. 2nd Artists' Rifles, O.T.C., Private Jan. 1917. 3rd G.B. Royal Welsh Fusiliers, attached 19th Rifle Brigade, 2nd Lieut. May 1917; Lieut. Nov. 1918. Attached H.Q., Palestine and Egypt.

GRANT, ALEXANDER LEWIS.
Burghead School. Highland Artillery Volunteers, Gunner 1907. M.B., Ch.B. 1912. R.A.M.C., Lieut. Feb. 1915-16. Mercantile Marine, Japan - Vladivostok and Australia, Feb. 1916 to April 1917.

GRANT, ANDREW.
Grantown-on-Spey School. M.B., Ch.B. 1913; D.P.H. (Camb.) 1918. R.A.M.C., Lieut. Jan. 1915; Captain Jan. 1916; Major June 1919. Wounded July 1916. M.B.E. (Military) June 1919.

GRANT, ANDREW.
Aberdeen Grammar School. M.B., Ch.B. 1902; D.P.H. (Edin.) 1904; D.T.M. Johore Military Forces, Surgeon-Lieut., attached Singapore Command, Sept. 1914; Surgeon-Captain March 1916. R.A.M.C., Lieut. July 1916; Captain July 1917; Acting Major June 1918 to May 1919. France Sept. 1916 to May 1917; Palestine April 1918 to June 1919. O.B.E. and Dispatches June 1919.

GRANT, A. R. S.
Student of Medicine. 9th Royal Scots (T.), Private.

GRANT, ARTHUR BALFOUR.
Student of Medicine, 1910-18; M.B., Ch.B. 1918. O.T.C. Medical, Feb. 1916 to Oct. 1918, Cadet Corporal. R.A.M.C., Lieut. Holland.

GRANT, COLIN.
M.B., Ch.B. 1909. R.A.M.C., Lieut. Oct. 1914; Captain April 1915. 70th Field Ambulance.

GRANT, DANIEL McDONALD.
M.B., Ch.B. 1909. R.A.M.C. (T.), Lieut.; Captain April 1915. 1st Highland Field Ambulance.

GRANT, DOUGLAS ALISTAIR.
Student of Law, 1910-12. 9th Royal Scots (T.), Private.

GRANT, EDMUND GEILS REGINALD.
Eastbourne College; First XV. O.T.C. 1911-14, Sergeant. Student of Medicine, 1913-15. O.T.C. Infantry, Oct. 1914-15, Cadet. 4th Royal Warwickshire Regiment (S.R.), 2nd Lieut. Sept. 1915; Lieut. July 1917. Wounded July 1919.

GRANT, GEORGE ALFRED.
George Heriot's School. Student of Law, 1897-9. Solicitor before the Supreme Courts, 1903. Irish Fusiliers, Vancouver, B.C., Captain Aug. 1914.

Record of War Service

GRANT, GEORGE REGINALD.
George Watson's College. M.B., Ch.B. 1913. O.T.C. Medical, 1909-12, Cadet. R.A.M.C. (S.R.), Lieut. Aug. 1914; Captain April 1915. Twice Wounded. M.C.

GRANT, GERALD WALLACE.
St Andrews College, Toronto. B.A. (Dalhousie). Student of Medicine, 1911-17; M.B., Ch.B. 1916. Anatomy Staff, 1916. O.T.C. Medical, Jan. 1913 to July 1916, Cadet Staff Sergeant. 11th Stationary Hospital, Rouen (Dresser), 1915. Canadian Army Medical Corps, Captain Nov. 1916. France. M.C. Aug. 1918.

GRANT, GORDON COUPER.
Aberdeen Grammar School. University O.T.C. Artillery, July 1917 to Jan. 1918, Cadet. Highland Light Infantry, 79th R.D. Battn., Private Jan. 1918. Royal Air Force, 3rd Air Mechanic, Feb. 1918.

GRANT, HUGH DUNCAN.
Dornoch Academy. Student of Law, 1913-15. R.N.V.R., Lieut.-Commander Feb. 1916. R.N. Air Meteorological Service Officer, Oct. 1916; Lieut., R.N.V.R., May 1917. Superintendent, Admiralty Meteorological Service, Aug. 1918.

GRANT, IAN MOUNT.
M.B., Ch.B. 1907; M.D. 1910. R.A.M.C., Lieut.; Captain April 1916.

GRANT, JAMES TAYLOR.
George Watson's College. M.B., C.M. 1893; M.D. 1895; B.Sc. (P.H.) 1894; F.R.C.P. 1903. R.A.M.C., Lieut. 1915; Captain June 1916; Major March 1919. Specialist Sanitary Officer.

GRANT, JOHN CHARLES BOILEAU.
Nottingham High School. M.B., Ch.B. 1908; F.R.C.S. (Edin.) 1913. Anatomy Staff, 1911. R.A.M.C., Lieut. 1914; Captain Oct. 1915. No. 18 Hospital, France, 1915. Dispatches 1916. M.C. 1917; Bar to M.C. 1918.

GRANT, JOHN PETER.
Winchester. Cadet Corps 1901-4, Corporal. M.A. (Oxford); LL.B. 1912. 2nd Lovat Scouts (T.), Oct. 1904; Captain Aug. 1914; Major Sept. 1916. Dispatches, Gallipoli 1915; Macedonia June 1916 and 1917. M.C. 1916.

GRANT, JOHN VICTOR LIVINGSTONE.
M.B., Ch.B. 1911. R.A.M.C. (S.R.), Lieut. Sept. 1914; Captain April 1915. Attached 15th "The King's Hussars." No. 13 Stationary Hospital; No. 4 and No. 9 Cavalry Field Ambulances. France Oct. 1914; The Rhine. Wounded Dec. 1915. M.C. Aug. 1918.

GRANT, JOSEPH.
M.A., 1914; B.Sc. 1915. R.E. (T.), 2nd Lieut. July 1916; Lieut. Jan. 1918.

Record of War Service

GRANT, LEWIS JOHN.
Glen Urquhart School. M.A. 1903. Schoolmaster, South Rhodesia. No. 4 Coy. Q.R.V.B., Royal Scots, 1900-3. South Rhodesian Defence Force, Captain. R.F.C., 2nd Lieut. Sept. 1917; Royal Air Force, Captain April 1918; Major July 1918.

GRANT, ROBERT.
M.B., Ch.B. 1912. R.A.M.C., Lieut.; Captain May 1916.

GRANT, ROBERT.
Townsville School, Queensland. B.A. (Queensland) 1915. Student of Medicine, 1915 and 1919. O.T.C. Infantry, Nov. to Dec. 1915, Cadet L/Corporal. Royal Highlanders (Black Watch), Dec. 1915, 2nd Lieut. Jan. 1916; Lieut. July 1917. King's African Rifles.

GRANT, ROBERT DONALD SUTHERLAND.
M.A. 1901. Schoolmaster. Munitions. Kincardineshire Volunteers, Sergeant; Musketry Instructor; Acting Sergeant Instructor.

GRANT, ROBERT WILLIAM LYALL.
M.A. (Aberdeen); LL.B. 1903. University Battery E.C.A.V., 1899-1901. Attorney-General, Nyasaland Protectorate. R.G.A. (T.), Captain 1904. Nyasa, Rhodesia Field Force, 1914-19.

GRANT, STANLEY NOEL.
Aberdeen Grammar School. M.A. 1919. 4th Gordon Highlanders, Private Sept. 1914 to Jan. 1915. Y.M.C.A., France. Ministry of National Service, March to Dec. 1918.

GRANT, WILLIAM HALLEY.
Merchiston Castle. O.T.C. 1910-14. Student of Arts, 1914-16 and 1918-20; M.A. 1920. Royal Fusiliers, Private May 1916. France 1916-17. Wounded at Arras, April 1917.

GRASSICK, WILLIAM LOGAN.
Ayr Academy; Dux; First XV. M.A. (Hons. Classics) 1914. Student of Medicine, 1915. Donaldson Auchairne Bursar, 1909; Crichton Bursar, 1915. O.T.C. Medical, Oct. 1916 to March 1918, Cadet. R.N.V.R., Surgeon Sub-Lieut. March 1918. H.M. Ships *North Star* and *Minion*.

GRAVES, DOUGLAS HENRY McDONALD.
George Watson's College. M.B., C.M. 1890. Indian Medical Service, Lieut. July 1891, Lieut.-Col. July 1911. Mesopotamia. N.-W. Frontier, India.

GRAY, ADAM PATTERSON.
Jedburgh Grammar School. M.A. 1899. R.G.A., 181st Siege Battery, Gunner April 1917; Bombardier Nov. 1917. Italy.

GRAY, ALEXANDER CHARLES EDWARD.
Edinburgh Collegiate School. M.B., C.M. 1890; M.D. 1898. R.A.M.C., Lieut. Oct. 1915; Captain Oct. 1916; Major March 1918. Fulham Military Hospital and Cerebro-Spinal Fever Wards, London District, 1915-19. O.B.E. June 1919.

Record of War Service

GRAY, ALFRED JOHN.
  M.A., B.Sc. 1908. R.F.A., 277th (Army) Brigade, 2nd Lieut.; Lieut. July 1917. France.

GRAY, ARTHUR HERBERT.
  Leys School, Cambridge. M.A. 1890. D.D. (Glasg.) 1919. Minister, U.F. Church of Scotland. Chaplain, 97th Infantry Brigade, Captain June 1915; Major April 1918 to Feb. 1919. France Nov. 1915-16.

GRAY, EDWARD PENROSE TWYFORD.
  Student of Medicine, 1912-14. O.T.C. Infantry, Aug. to Oct. 1914, Cadet. R.A.M.C. (T.). Scottish Horse Brigade Field Ambulance, Private. Scottish Horse, Lieut. July 1917.

GRAY, ELLA ORROK.
  Edinburgh Ladies' College. Student of Arts, 1914 and 1916-18; M.A. 1918. Women's Royal Naval Service, Senior Writer, Nov. 1918.

GRAY, GEORGE CECIL RHODES.
  Merchiston Castle and Larchfield; First XV. and XI. University O.T.C. Artillery, Feb. to Oct. 1917, Cadet Bombardier; Officer Cadet Oct. 1917. R.F.A., 88th Brigade, 2nd Lieut. March 1918.

GRAY, GEORGE MARTIN.
  M.A., 1909; LL.B. 1912. O.T.C. Infantry, March 1910 to Feb. 1912, Cadet Sergeant. 5th Gordon Highlanders, Captain June 1916.

GRAY, HENRY.
  Boroughmuir School. Student of Arts, 1915-16. O.T.C. Infantry, 1915, Cadet. 9th Royal Scots (T.), Private Dec. 1915; Acting Sergeant Nov. 1917. France Sept. 1916 to April 1917.

GRAY, JAMES.
  M.B., Ch.B. 1894. South African Campaign, 1902. Australian Army Medical Corps, Captain Oct. 1915. No. 2 Australian Hospital, Gheyirah Palace, Cairo, 1915. Wounded Sept. 1916.

GRAY, JAMES.
  Ballymoney School. M.B., Ch.B. 1911. R.A.M.C., Lieut. April 1916; Captain April 1917. India April 1916-18; Palestine April 1918 to Sept. 1919.

GRAY, JAMES M.
  Kingussie School. Student of Arts, 1918. Royal Air Force, Cadet, June 1918.

GRAY, JOHN.
  George Heriot's School. O.T.C., 1915-18. Student of Medicine, 1918-19. 4th Highland Light Infantry, Private April 1918.

GRAY, JOHN ALEXANDER.
  George Watson's College. M.A. 1898; M.B., Ch.B. 1903. R.A.M.C., Captain Aug. 1914. France March 1917 to Dec. 1918.

Record of War Service

GRAY, JOHN WILLIAM.
  Campbeltown Grammar School. M.A. 1907; M.B., Ch.B. 1911; B.Sc. (P.H.) 1914. R.A.M.C. (S.R.), Lieut. Dec. 1911. Mobilised Aug. 1914; Captain April 1915; Acting Major June 1918. France 1914 to Nov. 1919. Dispatches Jan. 1916.

GRAY, MAURICE WISHART.
  Kirkwall Grammar School. M.A. 1911; B.Sc. 1913. Research Scholar, 1913. O.T.C. Infantry, 1909-12, Cadet L/Corporal. Lothians and Border Horse (T.). 1/1st Scottish Horse Brigade, 2nd Lieut.; Lieut. July 1917. Egyptian Army, July 1917; Captain; Major. Salonika.

GRAY, OLIVER.
  Daniel Stewart's College. Student of Medicine, 1913-16 and 1918-19. O.T.C. Infantry, Oct. 1913 to Jan. 1916, Cadet L/Corporal. R.N.V.R., Surgeon-Probationer, May 1916 to Oct. 1918. H.M. Ships *Cockatrice* and *Atherstone*.

GRAY, OLIVER.
  Glasgow Academy and Bootham School, York; First XI., Cricket and Football. University O.T.C. Artillery, Feb. to March 1917, Cadet. British Ambulance Unit, Italy, six months. R.N.V.R., Midshipman, Jan. 1917; Sub-Lieut. Nov. 1918. H.M. Ships *Lark*, *Murray*, and *Telemachus*.

GRAY, THOMAS PAUL.
  M.B., C.M. 1886; M.D. 1898. South African Campaign, Civil Surgeon, 1900-1. R.A.M.C., Lieut. April 1915; Captain April 1916. 24th Division, R.F.A.; 2nd Dragoon Guards. Aldershot Hospital.

GRAY, WILLIAM ADAMSON.
  George Watson's College. Student of Medicine, 1912-18; M.B., Ch.B. 1918. O.T.C. Infantry, May 1915 to March 1916, Cadet. R.N.V.R., Surgeon-Probationer, March 1916. Royal Navy, Surgeon-Lieut. April 1918-19.

GRAY, WILLIAM BAIN.
  George Watson's College. M.A. 1908. Examiner in Scottish History, 1914. 6th Royal Scots (T.), 2nd Lieut. Feb. 1912. Mobilised Aug. 1914; Lieut. Nov. 1914; Captain Sept. 1916. General Staff Officer (3rd Grade), Dec. 1918.

GRAY, WILLIAM BIRRELL.
  George Heriot's School. Student of Science, 1912. South African Campaign, 1900-2. Nigeria Land Contingent, Sept. 1914; Major and O.C. July 1915 to 1918.

GRAY, WILLIAM FORREST McARTHUR.
  Fettes. O.T.C. 1914-17. University O.T.C. Artillery, Dec. 1917 to Aug. 1918, Cadet. R.F.A., Officer Cadet Aug. 1918.

GRAY, WILLIAM GEORGE.
  George Heriot's School. Student of Science, 1915-16. 6th and 7th Argyll and Sutherland Highlanders, Private March 1916; 2nd Lieut. May 1918. Attached 1/2nd London Scottish. France, 51st Division. Gassed at Arras May 1917.

Record of War Service

GRAY, WILLIAM HAMILTON.
Daniel Stewart's College. Student of Law, 1899-1901. Chartered Accountant, 1902. 4th and 17th Royal Scots, Lieut. and Quartermaster Dec. 1914; Temp. Captain Sept. 1915. France.

GRAY, WILLIAM LEWIS.
Glasgow Academy and High School. M.B., Ch.B. (Glasg.); B.Sc. 1888. R.A.M.C., Lieut. Feb. 1887. South African Campaign, 1900-1. Lieut.-Col. 1910; Col. 1915. Dispatches July 1916 and Jan. 1917. C.M.G. Jan. 1917.

GRAYSTON, JOHN WILLIAM.
United College, Bradford. Student of Arts and Divinity, 1911-14; M.A. 1914. R.G.A., 147th Heavy Battery, 2nd Lieut. Sept. 1914; Lieut. Nov. 1915; Captain Sept. 1917; Acting Major April 1918. France Feb. 1915 to June 1919. M.C. June 1918.

GREATOREX, ROBERT WILKINSON.
M.B., Ch.B. 1909. Volunteer Medical Staff Corps, 1904-7, Private. R.A.M.C., Lieut. Jan. 1915-16 and Oct. 1917; Captain April 1918.

GREAVES, FRANCIS WOOD.
Harrison College, Barbados. First XI. M.B., Ch.B. 1908; D.T.M. (Liverpool) 1908; D.P.H., R.C.P. & S. (Edin.) 1909. No. 4 Coy. Q.R.V.B., Royal Scots, 1904-6. Trinidad Medical Service, Surgeon-Lieut. Oct. 1914 to Sept. 1918. Attached Trinidad Mounted Infantry. H.M. Transport *Magdalena*.

GREEN, ARTHUR CAMPBELL VAUGHAN.
George Watson's College. O.T.C. 1910-11. M.B., Ch.B. 1912. O.T.C. Medical, 1909-12, Cadet. Royal Navy, Surgeon-Lieut. Aug. 1914. West Indies 1914; Northern and Dover Patrols 1915-18; Ostend and Zeebrugge, North Russian Exp. Force 1919. Dispatches 1918.

GREEN, HERBERT MELVILLE.
Clifton College. M.B., C.M. 1894; M.D. 1898; L.R.C.P. & S. (Edin.) and L.F.P.S. (Glasg.) 1893. No. 4 Coy. Q.R.V.B., Royal Scots, 1888-91, Sergeant. R.A.M.C., Lieut. Oct. 1915; Captain Oct. 1916. St John's Hospital, Malta; 64th General Hospital, Salonika. France.

GREEN, JOHN JOSEPH.
Holy Cross Academy, Leith. Student of Arts, 1915 and 1919. R.F.A., 187th Brigade, 41st Division, Gunner March 1916.

GREEN, JOHN LIGERTWOOD.
George Watson's College. M.B., Ch.B. 1900; M.D. 1907. Marchhall R.C. Aux. Hospital, Edinburgh, 1915-17. R.A.M.C., Lieut. May 1917. France. Invalided out April 1918.

Record of War Service

GREEN, JOSEPH.
　　Norwich Grammar School. M.B., Ch.B. 1905; M.D. and D.P.H. 1911. R.A.M.C. (T.), Lieut. April 1915; Captain Oct. 1915. 54th East Anglian Casualty Clearing Station; Military Hospital, Imtarfa, Malta. 1/6th Royal Welsh Fusiliers and 53rd Division, Ammunition Column, R.F.A. M.B.E. 1918.

GREEN, STEPHEN.
　　Fettes. O.T.C. 1909-10. Student of Arts and Divinity, 1910-16; M.A. 1914. R.A.M.C., Private Dec. 1915.

GREEN, THOMAS ARTHUR.
　　Skipton Grammar School. M.B., C.M. 1890; M.D. 1897; F.R.C.S. (Edin.) 1904. R.A.M.C. (T.), April 1908; Captain Oct. 1911; Major Nov. 1914; Lieut.-Col. Aug. 1916. 1/3rd South Midland Field Ambulance. France and Italy Feb. 1915 to June 1919. Dispatches Jan. 1917 and Jan. and May 1918. D.S.O. June 1918.

GREENBERG, MAX.
　　South African College, Cape Town. First XV. and XI. M.B., Ch.B. 1910; F.R.C.S. (Edin.). South African Medical Corps, Captain Oct. 1914.

GREENFIELD, JOSEPH GODWIN.
　　Merchiston Castle. B.Sc. 1906; M.B., Ch.B. 1908. R.A.M.C., Lieut. Aug. 1914; Captain Oct. 1917. France.

GREENFIELD, THOMAS CHALLEN.
　　Merchiston Castle. O.T.C. 1907-11, Cadet Corporal. Student of Science, 1911-14; B.Sc. 1914; A.M.Inst.C.E. 1919. O.T.C. Engineers, Dec. 1911 to Oct. 1914, Cadet Corporal. R.E., 2nd Lieut. Dec. 1914; Lieut. July 1915. France. Wounded Nov. 1915. Invalided out April 1917.

GREENHILL, JAMES KENNETH.
　　B.A.; LL.B. 1913. Advocate 1913. R.A.M.C., Lieut.

GREENHILL, JOHN CLAPPERTON.
　　Edinburgh Academy and Sedbergh. O.T.C. 1907-8. Student of Law, 1912-13. Chartered Accountant, 1917. 12th Argyll and Sutherland Highlanders, 2nd Lieut. Sept. 1914; Lieut. Jan. 1915; Captain June 1915. France and Serbia 1915; Egypt 1916. Invalided out May 1916.

GREENLAW, EBENEZER WATT.
　　Greenock School. M.A. 1904. Schoolmaster. 6th V.B. Royal Scots, 1900-1, Private. City of Edinburgh Volunteers, Private March 1917-19.

GREENLEES, THOMAS DUNCAN.
　　Ayr Academy. M.B., C.M. 1882; M.D. 1901. South African Campaign, 1899-1902. R.A.M.C. (T.), Major Jan. 1915. Dorset and Wiltshire R.E. (T.). Invalided out Sept. 1917.

Record of War Service

GREENSHIELDS, WILLIAM SOMERVILLE.
M.A. 1911. A.S.C., Lieut.

GREENWAY, ALEXANDER STEVENSON.
M.B., C.M. 1874; M.D. 1880; M.R.C.S. (Eng.) 1878. Vol. Medical Staff Corps, 1887. R.A.M.C. (T.), Lieut.-Col. 1908. 4th London Field Ambulance, Aug. 1914 to March 1919. T.D. 1908.

GREENWOOD, ROBERT ALFRED.
Mark Bridge, York. M.B., Ch.B. 1912. O.T.C. Medical, April 1908 to June 1911, Cadet Sergeant. R.A.M.C. (S.R.), Lieut. 1912. Mobilised Aug. 1914; Captain Dec. 1914; Acting Major Jan. to Dec. 1918. 10th Royal Hospital, Rouen, Dec. 1914. Dispatches June 1916 and Jan. 1918. M.C. June 1918.

GREENWOOD, THOMAS PARKER.
Skipton Grammar School. B.Sc. 1891; M.B., C.M. 1897; M.D. 1903. R.A.M.C., Temp. Captain July 1918. Nottingham County War Hospital.

GREER, WILLIAM NIVEN.
Foyle College, Londonderry. Student of Medicine, 1911-16; M.B., Ch.B. 1916. O.T.C. Medical, Oct. 1914 to July 1916, Cadet L/Corporal. R.A.M.C., Lieut. Aug. 1916; Captain Feb. 1917. O.B.E.

GREER, WILLIAM WELLS.
Brisbane Grammar School. First XV. M.B., Ch.B. 1904; M.D. 1906; F.R.C.S. (Edin.) 1914. R.A.M.C. (T.), Lieut. Sept. 1914; Captain March 1915; Major Jan. 1918. 3rd London Field Ambulance. Egypt. M.C. Dispatches March 1917 and Jan. 1918.

GREGOR, DAVID CLUNIE.
Edinburgh Academy; First XI. O.T.C. University O.T.C. Infantry, Jan. to June 1918, Cadet. Royal Air Force, Officer Cadet June 1918.

GREGOR, JAMES WYLLIE.
Edinburgh Academy; First XI. O.T.C. 1914-17. University O.T.C. Infantry, Jan. to June 1918, Cadet. Royal Air Force, Officer Cadet June 1918.

GREGORSON, ANGUS MACLAINE.
Student of Law. Writer to the Signet, 1893. 9th and 4th Royal Scots (T.), Lieut.; Captain Oct. 1914. Army Recruiting Staff, Ministry of National Service.

GREGORY, DAVID ALEXANDER.
Rossall. O.T.C. 1915-17. Student of Medicine, 1918-19. R.G.A. (T.), 2nd Lieut. Aug. 1918 to Jan. 1919. France Nov. 1918 to Jan. 1919.

GREGORY, JOHN BONAR.
Glasgow Academy. O.T.C. 1911-14. Student of Arts, 1914-15 and 1918-19. O.T.C. Infantry, Jan. to Oct. 1915, Cadet. Argyll and Sutherland Highlanders, 2nd Lieut. Oct. 1915; Lieut. April 1917. Attached 1st London Scottish 1916; 51st Division (Highland), 1917, and 59th Division (M.G.C.) 1918. France; Somme, Vimy, Roeux, Ypres, and Cambrai. Dispatches Oct. 1918.

Record of War Service

GREIG, DAVID MIDDLETON.
　M.B., C.M. 1885; F.R.C.S. (Edin.) 1890. Lecturer on Clinical Surgery, St Andrews University. R.A.M.C., Major Dec. 1904. T.D.

GREIG, EDWARD DAVID WILSON.
　Edinburgh Academy. M.B., C.M. 1895; M.D.; B.Sc.; D.Sc. 1909. Indian Medical Service, 1899, Captain; Major Jan. 1911; Lieut.-Col. Jan. 1920. D.A.D.M.S. Tigris Corps, Mesopotamia, March to Aug. 1916. C.I.E.

GREIG, EUGÈNE FRANKLIN.
　Lycée Charlemagne, Paris. B.Sc. 1909. Bachelier ès Sciences (Paris). O.T.C. Infantry, Sept. to Oct. 1914. R.G.A., 2nd Lieut. Oct. 1914; Lieut. March 1916. France Oct. 1915 to Dec. 1916, and Sept. 1917 to Oct. 1918.

GREIG, JAMES HENRY.
　George Heriot's School. Student of Arts, 1915-16 and 1918-19. O.T.C. Infantry, 1915-16, Cadet. 3rd Gordon Highlanders, Private June 1916; L/Corporal. Detective Branch, Military Police. France Oct. 1916 to March 1917.

GREIG, P. R.
　Student of Medicine. 2nd Lieut. in the Army.

GREY, GAVIN.
　George Watson's College. M.A. 1894. No. 4 Coy. Q.R.V.B., Royal Scots, 1889-1900, Colour-Sergeant. 1st Highland Light Infantry, 2nd Lieut. May 1900. 3rd attached 11th King's Liverpool Regiment, Captain June 1909; Temp. Major Dec. 1917 to April 1918. Commandant Prisoners of War Camp. France May to Sept. 1915; Salonika Jan. 1917 to April 1919.

GREY, JOHN OGILVIE.
　George Watson's College. Student of Law, 1887-90. Solicitor before the Supreme Courts, 1898. Q.R.V.B., Royal Scots, 2nd Lieut., 1893. 11th Royal Scots, Captain Sept. 1914; Major Nov. 1918. France for five years.

GREY, WILLIAM LILBURN.
　N.E. Co. School, Barnard Castle. O.T.C. 1912-14. Student of Science, 1915. O.T.C. Engineers, 1914-15, Cadet. Lancashire Fusiliers, 2nd Lieut. June 1915.

GRIERSON, HENRY JAMES.
　Glenalmond; First XV. Cadet Corps 1881-7, Corporal. B.A. (Camb.) 1890; Student of Law, 1895-6. Writer to the Signet, 1896. 6th Royal Highlanders (Black Watch) (T.), 2nd Lieut. Oct. 1914; Lieut. 1915; Captain June 1916; Major June 1918. France Nov. 1916.

GRIERSON, JOHN DARBYSHIRE.
　Hoe Grammar School, Plymouth; First XI. Student of Medicine, 1915-17 and 1918-19. O.T.C. Infantry, 1915-17, Cadet Corporal. 7th Seaforth Highlanders, 2nd Lieut. April 1917. France Oct. 1917 to Feb. 1918.

Record of War Service

GRIERSON, WILLIAM GOLDSWORTHY.
    Hoe Grammar School, Plymouth. Student of Medicine, 1915-16 and 1919. O.T.C. Infantry, Oct. 1915 to Jan. 1916, Cadet. 2nd Royal Highlanders (Black Watch), 2nd Lieut. Jan. 1916; Lieut. July 1917; Captain Aug. 1919. Mesopotamia Jan. 1917-18; Palestine, Syria, and Egypt, Jan. 1918-20.

GRIEVE, ALEXANDER BARRIE.
    Breadalbane Academy, Aberfeldy. M.A. (Camb.); M.A., B.Sc. 1907; D.Sc. 1912. Lecturer in Mathematics, London University. Royal Navy, Instructor-Lieut., Jan. 1916 to May 1919. H.M. Ships *President* and *Marlborough*. Jutland Battle, May 1916.

GRIEVE, GEORGE ANDREW.
    Student of Arts, 1906-9 and 1918-20; M.A. 1920. 2/1st Highland Cyclist Battn., Sergeant; Lieut. and Quartermaster Nov. 1914; Captain and Quartermaster Nov. 1917. 1/4th Gordon Highlanders, July 1918. France.

GRIEVE, GEORGE THOMAS WILSON.
    George Heriot's School. O.T.C. 1913-16, Cadet Sergeant. Student of Science, 1918-19. O.T.C. Artillery, Oct. 1916 to April 1917, Cadet Bombardier; Officer Cadet April 1917. North Scottish R.G.A. (T.), 2nd Lieut. July 1917; Lieut. Jan. 1919. France, March 1918 to Jan. 1919.

GRIEVE, HUGH.
    Student of Medicine, 1914-15. R.F.A. (T.). 4th Sussex Brigade, 2nd Lieut.; Lieut. June 1916.

GRIEVE, IAN MARTIN DONALDSON.
    Breadalbane Academy, Aberfeldy. Student of Medicine, 1918-20. 14th London Regiment (London Scottish), Piper Aug. 1914. France 1914. Wounded.

GRIEVE, JOHN.
    George Heriot's School. M.A. 1906. Schoolmaster. R.E., Corporal; Dispatch Rider.

GRIEVE, JOHN.
    Edinburgh Institution. Student of Law, 1898. Writer to the Signet, 1904. A.S.C. (T.), 52nd Lowland Division Train, 2nd Lieut. March 1911; Lieut.; Captain Aug. 1914; Major Feb. 1917. 10th (Irish) Division, A.S.C. Egypt June 1915; Serbia Oct. 1915; Macedonia Dec. 1915; Palestine Sept. 1917 to May 1918. Dispatches.

GRIEVE, JOHN CALDWELL.
    Dumfries Academy. M.B., C.M. 1905. R.A.M.C., Lieut. Jan. 1914; Captain April 1915; Acting Major Jan. 1918. 1st North Midland Field Ambulance. M.C. Jan. 1918.

Record of War Service

GRIEVE, JOHN WATKIN.
Bradford Grammar School. O.T.C. 1914-17, Cadet Sergeant. Student of Science, 1918. R.G.A., No 1 Siege Artillery Reserve Brigade, Jan. 1918; 2nd Lieut. July 1918.

GRIEVE, KELBURNE KING.
M.B., Ch.B. 1906. West African Medical Staff, Lieut. Cameroons Exp. Force, South Nigeria.

GRIEVE, WILLIAM.
George Heriot's School; First XV. and XI. M.A., B.Sc. 1907. Karachi Artillery Volunteers, 1915. 38th Dogras (I.A.R.O.), 2nd Lieut. Oct. 1916; Lieut. Oct. 1917; Acting Captain Feb. 1919. 56th Punjabi Rifles, Frontier Force.

GRIFFIN, ERROL FLEMING.
Pietermaritzburg College. Student of Medicine, 1912-14 and 1916-19. 7th Royal Scots Fusiliers, 2nd Lieut.; Lieut. Attached Royal Air Force.

GRIFFITH, WILLIAM.
St Peter's School, Weston-super-Mare. M.B., C.M. 1891. R.A.M.C., Captain Sept. 1915; Major. Attached R.G.A., 1915.

GRIFFITHS, ALFRED.
M.B., C.M. 1888; F.R.C.S. (Edin.) 1904. R.A.M.C., Lieut. Oct. 1915; Captain March 1916; Major March 1918. Mention 1916.

GRIFFITHS, DAVID JONATHEN POSTHUMOUS.
West Monmouthshire School, Pontypool; First XI. Student of Medicine, 1918. 4th Reserve Battn. Royal Welsh Fusiliers, Private May 1918.

GRIFFITHS, EVAN JOHN.
Llandovery School; First XI., Football. M.B., Ch.B. 1904; D.P.H. (Wales). R.A.M.C., Lieut. June 1915; Captain June 1916. Foreign Service for three and a half years.

GRIFFITHS, JOSEPH.
M.B., C.M. 1885; M.D. 1890; D.P.H. (Camb.) 1887; F.R.C.S. (Eng.). R.A.M.C. (T.), Colonel May 1908. 1st Eastern General Hospital. C.M.G.; T.D.

GRIMSTON, EDWARD ROBERT TYMON.
Student of Arts, 1913-16. 8th Royal Scots (T.), Private.

GRISTWOOD, THOMAS JAMES.
Boroughmuir School. Student of Arts and Science, 1916-17 and 1919. R.G.A., Gunner April 1917; Bombardier Nov. 1917; Corporal Sept. 1918; Officer Cadet Oct. 1918. France.

GROGAN, ANDREW WAUCHOPE.
Cheltenham. Student of Law, 1910-14. Scottish Horse (T.), 2nd Lieut. Sept. 1909; Lieut. July 1912; Captain June 1916.

Record of War Service

GROVES, CHARLES.
George Heriot's School. Student of Arts, 1913-14. 5th Royal Scots (T.), Private Sept. 1914; 2nd Lieut. Oct. 1916; Lieut. April 1918. Gallipoli and France. Invalided out Dec. 1918.

GROVES, ERNEST JOSEPH CLIFFORD.
Bedford Modern School; First XV. and XI. M.B., Ch.B. 1905. No. 4 Coy. Q.R.V.B., Royal Scots. R.A.M.C. (T.), Lieut. Aug. 1914; Captain April 1915. 2nd South Midland Field Ambulance. Invalided out 1918.

GRUMMETT, EDWARD FALKNER.
George Heriot's School. O.T.C. 1914-16. University O.T.C. Infantry, 1917-18, Cadet Corporal; Officer Cadet Sept. 1918. 4th Gordon Highlanders, 2nd Lieut. May 1919.

GUEST, EDWARD.
Allan Glen's School, Glasgow. Cadet Corps 1915-17, Sergeant. University O.T.C. Infantry, March 1917, Cadet L/Corporal; Officer Cadet. 5th Highland Light Infantry, 2nd Lieut. Jan. 1918; Lieut. April 1919. France.

GUILD, DAVID ALEXANDER.
Edinburgh Academy. M.A. 1907; LL.B. Advocate, 1909. R.F.A., Gunner March 1916; 2nd Lieut. June 1916; Lieut. Dec. 1917. France. Wounded near Rosières, Aug. 1918.

GUILDFORD, CHARLES JAMES.
Student of Arts, 1915-16. 3/6th Royal Sussex Regiment (Cyclist Battn.), Private Dec. 1915. 10th Essex Regiment, 2nd Lieut. March 1917; Lieut. Sept. 1918.

GULLAND, GEORGE LOVELL.
Royal High School. M.A. 1881; B.Sc.; M.B., C.M. 1886; M.D. 1890; F.R.C.P. (Edin.) 1890. Professor of Medicine. R.A.M.C. (T.), Major. 2nd Scottish General Hospital, 1910. Army Medical Service, Colonel July to Dec. 1915. Malta. C.M.G. and Mention 1916.

GULLAND, JOHN MASSON.
Edinburgh Academy. O.T.C. 1913-17, Cadet Officer. Student of Science, 1918. R.E. Signal Service, Officer Cadet April 1917; 2nd Lieut. Nov. 1917 to Jan. 1919. France 1918.

GUNN, ALBERT ALEXANDER.
Edinburgh Academy. M.B., Ch.B. 1898. R.A.M.C. (T.), Lieut. May 1909; Captain Dec. 1912. 1st East Lancashire Brigade and 210th Brigade, R.F.A. 41st Stationary Hospital, France. Egypt, Gallipoli, Palestine, and France Sept. 1914 to Dec. 1918. Dispatches July 1917.

GUNN, ALEXANDER WILLIAM.
Student of Medicine, 1910-15; MB., Ch.B. 1915. O.T.C. Artillery, March 1909 to Feb. 1912, Cadet. Royal Navy, Surgeon July 1915.

Record of War Service

GUNN, ANDREW RUGG.
M.B., Ch.B. 1907. R.A.M.C., Lieut. March 1915; Captain March 1916. Ophthalmist, 16th (Indian) Division, 1916-19. Gallipoli 1915. India 1916-19.

GUNN, ELIZABETH CATHERINE.
M.B., Ch.B. 1903; L.M. (Dublin). New Zealand Medical Corps, Captain Oct. 1915.

GUNN, GEORGE.
Student of Medicine. Seaforth Highlanders, 2nd Lieut.

GUNN, GEORGE HERBERT.
Thurso Academy; First XI. Student of Medicine, 1913-18; M.B., Ch.B. 1918. O.T.C. Medical, Oct. 1916 to Dec. 1918, Cadet Staff Sergeant. 5th Seaforth Highlanders, Piper Nov. 1910. 1st Gordon Highlanders, 2nd Lieut. 1914. Invalided out July 1915.

GUNN, HUGH.
M.A. 1893. Argyll and Sutherland Highlanders, Lieut. South African Campaign. 28th Northumberland Fusiliers (Tyneside Scottish), Captain 1915-16. Ministry of Munitions.

GUNN, JAMES ANDREW
M.A. 1901; B.Sc. 1903; M.B., Ch.B. 1905; M.D. 1907; D.Sc. 1909. Assistant Materia Medica Department. Professor of Pharmacology, Oxford University. R.A.M.C., Lieut. Feb. 1915; Captain June 1915. 3rd Southern General Hospital, 1915-17. Research, Ministry of Munitions, 1918-19.

GUNN, J. C.
Student of Science. 4th Royal Scots (T.), 2nd Lieut.

GUNN, JOHN CAMERON.
Student of Medicine, 1909-11. O.T.C. Artillery, Feb. 1910 to Nov. 1912, Cadet. Malay States Vol. Rifles, Private 1914.

GUNN, JAMES MARSDEN LOWER.
George Watson's College. O.T.C. 1906-11; Cadet Colour-Sergeant. Student of Arts, 1911-15; M.A. 1915; O.T.C. Infantry, March to Oct. 1913, Cadet. 5th Royal Scots (T.), 2nd Lieut. Jan. 1914; Lieut. May 1915; Captain Nov. 1917. Machine-Gun Corps.

GUNN, JAMES TURNER.
Royal High School; First XV. and XI. M.B., Ch.B. 1905; F.R.C.S. (Edin.) 1908. R.A.M.C., Lieut. Feb. 1915; Captain Feb. 1916. 51st General Hospital. No. 7 British Field Ambulance, April 1915; 18th Brigade, R.F.A. (Lahore Division), May 1915. France. Wounded at Somme, Aug. 1916.

Record of War Service

GUNN, JOHN.
: Daniel Stewart's College. Student of Medicine, 1911-12. 1st Canadian Regiment, Private Aug. 1914. 7th Royal Scots, 2nd Lieut.; Lieut. July 1917; Acting Captain Oct. 1918. Invalided out May 1919. M.C. Sept. 1918 and Bar Jan. 1919.

GUNN, JOHN DONALD.
: Loretto; First XI. B.A. (Camb.) 1905; First XV. MB., Ch.B. 1910; M.D. 1914; F.R.C.S. (Edin.) 1914. R.A.M.C., Lieut. April 1915; Captain May 1916; Acting Major June 1918; 42nd General Hospital, Salonika, Caucasus, and 82nd General Hospital, Constantinople.

GUNN, JOHN PETERSON.
: George Watson's College. Cadet Corps 1908; Cadet Sergeant. M.A. (Hons. Maths), 1912; B.Sc. 1913. O.T.C. Infantry, Oct. 1908-11, Cadet. 5th Royal Scots (T.), 2nd Lieut. 1911; Lieut.; Captain Jan. 1915. 1st King George's Own Sappers and Miners, I.A.R., Lieut. Aug. 1916; Captain Nov. 1917. Mesopotamia.

GUNN, JOHN WILLIAM CORMACK.
: Kirkwall School. M.A. 1908; M.B., Ch.B. 1912. Assistant, Materia Medica, 1913. R.A.M.C., Lieut. Dec. 1914; Captain Dec. 1915; Acting Major Jan. 1918, 19th General Hospital, Dec. 1917 to June 1919. 21st General Hospital, Alexandria. Dispatches April 1917.

GUNN, JOHN WILLIAM MILLER.
: Wick High School. Student of Arts, 1915-16. R.G.A., Gunner Dec. 1915; Bombardier; Acting Corporal. Gassed April 1918.

GUNSON, EDWARD BURTON.
: M.B., Ch.B. 1910; M.D. 1911; M.R.C.P. (Lond.) 1913. R.A.M.C., Lieut.; Captain, Feb. 1916; Acting Major Jan. 1918.

GUNSON, EDWARD CARWARDINE.
: Chelmsford Grammar School. M.B., Ch.B. 1902. R.A.M.C., Lieut. Oct. 1914; Captain Oct. 1915 to Feb. 1919. Wounded May 1917. D.S.O. July 1916.

GUNTER, FRANCIS ERNEST.
: Dover College; First XV. L.R.C.P.& S. (Edin.) and L.F.P.S. (Glasg.) 1891; M.B., C.M. 1893. R.A.M.C., Lieut. July 1895; Captain July 1898; Major May 1907; Lieut.-Col. March 1915; Temp. Col. June 1916. A.D.M.S. Aug. 1918. 83rd General Hospital, France. D.S.O. Jan. 1917. Dispatches Jan. 1917 and Jan. 1918.

GUPPY, HENRY BROUGHAM.
: Sherborne, Dorset. M.B., C.M. 1876. 2nd Devon Vol. Regiment, Private 1915-17.

GURNEY, ARTHUR LEOPOLD.
: M.B., Ch.B. 1901. South African Medical Corps, Captain Feb. 1914; Temp. Major April 1917 to Dec. 1918. R.M.O. 5th South African Infantry, East Africa, Jan. to Nov. 1916.

Record of War Service

GUSH, HOWARD WALTER.
St Paul's House, St Leonard's-on-Sea. M.B., Ch.B. 1903. Volunteer Medical Staff Corps, 1896-1903, Staff Sergeant. West African Medical Staff. R.A.M.C., Lieut. June 1916; Captain June 1917. France; Somme, and Arras, June 1916-17. German East Africa, 1917. Wounded Nov. 1917.

GUTHRIE, HUGH LIVINGSTONE CLARK.
George Watson's College. Student of Law, 1912-14. O.T.C. Infantry, 1914, Cadet. 1/9th Royal Scots, 2nd Lieut. Aug. 1914; Lieut. July 1917; Acting Captain; Acting Major. 1/7th Royal Highlanders (Black Watch), June 1916. Machine-Gun Corps, 1917 to Feb. 1919. France 1915-18. Dispatches Jan. 1917.

GUTHRIE, JAMES BRAID.
Leven School. Student of Arts, 1910-15; M.A. 1915; B.Sc. Schoolmaster. 6th Royal Scots (T.). Mobilised Aug. 1914; R.Q.M.S. Nov. 1914.

GUTHRIE, JOHN CRAIG.
M.A. 1900. R.G.A., Captain.

GUTHRIE, ROBERT LYALL.
Dundee High School. M.A. 1888; M.B., C.M. 1892; M.D. 1901. R.A.M.C. (T.), Lieut. Dec. 1914; Captain June 1915; Major July 1916; Brevet Major June 1917; Acting Lieut.-Col. Aug. 1917. France Aug. 1915. O.B.E. June 1919.

GUTHRIE, THOMAS MANSFIELD.
Edinburgh Academy. M.B., Ch.B. 1904. No. 4 Coy. Q.R.V.B., Royal Scots, 1897-1901, Private. R.A.M.C., Lieut. Dec. 1916. 68th Field Ambulance, Salonika.

GUTHRIE, THOMAS MAUL.
Brechin High School. Student of Law, 1889-92. Law Agent, 1895. 5th Royal Highlanders (Black Watch) (T.), 2nd Lieut., 1896; Lieut. 1899; Captain 1908; Acting Major 1916.

GUTHRIE, WILLIAM A.
Leven School. M.A. 1896. 5th and 7th Royal Highlanders (Black Watch) (T.), Oct. 1906; Temp. Major 1914; Temp. Lieut.-Col. April 1916; Major Oct. 1916. Dispatches June and Dec. 1916 and June 1918.

GUY, JAMES CAMPBELL MORRISON.
Edinburgh Academy. O.T.C. 1909-11. Student of Arts and Law, 1911-14 and 1918-19; M.A. 1915. O.T.C. Artillery, 1913-14, Cadet. R.N.V.R., Royal Marine Artillery, R.N. Division, Sub-Lieut. Aug. 1914; Lieut. July 1916. Antwerp. East African Exp. Force, Dec. 1915 to Sept. 1917. Invalided out April 1918. Dispatches Oct. 1917. M.C. March 1918.

GUY, JOHN AGNEW CAMPBELL.
Edinburgh Academy. Student of Medicine, 1910-16; M.B., Ch.B. 1916. O.T.C. Artillery, 1912-14, Medical 1914-15, Cadet. R.A.M.C. (S.R.), Lieut. July 1916; Captain Jan. 1917. 8th London Mounted Brigade Field Ambulance, Salonika, Aug. 1916; Egypt June 1917; Palestine July 1917; France June 1918.

Record of War Service

GUY, WILLIAM.
Norwich Grammar School. Student of Medicine, 1878-81; L.R.C.P. & S. (Edin.) 1884; F.R.C.S. and L.D.S. (Edin.) 1892. R.A.M.C. (T.), Captain 1908; Brevet Major June 1917. Specialist, Face and Jaws, 2nd Scottish General Hospital; O.C. Principal Dental Centre, Scottish Command.

GUYER, RONALD BRETT.
Edinburgh Institution; First XV. 1st Highland Cadet Battn., 1912-15. Student of Science, 1918-19. O.T.C. Infantry, March to Aug. 1918, Cadet Corporal. 4th Seaforth Highlanders, Officer Cadet Aug. 1918.

GWYTHER, ARTHUR.
M.B., C.M. 1893. Indian Medical Service, Lieut.-Col.

GYLE, JOHN BURNSIDE.
Perth Academy; First XV. Student of Medicine, 1914-15 and 1917-19. O.T.C. Infantry, Feb. to May 1915, Cadet. 14th Argyll and Sutherland Highlanders, Private May 1915. 6th Royal Highlanders (Black Watch), 2nd Lieut. Nov. 1915; Lieut. July 1917. Seconded, Machine-Gun Corps, Aug. 1916 to April 1918. France. Wounded near Monchy-le-Preux April 1917.

HADDON, DAVID ALEXANDER ROSS.
Fettes College. Student of Medicine, 1908-14; M.B., Ch.B. 1913; M.D. 1919. 9th Royal Scots (T.), 1906; Lieut., Aug. 1914 to Jan. 1915. R.A.M.C. (T.), Captain May 1915; Major Aug. 1918. France Feb. 1915 to March 1919. Wounded at second Ypres, 1915; Arras 1916; Passchendaele 1917. Dispatches Dec. 1916. M.C. Sept. 1917.

HADDOW, JOHN REID.
Daniel Stewart's College. 1st Highland Cadet Battn., 1912-13, Cadet Corporal. Student of Science, 1914-15. Royal Scots Greys, Trooper Nov. 1914. 17th Royal Scots, Lieut. Oct. 1917. Attached Royal Air Force, 1918.

HADDOW, ROSS T.
Falkirk High School. Student of Arts, 1913-14 and 1918-19. O.T.C. Artillery, Aug. to Nov. 1914, Cadet. R.F.A., 2nd Lieut Nov. 1914; Lieut. June 1916; Acting Major Aug. 1918. 4th Northumbrian Howitzer Brigade. 317th Brigade, 63rd R.N. Division. M.C. Oct. 1917.

HAIG, PATRICK BALFOUR.
Loretto; First XV. M.B., C.M. 1889; M.R.C.S.; L.R.C.P. (Lond.). President, Royal Medical Society. Resident, R.I.E. and Sick Children's Hospital. Indian Medical Service, Lieut. 1892; Lieut.-Col. 1912. Waziristan 1894-5; N.-W. Frontier 1897-8; Uganda 1899-1900. Hospital Ships, 1914-16; Field Ambulance, N.-W. Frontier, India, 1916 and 1917. Dispatches Feb. 1917 and March 1919. C.B. Feb. 1917.

Record of War Service

HAIG, WILLIAM.
M.B., C.M. 1894. R.A.M.C. (T.), Oct. 1900; Major July 1912. O.C. Ambulance Train. France. D.S.O. Jan. 1917. T.D.

HAINE, ARTHUR WILLIAM PRESTON.
Alloa Academy. Student of Medicine, 1914-16 and 1917-20; M.B., Ch.B. 1920. O.T.C. Medical, 1914-16, Cadet. Royal Naval Auxiliary Sick Berth Reserve, Feb. 1916. R.N.V.R., Surgeon-Probationer, Oct. 1916.

HAINE, JOHN EDGAR.
Boroughmuir School. Student of Medicine, 1915-20; M.B., Ch.B. 1920. O.T.C. Medical, Oct. 1916 to April 1919, Cadet. 7th Royal Highlanders (Black Watch), Private Aug. 1916. R.N.V.R., Surgeon-Probationer, March 1918.

HAINES, MAURICE COLTON.
Ulverston High School. Student of Science, 1897-8. 1st V.B. Royal Lancaster Regiment, 1895; Captain 1903. 1st London Regiment, Royal Fusiliers, 1904; Temp. Major Jan. 1915. Ministry of Munitions, April 1917.

HAKE, CYRIL MARRIOTT.
Student of Science, 1912-15 and 1919-20; B.Sc. 1920. O.T.C. Engineers, 1912-14, Cadet. R.E. (T.), City of Dundee Fortress, 2nd Lieut. Oct. 1914; Lieut. June 1916.

HALDANE, DAVID.
Warrender Park School. Student of Science, 1910-15. 9th, 15th, 2nd, and 11th Royal Scots, Private 1909; Q.M.S. June 1915; 2nd Lieut. June 1917; Lieut. Nov. 1918. Instructor, Machine-Gun School, Barry. France.

HALL, ANDREW ALEXANDER.
George Watson's College. M.A. 1899; M.D. (Gold Medallist), 1905. 9th Canadian Field Ambulance, Private 1917. R.A.M.C., Lieut. Feb. 1918. 2/2nd London Field Ambulance.

HALL, ARTHUR CROWDER.
Calday Grange Grammar School. University O.T.C. Artillery, 1917, Cadet; Officer Cadet Jan. 1918. R.F.A., 2nd Lieut. Sept. 1918.

HALL, DONALD GEORGE.
Edinburgh Academy; First XV. and XI. M.A. 1904; M.B., Ch.B. 1900, and M.D. (Camb.) 1904; L.R.C.P. 1900; M.R.C.P. (Lond.) 1904; M.R.C.S. (Eng.) 1900. R.A.M.C. (T.), Major 1908. No. 2 Eastern General Hospital.

HALL, EDMUND ALEXANDER WILLIAM.
M.B., C.M. 1886. Indian Medical Service, Lieut.-Col. 1912.

HALL, HENRY BAKER.
Malvern College. M.B., C.M. 1891. Royal Navy, May 1892, Fleet Surgeon, May 1908. Retired Feb. 1915. H.M.S. *Challenger*.

Record of War Service

HALL, IAN SIMSON.
George Watson's College; First XV. Student of Medicine, 1914-15 and 1918-19. O.T.C. Artillery, Oct. 1914 to Aug. 1915, Cadet. R.F.A. (S.R.), 2nd Lieut. Sept. 1915; Lieut. Oct. 1917. France April 1916 to Sept. 1918.

HALL, JAMES THOMAS.
National School, Ballybay, Ireland. M.A. 1907; B.D. 1910. Minister, Church of Scotland. Chaplain, Captain, Dec. 1915. 8th Casualty Clearing Station, France, Dec. 1915 to Oct. 1916. 2nd King's Own Scottish Borderers, Oct. 1916 to March 1918. Dispatches May 1918. O.B.E. (Military) June 1918.

HALL, JOHN FORTUNE.
George Heriot's School. Student of Law, 1912-14. Chartered Accountant, 1919. 4th Royal Scots (T.), Private 1908; L/Corporal 1913; Sergeant Nov. 1914; C.Q.M.S. May 1915.

HALL, JOHN ROBERTSON.
Edinburgh Academy. M.B., Ch.B. 1907. Medical Examiner, Recruits; V.A.D. Hospital, Morton House, Co. Durham. R.A.M.C., Lieut. April 1916. France. Wounded, Somme, 1916.

HALL, JOSIAH FIELD.
King Edward VI. School, Birmingham. M.B., C.M. 1892. Vol. Medical Staff Corps, 1886-7, Private. R.A.M.C. (T.), Captain Nov. 1914. M.O., 2/22nd Battn., London Regiment, France, 1916-17.

HALL, PETER TAYLOR.
George Watson's College. M.A. 1896. Minister, U.F. Church of Scotland. Chaplain, Captain, Dec. 1915. Dispatches May 1917.

HALL, ROBERT.
Grant School, Riverside, California. Student of Medicine, 1912-13 and 1918-19. R.F.A. (T.), 276th Brigade, 2nd Lieut. 1913; Lieut. 1915. R.F.C., Captain April 1917. R.F.A., Captain Dec. 1918. France Sept. 1915 to Dec. 1917. Wounded at Nieuport July 1917. Dispatches April 1917. M.C. July 1917.

HALL, SIDNEY HERBERT.
M.B., C.M. 1894; M.D. 1919. R.A.M.C., Lieut. April 1915; Captain April 1916. Malta 1915-16; Palestine and Syria 1917-18; Egypt 1919.

HALL, WILLIAM TELFORD.
George Heriot's School. Student of Science, 1913-14 and 1918-20; B.Sc. 1920. 6th Royal Scots, Private Aug. 1914. 4th Royal Irish Fusiliers, 2nd Lieut. April 1915; Lieut. Feb. 1917; Captain March 1918. Attached Machine-Gun Corps. France; Salonika 1916. Wounded in Flanders May 1918.

HALLAM, ARTHUR RUPERT.
Sheffield Grammar School. M.B., Ch.B. 1901; M.D. 1905. R.A.M.C. (T.), Lieut. 1906; Major Nov. 1909. 3rd Northern General Hospital, Sheffield.

Record of War Service

HALLCHURCH, WALTER WILLIAM.
Wolverhampton Grammar School. Student of Medicine, 1909-14; M.B., Ch.B. 1914. R.A.M.C., Lieut. Dec 1914; Captain Dec. 1915. 343rd Field Ambulance. S.M.O., Brigade H.Q., Enniskillen. O.C. Hounslow Military Hospital.

HALLEY, FRANCIS MURRAY.
Crieff Academy and Daniel Stewart's College. Student of Medicine, 1910-15; M.B., Ch.B. 1915. Demonstrator of Anatomy, 1914-15. O.T.C. Medical, Dec. 1914 to Aug. 1915. R.A.M.C. (T.), Lieut. July 1915; Captain Jan. 1916. 2nd Scottish Horse Field Ambulance, Salonika. Mesopotamia Jan. to Dec. 1918.

HALLIDAY-CROOM, DAVID.
Edinburgh Academy. B.A. (Camb.) 1898; M.B., Ch.B. 1903; M.D. 1906; F.R.C.P. (Edin.) 1910. R.A.M.C., Lieut. April 1917; Captain. France.

HALLIWELL, BASIL T.
Epsom College and Warwick School. Student of Medicine, 1912-14 and 1918-19. O.T.C. Artillery, Oct. 1913-14, Cadet. R.F.A., 86th Brigade, 2nd Lieut. Oct. 1914; Lieut. Dec. 1915; Acting Captain Dec. 1916; Temp. Captain March 1918. France July 1915 to June 1918. Dispatches Feb. 1918. M.C. Aug. 1917.

HALTON, HENRY.
Giggleswick. M.B., C.M. 1895; M.D. R.A.M.C. (T.), 1900, Captain; Major April 1915. Salonika and India. Kohát, Afghan Frontier.

HAMILTON, ALEXANDER GEORGE.
M.B., Ch.B. 1898. No. 4 Coy. Q.R.V.B., Royal Scots, 1893-8, Corporal. Chester Vol., Surgeon-Captain. 1/1st Welsh Border Mounted Brigade Field Ambulance, 1900. R.A.M.C., Lieut.-Col. July 1913. Mobilised March 1917. 231st Field Ambulance. Egypt, Palestine, and France. Dispatches (Jerusalem). O.B.E.

HAMILTON, ANDREW ROWAN.
Campbell College, Belfast; First XI. Student of Medicine, 1909-14; M.B., Ch.B. 1914; D.P.H. (Belfast) 1917. R.A.M.C. (S.R.), Lieut. Oct. 1914. 13th Royal Irish Rifles.

HAMILTON, ANDREW STEWART LOUDON.
Giggleswick; First XV. and XI. O.T.C. 1911-15, Cadet Officer. University O.T.C. Artillery, Sept. 1915 to Feb. 1916, Cadet. Royal Military Academy. Feb. 1916. R.F.A., 2nd Lieut. Aug. 1916; Lieut. Feb. 1918 to Sept. 1919. France. Wounded Sept. 1918. M.C. May 1918.

HAMILTON, ARCHIBALD GORDON.
Glasgow Academy; First XI. University O.T.C. Artillery, 1916-17, Cadet; Officer Cadet June 1917. R.F.A., 2nd Lieut. Feb. 1918. 58th Division. France.

HAMILTON, ARNOLD ANGUS.
George Watson's College. Student of Medicine, 1915-16. O.T.C. Artillery, 1916-17, Cadet. R.N.V.R., attached R.N.A.S., Sick Berth Reserve, Aug. 1917. Haslar and Chatham Naval Hospitals. Munitions.

Record of War Service

HAMILTON, BROWN.
M.A. 1905. His Majesty's Inspector of Schools. Private in the Army.

HAMILTON, EBEN STUART BURT.
Campbell College, Belfast. M.B., Ch.B. 1910; F.R.C.S. (Edin.) 1919. O.T.C. Medical, April 1908 to Jan. 1910, Cadet Sergeant. R.A.M.C. (S.R.), Lieut. 1910; Captain July 1914. Prisoner of War for five months, 1914-15. France, Mons, 1914. M.C. 1916.

HAMILTON, FERGUSON.
Carriden School, Bo'ness. M.A. 1907. Schoolmaster. R.G.A., 228th Siege Battery, Gunner (Observer), May 1916. Officer Cadet Aug. 1918.

HAMILTON, GEORGE.
Auchinleck, Ayrshire. M.A. 1906. Schoolmaster. George Heriot's School O.T.C. 1915-16, Lieut. and O.C. Royal Scots, Lieut. Jan. 1916; Temp. Captain.

HAMILTON, HENRY FLEMING.
M.B., Ch.B. 1909; F.R.C.S. (Edin.). West African Medical Staff, Captain, Cameroons Exp. Force, Gold Coast.

HAMILTON, JAMES KIRKLAND.
Royal Academy, Tain. M.A. 1902; M.B., Ch.B. 1908. R.A.M.C., Lieut. June 1917; Captain July 1918.

HAMILTON, JAMES OLIVER.
George Watson's College. M.B., Ch.B. 1908. R.A.M.C. (S.R.), Lieut. 1910; Captain Sept. 1914. France 1914-17. Invalided out Feb. 1917.

HAMILTON, JOHN ARCHIBALD.
George Watson's College. M.B., C.M. 1892; F.R.C.S. (Edin.) 1903. Indian Medical Service, Lieut. 1895; Lt.-Col. July 1914; Acting Colonel Dec. 1917. China, 1900. Indian Corps, France, Oct. 1914 to Dec. 1915. Mesopotamia from Jan. 1916. Dispatches Dec. 1915 and June 1919. C.M.G. Jan. 1916.

HAMILTON, JOHN ARNOTT.
M.A. 1912; B.D. 1917. Minister, Church of Scotland. O.T.C. Infantry, Nov. 1909 to April 1913, Cadet. Assistant Chaplain, Cromarty.

HAMILTON, ROBERT.
M.B., Ch.B. 1901; M.D. 1909. R.A.M.C., Lieut. May 1915; Temp. Captain May 1916. South Wales Borderers, 115th Brigade, France.

HAMILTON, WILLIAM.
Student of Arts, 1911-15; M.A. (Hons. Ment. Phil.) 1915. O.T.C. Infantry, Sept. 1914 to March 1915, Cadet. 9th Royal Scots (T.), Private March 1915, France. Invalided May 1916. R.A.M.C., Nigg, April 1917.

Record of War Service

HAMILTON, WILLIAM HUGH.
Edinburgh Institution. Student of Arts and Law, 1891-9; M.A. 1895. Writer to the Signet, 1899. Army Pay Corps, Acting Paymaster, Scottish Command Nov. 1915.

HAMILTON-GRIERSON, PHILIP FRANCIS.
Edinburgh Academy. B.A. (Oxford). Student of Law 1905-7. Advocate, 1907. 1/4th Royal Scots, Aug. 1914. 5th Royal Scots Fusiliers (T.), Acting Lieut. Oct. 1914; Acting Captain July 1915; Lieut. June 1916; Captain Dec. 1917; Staff Captain Dec. 1917 to 1918. Seconded to Egyptian Army, March 1919. Sudan. Dispatches 1916 and 1918. M.B.E. (Military) Jan. 1919.

HAMMAN, DIRK JACOB HUGO.
M.B., Ch.B. 1902; F.R.C.S. (Edin.); L.M. (Dublin). South African Medical Corps, Captain Oct. 1917.

HAMMOND, THOMAS B.
Student of Medicine, 1887-91. 13th London Regiment (Princess Louise's Kensington), Private.

HAMOND, FREDERICK JAMES.
George Watson's College. M.A. (Hons. Classics) 1907. Schoolmaster. R.N.A.S. (Armoured Car Division), Petty Officer; Air Mechanic Oct. 1914; Chief Petty Officer Aug. 1916. Dispatch Rider. German South-West Africa 1915, and East Africa 1915-17. Invalided out July 1917.

HANDASYDE, ALEXANDER KINCAID.
Edinburgh Academy. Student of Law, 1911-12. Chartered Accountant, 1914. R.A.M.C. (T.), Private Nov. 1914; Acting R.Q.M.S. 1918. 3rd Lowland Field Ambulance.

HANDFORD, HENRY.
Atherstone Grammar School. M.B., C.M. 1878; M.D. 1882; M.R.C.S. (Eng.) 1878; D.P.H. (Camb.) 1884; F.R.C.P. (Lond.) 1889. R.A.M.C. (T.), (Sanitary Service), Major 1909. Mobilised June 1915 to May 1916.

HANDYSIDE, PATRICK BRODIE.
Edinburgh Academy. M.B., C.M. 1883. Royal Navy, Surgeon-General, April 1917; Surgeon Rear-Admiral. Sierra Leone, West Africa, 1898-9; R.N. Hospital, Chatham. C.B. June 1918; Imperial Japanese Order of the Sacred Treasure (2nd Class) Nov. 1918; K.B.E. June 1919.

HANMER, HASSAL.
Wallasey Grammar School. M.A. 1913. Minister, Congregational Church. 17th King's Liverpool Regiment, Private Sept. 1914; Sergeant Sept. 1915; Colour-Sergeant Nov. 1917. France Nov. 1915 to Sept. 1918; North Russia Oct. 1918 to June 1919. Dispatches June 1919.

Record of War Service

HANNA, GEORGE HENRY.
Fulnech, Leeds. M.B., Ch.B. 1900; M.D. 1911. R.A.M.C., Lieut. 1916.

HANNA, JAMES BOWMAN.
Bangor Grammar School. Student of Medicine, 1911-17; M.B., Ch.B. 1917. O.T.C. Medical, 1916-17, Cadet. R.A.M.C., Lieut. May 1917; Captain May 1918; Acting Major Jan. 1919. Salonika June 1917-18; Black Sea 1919.

HANNA, WILLIAM G. C.
Loretto; First XV. Student of Law, 1899. Chartered Accountant, 1904; F.C.I.S. Scottish Horse (T.), 2nd Lieut. Aug. 1914. 4th Seaforth Highlanders, Lieut. July 1917; Staff Captain (Temp. Captain) June 1918 to March 1919. France 1916-19. Dispatches 1918 and 1919. O.B.E. 1919.

HANNAH, PERCY.
Student of Arts, 1915-16. R.A.M.C., Private. 1st Welsh Field Ambulance.

HANNAH, ROBERT.
M.B., Ch.B. 1908; D.P.H. (Edin.) 1910. R.A.M.C., Lieut. Sept. 1914; Temp. Captain Sept. 1915. M.C. July 1917.

HANNAY, HARRY.
Ewart High School. Student of Science, 1901-8. Associate, Institute of Mining and Metallurgy. O.T.C. Infantry, May 1915, Cadet. 5th King's Own Scottish Borderers, 2nd Lieut. May 1915. R.E. (T.), Lowland Division, Lieut. Nov. 1916; Acting Captain Jan. 1916; Acting Major Oct. 1918 to March 1919. M.C. June 1916. Dispatches May 1918.

HARCUS, ROBERT.
George Watson's College. University O.T.C. Artillery, 1917-18, Cadet Bombardier; Officer Cadet May 1918. R.F.A., 2nd Lieut. Feb. 1919.

HARDIE, JOHN ANDREW.
George Heriot's School; First XV. and XI. M.A. (Hons. Maths.) and B.Sc. 1908. O.T.C. Infantry, 1914-15, Cadet L/Corporal. George Heriot's O.T.C., 2nd Lieut. June 1915. 4th Royal Highlanders (Black Watch), 2nd Lieut. Sept. 1918 to Jan. 1919.

HARDIE, ROBERT.
George Watson's College. M.B., C.M. 1882; M.D. 1905. Royal Navy, Surgeon March 1887. Retired 1908. Mobilised, Fleet-Surgeon, Aug. 1914; Surgeon-Commander; Surgeon-Captain, Nov. 1918. Retired Dec. 1918. Ministry of Pensions. Mention Nov. 1914. O.B.E. Jan. 1919.

HARDIE, RONALD W. W.
Edinburgh Institution; First XV. and XI. Cadet Corps 1913-17, Sergeant. Student of Medicine, 1918. R.N.A.S., Sub-Lieut. April 1917. Royal Air Force, Lieut. April 1918; Captain and Pilot Feb. 1919.

Record of War Service

HARDING, HOWARD.
Merchant Taylors; First XV. M.B., Ch.B. 1902. R.A.M.C., Lieut. Jan. 1904; Captain July 1907; Major July 1915. India. Dispatches Jan. 1916.

HARDWICKE, LAWRENCE CAMPBELL VIGOR.
M.B., Ch.B. 1904. R.A.M.C. (T.), Major July 1917. O.C. 3/3rd London Field Ambulance.

HARE, ARTHUR WILLIAM.
Oliver's Mount School, Scarborough. M.B., C.M. (Hons.) 1882; M.R.C.S. (Eng.) 1886; F.R.C.S. (Edin.) 1886. President, Royal Medical Society. Assistant in Surgery, 1884-8; Professor of Surgery, Manchester University. R.A.M.C., Lieut. April 1915.

HARE, EDWARD.
Leith Academy. M.A. 1910; (Hons. Hist.) 1913. Schoolmaster. Seaforth Highlanders, Private Nov. 1915; L/Corporal; Sergeant.

HARKNESS, JOHN.
Wallace Hall Academy, Dumfriesshire. Student of Arts and Divinity, 1910-16; M.A. 1914. 9th Royal Scots (T.), Private Nov. 1915-19. 1st King's Own Scottish Borderers, Aug. 1916. France. Wounded at Ginchy, Somme, Jan. 1917.

HARKNESS, ROBERT COLTART.
Dumfries Academy; First XV. M.B., Ch.B. 1909; F.R.C.S. (Eng.); F.R.C.P. (Lond.). R.A.M.C., Lieut. Feb. 1916; Captain Feb. 1917; Acting Major Aug. 1918.

HARLEY, JAMES.
George Heriot's School. Student of Arts and Science, 1910-15; M.A., B.Sc. 1915. Schoolmaster. R.E. (Special Brigade), Corporal July 1915; Acting Sergeant Jan. to March 1919.

HARLEY, JAMES LAWSON.
Dunfermline High School. Student of Medicine, 1918. R.A.M.C., April 1916. Optician, 3rd Scottish General Hospital, Glasgow. France.

HARLEY, JOHN LAING.
George Heriot's School. O.T.C. 1912-15, Cadet Corporal. Student of Science, 1918. 9th Royal Scots, Private Oct. 1915. R.E., No. 3 Special Coy., Pioneer July 1916. France. Wounded at the Somme, Aug. 1916, and Ypres, July 1917.

HARMER, JOHN DANIEL.
Towcester Academy. M.B., Ch.B. 1905; F.R.C.S. (Edin.) 1909. R.A.M.C., Lieut. Dec. 1914; Captain Dec. 1915. N. Rhodesian Medical Corps, 1917. France 1915-16. India and Mesopotamia 1916-17.

Record of War Service

HARPER, ALEXANDER.
George Watson's College. Student of Law, 1900-3. Writer to the Signet, 1905. 14th Argyll and Sutherland Highlanders, Private May 1915; L/Corporal. 4th Royal Scots, 2nd Lieut. France, Beaumont Hamel, Arras, and Bourlon Wood, June 1916 to March 1918.

HARPER, FRANCES MARGARET.
M.B., Ch.B. 1903; D.P.H. (Camb.); D.T.M., R.C.P. & S. (Eng.). Attached R.A.M.C., No. 2 Malta Coy., Tigné, and St Andrew's Military Hospitals, Malta, Aug. 1916 to May 1919. M.O., Lady Muriel Paget's Mission to Czecho-Slovakia June 1919.

HARPER, FREDERICK GEORGE.
George Watson's College. M.B., Ch.B. 1907; M.D. 1910. R.A.M.C., Lieut. March 1915; Captain Sept. 1915. M.C. 1918.

HARPER, GEORGE.
Leith Walk School. Pathology Department. R.A.M.C., Private Aug. 1914; Corporal July 1916; Sergeant Feb. 1917. 13th Field Ambulance, 14th Stationary Hospital Laboratory, Boulogne Base. France 1914.

HARPER-NELSON, JOHN JOSEPH.
Coopers Company School, London. M.B., Ch.B. (Hons.) 1907; M.D. and F.R.C.S. (Edin.) 1913. Indian Medical Service, Lieut. 1908; Captain 1911; Major May 1918. Dispatches May 1915, Oct. 1917, Oct. 1918, and Feb. 1919. M.C. Oct. 1917. O.B.E. Feb. 1919.

HARRIES, THOMAS LAVELLIN PAXLEY.
Student of Medicine, 1911-17; M.B., Ch.B. 1916. Royal Navy, Surgeon-Probationer, Dec. 1914; Surgeon April 1917.

HARRINGTON, ARCHIBALD CHAPMAN.
Glenalmond. O.T.C. 1913. University O.T.C. Artillery, 1917-18, Cadet Corporal. R.G.A., Officer Cadet June 1918; 2nd Lieut. March 1919.

HARRIS, ARTHUR TREVENNING.
Grahamstown School, South Africa. O.T.C. 1906-12. Student of Medicine, 1914-15 and 1917-19; M.B., Ch.B. 1919. O.T.C. Medical, 1915, Cadet. 1st Argyll and Sutherland Highlanders, 2nd Lieut. Oct. 1915 to April 1917.

HARRIS, CHARLES EDWARD SMITH.
M.B., Ch.B. 1899. Royal Navy, Surgeon-Lieut., Aug. 1914. H.M. Ships *Fearless* and *Endeavour*.

HARRIS, CHESTER.
Newfoundland. Mount Allison University, Sackville, N.B., Canada. B.A. 1910; M.B. Ch.B. 1916. University O.T.C. Medical, 1914-16. R.A.M.C., Lieut. April 1916; Captain April 1917. 9th Battn. Royal Sussex Regiment. France 1916-18; Salonika and Bulgaria 1918-19. M.C. 1918.

Record of War Service

HARRIS, HERBERT REGINALD.
Fort William High School. Student of Medicine, 1918. R.N.V.R., Signalman June 1916.

HARRISON, ALEXANDER.
Merchiston Castle. O.T.C. 1904-7. Student of Law, 1911-14. Chartered Accountant, 1914. 7th Royal Scots (T.), 2nd Lieut. Sept. 1914; Lieut. June 1915; Captain July 1916; Major. Attached Machine-Gun Corps, Feb. 1918.

HARRISON, JAMES LEES. (See p. 749.)

HARRISON, WILLIAM ATKINSON.
Queen Elizabeth Grammar School, Penrith. M.B., C.M. 1880; B.Sc. (P.H.) 1883. Australian Army Medical Corps, Captain July 1915.

HARRISS, STANLEY ARTHUR.
M.B., C.M. 1891; M.R.C.S. (Eng.) and L.R.C.P. (Lond.) 1893; D.P.H. (Camb.) 1894. Indian Medical Service, Major; Lieut.-Col. Jan. 1914.

HART, FREDERICK G.
Edinburgh Academy. Student of Law, 1906-8. 8th Seaforth Highlanders, Lieut. Sept. 1914; Captain Jan. 1916. M.C.

HART, FREDERICK JOHN ABT.
George Watson's College; First XV. O.T.C. 1908-14, Cadet Sergeant. Student of Science, 1914-15. O.T.C. Artillery, Oct. 1914, Cadet. R.F.A., 2nd Lieut. Oct. 1914; Lieut. Dec. 1915; Acting Captain Feb. 1917 to March 1920. Egypt March 1915. Gallipoli April 1915; France March 1916 to June 1919. Thrice Mentioned in Dispatches.

HART, JAMES ARCHIBALD.
George Watson's College. Student of Arts and Medicine, 1912-15 and 1918-19; M.A. 1915. O.T.C. Infantry, 1914-15, Medical 1918-19, Cadet. R.A.M.C. (T.), Private May 1915.

HARTLEY, JAMES NORMAN JACKSON.
M.B., Ch.B. (Hons.) 1913; F.R.C.S. (Edin.). R.A.M.C., Lieut. Dec. 1915; Captain Dec. 1916. Edinburgh and Border War Hospital, Dunkirk, 1915; Surgical Observation Hut, Etaples, 1917-18. France. O.B.E. (Military) 1919.

HARTY, GARNET WILSON.
M.B., Ch.B. 1903; F.R.C.S. (Edin.) 1905. N.Z. Medical Corps, Temp. Major 1916. O.C. No. 4 Field Ambulance, and Ophthalmic Surgeon, N.Z. Exp. Force.

HARVEY, ALEXANDER WILLIAM MONTGOMERY.
Arbroath High School. M.B., Ch.B. 1902. Indian Medical Service, Lieut. 1903; Captain 1906; Major Aug. 1915; Brevet Lieut.-Col. June 1917. France Sept. 1914 to Dec. 1915; D.A.D.M.S., 1st Indian Army Corps. Mesopotamia, Feb. 1916 to March 1919; North Persia 1919. Dispatches Feb. 1915 and Aug. 1917.

Record of War Service

HARVEY, ARTHUR.
Student of Arts, 1913-15. O.T.C. Infantry, Nov. 1914 to March 1915, Cadet. 15th and 23rd Northumberland Fusiliers, 2nd Lieut.; Captain and Adjutant March 1918. France.

HARVEY, DAVID STANGER.
M.B., Ch.B. 1910. R.A.M.C., Lieut.; Captain Oct. 1915.

HARVEY, GEORGE WADDELL.
Edinburgh Academy. O.T.C. 1914-15. University O.T.C. Artillery, April 1916-17, Cadet Bombardier; Officer Cadet April 1917. Forth R.G.A., 2nd Lieut. June 1917; Lieut. Dec. 1918.

HARVEY, WILLIAM FREDERICK.
Dollar Academy. M.A. 1893; M.B., C.M. 1897; D.P.H. (Camb.) 1899. Indian Medical Service, Lieut. 1899; Major Jan. 1911; Mobilised Dec. 1914; Lieut.-Col. Jan. 1919. Indian Exp. Force. France 1915; Mesopotamia. Invalided home May 1917. Dispatches Aug. 1917 and July 1919.

HASELL, GODFREY SINCLAIR.
Rossall. Cadet Corps 1903-6, Cadet Corporal. B.Sc. 1912. A.M.I.C.E. O.T.C. Engineers, 1909-12, Cadet Sergeant. R.E., Lieut. Jan. 1915; Captain Feb. 1916; Acting Major June 1918; Major Oct. 1918; Adjutant R.C.E. and O.C. 262nd Coy. R.E., Aug. 1916 to March 1919. France. Dispatches 1918 and 1919. M.C. 1919.

HASLAM, JOHN FEARBY CAMPBELL.
Dollar Academy. M.B., Ch.B. 1912. O.T.C. Infantry, Oct. 1908-12, Cadet Sergeant. R.A.M.C., Lieut. July 1915; Captain July 1916. Salonika and France. Dispatches Nov. 1917. M.C. Jan. 1918.

HASTIE, STUART HENDERSON.
George Heriot's School. B.Sc. 1911. O.T.C. Infantry, 1909-12 and 1914-15, Cadet Corporal. 4th Highland Light Infantry (S.R.), 2nd Lieut. April 1915; Lieut. July 1917. Tank Corps July 1916, Acting Major Feb. 1918. M.C.; O.B.E.

HASTINGS, HARRY.
George Watson's College. O.T.C. 1909-10. Student of Medicine, 1914. 9th Royal Scots, Private Aug. 1914. 13th Highland Light Infantry, 2nd Lieut. July 1915. 5th and 8th Lancashire Fusiliers, Lieut. June 1916; Acting Captain April 1916. France 1915 and 1917-18. Prisoner of War 1918.

HASTINGS, THOMAS ERNEST.
St Lawrence College. First XI., Football and Hockey. O.T.C. 1908-12. Student of Medicine, 1912-14 and 1918. O.T.C. Medical, 1912-14, Cadet L/Corporal. 5th Royal Inniskilling Fusiliers, 2nd Lieut. Sept. 1914; Lieut. Jan. 1915; Captain Oct. 1915. Gallipoli 1915; Serbia 1915; Macedonia 1915-17; Palestine 1917-18. Wounded Aug. 1915. Dispatches Nov. 1917. M.C. Jan. 1918.

Record of War Service

HASTON, ALBERT.
Bathgate Academy. Student of Arts, 1918. Machine-Gun Corps, Private.

HASWELL, CYRIL WEBB.
Kingsmead School, Cheshire. University O.T.C. Artillery, Jan. to April 1917, Cadet. 2nd Artists' Rifles, Private April 1917. 2/17th London Regiment, L/Corporal Sept. 1918; Sergeant Dec. 1918. British Military Mission, U.S.A., Sept. 1917 to March 1918. France March 1918 to July 1919.

HASWELL, JOHN FRANCIS.
Leys School, Cambridge. M.B., C.M. 1886; M.D. 1898; M.R.C.S. (Eng.) 1890. 4th Border Regiment, 1886, Lieut.-Col. Oct. 1914. Transferred to R.A.M.C., Lieut.-Col. July 1917. Dispatches (India) 1917. V.D.

HATHAWAY, FRANK JOHN.
Aldenham. M.B., Ch.B. 1899; M.D. 1902. Volunteer Medical Staff Corps, 1895-9, Private. South African Campaign, 1900. R.A.M.C., Captain 1916.

HAULTAIN, WILLIAM FRANCIS THEODORE.
Edinburgh Academy; First XV. O.T.C. 1908-11, Cadet Sergeant. B.A. (Camb.). Student of Medicine, 1910-16; M.B., B.C. (Camb.) 1916. Cambridge University O.T.C. Medical, 1911-14, Cadet Corporal. Resident Dresser, 2nd Scottish General Hospital, Aug. 1914 to April 1915. R.A.M.C., Lieut. Aug. 1916; Captain Feb. 1917. 29th Lancers (Indian Army). Palestine. M.C. Jan. 1919; O.B.E. and Dispatches June 1919.

HAUPTFLEISCH, FRANCOIS JOUBERT.
High School, Lower Paarl. Student of Medicine, 1911-16; M.B., Ch.B. 1916. O.T.C. Medical, Nov. 1914-15, Cadet. South African Medical Corps, Captain Oct. 1917.

HAWICK, JOANN BARBARA.
Trinity Academy, Leith. M.A. 1908. Cataloguer, Edinburgh University Library. W.R.N.S., Senior Writer, Sept. 1918. Granton Naval Base.

HAWKES, ERNEST STANLEY.
Student of Medicine, 1909-16; M.B., Ch.B. 1915. O.T.C. Infantry, May 1909 to April 1913, Cadet. R.A.M.C. (S.R.), Lieut.

HAWKINS, FRANCIS HENRY.
M.B., C.M. 1882; M.D. R.A.M.C., Lieut.-Col.

HAWLEY, ALBERT.
Musselburgh Grammar School. Student of Law, 1913-16. O.T.C. Infantry, June 1915 to Jan. 1916, Cadet. Gordon Highlanders, 2nd Lieut. Jan. 1916; Lieut. July 1917; Captain July 1919. 8th Welsh Regiment, Mesopotamia.

HAWLEY, GEORGE.
Musselburgh Grammar School; First XI. Student of Arts, 1909-10. O.T.C. Infantry, Oct. 1912 to Feb. 1916, Cadet Sergeant. Royal Air Force, 2nd Aircraftsman Feb. 1918; 1st Aircraftsman Dec. 1918.

Record of War Service

HAWORTH, WALLACE ELLWOOD.
Canterbury College, N.Z. University. M.B., C.M. 1892; B.Sc. (P.H.) 1893. Rhodesian Native Regiment, Surgeon-Captain, Aug. 1917 to March 1919. German East Africa and Portuguese East Africa.

HAWS, GEORGE WILLIAM.
St Chad's College, Denstone, North Staffordshire. Cadet Corps 1906-7. Student of Medicine, 1910-14 and 1918-19. 9th Royal Scots (University Coy.), Oct. 1911 to Aug. 1914, Acting L/Corporal. 7th Royal Scots (T.), 2nd Lieut. Aug. 1914; Temp. Lieut. Sept. 1914; Temp. Captain Nov. 1914; Lieut. March 1916. Gallipoli 1915. Wounded July 1915. Invalided out Aug. 1916.

HAY, FREDERICK WILLIAM.
George Watson's College; First XV. M.B., Ch.B. 1908. Indian Medical Service, Lieut. Jan. 1911; Captain Jan. 1914. Croix de Guerre (French) 1917. Twice Mentioned in Dispatches 1918.

HAY, JAMES.
Daniel Stewart's College. B.Sc. 1896; A.M.I.C.E. 1st Lovat Scouts, Lieut. Sept. 1914. R.E., Captain May 1915; Major May 1917. France 1915. M.C. June 1917.

HAY, MATTHEW.
Dollar Academy. M.B., C.M. 1878; M.D. 1881; LL.D. Professor of Materia Medica, Aberdeen. R.A.M.C. (Sanitary), Lieut.-Col. Jan. 1909.

HAY, PERCIVAL JOHN.
M.B., Ch.B. 1901; M.D. 1904. Clinical Lecturer, Ophthalmology, Sheffield University. R.A.M.C. (T.), Lieut. June 1917; Captain June 1918. Ophthalmic Specialist, Aldershot Command.

HAY, ROBERT.
George Watson's College. M.B., Ch.B. 1912. Indian Medical Service, Lieut. Sept. 1914; Captain March 1915. Attached 1/6th Royal Scots. Mesopotamia Exp. Force, attached 87th Punjabis. France, first and second Ypres, Somme, 1916; Egypt and India. Wounded.

HAY, WILLIAM.
Robert Gordon's College, Aberdeen. Student of Science, 1913-14. M.R.C.V.S. 1915. O.T.C. 1913-15. Army Veterinary Corps, Lieut. Jan. 1916; Captain, Jan. 1917. France and India. Dispatches April 1918.

HAYCRAFT, JOHN BERRY.
M.B., Ch.B. 1909. R.A.M.C., Lieut. Aug. 1914; Captain Aug. 1915; Acting Major Jan. 1918. No. 1 Casualty Clearing Station, May 1915 to Dec. 1918. France. Dispatches June 1915. M.C. June 1918.

Record of War Service

HAYES, HENRY DOUGLAS.
George Heriot's School. O.T.C. 1913-16. Student of Medicine, 1916-17 and 1918-19. O.T.C. Infantry, May 1915 to Sept. 1917, Cadet. R.F.C., Private Sept. 1917; 2nd Lieut. Jan. 1918. France.

HAYES, VINCENT LEO PATRICK.
St Patrick's College, Ballarat. Student of Medicine, 1914. O.T.C. Artillery, Oct. 1914 to Dec. 1915, Cadet. R.F.A. (S.R.), 2nd Lieut. Jan. 1916. France.

HEARDER, FREDERIC POLLINGTON.
Queen Elizabeth Grammar School, Carmarthen. M.B., C.M. 1893; M.D. 1897. Volunteer Medical Staff Corps, 1889-93, Sergeant. R.A.M.C., Lieut. June 1918; Captain June 1919. Neurologist.

HEARNE, KENNETH GOODALL.
M.B., Ch.B. 1911. R.A.M.C., Lieut.; Captain Dec. 1915.

HEATH, DOUGLAS ALBERT GORDON.
Dunbar School. Student of Arts, 1918. 1/8th Royal Scots (T.), L/Corporal Aug. 1914. France 1914-18.

HEATHCOTE, GEORGE FRANCIS PALMER.
Grahamstown School. B.A. (Cape); M.B., Ch.B. 1914; D.P.H. 1920. R.A.M.C., Lieut. Aug. 1915; Captain Aug. 1916. 16th Manchester Regiment and 2nd East Lancashire Regiment. Croix de Guerre with Palms, April 1917. M.C. May 1918.

HEDDERWICK, ROBERT JAMES.
Fettes. O.T.C. 1916-17. University O.T.C. Artillery, 1917-18, Cadet; Officer Cadet March 1918. 2nd Scots Guards, 2nd Lieut. Aug. 1918. France Oct. to Nov. 1918. The Rhine Dec. 1918 to March 1919.

HEDDLE, MALCOLM.
Kirkwall Burgh School. B.Sc. 1909. A.M.I.C.E. R.G.A., 2nd Lieut. Nov. 1914; Major Oct. 1917. D.S.O. June 1918; M.C. Oct. 1918. Dispatches June 1918.

HEDLEY, WALLACE TYNEMOUTH.
Edinburgh Institution. M.B., C.M. 1896; L.R.C.P. & S. (Edin.); L.F.P.S. (Glasg.) 1893. R.A.M.C., Lieut. April 1915; Captain April 1916; Major March 1918.

HEMPHILL, ROBERT.
Robert Gordon's College, Aberdeen. Student of Law, 1894-6. Chartered Accountant, 1899. Union of South Africa, Rand Light Infantry, Lieut. Feb. 1910; Captain 1915.

HENDERSON, ADRIAN BETHELL.
George Heriot's School; First XV. O.T.C. 1913-16, Cadet Corporal. University O.T.C. Artillery, 1917, Cadet B.Q.M.S. R.F.C., 2nd Lieut. (Pilot Officer, Observer) Nov. 1917. France. Prisoner of War in Germany Aug. to Dec. 1918.

Record of War Service

HENDERSON, AENEAS ALEXANDER.
    Stirling High School. M.A. 1910. Schoolmaster. R.G.A., Gunner Nov. 1916. 3rd Argyll and Sutherland Highlanders. France Nov. 1917 to Jan. 1919.

HENDERSON, ALASTAIR.
    George Heriot's School. O.T.C. 1913-16, Cadet Pipe-Major. Student of Science, 1918. Rifle Brigade, Officer Cadet Jan. 1917; 2nd Lieut. June 1917. Twice Wounded.

HENDERSON, ALEXANDER.
    Dunfermline High School. M.A. 1906. Schoolmaster. R.F.A. and Anti-Aircraft, Gunner Dec. 1915. France.

HENDERSON, ALEXANDER BAIN.
    Clyne School, Sutherland. M.A. 1907. Schoolmaster. Cameron Highlanders, Private Dec. 1914; Corporal Feb. 1915; Sergeant March 1915; C.Q.M.S. May 1915; 2nd Lieut. Dec. 1915; Lieut. July 1917.

HENDERSON, ALEXANDER ROY MILNE.
    George Watson's College. O.T.C. 1912-15, Cadet L/Corporal. University O.T.C. Infantry, 1917, Cadet; Officer Cadet April 1917. R.F.C., 2nd Lieut. Aug. 1917; Royal Air Force, Lieut. April 1918. France.

HENDERSON, CHARLES LAMOND.
    Aberdeen Grammar School. 4th Gordons (T.), Aberdeen, 1913-14, Private. Student of Arts and Law, 1916-17 and 1918-19; M.A. 1919. 5th Bedfordshire Regiment, Lieut. and Adjutant May 1913. 68th Prov. Battn. Invalided out March 1916.

HENDERSON, DAVID.
    Robert Gordon's College, Aberdeen. M.A. 1904 (Hons. Engl.) 1905. 4th Royal Scots (College Coy.), 1903-5, Private. Australian Light Horse, May 1917. Transferred Australian Army Medical Corps. Invalided out Oct. 1917.

HENDERSON, DAVID KENNEDY.
    Royal High School. M.B., Ch.B. 1907; M.D. 1913. R.A.M.C., Lieut. July 1916, Captain July 1917; Major July 1918. Dunblane War Hospital.

HENDERSON, DONALD J. D.
    Dale College, King William's Town. O.T.C. 1915-16, Corporal. Student of Medicine, 1919. Royal Air Force, June 1918; 2nd Lieut. Jan. 1919.

HENDERSON, ERNEST J.
    Anatomy Department. R.A.M.C. (T.), Q.M.S. No. 7 Prisoners of War Hospital, Tel-el-Kebir, Egypt.

HENDERSON, FRANCIS.
    Durham School. Student of Medicine, 1909-14; M.B., Ch.B. 1914. R.A.M.C., Lieut. Aug. 1914; Captain Aug. 1915; Major Sept. 1918. No. 18 Ambulance Train, France, and No. 8 Field Ambulance. M.C. July 1918; Bar to M.C. Feb. 1919.

Record of War Service

HENDERSON, GEOFFREY ALEXANDER PHILIP.
Daniel Stewart's College. Student of Arts and Science, 1909-15; M.A. 1912; B.Sc. 1915. R.E. (Special Brigade), Corporal July 1915; 2nd Lieut. Feb. 1916; Staff Lieut. March 1917; Lieut. May 1917; Acting Captain Nov. 1917 to April 1919. France July 1915 to Nov. 1918. Wounded at the Somme Aug. 1916.

HENDERSON, GEORGE.
M.A. 1892; M.B., C.M. 1895. R.A.M.C., Lieut. Oct. 1915.

HENDERSON, GEORGE FRANCIS.
Loretto. Student of Law, 1894-7. Writer to the Signet, 1899. 3rd Scottish Horse (T.), Lieut. Aug. 1914; Captain June 1916; Temp. Major June 1916 to Sept. 1917. Attached 10th (Lovat Scouts) Battn. Cameron Highlanders, Oct. 1916. Gallipoli Aug. to Nov. 1915; Egypt Jan. to Oct. 1916; Salonika Oct. 1916 to June 1918; France June to Dec. 1918. M.C. June 1919.

HENDERSON, HESTER MORRIS.
Ladies' College, Cheltenham. M.B., Ch.B. 1908; L.M. (Dublin). Red Cross and Canteen Work, 1914-15. Auxiliary, R.A.M.C., attached Q.M.A.A.C. Recruiting Medical Controller, Warrington, Oct. 1917. Q.M.A.A.C., Abbeville, France, and Wear Bay Hospital, 1918-19.

HENDERSON, HUGH PRICE.
George Watson's College; First XI. Student of Science, 1918. 9th Royal Scots (T.), Private Sept. 1914. 7th Royal Highlanders (Black Watch), 2nd Lieut. June 1915; Temp. Lieut. Jan. 1917; Lieut. July 1917. 6th Machine-Gun Corps. France 1917-18. Wounded.

HENDERSON, JAMES.
George Watson's College. Student of Arts, 1917-19. 3rd Scots Guards, Private; Signaller April 1918 to Jan. 1919.

HENDERSON, JAMES ABBEY.
George Watson's College. Student of Science and Medicine, 1907-12 and 1913-16; M.B., Ch.B. 1913; B.Sc., P.H. 1915. R.A.M.C. (T.), Captain Aug. 1914; Major Nov. 1919. 3rd Lowland Field Ambulance, Aug. 1914. Attached Scottish Command, April 1916. 2/1st Home Counties Division, Sanitary Section, Jan. 1917. Egypt Aug. 1917; Jerusalem Nov. 1918. D.A.D.M.S., Jerusalem, Nov. 1919.

HENDERSON, JAMES ELMSLIE.
Morrison's Academy, Crieff. Student of Arts, 1907-12. President, University Union. O.T.C. Artillery, Oct. 1908 to March 1914, Cadet Sergeant. R.F.A., 2nd Lieut. Sept. 1914; Lieut. Feb. 1915; Captain April 1916; Staff Captain Jan. 1917 to April 1919. France. M.C. June 1918. Dispatches June 1916, Jan. 1917, and March 1919.

Record of War Service

HENDERSON, JAMES MERCER.
Stirling High School. Student of Arts, 1914-16. O.T.C. Artillery, Oct. 1915 to Dec. 1916, Cadet; Officer Cadet Jan. 1917. R.G.A., 2nd Lieut. April 1917; Lieut. Oct. 1918. France Aug. 1917 to June 1919. Wounded at Zonnebeke Oct. 1917.

HENDERSON, JOHN.
Edinburgh Institution. B.Sc. 1893; D.Sc. 1899. M.I.E.E. R.E., Lieut. Oct. 1915; Captain July 1918. Experimental Officer, Signal Service. War Office, March 1919.

HENDERSON, JOHN.
Durham School; First XV. and XI. M.B., Ch.B. 1909. R.A.M.C., Lieut. Oct. 1914; Captain Oct. 1915.

HENDERSON, NORMAN JOHN DEWAR.
M.A. 1913. 6th Royal Scots (T.), 2nd Lieut.; Lieut. Nov. 1916.

HENDERSON, NORMAN KEANE.
Student of Medicine, 1912-16; M.B., Ch.B. 1916. O.T.C. Medical, Nov. 1914, Cadet. R.N.V.R., Surgeon-Probationer; Royal Navy, Surgeon, July 1916.

HENDERSON, PATRICK HAGART.
Dollar Academy; First XV. and XI. M.B., Ch.B. 1899. R.A.M.C., Lieut. June 1900; Major Dec. 1911; Brevet Lieut.-Col. June 1917; Lieut.-Col. Dec. 1917; Temp. Colonel June 1917. France. No. 9 Casualty Clearing Station, Dec. 1914. D.A.D.M.S., 7th Division, Jan. 1915. Egypt Oct. 1915; Macedonia Nov. 1915. 28th and 27th Divisions; Russia Dec. 1918. A.D.M.S., 27th Division. D.S.O. June 1916. Dispatches Jan. and June 1916, July 1917, and June 1918.

HENDERSON, PERCY SYME.
Edinburgh Academy. O.T.C. 1915-17. University O.T.C. Artillery, June to Nov. 1918. K.O.S.B., 2nd Lieut. Aug. 1920.

HENDERSON, ROBERT SAMUEL FINDLAY.
Fettes; First XV. M.B., C.M. 1882. First XV. and International, 1882-5. R.A.M.C., Lieut. Aug. 1884; Colonel Jan. 1914; Hon. Major-General Dec. 1917. Suakin, 1885; Burmese War, 1886; Malakand, 1897; South Africa, 1901-2. A.D.M.S., Quetta Division, Feb. 1915, and 17th Division, April to July 1915. Director-General, N.Z. Medical Services, Aug. 1915 to March 1919. K.H.P. Dec. 1910. C.B. 1917. K.C.M.G. Oct. 1919.

HENDERSON, SELBY HERRIOT.
M.B., C.M. 1882. Indian Medical Service, Lieut.-Col. March 1912.

HENDERSON, THOMAS.
M.B., C.M. 1886. R.A.M.C., Lieut.

Record of War Service

HENDERSON, THOMSON.
George Watson's College. M.B., Ch.B. 1900; M.D. 1903. No. 4 Coy. Q.R.V.B., Royal Scots, 1894-9, Sergeant. R.A.M.C., Lieut. Aug. 1914; Captain Aug. 1915. Ophthalmic Specialist, Royal Victoria Hospital, Netley.

HENDERSON, WILLIAM JOHN GILMOUR.
Foyle College, Londonderry. M.B., Ch.B. 1912. R.A.M.C., Lieut. May 1915; Captain May 1916-19. Egyptian Exp. Force, July 1915 to May 1919.

HENDERSON, WILLIAM JOSEPH.
Ayr Academy. Student of Arts and Law, 1913-16; B.L. 1916. London Scottish, Private Aug. 1918.

HENDRIE, ALFRED STIRLING.
Dumfries Academy. M.B., Ch.B. 1905. R.A.M.C., Lieut. Sept. 1915; Captain Sept. 1916. 147th Brigade, R.F.A. Wounded March 1918.

HENDRIE, JOHN GAIRDNER WHITE.
Ayr Academy; First XV. Student of Arts and Divinity, 1906-10 and 1912-14. M.A. (Hons. Engl.) 1910. President, Dialectic and Theological Societies. O.T.C. Infantry, 1909-10, Artillery, 1912-14, Cadet Bombardier. Ayrshire R.H.A. (T.), and R.F.A., 2nd Lieut. Oct. 1914; Lieut. June 1916; Acting Captain Sept. 1918. France May 1916 to July 1919. Croix de Guerre (Belgian) 1917; M.C. 1918.

HENDRIE, JOSEPH.
Broughton School. Student of Arts, 1914-16 and 1919; M.A. 1919. Schoolmaster. R.N.V.R., Signalman, April 1916. South Atlantic Convoy Duties.

HENDRIE, KELVIN GLADSTONE PETER.
George Heriot's School; First XV. O.T.C. 1913-16, Cadet Sergeant. University O.T.C. Infantry, Dec. 1916, Cadet. R.F.C. April 1917, Pilot; 2nd Lieut. June 1917; Royal Air Force, Lieut. April 1918.

HENDRY, CHARLES VICTOR.
Daniel Stewart's College; First XV. Cadet Corps 1912-15, L/Corporal. Student of Medicine, 1918. 2nd Royal Highlanders (Black Watch), 2nd Lieut. Aug. 1915; Lieut. July 1917; Acting Captain Nov. 1918. Mesopotamian and Egyptian Exp. Forces.

HENDRY, G. P.
Student of Arts. R.H.A. (T.), Ayrshire Yeomanry, 2nd Lieut.

HENDRY, PATRICK.
Daniel Stewart's College. B.Sc. 1909. South African Imperial Light Horse, Trooper Sept. 1914. R.F.A., 2nd Lieut. Oct. 1915; Lieut. July 1917. M.C. March 1917.

HENDRY, RIDLEY. (See p. 749.)

HENDRY, ROBERT.
Merchiston Castle. Cadet Corps 1891-3. Student of Arts and Law, 1895-1900; M.A. 1900. Advocate, 1901. 9th Royal Scots (T.), Lieut. Oct. 1914; Captain June 1916. France.

Record of War Service

HENDRY, WILLIAM.
Daniel Stewart's College; First XI. and XV. M.A. 1909. Schoolmaster. No. 4 Coy. Q.R.V.B., Royal Scots, 1906-8, Sergeant. O.T.C. Infantry, Dec. 1908 to April 1910, Cadet L/Corporal. 5th Royal Irish Regiment, Aug. 1915; Captain July 1917. Serbia, Salonika, Egypt, Palestine, and France.

HENRY, ALEXANDER ALLAN.
George Heriot's School. Student of Science, 1912-14. R.E. (T.), City of Edinburgh Fortress, April 1908; Corporal Aug. 1914; Sergeant Dec. 1914; C.S.M. Feb. 1917. 188th (Special Coy.) France. R.F.A. (S.R.), 2nd Lieut. Sept. 1917; Lieut. March 1919. France.

HENRY, J. A.
Student of Science. 10th Royal Scots (T.), 2nd Lieut.

HEPBURN, CHARLES MICHAEL.
Alloa Academy. Student of Arts and Divinity, 1912-15 and 1918-19. M.A. 1915. O.T.C. Infantry, Oct. 1914-15, Cadet L/Corporal. 7th Argyll and Sutherland Highlanders (T.), 2nd Lieut. July 1915; Lieut. Jan. 1917; Captain. Machine-Gun Corps.

HEPBURN, DAVID.
Brand's School, Milnathort. M.B., C.M. 1881; M.D. 1891. Volunteer Medical Staff Corps, 1886; Captain and O.C. Lecturer, Demonstrator, and Examiner in Anatomy. Professor of Anatomy, University College, Cardiff. R.A.M.C. (T.), 1886. Colonel and O.C., 3rd Western General Hospital, 1908. C.M.G. V.D. Twice Mentioned in Dispatches.

HEPBURN, JAMES.
Dunfermline High School. Student of Medicine, 1910-15; M.B., Ch.B. 1915. O.T.C. Infantry, Oct. 1911 to April 1915, Cadet L/Corporal. R.A.M.C., Lieut. Aug. 1915; Captain Aug. 1916.

HEPBURN, WILLIAM ALLAN FORSYTH.
Kirkcudbright Academy. M.A. (Hons. Engl.) 1913. 4th Royal Scots (T.), Private Jan. 1910; Corporal. 3rd Gordon Highlanders, 2nd Lieut. Jan. 1918. Attached 14th Argyll and Sutherland Highlanders. M.C.

HEPPLE, ROBERT ALEXANDER.
Ballymena Academy. M.B., Ch.B. 1913. Boxing 1910. O.T.C. Medical, Jan. 1909 to June 1912, Cadet L/Corporal. R.A.M.C. (S.R.), Lieut. June 1912. R.A.M.C. (Reg.), Lieut. Aug. 1914; Captain April 1915; Acting Major Jan. 1918. M.C. Aug. 1918; Bar to M.C. Feb. 1919. Dispatches 1919.

HERD, GEORGE GROSVENOR.
Edinburgh Academy; First XV. and XI. O.T.C. 1913-15. Student of Medicine, 1915-17 and 1919. O.T.C. Infantry, 1916-17, Cadet. Artists' Rifles, Private April 1917. 7th and 8th Royal Highlanders (Black Watch) (T.), 2nd Lieut. Nov. 1917; Lieut. May 1919. France. Wounded at Meteren July 1918.

Record of War Service

HERD, WALTER.
Kirkcaldy High School. M.A. (St Andrews); LL.B. 1912. Solicitor, 1912. 7th Royal Highlanders (Black Watch) (T.), 2nd Lieut.; Lieut. 1915; Captain Sept. 1916. M.C. 1918. Dispatches 1919.

HERDMAN, RONALD TYDD.
Collegiate School, Edinburgh. M.B., C.M. 1894; M.D. 1910; D.P.H. (Camb.) 1910. R.A.M.C., Lieut. May 1915; Captain May 1916. Dispatches Dec. 1916.

HERDMAN, THOMAS ANDERSON.
Edinburgh Institution; First XV. O.T.C. 1908-15, Cadet Corporal. University O.T.C. Artillery, Oct. 1917 to May 1918, Cadet Bombardier. Royal Marine Artillery, Oct. 1916. R.F.A., 2nd Lieut. Feb. 1919.

HERMON, JAMES MILNE.
M.B., C.M. 1890; M.D. 1899. R.A.M.C., Lieut. Dec. 1915-16. Military Hospitals, Grantham and Millbank. H.M. Hospital Ship *Panama*. Invalided out.

HERON, DAVIS.
M.B., Ch.B. 1900; F.R.C.S. (Edin.) 1912. Indian Medical Service, Major July 1914. C.I.E.

HERON, JOHN.
Boroughmuir School. Student of Medicine, 1918. 4th Royal Scots, Private Sept. 1916.

HERON, WILLIAM SAMUEL.
M.B., Ch.B. 1907. R.A.M.C., 28th Field Ambulance, Lieut.

HERRIDGE, DAVID RUSSELL.
Hampton Grammar School. Student of Law, 1913-15, O.T.C. Infantry, Jan. to Feb. 1915, Cadet. A.S.C., 2nd Lieut. March 1915; Lieut. June 1915; Captain Jan. 1916; Major April 1918. Ships' Accountant, Dardanelles. Egypt July 1915; Palestine. M.C. (Jerusalem) April 1918. Dispatches June 1918.

HERRIOT, THOMAS PEARSON.
Fettes; First XV. and XI. M.B., Ch.B. 1912; M.D. 1920. R.A.M.C., Lieut. Feb. 1915; Captain Feb. 1916. Jullundur Brigade, 1918-19.

HERVEY, GERALD CHARLES IRVIN.
Student of Medicine, 1913-14. 9th Leicestershire Regiment, Captain and Adjutant Sept. 1915; Major June 1918.

HETHERINGTON, WILLIAM MAXWELL.
Edinburgh Academy. O.T.C. 1913-16, Cadet L/Corporal. Student of Medicine, 1916 and 1919. O.T.C. Artillery, May 1916 to June 1917, Cadet B.Q.M.S.; Officer Cadet June 1917. R.F.A., 2nd Lieut. Nov. 1917. Egypt 1918-19.

Record of War Service

HEWAT, ANDREW FERGUS.
Edinburgh Academy. M.B., Ch.B. 1907; F.R.C.P. Assistant to Professor of Tuberculosis. R.A.M.C., Lieut. Oct. 1915; Captain Oct. 1916. Royal Victoria Hospital, Netley, Physician. Mention March 1919.

HEWAT, AUBREY MIDDLETON.
Fettes. M.B., Ch.B. 1907; M.D. 1911; D.P.H. (Edin.) 1908. R.A.M.C., Lieut. July 1917; Captain July 1918. France 1917-19.

HEWAT, HARRY AITKEN.
Loretto. Student of Medicine, 1910-15; M.B., Ch.B. 1915. O.T.C. Medical Nov. 1914 to April 1915, Cadet Sergeant. Royal Navy, Surgeon, April 1915. Royal Air Force Medical Service, Captain Sept. 1918; Acting Major Oct. 1918.

HEWAT, JOHN.
George Watson's College; First XI. M.B., Ch.B. 1909. Anatomy Staff, 1914. R.A.M.C., 1914; Captain March 1917. King's Royal Rifles. Mesopotamia and 33rd General Hospital, India.

HEWAT, SIR JOHN.
George Watson's College. M.B., C.M. 1887. South African Defence Forces (Volunteers), 1888. Mobilised 1914, Lieut.-Col.; Colonel 1918. German South-West Africa. Dispatches 1916. Knighted for Service as A.D.M.S.

HEWAT, JOHN.
South African College, Cape Town. M.B., Ch.B. 1911; M.D. 1913. R.A.M.C., Lieut. Aug. 1914. Attached British Indians. South African Medical Corps, Captain 1915. France.

HEWISON, JAMES KING.
Morton Parish School. M.A. 1874; D.D. 1900. Minister, Church of Scotland. Chaplain, 4th Highland Brigade, R.G.A. (T.), Captain Dec. 1910.

HEWLETT, GEORGE.
Giggleswick. M.B., C.M. 1883. Royal Navy, Surgeon, Aug. 1887; Fleet Surgeon 1901. Mobilised Oct. 1914. P.M.O., H.M. Dockyard, Portsmouth, 1914-17. S.S. *Sardinia*, Nov. 1917 to July 1918. Torpedoed. Ministry of Pensions, Sept. 1918 to May 1919.

HEWLETT, JAMES EDGAR.
M.B., C.M. 1894. R.A.M.C., Lieut. May 1915-16.

HIGGINS, WILLIAM GORDON.
Student of Science, 1917-19. C.D.A. (Edin.). O.T.C. Artillery, Aug. 1918 to May 1919, Cadet. 4th Royal Scots (T.), Private Oct. 1914.

HIGNETT, LIONEL WATSON.
King's School, Chester. M.B., C.M. 1896; M.R.C.S. (Eng.) and L.R.C.P. (Lond.) 1892; D.P.H. (Camb.) 1909. R.A.M.C. (T.), Lieut. Feb. 1915; Captain Aug. 1915. Egypt and Suvla Bay, Gallipoli, Aug. 1915. Invalided home Nov. 1915.

www.ingramcontent.com/pod-product-compliance
Lightning Source LLC
Chambersburg PA
CBHW080405230426
43662CB00016B/2324